7ᵗʰ Town / Ameliasburgh Township

Past & Present

Compiled by:
7ʰ Town Historical Society

Revised Edition, 1999

GL⬥BAL

Global Heritage Press Inc.

7th Town / Ameliasburgh Township Past and Present

Originally published by 7th Town Historical Society, Ameliasburgh, ON 1984
Revised Edition by Global Heritage Press Inc., Milton, ON 1999
Second printing by Global Heritage Press Inc., Campbellville, ON 2005

ISBN   1-894378-30-X

Canadian Cataloguing in Publication Data

Main entry under title:

> 7th Town/Ameliasburgh : past & present

Reprint of the edition published Ameliasburgh, ON : 7th
> Town Historical Society, c 1984
Includes bibliographical references and index.
ISBN 1-894378-30-X

1.   Ameliasburgh (Ont. : Township) - - History.
2.   2. Ameliasburgh (Ont. : Township) - - Biography. I 7th Town
3.   Historical Society.

FC3095.A47S49 1999   971.3'587   C99-900747-5
F1059.A47S49   1999

Additional copies available from:
Global Heritage Press Inc.
43 Main Street South
Campbellville, Ontario, Canada L0P 1B0

Tel.: 800 361-5168
Internet: www.GlobalHeritagePress.com

Made in Canada.

Preface - 1999 Edition

7th Town/Ameliasburgh Township
Past & Present

7th Town/Ameliasburgh, Past & Present was originally complied in nineteen eighty-four by a group of dedicated members of the Seventh Town Historical Society. The self-published volume contains a storehouse of information on Ameliasburgh Township, from its earliest times until the present (1984). The first edition sold out quickly. Those who are interested in the community and its families recognize the value of the book as a historical record and genealogists prize the detailed information about their ancestors and extended families.

This revised edition contains a facsimile reprint of every page of the original book plus new material. Of great value is a new and extensive index to the original book, which was compiled by the late Murray Clapp of Picton, with assistance from Larry McQuoid of Belleville. The index is a windfall for family historians because it guides readers to over six thousand names linked to many thousands of valuable references.

Also new to this edition is additional information on The Carrying Place United Church, a contemporary sketch of Chief Rohuaro and an important new *Corrections to 1984 Edition* section, which immediately follows this Preface.

Corrections to 1984 Edition

PAGE

Map on front cover denotes 1859 not 1835 (not included in 1999 edition)

03   Caption for photograph "Late Paleo-Indian point, about 8,000 B.C. made from Ohio chert, the oldest point found thus far in the County."

14   Photograph of Chief Rohiario, Kente Mission, 1668

17   Caption for photograph "Sulpician Brothers Trouve and Fenlon arriving at the Kente Mission 1668, by Rev. Bowen P. Squire."

34   9th Line down from top of page, should be "ordered" not "order."

35   Date should read "circa 1790" and not 1787.

37   10th Line from the bottom of page, should be "Lot 91" not "Lot 89".

52   3rd Line from the bottom of page, insert "Deputy Reeve Russel Thompson."

62   5th line down from the top of the page, name should read "Sir James Kempt."

63   5th line from the bottom of the page, should read "flagstone hearth."

66   Below 1st map, 3rd line should read "Lieutenant Governor Simcoe."

70   4th line from the bottom of the page, should be "usual considerate liberality,"

71   Passage from 1873 Lovells Gazetteer of British North America, "four store" should read "four stores."

73   Note; John A. Preston died in 1898, and not 1893 as stated.

100   6th line from the bottom of the page, William Marsh drowned 1897 not 1879.

104   10th line from the bottom of the page, should read "immense quantities of fish."

127   14th and 17th line from the top of the page, the name "Geyer" should be changed to "Goyer."

134   13th line from the bottom of the page, the description should read "This paved road went from Rednersville to the west end of Old Orchard Road." Also, 7th line from the bottom should read "Tomatoes were shipped…"

144   3rd line from the bottom of the page, remove the word "four"

169   8th and 18th line from the top of the page, "Ameliasburgh" should read "Ameliasburg"

185   2nd line from the top of the page should read "4,000 acres of farmland."

241   15th line from the top of the page, "Truman Fergsuon" should read "Truman Ferguson."

248   4th line from the bottom should read, "Mill on Baker's Island."

360   Caption in photograph, student in back row, third from the end should read "Norma Harris."

363   2nd line down from top of page, "1915" should be "1900."

395   Lower photograph, back row, 2nd from the end, name should read "B. Vaughan".

428   7th line from bottom of the page "Hoboken, New York" should read "Hoboken, New Jersey."

430   7th line from bottom of the page, Peter C. Dempsey was great-uncle (not Grandfather) of Gordon and Donald"

440   Under paragraph describing "The Dempsey Evaporator," 4th line from bottom should read "1915" and not "1910." Also, 7th line from the bottom of the page, name should read "W. C. Dempsey" and not Harry Dempsey.

444   Caption under photograph should only read "Dempsey Evaporator at Albury"

503   Delete the heading "The Howard Weese Canning Factory by Frances Weese." This is not applicable to these paragraphs. This heading

applies to information being given on page 504, beginning the second paragraph.

534   The last paragraph begins "Henry Stafford, who lived on lot 76, concession 3, Ameliasburgh". This should read Henry "Gilford" Stafford, he went by the name of "Gilford."

564   4th line from the top of the page, the body was that of her son, not her husband.

598   Richard Hall was of "Sophiasburgh" and not Hillier and Dr. Peter Martin was of "Deseronto" not Frankford.

635   The last line of the last paragraph of the section entitled "Third Concession Aleyas". Should read: "Norman (not Paul) stayed on the homestead and never married. Paul married Ilene Gampble and lived nearby on the 3r[d] concession with their four children Noreen, Wayne, Lois and Wanda. Mary (Tyler) married Douglas Bradshaw of Trenton and Lewis Tyler married Annabel Taylor of Hillier.

656   10th line from the bottom of the page, Helena (Calnan) (1857-1921).

671   11th line from the top of the page, should read "Holstein"

676   14th line from the bottom of the page, Ann (Gibson) (1852- 1922)
       6th line from the bottom of the page, Grace (Gibson) who married Charles Wood had five children the fifth being Ronald, who married Olive Mackey.

705   2nd Line above photograph name should read "John Bleeker" not Baker

739   2nd line from the bottom of the 2nd paragraph should read "Wesley Weese married Harriet Bryant, "their children were Fred, Pearl, Kenneth, Mary, Guay, Susie, Gladys, Harriet and Howard.

746   Paragraph entitled "The Margaret Wood Family", Vera was born 1894 and not 1849.

7th Town/ Ameliasburgh Township

Past
&
Present

Compiled by:
7th Town
Historical Society

CONTENTS

P̿REFACE

Seventh Town—Ameliasburgh

The title chosen for our book needs an explanation. When the disbanded troops and Loyalists arrived at the conclusion of the American War of Independence, free land was made available in what was then an unsurveyed wilderness, and it was necessary for surveys to be run in a hurry. The size of townships (or towns, as they were called) was determined, and then the surveys began, East and West of Cataraqui Town. There was no time for names— numbers were used. Thus there were two distinct ranges of townships, one upon the St. Lawrence numbering one to nine, and one upon the Bay of Quinte numbering one to ten. Our township was number 7 west of Cataraqui, and for years it was called Seventh Town. Later the situation was made less confusing when names replaced the numbers. Seventh Town was named Ameliasburgh, after the seventh daughter and fifteenth child of King George III.

7th Town was named after Princess Amelia- daughter of King George III.

viii

FOREWORD

When the Seventh Town Historical Society began, one of the purposes was to collect all the information available about the history of Ameliasburgh. Over the years, this has been done, and papers have been presented at our meetings dealing with family and village histories, and the history of farming, trade and commerce in the area. With the challenge of 'Bi-centennial'— and the assistance of a grant from the 'New Horizon Program' from Health and Welfare Canada— it was decided that this was the appointed time for compiling, editing and adding to this material. The result of all this is the book you now hold. We hope it will be informative, amusing and a source book for the future. As a committee, we are well aware of our proneness to human error. Writers of history may be frustrated or delighted when new items come to light, after their material has been published. Every effort has been made in searching out primary sources to get accurate information. We are deeply indebted to many citizens of the township and beyond, who have lent early documents, books and pictures for our use and, ultimately, ⌐ your enjoyment. Special tribute must be paid to Loral and Mildred We ⌐maker who put their very extensive archival and genealogical records at the committee's disposal, and who have edited much of the contents of this book. Many writers have compiled material, but, contrary to the old statement that a camel is a horse put together by a committee, we feel that the expanded committee who has prepared this book, had one purpose in mind, and, we hope you will agree that this purpose has been achieved.

DEDICATION

In Commemoration of those who pioneered the settlement of Ameliasburgh Township and all those who have followed and will follow in their footsteps, this work is dedicated in this Bi-Centennial year.

The Book Committee

Back Row— left to right: Bruce Graham, Harry Bisdee, Seymour Hamilton, W.D. Hanthorn, Julia Sager, Rev. Maurice McLeod.

Front Row— Nellie Montgomery, Evelyn Hamilton, Marion Calnan, Beth Nightingale, Mildred Wanamaker.

Absent— John and Daisy Wannamaker, Thomas Short and Loral Wanamaker.

With a grant from New Horizons

Special thanks to Bruce Graham for photography

CHAPTER 1

AMELIASBURGH TOWNSHIP

The Mississauga Indians were the main inhabitants of the area we know as Ameliasburgh Township until the arrival of the surveyors and subsequent settlement of the assigned lots in 1787. Prince Edward County had been named "Presqu'ile de Quinte", literally, "the almost isle of Quinte", by the French, and was renamed Prince Edward in honour of the son of George III in 1792.

Settlement and industrial development in Ameliasburgh has been shaped largely by its unique geographic position. It is tied to the mainland only by an isthmus a mile and a half wide on its western end. Even this isthmus has been severed by the Murray Canal. This gives the area a claim to fame that dates back even before the time of a written history of the area, for the Indians recognized this land as "The Carrying Place", across which goods and even boats had to be transported when travelling from the waters of Lake Ontario to those of the Bay of Quinte. A large part of the township is surrounded by water, the Bay of Quinte to the east and to the north, Weller's Bay on the west, and Consecon Creek and Lake Consecon on the south. Almost in the centre of the township is Roblin Lake. The land dips southward, so the water drains mainly toward Lake Ontario, rather than into the Bay of Quinte. Marsh Creek is the only stream of more than local consequence that reaches the Bay of Quinte.

The climate is affected by the proximity of water. Jacob Spelt in *Urban Development in South Central Ontario* wrote in 1955, "Even climate is affected by the peninsular position. In winter instead of warming the shores of the County, Lake Ontario retards spring temperatures, yet in the fall the number of frost-free days are lengthened." We know, however, though this is true for the parts of Prince Edward County closer to Lake Ontario, orchards in Ameliasburgh Township are in full bloom at least a week ahead of those at Wellington or Waupoos. The number of frost-free days in the fall varies in direct relation to the distance from the Bay of Quinte or other major bodies of water.

Precipitation ranges from 30 to 34 inches, and as some of the land has less than a foot of soil over the limestone bedrock, at least a part of the homesteads were used as pasture land. This contributed to the early and, indeed, spectacular rise of the dairy and cheese-making industries. The number of days of precipitation averages about 100 per year.

As we try to recall the days of the pioneer, we should attempt to put ourselves in the situation of a family surrounded with a forest out of which they had to wrest a home and a living. Another family, the nearest neighbour, would be so situated, with no easy means of communication. Sickness, disease, accidents, all could cause difficult situations with which the family would have to cope, largely, on its own. These people, of course, had the advantage of coming from a new country that was only a generation or so removed from pioneer days, and there was the added incentive for many of finally having land they could call their own, under a government and flag they had chosen.

The accessibility to water for the marketing of produce helped the area develop fairly rapidly. From 1800 to 1860 there was a good export market for wheat, both to Lower Canada and to Great Britain. In the years between 1860 and 1890, barley and rye for malting were grown in large quantities and exported to United States at premium prices. From the 1840's to the early 1900's hops were also grown and exported. These were real days of prosperity in the township.

Large quantities of lumber were shipped, also, and when the orchards began producing, apples found a ready market in Canada and overseas. With the coming of the railway, canned products, both fruit and vegetables, found another route out of the township.

Population:
1817— Gourlay estimated the population at 1068
1841— Smith's Gazetteer 2,115
1850— Census 2,881
1861— Census 1,789 males 1,697 females
1937— Population: 2,500 Area: 45,440 acres
1983— Township Records: 1,992 households
      Population: 4,850
      Township Roads: 80 miles
      Area: 19,635 hectares

Today, Ameliasburgh is increasingly a 'bedroom' community, where people live, eat, sleep and socialize, but go elsewhere to earn their living. Most farms are large industrial complexes, employing several people and incorporating several hundred acres. Smaller farms find the farmer going away to work part-time in order to supplement his income. The location and scenery that the township enjoys has been recognized by many who have built homes here, thus swelling the population, and at the same time changing and enriching the quality of life. A new wave of pioneer has come; his project is not to clear the land, but rather, to pay off the mortgage on his new home, that will, finally, let all around know that the land is his and his family's— free and clear.

CHAPTER 2

PRE-HISTORY

The History of Archeological Research in Ameliasburgh

Dr. Mima Kapches
New World Archaeology, Royal Ontario Museum

With the early settlement and land clearance of Ameliasburgh, many Indian sites were undoubtedly discovered. Archeological sites in Ontario are, as a rule, not deeply buried. Instead, they are found on or close to the modern soil surface. With cultivation, archeological materials are often brought to the surface. These mark the location of campsites or villages of the prehistoric period.

The study of the types of artifacts, where they are found on a site, and where the sites are located within a region, provides essential data for archeological research. Through the careful recording of these data, a synthesis or an overview of prehistoric events can be compiled. There have been several individuals who have conducted archeological work in Ameliasburgh.

The first was T.C. Wallbridge who in 1859 explored several mounds along the Bay of Quinte. The report of his activities was published in the *Canadian Journal* in 1860. The description of his excavations and the accompanying lithographs are very detailed. They provide scientific data on the mounds, their construction and their inclusions. This report is all the more worthwhile

Pink Prehistoric projectile found on Lot 65, Con. 3 by Seymour Hamilton.

since with continued cultivation and development, these mounds rapidly disappeared. So quickly that, in 1897, David Boyle, the first provincial archeologist, commented that few traces of the mounds were observable.

David Boyle, working from the Provincial Museum in Toronto, was in correspondence with people from the County who had artifact collections. Muriel Merrill of Picton corresponded with Mr. Boyle from 1901 for several years. The result was an article authored by Miss Merrill in 1912 on 'Indian Pottery of Prince Edward County' which appeared in the *Annual Archeological Report of Ontario*. She mentioned in her letters and in her article, finds of Indian artifacts throughout the County.

Another long time correspondent with David Boyle, commencing around 1900, was George G. Chadd. Mr. Chadd, an employee of the Central Ontario Railway, was stationed at Carrying Place. From there he collected extensively on sites in Ameliasburgh and elsewhere in the County. Reverend Bowen Squire, a youth at the time, remembers Mr. Chadd used to go collecting every day after work. Chadd's collection was eventually moved to Trenton where he built a stone building, which he described in a letter to David Boyle as "fire proof". Following Mr. Chadd's death, his collection was acquired by the Royal Ontario Museum in 1921. It forms an important part of the ROM's permanent collections, since Chadd documented the location of most of his finds.

Another substantial collection from the region was Wallace Havelock Robb's Abbey Dawn specimens. A major contributor to this collection was Fred Flindall of Trenton. Robb described several items in *Kingston History*, including some of Mr. Flindall's artifacts, which he donated to the Kingston Historical Society in 1965. Some artifacts from Abbey Dawn are currently at the Lennox and Addington Museum.

The next individual to conduct archeological work for a long period of time was a County resident, the Reverend Bowen P. Squire. Through an interest in native history, possibly stimulated by Mr. Chadd, the Rev. Squire conducted survey and excavation around Lake Consecon. His most significant recoveries related to the historic Kente Mission site. He reported on his work in several articles in *Ontario History* and in *Ontario Archaeology*.

The collections from his activities are stored at the Ameliasburgh Museum and the Hastings County Museum.

Other archeologists who have conducted limited research in Ameliasburgh are Paul W. Sweetman and Ken Swayze. Neither of these gentlemen published reports, although manuscripts on their projects were available for my study. In 1983 the Royal Ontario Museum conducted an archeological survey under my direction. A similar project will be conducted in 1984. My goals are to develop a several year project in the County, first identifying sites, than excavating selected sites, and finally writing a detailed prehistory of Prince Edward County.

There are several individuals in Ameliasburgh who have collections of Indian artifacts. Each of these, when analysed, becomes an important part in the development of the prehistory of the township. In the discussion that follows, the long and interesting prehistory of the County is described. This presentation is only an outline. There are hundreds of details within each period that cannot be discussed, they had to be overlooked for this brief chapter. With continued archeological research in Ameliasburgh and the County, more details will be known.

The Palaeo-Indian Period

The prehistoric past of Ameliasburgh commences some 12,000 years ago. At that time the County was newly freed from glacial ice and the floodwater of glacial lakes. The vegetation was quite different than that of the present. It was a barren landscape which was quickly colonized by scrub bushes and grasses. The climate was still quite cool, from the icy winds blown down from the huge glacial mass which was retreating gradually to the northeast. This environment, somewhat similar to that of northern Canada today, was a specialized habitat which offered resources to support unique species of wildlife. Herds of barren ground caribou, whose previous distribution had been to the south in the environmental zone along the glacial edge, moved north as their habitat receded with the ice sheets. Mastadons and mammoths adapted to the cooler glacial environment also travelled north.

These species were hunted by the Palaeo-Indians who were present in Ontario about 10,000 B.C. The caribou were an important game animal since they migrated along the same routes at least twice yearly, moving from the south to the north in the spring, and the north to the south in the fall. This predictability of movement was observed by the Palaeo-Indian hunters whose sites are often located near possible migration routes. Another advantage when hunting herd animals is that it is likely that several individuals would be killed, thereby increasing the economic rewards of the hunt.

Palaeo-Indians lived in small communities called bands. The size of the community was from 15 to 30 individuals. The band would not have lived in one settlement throughout the year but would have moved continually in the larger region.

The Palaeo-Indians made distinctive artifacts of chert, a stone similar to flint found in several Ontario localities, called fluted points. These lanceolate shaped points have a flake removed down the centre of the point resembling a channel. This is called the flute. These points were attached, or hafted, to wooden spears which were thrust or thrown short distances to kill.

To date, no fluted points are known from the County. However, one is known from Lennox and Addington County to the east and several are known directly to the west on the north shore of Lake Ontario. Therefore, it is anticipated that some specimens of this early period may yet come to light in the County.

After this period there was sporadic occupation of the County. Small bands of hunters, each with their distinctive type of projectile points, passed through. Some of these bands were from places as distant as Ohio. This is known because the chert that these points are made of is only found in that state.

The Archaic Period

The next period for which there is definite evidence of intensive use of the County is the Archaic (6000 BC to 1500 BC). In contrast to the preceeding Palaeo-Indian period, when hunters may have temporarily used the resources of the County, during the Archaic, there were people who were year-round residents. A major reason for this alteration in the use of the area was that the environment had changed. No longer the grasslands of the post-glacial period, nor the pine forests which were quickly established after the grasslands, instead, with increasingly warmer temperatures, there was modern vegetation. The County is in a very specialized southerly location which is moderated by the lake. Therefore, it had a more southern variety of trees and plants. These were all very conducive to human exploitation. Nut bearing trees, wild rice, and naturally occurring wild fruits such as strawberries were a significant addition to the diet. The plant foods were augmented by the great variety of animals present, mammals, fish and fowl.

The majority of the artifacts found from this period are of stone. As with earlier periods, it is known by analysing the used edges of the stone artifacts that a great variety of items and goods of wood, bone and skin were made. However, these fragile organic articles decompose under normal soil conditions over the years. As a result, the stone artifacts, are the only remnants of sites occupied by Archaic peoples. Typical artifacts are large stone axes, adzes, gouges and chisels. Made of dense rock such as granites and schists, these were primarily woodworking tools. There is evidence that Archaic peoples made dugout canoes. By felling a tree then using axes and gouges, they shaped and hollowed to form the canoe. The County has one of the highest densities of gouges in southern Ontario. With the surrounding lakes and many interior lakes it is likely that canoe manufacturing was an important local activity.

With the development of an advanced technique of water transportation, there was an increase in the exploitation of the County's water resources. The inner lakes could be fished with nets, spears and harpoons. Greater quantities of wild rice could be gathered more efficiently in the lakes.

The projectile points of this period were hafted onto spears. There is evidence of decoratively carved stone weights called bannerstones which would have been attached to spear throwers. These weights increased the speed of the spears as they were thrown, thereby increasing the penetration on impact. The projectile points are often made of cherts from Ontario sources. During this period, there apparently were bands of hunters and their families who lived in specific regions, or territories, in Ontario.

Importantly, there was continued interaction with peoples far beyond the County, to the east, to the north and to the south. From the St. Lawrence there

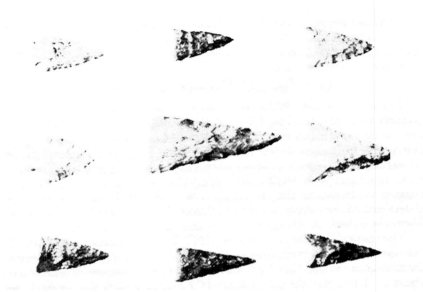

A selection of chert projectile points from Prince Edward County, the Chadd Collection, Royal Ontario Museum.

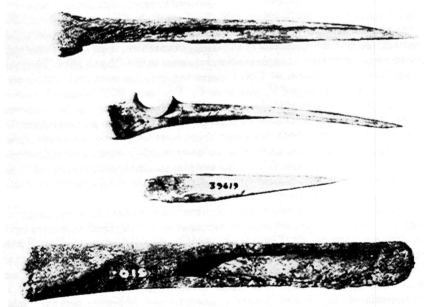

Bone artifacts from Prince Edward County, the Chadd Collection, Royal Ontario Museum.

was trade in well-made, delicately-notched points of slate. From the north, around Lake Superior, possibly via the Ottawa Valley, points, axes, and beads of native copper were traded. Conch shells from the Gulf of Mexico, made into long tubular beads and decorative breastplates called gorgets, are found on some sites in the County.

The Initial Woodland Period

During the Initial Woodland period a new technology appeared, the production of pottery. Clay was mined from creeks and rivers, grit was added, and the clay was rolled into coils which were then used to build a vessel. The exteriors of the vessels were decorated with many varieties of stamped motifs. As well, there is evidence of smoking with the presence of long tubular pipes of stone and pipes with small bowls called platform pipes. It is not known if tobacco was smoked at this early date. A very distinctive and uncommon pipe of this period is made of stone in the shape of exotic birds such as parrots. These were made in the central states and traded into Ontario.

This period commences around 1500 BC and extends until AD 500. Perhaps the major cultural developments of the Initial Woodland in Southern Ontario occur in the Rice Lake and Bay of Quinte regions of southeastern Ontario. Along the shores of these lakes, bays and rivers, mounds were constructed. As important people in the community, political leaders or religious leaders, died they were given elaborate and sacred burials in pits. Above these burial pits, mounds of each were constructed. Sometimes, after these mounds were built, other individuals were buried in the mound fill.

In the first half of this century there was a controversy surrounding the construction of these mounds. It was thought that they were built by the same peoples who built large complex mound systems in the Ohio Valley. The myth of the 'Mound Builders of Ohio' migrating into Ontario was a dominant theme in early archeological studies in the Province. With detailed research over the last 30 years this theory has been demonstrated to be incorrect. Instead, the mounds were built by local peoples. There was no mass migration of people into the Province. However, there was the sharing of symbolic ideas (including mound building and other religious motifs) which were traded over long distances. The Initial Woodland peoples in Ontario interacted with the Ohio peoples. The Ohio ideas were introduced into the distinctive Ontario culture which we call Point Peninsula.

One of the major reasons for the concentration of mound sites along these waterways was the high amount of naturally occurring food resources (wild rice, fish and waterfowl). These foods were hunted, fished and collected with greater efficiency to provide a large quantity of food which could support an increased group population. In contrast to the small bands of the Archaic period during the Initial Woodland several bands clustered together in communities of up to 100. Several concentrations of people occurred from spring to fall; apparently in the winter the smaller bands units dispersed to hunt.

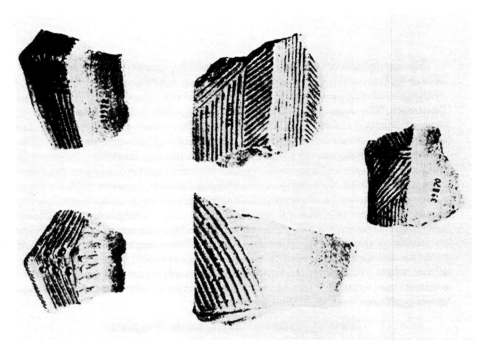

A selection of prehistoric Iroquoian rim shards from Prince Edward County, the Chadd Collection, Royal Ontario Museum.

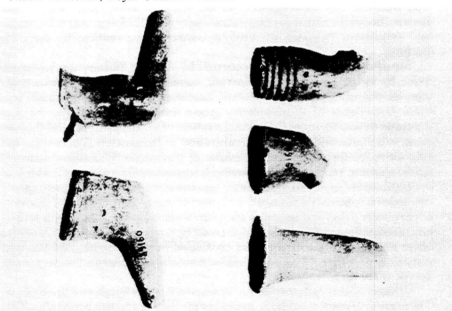

Prehistoric Iroquian clay smoking pipes from Prince Edward County, the Chadd collection, Royal Ontario Museum.

For the Initial Woodland and for the earlier periods, the Archaic and the Palaeo-Indian, it is not possible to make an identification of the ethnic affiliation of the peoples. It cannot be stated that they were Algonkian or Iroquoian. The reasons are that we are dealing with such an incredibly large time scale, over 10,000 years, during which there were periods of migration (when groups from many different regions moved through the area). The cultural developments were not smoothly continuous, therefore, it cannot be stated that one period's people automatically developed into the peoples of the subsequent period. The analyses of archeological data, types of artifacts, types of house structures and the physical attributes of the peoples based on the examination of the skeletal remains, leads to assumptions of cultural continuity between periods. The major difficulties concerning the data from the earlier periods are their limited nature. There are insufficient pieces of evidence to fit together the full picture. In the more recent period, from the end of the Initial Woodland to the Ontario Iroquois, many different kinds of evidence are available which allow for knowledgeable statements about specific cultures and their developments.

The Ontario Iroquois Period

From the archeological evidence, it is possible to state that late Initial Woodland peoples in southeastern Ontario were the ancestors of the Iroquois. The details of the developments of the Iroquois before A.D. 800 are still sketchy but archeologists are confident that from AD 500 to AD 800 changes and transitions occurred in southern Ontario that resulted in the early Iroquois.

Significant innovations had occurred by AD 800. Pottery was no longer made by the coiling technique. Instead, vessels were modelled from a single mass of clay using a paddle and anvil. Smoking pipes of clay were made and there is evidence of tobacco being grown and smoked. Perhaps the most dramatic development occurred in the sphere of subsistence. Around this time there is definite evidence for the cultivation of Indian corn (Zea mays). The cultivation of corn altered the lifestyles of the people. With the clearing of fields, planting, tending and harvesting, it was essential for some individuals of the community to remain stationary from the spring to fall. The advantages of this sedentary status were reaped with the harvest of corn. Sufficient amounts of corn were dried and stored to allow for a settlement, a village with several houses of perhaps 150 people, which could be occupied year round. Of course other members of the community continued hunting, fowling, fishing, and gathering, as before. These foods added essential nutrients and variety to the diet of these early Iroquois.

Villages of this early period are known in Ameliasburgh and the County. There are also small temporary campsites for fishing and fish processing. This was not a time of massive land clearance for cultivation, instead around the sites there were small areas cleared for fields.

The early Iroquois period continued until about AD 1250. After this date new cultigens, beans and squash were introduced. Corn and these two new plants were placed together in small mounds of earth called corn hills in the fields. These three plants, called the Three Sisters in Iroquoian mythology, provided a stable nutritious source of food. The result of the adoption of the Three Sisters was felt in population increases in all Iroquois communities.

Small villages could no longer contain the population growth, large villages, 3 to 5 acres in size, appeared. This is called the middle Ontario Iroquois period and spans AD 1250 to AD 1450. The villages were surrounded by rows of posts creating a defensive palisade. Inside this fence were several longhouses. The average longhouse was 70 feet long by 26 feet wide, but within each village there was always variation in length. The width of longhouses remained fairly constant between 22 to 26 feet.

The houses were built entirely of wood. Pointed and fire-hardened wooden posts were placed in the ground. The tops of these posts were bent and the posts from either side were joined, with extra posts added as necessary, to form the roof. The size of the saplings used to build the superstructure, their height 10 to 15 feet, and diameter 5 to 6 inches, assured flexibility and consequently restricted the width dimensions of the house. Shingles of bark, elm was preferred, were placed on the exterior. Within each house lived several families. There are some villages of this middle Ontario Iroquois period in Prince Edward.

The late Ontario Iroquois period, spanning AD 1450 to about AD 1550, is represented by several village sites in the County. These large villages were occupied by Huron-speaking Iroquois who fished, hunted, collected, and very efficiently planted and harvested the Three Sisters. Large areas of land around the 3 to 5 acre villages were cleared for planting.

These late Iroquois traded to the east, with the St. Lawrence Iroquois, and to the west, with the Humber and Markham Huron Iroquois. These were all Ontario Iroquois. During this period, there is little evidence of interaction, either peaceful or aggressive, with the New York Iroquois. The Ontario Iroquoian-speaking tribes evolved independently from the New York Iroquois The New York Iroquois tribes, which later amalgamated to form a powerful political alliance called the League of Confederacy, consisted of five tribes. These were from east to west, the Mohawk, the Onondaga, the Oneida, the Cayuga and the Seneca.

The several Iroquoian villages occupied in Prince Edward were abandoned soon after 1550. The County was vacated of Ontario Iroquois occupants as these Huron-speakers moved to the northwest to settle, with other migrant groups as tribes in the Huron Confederacy, in the Penetang peninsula. Other areas of southeastern and southcentral Ontario were similarly vacated during this time. The St. Lawrence Iroquois moved northwest along the Trent waterway system towards Huronia. The Iroquois in southcentral Ontario, along the Humber river and in the Markham region, also moved north to Huronia. This movement was not a displacement, these Iroquois were not replaced by other peoples. Instead, the areas vacated were left empty, a no-man's territory.

There are various explanations for these migrations. Around 1550 AD there are great quantities of mistreated human bone in villages. The presence of this material indicates increased aggression and the torturing of captured prisoners. The palisades around the villages became quite massive, consisting of many rows of posts, showing a greater concern for protecting the village inhabitants. The warfare was conducted on two fronts, the St. Lawrence Iroquois to the east, and the League Iroquois to the south.

Why does aggression appear at this time, and why did it escalate in the late 16th and early 17th centuries? Although there were no Europeans in Ontario until after 1615 AD, the effect of the European presence on the St. Lawrence and in Chesapeake Bay were felt early in southern Ontario. The trade of European goods, copper kettles, iron axes and glass beads, preceded the historic period. These goods were traded from one native group to another. The introduction of European items altered the delicate balance of the exisiting political alliances between the Ontario and New York Iroquois tribes. It created an imbalance, where the Huron became the powerful trading group with the French. Other groups, jealous of this monopoly, waged war.

In the archeological record, the first major indications of strife are the migrations around 1550 AD. The Huron-speaking Iroquois in southcentral Ontario moved north to consolidate and strengthen their forces in Huronia.

The sites and fields that were abandoned, including those in the County, were rapidly overgrown. These territories were used by Iroquois hunting and fishing parties, or on their way to New York State. It is possible that Algonkians seasonally used the many environmental resources of the County. However, there were no permanent settlements until the late 17th century.

The history of the Ontario Iroquois after the arrival of the French in 1615 is very dramatic. They had several years of successful and intensive trading activities then the League Iroquois began to systematically attack their villages. By 1652 the Huron, the Petun and the Neutral were annihilated as cultural entities in Ontario, their remnant population were either driven out of the province or adopted by the New York tribes.

The Post Iroquoian Period
in Southeastern Ontario

With the end of the Ontario Iroquois, southeastern Ontario became territory for bands of Mississaugas and New York Iroquois who settled in a few scattered communities. Little is known about this period during which a small number of French traders established outposts where they continued to trade with local bands. This was at the request of Cayuga, New York Iroquois, who had settled in Ameliasburgh. The Kente mission and later periods of Ameliasburgh native history including the Mohawks, and the Grape Island mission, will be discussed later in this book.

Conclusion

The intent of this chapter has been to provide an outline of the events during the prehistoric period of Ameliasburgh and the County. The prehistoric period is very long and only sketchy details of each period were presented. With additional research, more information will be known and the knowledge of developments within each of the -periods will be further expanded.

Chief Robiario, Kente Mission 1668

CHAPTER 3

EARLY HISTORY

The Historic Indian Period

The first references to the Bay of Quinte area on the pages of history were established when the noted French explorer and geographer, Samuel de Champlain in 1615, accompanied by other Frenchmen and Father Joseph le Garon, a Franciscan (Recollet) missionary to the Hurons, travelled from Quebec, up the Ottawa River into Huron country, in the Georgian Bay area.

The Indians were friendly toward Father Joseph and built him a cabin apart from the village, where he might offer to God the sacrifice of the Mass. Unfortunately, the development of the mission was thwarted by the Huron-Iroquois struggle which ensued.

Champlain had arrived in Huron country in time to join a war-party of some 3,000 Indians, who paddled their canoes through the Severn River to Lake Couchiching and Lake Simcoe, from there up the Talbot River to Balsam

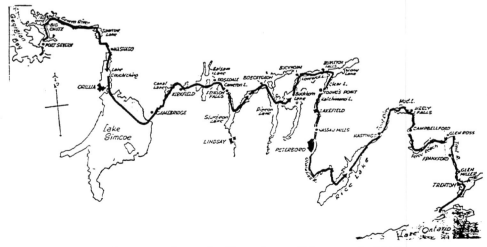

Champlain's trip down the Trent-Severn Waterway in 1615.

Lake, then east to Sturgeon Lake, following down the Otonabee River to Rice Lake, from which they entered upon the rivers and lakes of the Trent River system, into the Bay of Quinte and eastward to cross the Lake of the Entouhonorons (Lake Ontario). It is believed Champlain and his Frenchmen were the first white men to see Prince Edward County and especially the Ameliasburgh shoreline, but there is no record of his ever setting foot upon it.

On October 10, 1615, they were ready to attack the Onondaga nation, near the present site of Syracuse, New York, in what Champlain thought would be a short engagement. In the unsuccessful attacks which the Hurons launched against this tribe of the Iroquois Nation, Champlain was twice wounded, which necessitated his remaining in the region of the Bay of Quinte for some weeks upon his return. In the diary which he kept, he described the natural beauty of the area, the abundance of wild animals, beautiful birds and grapevines and how the Indians trapped. Bishop Morris in *Champlain, The Life of Fortitude* (Toronto, 1963) wrote: "All this lovely region was uninhabited, for its Indian population had abandoned it in fear of Iroquois raiders." For reasons unkown, Champlain stayed in the area until July, 1616.

As a consequence of Champlain's tragic first contact with the Iroquois, a situation was created where the French and Hurons were constantly at war with the Five Nations Indians, consisting of the Onondagas, Cayugas, Senecas, Mohawks and Oneidas.

With the passing of time, the natural hostility of the Iroquois was heightened to a fever pitch and a fierce competition for the monopoly of the fur trade developed. The Indians became suppliers of the resources of the country and consumers of European goods. Quoting from J.M.S. Careless in *Canada, A Story of Challenge*: "The conflict had been long developing, and it had not been caused merely by Champlain's unwise skirmishing with the Iroquois, nor by their desire for revenge. The whole pattern of the fur trade and of the relations of red man and white, had been more significant in bringing on war." In 1649-50, after 35 years of skirmishes, Huronia was devastated by the Iroquois and the Huron tribe was scattered, never again to form a nation.

The Indians were either allies and protectors or enemies and often sought the alliance of the newcomer in his struggle with other Indians, while the bases of Indian-white relations were economic and military. The fur trade almost came to a halt when the Iroquois began attacking neighbouring tribes, then began to menace French settlements. The colony of new France had reached a critical stage.

The outcome was that new settlement was encouraged and Iroquois raids discouraged by the gallant stand taken by Adam Dollard and his 16 comrades at the Long Sault, west of Montreal in 1660. France sent out a thousand troops who along with the colonial militia ravaged Mohawk lands and in 1667 they made peace. Now the Indian tribes who were afraid of being destroyed themselves by the French began to ask for missionaries.

A view of Indian life by Bowen P Squire.

THE SULPICIAN ORDER (PARIS)
Missionaries to the Cayugas

Prince Edward County, which throughout these vicious wars was uninhabited, now began to attract the Indians. A group of Cayugas of the Five Nations, moved to the County. They named their village Kentio, which the French missionaries spelled Kente or Quinte. On early French maps the name was used for a variety of locations. The exact site of the village remains a mystery. However, we do know that 150 years before the capture of Quebec, and nearly 170 years before Canada was settled, there existed at the Bay of Quinte an active mission of Roman Catholic Christianity, entrusted to the Sulpician Order (Paris).

KENTE— FROM 1668-1680

Translated by Daisy Wannamaker from an article on Indian Life Style by Prof. P. Rousseau in the Montreal Bulletin, 1930.

The main reason for the coming of the Sulpician Brothers was to indoctrinate the native people into their Christian way of thinking. Eight Brothers or Black Robes were at the Kente Mission from 1668-1680, off and on. Most of these men travelled throughout New France founding other missions, but to Kente went the distinction of being the first European settlement in Prince Edward County and they established firmly the first Christian teaching in the area.

The Indians themselves took the initiative, asking for instruction, pastors and the need for missionaries and undertook the trip to Ville Marie (Montreal). A Monsieur de Queylus gave them a warm welcome and in the ensuing period of negotiation, Fathers Trouve and Fenelon accompanied the Indians back to the area of the Kente Mission. The *Bulletin* makes mention of settlements that had been established on the north shore of Lake Ontario for about three years.

The mandate of the Sulpicians was to reshape the thinking of the natives instilled previously by the Company of Jesus (Jesuits). The Sulpicians and the Jesuits were rivals for the souls of men.

The priests set out with their Indian friends on the Feast of Guardian Angels, appropriately, October 2, 1668 from Lachine. After 26 days of back-breaking travel and fatigue, they came to a peninsula off the mainland, with broken coastline, deep bays and winding coasts. They went around the south and came upon two bays on the south side: little Sandy Bay and big Sandy Bay. The latter emptied into the west (West Lake). This is the route taken into the Bay of Quinte— with its large trees, coming into a fiord with sunny, sandy beaches. Here was the reserve of Kentio; the missionaries called it Kente, the English Quinte. Five times the maps of Ontario changed the name depending on the tribes that succeeded in the area: Hurons, Algonquins, Iroquois, French, Mississagas, Ojibway and English.

Waiting at Kente was Rohiario, the chief of the tribe. With great joy and celebration, cooking pots were set up and a feast served, consisting of fried pumpkin in grease, which the missionaries thought was great food, comparable to anything in Europe. M. Trouve mentions another meal— sagamite (a soup) a combination of Indian corn (all they could hold in their hand) vegetables, fish, fat and sometimes dog. It was boiled and, as a sign of honour, an old woman might add some salt.

A Cayuga village at Kentio, from painting by Rev. Bowen P. Squire.

Kente Village Cayuga family, from painting by Bowen P. Squire.

The priests began teaching the catechism to 50 children, but when they approached the tribe to baptize them, the Indians believed it would cast a spell which would bring death. Chief Rohiario said to Trouve, "Father, baptism will kill the children, and if our children die, we will say that you have come to destroy the village." Trouve answered, "Do not fear, we French are all baptized and we are many." "All right," said Rohiario, "do what you want, you are the boss."

The ceremony took place in front of all the curious Indians, who were attentive, silent, respectful and touched by the ritual. At the head of all the children came the only daughter of Rohiario, the Chief, baptized Mary, a name signifying the first fruit of their labours for the kingdom of God. (1669)

During the winter, instruction into the preparation of baptism and preparing the aged for death was the primary concern of Trouve and Fenelon, Father d'Urfe returned to the mission to join in the work. The winter of 1669-70 was long and severe. Hunger was evident in the Kente Mission. The hardship and deprivation and the Indian manner of coping with the situation caused the missionaries overwhelming sadness.

In 1671, the mission comprised three villages and served the shores of Lake Ontario, not counting the families isolated in valleys and river areas. There were seven missionaries, with four new arrivals. Main buildings in the villages served for the education of the children, the care of the sick, disabled and aged. DeBretonvilliers, (Superior of the Seminary of St. Sulpice, Paris) sent implements, animals, furniture and materials to assist the mission, until his death in 1676. Then Governor Frontenac decided to build fortifications at the present site of Kingston, (Fort Frontenac) and with unstable political activities funding of the mission became an issue.

In May 1677, plans for the abandonment of Kente began to take shape. Trouve and Cice were the only missionaries left. Tronson (Superior in Paris) cited the reasons for the failure as Trouve's departure, the lack of order, waste and the "instability" of the Indian. He did feel that the establishment at Kente was to the glory of God and it had served the people well, for the missionaries had brought the Indian people a humanity that was not there before. The salvation of the Indian was the sole reason for the Kente Mission.

In 1680 the mission closed, ending an era. One cannot help but be impressed by the courage, zeal and dedication of "the Black Robes."

THE SEARCH FOR THE LOST MISSION OF KENTE

Where is the Lost Mission of Kente that Historians refer to as simply "The Lost Iroquois Mission?" When Reverend Bowen Squire, a retired Baptist Clergyman and renowned artist of Ameliasburgh Township, asked, "Where is the site where once the Cayugas raised their village of Kente?" he began to

Rev. Squire with part of his Indian Collection. Photo courtesy The Trentonian.

Rev. Squire excavating on his farm at Consecon Lake. Photo courtesy The
Trentonian.

search for a pattern for a route of travel. Several maps made of the region in the
17th century never pin-pointed the exact spot. Its position was described as
east of the Carrying Place (The Great Portage), east of Lac de Kente (Weller's
Bay) and in the western part of the County. Old records suggested the site was
so many days' journey west from Fort Frontenac. Canniff, author of *The
Settlement of Upper Canada*, believed the site was near the Carrying Place, at

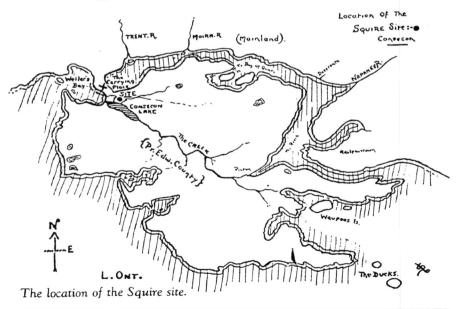

The location of the Squire site.

Bald Head Point, because relics of a religious nature had been found there. Many of the artifacts from Bald Head belong to the 'Chadd' collection now housed in the Royal Ontario Musuem, Toronto.

In 1957, Squire was given a small grant by the Archeological and Historic Sites Board of Ontario, to search out these suspicions. There was a definite lack of evidence on Bald Head, in Weller's Bay. Squire began looking elsewhere, working on the premise that the Mission was the central and largest village in a chain of villages on the mainland, stretching across the County of Prince Edward from the main Iroquois encampments south of Lake Ontario.

Armed with copies of original Jesuit recollects from France and records from British museums as aids, Squire set about a concentrated search.

West of the entrance to Hay Bay and across from the Long Reach was the source of a large, once navigable creek known as Allisonville or Pearsoll's Creek, which flows into Consecon Lake, which then was an inlet of Weller's Bay. Along this route Squire found sites three and four miles apart. By autumn 1959, within a ten-mile circle around Consecon Lake, he found the sites of six large villages and a number of burial grounds. The largest site, situated on the north side of the lake, on lot 96, concession four of Amelias-burgh Township, was Mr. Squire's own farm.

Kente Farm
c. 1798

Kente Farm
c. 1850

Excavating was done on the site from 1951 to 1964 and several hundred artifacts were discovered. Over 100 designs on pottery shards alone have been listed. Archeologists believe that several cultures from the pre-historic to the Canadian historic are represented.

Many of the artifacts were identified by Thomas Lee, a field representative from the National Museum of Man in Ottawa. The late Professor T.F. McIlwraith of the University of Toronto, who spent time at the site, was convinced that here was the site of the Lost Mission, even though the greater part of it is now under Consecon Lake because the lake is much larger due to the dams that were built circa 1806.

For some time the Squire Site was an interesting attraction for archeological students and tourists. It was always Mr. Squire's hope that government funding might help restore Kente in the same way that Huronia was developed, so there would be an historical site at each end of the Trent-Severn Waterway. He offered the site to any level of government that would open the log house that was on the farm, as a museum. No one was interested.

After 20 years of research and labour on the farm, the Squire family sold it. A plaque in the village of Consecon, a cairn in Wellington and the Ameliasburgh Public School, named Kente School, are reminders of the past. Not so much as a sign guards the former Squire site.

If one visits the Ameliasburgh Museum, you will see a part of the collection of artifacts from the Squire site. With his great talent for painting, Mr. Squire has preserved on canvas many historical events. Many of his paintings depict the life of the Indian and the history of the Kente Mission.

As Canadian poet Charles Sangster noted in the poem *The Red-Men*, in the Township of Ameliasburgh, "we seem to wander over hallowed ground."

The Red-Men[1]

My footsteps press, where centuries ago,
The Red-Men fought and conquered; lost and won
Whole tribes and races, gone like last year's snow,
Have found the Eternal Hunting Ground, and run
The fiery gauntlet of their active days,
Till few are left to tell the mournful tale:
And these inspire us with such wild amaze,
They seem like spectres passing down a vale
Steeped in uncertain moonlight, on their way
Toward some bourn where darkness blinds the day,
And night is wrapped in mystery profound.
We cannot lift the mantle of the past:
We seem to wander over hallowed ground:
We scan the trail of Thought, but all is overcast.

By Charles Sangster, 1822-1893

[1] *Kingston Hist. Soc. No. 11, 1963*

Janet MacDonald holds an ancient war weapon which belonged to the Cayuga Indians. This relic was discovered by Bowen Squire on the north shore of Lake Consecon. Backed by a grant from the provincial Ministry of Culture and Recreation, she concentrated on the history of Ameliasburgh, particularly Indian Culture. Below: Artifacts from the township.

Janet MacDonald and a display for Indian Day at the Ameliasburgh Museum, 1978.

THE END OF FRENCH CONTROL IN QUINTE

Fort Frontenac, also known as Fort St. Louis, became the first French fort on Lake Ontario. It had originally been planned for the site of the Kente Mission which had been a listening post for the feelings and the movements of the Iroquois Indians.

Le Marquis de Denonville became the governor after Frontenac was recalled to France in 1682. He decided that some Iroquois tribes were too strongly in league with the British to be trusted. In 1687, he invited chiefs of the Iroquois to a feast at Fort Frontenac. There he seized about 50 braves, 80 women and children of the 'Kentes', tortured some and sent them as galley

Capture of Fort Frontenac in 1758 by Col. John Bradstreet. Painting by B.P. Squire.

slaves to France. In retaliation, the Iroquois slew several hundred people around Montreal and it was not until 1701 that peace was restored. The Iroquois Confederacy sided with the British and returned to their haven south of Lake Ontario. The Mississagas, a branch of the Ojibway tribe moved to the north shore of Lake Ontario and trading was resumed around the Bay of Quinte.

During the Seven Year War (1756-63), Canada became British, Fort Frontenac was burned and French control in and around the Bay of Quinte ended. A Royal Proclamation in 1763 invited British subjects to take up land in the new Dominion, but Ontario was out of bounds as reserved for Indians.

TROUBLE IN BRITISH NORTH AMERICA

The Treaty of Paris (1763) ended the Seven Years' War and gave Britain control over the eastern half of North America, a vast empire with many possibilities and problems.

For a time all appeared to go well, but urgent problems arose. The difficulty of reorganizing such a vast and complex empire was a cause for unrest. In Canada for example, the French-Canadians came into dispute with the English-speaking merchants. The British Government unwisely imposed trade restriction and taxes upon the Thirteen Colonies, who by this time felt strong and independent after a century of growth.

By 1773, radicals in the Thirteen Colonies began to openly oppose British regulations of 'Intolerable Acts'. The Quebec Act (1774), gave French-speaking Roman Catholics the usage of their laws, free exercise of their religion, language rights and all privileges and advantages of British subjects. These actions helped fuel the revolution, and the following spring the first shots were fired that ended in the division of the North American Empire and the creation of the United States.

The Revolution in the Thirteen Colonies had really been a civil war in which the population was torn with conflicting loyalties. Those who had remained loyal to the Royal Government during the war were treated harshly. Loyalist sentiment was strong and widespread and no one foresaw the exodus of thousands of new settlers who changed the course of Canadian History. Many became the ancestors of today's residents of the Township of Ameliasburgh.

LOYAL TO THE BRITISH CAUSE!

In 1774 Sir William Johnson, who had been a master of Indian diplomacy in the Johnstown area of New York and throughout the Mohawk Valley, died. His son John and nephew Guy assumed the leadership of the Mohawk Valley Loyalists, together with John Butler and Joseph Brant, the Mohawk Chief.

Because the Johnsons and their followers had stayed with the Royal cause, they had to retreat to Canada with Butler in 1776. Here at Montreal they organized the King's Royal Regiment of New York and the corps which became known as Butler's Rangers. As time passed, more and more fighting Loyalists of the north were forced to retreat, and by 1780 they were being received at camps in Three Rivers and Sorel. Here the Governor of the Province of Quebec, a Swiss professional soldier, General Frederick Haldimand, was making arrangements to feed and clothe the refugees and giving consideration to settling them on the land. As more and more exiles moved out of New York State and headed into Quebec province, a formidable task faced General Haldimand, but the British Government had pledged support.

Haldimand sent the Surveyor General, Major Samuel Holland, up the St. Lawrence in May 1783 to begin surveys to provide, not for the Loyalist, but for the Indian. However, the surveyors were so impressed by the 'fair lands' along the river and around the Bay of Quinte, that their report stated: "I think the Loyalists may be the happiest people in America by settling this country." Haldimand was made aware that the Indians were not adverse to the Loyalists living among them and would feel more secure from their enemies. Besides, there was plenty of land for all.

BARGAINING FOR LAND

Haldimand had to secure the Crown's title to land for the newcomers, and then arrange for its disposition. No private purchases were allowed from the Indians; formal treaties were to be made instead.

Each treaty was solemnized by the giving of presents. Canniff wrote: "Every man received two blankets, cloth for one coat and one pair of trowsers, two shirts, several small articles, besides a gun, ammunition, kettles and other things." The Indians went to Kingston annually to receive their presents from the government; sometimes there would be a hundred canoes.

In 1782, Sir John Johnson was appointed Superintendent General of Indian Affairs for British North America. He was to oversee the elimination of Native rights by purchases or treaties, where early settlement was beginning close to the St. Lawrence and Lake Ontario. In October 1783, the Crawford Purchase had secured land from the Mississaugas extending from Gananoque to the Trent. The Indians retained some land, including most islands in the Bay of Quinte, 1200 acres on Mississauga Point, one hundred acres on Bald Head Point, Weller's Bay and what is now the downtown section of Belleville. Other purchases were made at later times so Upper Canada maintained a friendly Indian Frontier.

One of the most important treaties made with the Mississaugas was transacted in Ameliasburgh Township, at The Carrying Place in 1787.

THE CARRYING PLACE

Carrying Place is located in the north west corner of the County of Prince Edward where a narrow isthmus connects it with the mainland. This isthmus separates the arm of Lake Ontario known as Weller's Bay from the Bay of Quinte. The distance between the two bays is 1¾ miles, and is famous as an old Indian Portage.

On Sept. 23, 1787, Sir John Johnson and other Government

representatives for the King, along with 600 Chiefs and Indians, met here for an important meeting.

The Gunshot Treaty, from a painting by Bowen P. Squire.

THE GUNSHOT TREATY
The Carrying Place, Sept. 23, 1787

Here at the Carrying Place, where that important meeting was held, the Gunshot Treaty was signed, by which the Indians released all their territory along the lakefront and northerly, supposedly as far as a firing gun could be heard or, more likely, it was because gunshot was among the gifts exchanged. In reality, thousands of acres of territory had been ceded away.

A report of the Gunshot Treaty read: "On Sept. 23, 1787, there met at the Carrying Place, at the head of the Bay of Quinty, all the Mississauga Indians, with Major Ross and Captain Louis Prottle and Nathaniel Lines and 'Wabukoyn, Neace and Parquan', (who signed by their totems). Presents were distributed and the north shore of the Bay of Quinty bought, following an agreement of Oct. 1783."

The cairn at Carrying Place.

On Oct. 16, 1934, the Historic Sites and Monuments Board of Canada erected a cairn to commemorate the signing of the Gunshot Treaty, on the spot where the Great Portage crosses Highway 33. A plaque on the cairn records in both English and French the following inscription:
"The Historic Carrying Place— Here 23rd September, 1787, Sir John Johnson concluded the treaty with chiefs of the Mississauga Indians, by which they ceded to the Crown, lands extending westward from the Bay of Quinte to Etobicoke River and northward from Lake Ontario to Lake Simcoe and Rice Lake".

CHAPTER 4

EARLY SETTLEMENT

When the American Revolution ended, the Thirteen Colonies which had belonged to Britain became the independent United States of America. Those colonists who had opposed independence and remained loyal to Britain called themselves Loyalists. All through the war Loyalists had made their way to Canada, and quite a number were in the army, but when the war ended, many were still in their homes. Their property was confiscated and they were persecuted so harshly that they were forced to flee with only the few possessions they could carry with them. Many sought shelter in New York City behind British lines. The British had held New York City since Sept. 15, 1776.

General Sir Guy Carleton, commander of the British forces in America, took charge of the evacuation of the British troops at New York, the German mercenaries who had been assisting them, and any of the Loyalists who wished to leave. Carleton gave out rations and clothes and transported many thousands by British ships to Nova Scotia. General Washington was urging Carleton to get out of New York, but Carleton refused as long as there were families making their way from the interior into the city. In fact, he did not yield it up to the Americans until Nov. 25, 1783.

Among those awaiting transportation out of New York was Michael Grass who had been a prisoner of war of the French at Fort Frontenac during the French and Indian War. He persuaded a group of refugees of the desirability of resettling in the Cataraqui area, then went to Carleton with the suggestion that they be transported there. He also approached another group under Peter Van Alstine, and they agreed to go to the Cataraqui area also. Carleton made ships available, and they set out for Quebec Province, under the escort of a British naval ship. At that time this part of Canada was included in the British province of Quebec. By the time they reached Quebec small pox and measles had broken out on board the transports. They proceeded up the St. Lawrence to Sorel, below Montreal, where they spent the winter of 1783-84 in huts and tents.

There were also wintering at Sorel many disbanded Loyalist soldiers and their families. At the close of the war the Colonial soldiers were serving on the northern frontier. In the fall of 1783 some of their wives and children from the Mohawk valley and the upper Hudson made their way through swamps and forests to Lake Champlain, where they were transported by boats to Sorel via

Lake Champlain and the Richelieu River. Not all the families came at this time. In many cases the disbanded soldiers took up their lots, and later returned to the States, risking imprisonment, to get their families.

In the spring of 1784, both groups started for Cataraqui in large flat-bottomed boats called batteaux, which were propelled by men with poles. They travelled in convoys of 12 boats, with four or five families in each boat. It was a long and arduous journey because of the many rapids.

The plan was for ten towns (townships) to be surveyed from Cataraqui west to the head of the Bay of Quinte, but only five were undertaken in 1784. The survey was started in September of 1783 under Surveyor General Samuel Holland. Holland and his men worked furiously to get enough lots measured and marked before the settlers arrived.

First Town was Cataraqui, settled by Grass and his New York band of associated Loyalists. Second and Third Towns were settled by the disbanded Loyalist soldiers and their families. Van Alstine and his party settled in Fourth Town, landing at Adolphustown on June 16, 1784. British soldiers and a few discharged German soldiers settled in Fifth Town (Marysburgh). Some of the Loyalists who settled the first four townships in 1784 later came to Sixth and Seventh Towns.

The Loyalists received their land grants by lot. The number of each lot was written on a separate piece of paper, and all were placed in a hat and well

Drawing Lots, Painting by Rev. Bowen Squire

Seventh Town/Ameliasburgh

shaken. Each one to receive land drew a piece of paper from the hat, and the number he drew was the number of his lot. The Surveyor acted as a land agent, arranging the time and place for the settlers to draw. The Surveyor had a plan of the township, and as each drew his lot, his name was written immediately upon the map.

Each married man was allotted 100 acres, and 50 acres for each member of his family. Single men were granted 50 acres, privates 100 acres. Officers received more, according to their rank.

Other Loyalist families were coming in overland, singly and in small groups. They came on foot, by ox-cart, and by river and lake. The most commonly travelled route was to follow the Hudson River to the point where it divides, then to take the west branch (the Mohawk River) and from thence, by portaging, reach Lake Oneida and on to Lake Ontario by the Oswego River. Others followed the Lake Champlain route, or routes which brought them to the present day Cornwall or Ogdensburgh. At Cornwall, the Loyalists could swim their horses or cattle across the river. Often families about to come to

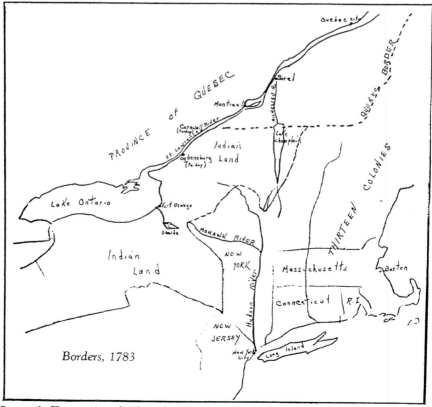

Borders, 1783

Canada would build Schenectady boats to traverse the rivers and lakes. These were small, flat-bottomed boats rigged with a sail.

The Loyalists also came north in the winter, several families travelling together in a train of sleighs. As well as clothing, bedding and a few treasured possessions, they had to carry sufficient provisions for themselves and the horses for the journey. The 'French train' was also used by the winter travellers. It consisted of a long, rough sleigh with several horses driven tandem style; this allowed passage through the trees to be made more easily.

Early in the year of 1785, Lieutenant Kotte was order by Major Holland to start a survey at the very top of South Bay (Picton Bay) and follow the High Shore eastward to Green Point, laying it off in 44 lots of 200 acres each; thence around this point and commencing at Grassy point to begin a survey along the Bay of Quinte westward 64 lots to form the Sixth town, where a road allowance was to be left between Sixth and Seventh town. To continue with Seventh town, the survey party had to move north and start at the Bay of Quinte at Lot 65, continuing westward to Lot 106. Later five more lots were surveyed from Lot 65 east to the Point (Rossmore). A base line was established along the waterfront. All that was done in that first survey was to measure 20 chains width across the frontage, and leave a stake or blaze to mark the lot boundary. Each lot was to contain 200 acres with a frontage of 1320 feet and a depth of 6,600 feet (1¼ miles). The surveyor's chain was 66 feet long, made up of 100 links, each measuring 7.92 inches.

There were many inaccuracies. Because of the irregularity of the shoreline, many lots contained much more than the 200 acres intended. It often happened that the base line, running from one cove of the Bay to another, left a large strip of land between it and the water. This 'broken front' belonged to the adjacent 200 acres, so some fortunate settlers often received 50 extra acres or more.

At first only the lots along the water were marked out. Later the second line was laid out at a distance of a mile and a quarter from the first. The distance from one line to the next was called a concession, a term derived from the French. At the front line there was an allowance of 60 feet for a road, and at the second line for one of 40 feet. Between every six lots, a strip of 40 feet was supposed to be left for a crossroads. In their haste in Ameliasburgh, the surveyors omitted three crossroads. It was 1787 before the survey of the front of Ameliasburgh was completed.

A muster roll of the various townships in October 1784 in the Public Archives, Ottawa, shows the following for Seventh Town:

Lewis Mosher	1 man	1 woman	no children	man on land
Nathan Brown	1 man	1 woman	no children	gone to Cataraqui
John Bradford	1 man		has never joined	
Peter Hegedorn	1 man		has never joined	

So only one man, Lewis Mosher, was on his land in Seventh Town in the fall of 1784, and he settled later below Kingston.

As an additional bounty to Loyalist soldiers, on June 4, 1787, Lord

Survey of 1st Concession 1787

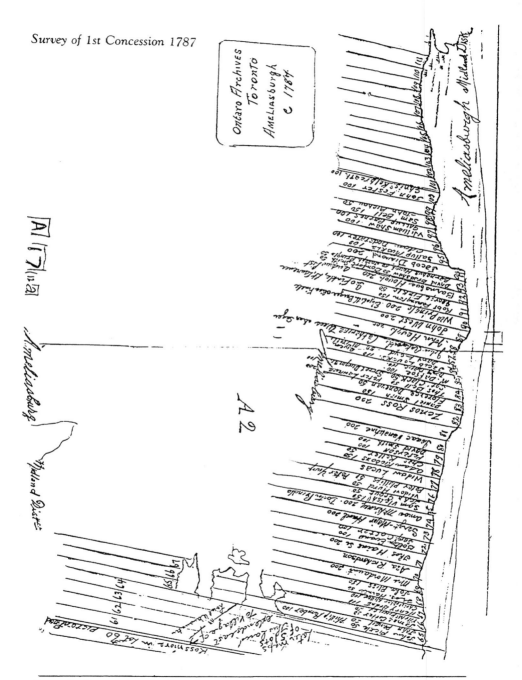

COPY OF ORIGINAL MOTION

"At the Council Chamber at Quebec, --Monday 9th November, 1789
Present:
His Excellency the Right Honorable Lord Dorchester.
The Honorable William Smith, Chief Justice,

Hugh Finlay,	George Pownall,
Thos. Dunn,	Henry Caldwell,
Edwd. Harrison,	William Grant,
John Collins,	Francois Baby,
Adam Mabane,	Chas. Delanaudiere,
J. G. C. Delery,	Le. Cte. Dupre

"His Lordship intimated to the Council that it remained a Question, upon the late Regulation for the Disposition of the Waste Lands of the Crown, whether the Boards, constituted for that purpose were authorized to make Locations to the Sons of Loyalists, on their coming to full Age and it was his wish to put a Mark of Honor upon the families who had adhered to the Unity of the Empire, and joined the Royal Standard in America before the Treaty of Separation in the year 1783.

"The Council concurring with his Lordship it is accordingly Ordered, That the several Land Boards take Course for preserving a Registry of the Names of all Persons falling under the Description aforementioned to the End that their Posterity may be discriminated, from future settlers, in the Parish Registers and Rolls of the Militia, of their respective Districts, and other Public Remembrancers of the Province, as proper Objects by their persevering in the Fidelity and Conduct, so honorable to their Ancestors, for distinguished Benefits and Privileges.

"And it is also ordered, that the said Land Boards may in every such case provide not only for the Sons of those Loyalists, as they arrive to full Age, but for their Daughters, also of that Age, or on their Marriage assigning to each a Lot of Two hundred Acres, more or less, provided nevertheless that they respectively comply with the general Regulations, and that it shall satisfactorily appear that there has been no Default in the due Cultivation and Improvement of the Lands, already assigned to the Head of the Family of which they are Members.

J. WILLIAMS, C.C.

Copy of Order-in-Council

Mary (Babcock) Wanamaker —
"U. E. having preferred to this Board a Petition addressed to his Excellency the Governor in Council for a Grant of Two Hundred Acres of Land, in the Township of *Ameliasburgh Twp* in the District of *Mecklenburgh* under the foregoing Order, we have examined into *her* Character and Pretensions, and find that *She* is duly entitled to the benefit of the said Order, being the *daughter* of *John Babcock - Ensign* ——— U.E."

Daughter of a Loyalist U.E. receiving grant

Seventh Town/Ameliasburgh

Dorchester, Governor-in-Chief of Quebec, by Order-in-Council conferred an additional 200 acres, free from any expense whatever, on those who had joined the colours in America previous to the Treaty of Separation in the year 1783. A later Order-in-Council on Nov. 9, 1789 conferred a mark of honour upon the families who had adhered to the Unity of the Empire and joined the Royal Standard in America before the Treaty of Separation. They were entitled to use the Mark of Honour, U.E. affixed to their name. The Land Boards were instructed to preserve a Registry of the names of all persons entitled to this Mark of Honour. This Order-in-Council also conferred 200 acres to each of the sons and daughters of those Loyalists falling under the description aforementioned, as they arrived at the age of 21, or the daughters at their marriage, providing the head of the family had not defaulted on his land. To prove they were truly U.E.'s, these soldiers had to appear before a Quarter Session of Magistrates with documents such as a discharge certificate or an affidavit from the officer under whom he had served. This qualification was necessary if he and his children wished to receive their Dorchester Bounty. The children also received their land free of all charges.

The first permanent settler in Seventh Town was John Weese in 1787. Weese, as a private in the King's Royal Regiment of New York, was mustered out and given 100 acres of land, ½ of Lot 6 (with his son John Jr. receiving the other ½ Lot 6), concession 2, 3rd Town (Fredericksburgh) where he settled in 1784 and improved his land. As a family man with a wife and five children, Weese was also allowed 300 acres, Lot 89, 1st Concession of Seventh Town as family land. In 1787 he moved from Third Town to the Bayshore of Seventh Town and settled on the property where his descendants still reside. Having improved his first land in Third Town, he also received in 1787 his Dorchester Bounty— 200 acres, Lot 89, 2nd concession of Seventh Town. It would appear Weese lost the 200 acres in the 2nd concession, not having made improvements on same, for we find it under the name of the Honourable Richard Cartwright in June of 1794. Weese is said to have assisted with the survey of Seventh Town.

Thomas Dempsey was the second permanent settler in the township. Dempsey came to Canada by Oswego in 1788, accompanied by his wife, three children and his wife's parents, Mr. and Mrs. Peter Lawson. They spent a year at Napanee, then came to Seventh Town in 1789 and settled on the east ½ of Lot 89, concession 1, which Dempsey had purchased from John Finkle. Dempsey's wordly goods consisted then of a cow which they brought with them, seven bushels of potatoes and a French crown, also a half acre of wheat which Finkle had sowed. During the first years they were in great distress. A tablespoon of flour boiled with milk, or grain shelled by hand, formed their daily meals. The clothing consisted of blankets obtained from the Indians for the women, and buckskin pants and shirts for the men.

Dr. Canniff gives the following account: "At one time there arose a wide spread alarm that the Indians were, upon some fixed nights, going to massacre the settlers. This arose from some remarks let fall by a half-drunken Indian.

Mrs. Dempsey gathered up what she could, and with her children, including a day old baby, crossed in a canoe to Eighth Town (Sidney). On another occasion when her husband was absent, Mrs. Dempsey saved her life and the children's from drunken Indians by rushing up a ladder with them into the garret, which could only be reached by a small opening through the ceiling, and then hauling the ladder up. The Indians endeavoured to assist each other up and through the entrance, but she, having a knife, succeeded in keeping them back by cutting their fingers when they attempted to get up. These hostile acts were exceptions, and always the result of intoxication."

The County, as it was first laid out, was made up of only three townships- Fifth Town (Marysburgh), Sixth Town (Sophiasburgh) and Seventh Town (Ameliasburgh). Seventh Town included all of what is now Hillier and a small part of Hallowell, as well as all the present Ameliasburgh.

Canada was not known as 'Canada' in 1784— the British called it "Our Province of Quebec in America." In 1777 civil and criminal courts had been established in Quebec. After the arrival and settlement of the Loyalists, additional Justices of the Peace were appointed in the western portion of the Province, but without provision for any Courts. In all but minor matters, recourse had to be in the Courts of Montreal, which was a great inconvenience.

The Loyalists had been accustomed to British laws and local self-government in the Colonies. They objected strongly to the existing conditions and demanded separation from the French. At length on July 24, 1788 the Governor-in-Chief, Lord Dorchester, issued a proclamation dividing the new settlements to the west of the French limits above Montreal into four districts, given the German names of Lunenburg, Mecklenburg, Nassau and Hesse. Seventh Town was in Mecklenburg, which extended from the mouth of the Gananoque River as far westerly as a north-south line intersecting the mouth of the Trent River. In each of the districts, authority was given for establishing a Court of Quarter Sessions. These Courts went into operation in 1789. In Mecklenburg, Richard Cartwright, a prominent Kingston political and business man, was named judge.

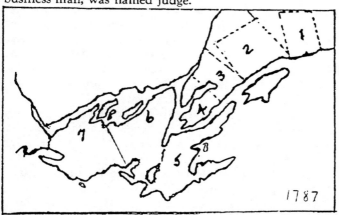

1787

Map of first
7 towns

The Constitutional Act of 1791 further satisfied the Loyalists as it divided Quebec into Upper and Lower Canada, with the settlers in Upper Canada to have their own legislative assembly and freehold land tenure.

On Feb. 3 1791, the Surveyor General gave instructions to "Survey and run the Second and Third concessions in the Townships of Marysburgh, Sophiasburgh and Ameliasburgh and Fix the boundaries of the said lots in said concession, to cost:

1 surveyor	60 days @ 7/6 per diem	£ 22 10s
10 men	60 days each @ 1/4 per diem	£ 40

One third of the land in each concession was reserved for Crown and Clergy. In the first concession, the Government reserved the 5th, 15th and 20th lots, and the Clergy the 3rd, 10th, 17th and 22nd. In the second concession the Crown reserved the 4th, 11th, 21st and 23rd; and the Clergy the 2nd, 9th and 16th. Thus in every two concessions the Crown would have three lots in one and four in the other, or seven in all, and the Clergy the same. This made it very hard for the settlers who had to open roads across these empty lots.

Many settlers began to take up land in Seventh Town in the 1790's. Some were not content with their first locations, like Robert Young who came to the Carrying Place from New Brunswick, or Robert Wilkins who settled in Nova Scotia before coming to Seventh Town. Others who had lived for several years in one of the first four Towns later moved to Seventh Town, like John Babcock who settled in Fourth Town in 1795, then came to Seventh Town in 1798, or Henry Redner who came up from New Jersey in 1791 but did not come to Seventh Town until 1798.

Loyalist sons and daughters came of age and took up their grants in Sixth and Seventh Towns. People continued to arrive from the United States. Sometimes they would tarry a while in the older townships and 'work out' or rent land, and later move to permanent locations in the more remote townships such as Seventh Town. Some of those who settled in Seventh Town in the 1790's were John Bleecker, John Post, David Sager, James Peck, Jacob Bonter, Lewis Brickman, Owen P. Roblin, Peter Crouter, six Wanamaker brothers— Peter, Jacob, Henry, Andrew, Thomas and Harmanus, Elias Alley, Henry Herman, Benjamin Gerow, Philip Reddick, Jacob Corbman, and James Henessey. Many others arrived in the early 1800's as Godlove Mikel in 1801, Henry Tice in 1803, Elijah Wallbridge in 1804 and William Anderson in 1806.

These pioneers endured great hardships and privations. Their first homes were log cabins, hewn out of the forest. The windows often were covered with oiled paper. Chairs, tables and beds were fashioned by hand from rough wood. When clothing wore out, the settlers had to make clothes of deerskin, like the Indians. Clearing the forest with axe and fire was a slow and difficult task. The following account relates some of the difficulties of pioneer life:

"My great grandmother was born here in 1791. As a little girl I sat on a stool close to her, and asked her all sorts of questions about life in the wilderness.

Stump Pulling, Painting by Rev. Bowen Squire

She said it was all forest, and they had no stoves, just fireplaces. She said they had no matches, so they tried not to let the fire out. They would bank the coals all up good, and if the fire did go out they would have to go through the woods for coals to someone else's home, maybe a long way off. I said, "Well, Grandma, you must have been scared for fear of getting lost. How did you ever find your way home?" "Oh", she said, "We blazed the trees, so we could find our way." She said they had no lamps. I said, "How did you see?" "Well", she said, "We had candle moulds and made candles from tallow." She told me how wolves used to roam about at night, and she was very afraid of them too. If they saw a window lighted up at night, they would howl around the house. They had no clocks but they got very good at telling time by the sun. When the sun was in the middle of the sky, they knew the day was half gone. Grandma said there were no schools. Of course, that was bad as they could not read the Bible, so her father or mother read it to her. Then she told me about sewing. They had to make everything by hand— quilts and all their clothes. Then she said they had no sugar, only what they made from maple trees. They had to make their own soap, and carry all the water. Life was very hard when Grandma was a little girl."

The Loyalists were a mixture of nationalities, cultures and religions, representing all the people who settled in the Thirteen Colonies. Most of them were farmers, but there were also millers, blacksmiths, carpenters, shoemakers, tailors and tanners. They made an impact out of all proportion to their numbers. This part of Canada would very likely have been taken over by the Americans had it not been for the settlement of the Loyalists.

Cradling Grain,
painting by
Rev. Bowen Squire.

For years there was plenty of land to be had for a small sum or a horse or cow. There were those who drew land and never saw it; it was thoughtlessly sold for little or nothing. Others became discouraged with the hardships of life in the wilderness, and were willing to sell their land for very little. A few did not keep their lands because they were located in the rear concessions, and so were regarded as hardly worth having. Sometimes settlers upon the front, who had drawn land also in a more remote area, disposed of the latter to obtain the immediate necessities of life, such as clothing, stock or seed grain. There were persons in prominent positions who realized the future value of these lots and stood ready not only to accept offers to sell, but to induce the careless and ignorant to dispose of their claims. Richard Cartwright was one of those who bought up any lots available. At his death in 1815, Cartwright owned 27,552 acres, 3,100 acres of which were in Ameliasburgh Township, consisting of the following:

#95	1st concession	400 acres	# 2	3rd concession	200 acres
# 5	2nd concession	100 acres	# 3	3rd concession	200 acres
# 6	2nd concession	200 acres	#61	3rd concession	200 acres
#86	2nd concession	200 acres	#62	3rd concession	200 acres
#89	2nd concession	200 acres	#63	3rd concession	200 acres
#94	2nd concession	200 acres	#65	3rd concession	200 acres
#96	2nd concession	200 acres	# 7	lake side	200 acres
#97	2nd concession	200 acres			

John Graves Simcoe was named the first lieutenant-governor of Upper Canada. In 1792 he divided Upper Canada into 19 counties. Prince Edward was named for the fourth son of King George III, Edward, Duke of Kent. Simcoe also changed the names of the districts, so that Mecklenburgh became the Midland District. Believing that there were many Loyalists still in the United States, Simcoe offered free land to all those who would take a loyalty oath, build a house, clear at least five acres, and make a road across the front of their land. This offer attracted may late settlers to Upper Canada.

In 1795 the first Registry Act was passed, under the title of an "Act for public registering of deeds and conveyances, wills and other encumbrances which shall be made or may affect any lands, tenements or hereditaments within the Province."

English standards for weights and measures were established also in 1795. The magistrates at Quarter Session were required to appoint an Inspector to stamp the various measures in commercial use. From time to time powers and duties of the Courts of Quarter Session were enlarged until they covered quite a variety of subjects, even the amount to be charged for a loaf of bread, as we see from the records of a Session at Kingston, September 1796.

"The average price of flour being 20 shillings, it is ordered that the assize of Bread for the four pound loaf of fine wheaten flour be 9 pence currency, and a brown loaf weighing six pounds be 9 pence currency. The bakers are ordered to mark the loaves with the initials of their name."

In 1798 the original districts were sub-divided. Midland District was composed of the Counties of Hastings, Prince Edward, Lennox and Addington and Frontenac. Each district had its own Quarter Session Court and Justices of the Peace to administer the affairs of the municipalities.

Because of many problems with survey posts, the second Provincial Parliament in July 1798 made it a Capital Felony to disturb survey monuments. The Act reads as follows— "That if any person or persons shall knowingly and wilfully pull down, deface, alter or remove any such monument so erected, he or she, or they, shall be adjudged guilty of a Felony and shall suffer death without benefit of Clergy."

In 1797, parts of Fifth, Sixth and Seventh towns were set aside to produce Hallowell. Both the 1825 survey plan of Sophiasburgh and that of Hillier state: "... when the late Surveyor General, the Honourable David William Smith, formed the Township of Hallowell out of the Townships of Sophiasburgh, Marysburgh and Ameliasburgh... 22 October 1825 W.C."

By an Act in 1823 a Township was separated from the Township of Ameliasburgh and named Hillier Township, to come into effect on Jan. 1, 1824. The division was established between concession 4 and 5, with Ameliasburgh being Bay side concessions No. 1 to and including No. 4 concession, and Hillier to be concession No. 1 Lake side to and including concession No. 5.

CHAPTER 5

Municipal Affairs

Counties were created in 1792, but only for the purpose of organizing militia battalions, registering land titles, and electing members of Parliament. The districts administered local government through Justices of the Peace in Courts of Quarter Session. The J.P.'s were appointed by the Governor and were in no way responsible to the people. In the Midland District they met twice yearly in Adolphustown and twice yearly in Kingston. They levied and disbursed the taxes, built roads and bridges, court houses and gaols, granted licences to tavern keepers and ferry operators, set the ferry rates and paid the wages of members of the House of Assembly. They sometimes remained in session for a week.   In July 1793 the Municipal Act was passed authorizing the town meeting form of local government. However the authority to call a public meeting rested with the J.P.'s. The town meetings were held annually to elect a township clerk, a tax collector, two assessors, a pound keeper, and overseers of roads and fences.

For a number of years (from 1809 until 1817 at any rate) Ameliasburgh was linked with the County of Hastings rather than with the rest of Prince Edward County for representation in the Legislative Assembly. From the Quarter Sessions held at Kingston, 25th April, 1809 we have the following: "It is ordered by the Magistrates in Sessions that the sum of twenty-three pounds be allowed James Wilson member of Parliament for the County of Prince Edward, excepting the Township of Ameliasburgh. It is ordered that the sum of eighteen pounds ten shillings be levied from the County of Hastings and the Township of Ameliasburgh for James McNabb Member of Parliament."

Elections were very exciting affairs in the early days. Instead of several polling booths throughout each township as we have now, there was only one in the whole electoral district and people came 'pouring in' from all parts of the district. The open vote and the presence of whiskey gave rise to many heated discussions and fights.

In 1830 John P. Roblin of Ameliasburgh was one of the two members from Prince Edward County elected to the Legislative Assembly, Asa Werden being the other one. Roblin was elected again in 1835, defeated in the next election, but elected again in 1841 and in 1844. He was a prominent member of the old Reform party. In 1831 Prince Edward County separated from the Midland District and became a separate Prince Edward District. In 1841, Roblin went to the first session of the United Province of Canada.

In 1841 the District Councils Act was passed which reduced the authority of the Court of Quarter Sessions and gave some control of municipal affairs to the municipalities themselves. The Warden, Treasurer and Clerk were Crown appointees but each township was entitled to send one councillor to the District Council for every 300 freeholders and householders. In 1842 Ameliasburgh sent two members to the District Council— William Dempsey and Owen Roblin. The district councils had the authority to enact by-laws concerning schools, roads, bridges and public buildings.

In 1849 the Municipal Corporation Act was passed, which provided for the incorporation of counties, townships, towns and villages, with power to elect councils, appoint officers and conduct local affairs. Township councils were to be made up of five members, one of whom would be elected reeve by the others. Thus it was that the Township of Ameliasburgh was incorporated in 1849 and divided into five wards, each electing a councillor.

The first meeting of the Municipal Council of the Twp. of Ameliasburgh was held on Jan. 21, 1850 at the house of David Coleman. The councillors for their repsective wards were:

Carrying Place Ward— Reuben Young
Center Ward— William Dempsey
Roblin Lake Ward— Owen Roblin
Consecon Ward— Thomas G. McGrath
Rednersville— Samuel S. Wallbridge.

Wm. Dempsey was appointed reeve and R.C.H. Cotter appointed clerk. Assessors, tax collectors, overseers of roads, fence viewers and pound keepers were appointed.

The second meeting, Feb. 4, 1850, was held at John Pulver's in Rednersville, where it was decided to hold the sessions of Council alternately at Rednersville and Consecon. The township was divided into road divisions and the several overseers of roads were furnished with their road list and instructions. By-laws were passed for the regulation of fences and for the regulation of horses and cattle running at large.

Both the January and February Council meetings of 1851 were held at David Coleman's, likewise the first meeting in 1852. In May of '52 it was moved that the sum of 15 shillings be paid David Coleman "for attendance on the Council and candles furnished." Some of the meetings were held elsewhere in the years following, one in 1854 was at the house of Hector Howell, and one in 1855 at the house of John Carnrike.

The system of five wards continued until 1866. In December of that year a place of nomination was designated for the nomination of candidates for the office of reeve, deputy-reeve and three councillors.

The 1898 Ameliasburgh Township Council, standing: James P. Benson—clerk, Wm. A. Brickman— treasurer. Seated: Daniel Howe— deputy-reeve, Byron Frederick— councillor, Edward Anderson— reeve, John H. Parliament— councillor, David Stafford— deputy-reeve.

For some reason the 1863 Council decided that both the Clerk and Treasurer must be residents of Roblin's Mills. The minutes of Dec. 1863 read: "Whereas it is the opinion of this Council that the Clerk of this municipality do live at Roblin's Mills, it being the most convenient place, it is therefore moved by W. Whittier, seconded by P. Roblin, that Chas. Drewery do act as Clerk in the place of S. Meacham, and that the Council do now dispense with the services of S. Meacham.

"Moved by W. Whittier, seconded by P. Roblin that the Council dispense with the services of Jas. Redner as Treasurer of the Municipality after the books of the Township are audited, and that J. Sprague do act as Treasurer in the place of said Jas. Redner."

The matter of building a Town Hall was brought up many times, but it was not until 1874 that action was finally taken. A site was purchased from David Coleman and the hall built, as described in the chapter on Roblin's Mills. From that time on Council met in the Township Hall.

Work on the early roads was carried out by statute labour. Each inhabitant was required to work several days a year on the roads, this work being supervised by the pathmasters. In Ameliasburgh, statute labour was abolished in 1928 by Council under Reeve W.H. Montgomery and Deputy-Reeve Earl

Will McFaul drawing gravel for statute labour c. 1910.

Statute Labour on Bryant sideroad.

It took several teams to pull Ernest Wallbridge's V snow plough through the drifts on Huff's Island road c. 1936.

Bonter. They purchased a power maintainer which was kept busy scarifying, re-shaping and widening township roads. In 1930 a crusher and bin was purchased. Since then many pieces of road equipment have been added and large buildings erected to house them.

Building Bonter's Sidewalk (Rednersville Road) in 1930.

The first Ameliaburgh Township dump truck c. 1940.

William Nightingale, township clerk 1963-1977.

Ameliasburgh Clerk-Treasurer 1984, Jary Plamondon.

Mrs. Verna J. Sills, treasurer 1961-1971.

Ameliasburgh Township Barns, 1984.

In 1966 an addition was built on the township hall, consisting of clerk's office, vault, washrooms and kitchen. Previous to 1966 the clerk's duties were carried out in his own home. The official opening of the addition was held in June 1967 in connection with the Township's Centennial celebrations and the opening of its Centennial Park. This land was formerly used as fair grounds but had not been used for years. The grounds were levelled, hundreds of tons of sand dumped on the beach, a play area with swings and slides provided as well as a flood-lighted ball diamond and bleachers. This was the township's project for Canada's Centennial, under the reeveship of George Cunningham.

Garbage collection began in Ameliasburgh Township on Feb. 16, 1970, with Quinte Sanitation having the contract. In February of 1971 the township bought its own garbage truck.

In 1980 another addition was put on the Township Hall. This provided new office space and council chambers. The official opening was Aug. 20, 1980 and the expanded offices were dedicated to the former clerk, William Nightingale.

Ameliasburgh Township Hall, 1984.

Clerks of the Township of Ameliasburgh

R.C.H. Cotter 1850-1852
John Platt 1852-1854
Simon Meacham 1854-1863
Charles Drewery 1864-1871
John C. Richards 1871-1874

Henry Webb 1875-1877
James Benson 1877-1907
Fred File 1908-1951
Tom Walker.......... 1951-1963
William Nightingale 1963-1977
Jary Plamondon 1977-1984

Treasurers of the Township of Ameliasburgh

William Brickman 1850-1859
James Redner 1860-1863
John Sprague 1864-1875
William Delong 1875-1886
W.A. Brickman 1886-1900

James E. Glenn.......... 1901-1930
T. Ashton Sills 1931-1961
Verna J. Sills........... 1961-1971
Brian Smith 1971-1973
James Boyce 1974-1975
Jary Plamondon 1976-1984

Reeves and Deputy Reeves
of Township of Ameliasburgh, 1850-1968

Year	Reeve	1st Deputy	2nd Deputy
1850	Wm. Dempsey		
1851	Wm. Dempsey		
1852	Owen Roblin	Clark Whittier	
1853	Owen Roblin	H. Weese	
1854	Sylvanius Sprague	James Jacques	
1855	Sylvanius Sprague	James Jacques	
1856	Sylvanius Sprague	James Jacques	
1857	Sylvanius Sprague	James Jacques	
1858	Sylvanius Sprague	James Jacques	
1859	Sylvanius Sprague	Peter Dempsey	
1860	Peter Dempsey	Samuel S. Wallbridge	
1861	Peter Dempsey	Edward Brady	
1862	Sylvanius Sprague	Philip Roblin	
1863	Sylvanius Sprague	Philip Roblin	
1864	Sylvanius Sprague	Wm. B. Whittier	
1865	Sylvanius Sprague	James Young	
1866	Sylvanius Sprague	James Young	
1867	Sylvanius Sprague	Philip Roblin	
1868	Sylvanius Sprague	George Roblin	
1869	Henry B. Hunt		
1870	Wm. Anderson	Wm. R. Dempsey	
1871	Wm. Anderson	Reuben Young	
1872	Wm. G. Stafford	James M. Squires	
1873	Wm. G. Stafford	James M. Squire	
1874	Wm. G. Stafford	Wm. R. Dempsey	
1875	Wm. R. Dempsey	Joseph Nightingale	
1876	Wm. R. Dempsey	Joseph Nightingale	
1877	Wm. R. Dempsey	Joseph Nightingale	
1878	Joseph Nightingale	James A. Johnson	
1879	Joseph Nightingale	James A. Johnson	
1880	Wm. Anderson	Royal Hermon	
1881	Wm. Anderson	Peter V. Beech	
1882	Wm. Anderson	Peter V. Beech	James Glenn
1883	Wm. Anderson	Peter V. Beech	James Glenn
1884	Wm. Anderson	J. Benson Morden	Samuel Gilbert Way
1885	Peter V. Beech	R.H. Hunt	Wm. Peck
1886	Peter V. Beech	James Glenn	Harmon W. Weese
1887	Wm. R. Dempsey	James Glenn	Harmon W. Weese
1888	Wm. R. Dempsey	Harmon W. Weese	John Nightingale

Year	Reeve	1st Deputy	2nd Deputy
1889	Harmon W. Weese	John Nightingale	
1890	James E. Glenn	John Nightingale	D.E. Minns
1891	John Nightingale	Wm. E. Delong	Thomas Wadsworth
1892	John Nightingale	Wm. Peck	Wesley Weese
1893	Wm. Peck	James E. Glenn	Wm. E. Anderson
1894	Wm. E. Anderson	James E. Glenn	S.W. Dempsey
1895	Wm. E. Anderson	David W. Robinson	Wm. C. Killip
1896	Wm. E. Anderson	David W. Robinson	Wm. C. Killip
1897	David W. Robinson	Daniel A. Howe	John G. Peck
1898	Wm. E. Anderson	Daniel A. Howe	David F. Stafford
1899	Wm. E. Anderson		
1900	Wm. E. Anderson		
1901	David W. Robinson		
1902	Daniel A. Howe		
1903	Daniel A. Howe		
1904	David Adams		
1905	Wm. W. Anderson		
1906	Wm. E. Anderson		
1907	Harry Dempsey		
1908	Harry Dempsey	W.A. Tont	
1909	Harry Dempsey	Wm. Nethery	
1910	Wm. S. Nethery	John H. Parliament	
1911	Wm. S. Nethery	John H. Parliament	
1912	Wm. S. Nethery	John H. Parliament	
1913	John H. Parliament		
1914	W.W. Anderson	W.W. Ward	
1915	W.W. Anderson	George Cunningham	
1916	W.W. Anderson	George Cunningham	
1917	W.W. Anderson	Fred Chase	
1918	Fred Chase		
1919	David W. Robinson	R.H. Fox	
1920	David W. Robinson	R.H. Fox	
1921	David W. Robinson	Jas. E. Robinson	
1922	David W. Robinson		
1923	David W. Robinson	John A. Weese	
1924	John A. Weese	W.J. Reddick	
1925	John A. Wesse	Geo. S. Wallbridge	
1926	John A. Weese	Geo. S. Wallbridge	
1927	Fred Chase	W.H. Montgomery	
1928	W.H. Montgomery	E.E. Bonter	
1929	W.H. Montgomery	E.E. Bonter	
1930	E.E. Bonter	C.H. Cook	

Year	Reeve	1st Deputy
1931	E.E. Bonter	John A. Walker
1932	Fred Chase	Robert Zufelt
1933	R.H. Zufelt	James Barber
1934	R.H. Zufelt	James Barber
1935	James Barber	S.M. Peck
1936	James Barber	S.M. Peck
1937	James Barber	S.M. Peck
1938	James Barber	C.S. Peck
1939	James Barber	Howard Weese
1940	Howard Weese	J.A. Dymond
1941	Howard Weese	Earl Onderdonk
1942	Howard Weese	Earl Onderdonk
1943	Earl Onderdonk	I.A.E. Nightingale
1944	Earl Onderdonk	Jerald Anderson
1945	Earl Onderdonk	N.E. Whitney
1946	N.E. Whitney	Harry Redner
1947	N.E. Whitney	Thomas Walker
1948	N.E. Whitney	Thomas Walker
1949	N.E. Whitney	Thomas Walker
1950	N.E. Whitney	Thomas Walker
1951	Thomas Walker N.E. Whitney	Melvin Pulver
1952	Melvin Pulver	Wm. Nightingale
1953	Melvin Pulver	Wm. Nightingale
1954	Melvin Pulver	Wm. Nightingale
1955	Melvin Pulver	Clifford Smith
1956	Melvin Pulver	Clifford Smith
1957	Melvin Pulver	Clifford Smith
1958	Melvin Pulver	Clifford Smith
1959	Clifford Smith	Harmon Montgomery
1960	Harmon Montgomery	Arthur Miller
1961	Harmon Montgomery	Arthur Miller
1962	Harmon Montgomery	Arthur Miller
1963	Arthur Miller	Harold Bonter
1964	Harold Bonter	George Cunningham
1965	Harold Bonter	George Cunningham
1966	Harold Bonter	George Cunningham
1967	George Cunningham	Laird Adams
1968	George Cunningham	Laird Adams
1969	George Cunningham	George Cunningham
1970	Russell Thompson	Norman Post
1971	Russell Thompson	Norman Post

Year	Reeve	1st Deputy
1972	Russell Thompson	Norman Post
1973	Russell Thompson	Roger Redner
1974	Russell Thompson	Roger Redner
1975	Arnold Wetherall	Gordon Babbitt
1976	Arnold Wetherall	Gordon Babbitt
1977	Gordon Babbitt	Paul Boyd
1978	Gordon Babbitt	Paul Boyd
1979	Paul Boyd	Klaus Werkhoven
1980	Paul Boyd	Klaus Werkhoven
1981	Dan Brady	Klaus Werkhoven
1982	Dan Brady	Klaus Werkhoven
1983	Dan Brady	Ronald Carter
1984	Ronald Carter	Bill Bonter

Ameliasburgh Wardens of Prince Edward County

1842-1847 . . . . Jacob Howell	1919 . . . . R.H. Fox
1850 . . . . John Howell	1926 . . . . John A. Weese
1876 . . . . W.R. Dempsey	1929 . . . . W.H. Montgomery
1884 . . . . William Anderson	1937 . . . . James Barber
1889 . . . . Harmon Weese	1944 . . . . Earl Onderdonk
1894 . . . . James E. Glenn	1950 . . . . Norris Whitney
1898 . . . . William G. Killips	1957 . . . . Melvin Pulver
1901 . . . . Peter V. Beech	1961 . . . . Harmon Montgomery
1903 . . . . D.W. Robinson	1966 . . . . Harold Bonter
1909 . . . . Harry Dempsey	1973 . . . . Russell Thompson
1917 . . . . W.W. Anderson	

Ameliasburgh Members of Legislative Assembly

Term of Office

John P. Roblin	1830-1835	Nelson Parliament	1914-1919
	1835-1836		1919-1923
	1841-1844	Norris Whitney	1951-1955
	1844-1847		1955-1959
William Anderson	1862-1863		1959-1963
	1870-1871		1963-1967
Wm Ryerson Dempsey . .	1862-1863		1967-1971

Ameliasburgh Member of the Federal House

John Aaron Weese 1930-1935

CHAPTER 6

'THE' CARRYING PLACE

The Carrying Place Centennial Float, 1967

The Carrying Place

The narrow isthmus that joins Prince Edward to the mainland at the Carrying Place is about a mile and three quarters wide. This separates the Bay of Quinte from Lake Ontario. Here it was that from time immemorial, travellers followed a road which leads, to this very day, from water to water. The Mississaugas called this portage "de-ga-bun-wa-kwa", meaning in English, "I pick up my canoe." The Iroquois named it "Chappatagan". It was the "Holiest of Holies" to the Indians.

Here in the northwest corner of Ameliasburgh township, this mocassin-worn trail, this busiest thoroughfare in the country, even though there were other carrying places, became for all time *the* Carrying Place.

Our Village
by Lillian Leveridge

Carrying Place— a simple village now
That looks upon the world with kindly eyes.
No mill or factory clamours break the peace,
The quietude that round about her lies.
Hers are the unassuming country ways,
The still, blue nights, the cheerful, busy days.

She hears a far-off echo of the thunder
Of armies in collision, grim and dread;
Nearer, with note of challenge and of wonder,
The droning air-planes flashing overhead.
This is today. And yet her dreams are deep
Of days long gone and valiant hearts that sleep.

This winding street between two placid waters,
Ontario and Quinte, was a trail
Followed by Indian braves, a shadowy portage
Where birds and wild flowers beautified the vale.
Before Columbus came, it well may be,
The Redmen trod this trail untrammelled, free.

The wheels of change revolve relentlessly:
Hither the pioneers of empire came.
With avid eyes they viewed the lovely land
Far reaching, and on these fair leagues laid claim.
Here where the cairn now stands, the chieftains met
And signed the Gunshot Treaty, valid yet.

The wheels of change and chance are never still.
Once it was thought to build a city here,
The capital, perhaps, of this domain.
But destiny was pointing otherwhere:
So while Toronto blossomed into fame
The quiet village kept its own quaint name.

In still blue nights when not a sound is heard,
Come there not softly up the moonlit street
Pale Presences with dusky waving plumes,
That round the cairn and in the old church meet,
Whispering, whispering of long-dead days
Harmlessly haunting the old Carrying Place?

Carrying-Place, at the Head of the Bay of Quinte.

This 1830 drawing is from the centre of Carrying Place, looking south west on the Portage Road. It is the dividing line between Ameliasburgh township in Prince Edward County on the south side, and Murray township in Northumberland on the north side. Here at the Carrying Place was the 'turnabout' for William Weller's 'Coach and Four' running from York to Prescott. On the right side of the drawing one may see the sign of the tavern kept by Benjamin Young, and further along the spire of St. John's Anglican Church. The white house on the left belonged to Peter Harris.

Head of the Bay of Quinte, from the Carrying Place

An 1830 drawing on the east end of the Portage. The first house on the left is that of Charles Biggar. The last house on the left, next to the bay, is that of Capt. Robert Wilkins. Indian Island is closest to the shore.

The southwest end of the Portage, looking toward Weller's Bay, named for the enterprising teamster, Asa Weller. The log blockhouse on the right of the drawing was built on an elevation for a good view of Lake Ontario, in order to protect this strategic position.

The three water color drawings were done by Capt. Thomas Burrowes, R.E.D., Overseer of Works for the Government of Upper Canada. He had overseen the construction of the Rideau Canal, and in his travels about the St. Lawrence River and Lake Ontario made drawings of the various areas.

Three Weller Houses

Because of its position, The Carrying Place was considered to be a settlement with a future. Asa Weller, one of its first white settlers, foresaw the potential and founded a boat-hauling business that took bateaux across The Carrying Place on low-wheeled trucks drawn by oxen. In 1805, along with his son, he expanded his operation into one of the first stage lines in Upper Canada running from Prescott to York, and including sections of the Bay of Quinte to Weller's Bay, the western end of the Portage.

About 1806, Asa Weller considered building himself a good sturdy house. It would be of brick, the first one at The Carrying Place, with a stone foundation, and situated on the north side of the Portage Road. It would be a simplified country style, two storeys, the facade having five windows above, and two on each side of a plain front door. At each end would be a fan window lighting the attic. A brick lean-to at the back was to be used for a summer kitchen. The fireplaces were to be downstairs only, their mantels having sunburst' patterns after the designs of Robert Adams. To complete the

The first Asa Weller permanent home 1808.

Asa Weller's 'Tap House' or 'Middle House', 1810.

building required nearly three years. Today Mr. and Mrs. Frederick Quinn occupy this first historic house of Asa Weller, and they are hoping to restore it.

On completion of his own house about 1808, with the increased activity along the Portage Road, and the looming prospects of war, Asa Weller and his son decided to construct an inn and taphouse for travellers. This time he located a little to the east of his own house and on the south side of the Portage, again building of stout brick. An elegant Greek Revival plan was chosen, having a two-storey, square-fronted central section with Greek-arched roof-line. A splendid door topped with an arch was centred between one window on each side, with three windows at the second level, and a graceful fan window above. A one-storey wing on each side extended the house and added four more windows to the first floor. The central section contained numerous bedrooms, and an upper ball-room. The tap room and dining room were on the lower floor, the side wings reserved for parlours and sitting rooms, each with a fireplace. An urgent need for its use commercially speeded up its construction which was accomplished about 1810 in time for the traffic and business created by the War of 1812. Thereafter, this second house became known as 'The Tap House'. Presently the owners are Mr. and Mrs. Thomas Quinn, who are restoring it.

The Miskin-Weller House, 1828

The third house with an Asa Weller connection is the one known as the Miskin-Weller house, or locally, the Corrigan house, now occupied by Mrs. Emil Klingspon. Located east of 'The Tap House' on the Portage Road, it was built in 1829 by Richard Miskin, a ship's carpenter, for his bride Sarah Weller, the first white child born at The Carrying Place, and daughter of Asa Weller. It is considered an outstanding example of fine country Georgian architecture of the 1820's, long and shallow, of red brick, its chimneys balanced at each end of the house, with five windows at the second level, and four at the first separated by a centre hall and doorway.

Mr. Miskin sheltered his doorway with a neo-classical porch. In 1869 a one-storey kitchen to the west was added. A regional detail peculiar to Prince Edward County is the style of doors on the second floor, each having five panels. On the building of this third Weller house, 'The Tap House' became known as 'The Middle House'; another version has 'The Middle House' so-named because it was midway on the Portage road.

An excursion to these three homes is, indeed, a pleasant experience, reminding us currently of Asa Weller, Carrying Place's far-sighted pioneer who initiated the first stage lines in Upper Canada.

Weller's Coach and Four at The Carrying Place, 1830

The Carrying Place Turnabout

Asa Weller was one of the first stage-coach operators in Upper Canada. Coming into contact with the travelling public and noting their needs, he and his son, William, established a bi-weekly stage-coach service between the Carrying Place and York, about 1830. It connected with the steamer 'Sir James Kemp', which left from Wilkins wharf at the eastern end of the Portage and carried passengers on to Prescott.

William Weller advertised in *The Christian Guardian*, June 12, 1830: fine new coaches with four horses, carefully driven, horses and drivers changed every 15 miles, their 'turnabout' at the Carrying Place.

A description of the stage-coach era is given in *Pioneer Life Among the Loyalists in Upper Canada* by W.S. Herrington, K.C., who was born in Ameliasburgh:

"The very term, stage-coach, suggests to our minds a spanking four-in-hand, in brass-mounted harness, attached to a gayly-decorated conveyance. We picture them dashing through a village under the crack of the coachman's whip. Away they go, rattling over the bridge, down the turnpike, and with a shrill blast of the guard's horn, they haul up at the wayside inn, where a fat and smiling landlord escorts the passengers in to a hot dinner. Such were not the stage-coaches of our forefathers: they were simply lumber wagons without springs, and covered with canvas like the prairie schooners, or plain wooden enclosures with seats suspended by leather straps. Just think of being cooped up in such an affair from sunrise to sunset— the clumsy 'coach' jolting over the rough roads, dodging stumps, rocks and fallen trees, plunging down a steep embankment, fording rivers and streams, and sinking now and then to the axles in mud!

"During the summer months the mosquitoes and black flies added to the misery of the travellers. Even so, in this, as in all things, the pioneers looked not so much on the dark side of life as on the bright. The distance had to be covered; every jolt and bump brought them nearer their destination. The tales of the fellow travellers were entertaining and helped to shorten the way. Perhaps one was a legislator just returning from a meeting of the House, perhaps a merchant on his way to Montreal to make his year's purchase of goods, or a young adventurer from the old country spying out an opportunity to better himself in the New World. The forest had its charms, although the insects at times were abominable. As the coach passed through a clearing the yeoman, with a swing of his hat, would wish the travellers God-speed. The monotony was broken, time and again, by a glimpse of a bay or lake; and the road, in places followed the beach, where the waves broke under the horses' feet. Awaiting them at the journey's end were the rest and peace which the home alone can afford, that bright welcome of the fireside built with their own hands, and the smiles of the loved ones who had shared all their trials and victories."

William Weller was proud of his timetable record. In 1840, at the request of Governor-General Lord Sydenham, a dash to Montreal, 350 miles away, in order to reprieve a man from the gallows tested his reputation. He completed the journey in 35 hours and 40 minutes, in time to deliver the governor-general and save the man's life.

The Robert Young Homestead

Late in 1792, Robert Young, ex-captain and engineer in the British Navy, arrived on the Carrying Place Portage from Nova Scotia leaving the Loyalist settlement of Annapolis to take up land. He was the second permanent settler, preceded by Asa Weller who had been living on the trail a couple of years.

Cap't Young was a personal friend of John Graves Simcoe, first Lieut. Gov. of Upper Canada, and as a Justice of the Peace he was entitled to a land grant of 1200 acres in order to establish himself. Lieut. Gov. Simcoe encouraged his friend to take his land along Yonge Street in the present Toronto, an area for which a bright future was prophesied. But Young favoured the site at the Carrying Place and took part of his acreage there on the south side of the trail reaching west to the bay, establishing his family in a temporary log house across the road from the log quarters of his neighbour, Asa Weller. His remaining acres he took along Lake Ontario and Pleasant Bay.

Throughout the 1790's and early 1800's there was ever-increasing traffic and business along the Portage. Asa Weller's bateaux were kept busy transporting boats over the isthmus. The North West Company chose the route to send some of its canoes of furs to the east. The Weller stage coach was carrying travellers and mail. All this activity gave rise to employment and new businesses.

There was need for hostelries. Already, Asa Weller was accepting guests in his log quarters, while planning a new house. About 1805, Cap't Robert Young, close to 70 years of age, along with his son, James, who had married Asa Weller's daughter, Catherine, in 1804, considered building their permanent house. From time to time they had reason to entertain members of the militia, and other prominent passers-by. Then, too, Cap't Young had been made a justice of the peace, was performing marriages, and needing appropriate facilities. No longer was the log house adequate for the expanding family and its requirements.

Plans were made for a spacious home of frame, within sight of the bay. The space for its cellar was excavated by Young's own slaves. Over the next three to four years the house gradually took shape. Its kitchen was located in the cellar, Dutch-style, its large fireplace having a swinging crane, and on one side a bake oven. A pine floor and a flagstone were in an addition attached to the west end of the house, and reached only by way of the cellar kitchen or an outside door. On the main floor there were two more fireplaces having handsome mantels. For his parlour ceiling Mr. Young chose an extraordinary moulding done in plaster. A Dutch-style verandah ran the length of the main house with an enclosed gable-porch in the centre at the second storey level, from which one could view the activities on the bay and up and down the Portage road. The house was finished in 1808.

The Youngs were noted for their hospitality in their home. As justice of the peace, Robert Young was popular, marrying couples from far and wide. All of his sons became officers of the militia. As well, James became a member of Parliament. One can imagine the entertaining that ensued.

Robert Young House, 1808

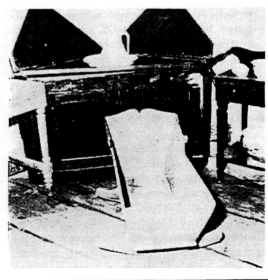

*Furniture in
Robert Young House*

Seventh Town/Ameliasburgh

During the War of 1812, the house and its property was a haven for troops and officers using the Portage short-cut. At one time, two regiments of as many as 2,000 troops met and camped on the Young farm. The area was also used to billet prisoners captured in battle at Queenston and being transferred to Kingston. Among the several outbuildings were a tannery and blacksmith shop. The original log home became a store. Business flourished at the Young homestead.

Robert Young conveyed his property to his son James in 1809 before the war. James and his wife, Catherine Weller, who raised their family on the farm, both died in 1831, the house and farm passing to their eldest son Reuben, born in 1805. Today, Blake Young's family, Marjorie, Ted and Elmer, would call Reuben their great-great grandfather and could boast of their ancestors, both Robert Young and Asa Weller, the two first families to settle at the Carrying Place. For more than 150 years the homestead was occupied by the Young family.

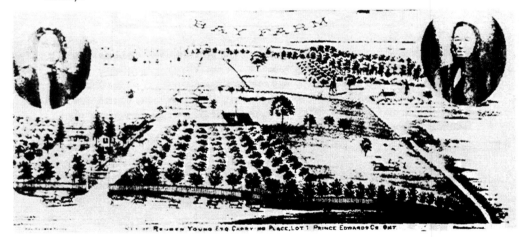

From Belden's Atlas 1878

The Empey Hotels

The first Empey Hotel at the Carrying Place was busy during the building of the Murray Canal. Sir John A. MacDonald stayed there while in the area to turn the first sod in 1888 for the construction of the canal. According to *The Trenton Courier* of Feb. 21, 1899, "On Tuesday morning the Empey Hotel at the Carrying Place was destroyed by fire."

A new Empey House (Hotel), shown in the accompanying picture, was built on the southwest corner of the intersection with the present Highway 33, just west of the present Post Office. The Empey family is shown on the front porch; the little girl became Mrs. Ernie Bonter. Mrs. Empey married James

Hendricks later. For awhile James Snider ran the hotel, before it burned in 1925, when it was owned by a Mr. Martin.

Sept. 19, 1907— Carrying Place: Mr. Stanley Empey is spending a few days at his home.

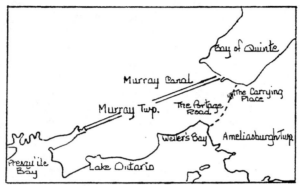

The Portage Road at the Carrying Place. Note the Murray Canal in relation to the Portage Road. As early as 1800 there were proposals for a canal, which Governor Simcoe considered very necessary. It was the first canal ever contemplated in Canada, and in early reports was referred to as the Simcoe Canal. Work started on the Murray Canal in 1888. With the completion of the canal, traffic and business shifted from the portage Road and by-passed the Carrying Place.

The second Empey Hotel

The Carrying Place School

School Section No. 1 Murray and No. 5 Ameliasburgh

The Hallowell Free Press noted in an article of October 27, 1834 that the population of the Carrying Place was about 200 and that the village had "a school-house which was occasionally used for religious purposes by the tribes of wandering priests of every denomination by whom this Province is thronged".

In 1841, grants were given to counties for educational purposes and in 1843 the townships were divided into school sections. The log school houses of former times began to be replaced and records preserved. The school records in the Carrying Place were fairly continuous after 1852. In that year, R.C. Dyre was the teacher with a salary of 40 pounds, and the school term ran from March to December.

In 1858 a monthly tax of one shilling was levied on every pupil, but this ended in 1859 with free schooling and a property tax. Each family with children contributed a cord of wood, cut and ready for the stove.

A new school was planned for 1873. To finance the building, $400 was borrowed from Murray Township and $400 from Ameliasburgh Township, since the old Portage Road divided the Carrying Place into two school sections. Debentures were issued and retired in five years. By 1884 a partition was put across the one large room, and the Carrying Place had a two-room school.

By the 1950's the old school had become hard to heat, too costly to maintain, and was overflowing with pupils. A new school was opened in 1954, located to the east of the old one in Murray Township and along Highway 33. St. John's Anglican Church purchased the old school for $1.00 and used it for awhile. Again, upkeep was too expensive, and so it was demolished. After the introduction of County School Boards in 1969, there was a re-shuffling of students, some to Murray Centennial. The school population generally declined through the 70's, and the Carrying Place school was no longer required; it closed in 1977.

In some old records, the first caretaker listed is Robert Newman in 1878 at the salary of 6 Dollars for one year". A long list of teachers, beginning in 1861 through to 1939, indicates that many of them stayed only one to two years, with very few exceptions. From September 1920 to December 1928, Charles L. Jones taught, studied for a university degree, and left to teach in Toronto at East York Collegiate. Lela Black (Mrs. Cecil Blakely) spent nine years from 1930-1939. Elsie Fitchett (Mrs. Vernon Westfall) began her teaching career in the Carrying Place in 1924, continued to 1927, then moved to Young's School, S.S. 10 Ameliasburgh where she spent nine more years. She returned to the Carrying Place in 1936 and remained until she retired, after more than 40 years of teaching. The last principal, Gwen Smith (Mrs. Pat Herrington), commenced in 1954 and completed a span of 23 years when the school was closed in 1977.

1929 Entrance Class, Carrying Place School

1950-51 Carrying Place School

Early History of St. John's Anglican Church

It was in 1824 that an Irishman, Rev. John Grier, established the first local parish of the Church of England at the Carrying Place. Also, he conducted services at Picton, Rossmore, Wellington, Hillier, Consecon, the Trent and Brighton. In 1841 he left the Carrying Place for Belleville to St. Thomas's.

St. John's Anglican Church

The first church, a frame building, was struck by lightning and burned in 1885, and a new church was built. The progress of the re-building of the new church was reported in the *Trenton Courier:*

October 29, 1885— "This ancient wooden specimen of no order in architecture has been levelled with the ground, much to the regret of the aged inhabitants of the neighbourhood in whose eyes it seemed to be a necessary element in the landscape. It was an uncouth structure, and therefore it is well that it should have been made to yield to the spirit of progress under whose inspiration a gothic successor is rapidly rising from the old foundation. That correctness of architectural detail, beauty of form, and harmony of parts have been insured needs no further proof than the fact that the architect whose plans are closely followed is Thomas Fuller, Esq. author of the Central Department of the government buildings at Ottawa and generally known as an English ecclesiastical architect of eminence.

"On Thursday last 22nd inst, Oct., at noon aided by several clergymen and as well as very kindly by the choir of St. George Church, Trenton, the corner stone of the new building was laid by Reuben Young Esq., to whose generous liberality joined to that of Mrs. Cochran of Belleville, and late of Trenton, the congregation acknowledge themselves as mainly indebted for a church which when completed will bear comparison with any other in a rural parish in the diocese.

"The materials of the old building are being integrated into the new, a veritable reformation, when veneered with red and white brick, and the new tower, embracing the entrance in the south-west corner and specially erected to carry the bell, large and sweet toned, is completed, the effect will be extremely pleasing to the eye. The interior roof is open and ceiled with ¾ inch tongued, grooved and beaded strips diagonally, which together with the massive timbers, cross ties, etc. will be stained and varnished. A large and commodious chancel affords ample space for extraordinary services. The nave will easily seat 250 persons. The building committee are thus far fortunate in the contractor for the wood work, as well as the masonry, the latter being done by Mr. Jas Burr of Brighton. The respective works are being energetically pushed forward to completion to enable the congregation to occupy the building in two or three week's time. The ladies, ever alive, wise in their generation, and never sparing of effort, utilized so far the opportunity presented by the large gathering to witness the laying of the Corner stone as to realize a sum ultimately it is expected not far from one hundred dollars. They have undertaken the work of providing all interior furnishings.

"Many a grateful thanks are tendered to several kind friends among Methodist families of the neighborhood for the warm interest manifested in large contributions of provisions. Their presence at the tables, which seated some 300 persons, and participation in the hospitalities which they bountifully contributed to promote afforded much pleasure to all the Church members. A favorable augury, let us hope of a near and more real union in faith, worship and discipline, no doubt mutually hoped for and certainly being consummated."

October 29, 1885— "A CARD- The Rev. L.A. Morris, Rector of Ameliasburgh desires to acknowledge very gratefully the receipt of fifty dollars from D. Gilmour Esq., in aid of the building of St. John's Church, Carrying Place, now in course of erection."

October 29, 1885— "LOCAL NEWS - The new Anglican Church at the Carrying Place can be seen from our mountain."

November 26, 1885— "This really handsome building will, we are informed, be formally opened for Divine Service on Thursday, 17th of next month, December, at the hour of two o'clock p.m. There will be a full choral service rendered by a large choir, that of St. George's Church, Trenton. The service will be by the venerable the Archdeacon of Kingston, followed by short addresses by several clergymen. We believe that the Central Ontario Railroad, with its unusual considerate liberality, will take passengers to and from the Carrying Place at a single fare. The service will be so timed as to enable passengers to avail themselves of the 1:25 p.m. train from Trenton, and of the 5:55 p.m. train returning. This new church is worth a special visit as a model

THE CARRYING PLACE UNITED CHURCH

It is estimated that the first Wesleyan Methodist Church at the Carrying Place was built 1834-38, on land probably donated by the Charles Biggar family who were influential parishioners. Located on the north side of the Portage Road, it was a large white frame, with its parsonage across the road on the south side, in Ameliasburgh. The church was part of the Murray circuit established in 1833-34 and extending from Brighton to Picton.

A devastating fire around 1907 destroyed much of the Carrying Place including, the by now, Methodist Church. However, the congregation rallied and a new church of cement blocks arose on the same site, its corner stone laid in 1909. Again, the Biggar family, this time J. L., donated $500.00, and a stained glass window. Sheds beside the church later became a de-tached hall. The building began to settle and in 1913 buttresses were added to strengthen the walls. The strain of meeting bills became so great that in 1917 it was decided to close the church, although the congregation had just finished paying for it.

Nevertheless, the Ladies' Aid continued to meet, held socials, bazaars and suppers, and with a persistent dedication petitioned for re-opening. This, accomplished in 1931, the Carrying Place United Church, joined the charge along with Salem, Hillier and Consecon.

Financial problems dogged the church until, in 1943, it had to close again. But, re-opened in 1951 with a capacity crowd, the church has progressed continuously these last thirty years and more.

"The Trenton Courier", September 26, 1907,
The Carrying Place

Hurrah for the Harvest Home Dinner the Ladies' Aid intend holding on Mr. A. C. Pierson's lawn on October 1st in aid of the Building Fund of the Methodist Church.

Carrying Place United Church

of what a country church ought to be, not a mere agglomeration of building material but a poetic embodiment of the spirit of solemnity and devotion."

Former Anglican rectory. The first rectory was a log building facing on 'The Carrying Place' road. When the first storey of the present brick edifice was added on, it became the kitchen, which is why the addition did not face the street. In 1904, the Rectory was enlarged by raising the height to two storeys as shown by the distinct line of demarcation between the two types of brick.

Mar. 19, 1885— The ladies of St. John's Church, Carrying Place will give a tea on Friday, the 27th inst., in Row's Hall for the benefit of the Sabbath School. A good programme. All cordially invited.

1873 from *The Gazetteer of British North America*— In Murray or the Carrying Place there were two tanneries, a hotel, four store and a Church plus 200 people.

The Naming of The Carrying Place Post Office

Up to the year 1913, there was no such thing as The Carrying Place Post Office. From the day it was opened (the records before Jan. 1, 1857 are not available), the post office was known as 'Murray'. Its first postmaster appears to have been Reuben Young, but no date was given. The record of postmasters is as follows:

January 1, 1857, James L. Biggar
October 1, 1861, R.O. Dickens
January 1, 1874, Peter Rowe
February 1, 1877, R.J. Corrigan

October 1, 1885, T.J. Spafford
May 1, 1893, John A. Preston
February 1, 1894, Agnes F. Preston
September 1, 1899, Harry A. Boyce
March 17, 1911, C.M. Westfall

In 1911, when C.M. Westfall was appointed postmaster, he began an appeal for a change of name for the post office from 'Murray', which was the name of the township in which half of the village was located, to 'The Carrying Place' with its historical background. He solicited the help of Carrying Place born W.H. Biggar, K.C., General Counsel for the Grand Trunk Railway Company of Canada.

The following letter is Mr. Westfall's copy of one sent by Mr. Biggar to Hon. L.P. Pelletier, Postmaster General, requesting the change of name:

March 7, 1913

Hon. L.P. Pelletier,
Postmaster General, Ottawa
My Dear Minister:-

I have just received a letter from the Postmaster of Murray Ont., stating that a petition is before you asking that the name of this post office be changed to 'The Carrying Place'. As I was born at 'The Carrying Place' and both my Grandfather and Father for years filled the position as Postmaster, I naturally have considerable interest in the matter. I have often felt in my own mind that 'Murray' was not an appropriate name for the post office, that being the name of the surrounding township in which several other post offices are located. I presume, however, that the post office at 'The Carrying Place' was the first one established in the township. It certainly dates a long way back, as I have in my possession a letter addressed to my Grandfather then Postmaster which bears date 15th, February, 1825. You no doubt have been informed of the reasons why the name 'The Carrying Place' was given to the isthmus which connects the Counties of Northumberland and Prince Edward and lies between the Bay of Quinte and what is known as Weller's Bay. The latter even within my recollection was landlocked with exception of a narrow channel, but long ago the beach between it and the Lake began to wash away and today the outlet is probably between one and two miles wide. I have always understood that in the early days it was much used as a portage for the reason that it not only formed a safer means of communication between the east and west by avoiding the dangers of navigation around the County of Prince Edward, but was also shorter. Be that as it may, the name 'The Carrying Place' is that by which the way across this isthmus has for a very many years been known, and to my mind if you were to approve and authorize the change in the name of the post office, you would be only doing that which should have been done before. 'The Carrying Place' has a distinctive place in the history of Upper Canada and a post office bearing the name could be immediately located by any student of history; while on the other hand to such a student the present name means nothing. Personally I need not assure you that the position has my most cordial support and I feel certain that all the surviving members of our family would take the same view.

Yours faithfully,
(Sgd.) W.H. Biggar

Apparently Mr. Westfall's petition and Mr. Biggar's personal appeal impressed the Postmaster General sufficiently, for 'The Carrying Place Post Office' became a reality.

Murray Post Office and General Store c. 1900

Murray P.O.

The post office and store was kept by Agnes (Hele) Preston and her husband, John A. Preston, until his death 1893. Later it was known as the Boyce Store when she married Harry Boyce in 1889. At this point the 'Middle House' was owned by the Boyce family. Agnes and Harry moved to Kingston where he became a medical doctor.

This building was across the road from the present post office. There was a boardwalk between the store and the Buchanan farm which was west of St. John's Anglican Church. The store burned c. 1911.

St. John's Community Hall, Carrying Place

By W.D. Hanthorn

Although this hall was sold to Vernon Westfall in 1968 and demolished to provide parking space, it played such a large part in the lives of all in this area that it holds many happy memories for all that attended the parties and dances held there. It certainly does for me.

It was built in 1910 from timber cut from the farm of Henry May in the English Settlement across the Murray Canal with labour supplied by elders of St. John's Anglican Church: the Wellers, Allisons, Alyeas, Chases, Pecks, Russells, Rowes and Youngs. Others also contributed. For any project of this nature a bee was held and the women provided food for the men that worked. This was a very common practice of those days and always a happy labour of love.

This building was erected on property that had been granted to the

Anglican Church in Ameliasburgh Township called the Glebe. It was almost across from the Methodist Church which had been rebuilt in 1909, after having been destroyed in the big fire. There is no doubt that members of other denominations helped with both buildings. Politics were often considered more important than religion. Almost all functions by all factions were held in this hall and many young people met their life's partners there.

A list of activities held there would include minstrel shows, medicine shows, plays with local talent, bridal showers, wedding receptions and anniversaries, sewing and quilting bees, benefits for burned-out and needy families, political meetings, voting, A.Y.P.A., meetings against the use of alcohol, euchre parties, bake sales, banquets and innumerable dances. Parcels were wrapped for overseas for both World Wars. The first Ladies' Legion Auxiliary was organized there, but later moved to Consecon.

Yourself and lady are requested to attend

A Dance

to be given in the
Carrying Place Hall

Friday, January Thirty-First
Nineteen Hundred and Nineteen

Gentlemen $1.00
Ladies a Cake

Cooper's Orchestra in Attendance

COMMITTEE

H. Latour	A. Hayes
H. Maitland	R. Chase
H. Young	G. Church

Kindly Present This at the Door

The dances hold a special memory for me as I helped promote some of them. Bands such as Hugo Diggins, Knobby Jones and Bert Niosi provided music, as did local fiddlers and musicians of all kinds.

In the winter of 1921 or 1922, a group of Trenton's prominent citizens entertained us with a concert. My only recollection of this was the rendering of 'The Twelve Days of Christmas' and a solo by Mrs. Gill of the lumbering firm of Gill and Fortune. I had never heard such a high-pitched voice. The rafters shook when she hit the high notes. She sang 'When the Apples Grow on the Lilac Tree'. The thought occurred to me that no ladder would be required to pick those apples. Her song would have brought them tumbling down. It was right after that they put in long truss rods to keep the walls from buckling. I remember how we boys used to skin-the-cat and chin ourselves just to show off for the girls.

It was, perhaps, that same winter that Chas. M. Westfall, Art Hayes and others took a big gamble and engaged Ben Hokea and his Hawaiian Troupe to play. It was a miserable cold winter night and at the opening time the hall was empty, but soon they could not all get in. Alice Hayes tells me how worried they were until the crowd came. Those outside tried to keep the door open so they could hear but those inside tried to keep it shut to keep out the cold. I, for one, had never heard melody to compare with it. Price of admission was $3.00, an unheard of price, which I borrowed from Charlie Westfall promising to repay by helping to put in his ice.

Dances were held almost weekly. Square dancing was most popular with callers such as Webb (Windy) Taylor, Gordon Bonter and Ross (Slim) Alyea. Two Step, Fox Trot, Polka and the Waltz were played occasionally for variety. The Frug, Turkey Trot, and Black Bottom dances were short-lived, but no stranger than the Bird dance in vogue in 1983. Some of the more radical boys would have black cuffs sewn on their wide-bottomed sailor-type pants. Trousers in those early years were narrow, short, with cuffs. They changed to wide Bell Bottoms for a short time. Once a girl caught her spiked heel in the cuff of the only pair I ever owned and took us both to the floor. I was sure I would lose them before I got loose. Some came in Zoot suits, but they were soon gone. I never owned one but I did have a purple tie with matching pocket kerchief then in vogue. I also wore spats. This was in the so-called flapper era when the Charleston was very popular and the girls wore their skirts short and shorter. Button shoes had long before given way to spiked heels and many girls wore jazz garters above or below their knees or rolled their silk stockings down. The old hall heard a lot of laughter, saw a few fights (mostly outside by jealous lovers or drunks). No drinking was allowed inside, no bars, no bottles sitting on top or under tables, not that there wasn't lots consumed outside or even in the woodshed.

Caretakers that I remember were Jack Clarke and Ross Chase. Living as close as I did, I was often called on to light the fires in the three wood stoves and it took a long time to warm it in cold weather.

Carrying Place Union School 1 and 5 served a large area of Ameliasburgh and Murray Townships. Although the school was located in Murray, the yearly Christmas concerts were held in the hall. This hall also served as a school while additions or alterations were made to the school in Murray. The first time I recall being in this hall was for the Christmas concert of 1921. We had just moved to Carrying Place that fall and my brother and sisters were taking part in it. What followed was a typical format for all the Christmas concerts held there until regional school busing created such a rift in our community and they became a thing of the past. The place was jammed with excited kids, anxious parents and worried teachers. Every child had a part to play even if it was only to sing in the chorus. No parent would think of missing it. An M.C. (usually a preacher, but not necessarily an Anglican) made an opening speech. He would tell a supposedly humorous story, order the curtain raised and introduce the items of the program in their proper order. A prompter was often needed as many forgot their lines. The curtain, on a large roller, was adorned with various-sized ads mostly paid for by Trenton merchants. When it came down for the final time both parents and teachers raised a sigh of relief. Right after the applause subsided a noise of Bells would be heard outside the door which would be opened to admit Santa. He was immediately the focus of attention in his red suit and white beard. With a HO, HO, HO he was ushered to the gaily decorated tree. Most children got a present from their parents as well as one from their teacher. Often a teacher would spend a good portion of the month's salary just to see the happy faces of their pupils. Even I got a present that year which I presume came from the teachers for helping with the tree. The school board provided a bag of candy for all kids regardless of age. The reason I mention the concerts and activities that took place in our hall is that now it is gone there is not the community spirit as before. Where most all were on a first-name basis, it is now a collection of segregated strangers.

It is not possible for me to write about this hall in an impersonal manner. It holds too many memories for me. I think about my old friends, Frank Wilson and his Black Face comedians. About Freddy Elliott and his step dancing. About how Bus Lesperance loved to pound his drums. About the dances I helped promote and the old friends no longer here. I think about how proud I was at our wedding reception and shower, also when my children and grandchildren appeared in the Christmas concerts, the humorous things that happened there that made us laugh.

The old hall was declared to be unsafe and activities were held in the old abandoned school on the Murray side, but it did not last long. The loss of our hall was a severe blow to this community. Carrying Place has never been the same since.

From *The Trenton Courier*, Jan. 2, 1896— On Thursday December 26th the English Church Sunday school had its Xmas tree entertainment in Rowes Hall. The children received their presents and part of the programme was given. The night was so terrible that few dared venture out, yet a pleasant evening was spent. The tree looked very pretty, brilliant with many coloured wax candles, festooned with popcorn while peeping out dolls and the various presents for the children. The special prize for the whole school was taken by Edith Corrigan. Conduct prizes were given to Ada Brooks, Ella Rowe, Edith Corrigan, George Corrigan, and Willie Herrington. (Could this have been the same hall?)

The Carrying Place
"Passed is all its greatness"

Highway #33 passes in front of Hanthorn's Garage; St. John's Hall is now gone; Westfall's store is operated by Elvin Higgins; The 'Manse' and 'Parsonage' are private homes; The United Church is still used.

The Portage Road remains; Lower Left— foundation of Empey Hotel; 1934 cairn unveiled to commemorate Gunshot Treaty; 1873 the Union School #1 Murray and #5 Ameliasburgh; 1885 St. John's Church— not stuccoed. Note remains of board walk, and lilac hedge planted by the Corrigans in front of St. John's Church.

The Young Families of Carrying Place
The Joseph Young Family

Marjory & Keith Young

Young is a family name connected with the Carrying Place. Joseph Young and Mary Weeks were married in the United States and came to Upper Canada where she lived to the age of 99 years and one day. Their son, John Young (1812-1893), married Susan Nix (1818-1917) and their son Marshal Young of Gardenville likewise lived a long life (1851-1943). It is to him that we are indebted for much of the early history of The Carrying Place and surrounding area.

Marshall Young married Rosa Vail and to them three sons were born. Ernest, was killed overseas in World War I; Clarence went to Chicago; and Arnot remained at Gardenville. His mother died when he was born and his father married Alvina Merrick and after she passed away he married a third time to Lillian Cape.

Marshall Young was a commercial fisherman and on his excellent garden land grew fine patches of strawberries. In his later years he often rode his large tricycle along what is now Highway 33 into Trenton. He suffered a stroke and his last years found him confined to a wheel chair.

Arnot, Marshal's son, stayed in Gardenville and married a local girl, Maud Snider, whose family also resided in Gardenville. Their home was a lovely place across from the Gospel hall. For a living, Arnot was a commercial fisherman, a barber, and a gardener and fruit grower. Their son is Keith Young who resides in Gardenville in his grandfather Marshal Young's house.

The Blake Young Family

Edward Blake Septimus Young and his wife Sadie Deveny had made their home in Trenton. They had a young daughter Marjorie who was three when they decided to move back to the Young 'Homestead' at the Carrying Place. Three younger sons were born there, Ted who lives in Belleville, Don who is deceased and Elmer who lives in California.

The Young children must have had many a pleasant time romping on the spacious grounds, or hiding away in one of the 14 rooms of their historic home with its three fireplaces, antique furniture and wide verandahs.

In 1937 Marjorie Young, daughter of Blake Young, was united in marriage to Keith Young, son of Mr. and Mrs. Arnot Young. Although both have the surname Young, they claim no relationship. To this union was born one son Mansfred who has a daughter Shelley and are now the only descendants of either Young family living at the Carrying Place.

In 1944 Marjorie and Keith Young bought the home which had belonged to Keith's grandfather, Marshall Young. They still live there and have an antique shop. Their home is very close to the Robert Young home as it is still known about the Carrying Place, so Marjorie still must feel a part of the history of the place.

The Memoirs of Marshall Young (1851-1943)
Gardenville History

About 1800 what is now known as Gardenville was a standing forest of large trees, such as soft maple, ash, elm and oak. A man by the name of Greenwood bought the timber from Reuben Young, who owned a large block of land in the vicinity, and put men to work to cut the trees into cordwood. He built a small dock at a point of land called Pine Point, hauled the wood from the nearby woods, and loaded it on small schooners drawing eight or nine feet of water, for shipment to other parts of the province.

After this land was cleared there grew a vast raspberry patch and for two or three years thousands of pails of berries were picked. People came from far and near in all manner of rigs from one-horse buggies to wagons with hay racks, loaded to capacity with berry pickers. They also came by boat from Consecon and Brighton.

The first settler at Gardenville proper was William Andrew Young, his brother, Aaron, and Daniel Chase, who settled in the same year. Others kept buying lots and building homes until the place was pretty much as it is today.

During the 1870's, Gardenville became a booming place because the McMullen Brothers bought a block of land and built a roundhouse to accommodate eight engines, a machine shop with a tall brick chimney and a dock with a railroad track that ran the length of it, for the purpose of handling iron ore. They also built a nice boarding house and a fine barn.*

*See chapter on Railways.

All this was for nothing, as the ore was so full of sulphur it proved to be useless. I, Marshall Young, helped build those docks, and I was here when the roundhouse and other buildings were erected. I helped in loading vessels with ore for shipping to Cleveland and I lived to see the failure of the whole business venture, where hundreds of thousands of dollars were lost.

The Naming of Gardenville

The place in the beginning was called 'Toad Town', but when the little Gospel Hall** was built, the people of the place wanted to give the hall a name and they began to cast around for a more civilized name. I have the honour of proposing 'Garden' and Frank Chase chose 'Ville' and the hall was called Gardenville Gospel Hall, which may yet be seen with the date it was built '1897'. Soon after, Gardenville Post Office was established but closed when rural mail became the vogue.

Gardenville began with berries and has continued with berries and no doubt will continue in the berry industry for all time. We are cultivating the best varieties known to the public and we are keeping abreast the times in this respect. Strawberries are the main crop with red raspberries and long blackberries in that order. Of course we don't depend exclusively on gardening. Quite a few follow fishing as a sideline while others pack apples in the packing season.

Gardenville has its good and bad reputation, but I think it will compare favourably with other small villes. It has at present a grocery and a filling station owned and operated by Alf Dymond, our present Deputy Reeve. We have also a competent fish buyer in Harry Young who handles most of the fish caught. Down on the bay shore known as Pine Point there has been built a number of fine cottages, and this place may become a summer resort yet.

**See chapter on Churches

Strawberry field, Gardenville

Gardenville is becoming quite a flourishing little 'Ville' and may it continue to prosper is the wish of everybody.

From *The Trenton Courier*, Jan. 3, 1907— The Brethren of Gardenville held their annual feast on Sunday and Monday of this week.

Mar. 14, 1907— The Plymouth Brethren of Gardenville intend having revival meetings in Mr. H. Flindall's Hall beginning on Wednesday evening this week.

Nov. 30, 1905— The schooner Robert MacDonald is aground in Weller's Bay near Gardenville.

Morrey's 1906 Business and Farmers Directory of Gardenville
Union Publishing Co. of Ingersoll

	Freeholder, Tenant	Con.	Lot
Adams Carman	f		2
Alyea S. Mrs.	f	2	110
Bonter J.A.	f	2	111
Bonter J.A.	f	2	114
Bonter J.E.	f		3
Brickman Benjamin	f		3
Brummel Frank	f		2
Chase Abraham	f		1
Chase A.J.	f		28
Chase Mrs. D.	f		10
Chase Frank	f		4
Chase M.B.	f		6
Church George	t	2	111
Church M.S.	f	2	111
Church Reuben (Murray P.O.)	t	2	111
Church Mrs. W.	f		4
Clark G.H.	f		3
Clark G.N.	f		19
Cooper Andrew	t		10
Cooper Henry	f		10
Cross John	f		1
Curtis Dr. (Murray P.O.)	f	bh	
Diamond John	f		4
Houser Nelson	f		11
Humphrey C.G.	t		2
Humphrey Schiller	f		2
McMahon Hugh	t	1	111
Moines Isaac	f		3
Siddell Joseph	f		6
Siddell Robert	f		6
Snider Clarence	t	2	110
Snider Frederick	f		4
Snider Henry	f	2	110
Stapleton G.N.	t		4
Stapleton Stinson	f		4
Taft Gilbert	t		3
Taylor F.G.	t	1	112
Taylor G.E.	f	1	113
Weese B.W.	t		2
Weese Hiram	f		5
White Frederick	f		111
Wilson Robert	t		2
Wright Walter	f		2
Young Aaron	f		3
Young J.L.	f		2
Young Selina	f		3

The George Snider Family Of Gardenville

The Geo. Snider home— first frame home in Gardenville

When Gardenville was still woods and swamp and Indians inhabited the place, George and Mary (Moynes) Snider built the first frame house there and lived in it for many years, before retiring to Brighton. It was located close to Weller's Bay where the Jack Wilson home is now.

George and Mary Snider were the parents of five sons, namely Isaac, Harry, Frank, James and Fred. James managed the Empey Hotel at the Carrying Place prior to his moving to Brighton, where his brother Harry had a store. Frank and Harry died young. Fred was the son who remained in Gardenville.

There was a small cottage on lots 4 and 5 that had been built by John Wannamaker. It was to this cottage that Fred Snider brought his bride, Loretta Clark, daughter of Mr. and Mrs. Elias Clark from the north shore of Consecon Lake. Their Gardenville cottage was small so they hired Herbert Herrington, a local carpenter to build on a large addition. In this beautiful home Cecil Snider was born over 80 years ago. It was to this same home that he took his own bride, Margaret Cruikshank from Scotland in 1924.

Cecil Snider easily recalls the trips he and his father made to Belleville market with horse and carriage to sell the produce from their farm which consisted of several kinds of berries, and vegetables. The 17-mile trip to Belleville took them over the toll bridge, where the horses had to walk slowly over the planks, giving them time to eat a leisurely breakfast, which they brought with them. Upon their arrival at the market, the horse was stabled and fed in a nearby livery, awaiting the homeward trip. Their fruit and vegetables always sold well and the price for strawberries was about four boxes for a quarter.

Fred Snider passed away in 1926 and his wife Loretta lived on for 16 years more with her son and his family until her death in 1942.

George Cruikshank, brother of Mrs. Snider and of Bella Herrington, built a garage in the Carrying Place, which was later bought and added on to by the Hanthorns. Cecil Snider worked there for awhile before becoming a civil servant for many years at the Canadian Forces Base in Trenton.

Cecil and Margaret Snider have two children. Their daughter Betty married Douglas Baxter and they live next door to her parents. Fred, their only son, has three children who live nearby.

The Henry Snider Family of Smoke's Point

Lot 110, Con. 2

George Snider, who built the first frame house in Gardenville, had a brother Henry who farmed on the Smoke's Point Road. He was the father of Clarence Snider who married Ada Chase. Their son Earl Snider married Keitha Henderson, a local school teacher. They had two daughters Jean and Helen.

When Earl Snider passed away, the farm was purchased by the Tenhove family from Holland and is one of the fine dairy farms in Ameliasburgh.

Dymond's General Store, Gardenville

William J. (Jackie) Dymond came from Bothwell near Chatham and worked in a basket-making business in Trenton with Adrian Forbes. He wove baskets, mainly for picking apples, from slippery elm wood sawed into strips, then hammered apart. He used a shingle horse and drawknife to smooth them. He was married to Mary Ann Chase. Everyone who knew her fondly called her 'Ma'.

Mr. and Mrs. W.J. (Jackie) Dymond had twins, a son J.A. (Alford) Dymond, and a daughter, Allie, who married William Kemp, owner of much land around Gardenville. Jackie had his first store in Jerry Kemp's house on the north corner of the crossroad in Gardenville. Then in 1898 he purchased 12 acres of land and the building across the road on the south corner and began his business there. Later he bought all the land from the corner to the Gospel Hall from Adam McKay of Trenton. In 'the good old days' this corner store also had a post office, but this was moved to the Carrying Place when rural mail routes were established.

Dymond's was a small store with a single, long counter. A glass candy case sat on the counter just inside the door. When it became too dark to see, coal-oil lamps that sat in brackets on the walls were lighted. Coal-oil was a commodity much in demand. White and brown sugar and rolled oats came in barrels. Prunes and raisins came in big boxes and had to be weighed out. A box stove heated the store and crates and benches could be pulled up for visitors to sit awhile and warm themselves. The Dymond store had no cash register. The money was kept in a drawer, fitted with little wooden change trays. The son

Allie Dymond
married William Kemp

William J. (Jackie) Dymond,
basket maker

Dymond's store

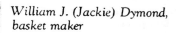

and his family lived in part of the attached house, while his parents ran the store. This location housed the family and the business for three generations over 58 years.

The Jeremiah Kemp Family

Jeremiah Kemp (1843-1921) might well be called the entrepreneur of Western Ameliasburgh, for he appeared to own land in many places, and indeed much of Gardenville. He went to auction sales and bought anything he thought marketable.

At one time Jeremiah and his wife Alfretta C. Brooks (1853-1916) lived in the log house that was on lot 101 concession 2, now at the Museum in Ameliasburgh. It was here that their only son William Kemp was born.

In 1906 Jeremiah Kemp traded lot 97 concession 2 for lot 106, now the Dan Brady farm, with Adelbert Snider, and the Snider family farmed there in the Snider cross road for many years. Kemp also owned a brick house which was across from and a little east of the present fire-hall. The Kemp family lived in and owned the house on the north corner of the road to the Gospel hall.

William Kemp grew up and married Allie Dymond, twin sister of Alfred Dymond and they had two daughters, Thelma and Ruth. William built what is known in Gardenville as the Baxter house across from Bert Pennings chicken farm, on one of his father's farms. Eventually, William and his family moved to Toronto and after Jeremiah's death the house was rented.

Freeman Hart was a carriage maker in Havelock. His son Webster and his Welsh-born wife Sarah Craddock came to the Carrying Place and settled on Old Orchard Road on the Smith place, later moving into the Jeremiah Kemp house which was then across from the fire-hall, and finally into William Kemp's house in Gardenville, which was bought later by the Baxter family.

Webster Hart and his wife Sarah had four children:

Stanley— in 1933 married Grace Dymond, niece of William Kemp's wife Allie. They had three children, Gwen, Jack and Bud. All have moved away. Stanley died in 1979, Grace remains in Gardenville in the home she and Stanley built near the Gospel Hall.

Dorothy— moved away.

Margaret— married into another Gardenville family when she married D'Arcy Stapleton. They had one daughter, Joyce, and reside in Brighton.

Albert— lost his life by drowning.

The Stapletons of Gardenville

The name Stapleton appears in the history of Consecon, where Joseph was a carriage maker until he moved to Brighton in 1899. His brother Stinson Stapleton came to Gardenville and worked as a commercial fisherman and gardener. His house, across from the oldest frame home there, had a wide verandah on two sides. He kept a gramophone with a big horn attached to it on the porch. When he had been imbibing he would crank up the machine and do a lively step dance all about the verandah, much to the merriment of the

Stapleton's Summer Resort, Gardenville

youth of the hamlet who watched from various vantage points.

The Stapletons also had a summer resort on their property very close to Weller's Bay. People came to pitch their tents and remain for a holiday. One might say that the Stapleton's pioneered the tourist business in Ameliasburgh.

Stinson Stapleton's wife was Adelaide Bonter and they had two children, May and Herbert. May (d. 1919) married Stillman Herrington while Herbert married Gladys Young. They had a son D'Arcy who was very young when his father died in 1915.

When D'Arcy grew up, he married Margaret Hart and they moved into the Joe Stapleton home in Brighton where they still live. They have a daughter, Joyce.

It is interesting to note that Gladys Young- wife of Herbert Stapleton— was one of nine children of James Young of the Carrying Place. Her sister Pearl married Tom Colletti who was a tailor and they retired in Gardenville. Her brother Leslie was an engineer on the train that ran from Trenton to Picton, while her sister Augusta married Jack Clark and they came back to Gardenville.

From *The Trenton Courier,* Mar. 26, 1885— Married. BONTER-CHASE (Adelaide Stapleton's parents)— On the 25 inst., by the Rev. G.W. Dewey, at the parsonage, Mr. George Sylvanius Bonter, of Ameliasburgh, to Miss Jessie Estella Chase of Murray.

April 9, 1885— A Torontonian writes that the Fenians are contemplating an invasion, and advises precautionary measures.

A Sequel to Marshal Young's History of Gardenville

By Marjorie Young

When I came to the Carrying Place in 1918, I recall visiting the Chadd house.* A man named Harry Chase who retired in Consecon operated the lighthouse. It was later used as a summer cottage by Harry Orser and finally destroyed by fire.

The center of the Gardenville Community was in reality the Gospel Hall. Suppers and religious services were well-attended as Sunday Schools didn't exist for some time in the two churches within the Carrying Place. Sophia and Horatio Grounds taught Sunday School while Oral Moynes and Alfred Dymond conducted services.

Gardenville boasted three barbers: Oral Moynes, Clarence Madigan and Arnot Young. A haircut was 25 cents. There was a general store owned and operated by Alf Dymond and his wife (Frankie Moynes). Many ball games were played in a field nearby the store and the Gospel Hall.

If you followed the road westward from Dymond's store, past the Hall and Arnot Young's home and beyond, you would come to the shores of Weller's Bay where Marshall, Arnot and Keith, three generations of the Young family, made their living by commercial fishing. Today there is no fishing carried on there.

Very few patches of Gardenville strawberries still remain to remind us of the years from the 1930's-1960's when people came from far away places to buy the late-maturing variety that flourished there. The selling price was four quart boxes for 25 cents. They grew so bountifully that strawberry gardeners took them to Toronto, Kingston and Peterborough to sell them. A great patch of long blackberries grew on the Oral Moynes property. They were prickly to pick, but so delicious to eat.

My father, Blake Young, now owned less than the farm originally contained, for about 1878, part was sold to Prince Edward Railway Company and another 125 acres leased to Edward Weller and used for a picnic area.

On the part that remained, there was an excellent stand of hard maples which my father tapped in March of each spring. He boiled the sap over a fire in the woods, gathering 40 gallons of sap to make one gallon of syrup which he sold for $2 per gallon. Tag alders grew profusely in the area and kept the children busy carrying it to the fire and because it disappeared so fast it was known as 'gopher wood'.

A part of this same property was known as 'The Company'. It was a very large pasture lot where area farmers pastured their cattle for the season.

The part leased to Edward Weller had a beautiful sand beach and he opened it up to the public for picnics and swimming. One of his four daughters stayed by the entrance gate every Wednesday afternoon and during the weekends and collected a 25-cent entry fee for each car. When Weller's lease

*See Ameliasburgh's First Museum.

ran out in the late 1920's, Charles Young, Blake's oldest brother, bought the property back for Blake. The depression came and Blake found it difficult to make payments, but in 1940 his brother gave him the deed to the land. Again for 25 cents per carload, the people returned to their favourite picnic and swimming area. On one Sunday, over 100 carloads of people came, and the Youngs operated a booth where candy, pop and ice-cream were sold.

In 1950, the T.H. Hancock Lumber Company of Toronto purchased this beautiful property from Young for $12,000. Hancock planned to dredge the harbour and resume the shipping of lumber to the United States from the original ore docks at the end of the spur line of the railway. Hancock also anticipated that the iron ore from the Marmoraton Mine would be shipped from the same dock, but his plans were changed when Bethlehem Steel built the iron ore dock on the High Shore below Picton.

Hancock went ahead with other plans. He hired men to build several buildings and a kiln for drying lumber. His firm turned out hardwood flooring and provided employment for several local people including my husband Keith and our son Mansfred. In 1952, Wm. Hanthorn of the Carrying Place was granted a franchise to operate a bus line to take people to and from work at the Hancock Mill.

Business boomed until two major fires and a declining demand for hardwood finally closed down the business.

A Story of Gardenville Happenings

By Fred Moynes

In 1884 'Pine Point' was a busy place with docking facilities for boats and iron-ore coming down from Coe Hill by rail to be loaded and shipped to smelters in Cleveland, Ohio.

Isaac Moynes lived near Coe Hill, but came down to Weller's Bay to begin work on a tugboat used to pilot schooners in through the channel from Lake Ontario into Weller's Bay. (This channel was closed by Hurricane Hazel in 1956). There were range lights on the shore to give sailors direction into the port. One set was at the end of the 'Portage Road' by a cottage then owned by Harry Orser, and another set was very close to the Robert Young house.

The large schooners, often loaded with coal, furled their sails when they came to the channel and the pilot boats brought them into dock to unload and re-load with iron-ore. O.G., as Oral Moynes was called, made frequent trips with his father to pilot the schooners into port.

Isaac's wife was Tryphina Eaton from Mill Island (now Baker's Island) in the Bay of Quinte, just off the Canadian Forces Base. Her father was a millwright and ran a big sawmill there. He was also an inventor and built a screw wheel in a case to replace paddle wheels on steamboats. He had blueprints ready to submit in order to obtain the patent but a man from New York State who visited him took the 'Eaton' invention home with him, removed the case and was granted the patent for it.

O.G. Moynes was born in the house where Henry Nelson lived, then his father bought the place where Frank Wilson lived, in the center of Gardenville. Later, he and his wife Izene Clapp (from Coe Hill) bought a big house from Jerry Kemp who owned a lot of property in Gardenville. This house was on the north corner across from the store owned by W. John Dymond. There they raised their family of a daughter, Lois, and three sons, William and twins Fred and Frank. They grew great quantities of asparagus, strawberries, raspberries and long blackberries.

Isaac Moynes died on Oct. 31, 1936. At that time the body rested at the home. Friends and neighbours came to pay their respect and some remained the night to join the vigil. Isaac's widow Tryphina had been persuaded to get some much-needed rest, but young eight-year-old Fred didn't plan to miss the Ghost stories being told by his uncle Alf Dymond.

Suddenly the doors and windows began to rattle, the dishes in the cupboard clattered, the stove lids shifted and everyone ran outside to hear an eerie sound. The birds began to twitter and fly about. O.G. Moynes and Alf Dymond, both deeply religious men, no doubt thought they had offended the Diety on High for they both turned ashen white. Grandmother Moynes appeared at this time and exclaimed, "It's an earthquake, we'll all be buried with Isaac!"

Fred's older brother often visited Jim Quackenbush, whose father was the caretaker at the old Carrying Place cemetery. That night a crevice opened in the rock there, where loads of debris have since been emptied. Fred Moynes easily recalls his grandfather's death on a Hallowe'en and earthquake date.

CHAPTER 7

CONSECON

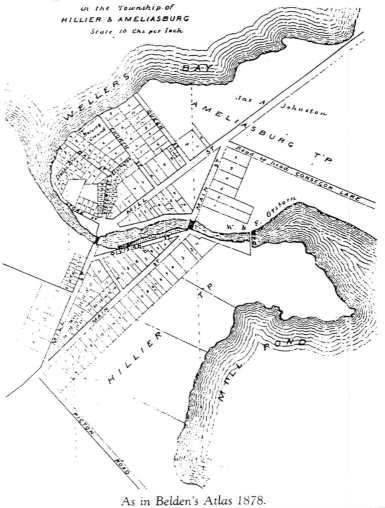

VILLAGE OF
CONSECON
in the Township of
HILLIER & AMELIASBURG
Scale 10 Chs per Inch

As in Belden's Atlas 1878.

Consecon looking down Mill Street.

Westerly on Mill Street.

Crossing the bridge on Main Street.

Consecon Lake

by Helen B. Anderson

A gem on Nature's breast it lies
Beneath the azure summer skies;
The years have come, the years have gone,
Unchanging, still its waves roll on.
The Red man on the peaceful shore
With swift canoe is seen no more,
Forgotten how his fisher's fame!
But no! he gave the lake its name.

Consecon is the Indian word for pickerel or 'big fish', that was found abundantly in those waters in pioneer days. Early in the spring when the heavy run-off is peaking, if one stands on the bridges at night, the eyes of the thousands of spawning pickerel sparkle like silver pennies in the sunshine.

Consecon Creek Watershed covers an area of 71.7 square miles and is the largest river system in Prince Edward County. However, during the drier seasons there is no flow of water from the watershed and the lake is fed from underground springs. For this reason, the lake is one of the last to freeze over in the fall and to open in the spring.

Consecon Lake was not always as it is today, seven miles long and a mile and a quarter wide. Previous to the building of the dams to produce extra water power to run the mills in Consecon, the lake was really a large river, having a small island known as Goose Island out from the original school,

Road by North shore of Consecon Lake where Hillier and Ameliasburgh Townships divide.

where John Jinks lives now. It was inundated. Smith's *Canada: Past, Present and Future*, circa 1850, states, "about two miles from Consecon is a small lake called 'Consecon Lake', about two miles in length. It receives the Consecon Creek and discharges its waters into Weller's Bay."

Throughout the early years there were two mills at the east end of Consecon Lake and from these mills loads of grain sailed up the lake to Consecon Village. There remains to this day a sunken barley boat in the middle of the lake, far down in its depths. Smaller craft were built in Melville and taken into Weller's Bay through Consecon Creek.

Mr. Ramsey, editor of the *Free Press* prior to Nov. 18, 1833, in his *Travels in Upper Canada* described the country as rich and fertile around Consecon. He noted that the finest wheat in the province grew there. He concluded with a description of the Consecon Lake area and noted that the northern side had long been settled.

Consecon Village he noted, was "prettily situated at the bottom of a rising ground and stands upon both sides of the stream which runs from Consecon Lake into Weller's Bay, an arm of Lake Ontario." At this time the population of the place was "200 souls". By 1847 Smith in *Canada: Past, Present and Future*, estimated Consecon's population at 400.

Prince Edward County Directory, 1865, states, "the largest lake vessels can safely ride at anchor during the most severe storms, being protected from the roughness of the lake by an extensive sandbank. The Government has decided, we believe, upon enlarging the mouth of the creek and dredging the harbour, which, when done, will add to the trade of the village by including many vessels to take advantage of its superior accommodations and winter there."

One of the docks on Weller's Bay.

In 1898 a Life Saving station was moved from Wellington to Consecon. It had been at Wellington since March 17, 1883. Sailing vessels were numerous in the early days and were sometimes driven on shore by high winds. Walter Locie was one of the original lifeboat crew. A Life Saving Station existed at Consecon, on Weller's Bay until June, 1918.

Consecon

by Julia Rowe Sager

The land in the Consecon area and around the lake was distributed by the government of Upper Canada between the years 1794 and 1866.

In 1794, Dr. James Latham received several lots of land both along the north shore of the lake and elsewhere, but his story remains a mystery.

It was shown on a map of 1796 that much of the land around Consecon was owned by Robert Charles Wilkins and William Marsh. West of Consecon, Captain John Stinson received every lot to Lake Ontario, hence, the name "Stinson's Block".

As early as 1804, Mathias Marsh, described as a wealthy Vermonter and owner of 1,000 acres at Consecon, had built in the village the first saw mill in Ameliasburgh Township. His son Archibald, one of 24 children, actually built the first grist mill and became an influential resident, partly through his generous sale of land for the building of the Methodist Church in 1829 (records show 30 pounds for the land). The *Hallowell Free Press* of Feb. 7, 1832, advertised a change of name of "that place formerly called Consecon" to Marshton, in honour of Mr. Marsh. In time, however, the name reverted to Consecon, derived from the Indian word 'con-con' meaning 'pickerel,' fish which were caught there in abundance.

By the middle of the century, Consecon was a village of 400, bustling with business. William Whittier had come from Maine in 1830 to operate a store

Saylor's Mill

and buy fish; his son, Clark, by the 1850's, had added a tinsmith shop, made carriages and sleighs, and issued marriage licences. John S. Barker sold dry goods, hardware, and groceries. Brady and Young, general merchants, handled white fish and salmon trout from Consecon's fishermen. Kirkland brothers had a general store, and William was the postmaster and Justice of the Peace. As well, there were two other Justices of the Peace listed in 1857-58 in the *Canada Directory*, namely, Joshua Cadman and Samuel Pennock. A half dozen names of boot and shoemakers assured a well-shod population; listed were Ambrose Wood, John Stoneburgh, Gibb Squires, Richard Cowan, James Jacques and Nelson B. Wood. As transportation depended upon the horse, generally, there were several businesses to provide the needs. John Hicks made harness; Levi Lochlan, William Lampson, John McGown and John Morrison made carriages. There were blacksmiths Peter Harris, William Kenny, Eliakim Squires, and John Bowerman who also made carriages. William Johnson was a wharfinger whose dock could accommodate the boats built by William Squires. Carpenters Charles Nix, George Hayes, Noel Humphries, and Miller and Squires depended on lumber from Martin Miller's saw mill. The grist mills were operating at full capacity, two distilleries were going. The Georgian-style tavern built by Richard Hayes around 1838 was being operated by the Pennocks; Abraham Marsh was known as a temperance inn-keeper; J.M. Wood was proprietor of the Prince Edward Hotel, and R.J. Clute had the Commercial Hotel and stage house. There were insurance agents, a land agent, a bailiff, a notary public, a baker, a tailor, a weaver, a stone mason, a cabinet maker. Dr. Joseph Lougheed practised medicine. The common school became 'The Consecon Grammar School' in 1852. Octavus Weld B.A., was principal, and Thomas Kelps, teacher in 1856. It appears that enterprising souls initiated businesses and services to fulfill almost every need of the village and community.

A generation later, Consecon of 1870-80 was described to Florence Bush by

James McConkey who was born in 1867: "My earliest memory of Consecon is when I was around ten years old. My father let me go with him to the little carding wool mill at the upper dam across Consecon Creek to get some wool carded into rolls for spinning into yarn. At that time most farmers kept sheep for the purpose of having wool made into either flannel or fulled cloth. The flannel was used for women's and girls' dresses and bloomers, while cloth, sheared and pressed down, was a thick, firm texture and used for men's and boys' pants and coats.

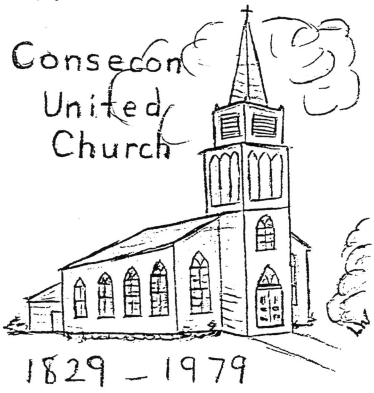

Consecon United Church

1829 – 1979

A drawing for a Christmas Card by Lily Walt

"There were three churches, Presbyterian, Church of England and Methodist. Daniel Garretsee ran one blacksmith shop, and William Kenny another. John Byers had a dry good store, Anson Whittier and James Squires were partners in another. One grocery store was run by Mother Robinson; Abraham Marsh ran another and also kept the post office.

"There were two grain storehouses with their docks for vessels to tie up and load barley. Vessels drawing 8 to 10 feet of water could navigate the bay and anchor at the docks. Barley was the farmers' main grain crop and sold for $1.00 to $1.25 a bushel. At times one could see team loads of 50 to 100 bushels waiting in line from the bay to the highway. James Johnson owned one dock and William Pierson the other.

"Also, there were two hotels. Ed Hogan managed the one on the north side of Consecon Creek, and Robert Porter the one on the south side. Both were licensed. There have been some hilarious times at those hotels, especially on holidays like the 24th of May, when a program of sports would be celebrated.

"About every summer, circuses visited Consecon. They were Cole's Menagerie and Robinson Circus. There was a merry-go-round with little wooden horses. It was operated by a man turning a crank near the centre pole. The boss played a concertina for the music. The tunes were *The Gypsy's Warning* and *The Poor Gypsy Queen.*"

In the 1920's, Consecon was described as a "booming village". Fishing was a thriving industry. Fish were bought by Herb McCabe, Wes Kizer, and Jim Eaton, packed in ice and shipped in boxes by train from Consecon Railway Station, mainly to the United States. Wm. Zufelt was an auctioneer and also operated a farm machinery and repair business. A barber shop and pool room opened under the ownership of Edgar Simonds. Adam Saylor's stone grist mill was operated in the 20's by Adam Burr, whose son, Ivan, drowned in the mill pond in 1923. The United Canners built a canning factory along Wellers' Bay in 1929. For many years it handled the local crops of peas, corn, tomatoes, pumpkin.

As for culture in Consecon, from the turn of the century Miss Frances McQuoid, a qualified piano teacher, instructed many of the young people of the community in learning to play the piano and, ultimately, to write examinations for the Royal Conservatory in Toronto. Another such teacher was Miss Muriel Howe. These two made a substantial contribution in this particular field of music for half a century.

There remains a story of Consecon over the last 50 years from the 1930's to the 1980's, but in the attempt to relate some history of the early village from its beginnings in 1794, events of this modern period seem out of harmony and more appropriate for use at some later date.

From *The Trenton Courier*, June 6, 1889:
Mrs. S.M. Searles, music teacher, Consecon, agent for New York and Canadian Pianos, Organs, Violins, and musical instruments of all kinds, Sewing Machines of all kinds, sheet music, etc. will take in exchange, farmer's produce, horses, stock of all kinds or approved notes. Also payment by instalments. Address, Mrs. S.M. Searles, Lake View Farm, Consecon, P.O.

Consecon— 1883

The united shows of Barnum, Bailey and Hutchinson came to Consecon Tuesday, June 22, 1883 and featured the famous Jumbo, "larger than two elephants." The "majestic, powerful, mastodonic, wonderful Jumbo" was unfortunately killed when he charged an oncoming steam locomotive in the Grank Trunk Railway yard in St. Thomas, Sept. 15, 1885. He was 12 feet high and weighed seven tons.— *courtesy Al Capon*

An advertisement in the Wednesday, August 5, 1857 edition of The Picton Gazette announces the visit to Consecon, Wellington and Picton of Van Amburgh & Co's. Menagerie and Circus.

Publicised as "the largest show in the world", the advertisement claims over 250 men and horses with the show presented as one consolidated exhibition under one tent for one price of admission.

The show featured "The great performing elephant, Tippo Saib", as well as the only pair of Royal Bengal tigers in America, "the largest ever captured alive."

A drove of trick ponies, a highly educated star troupe, "wonderful and intrepid exercises in the cages of lions, tigers etc. by Prof. Langworthy", as well as two great performing dogs and Herman Ludwig's Cornet Band, were added attractions.

An advertisement for a circus is recalled in The Picton Gazette.

1860— Real Estate For Sale

The June 1, 1860, *Picton Gazette* records nine properties for sale in the Village of Consecon as well as 30 building lots "in the most eligible parts of the village."

☐A large three storey brick hotel occupied by a Mr. Clute.

☐Store and outbuildings occupied by Mr. Brady; the building partly occupied

Carriage Shop on Division Street, formerly owned by Herchimer Tyler, later by Ben Hickerson. (Note Anglican Church in background).

by Mr. Sheriff as a grocery, and part of which was formerly a harness shop;
☐Dwelling houses occupied by J.W. Morrison, W.B. Whittier and a Mr. White.
☐A building and sheds formerly occupied as a Carriage Factory and in 1860 occupied by Mr. Morrison and Mr. Baird; and a dwelling house formerly occupied by Clark Whittier and later occupied by a Mr. Brady.

Consecon had its Fires!

From the *Trenton Courier* Files— 1873

The most disasterous fire that ever took place in Consecon happened on a Wednesday morning. About 2 o'clock, fire was discovered issuing from the store of John Byers, general merchant. The building being frame, the fire spread and soon the adjoining building, owned and occupied by John G. German, grocer was in flames. The wind being high at the time, the buildings across the street were soon subjected to the fiery element. People worked with a will, but there were no fire appliances in the village, and everything was at the mercy of the flames. The names of the losers are as follows:
John Byers, Gen. Merchant lost about $5,000 insured in the Royal for $4,000; John German, grocer, loss $1,000, no insurance; J.A. Johnson, Postmaster and commission merchant, loss about $200., no insurance; Anthony Crowter, tinsmith, loss small, no insurance; John Hicks, Harness-maker, everything saved; James Jacques, loss about $12,000, insured for $750; Several tenement houses belonging to S. Greenshields and Co., Montreal, insurance not known; and John Middleton, lost about $1,000, insured. The village presents a desolate appearance. Cause of the fire is not known.

From *The Trenton Courier*, Feb. 26, 1889:
Consecon
Jas. Arthur's carriage and blacksmith shop was burned last night at 11 o'clock, it was occupied by Mr. Thomas of Picton, carriage maker. The shop had a small insurance, contents pretty well covered.
The Fire brigade (men and pails) did good work and saved Wm. J. Robinson's grocery which was just opposite, his goods received some damage by removing.

A Consecon Millpond Tragedy

In the autumn of 1897, a railroad bridge was constructed over the western end of Consecon Lake. The Bridge construction no doubt changed the physical characteristics of the millpond. When William Marsh, aged 12 years, went out for a skate on Dec. 28, 1879, he accidentally drowned.

William was the son of Mr. and Mrs. Marshall Marsh and grandson of Archibald Marsh who had cleared the land and built the first mill in Consecon. Following is an account of the funeral:
Obituary of Willie Marsh
The funeral of little Willie Marsh age 12 years who was drowned in

Consecon Mill Pond

Consecon Creek was largely attended on Thursday of last week. The Sabbath School children turned out in a body and Rev. S.A. Duprau preached a very nice sermon to the children. Willie was very regular in his attendance at the Sabbath School, being there 51 Sundays last year.

> Little Willie's gone to Heaven
> Where his father went before
> And his dear old Grandma welcomes
> Willie on the other shore.
> A tender life cut short so quick
> No warning notes by being sick
> But in a few short moments passed
> To his reward in Heaven at last.
> Tho' sad his fate, yet joy to know
> He was prepared and fit to go.
> We here are taught the solemn truth
> Our God to love in early youth.
> And tho' he was to friends most dear
> And tho' he will be much missed here
> Yet taken for some purpose known
> To God above by Him alone.

From *The Trenton Courier*, Nov. 9, 1905:

Consecon— It is with feeling of sadness that we have to announce the death of one of the village boys, Mr. W.J. Marsh. Just three weeks ago the deceased was considered very ill, although he had been suffering from what he considered to be rheumatism, but which eventually turned into pneumonia. On Saturday

Beach on Weller's Bay with Consecon cemetery in background.

Drs. Kidd and Thornton performed an operation on his lung. The operation proved successful, but it was too late to be of lasting benefit, so about mid-night he passed quietly away. The Marsh family are among the oldest and most highly respected families of our village. The house in which the deceased died was the first frame house in Consecon. His grandfather being a U.E.Loyalist who made his home in Canada.

The deceased was also a nephew of James Kirland, Esq., a former resident of Trenton. The funeral took place from the family residence Monday at 2 p.m. The service was conducted by Rev. J.W. Whyte and Rev. J.A. Stewart, B.A. The remains were placed in Consecon cemetery beside his mother and father who died three years ago within a week or two of each other.

Yesterday's News - Today's History

From *The Trenton Courier*, Jan. 19, 1888:
James A. Johnston, Esq., left today for Southern California to sell an estate or ranch valued at $80,000. It belonged to a Consecon boy by the name of Weeks, son of the late Minard Weeks. Said boy was shot and the mother being heir at law gave Mr. Johnston full power of attorney to sell. I hope friend Jim will soon return as he will be missed in our little circle.

☐There was a great 'catch' of fish last week in the mill dam, about 500 pounds of pike and pickerel in about two hours.
☐R.R. Robinson and Colin Arthur have returned to old Queen's again after spending a pleasant holiday at home. The boys looked as if learning agreed with them.
☐Dr. Jacques bought the farm known as the Smith farm and cheese factory. Hope Doc. will come back to Trenton and go farming.

Feb. 9, 1888:

☐Mr. Thomas Spencer has started a barber shop in connection with his harness business. If anyone wants a good job done on harness, or a nice pompadour cut on their hair, he can do it.

☐Mr. Campbell, a lawyer from Lindsay, is here visiting Mr. Abraham Marsh. I guess "the Campbell will come" soon and take one of our fair girls.

☐Our Literary Society is in full blast. The debate this week will be "benedicks against bachelors". They always have choice readings, music and recitations.

Feb. 16, 1888:

☐Letters from J.A. Johnston, Esq., from San Diego state that the ranch he went to look after is valued at $51,000, besides a number of town lots in San Diego and a large stock on the farm. J.A. is well qualified to do the business for Mrs. Weeks.

☐Our temperance friends are going to rally again round the good old temperance flag and try for the Scott Act once more. Brother Holsey is working hard in the good cause.

Feb. 23, 1888:

☐The Salvation Army are going to have a big time on Wednesday night. Some babies to be baptized. Admission fee to see the christening, ten cents.

Mar. 1, 1888:

☐J.A. Johnston, Esq. left San Diego yesterday for home. Hope Jim will be back in time to vote.

☐The people are having quite a time about getting up a cheese factory. Don't know if they will succeed. Dr. Jacques owns the old one. Perhaps he will rent it to some person to run.

☐Mr. Rob't Porter is able to attend his own business now and has dismissed his bar tender.

☐John Holsey Esq., went down to Roblin's the other day to wake up the temperance folks there, who have been asleep this long time.

☐The Presbyterians have not succeeded in getting a settled pastor yet. The Rev. Mr. McLean very kindly preaches for them every Sunday.

Mar. 29, 1888:

☐J.A. Johnston does not like the climate of the much boasted Southern California as well as our dear old Canada.

☐Miss Belle Porter is very low yet, but hopes of her recovery are strong.

April 5, 1888:

☐We had a big fire at 2 o'clock this morning, the Prince Edward Hotel was burned to the ground, loss fully covered by insurance. It was owned by Mr. R.C. Clark, late of Brighton. So we have Scott Act on one side of the River at least.

☐Great talk to-day of the farmers around here organizing a company for a cheese factory, as the old Victoria is not going to be run this year. It is owned by Dr. Jacques.

May 10, 1888:

☐The Victoria cheese factory has been rented from Dr. Jacques. Mr. G.G. Davidson, cheese maker is to commence making cheese next week.

☐Mr. George Crane, Merchant, is very ill, but not considered serious.

May 31, 1888:

☐Captain J.A. Huyck has his nice little yacht in good trim, and will be pleased to carry pleasure seekers to the beach or Bald Head.

☐Some talk here of Mr. Robert Clark rebuilding the brick hotel. It would make a great improvement if he did. So far the fire made a big gap in the principal street.

July 5, 1888:

☐Mr. John Holsey has a goose that laid 52 eggs which he set mostly below hens and has over 40 goslings. Beat that who can.

July 19, 1888:

☐There seems to be plenty of water in the mill pond, as Mr. Saylor's mill keeps grinding.

Aug. 23, 1888:

☐Our quiet little village was thrown into a great excitement on Saturday by the shooting affray. The prisoners are at present confined at the residence of Constable Wesley Morrison. We have had newspaper reporters, lawyers and doctors, besides a great many strangers. The prisoners are father and two sons and they are quite unconcerned. I understand the trial will take place here, on Tuesday.

Sept. 28, 1888:

☐Mr. W. Killip is the happy father of another big boy. I tell you, Willi is doing well for Sir John's government.

Oct. 18, 1888:

☐Not much stir in grain yet. The farmers don't seem satisified with the price offered for barley.

☐Roblin's fair was not much better than Trenton, this year. I suppose, on account of the rain.

☐Mr. Saylor is putting up a boiler house. He intends if the water gives out to run his rollers by steam.

☐The fishermen here are catching immense quanities of fish— Trout in the Big Lake, Herring in the bay and Mudcats in the Consecon Lake.

☐Mr. John Holsey is shipping a few barrels of choice apples to his Father in England.

Nov. 8, 1888:

☐Mr. Saylor has got a steam engine, in case the water dries up this winter. He lost heavily last year by not having one.

Nov. 29, 1888:

☐The smoke stack of Mr. Saylor's big Engine, looms away up over our little village and gives it quite a business like appearance.

Porter Hotel

The Porter Hotel— Consecon

In 1837 when the rebellion between Upper and Lower Canada was flaring, an imposing Consecon landmark was taking shape. Richard Hayes was building his tavern known as 'Hayes Tavern' on one-half acre of land purchased from Nathan Marsh for 50 pounds. The County Land Registry Records contain a signature of Martin Miller, carpenter and joiner, as witness to the purchase, leaving one to imagine that they may have built or helped to build the tavern. It was located along the main street, also known as the Danforth Road, which ran through the middle of the Marsh property on the south side of Consecon Creek.

The building was a handsome one in Georgian style, white clapboard exterior, with a fanlight over the large front door. Hand-hewn timber was used when the tavern was built. The beams were held together with 'trunnels or tree-nails', and the wooden eavestroughs were held on with hand-wrought pins one-inch square by 27 inches long. Stove thimbles weighing around 75 pounds and chiselled out of limestone held the stove pipes in the walls. The original building measured 36 feet along the street by 30 feet deep. Like most building of that era, it was well made of choice materials, and expected to withstand years of use, as it did for 128 on that spot.

Richard Hayes did well in his new tavern, but according to the Land Registry Records he sold to George Hayes in 1841 "one-half acre land with building thereon erected, known by the name of Hayes's Tavern which said building is at present, occupied as an inn by the said Richard Hayes with all outbuildings consisting of barn, stables, shed, yards and all other appurtenances thereon". Again sold, in 1847, to the Pennock family, ownership of the tavern bounced about among Pennock members until 1869, with the exception of five years 1856-61 when records show transactions by a trio of Brown, White and Johnson and then a couple of Colemans. There was competition in the hotel and bar business in Consecon. In the Canada Directory of 1857-58, R.J. Clute operated the Commercial Hotel and stage house. Abraham Marsh was described as a temperance inn-keeper. J.W. Wood was associated with the Prince Edward Hotel.

The Pennocks sold to Robert L. Porter from Ireland in 1869, and from that time the 'Hayes Tavern' was known as the 'Porter Hotel'. In 1892 an addition was built, 30 feet along the street and 55 feet deep, more than doubling the capacity. An interesting story appeared in the *Trenton Courier* of Jan. 26, 1893 during Mr. Porter's period in Consecon. It seems, "A couple came from Colborne to get married. The only resident minister, Mr. Depew, was not at home, so the poor couple felt put out. One of Mr. Porter's boys found out their deplorable situation and took them to the residence of Mrs. McLean where Rev. Mr. Howie, a blind converted Jew, was stopping. He tied them strong enough to last for 50 years or more and received a handsome fee."

We might presume, also, that business was good at the hotel for the August 9, 1894 *Trenton Courier* reports, "Our little town is full of visitors, Americans and Canadians. Our scenery is fine, the air is pure and good, and we are proud of our nice village. Mr. Robert Porter has had a severe attack of rheumatism but is better."

In 1895 Mr. Porter sold his hotel to Charles Dade. For most of the next 25 years, the Porter Hotel was run by Paul Bruyea, the last to operate it as a hotel. He did an uproaring business in serving liquor over the bar, but prohibition and local option terminated this bonanza, and in 1920 he abandoned his Consecon interests, continuing in his hotel business in Trenton.

For the next nine years the Porter Hotel became a residence. Fred Weeks rented at one time, as did Mrs. Phoebe Wilson. Reuben Adams, who delivered mail around Consecon Lake, lived there with his family. One of his daughters, Mrs. Audrey Williams, recalls the parlour wainscot having oil paintings all around the room. Around 1921 the former dining room was used during the summer months for Saturday night dances.

The County Land Registry Records indicate that Jane F. Dade sold the hotel to Robert Kenny in 1929. Mr. Kenny's daughter, Mavis Halvorsen, along with her family were the last residents of the Porter Hotel. It passed its 100th birthday during their tenure, and when they moved out in 1955 it was well into its second century. For 11 years it awaited a revival, forever teetering on the edge of demolition. Then in 1966 its fortunes reversed, and it was sold to Roy Stevens of Waupoos to restore as a residence. Wm. Calver and Willis Metcalfe took it down and moved the material to its new site in Waupoos, where Mr. Stevens has restored the original Georgian-style structure as it was in 1838. He moved into his restored home on Dec. 24, 1983, 17 years after its dismantling in Consecon. The Porter Hotel has risen again!

Mr. Stevens reports some interesting discoveries while renovating: He has the siding from the 1892 addition on which the "Porter's Hotel" sign was painted, some 18 feet long. Under the layers of paint on the parlour wainscot he has found 17 oil paintings.

He found E. Gus Porter's school copy book dated 1868, in which the lad was required to copy over and over, "Wine is a mocker and strong drink is raging..." this for the son of a tavern owner.

A business card was found 'Canfield and Van Horn, Areolists and Jugglers, Season of 1907'.

One of the Planks supporting the second storey had the following written on it in a position that could only have been put there during construction, 'Richard Hayes, Esquire, Rogue and Liar'.

Another building of interest, which in all probability profitted from its location next to Porter Hotel in its heyday, is the one known as the 'honey house' today and used by Don Garrettsee for part of his apiary business. The house is a simple Georgian type, but its eye-catching feature was an unusual front porch tower, two storeys high, Italianate style, with round-top windows grouped in threes, an elegant and rather imaginative addition to a colonial home.

Lying to the east of the Porter Hotel and separated only by a nameless road allowance or lane, this house and its property was the site of a livery stable. Jim Searles owned and operated his livery from the long sheds behind the house and along the lane next to the hotel. There was a sign over the livery door, "Whip light, Drive slow, Pay cash or Don't go". Major Puffer was the last

Home of Jim Searles, who ran livery stable near Porter Hotel.

owner. Doubtless, visitors at the hotel availed themselves of the services offered at the adjacent livery stable. In addition, John German's son, George, owned a stage and provided transportation for hotel guests between the Porter Hotel and Consecon railway station. While the hotel boomed, both the livery and the stage profitted. But by 1920, when the hotel terminated its operation, and with the increasing popularity of automobiles, the need for these businesses would have waned. However, the recollection of the hotel and dependent businesses resurrects an interesting segment in Consecon's past.

From *The Trenton Courier*, Sept. 26, 1907:
Mr. and Mrs. Ide Rochester, left for their home after spending a time at Mr. Bruyea's hotel.
June 27, 1907— The baseball between Consecon and Crofton resulted in a victory for the Consecon boys. After the match the boys had tea at Mr. Paul Bruyea's Hotel.

James Eaton's Store in Consecon

by Julia Rowe Sager with a contribution by Bessie Smith
The red brick building one sees presently located at the bridge on the north side of Consecon Creek is the former James Eaton General Store, known originally as the Adam Saylor block. Mr. Eaton carried on his business there from around 1900 till his death in 1943.

In this main building he had his general store, as well as his upstairs living accommodation shared with his wife, Maggie. Also, there was space in one end rented to the Standard Bank which later became the Bank of Nova Scotia, and in addition an upstairs ice-cream parlour reached by an outside stairway. Here Chipper Clark entertained with his fiddle on occasion. On each end of this

Jas. Eaton store

Stores of Jas. Eaton and the Masonic Hall

same building, Mr. Eaton carried on more businesses, fish-packing, and egg-packing.

Two other adjacent buildings were used by Mr. Eaton. From the stone building, now owned by the Royal Canadian Legion, he sold furniture on the main floor and a few caskets (in which Mr. Eaton was found sleeping one evening after of day of merrymaking), and on the upper floor there was wallpaper and muresco. In the brick building across the road on the creek, known as the German building, he had stovepipes, hardware, paint, crocks, glass sealers, men's boots, coal oil.

All the while Mr. Eaton carried on his several enterprises he was a picture of sartorial splendour. He always wore a suit, a white shirt with a stiff collar, a tie, and a bowler hat. This was his year-round attire, rain or shine, cold or hot.

During the summer months only, a peddling wagon was dispatched throughout the surrounding countryside up and down the Third and Fourth Concession of Ameliasburgh, around Consecon Lake and up Stinson's Block. A team of horses was required to pull the wagon for it carried a great load of merchandise. For years Clarence Van Wart drove the team, then in later years it was the responsibility of John Viant, who was Mrs. Eaton's brother. Business was often done by barter, the weekly supply of farm eggs in return for rolled oats, sugar, flour and such necessities. It was good economics to cart the goods to the rural areas, for summer was too busy a time for the farmers to interrupt their work with shopping trips, and so the itinerant peddling wagon fulfilled their basic requirements, and also created a market for Mr. Eaton's wares.

Mrs. Bessie Smith of Consecon clerked in James Eaton's store from 1921-1924. Her wages were $7 per week working 8 a.m. to 9 p.m. Monday through Friday, and on Saturday till midnight. The following reminiscences are hers:

"The interior of the store was divided by an archway. It was groceries on one side, and dry goods on the other. Both rooms were heated by a pot-bellied stove that burned either wood or coal, coal being used when I worked there from 1921 to 1924. Coal oil lamps located on the walls were used for lighting as the store was open from 8 a.m. till 9 p.m. and on Saturday night it was usually

midnight, as farmers and their wives made Saturday night the social night of
the week. Outside the square would be filled with horses and buggies. The
women traded butter and eggs for groceries which were sold mostly in bulk. If
they had any money coming to them they didn't receive cash but were given a
due bill. Sugar was sold by 25¢, 50¢ or $1 worth. Bread was stored in a large
wooden cupboard in the centre of the grocery department and was baked at a
local bakery in the village, delivered unwrapped and sold for 10¢ or 11¢ for a
double loaf. The meat was kept in a large cabinet with ice in a compartment
over the top. Cheese in a 40 pound block sat on the end of one counter and the
same butcher knife sliced cheese, cut meat and cleaned fish. A large case of
candy displayed at the front of the store always caught the children's eyes. Two
suckers sold for a penny; also, licorice, hard candy and chocolate were real
cheap. Another glassed-in case at the rear of the grocery department contained
men's pipes, jack knives, watches. Buggy whips stood in the corner.

"At the front of the store, the shelves contained patent medicines, cigars and chewing tobacco. I recall a certain man coming real often for a plug of Briar.

"Through the archway into the dry goods department, bolts of prints and ginghams were stocked as most women made their own clothes besides using these yard goods to piece quilts. A large case with several drawers in it displayed spools of thread of all colours. White cotton thread was sold mostly in size 30 or 40. Crochet cotton and yarn were good saleable articles also. Women's shoes were another commodity, mostly black in colour. You could even buy women's corsets, handkerchiefs, gloves, cotton stockings. A few fancy jardinieres and dishes were displayed on a counter. There were stools that let down from the fronts of the counters to provide seating for the women. On Saturday nights these would be full.

"Mr. Eaton bought fish from the local fishermen, and Clayton Clark was kept busy cleaning them. They were packed on ice and shipped in wooden boxes the year round from Consecon railway station to the United States, one company in particular being Acme Fish Company of New York."

For more than 40 years, Mr. Eaton was a colourful figure in Consecon's history. Since his death on Christmas Day of 1943 there have been other proprietors of his main store, and business has been maintained continuously on that site.

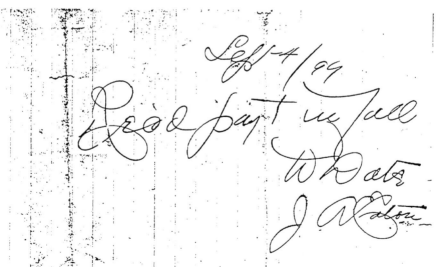

The Barber Shop and Pool Room

In the late 1800's, the pool room was a grocery store operated by George Crane, who built and occupied the home now owned by Douglas Bush. He was postmaster in the store there in 1900.

In the early 1920's, James (Jim) Eaton built a frame building adjacent to his

Post Office, Hardware of W.W. Miller across from Jas. Eaton store. Formerly owned by Elsworth Mastin.

general store for a barber shop and pool room. This eventually became a thriving business, as well as a social centre for the local farmers and villagers who enjoyed a friendly game of pool on winter evenings.

The proprietor was Edgar Simonds who put in a 12-hour day cutting hair for 25 cents, and a shave for ten cents.

When Jim Eaton died in 1943, Simonds purchased it from Jack Eaton, who continued to run the general store for several years. Mr. Simonds retired in 1947 at which time Karl Woof took over the building. Art Vandergraffe was the last to operate a barber shop and pool room there.

Good roads, fast cars, television and other diversions led to a falling off in the business and it never reached the peak of the 30's and 40's. Since 1969, Ted Carter has operated a variety store on the premises.

From *The Trenton Courier*, Mar. 19, 1885:
Mr. G.H. Crane of Consecon is selling his entire stock at wholesale prices to make a change in his business.
April 11, 1889— Mr. George Crane is selling at cost his stock of dry goods and groceries. Some say he is about to retire from business.

Apr. 11, 1889— Pretty near everybody here has got the Manitoba fever and a good many are going. One or two cars have left our station every week for some time. Crops have been so poor for the last two or three years, the farmers are getting discouraged.

Morrey's Business Directory for Consecon 1906

Population about 55

Alyea Herman— butcher
Burr M.B. and Son— flour mill
Chase Miss— dressmaker
Chase J.D.— livestock
Crane George— Post Master and Division Court Clerk
Dade C.R.— hotel
Eaton J.A.— general store
Garretsee Daniel— blacksmith
Goodmurphy G.R.— general store
Herrington I.N.— live stock
Johnston Bros.— blacksmiths
Johnson J.A.— grain, coal & appraiser
Canada permanent Mortgage Corp.
Ley Mrs.— dressmaker
MacDonald & Shourds— fruit evaporator
McQuoid F. Miss— music teacher
McQuoid J.F.— baker
Mastin Elsworth— implements & stoves
Spencer T.F.— harness
Thornton F.H.— physician
Weeks H.W. Mrs.— dressmaker
Weller's Bay Cheese factory

Memoirs of Some Consecon Oldtimers

Adam Saylor of Bloomfield bought the mill property and built a new stone mill circa 1882, and also the Saylor Block, which is presently the grocery store/Scotia Bank building. At that time the store was run by Vandewater and Ward. The part that is now occupied by the bank was the office of James Johnston, who loaned money and was treasurer of the Weller's Bay Cheese Factory. In 1891 there was some excitement when it was reported that a big sea serpent had made its way into Saylor's millpond. The monster was captured and proved to be a bill fish, four feet long and weighing almost 11 pounds.

There was a hall owned by William Killip west of the Saylor Block, which was destroyed by fire, and the hall was replaced by the Masonic Lodge which was dedicated in January 1905.

Across the street from Vandewater and Ward was a shop where the ladies could get their spring hats; it was operated by Mrs. J.F. McQuoid. There, on an adjacent lot a tailor made suits of clothes for men and boys. Earl Walt recalled that his first trousers were made here; previous to that his grandmother had made his clothes.

The property where the Methodist Church was built extended right to the corner. The Adam Burr house and the Will Chase home were built on church property.

In the 1920's Will Chase had a garage on the mill square. This was moved across the creek next the present post office. Harold Kenny was the proprietor for many years.

The Searles Livery Stable was behind the building known as the 'honey house' today. Behind the stable was a well, which when cleaned out was found to contain horseshoes, harness and other debris from the stable. It proved to be one of Consecon's best wells.

The gaoler lived where Sarah Cuyler lives today. There was a little room upstairs where the inebriated from the hotels were stowed away to sober up.

Mr. and Mrs. John German kept store in the brick building by the bridge.

The German store by the bridge.

There were two docks in Consecon, one down the street where the canning factory is, the other down the street beside the Anglican Church. Each dock had a store house for shipping barley. Joe Ward owned the dock across from the cemetery, James Johnson, the other.

Promoter Arthur Allen sold shares to build a factory along the Consecon Road across from the C.N.R. Station on land owned by Cyrus Humphrey. It was to be a "farmers' factory" with stock at $100 per share. It didn't run many years. It was bought by the Canadian Canners and removed.

May 2, 1889:
There has been a schooner in loading grain at Mr. Saylor's wharf.
May 30, 1889:
Folks have had quite a little excitement on Saturday on account of the voting

for the Bridge. We had sprigs of the law around shaking money which I think was not their own. We had merchants and money brokers; they worked hard to enlighten the poor heathen here, but it did not succeed, as only 13 voted and those few had little or no property to encumber.

1948 flood in Consecon.

Scotiabank in Consecon

Records in the Archives at Ottawa cover the year 1915 to 1984. The Bank of Nova Scotia opened its branch at Consecon on Dec. 16, 1915. During the previous two years the Bank had concluded amalgamations with two major chartered banks. In 1913 expansion took place in New Brunswick with the merging of the Bank of New Brunswick. The following year, more branches were added to the system when the Metropolitan Bank was merged with the Bank.

Arthur G. Noxon was appointed the first manager of this branch. Mr. Noxon had been with the Metropolitan Bank and at the time of amalgamation agreed to continue his banking career with the Bank of Nova Scotia.

Early premises for this branch were located on the east side of Mill St., specifically Lot 112. Banking operations were housed in a two-storey solid brick building containing also a general store and living quarters. Consecon continued to operate as a full branch until 1974 when it became a sub-branch of Trenton.

Managers through the years:
George Howard Eager— Sept. 7th, 1929-Sept. 30, 1949
James Alexander Treloar— Sept. 20, 1949-Dec. 1964

Scotiabank

Kenneth Hopwood— Jan. 4, 1965-May 1974
Eleanor I. Silver— June 1, 1974-present.
   J.H. Campbell, an officer at the branch, gave his life in the Great War 1914-1919.

   From *The Trenton Courier*, May 30, 1907— Mr. Hutchinson is taking the position of Mr. Clink in the Standard Bank.

Consecon Bank Robbery

   None of the residents noticed anything unusual that morning in Consecon, not even Ralph Brazzeau who was unloading groceries next door during the incident. He wasn't aware anything had happened until contacted by the newspaper a half hour after the incident.
   Kenneth Hopwood and Linda Haight, manager and teller, remained at the locked bank. Melvin Carnrike, garage manager, was the first to visit the bank, and was allowed in minutes after.
   The armed robbers were thought to be in the Crofton area. A rowboat was found floating in Belleville harbor 24 hours later. It had been stolen from a Rossmore cottage near the Bay Bridge where there was a roadblock. An account of the robbery appeared in the *Intelligencer*, May 27, 1969. The robbers were found in B.C. and sentenced.
   A second robbery took place on Oct. 10, 1981. Two young lads from Trenton were apprehended and sentenced.

James Benson & Kemilla Shuler, married in Consecon, 1860.

Marriage Certificate of the Shulers, who lived on the 3rd Concession pt. of Lots 103 & 104.

CHAPTER 8

R̄OSSMORE

In 1787 Louis Kotte was employed by the Government of Upper Canada to begin a survey in the Seventh Town (Ameliasburgh). Because so many settlers were squatting on land, he was also ordered to survey a portion of land at the mouth of the Saganaskia River— a community that later became known as Meyer's Creek, and which is known today as Belleville. At the mouth of the Saganaskia, now know as the Moira river were two islands named Zwick's Island and Bushy Island. Today these, with landfill, are known as Zwick's Islands Park— the west park incorporating Zwick's Island, and the east park is built around Bushy Island. Across from them, at around the south end of the Norris Whitney Bridge was the Point, variously called Wilkinson's Point or Ferry Point (so designated in *Belden's Atlas of 1878*) and much later the community became known as Ross More, and today— Rossmore.

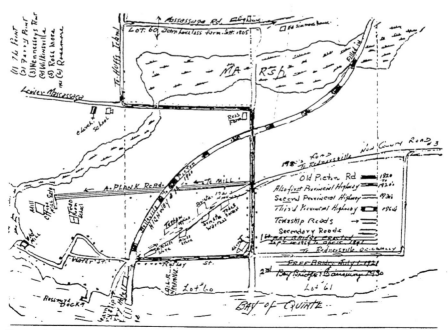

Ridley Street, Rossmore about 1900, looking west. Aunt Jane Brickman on back porch of house 1, Peter Weese with white whiskers, large man next, Wes Weese. In buggy, Ted Moy. House 2 and store (3) Jason Thompson's pictured elsewhere. House 4 Maria Teller. House 5 John Alyea- still standing, home of Mrs. John Hunt.

In 1790, Captain John Meyers built a saw and grist mill on the west bank of the Moira River, above the shallows of the river, and a village with stores and traders sprang up at Meyers' Creek. Access to this mill and stores was very important to the people of the Seventh Town, for the nearest mill until that time was the Government Mill opened for use to the public in 1787 in Napanee. Prior to that, grain had to go to Kingston to be ground. The other alternative was the use of the rather crude wooden mortar and pestle system of the Indian, where grain put in a hollowed-out log was pounded with a hardwood stick or pestle. Staples likes salt, imported sugar and tea were available in the stores or trading posts, along with sewing materials— thread, needles, and 'yard goods'. The first travel was by boat, from the point or elsewhere, but by 1803 a ferry was established. In the report of "Quarter Sessions holden at Adolphustown on the 25th day of January 1803", a ferry was allowed to Benjamin Gerow of the Township of Ameliasburgh at the following rates: "For every man 1 shilling; two or more persons 9 pence each; a man and a horse 2 shillings; span of horses with a carriage 2 shillings and six pence; a yoke of oxen 2 shillings and six pence; a cow 1 shilling; every sheep 3 pence; and every hog 4 pence."

The ferry crossing was evidently popular and lucrative, for by 1811 at the

Ferry house built by William Gerow; last owner, Mr. Ostrom. Note first bridge in the background and fishermen's net-drying reels. House removed when the present Highway #14 (62) was built in 1960's.

Home and store of J.E. Thompson general merchant and postmaster. Buildings on north side of Ridley street destroyed by fire.

January Quarter Session again "holden at Adolphustown" Benjamin Gerow's licence was renewed, and Phillip Zwick was also granted a licence for a ferry from "Thurlow to Ameliasburgh." The Gerow dock was on the property of Loral Wanamaker, five lots west of the Norris Whitney Bridge parkette. This ferry landed at the bottom of Sidney Street near the pumphouse in Belleville. It was a flat-bottomed boat propelled by sweeps or oars. Ferry Point— immediately east of the present bridge— became the later dock for the ferry, possibly even the Zwick's Ferry. A settlement sprang up around the dock— an inn, a trading post, and storehouses. Until the building of Highway 14 South in its present location, there was a large brick house built almost where the present road starts its climb to the Norris Whitney Bridge. This building was known as the Ferry house or the Ostrom House. Mr. Ostrom, the last owner, was responsible for the planting of many of the large trees which are found east of Highway 14, since all had disappeared during the tenancy of the sawmill in that area. The toll house for the second bridge occupied a corner of the hotel property. An earlier building on the same site was Hennessy's- built and operated by James Hennessy, a yeoman and tavern keeper. James Pierson either came or was sent from his home in Elizabethtown, N.J. to work for his uncle in the timber trade in Ameliasburgh Township. His mother came to visit the family and her son, and while here, met, fell in love, and married James Hennessy and for years assisted in the work of the tavern. Prior to this time, Benjamin Gerow kept a tavern in his house. On July 9, 1811 the Midland District Quarter session Court (at Adolphustown) heard the oath of Simon Palmateer that "on Sunday morning about four weeks ago I saw Benjamin Gerow at his house, where he keeps a tavern, playing cards with several others." Gerow, therefore, was charged with keeping a disorderly house. The jury heard the case and Gerow was declared "Not Guilty." Benjamin Gerow, as was noted above, was also the first recorded licensed ferry operator, with a licence granted in 1803.

The road west from Ferry Point followed fairly closely to the water— much in the direction of the present Ridley Street. This road stopped at where the first turn to the south now is, and proceeded on to Picton and Hallowell along the route of the Old Picton Highway, avoiding large rock outcroppings and marshes as much as possible. The road to Rednersville and west followed the water. In most cases, the journey between points was simpler, more comfortable, faster and safer by water than by road.

By 1850, the official name of the settlement was Wilkinsville, though it would seem that the name "Ferry Point" was well-recognized locally, even as late as 1885, the Quarterly Minutes of Rednersville Circuit refer to it as Ferry Point. By 1850, the village contained one store, one blacksmith shop and three taverns "where the vilest of whiskey is sold." Many of the residents were seasonal workers who were employed in the lumber trade. The first sawmills were established in 1864 by Page and Company. The mill had a capacity of

Seventh Town/Ameliasburgh

50,000 board feet a day. The mills were later taken over by B.F. Baker and Company who employed 75 to 100 hands each day in the season. These men were paid $4 to $5 a week. The last owners of the mill were the Rathbun Company with their operations centered at Deseronto. The area south of Ridley Street was marshy, with a large quarry in the center. This area, and to the east as far as the water, was the site of the mills, piled lumber, the first school and many of the millworkers' homes. A plank road ran east from the present three-way stop past huge piles of lumber and homes occupied largely by French families who worked in the mill. In a letter received in the fifties by the Wanamaker family from a daughter of one of these workers who took some of her elementary school training in Ferry Point, she lists some of the names of her neighbours there: names like Herbert, Goyer, LaViolette, Bevineau.

A large cottage-roofed house on high ground, near the present 'Bay Bridge Jeans' salesrooms, contained the mill offices. Nearby was a two-roomed, frame school. Mr. Howell was the principal, and Miss Letta Welsh was a teacher. This building was later dismantled, and re-erected as a Cooper shop just east of the church, and then moved again to become a drivehouse on the Herrington farm west of the village. The boiler room was nearer the water— in fact, the cottage built by Miles Hall was built on fill from the dismantling of the boiler room.

The first church record we have found is the minutes from the Rednersville Quarterly Board of 1885 when Ferry Point was made a part of the Rednersville Circuit. In 1888 a church was built on the east corner of the junction of Ridley Street and the Picton Highway— the first corner west of the Bridge. It was served first from Rednersville and then from Ameliasburgh Circuit. The name of the circuit was derived from the name of the place where the parsonage was located. Sunday School met each Sunday, and church services were held usually on alternate Sundays. This building was used until 1937 when it was destroyed by fire. The congregation rebuilt on the same site, and the church was supported by an active congregation for some time. With easier access to churches in Belleville and elsewhere, and with a change in population, it became increasingly evident that the church was no longer serving a viable purpose, so it was officially closed in 1968, and the building was eventually sold for a residence. Prior to the official closing, services had been held only occasionally for several years.

The development of the village of Rossmore is greatly dependent on the changing of the routes of roads through the area. We will thus look at the first road through the area— today known as Ridley Street, beginning in the present Park just west of the Norris Whitney Bridge and proceeding westward for one block. After 1921 this was the beginning of Highway 14 in Prince Edward County. Near the church was the store operated by Loral Gerow. He did a good business in this location until Highway 14 was rebuilt in the '30s. The new location— the present County Road 3— made the merchants on

Some Present Day Businesses in Rossmore.

Rossmore Trailer Sales, south of the village.

Elite Kitchen and interior cabinet designs, former Tatham building.

O'Brien Tree Service, Rossmore.

Don Hackett's Collision Service.

Magnus Construction Offices.

Tobe's County Gardens as it is today.

Lockwoods's Rossmore Upholstery.

Bob Wood Construction Company.

Middleton Transmission, Rossmore.

Percy Millard's Oil Furnace Business.

Bill Leeman's Ironworks, west of
the village.

Rossmore Food Market built by Rex
Alyea.

Becker's Milk as it is today, originally
Gerow's store.

Bay Bridge Jeans.

Technical Woodwork Office and factory,
makers of kitchen cabinets, vanities and
countertops.

DAC Furniture Refinishing today. The
former building was demolished when
the Bridge Approach was changed in
1980.

The Ross Farmhouse as it is today.

Ridley Street aware that much of the world's traffic was passing them by. Gerow literally picked up his store and moved it to a new location— at the junction of Highway 14 and Ridley Street. His family and himself slept in the large house he owned across from the store, but the store was heated by a large cookstove in the back where meals were prepared and eaten. There was no time off from work for meals, and the customer was free to interrupt the family meal to procure what was needed for the grocery shelves. Gerow later sold to Gunner Arnott who sold to Bob Mitchell, who added an excellent butcher shop to the service available. Today the building is a "Becker's" outlet, operated by Harold Prest.

For many years there was a bakeshop on Ridley Street— first opened in a building on the south side of the street by Joseph S. Thompson who came from Warkworth in the Mill days. Later, the shop was transferred to a building on the north side of the street. Three generations of Thompsons, Joseph, George (Judd) and his son Harold, baked bread in Rossmore until the bakery burned in the 1930's.

Ronald Sharpe built a large building and operated a garage in it for several years until the change in traffic routes. Then the building was transformed into a residence where he lived for some time. Next to this building is one erected by Percy Millard from which he operates an oil heating service. Following his demobilization in 1946, Rex Alyea built a house with a store attached, where he did an excellent business as a Red and White Store until the change in route of the highway. When this store burned, he rebuilt facing on the new County Road 3. This store was built in 1961 and has been later owned by Gordon Hamilton ('The Lucky Dollar Store'); then an IGA Store for a short time; then owned by Armon Quickert of Reid's Dairy and now called the 'Rossmore Food Market' owned by Frank Harnden.

The first commercial venture on the 'new' road was begun by the Tobe brothers of Belleville. It was known as "Tobe's County Gardens" opened in the late 1930's. The first building was a parked trailer where hamburgers, french fries, fried onions and hot dogs were prepared. A new idea was curb service. A waiter or waitress came to the car to take and deliver the order. This idea proved popular and more parking lot was built on— first a dance floor and snack bar, and eventually a large multi-purpose hall was added and the first building became a restaurant. Today, many visit the weekly flea market, and at least three nights a week the parking lot is filled to overflowing with the cars of the patrons of the bingo games. It is now operated by Ron and Barbara Cronkright.

Ralph Warren built a garage and service station just east of Tobe's which operated as such for many years. It was purchased by Don Hackett June 15, 1973 and became Hackett's Collision Service. Since that time the original building has had at least two additions.

Mr. Blondin built a garage just across from Tobe's and west of the quarry. Later Joshua Brant operated this as a garage and body shop for some years. It was purchased in 1975 by Bob Wood after it been empty for some time. The building now houses 'Bob Wood Construction' specializing in aluminum and vinyl installations of siding and eavetroughs.

East of the Quarry, Geyer and Shurtleff built a garage and a station selling Shell gas. With the opening of Rex Alyea's Texaco service at his store in 1961, four opportunities for buying gas were provided in a block, leading to the street being referred to by some as 'Gasoline Alley'. Geyer and Shurtleff sold to Moxam and Wood, who later sold to Howard Adams who operated the station for many years. In 1980 it was reopened by Bruce Middleton, the present owner, as 'Middleton Transmissions'. Today, the home owner who needs gas for his lawnmower must make the trip to Belleville, for there is nobody closer who sells gasoline anymore.

William and John Tatham, construction engineers, built his very attractive building east of the garage. From this building his business was conducted until his retirement. The building was then sold to 'Cornerstone Construction' owned by Brian Holmes who used the building for the same purpose until the completion of 'Century Place' in Belleville where his office now is located. 'Quality Woodwork,' makers of kitchen cabinets, vanities and specialty work, now occupy the office building, and what was once the storage building has been renovated to house the shop known as 'Bay Bridge Jeans'.

Just at the junction of the new and second Highway 14 is 'D.A.C. Furniture Refinishing'. It is a new building which replaces one that was torn down when the approach to the Norris Whitney bridge was moved east to the old Bridge approach.

With the changing of the location of Highway 14, also came the removal or relocation of buildings. The Argo Service station operated by Mr. Griffith was demolished when the bypass route as followed today was established in 1960. When the second bridge was built in 1927-1931 the house where Peter Martin Frederick had once kept store was moved. The bridge keeper's house was also moved from the West side of the new road to the east. A gas station was added to the front and also a small store. In 1960 this house was found to be in the way of the proposed highway, so once more it was moved— this time to the back of the lot, and the front additions were removed. Fate seemed to have a grudge against this house, for in the survey of 1979 for the Norris Whitney

Bridge, it was determined that the new approach would be through the front part of the house. Accordingly, it was offered for sale, and the purchaser cut the second storey off the building, thus being able to move it in two sections. It was moved to a site south of Picton, where, it is hoped, it can find a more permanent site.

Commercial fishing has also been a part of the scene in Rossmore over the years. The waters around Prince Edward County are zoned, and fishing licences have been sold to commercial fishermen— some of whom have lived in Rossmore. Dave, John and Daniel Belnap were the senior generation of fishermen. The next generation, Frank, Ed, Raymond and John Belnap drew their allotments around Massassaga Point. Arthur Alyea and his sons Jack and Rex fished in North Bay (Prince Edward County, that is) and Ted Gerow's licence called for the waters around Cow Island. With pollution in the Bay, both quality and quantity of fish suffered, and with it, commercial fishing is done elsewhere.

Today, Rossmore is a residential community in which there are also many small businesses. With the new Bridge, the potential for Industrial development is increased. Water traffic today is limited mainly to pleasure craft, with only a few commercial fishermen plying the waters of the Bay. Good roads with easy access to Freeways make travel easy, but with these advantages have come the change in community unity that was known to the pioneer.

CHAPTER 9

REDNERSVILLE

A History of Rednersville Village

Along the south shore of the Bay of Quinte almost midway between the Norris Whitney Bridge and the escarpment known as Onderdonk Hill is the present community of Rednersville; a community centering around Ward's garage and The Country Store at its center and the Primary School and Mike's— more properly known as Bill and Irma's grocery and coffee shop— at its easterly and westerly limits repectively. On the south is the United Church. Many residents commute to jobs in Belleville, Trenton or Picton.

As we look back to the past, we occasionally are reminded that there was a native civilization here before the arrival of the white man. Shards of Indian pottery and remains of Indian weapons have been found during excavation, or even in the routine working of the land. The documented history, however,

'The Brockville' at the Rednersville dock.

Ralph Stafford with a steam engine grading the street south of the store about 1912, looking north.

begins with the arrival of the Loyalist and his family in 1784. Surveyors laid out the land in 'towns' or, as we would say, townships, and land was assigned to those who had borne arms in support of the King against the rebels in the American Revolution. Land was also given to their children who had reached the age of majority, or to a daughter on her marriage. Ameliasburgh, being the Seventh Town west of Kingston (townships were assigned the same numbers as they proceeded east from Kingston as well), was thus not surveyed until 1787. The grant of scripts for lot 74 went to Amos McKinney and Doctor Prindle; for lot 75 to Sam Welsh and John Grout; for lot 76 to Widow Hurd (50), Peter Phillips (50) and Peter Young (100); for lot 77 to Widow Lucas (200). This covers the area from the school to Redner's Lane west of the village. This script gave the location of the land granted— the Crown Patent or Deed was purchased when the land was settled. Scripts were often traded or sold. On October 20, 1817, Crown patent for lot 76 (the land that lies west of the road running from the Bay south) was granted to Henry Redner, Jr. whose father Henry Redner Sr. had come to the land about 1798. Fredrick Swartfager received a script for Lot 75 on Aug. 10, 1801, and Henry Redner Jr. received his crown grant for Lot 77 on Nov. 25, 1802.

In 1835, Thomas McMahon bought a portion of bayshore, in all about two acres, on Lot 76. This he held until 1853. He built a dock and the settlement around became known as McMahon's Corners. A map of 1835 so lists the area. By 1850, the Methodist Conference Records speak of a "Chapel being built at Rednersville." When the name was changed is not known, but the name McMahon's Corners seems to have remained in the minds of some for quite a time.

First settlers cleared a site for their home very close to the water.

Descendants of the early settlers tell the family legend that only during the second year of habitation did they venture far enough from the water through the dense woods to be aware of the escarpment that rises south of the village. Only after several years of struggling to eke out an existence from land covered with virgin forest was a supporting settlement established.

Much travel was by water, so a settlement grew up around McMahon's dock. A trading post and storage facility for merchandise was built, and by 1810 Henry Redner Sr. was granted a licence for a tavern. The first postmaster in Ameliasburgh was Thomas McMahon, and in all probability the post office was near the dock. He was appointed in 1846. In 1854 James Redner succeeded as postmaster, and from then until 1915 the post office was located in the building we know today as The Country Store. The land on which this building is located first came into the Redner name in 1851, when a lot was purchased by James Redner. Whether this building replaced an earlier one is not known. Records of this present building start about 1854. In 1915 and until 1927, the Post Office was under the Postmaster Spurgeon Dempsey, and was in a building that he owned just east of the store. His wife Mary Ann sold candy and ice cream in season from this building. Some who were teenagers during that period recall going out at night to Peter Redner's melon patch, stealing muskmelons, hiding them in a building behind Spurgeon Dempsey's; then going into the store, buying ice cream and then going to a place of sufficient secrecy where they could enjoy the stolen muskmelon with ice cream.

From the early days the Methodist Circuit Riders held meetings at regular intervals in the home, and later in the log school. When the first chapel was

View of Rednersville following the advent of telephone.

Parsonage house at Rednersville about 1910. Built in 1861 by Thomas Wickett of Belleville for 283 pounds, 2 shillings 4 pence. Rev. and Mrs. Sexmith in the foreground.

built in Consecon about 1834, it meant that services were held more frequently, as there was a minister resident in the district. Further information about the building of the 'Chapel' at Rednersville in 1849 is in the chapter on Churches in the Township, but we can intimate here that the dedication came Feb. 17, 1850 with services at "10 and 6½ in the evening". From the files of the Brighton Ensign, Jan. 4, 1945, some light is shed on church life of that period. Mrs. Dulmadge gave an interview at that time. She had been a Miss Rogers who was resident of Rednersville until 1871. "Mr. Irvin Diamond led the choir which consisted of the Brickman girls, Roland Way, Dolf Benson, Calvin Cunningham and myself. In those days there was no organ in the church by common consent, but we were taught from a long narrow notebook which opened about 2½ inches in length. The tuning fork gave the note and the conducting was upper-beat, downer-beat, hither-beat, thither-beat and they could sing too. Later the church purchased an organ from one of the churches in Belleville. It had a fancy circular wheel sort of contrivance in the top— perhaps imitating the coming pipe organ. At that time organs were not plentiful and some of the older church members declared that 'Satan' had at last been brought into the house of worship."

About 1880 the high tower was removed as the weight was causing the west wall to bow out. Sometime about then a chancel was added to the east side to accommodate a choir and organ. In 1937 the Presbyterian Church in Demorestville was purchased, dismantled and transported to Rednersville where it was added to the rear of the stone building for a church hall. It also served as a school classroom from 1939 until 1958 when the new school was completed.

The first school was a one-roomed log building with benches around the sides so that pupils faced the wall. Teachers were often men who could not, or would not, look for other employment. Books were limited. Much was taught by rote. Often the Bible was the main textbook. Many years ago a 90-year-old lady taught me her mathematics lesson which she had learned in the middle 1840's. It goes as follows:

"Twenty pence is one and eight pence, this I got for going to school,
Thirty pence is two and six pence, and with this I bought a rule;
Forty pence is three and four pence, this I out in paper laid;
Fifty pence is four and two pence this I for a grammar paid.
Sixty pence is just five shillings who dare say it's not;
Seventy pence is five and ten pence; master this for entrance got.
Eighty pence is six and eight pence; just a lawyer's fee.
Ninety pence is seven and six pence as you can plainly see.
One hundred pence is eight and four pence; this I lent to Cousin Ben,
As he wanted nine and two pence I gave to him the other ten.
Wishing the amount ten shillings, I gave him ten pence more;
I told him never tease me, never borrow from me more."

This school was south of the Spurgeon Dempsey property and was used until replaced by a one-room stone building east of the village, built in 1855. The log school stood south of the house occupied by Roy Sherrard. The present school, now serving as a three-roomed primary school under the County Board of Education, was formally dedicated on March 7, 1958. In 1959

Rednersville school built in 1855, used until 1958.

The Cunningham stage from Ameliasburg to Belleville by way of Rednersville.

the old school— situated between the farms of Ross and Rae Roblin was sold to G. Ross Roblin for $600 on condition that it be torn down and the site levelled. Today a flagpole just west of the house where Ross Roblin's son, Gordon lives, marks the site of the second school.

The earliest road was the one between lots 75 and 76 from the docks southward. It was eventually completed through the County to Wellington and is often referred to as the 'Townline Road'. Although the survey maps called for road allowances, sometimes the old Indian trails were followed. The so-called Rednersville road followed the settlements along the bayshore, and then took the route of least resistance in ascending Onderdonk hill around the route known today as Old Orchard Road. In the 1930's, this road was greatly improved by the paving of one track. This was often referred to as "Bonter's Sidewalk" as Earl Bonter was the Reeve at the time. This paved road went from Carrying Place to Rossmore. We are still aware of it in the springtime, as often the center of the road will heave because of the 'sidewalk' that lies underneath. The Townline Road was very important to the early settler, for by it the stage from Ameliasburgh village to Belleville approached and stopped in Rednersville. By it the wagon loads of produce went to and from the docks, such as apples in barrels to be shipped or to be dried in the evaporator after it was built in 1911. Tomatoes where shipped to the canning factory which was built east of the dock in 1912. It operated until 1949 when it burned, just before the harvest season.

When barley and rye were grown to achieve the premium price the malters and distillers gave for the product, the road was in constant use far into the night in harvest season. Stories exist of lines of wagons waiting to unload in a line stretching far beyond the village limits to the south. In later years, coal was

Ward's garage and home built in 1931, replacing the 'Brown Store'.

Fire at Ralph Stafford's mill, August 1941.

Below: His house, and the saw and grist mill, which were erected in 1912.

The Phillips & Dempsey evaporator, Rednersville.

shipped in to the dock and delivered from thence. With a busy port and with the presence of sailors and citizens who worked up a thirst, and with the easy availability of thirst-quenching drink, a constable was appointed to maintain law and órder. One such man was a man named Mercer who lived in the house restored by Walter Holmes. Here he also kept a small store. Either the people were very orderly, or the records of their infractions were destroyed, for no records or reminiscences of his arrests have come to light.

The Country Store has been a focal point of village life since it was built. It served as a general store, post office, and at one time a tailor operated out of a back room. From 1854 until 1941, with the exception of the years 1915 to 1927, mail was received and dispatched from here. In 1941 the Post Office was closed, and the mail routes were rearranged to be handled from Belleville and Carrying Place. The store was built of local limestone. In 1889 it was badly damaged by fire, and the front was rebult in brick. Upstairs was reached by a stairway served by a separate door from the verandah; marked now by the most westerly window on the verandah. The upper storey was made into a hall known as Redner's Hall, and was used for dances, parties, suppers, elections, community meetings and lodge meetings. In 1898 the Anglican church rented it for an evening service each week. It was served by Rev. Forrester in 1898 and by Rev. E.F. Byers in 1899. Rent was set at 50¢ a meeting. On the night of July 9, 1926, initiation ceremonies for entrance into the Orange Lodge were being held in the hall. Lightning struck the building and followed along the pipes which fed the gas lights. John Wellington Bowers, age 53, a member of the order, and his son, William Harold Bowers who was being initiated into the Order, though on opposite sides of the building, were both killed. All others in attendance with the exception of Carl Williamson and Spurgeon Dempsey were knocked unconscious. These two bolted down the stairs and, ironically, the only car they could manage to start belonged to the Bowers family. It was an evening not soon forgotten in Rednersville. When Keith Redner bought the store in 1934, he made an apartment where the hall had been, and it has remained so ever since.

The Hermon House east of the village owned now by Harold Lightfoot. Mary Redner, daughter of Henry Redner Sr., married Henry Hermon. Their grandson, Royal Hermon, who surveyed the village lots in 1866 (the Hermon Plan), lived here. A brass foundry run by Searing Johnson was west of this.

During 'Barley Days' and until the toll was removed on the Bay Bridge, Rednersville was a busy community. On the north side of the lot just north of the church was a building which at one time was the local cider press. It was first operated by horsepower, a team on a sweep, and owned by George Gray Later it was operated by a gasoline engine. Frere Hermon bought it from Mr. Gray. Gallons of cider were made here each fall, and the cider barrel soon became the vinegar barrel when a culture— often called 'Mother'— was added. Earlier this building housed a tailor shop.

There are at least four sites of blacksmith shops in the village; one just south of Ward's garage, where the last shop to succumb to the demise of the horse as a work animal was located; another just two lots south where Moore's home now stands; and a third on a site where Roy Sherrard has an excellent garden each year. Gilbert French was a cooper or barrel maker, working in part of the building where Bill Eckhart had his blacksmith shop. The building was built in 1882 and demolished in 1940 by John Hall when he purchased the property. Today the property is owned by Harold and Betty Redquist. On the lot north of that one, now owned by Douglas Boyce, Emery Hubbs operated a carpentry shop in 1898. He also made buggies, and at one time operated a lime kiln at the south end of the village.

At one time there were three general stores in the village. The store we know today was in operation. On the opposite corner, where Ward's garage is today, was Alpress Ashton's store and butcher shop. It was often referred to as the brown store, as the clapboard was unpainted. On the north east corner was

Home presently owned by Mrs. June Lott. The central part contains an early cooking fireplace. The large window marks the site of the Standard bank which had office hours on Wednesday in the early years of the 20th century. John Elliott was bank officer. Ed Peters and Tom Thompson had a store in the east end of the building about the same time.

Restored to a house by Walter Holmes. Owned variously by Walter Mercer, town constable and later a baker, succeeded by Arthur Stewart; then a gas station operated first by Benjamin Howell and then by Harold Ward; then a bakery again operated by Lorne and Ralph Wilder who delivered bread in the winter on a covered sleigh inscribed 'Wilder Brothers'.

the 'Yellow Store' operated by the Ketcheson sisters— the specialty of the one was dressmaking, of the other was bootmaking. Just east of this Mr. Mercer, the town constable, had a small store for a time, but eventually he turned it into a bakery. Later it was run by Arthur Stewart. The village was the center for commercial, social and religious life for a large community. The two docks on the west and the east sides of the road were very busy all during the season of navigation. The boats carried away the produce for sale, and brought in the commodities and freight needed for the community. At least five times a day the whistle from an approaching boat would alert the inhabitants to its arrival at the dock. These boats also took passengers to Trenton and Picton or points in between. The Annual Sunday School excursion often went by water on one of the Excursion boats that made Rednersville a regular stop on her way to Twelve O'Clock Point or Massassaga Point. Overnight trips went as far as the Thousand Islands in the St. Lawrence.

Taverns were built in the Rednersville area from the earliest times. Henry Redner Sr., was granted a tavern licence in 1810. Probably this building was just south of McMahon's property and dock. By 1851 the following requirements were set down by the Township Council for Tavern Keepers: "1. A tavern proprietor must have character reference from 12 freeholders and the permission of the majority of ward electors.
2. Property of Tavern owner must be valued at one hundred pounds.

Hotel built 1882 by William Rose, later sold to Dr. Moran. Burned 1909, succeeded by the Evaporator.

3. Taverns must have at least 3 rooms and 3 beds for travellers (not including family quarters)

4. Taverns must have good yards, sheds, stables and stalls for six horses to be used by travellers.

5. There must be no unlawful assembly, cards, dice 'Mini-pins' or any other implement of gaming.

6. After 10:00 p.m. only boarders and travellers allowed on the premises.

7. Hour of closing on Saturday 7:00 p.m. except for Medicinal purposes to be authorized by a doctor or a Justice of the Peace."

In 1870 Mr. Pulver built a hotel on the lot just west of Ward's garage. This was operated in 1878 by Jake Sager, by Don Brewer in 1880, and Mr. McMullen in 1889. It burned down in 1892. These inns did not miss the censure of the Methodist church. At the Fourth Quarterly meeting for 1881 held on May 4 of that year the following motion is passed: "Moved and seconded that Bros. I. Langdon and Peter P. Dempsey prefer charges against Wm. Rose and wife for selling spirituous liquors and keeping a public house contrary to the Discipline."

The censureship notwithstanding, William Rose, listed as a blacksmith in 1854, built a fine hotel in 1882. This was on the north-west corner of the intersection, where a vacant lot provides parking space today. He later sold it to Dr. Moran for a residence and office. It burned in July, 1909.

The duality of the times can be seen from our vantage point, and succeeding generations will point out similar faults in us. We see the prosperity of the times which all enjoyed- the many fine buildings that were built, and the improved way of life that was made possible from the selling of barley and rye for premium prices to the American market for malting and distilling purposes. At the same time, the church, indirectly supported by this prosperity, was crying out against the liquor trade, and Letitia Youmans, first in Bloomfield, then throughout the County and beyond, was organizing the "Women's Christian Temperance Union" whose main purpose was to abolish the sale of intoxicants and tobacco.

William Canniff in *The Settlement of Upper Canada* first published in 1868 has an item of interest here. It is to be noted that until 1831 the performance of marriage ceremony was limited to a clergyman of the Church of England or a Justice of the Peace. Thus, in this area, those intending to marry went to Mr. Young at Carrying Place. On page 239 of the above-named book is the following:

"We have some interesting information from an old lady who settled in Ameliasburgh and still lives. Getting married at the beginning of the present century was a great event. The Carrying Place was the usual place of resort. They placed in a lumber wagon, a number of chairs, and each gallant was supposed to support his partner upon his knee, and thus economize room. 'Bitters' were indulged in, but no fighting allowed. If it began, the fighters were put out. Keeping good natured was a point of duty insisted upon. No old persons went to the wedding, but they joined in the dance, when the youngsters got back. A wedding without a dance was considered an insipid affair; and it was generally kept up two or three successive nights at different places. Francis Weese's was a halfway house between McMahon's Corners, (Rednersville), and the Carrying Place. Weese was a distinguished player upon the fiddle, and the wedding parties often stayed with him the first night."

During the years, the health of the residents has been well looked after. At least three doctors were residents here prior to 1920. They were Dr. T.S. Farncomb, Dr. Knight and Dr. Moran. Dr. Ethel Dempsey has carried on the old tradition of country doctor with house calls to patients on a 24-hour-call basis all during the years she had lived in Rednersville.

Today the village has become, to some extent, a part of suburbia, but with a difference. Much of the country atmosphere of friendly concern for a neighbour, and at least some aspects of country hospitality are still in evidence. The tearoom at The Country Store, and Mike's coffee shop are still places where the 'locals' gather to share news, views and ideas. The church during the week provides opportunity for many boys and often their parents to meet for Cubs, Scouts and Beavers; and on Sunday to Worship, yes, but also to meet and greet the neighbours, as worshippers have in the same place since 1849.

The Redner home, probably built in the 1840's, with only a cooking fireplace in the kitchen at the back. Photo by Concept Photo, courtesy County Magazine.

CHAPTER 10

ROBLIN'S MILLS

Now known as the village of Ameliasburg, the hamlet went by the name of Roblin's Mills for well over 100 years. Previous to 1838, it was called Way's Mill, for John B. Way built a flour mill there on the pond under the hill. He came to Canada from Albany, N.Y. where he had learned the trade of milling. In 1815 he bought the east half of Lot 72 on the lower third of Ameliasburgh, where he lived and died. On February 5, 1829 he purchased lot 81, third concession, from Jacob Cronk who had been granted the Crown deed to it in 1803. On lot 81, below the escarpment, Way built his flour mill at the east end of the mill pond. This pond received its water from the natural drainage from the west, and not from the lake above the hill. There was even a post office, opened October 6, 1832 with a Mr. Meacham as postmaster from 1832-35. Mrs. Verna Sills can recall three deserted houses below the hill when she was a child, and traces of their foundations can still be found west of the cemetery. East of the cemetery there was also a house which later became a barrel factory. The Elmore map of 1835 shows Way's Grist Mill and Way's Post Office.

In 1838, Way traded his land and the mill, all of lot 81, for Owen Roblin's

The mill pond c. 1910.

The Roblin mill as seen from the gorge.

property, lot 76, along the east side of what is now County Road 23. Owen Roblin also owned lot 77 on the west side of the road, where he lived (now the McFaul farm). He was the son of Philip Roblin of the Roblin's Mills of Green Point in Sophiasburgh, and grandson of Philip Roblin U.E. of Adolphustown.

In 1842, Owen Roblin built his stone mill on top of the hill, an impressive building of limestone, five stories high. It was powered by water from nearby Roblin's Lake. Roblin spent $1,000 in blasting powder alone to excavate a canal from the lake to the mill. Fish in the lake were so plentiful that a man was hired in the spring to net the fish entering the gates of the mill, to prevent them going through and jamming the wheel.

The same water used to run the flour mill was also used, at the bottom of the hill, to operate a sawmill, using one of the old-fashioned upright saws. There was also a cooperage mill, a shingle mill, and an ashery below the escarpment. Lye from the ashery was shipped to Montreal. An old map shows two roads going down the hill, one at the east end of the present village and the other just west of the mill.

One year, when the water in the lake was low, Roblin decided to convert to steam power. He built a tall brick chimney at the west end of the mill, but only used it one year. The water in the lake came up again, and he reverted to water power. During the mill's heyday it was never closed, except on Sunday. It shut down at five minutes to 12 Saturday night and started up again at six a.m. Monday morning. It shipped immense quantities of wheat and rye flour to Montreal. The Roblin Milling Company operated 24 four hours a day during the American Civil War, and part of the reconstruction period, producing about 100 barrels of flour a day. Two teams of horses, according to local

Owen Roblin's stone mill with carding mill and chimney on west side, office and shed at east end. Note the board sidewalk along south side of street.

history, were kept busy hauling flour to the Rednersville dock from which schooners sailed regularly to American ports.

West of the mill by the smoke stack was a lower building which was a wool carding mill. The Masonic Lodge met in one of the upper rooms of the carding mill. At the east end of the mill a low building housed the mill office and the post office. In 1845 Owen Roblin became the postmaster for the village, which by then was called Roblin's Mills, and held the post until his death at age 97, when he was said to be the oldest postmaster in Canada. At the far end of the office building was a shed for horses. In this same building coffins were made from wide pine and elm boards. Roblin also built a bakeshop across the road which operated under the name of Maple Leaf Bakery.

Owen Roblin built a fine, large home of limestone for himself across the road from the mill. It was this beautiful house which eventually became the main building of the Salvation Army Camp.

In 1860, as a wedding gift for his eldest son Edward and his bride, Roblin built, just west of his own home, a house of the very latest design— an octagonal house of limestone. It had a cupola on its roof, reached by narrow stairs and a trap door. Edward was a miller. Another son, Roger, purchased two acres from his father in 1879, the site of the present Masonic Hall, where he built and ran a store. Roger also operated a cider mill and an evaporator for drying apples at the east end of the mill pond.

Owen Roblin built several small houses for his workmen east of the mill. Across from the mill he erected a windmill which supplied water to the east end of the village through a system of buried wooden pipes.

The mill closed in 1920, and Harry Smith of Belleville bought the property and mill in 1947. In 1963 the mill was taken down and its machinery incorporated in the Roblin Mill at Black Creek Pioneer Village.

All the east end of the village belonged to the Roblins. All the west end belonged to the Colemans. In 1834 Robert Coleman received a grant of land, the 200 acres of lot 82, third concession Ameliasburgh. He divided his land among his five sons. His eldest son, David, a millwright, built in 1842 the house

Maple Leaf Bakery— baker Frank Thompson, Mrs. Thompson and daughter Vera, in the 1920's.

The Owen Roblin residence.

Above: Two views of the octagonal house built in 1860 by Owen Roblin as a wedding gift for his eldest son, Edward. Octagonal houses are rare in the County, and this one had a cupola on its roof.

Plaque erected on mill site in 1971 by the 7th Town Historical Society.

The James Coleman home built in 1844, now home of grandaughter Mrs. V. Sills.

John Irvine Coleman in undertaker's attire.

Stage driven by Irvine Colemn; picture taken in front of Heber Sager's (now home of Mrs. Cecil McFaul.)

which is directly across the street from the Township Hall. Before the hall was built, township council meetings were held in David's cellar kitchen which had a fireplace and an entrance from outside. Robert's second son, Charles, lived where Harry Bisdee now lives. He was a carpenter and wagon maker. His third son, James, in 1844 built the home where Mrs. Verna Sills resides. He was her grandfather, and built the blacksmith shop that was located at the west end of the village for many years. He operated the shop from the 1840's until his death in 1897. The fourth son, John, was a photographer and also had a wood-working and furniture shop in the house just east of the present museum. Robert Jr., the fifth son, remained on the homestead and operated the farm north of the village.

In 1868, James Coleman donated the land on which the Methodist Church was erected. His son, John Irvine, 17 at the time, drew all the water required for the building of the church from the lake in barrels on a one-horse cart.

John Irvine Coleman began an undertaking business sometime before 1892 and operated it until 1912. Originally he was in partnership with R.O. Roblin, son of Edward, who later sold his share to Mr. Coleman. Funerals cost from $40 to $90, most of them in the $40 to $50 range. The hearse, drawn by two black horses, was driven by Alfred Lundy, who lived across the street at the corner. Burials were as far away as Tweed and Stirling. The caskets were bought from the Globe Casket Co. of London, Ontario, and were lined by Mr. Coleman (assisted by his wife) using casket lining purchased in bolt form. The funeral room was on the north side of the barn next to the third concession road, and was called the 'Hearse room'. There were name plates with the name of the deceased engraved on them. Mr. Coleman did the engraving himself. He went to the home of the deceased to prepare the body for burial. Proper attire for the undertaker included top hat, long-tailed coat and striped trousers. White hat and white gloves were worn for a young person's funeral. The bearers wore either black or white gloves furnished by the undertaker.

In the 1870's Isaiah Coleman, son of David, delivered the mail to Belleville, using a two-seated democrat. Isaiah also had a harness shop, in what is now the Croft's garage. From 1919 to 1929, John Irvine Coleman delivered the mail to Belleville, leaving the village at seven a.m. and returning by 4 p.m.

Company One of the 2nd Battalion, Prince Edward Militia was located in Roblin's Mills. Company One included men from lot 81 to lot 101 in the third and fourth concessions. James Coleman held the rank of Ensign in 1852, was promoted to Lieutenant in the 1854 and Commanding Officer in 1862. Mrs. V. Sills has the roll of Company One for the year 1862, listing a total of 81 men.

Ameliasburgh Township Hall; note doors into storage room and jail.

In 1874 David Coleman sold five acres of land across the road from his home on which the Township Hall was built. The Hall was built by Elijah Sprague at a cost of $4000. Beldon's Atlas states: "The material employed is a beautifully tinted blue limestone, with Kingston gray cut-stone facings, with arched windows and doors— the whole of modern style, superior construction and considerable claim to architectural beauty." The basement contained a wood-house, storehouse and a lock-up, 20' by 12' with bars on windows and doors, in the north-east corner. It was only used on one occasion.

The Township Hall, from 1874 until the present, has been the centre of municipal affairs, as well as a place for meetings, concerts, dances, travelling shows, suppers, entrance exams and short courses by the Department of Agriculture. The 4th Division Court used to meet there four times a year. Township council meetings have been held there ever since it was built.

A Pigeon Shoot at the fair grounds in 1905, with round exhibition building in background.

The township grounds extended then, as now, to the lake. In 1875, Council granted the Ameliasburgh Agricultural Society the use of the public lands lying south of the town hall and paid the Society $100 to fence the grounds. In 1880, Council bought an additional 2½ acres adjoining Town Hall property from Edward Roblin for $200. In 1888 Council loaned the Society $500 to erect an exhibition building. A round two-story building with a balcony running all around it was constructed. This round building was used until 1928 when it was torn down and a rectangular structure built to replace it. The fair grounds were also used for horse races on Dominion Day and by the Gun Club for their fall pigeon shoot.

The Sprague family also played an important role in the history of Roblin's Mills. In 1856 Sylvanus Sprague purchased property from Roblin, on which he built a carriage shop on the north side of the road. Sprague's two sons, John and Elijah, operated the carriage shop in partnership until 1870 when John sold his share to William Delong. In 1879, Elijah bought out Delong, making him sole proprietor until his death in 1881. Buggies, democrats, wagons, cutters and sleighs were manufactured here. Elijah built the Township Hall, the Methodist church and his own house (now the Beebe home) where he boarded some of his shop workmen.

In September, 1882, Sam Allan and Wm. Hatch bought the carriage factory. Allan lived in the present Hamelink home, and also boarded some of

---

The Sprague carriage factory.

his help. In 1894 Hatch sold his interest to Allan, who operated it alone from then until fire destroyed it in 1894.

John Sprague, after selling his share in the carriage shop, bought property just to the east of it where he built and operated a general store. This is now Alfred Anderson's home. Upstairs over the store were rooms occupied by a tailor, William McElliott, and the Misses Stapleton, milliners. A telegraph office also operated from Sprague's store from the 1880's until 1930, with telegraph poles set along the north side of the street. Later owners of the Sprague store were Joseph Nightingale and then William Plews. Plews was the last operator of the telegraph office. Art Corfield ran a butcher shop from the same premises from 1930 till the mid 30's.

The first tailor in the village was Henry Delong who purchased ¼ of an acre from Owen Roblin in 1851, later designated lot 5, corner of Main St. and Taylor. Contrad (Coon) Delong also was a tailor, as was a John Taft. Two shoemakers were listed on the 1855 assessment roll— a Silas Cruper and James R. Henesy. Wm. H. Stafford ran a hardware business in the Delong house for a time, then Wm. Carnrike took it over and continued until the house burned in 1905. The present large frame home on lot 5 was built by Joseph Nightingale.

Roblin's Mills had two hotels. The first was built by Aaron Bryant circa 1851, and operated until 1887 when it was destroyed by fire, burning a house and a store west of it as well. A second hotel, called the Marsden House after its builder, Marsden Delong, was erected in 1889 on the site of the burned store. It had 12 bedrooms, a bar, reception room, dining room and sitting room, and was a stopover for travelling salesmen. The Marsden House was in business

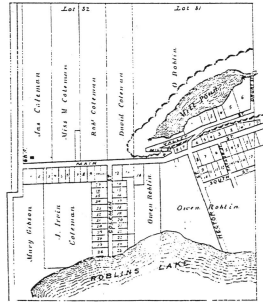

Plan of the village of
Roblin's Mills from
Belden's Atlas 1878

until 1928. The site is now the home of the resident care-taker of the Salvation Army Camp.

In 1870, Dr. File came to Roblin's Mills where he served the township as a dedicated country doctor for 60 years. His home was the last house on the north side of the road at the east end of the village. In the front room of his home he set up a small drugstore. The story of Dr. File and his family will be told elsewhere in this book, but the part they played in the development of the village must be recorded here.

The store, many will remember, is the File Bros. store. A brick structure, built circa 1895, it housed a general store downstairs and the lodge rooms of the Ancient Order of United Workmen upstairs. Two of Dr. File's sons, Fred and Albert, took over this store in 1908. Previous to that, Fred ran a grocery business for three years in the same front room of the File home that had served as a drug store.

File Bros. Store was in operation for almost 50 years. From Oct. 1912 till 1951, the village post office was located in this store, with Fred as postmaster. In 1957 Arthur Corfield took over the store for three years, then sold it to Ron Callow who ran it for eight years. Now remodelled, it is the Callow home.

Albert File, for many years, owned and operated Idlewylde. This property, purchased from Owen Roblin in 1856 by Sylvanus Sprague, later owned by his son Elijah, and then by a James Lewis, was taken over by Mr. File. He remodelled the building, changing partitions and laying hardwood floors. It was he who named it 'Idlewylde'. In reality it was a community centre for the township. Old and young alike came, to enjoy dancing to the music of many orchestras which were hired, including the Bon Ton of Belleville and Hugo Diggins, or even local girls who took turns playing the piano. Mr. File had his own orchestra too which consisted of: Piano— Fred Morton, Bass Viol—

Marsden Hotel.

File Bros. store.

Geoffrey File, First Violin— Fred Russell, Second Violin— Wm. Morton, Drums— Albert File.

Mr. File added an ice-cream parlour, canteen, a shoe repair and a barber shop, with Horace Calnan barbering evenings. Dr. Bradley had a dentist office there, open part time. Upstairs there was a pool hall, the tables purchased by File from the old Marsden Hotel. Art Corfield has his butcher shop there for a while also. Many functions were held in Idlewylde, such as checker tournaments, card parties, banquets, bazaars, fowl suppers and wedding receptions. Then its hey-day was over. For a few years Mr. and Mrs. Roy Smith used it as their home while he operated the grist mill across the way. When Albert File died in 1959, Idlewylde became the property of St. Alban's Anglican Church. The church board sold it to Elaine Wilson for an Inn and Art Gallery. After her dreams failed to materialize, Idlewylde, now in disrepair, was sold for taxes. The building was removed, and the vacant lot is now the property of the Township of Ameliasburgh.

Through the years, church and school played an important role in the lives of the residents of Roblin's Mills. The story of the Methodist church with its tall spire and St. Alban's Anglican Church with its bell is recounted in the chapter on Churches. Likewise the history of S.S. 12 is included in the chapter on Schools.

When the carriage factory burned in 1894, Albert Crosby bought the property and had a blacksmith shop there until 1901. Then he moved to the James Coleman shop at the west end of the village where his son, Grant, remained until 1932, then moved back to the Sprague factory site. When Crosby closed down his smitty, Art Corfield took it over and operated a grist mill there until 1943 when he sold it to Roy Smith.

Main Street Roblin's Mills c. 1907, looking west.

Harry Bisdee's Bakery,
Harry and Hilda Bisdee.

Masonic Hall 1983.

Metropolitan Bank.

Another earlier grist mill was located on the Bisdee property, run by Gilbert Choate c. 1904-1920. Then Choate sold to Grant Crosby who started a bakeshop. In 1935 Harry Bisdee bought the property and bakeshop. He had a peddling wagon on the road six days a week. The Bisdees baked white, whole wheat and raisin bread, and several kinds of buns. A single or half-loaf, as they were called then, sold for 5¢. In 1936 they added groceries to their business. An addition was made to the building in 1937; the building was divided and the bakeshop put in the rear. Because the flour dust affected their son, Eugene, the Bisdees had to give up baking, but continued the store and peddling

Folio 154

AMELIASBURGH, *Octr 1st* 1878.

Mr Joseph Nightingale

BOUGHT OF **E. SPRAGUE,**

CARRIAGE MAKER.

MANUFACTURER OF BOTH LIGHT AND HEAVY WORK.

1878

Jan	25	To side plate on runner 40, clip on beam 25, Welding brace 15		80	
		" Singletree 50, fix runner on sleigh 50	1	00	
Mar	1	" 1 bolster 100, pair crothes 125, 1 stake 50	2	75	
		" irons on bolster 50, rfl 2 singletree 40		90	
Apl	8	" setting rxles 100, rod in box 25, set springs 500	6	25	
		" fixing irons on gear 100, do demorest box 50	1	50	
		" 2 bed preces 100, spring block 75	1	75	
	26	" Painting Wagon 600, 1 cushion 150, 1 Clip 15	7	65	
May	25	" fixing buggy 20, June 3 fixing Circle 25	45	23	05
		To amt due		23	05

A bill from E. Sprague, Carriage Maker, listing 'light and heavy work' performed for a client.

wagon. In 1947 Norman Sword rented the store and carried on the business until his death in 1973. He was also the postmaster. Then Mrs. Morgan Sills took over the store and post office for three years, when she moved the post office to her own home and closed the store. From 1977 until January 1983, the building became a public library, but now stands empty as the library was moved to the township hall.

For a few years Roblin's Mills had a bank. From March 1906 to December 1915 the Metropolitan Bank was located in the Masonic Hall. For a short time in 1920-21 the Dominion Bank opened an office, also in the Masonic Hall.

A board walk, made of long planks, ran along the south side of the village street. This was gradually replaced by cement sidewalks, beginning with a section from Owen Roblin's home to the town hall in 1905, from Idlewylde to the east limits in 1906, and from the Town Hall to the west end in 1912. The last section to be done was from Idlewylde to the Roblin home in 1913. The story is told that the former contractor, not getting the job for this last section, showed his displeasure by walking the length of it before it was set.

Seventh Town/Ameliasburgh 157

Main St., Village of Ameliasburg, looking east, 1983.

Roblin stone in
Grove cemetery
under the hill

Main St., looking west, 1983.

There is a great deal more which could be told about Roblin's Mill, but space does not permit. What a busy, bustling hamlet it once was, with its mills, carriage factory, stores, hotels, blacksmith shop and other businesses.

History is never static. As this account is being written, the Prince Edward Region Conservation Authority is at work below the hill, bull-dozing and clearing along the shores of the mill pond to make a small park where the first village was located.

The Callow home, formerly the location of the File Bros. store.

A modern house on the site of the Marsden Hotel.

CHAPTER 11

M̄OUNTAIN VIEW

Loral Wanamaker, now residing in retirement at Rossmore, has made an extensive study of genealogy and local history. He spent his boyhood years living at Mountain View and remembers many people, and events that happened during his early years.

The following is his story of Mountain View as presented to the 7th Town Historical Society— 1972.

The 'Union'

Many people today are not aware of the location of the original Mountain View, which had at least three houses, a carriage shop, a blacksmith shop and a Post Office named 'Mountain View'. The location of this hamlet was on the east side of Highway 14, then known as the Picton Road, directly across the Highway from the intersection with the Second Concession of Ameliasburgh. The last of the buildings was demolished when the Highway was widened in 1960.

Looking directly west up the Second Concession at an early date when there were fewer trees, one could see the large outcropping of granite rock, similar to the rock which we see in North Hastings. This rock was known for many years as Young's Mountain and it is understandable that people living at the end of the concession road should refer to their hamlet as Mountain View because they did have a view of the Mountain.

The Second Concession starts at Highway 14 and meets the Rednersville Road at the old Centre Church and School (now Young's Antiques). Wellington Howell told me that this section was called Bunbury Road, and Harold Young of Young's Mountain confirmed this. West of the Rednersville Road (from Centre to Victoria), the concession road was known as the Palace Road.

I remember T.B. (Bo) Tillitson living in one of the houses, also George Nobles. I remember Royal Jones, who was the blacksmith in the other house and later Jim Cretney, also a smithy.

Being interested in the Post Office (30 years at Belleville Post Office as Letter Carrier, Senior Letter Carrier, and later Postal Officer in charge of Letter Carriers for 11 years), I received from the Post Office Dept. Ottawa a record of the Postmasters of Mountain View P.O.

(NAME OF OFFICE) *Tain View*	(ELECTORAL DISTRICT AND PROVINCE) *Prince Edward*

DATE OF ESTABLISHMENT — *1-3-1862* OFFICE CLOSED — *30-1-1932*
OFFICE RE-OPENED — *2-11-1936* *3-1-1948 for want of a postmaster*

CHANGES IN NAME

FORMER NAME .... DATE OF CHANGE ....

NAME OF POSTMASTER	MILITARY STATUS	DATE OF BIRTH	DATE OF APPOINTMENT	DATE OF VACANCY	CAUSE OF VACANCY
W. H. Way			1-3-1862	20-9-1880	Res.
J. B. Tifleston			1-4-81	20-5-84	Res.
John Potter			1-8-84	1909	
R. A. Frederick			9-12-1109	17-2-1913	Resignation
W. M. Hubbs			24-4-1913	26-4-1913	Resignation
James Grant Sprague		26-3-1868	20-11-1913	31-1-32	Closed
James Grant Sprague		26-3-1868	2-11-1936	30-10-1947	Resignation Closed

Post Office record of the Mountain View P.O., courtesy Loral Wanamaker.

The farm of John Potter, the new Postmaster, began about half a mile south of the intersection we have just discussed and ran south to the foot of the big hill where the road allowance divides the third concession from the fourth concession of Ameliasburgh. This road, now Highway 14, I believe is taken for the most part along here from the Potter farm. Just a short distance farther south from the start of the Potter farm was his home and a cheese factory, just where it is located today, in 1972. John Potter had three sons, and the eldest at this time began a greenhouse and a little later a canning factory on a part of his father's farm just a little south of the road to Huff's Island and which is operated today by his grandson Stanley Barber and his sons Willet and Robert Barber. This son was known as S.S. Potter (Stanley). A second son Wilfred Potter lost his arm in 1882 and consequently could neither help his father farm nor make cheese, which was done by a younger son Adolphus (Dolph) but he eventually moved to Seattle where he remained. His son Arnold and his daughter Addie often returned to visit.

Wilfred Potter, having lost his arm, looked for another occupation and about 1884 acquired a small store run by his Aunt Phoebe Thompson at the foot of the hill, and next to the cooper shop of Richard Exceen, who had his home south of the shop and on the very west corner of the Potter farm at the road allowance. The Dominion Census of 1871 shows this house of frame, but I don't remember the front part being anything but brick from, say, about

1900. My father made cans for Mr. Potter and I would take the little tins from the ends of the can, about the size of a penny, and Mrs. Potter would always give me a candy for same when I called on her. It would seem this house had been enlarged and bricked by whom I can't say. According to the memorial stone, R. Exceen had passed away by 1880 so it would seem logical that Wilfred Potter had taken this house over as a store and a Post Office and it was still called Mountain View, which at the foot of the big hill was a very appropriate name.

An early view of Mountain View showing the building which over the years has housed a store, post office and telephone system, and now apartments. Next is the twin towered church and next to that the school. The cemetery is pictured in the foreground.

It would appear that Wilfred Potter had the store and Post Office until he passed away in 1905. Byron Frederick purchased the store, and the Post Office was continued in this store and he appeared to me to be the Postmaster, but when John Potter died in 1909 you will note B.O. Frederick became the Postmaster while he had the store and until he moved to Belleville in 1913. In his late years, John Potter remarried and lived across from the store in what I knew as the Misses Fox house. It would appear that he, John Potter, was the Postmaster for 25 years, and during the term of his son Wilfred Potter and B.O. Frederick who were acting under him. Edward Hubbs bought the store and ran it for only a few months when it was purchased by J. Grant Sprague who made many additions to it. It was used as his Central for the Sprague Telephone Co. and he also carried a large stock at one time in the store. Today I can see they are building it over again and it is now apartments.

An early picture of the store and post office when operated by B. O. Frederick.

The same building after it had been taken over by Mr. Sprague for use as the Telephone Exchange.

Now this hamlet at the foot of the hill is called Mountain View, but all during my years it was known as the *Union* and even now the oldsters, call it the Union; long after the Mountain View Post Office was located here. After the first war it was seldom spoken of by any but a few as the Union, but I noticed in conversation only a short time ago with my brother-in-law Percy Parliament, he spoke of the Union, and I will speak about it a little from 1900 to 1950. Just at the foot of the hill is a road or allowance which ran east to the marsh and on the north side east of the store we had the barn and ice house then a new house built by Wilfred Potter where Mrs. Jay Sprague lives. Past this house was a lovely cold spring from which we carried water for the school, then woods, and a bit farther a big clearing or open field and here another lovely spring and this clearing was known to the older persons, when I was a lad, as the Camp Meeting Ground.

A clipping I found reads:—

"A Camp Meeting will be held for the Picton Dist. on the rear of Richard

Sprung's farm Township of Ameliasburgh near UNION SCHOOL to commence Thursday Sept. 6th, at 2 p.m. Application for tents to the Rev. I. Weldon not later than Sept. 1st at 2 p.m. Single tent three and double tent six, with plenty of good water and pasture."

Beyond this there were two houses built on the road which belonged to squatters and they had gardens alongside the houses which left just enough for a team and wagon to go through. These were lived in by George and Levina Nobles. Across from the squatters' houses was a fine orchard which would be on Don Jones' farm; and next a nice little house where I lived for a good many years with my father and mother, Grant and Letta. We rented this house from Wilfred Potter. There were about two acres here with an orchard on part. The next field going west on the south side of this road allowance was another good orchard on the Ferguson place, now the Motley farm. Another abandoned shack, once occupied by squatters, was about where Clarence Sprague's house is. Again the land west from here to the church shed was orchard (now old Sprague Canning Co.) and Wilfred Potter owned this, and we are back again to the Picton Road and this allowance had a name given to it by Grant Wanamaker "Turkey Run".

A view of the church showing a corner of the sheds once used for tying in horses.

The lovely old Country Church was built as "A Canada Methodist Church" in 1877. Early on it had a church shed all along the allowance, that is the north side of the church and also all across the back. Next, south, we have a lovely Stone School, built in 1855, and a bit larger than many country schools and just half way up the hill. This was used for a church, for funerals, for penny readings and just about anything going on in the Union previous to the building of the church. It was larger likely because it was a Union school, S.S.

11 & 7. It had been at one time a two-room school and the upper part of the partition was still in place many years after I went. I believe they spoiled it by plastering it over to make it warmer, and now it is in the process of being rebuilt into a home. East of the school house and half way up the hill we had the fine frame home of Jesse Sprung and east of him again another fine frame home of Clayton Sprung, father of Clark who now keeps it just the same, and just beyond a small frame house where a Mrs. Rush lived when I was small, and which is now gone.

Across from the school, that is on the west side of the Picton Road, we have the Union Cemetery on a gentle slope and here in the Tremaine map of 1863 is shown two houses. One of these would be on the lower part of the present cemetery and the other on what we called the garden or directly in front of the present small barn. It doesn't seem so, but these two homes, the Cemetery, the three homes east of the school, and the school and church are all in the fourth concession of Ameliasburgh.

Now continuing north we cross the driveway to the next house and this driveway is actually the road allowance but must have been closed years ago. Here there used to be a small frame dwelling of one storey where a Mrs. Fox lived. I often went there for our milk in a little tin pail at 5¢ a quart. My father purchased this lot from Elmer Doolittle and raised the roof of the house to a one-and-a-half storey. We sold to Edward Hubbs and he later sold to Uncle Henry Jason Parliament, who raised the roof to a cottage type, and this is where Alfred Post now lives (1972). Below and about opposite the old cooper shop, there was a blacksmith shop; the last smithy was Dave Duetta. Then the swamp. Alfred Post had a very old mulberry tree on this place and it was one of several large ones that I remember when I was a boy and this one does not seem to have changed any.

Loral Wanamaker

Further to Loral Wanamaker's history of the original Mountain View written in 1972, it would only be right to tell you of the Mountain View of 1984. Like many similar hamlets throughout Ontario, changes came slowly. The mills, blacksmiths and cooperages have long since gone. Even the one room school has been sold to provide a home. The original Sprague Canning factory has not processed tomatoes for several years. In the meantime a new factory is processing vegetables in a different way for a different life style. People living in the area have had employment at the Sprague's for many years. Firstly girls worked at the Sprague Telephone Exchange and over the years many girls were employed there as 'Hello' girls. Many farmers in the area grew tomatoes for Sprague's Canning factory and during the canning season a number of seasonal helpers were required. At the new modern plant operated by Roger Sprague, about 20 workers are needed. Some of the products canned are pork and beans, red kidney beans, white kidney beans, lentils, chick peas and lentil soup.

The original Sprague Canning Factory— operated by Grant Sprague and son Jay.

A modern plant for food processing owned and operated by Roger Sprague.

Potter's Greenhouses

Sometime in the late 1800s, John Potter, who built and started the Mountain View cheese factory, gave his son Stanley 14 acres of land on the corner of Highway 14 and Huff's Island Road. Stanley built an addition on the old house to the west to complete his home and started a small greenhouse on the southern side of the old house, along with a rather longish east and west one where he grew vegetables and flowers. He also constructed a building to be used as a canning factory where he canned peas, corn and pumpkin. Fred Potter and Grant Wanamaker made the cans used in the upper storey.

S.S. Potter (Stanley). It was Stanley Potter who started one of the first canning factories in Prince Edward. He also built greenhouses to grow vegetables and flowers. Old Potter Homestead— This is now the residence of Stanley Barber and Willet Barber.

I remember the farmers bringing in pea vines cut out of the fields on hay wagon racks and dumping them on the factory floor and the women sat and shelled the peas to be canned. He also put the husked corn through a corn-cutting machine. This was a rather risky procedure as the knives were quite sharp. The pumpkin was pressed through a pumpkin gun into the cans. He sold the most of the product on Belleville market along with vegetables he grew. Much of this was asparagus and grapes, along with cabbage. I went to help him 1922 and one of the early sales we made was a truck load of cabbage which we took to Kingston to sell. We got 28¢ per dozen for them so it wasn't a get-rich-quick scheme.

He died in 1930 at the age of 82, so his factory was among the earliest built around here. We have added on somewhat and torn down some to save the high cost of fuel.

'Barber Flowers' is now carried on by two Barber sons, Willet, living in part of the double house, and Robert, living in a new house erected on the property when he was married.

Stanley Barber

Mountain View Church

On the hillside overlooking the surrounding area stands the twin-towered church at Mountain View. This is a landmark which can be seen from some distance. The church was opened in 1878, built at a cost of $3000 and it was known as a Wesleyan Church but was called 'Union'. The congregation was associated with the Canada Methodist Church. In 1925 when the Methodist Church became part of the United Church of Canada, the church was thereafter known as Mountain View United Church. The congregation was part of the Ameliasburgh charge with the minister living at Ameliasburgh.

The site was donated by David Sprung and Mr. and Mrs. Cornelius Hubbs. The building of red brick has galleries, a large auditorium, with Sunday School room below; and what was once a furnace room and fuel storage room, is now a modern kitchen and nursery. The building, once heated with a wood and coal hot air furnace, has been electrically heated since 1960. A small addition on the north side built in 1972 provides washrooms and a small meeting room. In the early years, there were sheds to house the horses which were driven to church. The front, facing the road, has a beautiful rose window. Sunlight filtering through this window shines on the chancel in the afternoon.

When the congregations of Ameliasburgh, Massassaga and Mountain View were amalgamated in 1967, a new name was chosen and the church is now known as Wesley United Church— a part of the Prince Edward North Pastoral Charge. In 1955, Stanley Barber made a gift of an electric organ to the church in memory of his grandfather, Stanley Potter.

Two beautiful stained glass windows were donated for the sanctuary by Stanley and Margaret Barber in 1981. In the same year, as the cost of heat was increasing, it was deemed necessary to put insulation in the walls. While this work was being carried out, a severe thunderstorm passed through the area striking the bell tower. Damage was done to the tower and throughout the church. After some consideration it was decided to place the bell on a cement slab and it was located on the front lawn. The improvements and repairs cost some $29,000.

Across the road from the church is a pretty little cemetery where many of the pioneers and their descendants are buried.

Mountain View School

Years ago Mountain View was commonly called the 'Union'. At one time there were schools located near the site of the Barber greenhouse, and on County Road No. 2 near where Norris Gibson resided. Then a site at Mountain View was given for a new school. In 1855 when the new school was opened it was known as the Union school.

For many years this was a two-room school with about 90 pupils attending, pupils even coming from Huff's Island during the winter. In 1879 wood was purchased for the furnace at $2.70 a cord; in 1927 it had increased to $14 a cord.

The stone school erected in 1855.

Now in 1984 a cord of wood may cost as much as $100 delivered.

In 1940 some 400 acres of land was purchased for Mountain View Airport. This land was the Sophiasburgh part of the section, making Mountain View school no longer a 'Union' section, but wholly in Ameliasburgh.

Mountain View was one of the schools closed when the new central Kente School was opened in 1966.

Notes from the Tweedsmuir Book File

(as written by Lily Anderson)

1st school house at S.S. Potter's, another one on the Frank Lauder farm, then owned by Henry Snider who gave the land for the school house. Mr. Snider was also a local preacher. Another school house was on the high shore of Sophiasburgh. These three sections united and built the Union School at Mountain View. In 1855 when the Union school was opened, Lawrence Sprague and H.J. Parliament were the first to go in followed by Geo. Sprague and Miss Matilda Anderson. They had a spelling match that night and Aunt Tillie spelled the school down. Also they had a Polling Booth to elect a trustee at this Union school later on. Wilfred Potter and Wm. Henry Wood ran and Mr. Wood was elected.

Below the school house was a store run by Miss Phoebe Thompson. Wilfred Potter had the Post Office. There was also a store on top of the hill run by a Mr. Smith and when their baby was born Mrs. Sylvanus Sprague went down to help and before Mrs. Smith died she handed Mrs. Sprague the baby and asked her to care for it and bring it up. So Mrs. Sprague took the baby home, and when she took it in the house, her daughter Philena said, "What did you bring another baby for, there are eight of us already?" Her mother said that one more would not make any difference so they called her 'Baby' for a while and one day Mr. Sprague said the child has to have a name and he picked up a book called *Lena Rivers* and he said we will call the baby Lena Rivers Smith and she later on married Oliver Calnan.

Willet Way had the first Post Office in a rough cast house just across from, and a little south of, Jim Barber's; he also had one of the first carriage shops in the country, and a blacksmith shop in connection with a carriage shop. He made buggies, wagons and democrats. A man by the name of Captain Joseph Bunbury had a small store by the Post Office.

Mrs. John Potter doctored eyes and people came from all over to get their eyes doctored and would stay there until able to go home. She would have up to 25 staying at a time. Dolph Potter had one of the first cheese factories. Stanley Potter had one of the first canning factories, also he had a vineyard over on the farm where Jim Robinson lived and sold grapes. Lawrence Sprague, Virgil Thompson and Manly Howell grew hops. Barley was also in great demand. My father grew a lot of barley when he first bought his farm to make payments. It was shipped from the Pitching Place on the High Shore, also from Rednersville and there would be such a line of wagons all night and day to get unloaded. In the early days they had Camp meetings in George Anderson's woods. Later on I remember we had a Harvest Home dinner when they had a Congregational Meeting in the same woods in August. It was like a picnic: the whole family went and everyone had a good time together. Before the church was built they had church services and funerals at the school.

There was a child lost at Mountain View who was never found. The family lived in the Road Allowance from Potter's Grocery store. The child's name was Badgley. The whole neighbourhood turned out and looked for days in the woods and marsh. Some thought she might have been sold to the Indians. The child's mother afterwards married a Mr. Harding and they lived in the house where Clarke Sprung stores things, but she never told what happened to the child.

There was a place on the hill where they made potash. The bricks for our house were made on the farm. George Henry Sprung lived where Ben's lived and he had a race track on his farm. The house where Gilbert Ways lived burned down, and also the George Henry Sprung house burned and a child was burned to death there.

John R. Cunningham had a grist mill and a copperage factory by the mill dam. People used to sell their wood ashes.

George Anderson brought in the first Holstein cows at Mountain View.

William Anderson was a member of Parliament serving two terms. He was also Reeve, Warden and Justice of Peace.

H.J. Parliament born at Mt. View taught school at Victoria and boarded around at the different homes. He organized the first Sunday School at Victoria 1867, 100 years ago.

Mountain View is one of the largest churches in the County of Prince Edward, seats 300.

There was a child killed in a buggy coming down Mt. View hill, some of the harness broke.

Our Institute collected for the first hospital in Picton. Isabel Davern and I collected down Massassaga Road.

Two men traded wives.

The boys like to take boiled eggs to school so they could trade them for candies.

More About Mountain View

In the house at the bottom of the hill, on the west side of the road just below the cemetery and formerly known as Alfred Post's, lives a young lady who makes miniatures. Madeline Jobin Hope creates everything in miniature for entire rooms decorated in period settings. She has created doll houses, complete with all of the furnishings, a grocery store, various box rooms or shadow boxes each with appropriate accessories.

Mountain View Church— *An old picture of this church showing the beautiful rose window.*

Undoubtedly the large building at the foot of the hill on the east side of the roadway (just below the church) could tell many stories of its own. It has contained living quarters, a post office, store, telephone exchange and lately four apartments. We have pictures of this building with horses tied out front and we have pictures of the first cars parked beside it. To one generation it was popularly known as 'Spragues'.

Picture taken in 1912 showing the building containing store and post office and now the Telephone Exchange, Church and School on up the hill.

Mountain View is again increasing in population as several lovely new homes have been built, some along the top of the hill where there is a wonderful view, and others along the concession roads. On the third concession, west of Highway 14, is an unusual house built in octagonal shape. This is one of several built in the County. At one time, William Anderson, the member of Provincial Parliament, lived there.

Further up the Third Concession, Ameliasburgh Township has a large dump site where all of the Township waste is disposed of. Some people refer to this road as the 'Dump' road but residents living on top of the escarpment and using this road to get to Highway 14 refer to it with much grander title 'Valley Road'.

Old log house, once the home of Charles E. Lauder.

The log cabin pictured in this section, situated on County Road 2, was the home of Charles E. Lauder and his wife Amarilla Jane Cunningham, parents of Mrs. Edith (Lauder) Burkitt.

During an interview with Muriel Minaker she said that Lily Sprague remembered her grandparents living in the log cabin. She said how homey it always was with its bright yellow painted floors and colourful braided rugs.

In 1902, when Edith was four years old, a new home was built directly across the road by W.W. Fitzgerald of Wellington. Edith grew up here and after her father died, she and her husband Wm. Burkitt, moved back to the farm. The house is now occupied by daughter Muriel and her husband Grant Minaker.

Mountain View has had many road changes. Some of the buildings were built along the road allowance between the third and fourth concession. The church and school front on the old Picton Road. Highway 14 was built in 1924 and was much wider and without the sharp turn on the hill. In 1960 the Highway was again improved making a straighter roadway and again intersecting with County Road 2 at the top of the hill.

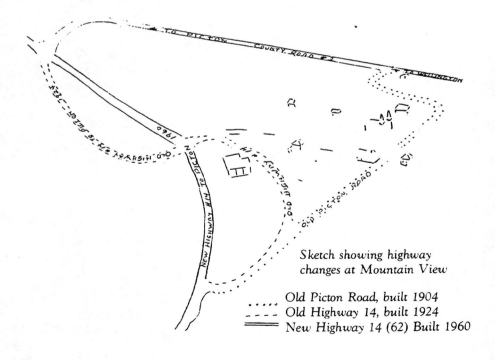

Sketch showing highway
changes at Mountain View

```
. . . . .   Old Picton Road, built 1904
- - - - -   Old Highway 14, built 1924
=======   New Highway 14 (62) Built 1960
```

J.G. Sprague— Founder of the Sprague Telephone System, Mountain View, 1898-1956.

The Sprague Telephone System

By D.K. Redner in the Picton Gazette, March 27, 1953
Copied from Rednersville W.I. Tweedsmuir Book

Alexander Graham Bell was a Scottish immigrant, born in Edinburgh. In 1870 he migrated to Canada where he conducted his first experiment with the telephone. In the following year he went to Boston where he became professor of vocal physiology. The first public exhibition of the telephone was made in 1876 at the Centennial Exposition in Philadelphia. By August of 1877 there were 778 telephones in use in the United States. With the first invention, only two persons could talk to each other (a 2-party line) but it was soon found that further parties could be connected and the line used by all with equally good results. In the same year of 1877, a man by the name of Gardiner Hubbard conceived the idea of a switchboard by means of which several lines could be connected, to allow conversation from one to the other and, thus, our telephone was born.

As soon as Grant Sprague had achieved a degree of young manhood he displayed his talents as an electrician and became interested in the telephone, eventually constructing a line from his home on Big Island to that of his uncle, James Longwell, some two miles distant. The first conversation was held on March 27, 1898, and it is fitting that this article should go to the press on March 27, exactly 55 years later. The two miles at that time was an almost incredible distance to talk, for few of the residents of the countryside had ever seen a telephone. Many visitors were admitted to witness its workings— some of whom had driven miles with old dobbin on the buggy or democrat.

Miss Lillian Sprague, who has served over 40 years in the capacity of secretary-treasurer of the company, recalled several amusing incidents of the early days. Many people conceived the ideas that the strength of their voice could be responsible for its being able to carry such a long distance, and the longer the distance the louder they shouted into the mouthpiece of that strange contraption hanging on the wall. The trials and tribulations of the first operators were many and varied. She laughingly told the story of one old lady, the mother of one of the line's first subscribers. She was near-sighted, and whenever she took down the receiver to answer she would invariably call to some of the other family members to bring her glasses so she could see who was on the other end of the line.

The present Sprague line is the third owned by the family, the first being developed from the first single line on Big Island which eventually became the People's Mutual System of Sophiasburgh. The care and upkeep of the line, however, became a case of that old adage "what is everybody's business is nobody's business", so after much difficulty had been experienced along this line, it was eventually absorbed into the Bell system. Then there was a second line in the Township of Hillier operating mostly to the north and west of Wellington with the central in Hillier village. That was in the time of the old horse and buggy days when quite too much time might elapse between a trouble call and a repair job. On this line the repair gang would leave home on Monday morning and often not return until Saturday afternoon. At its height of success, the line boasted about 100 subscribers. Mrs. Hardy kept central, and one day a frantic call came to the Spragues for help. She had broken her receiver and could take no calls. Ordinary business did not worry her to such an extent but it was those emergency calls— a fire, accident, a sudden call for the doctor— would they please come and fix it as soon as possible? The linesmen were all out on the road; the women at home could not readily locate them, so the secretary-treasurer contacted the next neighbour, Mabel Lauder (now Mrs. Norris Gibson) and proposed that she accompany her on the trip. The Sprague horses were all in use, so the two women walked a mile to Mountain View borrowed a horse and buggy from Joshua Dodd who lived where Alfred Post now lives, and drove to Hillier to make the repair themselves. The trip took all day. They had dinner with Mrs. Hardy and had the satisfaction of obtaining their objective.

The men on the construction and maintenance job used to camp wherever they worked. They had a bunk-house on a wagon with an upper and lower berth where four men could sleep. They had a cook-stove and got their own meals, but one day disaster overtook them and their abode burned to the ground. That incident took place along the lakeshore above Wellington. Soon after the line there was sold to the Bell, as it entailed too much driving for maintenance.

After the bunk-house burned, their means of locomotion for this type of work was a horse and democrat. As the years progressed, Fred became old

Sprague Telephone Company

Lease No. _____ Telephone No. _____

Order and Agreement for Connection with Sprague Telephone Company.

Connect my premises known as *W. H. Montgomery*

with other subscribers of the above exchange in this place for the period of *Five* year

at $ *10.00* from the date of connection, payable yearly in advance, and such connection to be continued upon the following conditions :—

The lines and instruments are furnished and maintained at a rental to subscribers payable yearly in advance.

The said Sprague Telephone Co. reserves the right to remove their instruments from any residence, store or office at any time if any subscriber makes any improper use of the instruments hereby leased, listening to conversations of others, profanity, etc, etc., or fails to pay rental in advance, or in case the instrument of any other company should be installed in the premises of the subscriber.

Subscribers will in no case allow any one to examine or handle the telephone in their premises and shall report any request to do so of any one to the Gen. Manager, failing to do so subscribers shall forfeit all rentals paid and the Company reserves the right to cancel lease and remove the telephone.

One battery renewal each year will be furnished, all extra renewals will be charged for.

All conversations limited to three minutes.

Subscribers must avoid using Telephones during a thunder storm.

Subscribers will kindly answer calls promptly.

All troubles on the line or to the instruments to be reported promptly to the General Manager.

All subscribers shall be responsible for any use of their telephone by non-subscribers or for non-subscribers' benefit and shall be required to pay for any and all conversations had by non-subscribers.

Each subscriber will before ringing on the line take down the receiver and say Hello, to ascertain if the line is in use by others, if in use by others immediately hang up receiver and try again in a few minutes.

Subscriber making call will please ring off one short ring when through with a conversation.

No subscriber will be allowed to make any change or alteration to wires or Telephones but make request to General Manager when any change is needed.

Messages transmitted by Messenger or vehicle or otherwise will be at the risk and cost of subscribers or non-subscribers.

The instruments are the property of the Sprague Telephone Co., and are not to be used for purposes other than for the exchange.

This contract not transferable without permission from the Company.

DATED, Big Island,

Aug 26th 190 *8*   *WHM* SUBSCRIBER.

J. Grant Sprague,
GEN. MANAGER.

_____
SUPT.

An order for a phone connection by the Sprague Telephone Company, 1908.

Mountain View, Ont., August 8th 1912

Mr. Lorne Brickman

Rednersville

To Sprague Telephone Co., Dr.

Interest Charged at the rate of 7% on overdue accounts.

1912					
August	1st	To one year's rent for Telephone			$10.00
		Trunk line messages			
Aug 29		Lorne Brickman	to B. J. Graham	Belle	.15
		"	" Wm. Falkner		.15
		Mrs	"		.15
					.15
		Lorne	" Mrs Trumpour	Well	.15
		Mrs	" Mrs Carl Bryant		.15
		Lorne	" Mr Carr	Belle	.15
		"	" Jean Fairfield		.15
		"	" Mrs Carl Bryant	Well	.15
			Total		$11.35

Will call Thursday Aug 15 1912

A customer's account

Fred, and he increased in wisdom and cunning, for Fred was a very wise horse and very efficient in the art of telephone line construction. He could be trusted to pull a pole and stop at a command at almost the exact spot. The same could be said of him when he was hitched to the democrat with a spool of wire slowly unwinding in the back. But old Fred had a few habits peculiar only to himself. He occasionally got tired of the strenuous life he was leading and would lay down for a short rest. When this happened it took an almost superhuman effort on the part of his driver to arouse him from his lethargy. In his spare time he was pastured on the Sprague farm on top of Mountain View Hill where Charlie and Miss Lillian still reside. One day he apparently became homesick when the linemen were working up the front road above Rednersville, so he took advantage of a lack of vigilence on their part and left for home with the democrat, leaving his master and helpers to their destiny. Several people along the way knew him and wondered at this unusal procedure although none took the trouble to stop him, so he achieved his ambition and when eventually caught up with, was standing looking over the bars into the pasture on the back of the Sprague farm.

When the line was started in Ameliasburgh, the only previous phone service was a few Bell phones spread over the entire area, and most of these were owned by businessmen or occasionally a very prosperous farmer. Owen Roblin had one at Roblin's Mills and Stanley Potter had another at Mountain

View where he ran the greenhouse and canning factory.

Grant bought the property in Mountain View where the exchange now is (1953) from Ed Hubbs who ran the store for a short time, having bought it from Byron Frederick. The latter drove one of the old-time peddling wagons around the countryside and accepted eggs as payment for groceries and dry goods. He bought the business from Wilfred Potter. Phoebe Thompson was the first storekeeper on the premises, and a story is told concerning some of the neighbouring farmers who occasionally had a few boiled eggs left over from a dinner and desired a change of diet for the evening meal. Accordingly the remnants of the boiled eggs were taken to the store and disposed of to Phoebe. The Spragues operated the store for a number of years, but eventually discontinued it in favour of the telephone business and the canning factory.

The first secretary-treasurer of the telephone company was Grant's father, John A. Sprague, but after his death the position was taken over by Miss Lillian who still shoulders the responsibility of that office. Her father, Lawrence, was one of the original share-holders of the company but eventually sold his interest to Grant.

The first Sprague Central was at their residence at Big Island, while the first switchboard in Ameliasburgh was at Ernest Redner's in Rednersville. Then it was moved to the home of Mack Lont in Centre neighbourhood where Mrs. B.L. Redner lives at present. It was then moved to Lawrence Sprague's where Annie Mae Salisbury and Myrtle Spencer were operators. After a short period it was moved to its present location at Mountain View in 1913. The central call used to be three rings, but this was afterward changed to one long. Then another important change was in the installation of the push-button which allowed only central rings to go to the switchboard and all others only on the line. And now there is the dial phone— but that is definitely in the future as far as the Sprague System is concerned, at least.

When the lines were first started, poles could be easily procured locally, but like many other changes through the years, that is no longer possible. Now they have to be imported from wherever they can be obtained. Purchases have been made from the adjoining township of Murray but their supply is becoming very limited and the most recent ones have been acquired from the eastern counties in Ontario.

The Sprague Telephone Company today is one of the most successful independent companies in Central and Eastern Ontario. It has on its list 625 subscribers including those of several summer cottages which only use it for about six months of the year.

Grant owned one of the first, if not the first, automobile in Ameliasburgh Township. It was a chain-drive Model T Ford and was an open car with plenty of brass trimmings, but no doors; it did have a top and was used exclusively for pleasure. After its acquisition, the horse and democrat eventually gave away to the motor. To-day several trucks are operated in connection with the lines.

The greatest major expansion of the system took place in 1940 when the

Mountain View Airport was connected. It had its own local switchboard but all outside calls as well as long distance were taken care of by the Sprague Central. All underground cable had to be laid in the airport and this entailed months of labour.

Grant announced his resignation from active management in 1948 at a dinner-dance at Tobe's County Gardens and invested the responsibility upon the shoulders of his son Jay who is the present day president of the company. Grant died in 1952. To-day the efficiency of the service and maintenance are the highest on record. As the name of Alexander Graham Bell will be ever honoured for his invention, so will the name of Grant Sprague be honoured as the father of the independent telephone system in the north and western parts of Prince Edward.

Grant Sprague and son Jay showing their truck loaded with maintenance equipment.

Further to the Redner story— Jay Sprague took over the ownership of the system, a business that had no secrets for him since he had taken an active part in its operation "from the day he was old enough to walk" as he puts it.

In October 1954, Mr. Sprague wrote to his customers to inform them that the Sprague Telephone System had been sold to the Bell Telephone Company of Canada. Soon afterwards, Bell crews started to rearrange telephone lines to increase the number of individual and two-party lines and to reduce the number of customers sharing rural lines.

First phase of the conversion program was completed in February of this year (1956) when customers in Rossmore got dial telephone service from the Belleville exchange. Two months later, dial service from the Trenton exchange was extended to subscribers living in Carrying Place and Consecon. On June 1, the bulk of the conversion got under way as lines were transferred to Picton and Wellington and the remainder to Belleville. The changeover was completed on a line-by-line basis.

Coincidental with the completion of the large-scale project, a supplementary issue of the telephone directory was sent to all subscribers concerned. The supplement lists all former Mountain view subscribers in alphabetical order with their addresses, the name of the exchange by which they are now served, and their telephone numbers. The 1957 issue of the Belleville-Trenton directory will list these subscribers under the heading of the exchange by which they are now served.

CHAPTER 12

MASSASSAGA

Massassaga

Massassaga, Indian Legend,
Tells us of many a great pow-wow
Held upon your border region
Near where Quinte's water now
Laps upon our shore the same
As it did when wild game
Nested on its brow.

Once the eagle's pinions swept
Above the lofty wood,
And the deer its covert kept
Near where the Indian wigwam stood.
Indian birch canoe did glide
On the Quinte's summer tide
And in the springtime's flood.

Where a gloomy bridge does now
Those clear waters span,
Weedy marshes once did grow
And the beaver built its dam.
Oft the black bear came to drink
At its sloping sanded brink
And the marmot swam.

Dark-skinned maids with deer-clad feet
In unchecked freedom rove
Where the wood and water meet
Near the hickory grove
Free born children to the wood,
Heir to Nature's solitude
And to mother love.

Did the Massassaga braves
Painted and in warrior dress,
Bloody tomahawks up raise,
Gather scalps for wars' redress?
Came they through the silent night
To their teepees' pineknot light
After battles' press?

Did we know all Indian lore
We could tell by fireside, tales
Of how the white man came
With their friends and household bales
Hewing out their homes beside
The shores that kiss the Quinte's tide
And in forest vales.

Lost are these old legends now
Lost and gone beyond recall
Are the 'where' and 'when' and 'how'
Of these lands, both large and small.
Out of all the Indians' claim,
There is but this, the name—
Massassaga.

Written by E. Pearl Brummell

The late E. Pearl Salisbury Brummell had lived for many years in the Massassaga area. She was a talented poetess and a lady of many fine qualities. She passed away at the age of 91. Through the years many of her poems appeared in *The Picton Gazette*. She had published a book of poems entitled 'Home Poems'.

Phil Dodds, in a special tribute to Pearl Brummell, wrote: "The many inspirational poems in this book reflect the appreciation of life in all its phases, of things both large and small, and above all, a love of God, family and friends as well as of nature.".

Massassaga

Massassaga is actually an island, although few people realize it. Marsh surrounds a good portion of it, while the Bay of Quinte and other small bays surround the remaining shoreline. Highway 14 (now Hwy. 62)joins it to the mainland at the southwest corner and on the south a roadway across the marsh joins it to Huff's Island. A very narrow stream and marsh separates Massassaga from the mainland on the north side. At one time people referred to this place as the fordway.

Massassaga is located opposite the City of Belleville and is partially behind the point where Rossmore is located. It contains almost 400 acres of farmland. The eastern point is much like other points in Prince Edward County, the land becomes shallow and is best used for pasture or recreational purposes. Upper Massassaga is considered to be the area to the west served by old Highway 14, now known as County Road 28. The part to the east of this road is referred to as Lower Massassaga. It has a roadway close to the Bay and continuing on down to the Point. Fenwood Gardens is a very attractive housing development in the upper section. The church and school were located east of the old Highway on the north side. The church was closed in 1967 when the congregation amalgamated with Mountain View. The original school has had numerous additions and is now made up of five rooms and a portable classroom. The senior students attend Kente Central School. High school students have always gone to Belleville for their education. At one time there was a cheese factory serving the area. It was located on the north end of the cross road (running north and south across Massassaga). This factory was active in the days when milk was picked up with a team and wagon. After the factory closed it was used as a piggery, which eventually burned. Now a home is located on the lot.

The proximity to Belleville has made Massassaga a very desirable place to live. Both Upper and Lower Massassaga roads are built up with lovely homes. Peat's Point is a very densely settled area. At one time it was considered to be a cottage area, but now it is used for year-round living. Peat's Point is named after an early fisherman, 'Pete LaRue' who lived in a small cabin on the Point. His light was a beacon to other fishermen passing up or down the bay. Over the years the name has been spelled many ways and now on new maps it is spelled "Peat's". Since Massassaga Point has been opened up, again a housing development is emerging on the southern part at Long Point or Horse Point as it is shown on maps today.

There are two old cemeteries on Massassaga, both family burying grounds, one is the Simonds cemetery which is behind the home where the Revills live. It is said that one of the first persons buried in the Massassaga Burying ground, now known as Sniders or Simonds burying ground, was a young girl who had been struck by a rattler. The girl was said to be a Palmateer, as told to Loral Wanamaker by his grandmother, Phoebe Jane (Loveless) VanCott many years ago. It was later confirmed by the late Frank Belnap of Rossmore. The other cemetery is the Wallbridge burying ground of Lower Massassaga right beside the road on Lot 53. Asa Wallbridge was buried in this cemetery, and also the first Elias Wallbridge.

Most of Ameliasburgh township was supplied with newspapers from Picton and from Belleville— The Traveller, or Prince Edward Gazette, published every Friday by Cecil Mortimer, Editor and Proprietor; John Silver, Printer, 12s. 6d. per annum, in advance, commenced April 1836 and continued about four years, when the printing press was removed to Cobourg. In 1840, the Prince Edward Gazette appeared, J. Dornan, Publisher. It was continued under this name by Rev. Mr. Playter in 1847 and 1849, Thomas Donnelly became Editor and Proprietor, changing the name to *The Picton Gazette*, which name it still bears. *The Picton Sun* was established in 1841, it was removed to Cobourg in 1853. The following year 1854 Dr. Gillespie and R. Boyle started *The Picton Times* which ran for a long time.

Various newspapers were established in Belleville from 1831. *The Intelligencer of Belleville* was founded by George Benjamin in September 1834, who continued as its editor until 1848, when McKenzie Bowell, Esq., M.P., succeeded him.

The Intelligencer marks its 150th year of publication in 1984. It is Belleville's daily newspaper and fourth oldest in Canada west of Montreal. Several newspapers began operation before the Intelligencer but only survived for a short while. Even after publication began there were several rival newspapers and in 1930 W.H. Morton publisher of *The Ontario* purchased the Intelligencer and the paper was published under the name of *The Ontario Intelligencer*. In 1965 the newspaper was moved to its present quarters at East Bridge and Pinnacle streets, on the site of the old post office. In 1972 the newspaper was acquired from the Morton family by Thomson Newspapers. It continues under the name of The Intelligencer and is regularly read by the residents of this area.

The farm on the west portion of Upper Massassaga Road is owned by Al Weatherhead. The farm long ago was named 'Elbow Grove'. Many people will remember buying beautiful red strawberries there during the season.

Very early a family named Zufelt lived in a house on the south side of the road. The present house was built before 1876 and is a very attractive brick home with bargeboard and a belvedere on the top. Mr. Weatherhead said that there was a bell on the tower of this and that a rope hung down through a hollow wall into a very shallow cupboard in the living room where it could be rung when necessary without anyone having to go up to the tower.

Foster Marvin's wife and her cousin were alone in the house when a severe thunderstorm came up and they went up to the belvedere to watch the storm which they said was the worst storm they had ever seen. While they watched in terror they saw ten fires started by the lightning.

Walter J. Osborne, a school teacher, lived here for a short time. He vaccinated two little girls, Letta Simonds, daughter of Joe Simonds (Hobert Adams' grandmother) and Letta VanCott, daughter of James VanCott (Loral Wanamaker's mother). He took a needle and dipped it in the pox on the cow and vaccinated the arms of the girls. Mrs. Wanamaker had a large scar, as large as a quarter, on her arm which she showed in later years and told how she had been vaccinated.

James Halliday owned this farm too, and he sold it to Ernest Wallbridge. In a few years Mr. Halliday bought the farm back again and later he sold to Mr. Weatherhead. When a new source of water was needed for the Fenwood Gardens Water Supply, a new filtration plant was developed on the south side

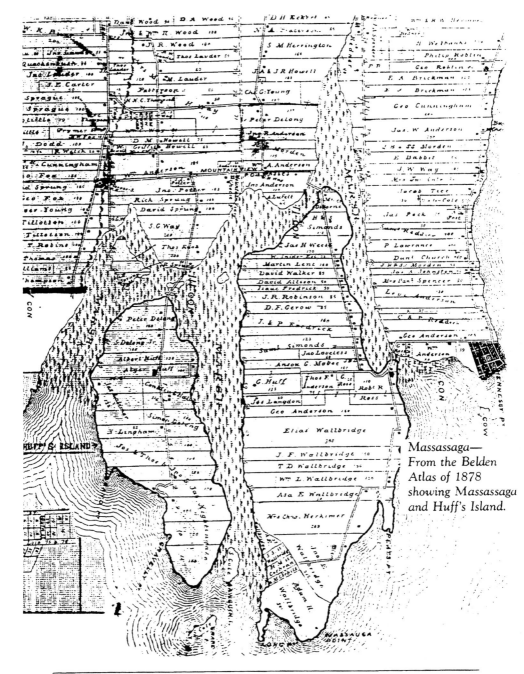

Massassaga—
From the Belden
Atlas of 1878
showing Massassaga
and Huff's Island.

of the farm in 1981 and it has proven very successful.

Russell Thompson came to Ameliasburgh Township in 1936 to work for John A. Weese, receiving wages of $20 a month for the summer and board for the winter months. At the end of four seasons, wages had increased to $25 a month.

In 1941 he married Miriam Keeble, whose parents came from England. Her father was one of the last veterans in this area who served in the Boer War in Africa. Mr. Keeble also served in the Imperial British Army in India.

The Thompsons took up residence at Mr. Weese's farm working it on shares. From there they rented and moved to the James Halliday farm, later they moved to the Wellington Howell farm where they lived for some 19 years. They purchased the Thomas Walker farm which included the farm to the east of it. It was necessary to build a new home, as the Walker house was on the north side of the road and not included in the farm sale.

Russell became interested in Municipal Affairs and became active on the Township Council where he served for some 12 years. He was the Warden for Prince Edward County in 1973.

Russell had a dealership for farm machinery. His son, Ben, started a business 'Quinte Speed & Custom' supplying automobile parts and doing repairs. The Thompson farm was sold to a German and Russell worked the land for three years after, and then built a new house for his retirement on a lot to the east of his former home.

The Walkers were once a very prominent family on Upper Massassaga. David Albert Walker moved from Sidney Township with his wife, Charlotte Fry, and three children in 1877 to the farm at Lot 64, Concession 2.

The children were Sybil Sarah, Fred and John A.; Sybil Sarah married Rev. Frank Anderson, a Methodist Minister who at one time preached on the Mountain View circuit. Fred went west, and John Albert farmed the homestead.

The great grandmother was Sarah Mason Sprung, born in Sophiasburgh. She married Joseph Walker and they lived in Hallowell, later going to Warkworth. Sarah Walker lived on the homestead in Ameliasburgh in her later years. Her two brothers David and Richard Sprung lived on the third concession where the Werkhovens and Loughs live now. Sarah died in 1892 at the age of 85.

Of the John Albert Walker family:
David Henry married Marjorie Bruce (Scotland). David was a Physicist at Chalk River in charge of Research of Nuclear Reactors for nearly 40 years. He is now retired and living at Deep River.
Sybil Wade married William S. Wills, Belleville.
Thomas Symons married Dorothy MacDonald. Thomas remained at home to farm and became interested in municipal affairs— first as Councillor and later as Township Clerk. When a new County Clerk was needed for Prince Edward, Thomas got the position and the family moved to Picton.

Among the early settlers on Upper Massassaga were the Absolom Lovelesses who lived in a log house on the south side of the road. They had a small garden with tomatoes, and when they got red, they were picked and put up on the fireplace mantel— but they were never eaten. They were called love apples and believed to be poisonous!

The names of some of the early residents of this area are Simonds, Giles, Mabee, Snider, Lent, Frederick, Gerow, Robinson, Walker, Brummel, Weese and Allison.

At one time a familiar sight on the Massassaga Road was the horse and buggy driven to school by the Brummel girls. The girls drove to Belleville every school day and tied their horse in at a blacksmith shop located behind Walker Hardware. At noon the girls dashed down to the blacksmith shop to give their horse its noonday meal.

Daniel Gerow's daughter, Julia Anne, married Wm. Belnap as her first husband and James Henry Weese for her second husband. Their first home was built near the marsh. A second unpainted, frame house was built on the site of Peter Koekman's home. Later Aaron Manley Weese built a cement block home beside the road where Russell and Dorothy now live.

John A. Weese served as Warden of Prince Edward in 1926 and as Member of Parliament in 1930. About 1936-7 he built the greenhouses. He grew tomato plants for many farmers and managed several canning factories. He also managed the farm until 1968. In 1982 a family named Dekker bought the greenhouses and property surrounding them. The barn was torn down and a new home was built on the location.

Hobert Adams, who had grown up on Massassaga and farmed, sold land to the developers who built the beautiful subdivision known as Fenwood Gardens. Hobert was a carpenter as well as farmer and he built several houses along old Highway 14 in addition to the one he lives in.

One William Anderson came from County of Monoghan, Ireland; in 1806 he married John Way's daughter, Mary, and bought land at Massassaga and started lumbering (the only other people there then were the Wallbridges). He raised a large family of six daughters and six sons. A son, George remained at home and farmed. John farmed where Harold Werkhoven lives now; William farmed on the farm known as the Mike Levine place; Levi settled west of Rossmore near the Hayes sideroad; James W. operated a boat crossing the Bay to Belleville. He lived where the Babbitts live on the Rednersville Road. The daughters married and lived nearby.

From the book *The County*, we quote— "An ingredient for a successful bee, for many, was a good fight. A good host was a man who never minded his guests fighting. Seventh Towners were the most notorious fighters in the whole Midland District. Old William Anderson at Massassaga Point told Dr. Canniff in 1867 that Sixth Towners were more mannerly in everything they did and never had so many fights as Seventh Towners."

The original Anderson farm was later sold to Benjamin Osborne and his son, Wilbert. In 1880 the Osbornes built a 17-room brick home with attic and a

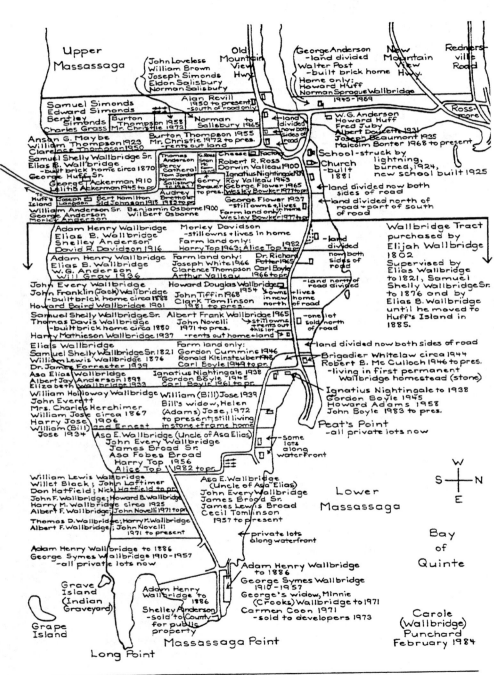

Upper
Massassaga

John Loveless
William Brown
Joseph Simonds
Eldon Salisbury
Norman Salisbury

Old
Mountain
View Hwy.

George Anderson
-land divided
Walter Post
-built brick home
Home only:
Howard Huff
Norman Sprague Wallbridge
1945-1969

New Mountain
View Hwy.

Redners-
ville
Road

Samuel Simonds
Edward Simonds
Bentley
Simonds   Burton
Charles Grass Thompson 1958
           Mr. Christie 1972

Alan Revill
1950 to present
-south of road only

Norman   to
Salisbury 1965

-land
divided
now both
sides of
road

W.G. Anderson
Howard Huff
Fred Juby
Albert Doucette 1931
Joseph Beaumont 1925
Malcolm Bonter 1968 to present

Ross
more

Anson G. Maybe
William Thompson 1923
Clarence Thompson 1950
Samuel Shelly Wallbridge Sr.
Elias B. Wallbridge
-built brick home circa 1870
George Huff Sr.
George A.Ackerman 1910
Edith G.Ackerman 1945 to pr.

Burton Thompson 1955
Mr. Christie 1972 to pres.
-rents out land

Thomas
Anderson
Percy
Cockeral
Tom Jordon
Norman
Salisbury
Sid Johnson

G.Rev. Cheese Factory
Stan   D
Pyle
Robert R. Ross
Dorwin Valleau 1900
Ignatius Nightingale
Gerry Roy Valleau 1945
Brauer Kelsey Flower 1977 to pr.
Wesley Bowker

School-struck by
             lightning,
Church   burned, 1924,
-built   new school built 1925
1881

-land divided now both
sides of road

Huff's
Island Joseph ☐ Bert Hamilton Brethour
        Langdon Sid Johnson 1918 1983 to pr.
William Anderson Sr. Benjamin Osborne 1900
George Anderson   Wilbert Osborne
Morley Anderson

Gerry
Brauer Audrey
        Judson

George Flower 1937
-still owns + lives
Farm land only; home
Wesley Bowker 1977 to pr.

-land divided north of
road + part of south
of road

Adam Henry Wallbridge
Elias B. Wallbridge
Shelley Anderson
David R. Davidson 1916

Morley Davidson
-still owns + lives in home
Farm land only;
Harry Top 1963; Alice Top   1982

☐ -land
divided

Wallbridge Tract
purchased by
Elijah Wallbridge
1802
Supervised by
Elias Wallbridge
to 1821; Samuel
Shelly Wallbridge Sr.
to 1876 ond by
Elias B. Wallbridge
until he moved to
Huff's Island in
1885.

Adam Henry Wallbridge
Elias B. Wallbridge
W.G. Anderson
Will Gray 1936

Farm land only:
Joseph White 1966
Clarence Thompson
Arthur Valleau   1966 to pr.

Dr. Richard
Potter 1965
Carl Boyle

now both
sides of
road

John Every Wallbridge
John Franklin (Jack) Wallbridge
-built brick home circa 1888
Howard Baird Wallbridge 1901

Howard Douglas Wallbridge
             1954
John Tiffin 1968
Clark Tomlinson
1981 to pres.

-land north of
road divided

-owns
+lives
in new
home
north
of road

Samuel Shelly Wallbridge Sr.
Thomas Davis Wallbridge
-built brick home circa 1880
Harry Mathieson Wallbridge 1937

Albert Frank Wallbridge 1965
John Novelli
1971 to pres.

-still owns
+ rents out
this lot

-one lot
sold south
of road

Elias Wallbridge
Samuel Shelly Wallbridge Sr. 1821
William Lewis Wallbridge 1876
Dr. James Forrester 1939

Farm land only:
Gordon Cummins 1946
Ronald Kleinsteuber 1948
Carl Boyle 1949 to pr.

-land divided now both sides of road

Brigadier Whitelaw circa 1944
Robert B. Mc Culloch 1946 to pres.
-living in first permanent
Wallbridge homestead (stone)

Asa Elias Wallbridge
Albert Jay Anderson 1898
Elizabeth Wallbridge 1933

Ignatius Nightingale 1938
Gordon Boyle 1945
Carl Boyle 1961 to pr.

Ignatius Nightingale to 1938
Gordon Boyle 1945
Howard Adams 1958
John Boyle 1983 to pres.

William Holloway Wallbridge
John Everett
Mrs. Charles Herchimer
William Jose circa 1867
Harry Jose 1906
William (Bill)
Jose 1934 and Ernest

William (Bill) Jose 1939
Bill's widow, Helen
(Adams) Jose, 1972
to present;still living
in stone +frame home

Peat's Point
-all private lots now

Asa E. Wallbridge (Uncle of Asa Elias)
John Every Wallbridge
James Broad Sr.
Asa Fobes Broad
Harry Top 1956
Alice Top 1982 to pr.

-some
lots
along
waterfront

William Lewis Wallbridge
Willet Black ; John Lattimer
Don Hatfield ; Nick Hatfield to pr.
John F. Wallbridge; Howard B. Wallbridge
Harry M. Wallbridge circa 1925
Albert F. Wallbridge; John Novelli 1971 to pr.

Asa E. Wallbridge
(Uncle of Asa Elias)
John Every Wallbridge
James Broad Sr.
James Lewis Broad
Cecil Tomlinson
1957 to present

Lower
Massassaga

Bay
of
Quinte

Thomas D. Wallbridge; Harry M.Wallbridge
Albert F. Wallbridge ; John Novelli
             1971 to present

-private lots
along waterfront

Adam Henry Wallbridge to 1886
George Symes Wallbridge 1910-1957
-all private lots now

Grave
Island
(Indian
Graveyard)

Adam Henry
Wallbridge
to 1886
Shelley Anderson
-sold to County
for public
property

Adam Henry Wallbridge
to 1886
George Symes Wallbridge
1910-1957
George's widow, Minnie
(Crooks) Wallbridge to 1971
Carmen Coon 1971
-sold to developers 1973

Carole
(Wallbridge)
Punchard
February 1984

Grape
Island

Long Point

Massassaga Point

ladder from the ceiling so one could climb out on the roof for a view. The roof-top area had an iron railing around it. In 1937 this house burned and Mrs. Osborne moved to Belleville.

The farm passed on to George Flower; he and his wife Kay built the present house. George bought the land in connection with the Valleau farm to enlarge his holdings. He in turn sold all of the farm to a Mr. and Mrs. Bowker from Quebec. They built a new house for themselves to the west of the Valleau barn.

When research for this project began, the committee was unanimous that there would be no genealogies but after reading several interesting stories it is difficult to not include some of the family history. It is quite by chance that one works on several family stories at one time and the relations between families is most incredible, as I have read that in Prince Edward, "If you scratch one they all bleed".

A bit of history concerning an old Ameliasburgh family has turned up and, while the persons bearing the family name have disappeared, there are still descendants. One David Glenn was born in the late 1790's and was a weaver by trade, coming from County Cavan, Ireland. He and his wife and two sons sailed for Canada about 1820 and the trip took six weeks. The family settled in the Hay Bay area, the father continuing the weaving trade profitably for ten years. Then they moved to Ameliasburgh, where they took up land from the Crown for some $4 an acre, on the third concession. They had a family of six boys and three girls. The fifth son, David Glenn, married and had three children; a daughter, Ella Jane, married David H. Sprung, another daughter Addie May (Morley Davidson's mother) married David R. Davidson. One James Glenn was the Treasurer of the Township of Ameliasburgh for a long time but the family name seems to have disappeared.

David Richmond Davidson moved from Brighton Township with his family in 1916. They purchased from Shelly Anderson the west half of Lot 57, Concession 1 and 2 on the Massassaga Road. One son, Raymond Glenn became a doctor after serving overseas. He practiced in Kenora. A daughter, Emma Marjorie, married John Bell, an Electrical Engineer, employed by the Canadian General Electric, Peterborough.

It was Morley Richmond who remained on the family farm where they carried on a mixed farming operation, a dairy herd, pigs and some cash crops. The Davidsons bred Holstein cattle and went on to improve the herd, which was accredited.

Morley married Anne Brown of Thurlow, who was a teacher at the Ontario School for the Deaf (O.S.D.) now Sir James Whitney School. She taught until her son David was born. Later they had two daughters, Judith (now Mrs. Richard Woodley of Belleville), and Jane who married Mitchell Lavery, a geologist now living in Timmins. David discovered that he had an allergy and could not be around cattle, so he applied and was accepted at the Royal Bank.

About this time the Davidsons decided to sell the farm. A neighbour, Harry Top, made a deal for the property south of the travelled road. Later four lots were sold off the remaining property which fronted on the Bay.

The Wallbridges, who were of English descent, were among the first to settle in America, located first at Dedham, Massachusetts, in 1685 and later at Preston, Connecticut. Zebulon, grandson of the original settler, Henry, and his two sons Elias and Elijah bought farms in upper New York State. Another son, Asa, having served with the British against the Rebel Colonists, at the end of the war went with thousands of Loyalists to settle in Nova Scotia in a part which later became New Brunswick. He cleared land and built a saw-mill. About 1792 he made his way to the Quinte Area and settled in a log cabin at Singleton's Creek on the bank of what is now the Moira River, a short distance below Dundas Street. Here he spent a year trading with the settlers and buying furs. Asa Wallbridge was unmarried and one of the first pedlars, eccentric and shrewd. He contributed much to the comfort of the early settlers. It was he who brought in many of the first fruit trees. He brought seeds from the States and planted them. It has been said that many of the old orchards in Prince Edward came from his plantings.

Asa wrote to his brother, Elijah, who came to Canada in 1800 with his son Wm. Holloway and others of the family. In 1802 one David William Smith for some 300 Pounds of lawful money sold some 1,200 acres of land to Elijah Wallbridge. A lease for 999 years was signed for the property. In the book *Pioneer Life on the Bay of Quinte*, it states that the Wallbridge tract of land was some 2,000 acres; probably this was arrived at from a later survey. The land stretched eastward from the Anderson place (third farm below the church), included Long Point, and extended from the Bay Front to the marsh in the rear. Elijah divided it up into five farms of about 300 acres each, one of which he gave to each of his children who were all, with the exception of one daughter, comfortably settled there by the year 1812. A further lot of 500 acres he reserved for a common pasturage, as was the custom in the American colonies. These farms were the first proper homes of the Wallbridges in Upper Canada. For many years they were possessed by the descendants of the Wallbridges.

The first Wallbridge home at Massassaga was a small frame house located west of the stone house now owned and occupied by Robert McCulloch.

The John Franklin Wallbridge house on the west half of Lot 56 was built in 1890. It is a large brick home on the south side of the road. The farm was named by Mrs. Wallbridge 'Locust Hedge Farm'. When their son Howard B. was married, a frame addition was built to the house so it could be divided. In 1969 Douglas Wallbridge sold to a family named Tiffin who later sold to Clark Tomlinson, who is a descendant of Elijah Wallbridge through his mother. Hannah Wallbridge who married James Broad was Clark's great grandmother.

The house and lot on the north side of the road where Douglas lives is the

John F. Wallbridge house built in 1890 where three generations have lived.

First permanent Wallbridge homestead— circa 1820.

only property left in the Wallbridge name of the 2,000 acres originally settled by Wallbridges.

A brother of John Franklin, Thomas D. Wallbridge, built his home on the north side of the road on the east half of Lot 56. It also is a large brick building. This house has been divided also, and has been the home of Harry and his son Albert.

A more recent picture of the first permanent Wallbridge home.

The Asa E. Wallbridge who lived on the Carl Boyle farm was a grandson of Elijah, the original settler. Martha, one of William Anderson's daughters, married Asa E. Wallbridge and they had six daughters. They brought up a nephew, Jay Anderson, grandson of Wm. Anderson, and he continued to live there along with two of the daughters, Bessie, who never married, and Carrie, who married James Howatson and was widowed at an early age.

Ignatius Nightingale and his wife Dora lived there for a time. Gerald Sniders and the Ross Lotts also lived there. In 1945 the Boyle Family came to Lower Massassaga and have developed a large dairy farm. The Boyles acquired land from the McCulloch farm, the south side of the Gray (Dr. Potter) farm and part of Peat's Point.

Henry Jose's ancestors were originally from Spain. Following the fighting between the Spanish Armada and the English Navy in 1588, Henry's ancestors settled in England instead of returning to Spain.

In the early 1850's, Henry and his wife, Elizabeth (Bennett), their three toddlers and their six-week-old baby, sailed from Cornwall, England, to Canada. They settled in Holloway, Ontario, where their next four children were born and where they lived for the rest of their lives.

About 1867, their oldest child, William Jose, and his wife, Delacey (Prest) of Holloway, purchased a 274-acre farm from Mrs. Herkimer. The farm had a fine stone and frame home. This farm was located in the Wallbridge Tract of Lower Massassaga.

When William Jose, son of the first William who settled on Massassaga, was a little boy of six, the maple trees were planted on either side of the road from the old Valleau house up to Massassaga church.

Son Harry married Edith Seeley and they had three sons, Ernie, who did

The first Jose family to settle on Lower Masassaga. William and Delacey and five of their seven children.

Fred Reid driving the team and Harry Jose, with blocks of ice to store in their ice house.

Home of William and Delacey Jose purchased in 1867, now occupied by Helen Jose.

carpenter work, some droving for Charlie Scott, and lastly he worked in various plants in Belleville.

No doubt many people will remember Roy, who worked for the Belleville Creamery. The Joses had always had a dairy farm. They cut ice from the bay in the winter and packed it in sawdust for cooling their cream in summer. Roy took a course in Kingston and then operated the Belleville Creamery.

The third son, William, married Helen Adams and they continued to operate the dairy farm. Helen tells about seeing loads of hay being taken up the Bay on the ice. This hay was taken to Belleville Market for sale.

Two nephews, Robert and Ronald Locke, built homes on the Jose property next to the road.

Massassaga Point is the most easterly part of Ameliasburgh township. On the north and east it is bordered by the Bay of Quinte. On the south side of the point a large marsh separates it from Huff's Island. Over a century ago, a large summer resort hotel was built on this Point. Families would spend their vacation at such a resort enjoying the facilities, bandshell, top-notch dining room and spacious grounds where they could play croquet and badminton, swim, ride horseback, relax in mineral baths or sit on the verandahs. It was very popular during the late 19th and early 20th centuries. It was only four miles down and across the Bay of Quinte from Belleville. At one time it was considered to be a 400-acre resort. The exact age of the hotel is unknown. From a newspaper clipping of May 28, 1879, the hotel was advertised as having been "overhauled and enlarged for the accommodation of guests, board by the day or week, hot and cold water, swings and dancing platform. The Steamers 'Utica' and 'City of Belleville' call at the Point on the way to and from Picton. After the first of June the Steamer 'City of Belleville' will make a special run

Delacey Jose feeding her turkeys— about 1900.

every Tuesday and Friday, leaving here at 10 a.m. The 'Prince Edward' will bring parties home on those days, leaving the Point at 8 p.m."

Signed Geo. F. Pretty
Proprietor.

May 28 '79

Large regattas were staged on Big Bay with presentations made at the dance pavillion. In 1888 Senator Henry 'Harry' Corby (son of the founder of Corby's distillery) held a gala opening, with 2,000 people arriving by boat. Many postcards printed about 1905 show steamboats at the wharf dispatching passengers. The three-storey frame hotel with wide verandah facing the water had two wings on the west side. The high level table land was covered with trees, with open spaces reserved for outdoor sports, lawn tennis and croquet. The hotel was used as the headquarters for several yachting regattas. In the late 1890's, the hotel was managed by the Jenkins family who later ran the Quinte Hotel in Belleville.

Belleville businesses treated their employees to picnics at the Point, as did the Churches and Sunday Schools. There were many moonlight excursions with dancing at the pavillion. Children enjoyed the amusement rides and booths that sold soft drinks and ice cream (delicious, made with real cream). In 1912, the price of a ticket to the Point was 25 cents. The steamer 'Annie Lake' travelled between the Point and Belleville every hour; the 'Aletha' and 'Brockville' were larger boats. Boats docked at Rossmore, Rednersville,

Northport and Massassaga Point. Picnics attended by hundreds of people at Massassaga and 12 O'Clock Point were highly popular during this period. Other boats which docked at Massassaga Point were the Ometa, Alexandria and Verona. Excursion boats came from Rochester and toured the Thousand Islands. Local people drove buggies and surreys to the Point for picnics before they had cars. A dance hall was built about the time of the First World War, and music was provided by a small orchestra.

The Massassaga Park Hotel.

The 'Brockville' loading passengers at the dock, Massassaga Point.

The Wallbridge family owned most of the land on the Point. Douglas Wallbridge who lives on Massassaga Road said his cousin's uncle, George Wallbridge, became embroiled in a dispute with Shelley Anderson over the use of the road leading to the Point. The resulting lawsuit allowed Wallbridge to close the road to keep his cattle from roaming. As a result of the road being closed, most people lost interest in the cottages there and they soon became derelict.

Anderson demolished his dance pavillion at the Point, using the lumber to build a home in Belleville. The Massassaga Park Hotel fell into disuse during the depression. Prior to its sale in 1934 the hotel was boarded up. The Eggleton Brothers of Stirling bought the buildings for lumber. When the motorcar became popular, people travelled further for their picnics and many resorts fell into disuse.

In 1971 Prince Edward Conservation Authority bought 60 acres on the Point where the Massassaga Park Resort had been located and began a conservation area to attract people for picnics, swimming, nature studies and fishing. On the south side of the Point the Ontario Rock Company had taken out tons of limestone for nearly 50 years for the manufacture of cement. There are still remnants of a dock made of steel reinforced cement which was used during the time that the rock was being taken out.

Between Massassaga Point and Long Point is a pretty little bay known as Sand Cove where many boats drop anchor for the night and sometimes the passengers come ashore for a barbeque or just to enjoy a pleasant stroll along the shore.

CHAPTER 13

HUFF'S ISLAND

1800 to 1972

By Wm. Nightingale

Prior to the settlement of Huff's Island by Europeans, little is known of its earlier settlers. There was apparently a branch of the Mississauga tribe of Indians living in the area; *Pioneer Life in the Bay of Quinte* speaks of some 50 Mississaugas under Chief Jim Chippigaw as living on the Island at the arrival of Solomon Huff in 1803 or 1804. According to recent 'diggings,' it has been determined that various tribes occupied the Island for at least 2,000 years. After the coming of the French to Canada and the alienation of the Iroquois tribe by Champlain, Prince Edward became more or less no-man's land, since the Iroquois held sway south of the Lake and their frequent raids on the north shore kept other Indians further inland.

There is no knowledge of any settlers on the Island until after the American Revolution. In 1787 the 'Seventh Town' (Ameliasburgh) was surveyed and laid out in 200 acre lots numbering from east to west. The Anglican Church was the recognized church at that time and was responsible for the religious and educational well-being of the people and, to finance this, the Government decreed that every 7th lot should be set aside for the use of the church (Clergy Reserve). In earlier surveys this was found impractical and the custom was to leave the equivalent in blocks. This was done on the Island and the portion from the present crossroad east, some 900 acres, was left as a block and identified as Block 'B', Ameliasburgh.

Beginning at the westerly end of the Island where the Township was laid out in the original lots: Lot 62 & 63, the property now owned by Robt. Weese, in 1802 was deeded to Richard Cartwright. He held it until 1845 when it was deeded to Peter Delong. We presume they had some buildings, but their location is not known. In 1880 Peter Delong deeded the property to David Delong and about this time the present brick house was built and I suppose the barn about the same time. In 1889, the Delongs traded farms with John and Will Barber and the farm remained in the Barber name until 1965 when it was sold to Robt. Weese. During the time it was occupied by the Barbers, it became known as one of the most productive farms in the area. The house was sold to Geo. Gale by the Weeses, and then to Ronald Orr.

Lot 61, the next easterly, was also deeded from the Crown to Richard Cartwright in 1802, and in 1849 to Simon Delong and in 1893 to Simon Henry Delong, and in 1917 to Willet Black and it has remained in the Black name to

Solomon Huff's House— First house on Huff's Island, built shortly after 1802. This house was built of log and covered with clapboard— now gone. Timbers from it are in Reg. Barber's garage.

the present time. The Delongs built the original part of the present house during the time they occupied the land and had also erected a barn on about the same location that the present barn is situated. The farm was rented for some years before being purchased by the Blacks. Tenants were the Reids, Tripps, Ways, and possibly others. In the 1920s the Blacks tore down the old barn and erected the present steel-clad barn, and they have also erected a number of other barns.

Lot 60 was deeded from the Crown in 1811 to Angus McLauchlin, in 1814 to William Mitchell, in 1837 to James Forsyth, and in 1854 to Peter Huff. In 1868 Peter Huff split the lot between his two sons, Albert and Alger Huff.

In 1911 Ernest Wallbridge purchased the west half from Albert Huff, and

Alger Huff deeded the east half to George Huff. The west half has remained in the Wallbridge family since 1911. In 1945, Ernest Wallbridge purchased the east half from George Huff and in 1949 sold it to Allan and Margaret Wallbridge, the present owners. The house on the east half was built about 1854-55 and is likely the oldest house now standing on Huff's Island. The brick house occupied by Lottie Green and Frank Wallbridge was also built by the Huffs. While the property was not deeded to Peter Huff until 1854, on a survey map of 1849 he is shown as occupant, so we presume he had rented for some years before purchasing. About 1926 the frame barn owned by Ernest Wallbridge was destroyed by fire and was replaced with a modern steel barn.

As stated earlier, the balance of Huff's Island had been set aside as Clergy Reserve and was deeded from the Crown to King's College, Toronto, the forerunner of the present University of Toronto. In 1804 this block, known as Point 'B', was leased by the Crown to one John Huyck of Adolphustown for a period of 21 years; the rental to be 13½ bus. of wheat or 45 shillings per year for the first seven years; 27 bus. of wheat or 90 shillings per year for the second seven and 40½ bus. of wheat or 135 shillings per year for the remaining seven. We presume that he sub-leased to Solomon Huff, as in 1803 or '04 the Huffs moved from Adolphustown to the Island. Mr. Huff was a very active farmer and woodsman and cleared much of the land and logged off the pine and

Farmyard at Jas. Nightingale, circa 1880, later the farm of Jas. S. Wallbridge.

rafted it to Montreal. They also set out considerable orchard, and an 1849 survey of the Island shows some 428 acres cleared and worked either by the Huffs or by tenants of theirs. Most of this land was on the easterly end of the Island on property now owned by Reg. and Bill Barber, a block along the marsh at the rear of David Farmer's place with a dwelling there, another block north of the present school with a dwelling about where the Motley buildings now stand, and a block of some 30 acres on the south side of the Island occupied by Nelson Ockerman.

During the time the Huffs occupied the Island, they made numerous attempts to purchase or obtain concessions from King's College for the

Tobacco Field on the Will Barber Farm

Tobacco Barn on the Barber Farm

Tobacco Harvest circa 1910. Left to right: ?, David Dehaney, John Cairns, Reg Barber, Stan Barber, ?, Clift Barber, John Wanamaker, Will Barber, ?, ?, Robert Bowness.

improvements they had made to property, but were unsuccessful and in 1838 turned interest in the property over to James and Abraham Huff (sons) for the sum of 200 Pounds. In 1843, James and Abraham Huff made a lengthy Petition to the Students and Chancellor of King's College asking for compensation for the improvements made to the property. In 1845, Solomon Huff drowned while returning by boat from Belleville and was buried on the hill above their house, and later moved to Mountain View cemetery.

The Rev. Roaf must have had an inside track, for in 1850 he purchased the Point 'B' from King's College for some 1,800 Pounds and the same year mortgaged it to Charles Corser of Wolverhamshire, England, for the sum of 4,745 Pounds. Apparently the Rev. Roaf could not make good, for he was brought before the Magistrate for non-payment of debts and the Magistrate ordered the Point divided and the lots sold. The Point was then surveyed and in 1851 it was divided into 11 lots, and in 1855 sold by Public Auction in Belleville. The Roafs tried to hang onto the property as Roaf, the Younger, purchased nine of the 11 lots.

In 1857, John Dew and James Nightingale of York formed a partnership and purchased the nine lots from Roaf and later the other two lots from

This airplane landed in a field on the Motley farm, Sept. 8, 1918.

Herbert Topping. Later they divided them, John Dew taking Lots 1 to 5 and Lot 11, and Nightingale Lots 6 to 10. Nightingale later purchased Lots 5 and 11 from Dew.

John Dew had various tenants: one named Cook occupied the south end of Lots 1, 2 and 3, and raised horses for Dew, also it would seem that Lewis Conklin occupied the north end of Lot 1 as tenant, and that Mrs. Conklin was some relation to Dew. In 1874, Dew sold the south end of Lots 1, 2 and 3 to James Lattimer and he and his sons had the property until it was sold to his great grandson, Douglas Black, the present owner. In 1881, Conklin and Hall purchased the north end of Lot 1, and later Conklin became the sole owner and erected the present buildings. Lewis Conklin had 11 children: Frank, Garnet, Elgin, Wallace, Durwood, Hattie, Clara, Minnie, Bessie, Lily and Maud. After Lewis' death, Durwood carried on and owned the farm until it was sold to John Mason about 1969.

Larry Hall purchased the north end of Lot 2, and sold it to Will Hall in 1891. He kept it until 1917, when it was sold to Fred Motley, and it remains in the Motley name today. In 1934, the existing house was destroyed by fire and the Motley's built the present house, which has been added to in the years since.

In 1869 John Dew sold the north part of Lots 3 and 4 to Simon Delong and in 1891 it was deeded to his son Simon Delong. In 1893 it was deeded to Jake Ryerson Delong and in 1917 to Elwood Delong. Will Hall purchased from Elwood Delong and in 1919 sold to Ross and Irene Fairman, who kept it until 1963 when David Farmer purchased the 100 acres. Originally there was a frame house on the south side of the road with the barn in the present location.

This barn was destroyed in a wind storm and Mrs. Delong was killed by the falling timbers. The barn was rebuilt using many of the same timbers. Around 1890, the present brick house was built by the Delongs.

Dew sold the south part of Lot 4 to one John Lingham and he in turn sold to Will and Charlie Hall. The brick house now owned by Keith Schauer was built about 1913, the former house being frame and located to the rear of the present house. Edward Hall took over from his father Will and built a tenant house about 1940. Edward later sold the farm and tenant house to Cor. VanZoeren. The brick house has changed hands a number of times, being owned by Joel Mazier, Alex Young, Ernie Flindall, Burke Bremner and now by Keith Schauer.

By 1869 James Nightingale had acquired the seven most easterly lots on the Island and at his death in 1879 split it between his family: Lots 5 and 6 to John, 7 and 8 to Joseph, 9 and 10 to Thomas, and 11 to Hannah. During the time James Nightingale had the property, considerable building took place. When they moved to the Island in 1857 they occupied the frame house on the bay-shore built by the Huffs. In 1877 and '78 they built the brick house now owned by Reg and Annie Barber and somewhat earlier had built the rough cast house which stands on the bayshore behind the house occupied by Henry Wallbridge.

When John Nightingale obtained Lots 5 and 6 on his father's death, he set about building on them, and in 1881 and '82 built the present brick house and frame barn on the property that Wm. and Beth Nightingale now occupy. Joseph Nightingale who received Lots 7 and 8 had married Jane Preston and had three sons and four daughters, James, John, Joseph, Annie, Ella, Emily and Minnie. The father, Joseph, died of a heart attack on the Belleville-Rossmore ferry in 1882. Later the farm was divided and John and Joseph took Lot 7 and built the present buildings and in 1913 sold to John Hatfield, and it is currently owned by his grandchildren. Lot 8 was sold to James Wallbridge, who built the present barn and he in turn sold to his daughter and son-in-law, Annie and Reg. Barber.

Lots 9 and 10 went to Thomas Nightingale, who had married Annie Bowen, and they had one daughter, Gertrude. Thomas was not interested in farming and eventually sold the lots to his brother-in-law Elias Wallbridge. Hannah, Elias' wife, had received Lot 11 as her inheritance, so the Wallbridges then had the three lots. Elias Wallbridge died quite young and his family carried on, and later Lewis Wallbridge took over the farm and built the stone house and barn now located on the property. Henry Wallbridge retains the stone house and the old rough cast house.

One the north end of Lot 6 there is the remains of a lime kiln in which much of the lime was burned from the limestone to make the plaster and mortar for the brick houses on the properties.

School

Originally the Island was a part of the Union School Section at Mountain View and the residents went to the school located at Mountain View. Sometime before 1870 a school was located on the Island and a Miss Huff hired as teacher, the first school was located in a log house on Lot 7 across the road from the present Hatfield house, a notation in Thomas Nightingale's diary under the date May 11, 1869, states: "Louisa Huff started to teach this morning," and again in July 27, 1869: "Wm. Cook was here to get signers to have Louisa Huff continue her school." In 1887 Alger Huff deeded a lot across from the present school house for the purpose of erecting a school. One was built here and later enlarged, but in 1914 or '15 it was destroyed by fire and in 1915 the present school house was erected on a lot supplied by Lewis Conklin. The Island school has never been large and about 1907 and '08 had at times only one pupil (Sylvia White). In 1966 after the Kente School was built, the school building was purchased by the community as a community centre.

The Bridge

From the time the Island was permanently settled and the roads laid out, it was the wish of the people to have a road and bridge across the marsh from the Island to the Massassaga mainland. Numerous petitions were presented to County Council regarding the building of a road, but they had landed on deaf ears. After the Bay Bridge was built in 1891, the need for the shorter route to Belleville became more pressing and numerous meetings of the residents of the Island were held. Finally in 1898 it was agreed to call for tenders for the construction of the bridge and causeway; a grant of $350 was obtained from County Council, and various families on the Island pledged amounts towards the cost and a total of $1,325 was raised or pledged. Plans were drawn up for the causeway and the span for the stream and tenders called. Various prices were received ranging from $550 to $1,362. The tender of $550 submitted by Will and Charlie Hall was accepted. Alger Huff was appointed Treasurer, James Wallbridge, Secretary, and John Nightingale, Superintendent of Work.

The roadway was constructed of pine plank, 16 feet in length and 3" in thickness, the planks to be laid at right angles to the line of the road and to be spiked to stringers laid longitudinally with the road. The stringers were to be supplied from the local wood lots. The bridge was erected on four piers constructed of cedar logs and filled with stone.

The roadway and bridge was to be started not later than Jan. 29, 1899 and completed not later than the 1st of May, 1899. I think that most of the active people of the Island must have worked on the bridge that winter to complete the job, since it is three quarters of a mile across; and they must have been dedicated when you think that the Hall Bros. did the job for $550 and of that amount they had pledged $100 apiece, so actually they only received $350 and supplied all of the hardware for bolting the piers and spiking the planks to the stringers for the roadbed.

The bridge and roadbed was completed at a cost of $1,472 and was used for

*Clockwise from above: Audrey
(Johnson) Brethour standing
on old bridge; Walter Hamilton installing new tile under the causeway; a view
of the old bridge from Huff's Island to Massassaga; Betty Wallbridge standing
in a tile used for the roadway.*

a number of years as a floating roadbed. Eventually, however, the planks
started to break loose from the stringers and it was decided to cover them with
stone and sand; large stones were placed on the outside and the roadbed filled
with sand from the Conklin farm. Grants were obtained from time to time
from County and Township Council and the roadbed gradually improved.

During a period of extremely high water in the spring of 1957, the bridge
floated off the piers and broke up and the roadway was closed for a number of
years. The District Road Engineer at that time, Ewart Marsten, felt that three
8-foot tiles would carry the flow of water. Since the tile cost $980 a piece, the
Island committee felt it would try two tiles; Township Council agreed to
supply the gravel to fill the stream bed, Ken Motley and Willet Barber drew
the gravel at a modest cost and the stream bed was filled and the two tiles
placed and the road was again re-opened. As grants were received and money
became available, the roadbed was raised, and in 1968 Township Council took
over the roadway and the tile was replaced. Over a span of some 100 years the
dream of our forefathers has become a reality.

CHAPTER 14

COMMUNITIES

Fenwood Gardens

Fenwood Gardens subdivision is part of Lot 66, Concession 2, Ameliasburgh Township. Lot 66 has not changed hands many times since it was taken up from the Crown in 1804 by Eleanor Dusenbury. In 1808 John Dusenbury's name appears, and later John Covert.

Andrew P. Wannamaker became owner in 1818, until 1851 when his youngest son, Isaac, took over most of the property. They sold in 1869 to Samuel Simonds who in turn sold to his son, Joseph, in 1885. Mr. and Mrs. Joseph Simonds were owners until 1949 when their grandson, Hobert Adams, took over and managed the farm until it was sold and subdivided in 1954.

This land was sold by Hobert Adams to Cecil R. Goodison and a Registered Plan of Sub-division #19, was put on by Thomas Ransom Sr. in 1956.

The name Fenwood Gardens was given to this area by Mr. Goodison, who lived in Toronto on Fenwood Heights, and Taylor Drive was named after his partner.

Before any development was started, Mr. Goodison died and the property was purchased by John M. Parrott, President of Stanley Park Limited of Belleville, through Gerald Joyce Real Estate in September, 1962.

The original subdivision was approved for some 59 building lots to be serviced by wells and septic tanks, plus a park.

Before construction was started, the Department of Highways purchased the northern portion of the subdivision for the Highway 14 bypass, leaving only 54 usable lots.

Some 14 wells were drilled on the property— one to a depth of 104 feet— and none produced an adequate water supply. At this time the engineering firm of Geo. L. Totten and Associates was called in. The representative was Orville Chisholm from Markham, Ontario, who with the co-operation of Ameliasburgh Township requested the services of a water geologist from the Ontario Water Resources Commission to find an adequate water supply. An extensive survey of the area revealed that the marshland to the north of the sub-division was at one time a river.

Donaldson's well drillers were employed and a good water supply was found at a depth of 65 feet in the middle of the marsh. They eventually moved closer to the sub-division and drilled and reached a good supply of water at 25 feet.

Approval was obtained from the Ontario Water Resources Commission for the construction of the first pumping station and distribution system. The contract was awarded to Frank Archer Pumps Limited of Kingston, Ontario.

In June of 1964 a house was started on Lot 37. The builder was Eldon Robinson from Plainfield. This house was sold to Mr. and Mrs. Fred Hoven and was occupied in September, 1964. The second house was built on Lot 38—same builder and suppliers. This house was sold to Mr. and Mrs. Rowan Holt and at the time of writing they are still living in Fenwood Gardens.

Lot 39 was the third house built, then Lot 22 at the north entrance and Carl LaRoque purchased this house and still lives there. Some of the builders who bought lots were Arthur A. Sills and Son, Maurice Rollins Construction, Don Kellar, Mike DiMark Construction, Fred Pope of Bellewood Manufacturing Limited, and Albert Horlock.

Most of the lots had buildings on them by 1972. In May of 1976, the Ontario Water Resources Commission ordered the Township to take over the operation of the water system after Mr. Parrott discontinued the operation. In 1982 a new water system was installed with new pumping facilities located south of old Highway 14.

Most of the houses are built in what was an 18-acre hardwood forest, a picturesque setting for the homes that are located there.

It is interesting to note that, in the 20 years since 1964 when the first house was built, unit-prices have risen from $17,000 to $80,000, and the cost of the big brick farmhouse on this same land in 1902 was $2,600.

Eatonville

A mile south of Rednersville in a setting of tranquil beauty are three homes by a creek and marsh. Once this spot was a scene of considerable activity with much coming and going to a tannery and a blacksmith shop. The creek provided a source of water for a tannery which was built by Norris Bristol in the early 1830's. His brother Benjamin built a tannery c. 1819 near Picton. Norris married Mary Anderson, daughter of the pioneer William Anderson. Both the tannery and the Bristol home were situated on the west side of the road across from the present Douglas Redner home on land now occupied by County Road 23. In the tannery days the road was narrower and farther to the east. Bristol operated the tannery until 1845, then moved to Madoc, selling his business to William Stafford.

William Gardiner Stafford married Sarah Jane Redner, daughter of Peter Redner Sr. He bought the Bristol tannery and home and ran the tannery for 30 years, doing an extensive business in manufacturing harness, boots and shoes. The hides were brought in from all parts of the township and beyond. Stafford in turn sold the tannery to Isaac Eaton, and bought a nearby farm, lot 78, from Alpheus Brickman (now owned by James Staveley). Here he built a fine home and barn, planted an orchard and started growing hops. Ralph Stafford of Rednersville was a grandson of William G. Stafford.

Eatonville Tannery

Isaac Robinson Eaton was born in Sophiasburgh Township c. 1838. He is listed on the 1861 census of Sophiasburgh as a shoemaker. He ran a boot and shoe store in Stirling for a time before buying the tannery from Stafford. His wife was Abigail Way. The tannery did a big business for many years with Mrs. Eaton boarding the tannery help. The little hamlet became known as Eatonville.

Man has always used the skins of animals to protect himself from the weather. Curing and tanning hides to produce leather was one of the earliest arts practised by mankind. The skins of oxen, cows, horses, sheep, goats and deer were mainly used. Various substances were used over the years to remove the hair and tan the hides. Tanneries were of necessity located close to a good supply of water with which to fill the vats. 'Green' hides were soaked in water to remove blood and dirt. Then they were placed in large vats filled with a solution of salt and ashes, as well as slaked lime and sulphide of lime to cure them and remove the hair.

Tanning rendered the skins immune to decay and shrinking. Tannin or tannic acid was obtained from hemlock, oak and chestnut bark. The Eatons ground the bark in a machine operated by horses going round and round. Their tannery had four large vats, for the cured hides had to go through a series of vats containing successively stronger tannin solutions called liquors. It is said that the odours were most unpleasant in the vicinity of the tannery. The hides were dried in a stretched position. For boot and shoe uppers the hides were split into two or three layers. Later the Eatons used a liquor made from wheat which did away with the laborious process of gathering and grinding

The Betty Redner home at Eatonville built in the 1860's.

bark. As more modern methods of leather manufacture came into use, Eaton could not compete and the tannery was closed sometime in the 1890's. Jay Zufelt took over the building as a blacksmith shop, living in half of the Eaton house. Upon a brother's death, the Eatons moved to Melrose to take over his farm. The Zufelt blacksmith shop was short-lived, and the building gradually fell into disrepair until only parts of the walls remained, and these were bulldozed down when the highway was rebuilt in 1968.

There was an earlier blacksmith shop at Eatonville run by Levi Peters. He lived in the present Douglas Redner house and his shop was just to the south of it. It was built up on piles as the creek sometimes overflowed the road and surrounding area. The horses had to go up a ramp to enter the shop. Peters also ran a small grist mill in a building a short distance down the Spencer sideroad, with a windmill on the roof supplying the power.

Henry P. Redner was the first to live in this Redner house. After Peters a man named Wright lived there and kept bees. Mr. and Mrs. Douglas Redner have lived there since their marriage. Their daughter Betty, recently retired from the teaching profession, now lives in the white frame house next door where her great grandfather Rynard Redner and her grandfather David Wright Redner both lived. This is a century farm which has been in the Redner name since 1819. Betty offers a 'Bed and Breakfast' service in this lovely old home.

Across the road from Betty's house is the residence of Judge Russell Honey. It was built by Mac Lont. For a few years the Sprague telephone switchboard was in the Mac Lont home before it was moved to Lawrence Sprague's. The first Lont home was a frame house on the corner of the Gore road, where Mac's parents, Mr. and Mrs. Wm. Lont, lived. The Mac Lont home has had a number of owners through the years; Joshua Dodd followed the Lonts, then Wm. Farley Brickman; Burton Redner bought it in 1928, and Lyle Tweedy was owner previous to Judge Honey.

Mountain View Airport

Mountain View was one of the many rapidly constructed airports built during the Second World War. Although most of the property is just outside the Township of Ameliasburgh, the base has made a great contribution to its economy, while playing a vital part in training personnel for active duty.

The H.J. McFarland Construction Company, then of Deseronto, built the runways during the summer of 1940, this no doubt being the company's first big contract. Rock was crushed from the quarry located just to the west of the airport boundary, for the runway base.

The next phase of the construction was the excavation of the ground for sewers and water lines. On January 1, 1941, Charlie Cook came to what was to become the main entrance of the airport with an Armstrong Brothers' Construction truck from Brampton. The truck was loaded with drill steel. Armstrongs had the contract to dig for the sewers. Because of the marshy ground in the area, not well-frozen, the truck could go no farther. Four local men who had heard of the project and who were standing nearby were immediately hired to carry the load of steel in, about a quarter of a mile across

First class to graduate from Mt. View bombing and gunnery school, 1941.

the boggy ground. The steel was in 20-foot lengths and it was quite a test of strength to carry it along in bundles of four lengths while slipping in a foot or so of mud between the bogs.

A little blacksmith shop was built where the steel was piled near the spot where the drill hall now stands. Within a very few days the steel was being cut up into appropriate lengths and bits formed on the ends with a sledge hammer and a special tool for forming the bit.

In the meantime, a bulldozer arrived and surveyors set up stakes and the shallow soil was scraped off and two giant compressors, one with three jack-hammers, the other with two, began drilling in the rock.

In a short time, roads of a sort were built into where the hangars were to be located and Piggot Construction moved in to build the hangars.

Then came great loads of tile, bricks, British Columbia Fir timbers and lumber for the living quarters, mess hall, officers' accommodations, ground mobile equipment buildings; in fact everything for a complete airport with living accommodation for more than 3,000 military people.

By the end of May a water line had been dug down the hill to the bay, a pumphouse built and equipped, large wooden tanks installed on the airport and Armstrongs were moving their equipment to another job in Newfoundland.

Ontario Construction built all the smaller buildings, which were covered with wooden shingles. Work went on around the clock and the machinery was still roaring and grinding when the new station's first wedding was solemnized in the recreation hall. June 19, 1940 was the official opening.

For the next four years, R.C.A.F. Mountain View was the site of intensive wartime training activities. By March 1943, the station boasted a strength of two Harvards, 52 Avro Ansons, 26 Bristol Bolingbrokes and 19 Lysanders. 1943 saw station staff and students rack up over 47,000 flying hours.

The average strength of the station was about 2,000. Trainees numbered 500. At any one time the station's two school wings— No. 6 Bombing and Gunnery School and the R.C.A.F. Air Armanent School were conducting over a dozen courses, churning out navigators, air gunners, armament officers, bomb armorers, turret maintenance men, gun armorers, etc. Over 200 navigators for example, were in training at one time, with new courses starting every two weeks. There were Canadians, Britons, Poles, New Zealanders and Czechs in training.

Suddenly, in 1945, in the closing month of the War, activity dwindled and by 1947, Mt. View was only a holding unit for aircraft mostly by then obsolete, and instruments, electronic equipment and parts left from the war. Many types of aircraft have been stored at Mt. View, including in addition to those already mentioned, the CF100, T33, Sabre, CF104, Vampire, Comet, Argus, Lancaster, Musketeer and Chipmunk.

The following poem on Flying was written by T.F. Williams of Woodstock, the oldest licenced pilot in Canada, in 1981, aged 88. Williams was shot down by the Red Baron in the First World War and only recently hung

Airmen at Mt. View Airport in 1942 with Fairey Battle Bomber.

up his wings for good. He is an uncle of J. Russ Williams, who retired from the County Board of Education. The poem was distributed in a press kit for the Great Belvedere Air Dash of 1973 from the Mountain View Air Base. The poem compares flying of 1917 with that of today.

> I look back to the day when 'twas up and away
> With only a map to guide me.
> When I looped and spun in cloud and sun,
> With no controller to chide me.
> With the girl in my life (or some other man's wife)
> Snug in the seat beside me.
> It was flight by chance and the seat of my pants
> When a cloud could easily hide me.
> Today, they must know where I would go,
> And who I would have beside me.
> What I would fly and exactly how high,
> And from radar nothing can hide me.
> It's clatter from here and chatter from there,
> And probably somebody squawking.
> It's not freedom to me, like birds in a tree,
> But bound like a captive falcon.

Mountain View Airport today displays none of the feverish activity of the war years, but if you drive along Highway 14 past the base, you just may glimpse a few silent gliders in the air, because in the summer the Air Cadet Glider School conducts its annual courses there, as Robert Bradford says, "with a fine sense of respect for the old station."

The Founding of Quinte Shores

An Ameliasburgh Subdivision
Information Supplied by Sue Taylor

The Hancock Company sold part of the land nearest the shore of Weller's Bay for a housing development. It has been sold and resold to developers. In January 1969, a sales office was built which later was converted to a beautiful home for Clifford and Julie Taylor of Toronto. Now there are 25 year-round homes and eight cottages on Quinte Shores, serviced by telephone, hydro, school buses and garbage collection.

Hiscock Shores

By Tom Hiscock
assisted by Earle Rowe and W.D. Hanthorn

Old-timers in the area will tell you it was known as the island. It comprised some 365 acres fronting onto Weller's Bay and owned by Reuben Church. Adjoining this property and closest to Smoke's Point Road lived Reuben's two spinster sisters in a house sitting on about 50 acres of land. The old farmhouse, after having been vandalized, burned down. In days now past, the sisters Maude and Minnie were assisted by a brother George in tending their few head of cattle and working the farm. When George went to Toronto to live, work on the farm slowly came to a halt. The two sisters were highly respected and both being excellent cooks, did not lack for company.

Maude Church, Gladys Church, Mimmie Church

Reuben Church rented his island property out to local farmers who used it for pasture land. Every spring time, the farmers would bring about 130 head to graze throughout the summer months, returning to take them home in the fall. The farmers swam their cattle across the mouth of a stream that flowed from a point near the farm house and ended in a swamp as it neared the bay. The farmers forded the water on horseback. The pasture and swamp were also favorite hunting grounds, there being an abundant supply of rabbit, duck, partridge, muskrat and other small game.

At the other extreme end of Mr. Church's island, a stream known as Brandy Creek empties into Weller's Bay. This creek has its source somewhere in the farmlands about two miles north of the bay. Earle Rowe, who lived on a farm where much of this creek crossed, recalls his father hitching up the democrat, (a horse-drawn buggy with a seat up front and a box at the rear) and heading to the mouth of the creek in the spring when the carp were running up to spawn. He stood on the bank and filled the box with a pitchfork in a very short time. The creek was jammed full of fish swimming up from the bay. Earle's father would then take the fish to the railway station in Trenton where they were shipped to the United States.

And how did Brandy Creek get is name? While not too sure, Earle Rowe had been given to understand there were a couple of colourful characters who operated a 'still' in these swamps for several years and small rowboats could navigate some of the streams to get into Weller's Bay. A couple of Indians were navigating their canoe down the creek when it suddenly flipped over. To their dismay they lost a bottle of brandy they were carrying. As the writer sees it, the bottle probably contained evil spirits anyway.

When Reuben Church passed away, his will disclosed the property had been bequeathed to his wife, Mary. When Maud and Minnie Church passed away, their estate was sold to Cecil R. Cronkwright. He lived in the old farmhouse for several years, operating a small camp and boat-rental business. With the selling of the Reuben Church property, Mr. Cronkwright moved to Consecon where he became a successful builder in the area.

It seems near the mid 1960's, R.S. Hiscock (familiarly known as Reg.), a well-established builder from Toronto's east end, rented a cabin for a couple of weeks in two succeeding summers from Mr. Ketcheson on the south side of Weller's Bay. While out fishing on the bay, he often crossed to the opposite side and couldn't help wondering why such a large parcel of land lay idle. It can be assumed at this time that an idea and a vision of the future began taking shape in his mind.

Reg. Hiscock, being a man of strong desire, began a relentless search for the owner, which ended in Cleveland, Ohio, where he found Mrs. Reuben Church living with her daughter Gladys. When negotiations for purchase were finalized, Hiscock became the new owner in 1967.

Hiscock began the task of fulfilling his vision by obtaining plans for subdividing the land into 100 lots. At his own expense, he constructed almost 1¼ miles of roadway and put in his own hydro poles and line, including a telephone line. Right out on Sugar Point, as the southwest corner of the island is known, he kept three lots and built a large cottage on the center lot.

The construction of the road which passed across the mouth of the creek took tons of rock day after day, before it finally ceased to disappear under the waters of the creek to eventually form a solid base on which to lay a culvert under the road. Locals who watched the daily movement of heavy construction equipment brought in by a local company, considered it such a costly venture that they jokingly referred to it as 'millionaire road'.

Throughout the period of development of Hiscock Shores, the developer ran into many problems and trying situations. Finally the township office gave the go-ahead with the provision that the area be designated for seasonal dwelling. His own home, having been built on native land, was classified as a permanent dwelling. Other permanent homes had also been built with the hope that they could be used as such. The roadway had been turned over to the Township by Hiscock and the hydro and telephone lines to their respective companies.

It was now the fall of the year and the Hanthorns of Carrying Place had bought a new 72-passenger bus to transport children to school. At the request of the parents living at Hiscock shore, Mrs. Hanthorn drove the big bus in more than a half mile to find a roadblock. She backed the bus all the way out to the Smoke's Point road and discontinued pupil pick-up for awhile. While walking out to catch the school bus, two little girls were molested and once more the bus service was restored and is still operating today. Once more the road was closed off, but equipment from the Forces Base at Trenton was dispatched to allow its resident workers to commute.

The Ontario Municipal Board had a meeting at the Township Hall from Dec. 15 to Dec. 17, 1980, and the problem was resolved about residency. The Township granted a permanent residency status to all who had built prior to Nov. 23, 1979.

Today, after the many fustrations and due to the dogged determination of one man, there stands some 90 homes; more than 20 are used all year by permanent residents. Many others are built with an eye to the future as retirement homes.

Thus, from a pasture in the Township of Ameliasburg, was Hiscock Shores founded.

The Garden
By Tom Hiscock

Show me the man, without a yearn,
  For a fork and hoe, and some earth, to turn;
Who craves not the smell, of a spaded earth,
  The entrance of spring, and a garden's birth.

Show me the man, who would not spend,
  His time in a garden, for hours on end;
Who has no desire, nor the heart to confess,
  To the beauty of summer, and a garden's dress.

Show me the man, who would not care,
  To enter and harvest the bounties there;
Who seeks not the tang, of autumn's breath,
  The debut of fall, and a garden's death.

Yes; show me the man, that I might tell,
  Of the beauties which, in a garden dwell;
For though man has planted, and turned the sod,
  The garden itself, is a gift from God!

Editor's Note— Hiscock Shores is a beautiful place, as the poem by Tom Hiscock states in the final line.

CHAPTER 15

M̄ILLS

The Mills of 7th Town

Edited and abridged from A History of the First Mills of 7th Town, now
Ameliasburgh Township
by Loral Wanamaker, 1970

All of Ameliasburgh was a wilderness when our pioneer ancestors arrived
here. One of their first requirements was food. As soon as a shelter of logs was
built, they made a clearing and planted seeds among the stumps. At first only
Indian corn and a little wheat was harvested, but how was it to be made into
flour with no mill?

At first an axe was used to crush the grain on a flat stone, but a more
satisfactory method was the hominy block or plumping mill; this being a
mortar made from hardwood, usually an ironwood stump, hollowed out by
building a fire in the center and keeping the outside wet, or by the use of a red-

Making Flour— Plumping Mill and Sweep Pole, painting by Rev. Bowen Squire.

hot cannon ball. This mortar was partly filled with corn and using a pestle or beatle of the very hardest wood, the grain was tediously crushed into a poor-quality corn flour. At times a large mortar was built by attaching a sweep-pole to the bough of a tree. When the pole was loaded with rock, much less strength was needed to crush the grain.

Petition Respecting Mill of John W. Meyers

Ontario Historical Society- Vol. XXVI
The Petition of us whose names are hereunto Subscribed—
Humbly Sheweth
That your Honours petitioners being customers of Capt. J.W. Meyers Mills which are erected on Lot number five in the first Concession of Thurlow and the said Captain W. Meyers having been at considerable expense of Improving and fencing a pasture on Lot number four near the Landing for the purpose of keeping a Team (for our conveniency) to transport our Grain and flour to and from his Mills and as said Lot number 4 is a Reserve we pray it my be confirmed (for our Benefit) to the said Captain Meyers either by Grant or Lease as your Honour is your Judgment may think fit— And your Honours petitioners as in duty Bound will ever pray— Thurlow 21st December 1798.
Lot prayed for is an Indian Reserve—
The Petition is dismissed. P.R.

Cornelius Blount	Isaac Bluwvet
Ichabod Bowerman	Jacob Billue
Owen P. Roblin	Abraham Lawsom
Mathew Goslee	Isaac Johnston
Robert Young	Elisha Beman
John Lawson	Asa Weller
Alpheus Taft	Jesse Spoloin?
Abner Tildon	John Skinckle
Nathaniel Taylor	William Babcock
William Rightmyer	Benjamin Clapp
Thomas Jones	D. McG Rogers
Benjamin Gerow	James Peeck. Jr.
Jacob Tice	Benj'n Richardson
John Henesey	Caleb L. Purdy
Richard Henesy	Joseph Walker
Henry Heerman	Artemis J.A. Ross
Henry Rednor. Sen.	Elijah Hubble
Andrew Wannamaker	John Huff
Harmanus Wannamaker	David Harris
Peter Wannamaker	Martin Rush
Jacob Wannamaker	Lawrence Halsted
Peter Crouter	Stephen Halsted
Lewis Brickman	

The Honourable Peter Russell Esquire President
of His Majesty's Province of Upper Canada &c &c &c

In Council

The Petition of us whose names are hereunto
Subscribed — Humbly Sheweth

That your Honours petitioners being custom
-ers to Captain John W Meyers Mills which are
erected in Lot number five in the first Concess-
-ion in Thurlow and the said Captain W. Meyers
...
...
The Landing for the purpose of laying a ...
(for our convenience) is transport on grain ...
down teams from his Mills, and as said it ...
... we pray it may be confirmed
(for our benefit) to the said Captain Meyers or his
...
may think fit to — And your petitioners as in
duty bound will ever pray — Thurlow

21st December 1798
Cornelius Blount
Ichabod Bowerman   William Rightmyer
Owen P Roblin
Matthew Golla   Thomas ...
Robert Young
John ...   Benjamin Girvou
...   Jacob Pice
...   John Kinsay
...   Richard Kinsay
...   Henry ...

As the clearings grew larger, the pioneer began to harvest wheat which was more difficult to grind than Indian corn or wild rice. The grinding of wheat by these methods resulted in a coarse brown flour which made wholesome bread and cakes. Quite frequently, the work of making the flour was done by the women using hominy blocks, due to the difficulty in travelling to the nearest mill at Napanee, which was built in 1787. At Lake-on-the-Mountain a grist mill was erected about 1796, and according to Canniff, Captain John Meyers had already constructed a mill at Meyer's Creek, (now Belleville) by 1792. Guillet in *Pioneer Days in Upper Canada*, dates it as 1794. He noted the grain was dragged from as far west as Port Hope, "through the pathless woods on rough sleds", to Meyer's Mill. However, Meyer's Mill must have been much more convenient for the settlers of Seventh Town, as the petition respecting his mill mentions he kept a team for the petitioners' convenience and many of the signatures were those of Ameliasburgh settlers.

An editorial in *The Picton Gazette*, Canada West, Aug. 20, 1856 states: "no one can entertain any doubt of the immense advantages to be derived from having cheap and good milling power in a locality. There is no species of manufacture which commands a readier or more certain market than a barrel of flour."

Consecon and Roblin's Mills are two locations mentioned as having excellent and cheap milling power.

Mills at Consecon

Col. William Marsh, with his own family and in charge of a group of settlers and Loyalists, arrived in Seventh Town in June 1793, and petitioned for a grant of land in this manner— "a grant about five miles distant south-easterly of the south landing of the Carrying Place on a small stream of water, which discharges itself at the head of the Bay of Quinte into Lake Ontario, with permission to erect a sawmill upon the said stream". According to the Archival records (ref. #1801, Public Archives of Canada) this petition was granted, for the surveyor was directed to assign Mr. Marsh 650 acres of land. After petitioning for and receiving the land, lots #105, 106 and 107, Concession 4, Ameliasburgh, William Marsh returned to Vermont where he died.

Beldon's 1878 *Atlas* gives the credit for the first mill in Consecon to Matthias Marsh, son of William Marsh the pioneer, although he had settled very early in Eighth Town (Sidney Township). The book, *Pioneer Life on the Bay of Quinte*, 1904, lists a son of Matthias as Archibald Marsh, the builder (Matthias Marsh had 24 children). This Archibald Marsh took on the job of clearing the land at Consecon where he had taken up a grant of land around 1802, and laboured very hard to build a house and also the first grist mill and flour mill there, so it would seem that the Marshes built the first saw mill in Ameliasburgh and the first flouring mill in Consecon, in 1808. Archibald Marsh died at the age of 50 in 1834.

The Elmore map of 1836 shows the Marsh mills on one side of Consecon

Creek and the Wilkins Mills on the other side of the same creek, both on lot #106, concession 4, Ameliasburgh.

Robert Charles Wilkins came to Seventh Town in 1792 (aged 10 years), with his father and settled at the Carrying Place. On Aug. 3, 1795, Robert Wilkins petitioned for a grant of land and by an Order in Council dated March 13, 1810, he was granted lot 102, con. 4, Ameliasburgh. On this lot he built a mill, about a mile east of the mouth of Lake Consecon. This mill was credited with having the best location and facilities of all the mills in Prince Edward County.

Smith's *Canada: Past, Present and Future*, 1850, lists Robert C. Wilkins as miller, carder and fuller. In the 1851 *Dominion Census* for Ameliasburgh, Mr. Wilkins, aged 70 years, was listed as mill owner, with the value of the mill at 2000 pounds Sterling. It consisted of three run of stones and produced 10,000 pounds of flour per year. Wilkins also ran a distillery.

This seems to give the Wilkins family two mills over the years, possibly owned and operated by father and son. Today the one on Lot 102 would be under the water, as this is where the present Railway bridge crosses the lake. However, at that time in history, there was a sharp fall of water at this point and the actual lake was about half the size it is today. Barley boats, some built in Melville at the east end of the lake, travelled the navigable river as it was then, to the point where the creek flows into the Weller's Bay. In 1970, John Walt, a local farmer, investigated this spot by boat and found old forms and iron pins which may have been a part of Wilkin's mill. Following is data on Lot 102, 4th Con., from the Registry Office at Picton, which upholds Mr. Wanamaker's theory of two Wilkins mills.

Lot 102

Crown Patent. Nov. 20, 1811— Crown to R.C. Wilkins, 200 acres
Bill of Sale July 11, 1851— R.C. Wilkin to James McCutcheson, 200 A.
Bill of Sale Nov. 29, 1854— Jas. McCutcheson to Wm. Robinson, 200 A
Bill of Sale Apr. 17, 1879— W.J. Robinson & Wife to Prince Edward Railway Co. 66/100 in lots
Bill of Sale Nov. 1, 1879— Wm. Robinson & Wife to P.E.R.R. Co., 3 acres, his right of way
Q.C. Deed March 27th, 1882 and 31st, Oct. 1893— Peter Burr to Adam Saylor, this may affect water rights.

Here ends the tale of Lot 102.

With regard to Lot 106, from the memoirs of James McConkey, (1870-1880) there was a sawmill attached to the south side of Marsh's grist mill and farmers drew in their logs in winter and they were sawn into lumber in the spring when water power peaked. He also recalled a carding and fulling mill across the creek at the upper dam nearest the lake. These mills were owned by Lieut. Col. the Hon. Robert Wilkins.

Helen B. Anderson in her *Chronicles of Consecon*, 1930, states, "the Lieut. Col. the Hon. Robert C. Wilkins, son of Robert C. Wilkins an early settler, owned the first mill in Consecon." The following men operated the mill: Joshua Cadman, James Graham, Charles Chase, John Holmes, and Millar T. Osborne."

Records from the Picton Registry Office first mention the Marsh mill and mill dam in 1829, when the business and property passed from Archibald Marsh to his heirs, who operated the mills until April of 1834, when it was sold to Robert Charles Wilkins. In August 1834, Col. Wilkins transferred half of his mill property to E.D.S. Wilkins (the west part), and in November 1844, granted the other part to Robert Wilkins Jr.

About 1854, business must have declined or the Wilkins lived too lavishly, or for reasons unknown, perhaps due to failure of the winter wheat crop in 1857-58, they became indebted to Reverend George Romanus and to Hon. William Campbell and others. It was then by Sheriff's orders that the Wilkins Mills passed into the hands of their creditors, who in turn sold the property to Frederick James Osborne for $6,000.

Osborne operated the grist and flour mill, which had two sets of stones, while his hired man John Allen operated the attached sawmill. Farmers drew their logs in winter and left them to be sawed into lumber during the spring freshet.

In the years 1880 and 1881, the Osbornes sold the mill property, part to Alvin Marsh and the other part to W.H. Marsh, who in turn sold the property the following year to Adam Saylor and Mr. and Mrs. Peter Burr, who turned their share of the property over to Saylor. About this time (1882) the mill burned and was replaced by a new four-storey stone mill, built by Adam Saylor. It was outfitted with a splendid roller system, a boiler house and big

New Stone Mill at Consecon circa 1882, built by Adam Saylor.

steam engine to run the rollers when the water was low. In improvements to the mill he spent more than $7,000.

This mill was equipped with a 'Little Giant' water turbine which weighed two tons and generated 60 horsepower. The wheel was built in 1873 by J.C. Wilson Co. of Glenora. Its wooden bearings in the shaft were made of ebony, the hardest known wood in existence. The pinion was made from hard maple.

This two-ton wheel was removed from the mill in 1974 and transported to the Ameliasburgh Museum. Harry Bisdee, at that time Curator of the Museum, was the overseer of the project.

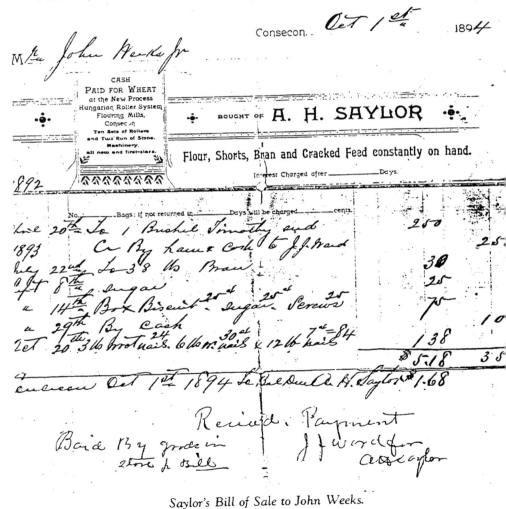

Saylor's Bill of Sale to John Weeks.

The Old Stone Mill in Consecon— destroyed by fire in 1931.

The James Grist Mill, 1932.

Ownership of the saw mill now passed down through three generations. Adam Saylor and his wife Matura (Cooper) had a daughter Mary who married Peter Burr and a daughter Phoebe who married Marshall Burr, who in 1894, took over the mill. In 1903 their son Adam Burr became owner of the mill, but his son Ivan Burr was drowned in the mill wheel, so the mill passed out of the family in 1923, when it was sold to Clayton French. There was a store attached to the west side of the mill at this time which was used as a butcher shop and later as a grocery store. Mr. and Mrs. French lived in the apartment over this store.

On April 25, 1931, Mr. and Mrs. William James and their son Roydon moved to Consecon from Frankford and stored their furniture in the store, for they were the proud new owners of the mill. That night the big mill burned. Only the mill wheels survived.

The James family built a metal and frame building for grinding feed, which ran mainly on water power. In their 17 years of ownership, Roydon made thousands of trips to the dam by the lake to raise and lower the logs to control the flow.

In 1945, Stephen Dempsey took over the management of the mill when he returned from overseas. Mr. and Mrs. Richard Baldwin purchased the mill in 1949 and operated it for 25 years. Water power and diesel engine now furnished the power, for milling.

Because of lack of storage space, the Baldwins built a grain elevator by the railway siding, so that western grain could be brought in or local grain in large

The Upper Dam near Consecon Lake.

Dick Baldwin— owner of Consecon Mill for 25 years.

The Baldwin Grain Elevator at Consecon Station.

quantities shipped out. They moved the unused freight shed from the railway station because it was a sturdy building "with a perfect hip," and reconstructed it on the mill site for a seed-cleaning plant. They added a tall part to the west side of the mill to house their electric power plant.

In the early 1960's, the dam went out and the creek bed was dry. The Baldwins, as a community gesture, donated all their water rights to the Ontario Water Resources Commission, on the condition that they rebuild the dam to maintain a pond in the village.

Work began on the project late in 1974 and the water in the creek was restored, improving the scenic appearance of both banks of the creek and providing a public park around the pond. One of the old grinding stones was imbedded in cement on the park— a fitting memorial to times gone by.

In 1974, an American family named Byreiter took over the mill for a period of time, until a local farm family living on Ameliasburgh's Second Concession decided to try their luck in the milling business. Consecon Feeds and Farm Supply, as Eric and Pat Bandy call their mill, is a healthy, thriving and exciting venture. They have added a store, tack shop and new equipment. They also employ local people, and farmers and villagers meet there to pass the time of day.

Consecon Mill Dam, circa 1960.

Consecon's Bush Mill

George Bush operated the first grist mill on the Ameliasburgh side of the creek in Consecon. In a building behind the evaporator, was his grinder, which was powered by a gasoline engine. He began grinding grain for area farmers in 1906, but later moved his mill across the road behind Miller's store to a two-storey building. The upstairs, he used for a shingle mill and there he made

Consecon Feed and Farm Supply Ltd. 1980. The tall part contains the electric machinery.

Official opening of New Office and Store, 1981. Robert Adams with Hereford Bull.

'cedar shakes'. Later on he bought a shop from Dan Garretsee, located down the street that is beside the Anglican Church, where he operated his mill until 1911, when he moved to his farm on the south side of Consecon Lake. George Lazier operated the mill for a time before replacing the building with a house.

The Mills of Ameliasburg Village

The first mill in what is now the village of Ameliasburg appeared on Elmore's map of 1835 as Way's Grist Mill and Way's Post Office. Their 1859 map shows it as Roblin's Grist Mill.

Way's Mills

The genesis of the early development is obscure, but in 1803 Jacob Cronk received Lot 81, Con. 3 by Crown Patent. In 1829 he sold the same lot to John B. Way who had learned the trade of milling before coming to Upper Canada. Way was responsible for erecting the first flour mill in the valley below the hill, in the place that today is called Ameliasburg, in 1829.

The village in the valley had an ashery, a shingle mill, a cooperage, a store and a number of homes. Today, foundations of some of those original buildings may be seen in the valley by the millpond, the site which was once known as Way's Mills.

The epitaphs on the tombstones in Grove Cemetery there, remind us of earlier days. Here one cannot help but reflect on the industries and the people who toiled here, some of them our very own ancestors.

Roblin's Mill

Owen Roblin, 1806-1903
Entrepreneur, the epitome of mid-century industry and enterprise. Founder of Roblin's Mills— Ameliasburg

Roblin's Mills, circa 1910.

In March 1838, Owen Roblin and John B. Way exchanged properties. There seems little doubt that Owen Roblin purchased or traded lots with John B. Way with the intention of building a better mill on the hill above the existing mill.

Philip Roblin, grandfather of Owen, had been a miller in New York but his property had been confiscated by the rebels. After severe hardships, the family reached Adolphustown where he was deceased in 1788. His eldest son, Philip Jr., in 1803 received a Crown Patent on land in Sophiasburgh known to us today as Roblin's Mills, but the Post Office was Green Point. There was excellent water power here for the Roblin's three mills and shipbuilding yard. Owen Roblin, the son of Philip #2, came from Sophiasburgh to Ameliasburgh and built a store and potashery five lots east of John B. Way's milling operation and began to export lye to Montreal.

There is no proof that the millpond in the horseshoe of the hill which powered Way's Mill received any water from the lake. Rather its water power originated from the drainage of land to the west. To quote *Pioneer Life on the Bay of Quinte*, "on taking possession of the Way property, Owen Roblin commenced to improve the water power; his first act was to excavate the present canal from the lake. The extent of this work may be estimated from the fact that the blasting powder alone cost the equivalent of $1,000... this busy man ran saw and carding mills and from his flour mill he shipped immense quantities of wheat and rye flour to Montreal; and during the Crimean War he exported day and night."

D.K. Redner in his account of Roblin's Mills, noted that a wooden flume carried the water for Roblin's enterprises. The flume near the mill which was 60 feet long, 15 ft. wide and 8 ft. deep was open at the top for several feet before passing under the road. Villagers came here for pails of water and farmers watered their horses at the spot. Loral Wanamaker and Bruce Ferguson, two local lads at the time, learned to swim in the canal where it joined the lake. They swam across the width of it. Wanamaker still recalls the loud roar the water made as it rushed under the road and over the embankment. According to Redner, a young girl named Lily Bowland slid into the flume and by a miracle was saved. Then the flume was covered as a safety measure.

As the demand for lumber increased, Roblin added another saw mill at the eastern end of the pond, while at the water fall from the canal on the edge of the hill he built his five storey stone mill in 1842. The water from the canal drove an overshot water wheel 30 feet in diameter. The wheel and gears were designed to take into consideration the volume and the speed of the water. This mill had a three run of stones and was latterly powered by a water turbine. The mill had a potential hydraulic head of about 75 feet.

To make good flour, the stones had to be kept in shape. Facing, as it was known, involved intricate hand work. Between the furrows on the surface of

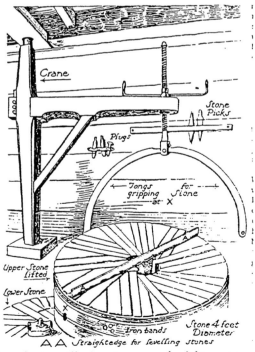

Interior of grist mill, showing crane for lifting upper stone.

the stone, 12 fine lines to the inch had to be cut. The picker who did this work often had scarred hands and when a picker came looking for work, the miller often asked him to 'show his metal', this being the gauge of his experience. Stones for making flour had to be accurately balanced so they didn't touch, lest the friction produce a scorched smell in the flour.

Grinding of grain was done by grooved mill stones six feet in diameter and about 18 inches thick. The top stone revolved and the bottom one remained stationary. There were holes in the sides of the top stone to allow lifting by crane for dressing the stones, the job of the millwright.

The late Ralph Stafford related that Royal Gerow was the person who dressed the mill stone in Roblin's mill and that his hands were badly scarred from the pieces of stone and steel which would fly during the process.

If the mill was busy the task of dressing the stones was done twice a month. To get access to the stones, a mechanism called a crane was used to lift up the upper stone to allow space for working. Chisels and hammers and picks were used and the picks were tempered with a solution made of the following ingredients:

water— 3 gallons, salt— 2 quarts, sal-ammoniac— 2 ounces, ashes from white ash bark— 1 shovel, which causes the Picks to scale clean and white as silver.

The interior of the mill was finished with pine lumber, with firm strong beams. In a small stone building attached to the east end of the mill was the office and at one time a post office. It was in this building, too, that Royal

Wesley and Francine Sager at the Hubbs farm on the Gore. (Notice the pump log made at Roblin's Mill.

Carding mill and Chimney, Roblin's Mill, 1910.

Gerow made pump logs which were used to pump water from wells.

A large stone building to the west of the mill proper contained the carding mill. A stationary steam engine was acquired when the lake level dropped. A huge brick chimney was built alongside this building. The lake level rose again and the chimney was only used one year.

Although the mill was outfitted with the best equipment of the day, all the gears and pulleys, endless belts and buckets did little to improve the working man's lot. There was always dust to breathe and heavy bags to lift.

R.E. Chrysler, wrote in an edition of *Watersheds,* "Like any enterprising business, Owen Roblin and his successor continually improved the mill by introducing newer equipment and methods. At the same time existing equipment was carefully maintained... the operation of the mill had been converted to the 'new process', which was introduced about 1870. This was known as the Evans Mill. Prior to 1867, most village mills operated on the American or flat-grinding system." This system ground as closely as possible to produce as much flour as possible at one grinding. The 'New or Evans Process', took off a minimum of fine flour on the first run and the 'midlings' that remained were reground, producing other types of flour. This process required an extra stone for the additional grinding of the midlings and a midling purifier.

By 1851 a tight community had established itself around the mill. According to the *Census* of that year, Roblin employed eight men. He had the highest assessment of anyone in the township. The village became known as Roblin's Mills but the post office was Ameliasburg.

Roblin's Mills— Merchant Milling 1838-1860 (Note Weigh Scales.)

The mill was used primarily for merchant milling from the time of its construction to about 1860. It had a total capacity of about 100 barrels daily and during busy periods it operated 24 hours per day. The flour, packed in barrels made in the Roblin Cooperage mill, was drawn to Rednersville or hauled to Belleville. Supplies of wheat and other grains were gathered on the return journey. Immense quantities of rye and wheat were shipped to Montreal during the American Civil War and the Crimean War. The failure of the winter wheat crop in 1857-58 and the development of the increasing barley market in the United States after the Civil War, however, drastically reduced the amount of hard winter wheat for merchant milling. Owen Roblin's mill was forced to restrict its activities to custom milling. Oats were rolled for oatmeal and some buckwheat flour was made.

The 1844-45 *Directory* lists Owen Roblin as having three sons, Edward, Donald and Roger. Two other children, Malcolm and Phoebe Jane, died young. Edward was the miller and he and his wife Ellen Cotter lived in the octagon-shaped house that Owen Roblin built for them. There was a myth that children born in this type of house would have a docile disposition.

The Roblins from the 'round house', as it was known in the village, had a

Seventh Town/Ameliasburgh

family of four. They were daughter Huldah and sons William H.C., Donald and Richard Owen (called RO), who settled in New York and had a candy factory. It was Wm. C. Roblin who became the miller.

Old timers in the village relate that fish came up the canal from the lake and dropped into the huge box where the wheel ran. At one time 500 pounds of fish were removed before the mill could be operated. Another time, the flume that conducted water to the mill needed repair where it passed under the road. In order to regulate the flow of water in this flume, a crank lifted or lowered planks. When the water was low, the flow could be cut off for awhile. Then, when the planks were lifted, power was provided for a few more hours. William Cotter Roblin, being a small man, with a rope tied around him for safety, crawled into the flume and repaired it.

A man named Taylor, who was a miller in Belleville, came to work at Roblin's Mills. He got a job for his friend Jacob Ferguson, too, and for many years he worked there. His son Truman Fergsuon, 3rd Concession, recalls his last trip down in the dark depths to dress the stone while young Truman remained apprehensively awaiting his return. "You won't have to worry again for that's my last trip my lad," were his father's words. He left the mill and drove the mail stage into Belleville for many years.

About 1920, the mill closed and for many years it stood abandoned, mute testimony to the busy, bygone days. Richard, was the last Roblin to own the mill. He died in Rochester, N.Y. in 1940.

Early in the 1930's, H.E. Fairfield purchased the mill, proposing to turn it into a cannery, but the depression years changed his plans. In 1947, Harry Smith of Belleville purchased the property. In 1962 a serious crack in the stone walls developed and it was reported the west end might fall. In 1963 it was sold by Mac Smith, at which time the millstones were in place and the wooden machinery still usable. On one of the upper floors was the old flour sifter with some of its silk screens containing flour. Then the mill was dismantled and taken to Black Creek Pioneer Village in Toronto.

When the Centennial Celebrations of 1967 began, fostering interest in preserving our history, the old Roblin Mill was gone. Today a plaque erected by the Seventh Town Historical Society marks the site.

Choate's Ameliasburgh Grist Mill

For a short time, Gill Choate ran a grist mill in a blacksmith shop on the property at the west end of the village where Harry Bisdee lives. His wife was able to tailor suits for the local young ladies.

The Arthur Corfield Grist Mill

About 1940, Arthur Corfield bought the blacksmith shop across from Idlewilde, and ran it as a grist mill. Business was brisk, so he made plans to move into the big Roblin Mill which hadn't been used for 20 years. After much planning and renovating by Corfield, the plan failed to materialize, so he continued his business for some years until it was taken over by the last miller in Ameliasburg, Roy Smith.

Mills on the Escarpment (Con. 4, Ameliasburgh)

On Lot 69, Con. 4, there is a ravine where a waterfall once powered a mill. Although Mr. Wanamaker lived a few hundred yards from the site, he was unable to find it marked on any Ameliasburgh map. He well remembers a very good wall of stone laid up in the ravine on which he supposed the mill was built and the water conducted to the mill from across the road to the south where the old dam can be easily followed to this day. Wanamaker reports that during an early spring flood, this mill washed over the hill and Manley Howell lost an eye as a result of the mishap.

Records from the Ontario Archives requested by Wanamaker produced no record of a mill, but a number of rental documents on this Clergy Reserve, as follows:

1817— Benjamin Way had first lease for £ 50/0/0

1833 document from Jacob Wanamaker giving all claims, rights and title to the east half of Lot 69 to Nathan Reddick, for £ 200, in which he gave all roads, waters and improvements and buildings to him

June 1847— receipts from the Home Agency, Toronto. One being from Sylvanus Sprague, £ 2/10/0... rent in full for W/½ Lot 69, 4th Concession, Ameliasburgh.

Another receipt (same year) from David Gibson for £ 30/15/10, rent in full up to June 1847 for E/½ Lot 69, Concession 4, Ameliasburgh.

The difference in the amount of rent, would lead one to believe that here existed one of the earliest mills in the Township.

The last lot on Concession 4, Township of Ameliasburgh was numbered 65 on the first map of Ameliasburgh. The next lot east is 64 Sophiasburgh and Mt. View Airport is located here. On the line between Lots 64 and 65 and a few yards north of Highway 14 there is another ravine which has been cut through the escarpment in much the same way as that described for the preceding mill. Here again is a wall of cut stone laid up on the south bank of the ravine which would place the mill here.

The earth dam for a head for this mill was on the south side of the road. It is hard to spot the exact site as the land has been worked. Mr. Wanamaker has no knowledge of whether these were saw mills or if they had grinding stones. Again from township documents he procured from the Archives, he found that this lot 65 was Clergy property, and leased by John B. Way of Sophiasburgh Township, Oct. 6, 1818. He was the same person who bought Lot 81, Concession 3, from Jacob Cronk Feb. 5, 1829, and built what was later known as Way's Mill.

The Babcock Home— to the west on this same creek was Babcock's Mill. Now the home of Malcolm Hubbs. Painting by Donnah Cameron.

The Babcock Mill on the Gore

Loral Wanamaker, in his history of the Mills of Ameliasburgh, told of a teacher who taught at the Bush School at Victoria having trouble hearing pupils read because of the whine of the saws at the nearby Babcock mill.

To reach this mill site, travel west on the Gore Road (south of Rednersville) until the bridge that spans the creek is reached. Pause on the bridge and look west about 40 rods and, on the west half of lot 86 now owned by Gerald Fox, one can trace where the mill was located.

In 1816 this lot was granted to John Babcock, but John Babcock Jr. already had a mill there Jan. 19, 1816 by petition. On the Tremaine map of Ameliasburgh of 1863, John R. Babcock was listed on Lot 87, Con. 1, and John H. Babcock on Lot 86 Con. 1. This, then, was the location of the Babcock saw mill, which in all probability had a stone for grinding as well. This mill was powered by an overshot wheel with buckets attached. These filled with rushing water and turned the wheel.

Nathaniel Wilson, who years later owned the east half of Lot 86 where the Voskamps now have a large 'Broiler' farm, recalled that all the lumber for that home, the earlier Fox house and the Townsend house had been sawn at the mill. Lumber, sawn at this mill was also used to construct the house on the Lorne Brickman farm that was used as a canning factory, the house now owned by Malcolm Hubbs, then a Babcock home, and others which belonged to the Babcocks, as this was a virtual settlement of Babcocks. One spring an unusually large freshet resulted in an ice jam which destroyed the dam and it

'The Babcock House'— the north part was built over 100 years ago with lumber from Babcock Mill. The rafters were rough, hand-hewn logs.
Left to Right: Mr. and Mrs. John A. Wilson, Mr. and Mrs. Nathaniel M. Wilson.

never was rebuilt because of the damage to upstream farms which had been flooded.

The closing of the mill must have been regretted by those who came from miles around to have their logs made into lumber.

Mills at Rossmore

Opposite the mouth of the Moira River in Belleville on the Ameliasburgh Bay side is a point of land which through the years has had many names. It has been known as The Point, Ferry Point, Hennessy Point, Wilkins Point and Ross More (Rossmore), by which it is presently known.

Many logs came down the Moira to be sawed into lumber at the Eagle Mill, as it was known, according to William Belnap in conversation with D.K. Redner. Pine lumber from the mill was used to build the old school in Rossmore, which was sold when the mill closed down to Edward Gerow for a cooperage shop. Later it was moved to the Herrington farm and used as a machine shed.

According to Belnap, the mill was set up on a little island east of Hwy. 14, and was run by a man named Froman, who sold it in 1864 to Page and Company. In the heyday of the lumber boom the logs that floated down the rivers were fastened into booms and towed by tugboats. French men from Quebec were hired for their skill in riding the logs. Local men tailed the booms to loosen logs that stuck on shore or shoals.

Often seven or eight schooners and two barges were being loaded at a time with lumber to export to Oswego. These barges were towed by the tug Al

Summers, under Captain Blanchard. Men were paid 20 cents an hour to load lumber by hand, while the employees received $1.00 per day.

Belden's Atlas reports that the B.F. Baker Co. took over operation of the mill and employed between 75 to 100 men. A time of depression came and the lumber mill was closed down in 1877, but was running again in 1878 for awhile. By 1880 it was operated and owned by the H.B. Rathbun & Son. Co. who had headquarters at Deseronto.

Ralph Murray was the millwright in charge of the mill and lived in a large house in the mill yard known as the Murray House. W.H. Lake was the shipper and book-keeper. But the lumbering business was on the wane and when a main shaft in the mill broke one day, the business ceased to exist and the mill was dismantled and moved to Rathbun headquarters.

The Mirancy Redner Mill (Con. 2)

The water coming through the flume built by Owen Roblin and from land drainage about the mill pond flowed in a northeasterly direction toward a marsh and onward into the Bay of Quinte. In the course of its meanderings, it was again harnessed to a mill.

The location of this mill was on Lot 79, Con. 2, Ameliasburgh, now a part of Willowlee Farm owned by Clarence and Lyle Vanclief on the south side of the concession road a short distance out in the fields.

On the 1836 and 1859 Elmore maps it is noted as Roblin's saw mill, and on the 1863 Tremaine map it is listed as Garrett's mill. On one map the creek and pond appear on the west half of lot 79, while on another they appear on the east half, the more likely location.

From the County Registry Office, Picton, comes the following information:
Crown Patent 1797— Crown to Joseph Bunberry 200 acres
1828— Capt. Bunberry to Matthew Bell
1830— Matthew Bell to Phillip Roblin
1840— Phillip Roblin to John P. Roblin
1840— John P. Roblin to — Redner.. northwest corner, west half part north of of creek and 20 acres in 78 and 79— course omitted
1852— John P. Roblin and wife to Thomas Garrett— west part of sawmill on lot in connection with saw mill.

Lewis, grandson of Henry Redner, the pioneer, settled on Lot 78, Con. 2 in 1869 when his son Mirancy was 17. On Jan. 30, 1876, Mirancy Redner and Annie Frances Delong were married. He bought and ran the flour and grist mill located on the east side of the creek just a short distance up the road to the west of his father's farm. They lived in the house at the back of the mill, a most uncomfortable place. To quote from the Rednersville *Tweedsmuir History*, "Chains clanked, stovepipes rattled, dishes clattered, the beds would shake, the bed covers would even be pulled off the bed. The story goes that two Irishmen were hired for a certain sum to dig out the creek running from Roblin's Lake down to the mill for a greater flow of water to run the mill. One of them mysteriously disappeared; it is believed that one man killed the other that he might have all the money payment. Hence the 'haunt' and certainly strange things were seen and heard it that mill house. Mirancy sold the mill to a man named Pettit, who ran it until it burned down. The mill house also burned at a later date."

The late Ralph Stafford of Rednersville recalled that when he was a boy it was Pettit's grist and flour mill. He remembered that it had burned when Mr. Pettit was dressing the stone because the dressing tool flew from his hand and struck and upset the light he was using which caused the fire. This mill was never rebuilt.

After having been in the Napanee district for seven years, Mirancy returned to the 2nd Concession about 1900 and built a grist mill to the east of what we know as the Gerald Redner house. He bought one of the discarded boarding houses from Rossmore, built in the days of its lumber boom, and moved it to the home location. This renovated building served as his mill. It was run by a stationary steam engine.

Mirancy made shingles at the mill from the extremely large cedar trees that were cut from Herb and Morley Dempsey's burned over swamp. Mr. Stafford was particular to note the large size of the cedar trees, some being over four feet through. These trees made excellent shingles several years later. He also had a cider press at the mill and in later years sold many telephone poles to the Sprague Telephone Company.

When the mill was dismantled, Ralph Stafford bought the stationary engine and James Barber the grinder. Mirancy Redner died in 1929.

Halliwell's Mill on Roblin's Lake- 1893

Major John R. Cunningham lived on the south side of Roblin's Lake and owned the farm now in possession of Mrs. Milton Wood. He was a carpenter and millwright, and it was he who built the round barn on his farm on the fourth concession as well as the old round building that housed the agricultural exhibits at the fairgrounds.

In partnership with the Messrs. Halliwell who owned the Corfield property at that time, a sawmill from Brown's foundry in Belleville was being set up on the shore of the lake. The Major had been busily engaged in fitting it up and generally managing it.

On May 20, 1893, Major Cunningham, before leaving home had complained of not feeling well, but took his dinner and proceeded to cross the lake in his sail boat. About four o'clock in the afternoon he took his boat and started home. The newspaper that reported the incident stated that, "about midway over the lake a little daughter of Mr. Sopers, who lived on the same side of the lake, saw the Major fall into the lake. For several days the search for the body continued. A seine was dragged all day and charges of dynamite set off for two days. It was proposed to send to Picton for a cannon to fire shots over the water". The third day Bob Sopers and George Graves located the body by dragging an old horserake behind a boat. As Cunningham was an excellent swimmer, the newspaper article suggested he may have "been in an apoplectic fit." The mill was never operated after his death. Major Cunningham was the Great Grandfather of Muriel (Burkitt) Minaker of Ameliasburgh and Clifford Calnan, Carrying Place.

Front part of Old Saw and Grist Mill of R.G. Stafford, Rednersville.

Stafford's Mill at Rednersville

In the year 1906, Ralph Stafford bought property in Rednersville from Mrs. Gerow. As well as a house and barn, there was a small building 18'x24' on the property. The following year he turned this building into a grist mill and ran it by a traction engine. The farmers brought their grain from far and near to be ground. In 1912 this mill was torn down and replaced by a larger one.

The gravel used to build the cement wall was bought from Henry Redner and George R. Wanamaker helped build it. Logs were purchased from George Roblin, cut and sawed into lumber at the mill and Henry Brickman helped with the construction of the frame part.

A stationary steam engine was installed to run the mill as well as a planer and saws to cut and plane lumber. Among other things, material was cut for the making of tomato crates.

In 1917 an additional 30-foot extension was added to the mill. The metal roof for this part was put on in January, in —20 degree weather.

In 1926 Mr. Stafford bought a Rumley Oil Stationary Engine and ran the mill with it until Aug. 5, 1941, when the mill was destroyed by fire.

Stafford's Mill yard, Rednersville Church in background.

Lumber Sawing— Stafford's Mills

The newspaper that was printed in Rednersville, named the *Rednersville Clarion* carried the following advertisement, in the March 18, 1921, issue: **NOTICE:** custom grinding done every Tuesday; work done while you wait. Lumber-cutting done after Feb. 18. Your patronage solicited.

R.G. Stafford.

Mill or Baker's Island

Because so many Ameliasburgh people worked on this Island, we will include it in our story of mills.

Canniff noted that there were extensive sawing mills on what was commonly called Baker's Island. It was formerly called Meyers' Island after Capt. Meyers who lived adjacent to it. He paid rent to the Indians for it for many years.

Mill or Baker's Island, as it is known today, is in the Bay of Quinte opposite the Canadian Forces Base in Trenton. There was a very large saw mill there in the 1880's. There were loading docks on the west side and as many as 11 boats loaded at one time. There was a fair-sized village of about 1,000 people who lived in company houses on the east side of the Island. A company-built and owned school was built in the village. In the middle of the Island was a large boarding house which was run by Finley Gerow, where the single men lived. The married men had their own company houses. All buildings were of lumber sawn at the mill. There were two shifts in the busiest season. The large sawmill there was about the same size as the Rossmore Mill, and there was keen competition between the two mills.

In the 1880's, John Eaton, who was a millwright, inventor and assistant engineer, worked on the island. His daughter attended school there. He had

John E. Eaton—
Assistant Engineer,
Mill Island in 1880's.
Ancestor of the Dymond
and Moynes
family of Gardenville.

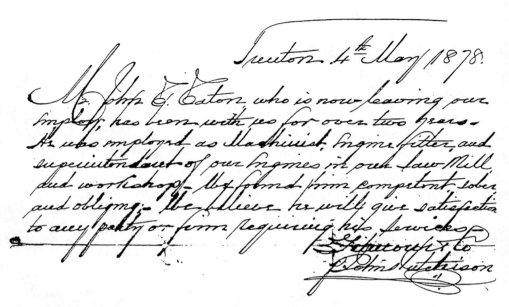

Reference— 1878— for John E. Eaton from Gilmour and Co., Trenton.

been an engineer for Flint and Yeomans in Belleville and for Page & Co., and he worked for Gilmour in Trenton in the 1870's. He invented a part for a steamboat, but a man from New York stole his patent. Later the Eaton family moved from the Island and lived in the 'middle house' in Carrying Place and for a long time it was known as the Eaton House.

Clayton Weese of Brighton recalls that his family supplied meat and vegetables to the people on the island. His father was James Francis Weese, and they lived on and owned the farm known today as the Summers Dawson farm along the Weese sideroad. Ryerson Dempsey, father of Harry and Grandfather of Gordon and Donald, had a slaughter house down on the bayshore and the Weese's one up on the hill. Both supplied meat.

There was one dependable deep well on the Island that was stoned up by George Weese, great-grandfather of Allan and Lyle Weese while their own grandfather, Randall Weese, worked at the mill.

From the Hastings shoreline, a flat bottomed scow ran back and forth to the Island to transport people. It was large enough to hold a horse and buggy.

A tugboat captained by a man named Doughby, hauled the huge barges named England, Ireland and Scotland, which carried up to 80,000 board feet of lumber to Oswego. The poor lumber sold locally at a cheap rate. The saws used were the muley saws which were like a crosscut saw that sawed up and down. Mr. Weese recalled a frosty March morning when a worker met his death by falling on the saw.

When the sawmill was at its busiest, so much sawdust was dumped at the east end of the island where the steam engines were that two little islands were joined. When the mill closed down, the buildings were demolished by the company that had built them and the place shortly became deserted.

Glenn Meyers of Trenton recalls that his Uncle Walton taught school there and his family pastured calves on the island after it was cleared. The old well and a trapper's cabin remained for some years until a man named Mr. Estes from Cuba, N.Y., bought the 17 acres in the Island. In 1929 the Canadian Government expropriated the island and Mr. Estes took less money than it had cost him.

Today the well has been filled in, a causeway has been built from the Base to the Island forming a beautiful protected harbour where dozens of fine yachts and sailing crafts are moored, for it has now become the C.F.B. Yacht Club. An attractive clubhouse graces the highest part of the Island where one gets a tremendous view of the Ameliasburgh shoreline.

CHAPTER 16

BLACKSMITHS

Blacksmiths and their Locations in Ameliasburgh Township

by Elmer Young

As a young person I remember quite a few blacksmiths and their locations, but when one starts to find the earliest ones it becomes more difficult. For a good number of the recorded shops I have had to depend on a few oldsters who remember so and so had a shop just where, and now there are no more blacksmith shops. There are no working horses and only here and there do we find a few riding horses and as these want shoeing they are usually done by a travelling smith with a truck.

From early writings it is at once noted that a blacksmith was one of the earliest requirements of the pioneer settlers, not so much to shoe the horses or the oxen but to make axes, saws, wedges and all tools for the felling of the solid mass of trees before any land could be planted. Quite often a shop was located at a road intersection with other shops located nearby, and we have the beginning of a village.

The Blacksmith Shop, painting by the Reverend Bowen Squire.

The James Coleman Blacksmith shop on the corner of Lot 82 with Will Coleman standing in the doorway.

One such village was Rossmore or Ferry Point and the earliest name I could find here was John Cassidy who ran a shop on the south side of Ridley St. and another one by George Chatterson on the north side of the same street, just west of Loral Wanamaker. These would be considered good stands as many horses would be passing here to go on the ferry, or later the bridge, to Belleville. C. Hazlett had a shop on one of the above locations and at perhaps about this time (1895) Mr. Cassidy moved to a shop on Lot 66, 1st Con., now the Purdy Place.

The earliest shop I can find in Rednersville was Dave Rose's carriage shop and blacksmith shop, which often go together. He was located about where Mr. Devries now lives and it was also told Dave Rose or his father had a shop on or beside where Allan Dempsey now resides. From here we find a George Russell had a shop about 1880-90 where Summer Dawson now lives. Also on the road south through Rednersville, George Brickman and Bill Urquart were blacksmiths on a lot about where John Hall resided. George Brickman moved to Belleville and Mr. Urquart opened a shop along side Hugh Weese's milk stand and he had the misfortune to drown in the bay about 1905. Going on, we find Billy Hutchinson had a shop where Jack Jones lives on Lot 88. Then on up the road a bit farther on Lot 95, just west of the school house at what is now known as Onderdonk's Hill, John Onderdonk came in from the U.S.A. and opened up a shop— he would have been the grandfather of Earl Onderdonk. There was also a blacksmith shop on Lot 106 at the 2nd Con., and now Highway #33 operated by George Hayes. On the Gore of Ameliasburgh there was once a shop on Lot 84 near Melvin Pulver's farm run by a Stephen Nix.

In the Village of Ameliasburg (Roblin's Mills) one of the earlier blacksmiths was James Coleman on the corner of Lot 82 where he worked from 1844 for many years. There was also a blacksmith shop in connection with the Sprague Carriage Factory, later the shop of Hatch and Allen, with L.R. Criss as paint stripe man. When the carriage factory burned in 1894, Albert Crosby bought the property and operated a blacksmith shop there until 1901. Then Crosby took over the Coleman shop where he and his sons, Grant and Harry, handled the work of the surrounding country for many years. He in turn sold out to Dick Soble who, after a number of years, had to sell out to the township for road widening. Soble then opened a shop behind his barn back of the old Marsden House Hotel.

When the Crosbys sold out to Soble, they returned to the Sprague factory site. Harry started the first garage in Ameliasburgh at that location, with a hand-operated gas pump.

We find carriage and wagon factories in the early days were usually run on a small scale by one or two persons and nearly always a blacksmith would be a part of such an operation. This was the day when a farmer was well-to-do if he owned a buggy, a democrat and a heavy farm wagon. We are told of a blacksmith shop run by J.R. Wood on the 3rd Con. Lot 74 in the 1870's on the north side of the road, later the Hartford Parliament farm, now owned by R. Lough.

A little farther east and north at the east end of the 2nd Con. at the intersection with Highway #14, we have an early blacksmith shop. The land was granted to Capt. Richard Porter in 1796 and shortly thereafter or about 1800 Edmund Murney and Joseph Locklin purchased 100 rods on which to build a carriage factory and a blacksmith business and later a Post Office and a small store there. Sam Allen and William Hatch also ran the carriage business until about 1890 when Thos. B. Tillotson appears to have had it for a short period; then Royal Jones from Bannockburn purchased it and was in business here for a good many years until 1921 when he sold it to George Johnson, a woodworker, with James Cretney a blacksmith. (Mr. Johnson was the brother of Mrs. Cretney.) Finally with work dwindling as the power machinery took over Jim sold out in 1958 when the highway bought it for widening purposes and demolished the two houses and carriage shop. In a good many of these blacksmith shops there was a hired helper, as Thomas Rowland worked for Royal Jones, and many worked and learned the trade.

At the foot of the Union hill there was a shop for many years. The last smith remembered was David Duetta— this was on Lot 68 Con 3, just below Alfred Post's house across the road from an old Cooper shop. I went over many of these shops with Ralph Stafford who was much older than I and he could remember when there was a shop run by one or two farmers for their own use, and when time was available they did custom work for others.

I note in the old Ameliasburgh directory that there were two blacksmiths in Consecon and at the same time only one in Ameliasburg.

From the 1865 and 1880 directories of Ameliasburgh I was able to find the following names as blacksmiths.

James Coleman	Pt. Lot 82 Ameliasburgh	3rd Con.
John T. Coleman	Pt. Lot 82 Ameliasburgh	3rd Con.
George Chaterson	Pt. Lot 60 Rossmore	1st Con.
James Clark	Pt. Lot 60 Rossmore	1st Con.
A.R. Hennessey	Pt. Lot 60 Rossmore	1st Con.
Andrew Graham	Pt. Lot 104 Consecon	4th Con.
Hiram Grannis	Pt. Lot 81 Ameliasburgh	3rd Con.
Stephen Nix	Pt. Lot 84 Rednersville	1st Con.
W.L. Peters	Pt. Lot 76 Rednersville	1st Con.
William Rose	Pt. Lot 76 Rednersville	1st Con.
Thomas Rowland	Ameliasburgh	
C. Hazlett	Pt. Lot 60 Ameliasburgh	1st Con.
Daniel Brisby	Ameliasburgh	a carriage blacksmith
Irving Coleman	Pt. Lot 82 Ameliasburgh	3rd Con.
G.T.B. Russell	Pt. Lot 76 Rednersville	1st Con.
John E. Carter	Pt. Lot 73 Ameliasburgh	4th Con.

Blacksmith shop, just east of old File store in village of Ameliasburg. The building has been gone many years. The blacksmith in the door is Ab Crosby.

Left: E. Wallbridge, thrasher and farmer, left, and J.F. Cretney, Blacksmith.
Right: Woodworking and blacksmith shop in 1922 when the road was being
built, owned at that time by Cretney & Johnson.

Hereford cattle near Blacksmith shop on way from Massassaga pasture to
Huff's Island in Fall 1945. Cretney blacksmith in background.

The Blacksmith Shop— Mountain View

By Mrs. Jas. F. Cretney

The land on which the blacksmith shop, woodworking shop and house stood is a part of the 200 acres given by the Crown to Captain Richard Porter around June 22, 1796 (Lot 68). In 1871, one hundred rods were taken off and that is the piece the present owner is occupying. The first owners were Edmund Murney and wife, and Joseph Locklin. Others were Samuel B. Way,

Mountain View Oct. 1st 1880.

Joseph Nightingale in Acct with Hatch & Allen

1879.				£	s	d	c
Nov	24	To 1 new Shoe 25. 3 Removes 30			5	5	
Dec	1	" Steel in Pick & Sharpening ends			4	0	
1880 Jan	30	" 5 new Shoes 1.25 3 Removes 30		1	5	5	
	6	" 12 Removes 1.20 6 links in Chain 30		1	5	0	
	"	" 2 Hooks in Chain 20 2 Rings in Yoke 20			4	0	
Mar	4	" Setting 1 Tire 50 1/2 Rim 75		1	2	5	
	13	" Sharpening Drag Teeth			6	0	
	"	" 1 new Tooth 25 6 Bolts 25			5	0	
	"	" Repairs Whiffle tree Hook 25			2	5	
	"	" Reversing Hooks 40 2 pieces in Frame 100		1	4	0	
	15	" 6 links in Chain & 1 Hook			4	5	
	"	" new end on Wagon Wrench			3	5	
	"	" Setting Lumber Tire			5	0	
	"	" 8 Spokes 1.60 3/4 Rim on Wheel 1.00		2	6	0	
	18	" Setting Lumber Tire 50 1 Spoke 20			7	0	
April	2	" 1 Reach 1.00 2 new Shoes 50		1	5	0	
	"	" Ring 10 1 Hook & 2 Bolts 20			3	0	
	24	" Fixing ferrule & Hook			2	5	
	"	" Fixing Tow Drag Draw-bar			3	0	
	30	" 1 new Shoe 25 1 Bolt 5 (May 1) 1 Bolt 25			5	5	
May	10	" Making Spear 75 (14) 2 new Shoes 50		1	2	5	
	14	" 4 Removes 40 Welding Cant hook 20			6	0	
	20	" 4, 14 inch Bolts 3/4 Iron		1	0	0	
June	2	" Drilling & Countersinking Holes			5	0	
	22	" Setting 2 Lumber Tire		1	0	0	
	"	" Whiffle tree Clevis 20 2 Bolts 10			3	0	
July	17	" Repairs on Reaper		1	0	0	

Joseph Nightingale's account sheet with Hatch & Allen shows the importance of blacksmiths in the 1880's.

in 1854; then Samuel Allan and William Hatch, carriage makers, and so on until 1890, when Thos. B. Tillotson was the owner. In 1890 Royal Jones from Bannockburn in Hastings Co. bought the property and carried on the business till 1921. He sold it to Geo. Allan Johnson, a woodworker, and Jas F. Cretney, blacksmith. Both were returned men from the Great War (1914-18) and were partners till 1921 when Mr. Cretney bought the business from his partner.

Mr. Cretney enlisted in the Canadian Mounted Rifles but was soon posted as 'Farrier' to the Medical Unit which had 125 horses. Officers of that Unit tried hard to get the display case of horseshoes he made in 1908 but his horsey friends took them over and kept them until after the war. The Case, pride of the blacksmith's heart, contains one forging of six beautifully made horseshoes joined together from one piece of steel. They shone like silver and the finish is as smooth as though they had been planed rather than laboriously hammered out by hand.

> The Blacksmith today is aged and tired
> Shoes no more horses, sets no more tires
> But a perfect example of a village smith
> A craftsman who is proud of his handiwork.

Blacksmith Shops of Carrying Place
By W.D. Hanthorn

The story has been told that on a Sunday morning in 1907, Miss Amelia Hayes, about to renew fresh flowers for the altar of St. John's church in Carrying Place, went to the vestry door and realized her father's blacksmith shop was on fire. She raised the alarm but it was too late to prevent the huge fire that consumed almost all of the buildings on the Murray side of the Village.

Destroyed in the fire was a hotel, a bakeshop, the Methodist Church, as well as several residences including that of Henry Hayes, the owner and operator of the aforementioned blacksmith shop. Spared by the fire was the Murray Post Office and a store operated by John and Ida Boyce. This building burned a short time after.

Since the fire did not cross the road, it left untouched the blacksmith shop of Wm. J. McLaughlin. However, in an almost unprecedented scandal of those days— Wm. J. McLaughlin ran off with the village belle leaving his tools to rust away and his shop to decay. This left Carrying Place with no smithy.

In 1921 due to the persuasion of C.M. Westfall. J.M. Hanthorn was induced to set up a blacksmith shop behind the residence he had bought from Harry Latour, just east of the Anglican rectory in Ameliasburgh Township. He and his 17-year-old son William D. blacksmithed in this shop until moving to the Murray side of Carrying Place in 1925. W.D. (Bill) Hanthorn continued his father's practice in conjunction with his motor repair trade in Murray Township until 1947.

At this time he purchased a partially built garage from George Cruickshank. This was in Ameliasburgh Township alongside Highway #33. Moving his shop and forge, he attached it to the south side of this building where he resumed doing all types of blacksmithing with the exception of horseshoeing. Due to the increasing use of tractors, this service was seldom required.

With the changing times so also did the means and methods of blacksmithing. Acetylene torches and electric welding made repairs faster and easier. Hard-surfacing and welding new points (pieces of car spring) to worn plough shares saved the farmers a lot of money. With the aid of Otaco Conversion kits, old cars with shortened frames and drive shafts were transformed into autotracs, a useful and cheaper method for a farmer needing a tractor to replace horses. Wooden wagon wheels were cut down and steel rims mounted with rubber tires which rode smoother and made wagons much lower and easier to load.

During World War II, Weller's Bay, near Bald Head in Ameliasburgh Township, was used as a practice bombing range. About 1948-50, salvage boats began dragging the area to recover the spent bombs for their valuable lead content. Mr. Hanthorn was kept busy from shortly after dark until about 2 a.m. most nights repairing the bent and broken teeth of the dragging rakes damaged by the rocks. This was a new and short-term source of income for this blacksmith. His forge was removed in 1967 when alterations were made to the garage building.

Like 'The Last of the Mohicans,' he was perhaps the last of the old time blacksmiths in Ameliasburgh Township. It seems there is no record of established shops in the Carrying Place Village previous to that of Henry Hayes. It has been stated that army personnel and travelling journeymen performed the necessary services, such as repairing wagons and shoeing horses and oxen.

A carved wooden likeness of J.M. Hanthorn at his anvil in Ameliasburgh Township, 1923, is on loan to the Ameliasburgh Museum, where it is on display.

Blacksmithing in Consecon

By Lily F. Walt

The only blacksmith shop on the Ameliasburgh side of Consecon Village was owned and operated by Daniel Garrettsee who lived in the house now occupied by his grandson, Donald Garrettsee, Consecon's well-known bee keeper.

The smithy was a frame building of wide, vertical pine boards across the street where Ross Chase has his garage now. Patrons waiting their turn to have a horse shod could put their animals in the adjacent shed of the Anglican Church. Mr. Garrettsee served the local farm population of both townships (Hillier and Ameliasburgh) for about forty years. He lived to a hale and hearty old age until about 1900; he suffered a heart attack while working in his apple orchard at the rear of his home.

In 1901 the smithy was purchased by George Bush who, with the help of Alva Miller, continued the business for a few years until he changed the building to be used as a grist mill. (Alva Miller at one time ran a blacksmith shop of his own in the hamlet of Melville.) The grist mill run by a gasoline engine was later sold to Geo. Lazier.

Other blacksmiths continued to ply their trade and to serve both townships, but they were located on the south side of the creek which is in the township of Hillier. The 'Kenny' shop was a small frame building just south of the Presbyterian Church. That church also provided accommodation in its shed, but in winter did not attract customers as it was open to the raw easterly wind. The 'Kenny' shop continued to be so called, but it was run by Kenny followed by Maybee then Johnson.

Consecon Creek provided water as a source of power for the local mill but water, too, was necessary for the cooling of the blacksmith's heated iron. So it is not suprising that from time to time a smithy was located at a spot on the south bank. The 'Brick' shop on property owned by miller Adam Burr did a thriving business with two forges and employed two men, one of whom was the aforementioned Alva Miller.

The Johnson brothers, Bert and George, lived in homes still standing not far from the creek. They operated the blacksmith shop which stood on the site of the old mill wheel today. (John Morrison had a small general store directly opposite the smithy, so with the mill, the smithy, a store, hotel, livery stable, Presbyterian church and manse, that location must have been an active area at the beginning of the century.) After George Johnson retired, his brother continued to operate the forge until it was sold to a man from Trenton who employed a man by the name of Baxter.

The new operator did not find it a paying business, so after a short time it was sold to George Peters who worked for many years at the shop. He was a skilled blacksmith but times were changing.

By that time the motor car was replacing the horse and buggy; tractors did not require iron rims to be replaced on wooden wheels. After Mr. Peters, the last of the blacksmiths, retired, the dilapidated smithy stood by the creek until 1967 when we were celebrating the birth of our Dominion. It was torn down when the council wisely decided to beautify the banks of the creek.

In the days before mechanics and welders became specialized, the old blacksmith was a master of his trade. He not only fashioned iron shoes and expertly shod the dainty hooves of driving mares and heavy plough horses; he fashioned wrought iron square-headed building nails, repaired broken pieces of machinery and even invented contrivances which were never patented. He could make a ring from a horse shoe nail, or a shiny chain for a necklace. We cannot claim the inventor as being a local blacksmith but it is said that the first set of false teeth was produced by a blacksmith and he used the flat heads of some horseshoe nails!

Compiled by Lily F. Walt from information obtained mostly from Douglas Bush.

Blacksmithing 1984

Fred O'Brien, whose home is in Ameliasburgh Village, has been a blacksmith for some 15 years. He shoes the horses of Standardbred owners. In the winter he works at the Windsor racetrack, and when he comes home, he shoes Standardbreds for Quinte area horsemen who are racing this winter. On an average day he may shoe 11 horses, sometimes he does as many as 16. This is a trade Mr. O'Brien learned from his grandfather in Nova Scotia and one which he enjoys. He also works with a number of saddle horses in the area.

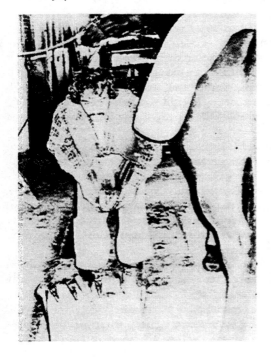

Fred O'Brien shoeing a horse.

CHAPTER 17

FERRIES & BRIDGES

We cross the Bay of Quinte from Rossmore to Belleville so quickly and easily today that we can hardly visualize what it was like for our ancestors. For the early settlers scattered along the shoreline in Seventh Town, the Bay was their highway and their lifeline. Across the Bay at the mouth of the Sagonaska (Moira River), William Bell had a trading post as early as 1787 where they could obtain tools, seeds and tobacco. Bell procured his merchandise from a Kingston merchant, who in turn was supplied by Montreal merchants. In 1790, Captain John Meyers built a saw mill on the river, and later a flour mill to which the pioneers took their grain for grinding. Shortly after 1800 the McNabbs also built mills and a small cloth factory on the west bank of the Sagonaska. Meyers' Creek (renamed Belleville in 1816) quickly became a village with mills, blacksmith shop, tavern and stores where furs, potash and wheat could be traded for such staples as sugar, salt and tea. So the settlers of Seventh Town from earliest times had good reasons for crossing the Bay.

The shortest distance across the Bay from Seventh Town to Meyers' Creek was from the Point, where we still cross today in Rossmore. Early residents at the Point— the Henneseys, Moons and Benjamin Gerow— found a good business in ferrying passengers and goods across the Bay by canoe or rowboat. The Point became known as Ferry Point; it was also called Hennesey's Point or Moon's Point. As the population increased on both sides of the Bay, so did the passage of people, goods and livestock. Larger flat-bottomed boats or scows, propelled by sweeps, were required to transport horses, cows and hogs to or from the Belleville market. The next step was to even larger boats powered by a horse treadmill.

In 1797 an Act was passed which authorized the Justices in Quarter Session to set the rates for persons operating ferries, such fees to be posted at the ferry docks. The Midland District Quarter Court in January 1803 allowed a ferry licence to Benjamin Gerow of Ameliasburgh at these rates:

	Shillings	Pence
Every man	1	
2 or more		9 each
Man and horse	2	
Span of horses and carriage	2	6
Yoke of oxen	2	6
Cow	1	
Every sheep		3
Every hog		4

The fact that Gerow was the licensed ferry operator did not stop other boat owners from trying to get a share of the ferry business, with the result that there were many altercations. Gerow was involved in several court cases. One of these, heard by the Quarter Session Court at Kingston on Jan. 8, 1807, was the case of James Hennesey vs. Benjamin Gerow. Jury foreman was Thomas Dempsey, and among the jury members were Henry Redner, John Babcock, John Bonter and John Huff. The decision was 'Guilty' and Gerow was fined two shillings and six pence.

In 1811 the Quarter Session Court granted Benjamin Gerow the licence to ferry from Ameliasburgh to Thurlow, but allowed Philip Zwick the licence to ferry from Thurlow to Ameliasburgh. Again the rates were set, with every cwt. of luggage to cost 2d. The Gerow and Zwick ferries docked on the west side of the point on the property where Mr. and Mrs. Loral Wanamaker now reside. Traces of the timbers filled with rock can still be seen in low water. On the Thurlow side they landed at what is today the Water Filtration Plant where the remains of an old dock were discovered in 1974.

By 1814, David Hennesey was the licensed ferry operator. He had a certificate from Richard Cartwright, Colonel commanding the Militia of the Midland District, exempting him from military service as the ferry was necessary for His Majesty's Service, the War of 1812 still continuing at that time. The ferry continued to be operated by Hennesey and then by his widow until 1825 when her seven year licence expired. She petitioned for another seven year term; John Moon of the point also petitioned that he be granted a licence to operate the ferry. Neither of them got it because of a petition of inhabitants of the Town of Belleville and the Township of Ameliasburgh complaining of the poor ferry service offered by Mrs. Hennesey and requesting that Henry W. Yager be granted the licence as he had purchased a Horse Boat of sufficient power to cross at any time during the season. Their petition was heeded and Yager was granted the lease for the next seven years.

In June 1832 there were four petitioners seeking the ferry licence: James Hennesey offering £5 5s. per annum, Henry Moon offering £80 for seven years, John Moon offering £8 per year and Alexander Oliphant Petrie with an offer of £15 12s. 9 pence annual rent. Perhaps because his bid was highest, Petrie was given the seven year licence to operate the ferry. In October of that year Petrie applied to the Quarter Session Court at Kingston to have certain fees established at the ferry between Hennesey's Point and Belleville. The court approved the following rates:

- single man and horse 2/6
- span of horses, carriage and drive 5/
- foot passenger 1/
- potash, per barrel . . . . /10
- barley, per bushel . . . . /1

Petrie had only been operating the ferry for a year when he had a charge of armed robbery laid against him by Jeremiah W. Parker. He was tried in August 1833 at the Assizes for the Midland District at Kingston. According to an account in the Kingston Chronicle and Gazette at that time, Jeremiah W. Parker, an American with an exhibition of wild beasts and stage dancers had applied to Petrie for service to Belleville, coming from Hallowell (Picton). The rate was 15 s. Petrie waited around for them for 2 or 3 days. When Parker finally did come he selected a boat operated by Hennesey, rather than Petrie's, since "the wind was high" and Hennesey's boat larger. A few days afterward, while crossing the bridge in Belleville, the two met. Petrie pointed a loaded pistol at Parker and demanded three dollars, told Parker he must pay him whether he crossed on his boat or not because he held the lease. Petrie was given the money, a receipt was requested, and the two went into a tavern to make it out. Several persons witnessed the incident. The jury retired for a few hours and brought in a decision of "Guilty." Petrie was sentenced to death by Justice James B. Macauley, Judge of the Assizes.

Petrie's cause was taken up by Belleville citizens and the Kingston press and he was eventually pardoned. He returned to his ferry service, but in March 1834 petitioned for a few months in which to make up arrears because of low business and his own imprisonment. He mentioned rival operators who were cutting into his business, "they having been accustomed to do this from earlier days."

In 1835 Henry Yager petitioned for the licence again, submitting many names, and criticizing the service supplied by Petrie. Yager had fitted out a boat of two horse power at a cost of £200 "to stand the storms that would naturally arise in crossing the Bay." Yager was refused since the ferry was licensed to Petrie for seven years. In 1837 Augustus Bennett of Belleville petitioned for the ferry licence, also complaining of the inefficient manner in which the ferry was managed. He too was refused.

In the 1850's the ferry was operated by a Moon of Rossmore. The ferries continued to be horse-powered until 1858 when the first steam ferry began operation. In 1858 the Town of Belleville was granted a licence for 25 years to operate a ferry between the town and Ameliasburgh. They sub-let the lease to John Redner for a 10-year term. Redner had a steam ferry, the H.P. Redner, which ran, weather permitting, seven trips a day between Belleville and Ameliasburgh except on Sunday when only two trips were made. Foot passengers were charged 4 pence, horse, buggy and driver 1 shilling, all cattle 1s each, pigs, sheep and calves 4d. each, barrels with contents 3d. each. Passengers wishing to cross after hours were taken over in a skiff for one shilling each.

In 1868 the contract was given to A.L. Bogart who had just purchased a new, larger steam ferry which he named the 'Prince Edward.' A new dock was built to accommodate it just east of the point in Rossmore. The April 24, 1868 issue of The Intelligencer contains an account of the Prince Edward: "This steam ferry, which was built purposely to run between Belleville and Prince Edward County, left St. Catharines on Sabbath afternoon at 3 o'clock and arrived at this port at 9 o'clock Monday evening. She has been visited today by large numbers of our citizens naturally having a curiosity to see a boat in which they have such a large interest. We venture to say that there were few who were not agreeably surprised, the size and appearance of the vessel being so much larger and grander than they had any idea of. The Prince Edward is what is called a 'double-ender' having wheels at each end. She is 90' in length, breadth overall 36', and has a carriageway on each side of the engine 8'8" in width. The awning deck, which extends from stem to stern, is 13' 4" high, giving ample room for the largest loads of hay. On each side, on a line with the outside wheels, are cabins, and above them will be placed rows of seats for the passengers. It is so arranged that a floor can be laid from side to side, connecting with the platform above the engine, giving a fine promenade deck on occasions of excursion parties, picnics, etc. There is room for 20 teams and 100 passengers, and, without teams, from 2 to 300 passengers could be comfortably accommodated. She is driven by a low pressure condensed engine of 76 horse-power and will easily make 12 miles an hour. She draws, without a load, 3½ feet. The Prince Edward was built by Simpson of St. Catharines, and is a staunch, well-built craft possessing all the latest improvements. Let us hope that she may be not only a source of profit to her owner, A.L. Bogart Esq., but a means of greatly increasing the trade between the Town and the County of Prince Edward."

In June 1868 the St. George's Society of Belleville advertised a Pic Nic at Massassaga Point "having engaged the new and commodious Prince Edward." The steamer was to make three trips to the Point, leaving at 9, 10½ and 12½, returning at 6 p.m. Such excursions occurred frequently, causing great dissatisfaction among those who waited in vain at the ferry docks. There were many complaints about the service and the rates charged.

So great was the dissatisfaction that the Township of Ameliasburgh in 1879 issued a licence to James Anderson to operate a steam ferry between the Township and Sidney. Anderson and Captain J. Porte built a ferry which they named the Mary Ethel. The Mary Ethel had room for seven teams or rigs on each side, and was noted for its ice-breaking capacity. Anderson crossed from his own dock on lot 70 to Jones' Creek on the Sidney shore. This resulted in a court case with Anderson being sued by John Jellett who had leased the Prince Edward from Bogart. The court decision ruled that Anderson's ferry interfered with the original ferry and should not operate.

The Mary Ethel and her captain, James Anderson.

In 1882 Belleville applied for a renewal of its ferry licence, but the government granted the new licence to the Township of Ameliasburgh. So the Mary Ethel went back into service, but this time crossing from Rossmore to Belleville, where she continued to operate until the bridge was built.

The ferry service continued to be a very undependable and unsatisfactory method of crossing the bay. Strong winds and ice played havoc with time-tables. There were times in the spring and fall when the ferry could not run at all, when passage across the bay was impossible, except on foot or iceboat. Isaiah Coleman who drove the mail from Roblin's Mills to Belleville in the 1870's occasionally had to walk across, dragging the mail bag behind him, when the ice was too thick for the ferry to run but too thin to support the horses. Many harrowing trips were made across when there would be 5 or 6 inches of water over the ice. However, even after the bridge was built, the ice was much driven in winter, not only to save the toll but because the plank floor of the bridge was not good for sleighing. Bert Redner started across the ice one January day with a load of hogs bound for the stockyards in Belleville. The farther he went the deeper the water over the ice became until finally the pigs started floating about. Abandoning them, he and his companion headed back towards the Ameliasburgh shore on the horses' backs, Redner taking the more mettlesome one, which promptly threw him off. However, horses and men reached shore safely where several who had observed their difficulties had gathered. The pigs were rescued with a punt, but it took a month to get them back to market weight again.

THE FIRST BRIDGE

A bridge had been talked about for many years. About 1873 an engineer was employed to make a series of soundings between Bushy Island and Rossmore. Founded thereon was his estimate of $125,000 for a wooden bridge. As this sum was thought impossible to raise, the subject was dropped for a few years. Finally in 1887 a group of Belleville businessmen formed the Bay of Quinte Bridge Co. and petitioned the Dominion Goverment to grant permission for the construction of a bridge between the Counties of Hastings and Prince Edward, at or near Belleville. The two principals of the Bridge Company were wealthy entrepreneurs of that time: Senator Harry Corby, owner of Corby Distilleries, and Thomas Ritchie, an affluent Belleville merchant. On June 23, 1887, an Act was passed incorporating the Bay of Quinte Bridge Co. with power to construct and maintain a toll bridge, with a swing section of not less than 100 feet for passage of vessels. The bridge was to be commenced within three years and completed within six years. The company began to raise capital by selling shares. Private individuals subscribed over $26,000. The City of Belleville purchased $30,000 worth of stock, and the Township of Ameliasburgh $15,000.

The first Bay of Quinte Bridge.

The swing section open with the Alexandria passing through.

The toll-house at the Rossmore end of the first bridge and J.I. Coleman drawing the mail from Belleville.

Actual construction of the bridge began during the summer of 1889 with dredging of the marsh between Bushy Island and the Belleville shore. The crib foundation for the north abutment of the bridge was sunk on September 14, 1889, and the masonry work on it commenced a month later. Pile driving for the pier foundations began in February 1890. Building the great steel super-structure was contracted to Brown Manufacturing of Belleville. The erection of the superstructure, which consisted of 17 spans of steel, began on Nov. 10, 1890, and was completed on April 15, 1891. The bridge was ready for traffic as soon as driving the ice became unsafe. The continuous truss span was not only the wonder of the Quinte area, it was the longest highway bridge in Canada at the time. From the Rossmore side the first span was 63 feet; the swing span next was 238 feet, then two spans of 148 feet each; the balance of 13 spans were 98 feet each, making a total steel bridge over water of 1871 feet. There was a short causeway to Bushy Island of 800 feet, and then through the marsh a distance of 2600 feet, making about a mile of bridge and causeway. Officers of the Bridge Co. in 1891 were: Thomas Ritchie, Pres.; H. Corby, Vice-Pres.; U.E. Thompson, Sec.-Treasurer; Directors— Harmon Weese, A. Sutherland, E. Guss Porter.

This first bridge was built for horse and buggy and was quite narrow. It had a plank deck which had to be replaced often because the horses' shoes slivered it up. The swing was turned by hand from the deck of the span, requiring two men to open it. In winter the ice around the piers had to be cut continually or it would shift them, which it did on occasions.

The maximum toll rates were set in the Act of Incorporation: for every person on foot five cents, children under six years of age accompanied by parent or guardian, free: for every horse and single carriage, wagon, cart or other vehicle and driver, ten cents; for each additional horse five cents; for every horse and rider, ten cents; for horses and cattle singly, ten cents each; in droves of three or more, five cents each; for calves, sheep or swine singly, five cents each; in droves three cents each; for every handcart or wheelbarrow and attendant, five cents.

The bridge was let by tender to the highest bidder. He had to collect the toll, swing the bridge for boats, keep the bridge planked and the ice cut around the piers. During very cold weather this was a big order. In 1895 the Bridge Co. accepted the tender of Richard C. Arnott for the bridge tolls. His tender was $4,510 over the amount received by the company for the previous year. The toll house was on the Rossmore side.

In 1917, extensive repairs had to be made to the bridge with four of the piers and plank decks replaced. By the 1920's the bridge that had been built for horse-drawn vehicles was proving inadequate for the increasing number of cars and trucks travelling across it.

As the years passed there was agitation for the tolls to be lifted. Belleville Fair directors even felt the tolls were cutting attendance at their annual exhibition. The government was pressured to purchase the bridge and make it toll-free. Finally in Oct. 1920 an agreement was reached by which the Ontario Government, the County of Prince Edward and the City of Belleville would purchase the bridge for $85,000 and make it a free public highway. The Province paid $35,000, the County $20,000 and Belleville $30,000.

On July 1, 1921, the Bay Bridge was declared free, and was taken over by the Ontario Government. A large crowd was present, and music was provided by the Rednersville Band under bandmaster Ralph Stafford. The speakers were Belleville Mayor E. Hanna, the Hon. Nelson Parliament and George Hogarth, Provincial Engineer. The last motor vehicle upon which toll was paid was driven by T.G. Thompson, a baker from Rossmore. The last nickel paid by a pedestrian was collected from A.E. Phillips of Ameliasburgh.

THE SECOND BRIDGE

By the mid 1920's, because of the deterioration of the piers and the need for a wider roadway on the bridge, the Ontario government decided to rebuild it, replacing most of the continuous truss span with solid causeway. It was completely rebuilt between 1927 and 1931.

The *Daily Intelligencer* of February 4, 1927 reports: "The Bay Bridge will open for traffic early in the spring, the ground work of the alteration being completed by then," Mr. Russell of the Russell Construction Co. says. At the present moment the company is engaged in filling in between the piers, and traffic across the bridge is impossible. In consequence the traffic is being directed across the ice. "Just like the days gone by when people welcomed the coming of winter that they might cross the ice and avoid the toll charged for using the bridge," an old-timer observed as he watched a horse-drawn vehicle followed by two motor cars make an easy passage on the wind-swept ice.

From the *Daily Intelligencer* of March 7, 1927: "The filling in by putting gravel on the stone will be completed tomorrow night and the bridge, closed since the 26th of January, in use once more. This announcement will be hailed with great relief by both Bellevillians and Prince Edward County people who have looked with alarm on the fast disappearing ice by which they have crossed since the closing of the bridge."

The bay ice was driven for two winters, the route being marked by ever-greens. Traffic went on the ice on the west side of the bridge in Rossmore and off at Zwick's Island. In the summer, temporary wooden ramps were used to allow one lane of traffic while the work on the causeway proceeded. All the centre spans were replaced by the causeway. The piers themselves were left and the causeway built around and over them. This later led to humps and dips on the bridge road as the rest of the causeway sank somewhat but the old piers did not.

At the north end, a channel was left with a fixed steel bridge on two spans. The Frontenac Dredging Co. of Kingston had the contract to rebuilt the piers and place two new spans here. A tragic accident happened while they were working at the piers in December of 1929. Their scow had been loaded in Point Anne four weeks previously and brought up to the bridge site. It was built in four sections and was filled with sand and stone to make ingredients for the cement which was to be poured into the piers. The sand was heated before using by placing a steam pipe in the section containing it. On Dec. 16, Winston Brant, 18, and another workman by the name of Weller were in one section loosening the frozen sand from around the edges and throwing it into the centre where it could be treated by the steam. In some unaccountable manner, one of the dogs which held the bottom together released and allowed the bottom to swing open, carrying Brant and Weller down into the bay along with the 25 tons of sand in that pocket. Weller could swim but Brant could

The second bridge and causeway.

not and he drowned. Weller managed to paddle water and come up within the scow where he grabbed one of the large chains. Another man reached down with a shovel which Weller grasped and was pulled to safety. Brant's parents watched for days hoping his body would be found, but it never was.

Frontenac Dredging Co. also had the contract for replacing the three fixed spans and the swing span over the navigation channel on the Prince Edward side. The new spans were wider than the previous ones and had a sidewalk along the east side. Two houses on the west side of the bridge approach were moved because of the wider bridge requirements. The old piers were enlarged and reinforced by cribbing them up with timbers and then filling in all the space with large flat stones, which were obtained from farmers in Ameliasburgh. Clifford Hillman recalls drawing loads of flat stones with horses and wagon to Rossmore where they were stockpiled over winter, each man having his own pile. They were paid by the yard; his wagon held two yards. In the spring they had to reload the rocks, drive out on the bridge and throw them in around the piers.

The bay bridge was closed for four days in June 1930 while the old swing span was removed and replaced with a new one. The *Ontario Intelligencer* for Thursday June 26 states: "At 9 a.m. this morning the bay bridge was re-opened for traffic after having been closed since Sunday morning with the replacement of the old span by the modern span. It was expected the work would be completed last night, but the workmen were so harassed by the armies of mosquitoes that they were compelled to cease operations until this morning."

Mrs. Angus Poirier (nee Verna Belnap of Rossmore) remembers well the building of the second bridge, as she walked across the bridge to work every day. When the swing span was being replaced she had to go down a ladder, cross over the water on a two-plank walkway, then go up a ladder on the other side.

For two weeks in December 1930, the swing span was put in the open east-west position so the steel workers and bridge gang could work on it. Traffic, meanwhile, was able to proceed through it over temporary spans stretching from pier to pier. The deck or floor of the swing was constructed of creosoted planks on steel, this floor alone weighing 30 tons. Upon this another deck of elastite, one and a half inches thick, was laid. The bridge was only closed to traffic from midnight Saturday Dec. 20 until midnight Sunday night while the central portion, over which traffic had been moving, was completed. Then the swing was moved back into its closed position to link up with the bridge driveway.

An old pier on the north side was later taken out, making the channel 80 feet wide on that side. The swing was no longer operated manually from the deck, but by electrical controls from a house at the top and centre of the swing span. The bridge was completed in February 1931.

The old toll house was moved to the west side of the bridge and continued to serve as a bridge house for the bridgemasters. Nelson Vanclief, who worked on the bridge from 1936 to 1945, started at 25¢ an hour which was raised to 35¢ after a few years. He worked a 12-hour shift from noon until midnight, with his co-worker, Roy Valleau, taking the other 12 hours. The bridge was opened on demand, for boat traffic was given first consideration. During his term of service the little park on the west side of the bridge approach was begun, trees and perennials planted, grass cut and a flag-pole erected.

Other long-term bridgemasters were Bill Burkitt, 15 years; Frank Keene, 15 years; Art Weir, 20 years; and Art Adams, 12 years. The navigation season opened April 1 and continued as late in the fall as the weather allowed. Mr. Keene recalls working until December 23rd one year, but it usually closed in November. By the time he started in 1959, there were three shifts of eight hours each. Duties included swinging the bridge, maintenance and greasing of the swing mechanism, looking after the grounds and putting the flag up and down. On a holiday or weekend as many as 100 boats might pass through the bridge. Mr. Burkitt, who was on the bridge from 1948 to 1962, recalls losing a lot of caps in the bay as he climbed the ladder from the road level to the control house.

He also remembers letting an airplane through once. When landing at Point Anne, rocks had torn holes in its pontoons. A canoe had been fitted on the damaged pontoon so it could still skim along the water but could not take off. The owner asked how wide the bridge was and Burkitt told him 80 feet. That was wide enough to let it through. On another occasion the power went off when the bridge was in open position and stayed off for an hour, while the traffic piled up in both directions. A 25 horsepower electrical motor moved 150 tons; manually it would have required several men.

Twenty-four hour coverage continued as long as coal boats came to Trenton Airport; they were the last commercial boats. After the Airport converted to oil, the bridge was manned only from 6:30 to 10:30 with two eight-hour shifts. The last few years the navigation season started later also, beginning the middle of May and ending Sept. 15. Since about 1975, the swing was opened on a timetable, rather than on demand with openings at 7, 9, 10, 11, 11:45, 12:30, 1:15, and then on the hour except at 5 until 10 p.m.; also 10:20 if there was a boat. A new bridge-house was built in 1964 on the east side of the bridge approach.

THE NORRIS WHITNEY BRIDGE

As the decades of the 1900's rolled around, there was a tremendous increase in motor traffic over the bridge and boat traffic through the swing section. During the summer boating season there were many traffic tie-ups. Occasionally break-downs in the swing mechanism caused long delays, or repairs to the bridge restricted traffic to one lane. For years there was talk of the need for a new high-level bridge. There were petitions to the Ontario Government, feasibility studies, reports and meetings. Norris Whitney, M.L.A for Prince Edward-Lennox, his successor James Taylor, and Dr. Richard Potter, member for Quinte riding, were among the active supporters of a new

Norris Whitney Bridge from Zwicks Island, showing causeway and fixed steel bridge over channel. Courtesy: The Intelligencer

Twin concrete towers under construction. Courtesy: The Intelligencer.

Aerial view of Norris Whitney Bridge and the old bridge. Courtesy: Lyle Webb.

View of Norris Whitney Bridge from Rossmore, east side.

Work crews demolish old bridge and part of the causeway. Courtesy: The Intelligencer.

bridge. Finally in August of 1974 the Honourable John Rhodes, Minister of Transportation and Communication, during a visit to the site announced that a bridge would be built. Controversy then arose over the location. Ameliasburgh Township Council recommended that the bridge be built one and a half miles west of the existing bridge to give direct access to Highway 401 via the Wallbridge-Loyalist Road, while the City of Belleville naturally wished it to remain near the existing structure. A study team was sent in to decide on the best location. Its recommendation was that the bridge be built at the present location as it would be the most economic to build there, would have least impact on the environment and would best service local traffic.

It was James Taylor's suggestion that the new bridge be named the Norris Whitney Bridge in memory of one of its first promoters and the member for Prince Edward for over 20 years. This suggestion received government approval.

It was not until August 1980 that tenders were called, and October 1980 when the contract was awarded to Cliffside Pipelayers Ltd. of Toronto whose tender was $13,313,719, but it was an associated company, Pitts Engineering Construction Ltd., which actually did the construction. A start was made on the northern approach in the late fall of 1980, with the rock fill for the ramp trucked from a new quarry opened just a short distance out of Rossmore.

In the spring of 1981 dredging of the Bay began, to prepare the way for pile driving into the bedrock. Ten huge piers of steel and concrete were

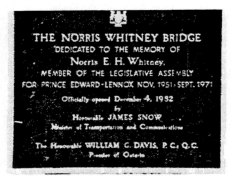

The bronze plaque.

constructed, anchored to the bedrock by steel piles to a depth of 18 inches. On each pier two massive supporting columns were built and capped, ready to carry the superstructure of the bridge. In November the first steel span was placed on the north end of the bridge. Work on the bridge resumed in the spring on 1982. Huge steel girders up to 166 feet in length and weighing nearly 80 tons were delivered to the site by long tractor-trailers. All the spans were completed by July 1982 except the one by the swing section of the old bridge, which could not be put in until the end of the navigation season. The concrete deck was proceeding span by span as well. To finish the job before winter, the old bridge was closed to navigation on September 8 and the final span completed.

The bridge was officially opened on December 4, 1982 by the Honourable James Snow, Minister of Transportation and Communication, who described the new bridge as a vital link connecting Prince Edward County and Belleville. A bronze plaque commemorating Norris Whitney, on the east wall of the pedestrian walkway at the Rossmore end of the bridge, was unveiled by Mrs. Lewis Lont and Mrs. Morgan Sills, cousins of Mr. Whitney. Several minutes later the old bridge was closed off and traffic started using the new one. Walter Hamilton was the first one across the new bridge.

The bridge was built 100 feet east of the old one. It has a total length of 2940 feet, a roadway width of 33 feet, and a sidewalk on the east side. At the navigation channel it has a vertical clearance of 75 feet, sufficient to accommodate the tallest craft now on the Bay. To avoid a long approach ramp on the Rossmore side, the navigation channel was moved to the channel at the fixed bridge span at the north end of the old bridge; this was deepened and widened. In 1983 the old fixed span, the swing span and part of the causeway were removed. The remainder of the causeway was left to form a breakwater for Belleville harbour. To remove the bridge spans, a barge was filled with water until it was lower than the bridge, floated under, and the water pumped out. As the barge rose, the bridge settled on it and was taken to shore.

A top course of pavement was laid on the bridge deck in 1983. Traffic signals were installed at the intersection of Highway 14 and the County Road at Rossmore. The parkette at the Rossmore approach was sodded and landscaped. A new rock monument made from a piece of the armour stone from the old causeway and, bearing a bronze plaque, was placed beside the stone marker erected in 1890.

CHAPTER 18

NAVIGATION

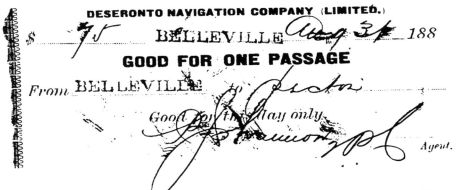

Ticket from the Deseronto Navigation Company of the 1880's. A Rathbun Enterprise.

A family's steam propelled boat anchored for the family to have their picnic lunch.

Steamer Alexandria.

The 'Alexandria' before and after it was refitted in 1883 as a passenger liner or the Bay of Quinte and Lake Ontario.

Aletha

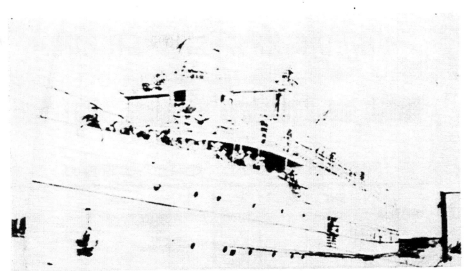

The Geronia

An excursion boat leaving the Dock at Rednersville.

Sunday School Picnic, Consecon Lake.

✦ MANAGER'S ✦ STATEMENT. ✦

Receipts and Expenditures of Steamer "Mary Ethel."

T. & B. Q. N. CO.

SEASON OF 1882.

DR.	$ c	CR.	$ c
1882 To bal. due Manager '83..........	605 12	1882 By bal. due Manager '81..........	144 88
		" Petty account.............	45 37
		" Comp. "	394 87
		" Fuel "	18 00
		" Postage "	2 00
	605 12		605 12

SEASON OF 1883.

DR.	$ c	CR.	$ c
1883 To Fares collected season '83	4524 16	1883 By Bal. due from '82.............	605 12
" Bal. due Manager.............	108 38	" Petty expense................	298 48
		" Fuel.....	1638 76
		" Wages	1363 01
		" Dock.....	31 97
		" Printing, &c.,...........	20 25
		" Insurance.............	75 00
		" Comp. account	243 45
		" Wood on hand,.............	356 50
	4632 54		4632 54

AUDITORS' REPORT.

We hereby certify that we have examined the Books, Cash Account and Vouchers produced, and find the same correct.

WM. G. STAFFORD, }
J. B. MORDEN,   } AUDITORS.

✦ ASSETS AND LIABILITIES. ✦

Capital Stock of the Company,...........$8,500		Amount Stock collected by Treasurer,....$8,340	
		Balance due on Stock 160	
	$8,500		$8,500

CHAPTER 19

RAILROADS

The Prince Edward County Railway

To isolate the story of the railway in Ameliasburgh from the remainder of Prince Edward County is impossible, but if it had not been for the foresight of Ameliasburgh's first reeve, the Prince Edward County Railway might never have existed.

From the 1830's, plans were being made for railroads. Every town in Ontario which was located on a railway prospered, for the railway created new business and employment for many. It too, was a convenient way to travel with its coaches warmed by wood or coal stoves, in contrast to a stagecoach.

While the Tory railway supporters talked of the industry that the railway would bring to Prince Edward County, the Grits played down its importance with the talk of the expense, the danger and the excellent shipping facilities by water which already existed.

In the 1870's serious talk of a railway began when a group of promoters

A COR train passes under a roadway, with a well-dressed couple watching, circa 1899.

headed by Charles Bockus of Picton, who had been a member of parliament for the County, received from Charles Legge, a Montreal civil engineer, a report on various routes connecting Picton with the Grank Trunk Railway. Even back in the 1850's, Picton's first Mayor, Philip Low, had succeeded in getting a cable across the Bay of Quinte, so Picton already had Grand Trunk telegraphic facilities.

County Council in 1872 passed a bylaw granting $87,500 toward construction, if it were to begin in nine months. It didn't. Council withdrew its grant. County Council met again in 1878 and passed a new bylaw, with the understanding that a 34 mile line between Picton and Trenton be completed by October, 15, 1879, to qualify for the grant of $60,000. This decision was won by a single vote because W.R. Dempsey, Reeve of Ameliasburgh, (which was anti-railway,) believing sincerely that the County generally in the end would benefit, 'crossed the floor' to allow the bylaw to be passed. Dempsey, as a result, was accused of taking a bribe, as others also were. He was defeated at the next election.

Two years later this accusation was cleared and Dempsey was again elected Reeve. Rev. George McMullen, a railway supporter, upheld his decision at an Ameliasburgh Nomination meeting. Later W.R. Dempsey became a member of the Ontario Legislature.

The Prince Edward Railway, incorporated in March 1873, began with very little capital— only $10,200 and some promises of bonuses. Alexander Manning, a Toronto financier, took on the work. From the 'Empress of India,' docked in Picton harbour, he removed 32 horses, some carts, scrapers, wagons and other tools and began to work. By the end of 1878, 15 miles had been graded, it had been decided on which side to pass Consecon Lake; land had been purchased for the right-of-way there from William Robinson, and as well from Reuben Young at the Carrying Place. Trenton had granted the railway a $10,000 bonus and a right-of-way through the village.

During that winter many carloads of new British 42 pound steel rails were unloaded at the Grand Trunk station north of the village and the engine house was soon ready for the first steam locomotive, which travelled between Trenton Junction and downtown Trenton station in June, 1879. The Newspaper *The Bay of Quinte Advertiser*, in its May 22, 1879 issue had this to say: "The steam mill at Dead Creek is running day and night cutting ties for the railroad. Gangs of men are building culverts along the road and making ready for laying ties and rails. The connecting switch at the Grand Trunk has been made and the laying of the rails is progressing from that point. Thirty-eight carloads of rails and 18 carloads of ties have been delivered at the Grand Trunk station for the road." At the same time a long, low pile trestle (1000 feet) was being built across the west end of Consecon Lake. This was the costliest part of the project, because it disappeared and another was constructed on a narrower crossing to the west (140 feet).

Stations, some manned by station agents and some flag stations, had already been built, including Trenton, Carrying Place (a flag station),

Consecon, Wellington, Bloomfield and Picton. By the end of September everything was completed to the point it could be used— a remarkable accomplishment using horses and manpower. John Haney, who was in charge of completing the railway, was appointed general manager.

The Courier of Oct. 16, 1879 made an announcement: "The first excursion from Trenton to Picton takes place next Tuesday. This will be a fine opportunity to view the hitherto isolated county of Prince Edward. The railroad runs across Consecon Lake and the view of Lake Ontario, and the trip on the whole will be a most enjoyable one."

Crossing Consecon Lake.

The trip was highly successful and there was much celebrating and that first train had Robert Hamilton as conductor, George Berry as engineer and George Neun as fireman. The company owned two small woodburning, steam engines, the *Trenton* and the *Picton*, two baggage cars and two flat cars. It ran three trips a day, with as many as seven passenger cars on Saturdays. Even though the train was proving its usefulness, there were those who remained apprehensive about the dangers of the railroad. Editor Young, in an 1879 issue of the Courier wrote the following editorial: "We have again and again sounded the note of warning in these columns, regarding the danger our youth are in from the railroad. Some make it a practice to get on the cars and ride out towards Consecon. Some have amused themselves with placing pins on the track to see them flattened. Others have been noticed striking each car as it passed. The variety of ways in which they risk being caught and crushed are many and our fear is that we will have to chronicle the sorrow of some family

*George Collins was general manager of the
Central Ontario Railway in the early years of the
century. A native of Ameliasburgh, he was
educated in Trenton and then went to work for the
railway. His father and mother came to this
country from Ireland.*

for the loss of their little boy or girl. Will parents see to it that their children do
not go near the railroad?"

Owing to the light rails used in the construction, the narrow cuts and lack
of a snow plow, the company was plagued with snow problems during the
winters. Sometimes the train was held up for days, resulting in no mail, papers
or express. Then too, there was no turntable in Picton and the engines were
unable to turn about, until sometime in 1881 when a hand-operated, roofed-in
one was built. The roof had a hole in the top for smoke to escape. Now the
engines could be turned about. This year also saw a change in ownership of the
Prince Edward Railway. The McMullen Brothers bought it. They widened out
the cuts where the snow drifted in badly so there were fewer delays. H.M. Love
of Picton was the McMullens' telegraph operator.

In 1882, the name of the railway was changed to Central Ontario Railway
and head office was shifted from Trenton to Picton. This was the year that the
first shipment of canned goods was made from Wellington Boulter's canning
factory in Picton, consigned to Winnipeg. In 1885, Boulter shipped out a solid
train of 17 cars of canned goods consigned to Victoria, B.C. Each car carried
two Union Jack flags.

About the same time, farmers in the County began shipping cattle to the
stock yards in Toronto and Montreal. Through the years, many carloads left
the Consecon station because it became a central shipping area. Mr. Marrow
was Consecon's first station agent.

Because of the business upswing with the railroad and to meet the needs of
a mining establishment in Coe Hill, which had already been linked to Trenton
by rail, the McMullen Brothers expanded their interests in Ameliasburgh.
They bought land from Reuben Young at 'Pine Point' on Weller's Bay (where
Hancock Lumber is located now), and built a roundhouse to accommodate
eight engines, a machine shop with a fine, tall chimney (which never smoked)
and a thousand foot dock made of three inch plank, studded with piles by the

thousand. A railway track ran from one end to the other, for the purpose of handling iron-ore from Coe Hill. The harbour was dredged so boats could enter. Alongside the dock was a fine boarding house and a barn.

Circa 1910: Section men prepare for action in front of the downtown Trenton station.

On June 2, 1884, the first ore train steamed over the roughly laid mine track to Weller's Bay. Two barges lay at anchor ready to pick up the ore, which was shipped direct to a smelter in Cleveland, Ohio. By late August that year, 12,000 tons of ore had been shipped from Weller's Bay. Because of the excess of sulphur in the ore, the mine had to close down and the McMullens lost heavily in that hapless adventure. The waters of the bay rose and inundated the dock and it was some years before it emerged again, only to be dismantled and sold

Left: Grand Trunk railway station, Trenton, from a postcard view. Right: Another postcard view, circa 1907, 'Clearing the Tracks, an electric snow plow in Canada'.

Left: Downtown Trenton Station, used by many Ameliasburgh people who stopped there. Right: Postcard view of the Flight of International Limited, Grank Trunk Railway system.

Right: Central Ontario Railway roundhouse and machine shops, Trenton.

by the railway company. Today, only a few piles in the water remind one of that day in history.

George Collins, whose parents Mr. and Mrs. James Collins farmed in Ameliasburgh, went to work as a clerk for the Central Ontario Railway in 1882. Later he was promoted to Manager and Director for the remainder of the Central Ontario Railway's existence. About the same time an industrialist from Ohio, Samuel J. Ritchie, was buying mineral rights in North Hastings including a partnership in the Coe Hill mine. Ritchie and the McMullens entered into a partnership of the railway. They bought three new locomotives; one appeared on the Picton run. After 31 years of service, it was scrapped in 1913. Now it became known that the railway passed into American management; the McMullens had sold out.

For a while the Central Ontario Railway Company tried to expand its facilities northward, but lack of finances, poor grade ore, a strike, difficult construction, competition from other companies and operational difficulties hampered progress.

By 1896 the railroad was extended to Marmora by an independent company, providing transportation for the Gilmour Mill employees from Trenton, as well as logs and timber from the Rathbun Mill from Marmora. George Collins announced that cheese was being exported to Britain. Passenger excursions were becoming popular. A fall fair in Picton had required 15 coaches to accommodate the people.

In 1901, Collins ordered new, heavier rails of 56 pounds for the Prince Edward line and planned to use the lighter rails for sidings to factories. By 1905 the heavier rails were laid. Monday Dec. 23, 1903, was the grand opening day of the Trenton Station. The winter of 1905 was a very stormy one, for the train didn't run through Prince Edward for five days. The snow was nearly to the telegraph wires that ran parallel to the track.

Apples grown in the County had previously been shipped by boat, but by 1905 they were beginning to go by rail. Thousands of barrels were shipped to Britain. By 1908, another snowy winter, Collins began to negotiate for a bigger, better roundhouse. By 1909 the train with coach and baggage car went three times daily to Picton.

Life in the community with the coming of the railway became more intimate. Around the station everyone became friendly, and the station agent, who was also a telegrapher, was known by all. In those days all trains were dispatched by the use of 'Morse Code' which was transmitted on wires and came into the station on a telegraph key, in a series of dots and dashes which the agent decoded to get the message. He could operate the key to send out messages as well. Today trains are dispatched in a different manner, with a system of lights being used.

The station was heated by a huge, pot-bellied stove and gave comfort to all who sat around waiting for the train. Here was a place to discuss local issues of the day. If the train was an hour late, it really didn't matter.

The station platform was loaded with produce, mailbags, boxes of fish

A *steam locomotive*

Left: *Baldwin's grain elevator and freight shed in Consecon.*
Right: *The Marmora to Picton Ore Train, 1969. Courtesy: The Trentonian*

packed in ice, and miscellaneous baggage loaded on small wagons. When the train pulled into the station, with bell ringing and brakes creaking, the puffing and hissing of the big steam engine meant that someone had to stand guard by the horses with their buggies or democrats, lest they should run away from the frightening iron monster.

It was a thrill to see the conductor in his uniform step down from the rear platform, with its shining handrails, to welcome the passengers. The brakeman helped the passengers aboard with their luggage and a warning to "watch your step." You took your seat, looked out the window to see the baggage being wheeled along the platform to the baggage car, then noticed the conductor checking his gold pocket watch. In a moment he called a-l-l-a-board! and stepped up into the coach, the locomotive whistled, and you were off.

Steam engines were hazards too, as sparks from the smokestack often ignited grass fires along the tracks. Over the years Ameliasburgh residents responded to requests for assistance to fight railway fires. There was a flag station at Weller's Bay until sparks from a locomotive set fire to the wooden shingles of the roof and it burned down. It was replaced. There were collisions too between the train and cattle that strayed onto the rails and even a few railway crossing accidents that proved fatal to humans, because there were no warning signals as we have today.

It was 1911 before Collins' request for a new roundhouse was granted. It was decided to build at the foot of Dufferin Avenue in Trenton instead of at the Weller's Bay location. A huge concrete building, with very high ceilings, covering 40,000 square feet, was erected. It contained machine shops to service 15 locomotives. As the engines arrived they were put on a turntable that swung them into a stall. Many local men were employed there until the depression of the Thirties, then the roundhouse and its shops closed. It was at the height of the train era, a very important facility, operated by the Central Ontario Railway and later by the Canadian Northern, which bought the former in 1909. Head offices moved from Trenton to Toronto and by 1912 all equipment had been lettered 'Canadian Northern.'

Canada's first gas-electric car came to Prince Edward County in April 1912. It was the forerunner of our sleek diesels of today. It carried from 30 to 40 passengers and Ameliasburgh residents recall that a journey from Trenton to Picton took about 45 minutes. The return fare was 25 cents. Teachers to Carrying Place school and students to local high schools also commuted by it. Indeed, Adam's School section in the township advertised for a teacher, noting

October 14, 1918: Explosion at the British Chemical Co., courtesy Trenton Library.

the station was near. However, engineers didn't enjoy driving this train because it was not entirely reliable, so it was removed from service.

Then came World War One and the Canadian Northern carried our Prince Edward County servicemen to Trenton Junction for transfer to other trains. County produce continued to be shipped from every station along the route. Freight charges went higher, passenger timetables were confusing in that they were not synchronized. On Oct. 14, 1918, a fire started at The British Chemical Co. in Trenton. By evening it was evident that the plant would be destroyed. Explosions occurred throughout the night and would have been more hazardous had not a railroad engineer named Joseph Barry driven his engine into the explosion area to haul out two box cars loaded with TNT and remove them to the roundhouse.

We have neglected to mention the section men with their jitneys, propelled along the tracks by hand, or the gas cars putting along the tracks with no protection from the elements, but transporting the men with their picks and shovels, who kept the tracks safe and in good repair. Nor are we unmindful of the close encounters experienced by these same people. One incident brought to our attention happened on the Consecon Lake trestle when a train suddenly confronted a gas car driven by William VanWart and his crew of Andy Donald, Ernest Elmy and Arnott Anderson. Sensing the inevitable, the latter three quickly left the car to slide none-too-gently down the embankment to the edge of the water. However Bill stayed with the car and survived while his crew was busy venting their wrath with choice language. Ernest's lunch bucket was 'flat as a pancake.'

We recall others in Ameliasburgh who depended on the trains. Local fish merchants, Jim Eaton, Wesley Kizer and Herb McCabe, to name a few, shipped thousands of boxes of fish packed in ice. Franklin G. Zufelt, who for many years was a stock drover, had a fenced stock yard where Baldwin's elevator now stands. His son William V. Zufelt began a Massey-Harris machine dealership in Consecon and all the new equipment came in by rail to the Consecon station. For many years Fred Ward carried on a coal business from the sheds he had at the station. With a large delivery wagon pulled by big, strong horses, he delivered coal by the ton or by the bag. He also sold cement, salt, binder twine, wire and lumber that came in by rail. In later years Dick Baldwin, mill owner in Consecon, built a tall grain elevator near the station and farmers brought great loads of grain that were shipped from there by rail. Also Baldwin purchased western grain for his mill customers, that was brought in to the elevator by rail.

By an order-in-council on May 17, 1956, the Canadian Northern Railway became a part of the Canadian National. Today this great system owns and operates the one and only Prince Edward Railway.

On May 12, 1959, the last steam engine to work in the County was retired. In 1964 the beautiful Central Ontario station in downtown Trenton was torn down and the A and P store located where that impressive building was. The freight sheds too, were demolished in 1982. By 1966, the small country stations were obsolete. In 1967, during the Centennial Celebrations, the once busy, important Junction Station was torn down and replaced with a bus-stop enclosure. Few passengers leave from what was once a busy station.

Shortly after the second World War, Bethlehem Steel began to work an open pit mine near Marmora. The mine produced large quantities of iron ore, which was shipped in pellet form in ore carriers over the Prince Edward rail line to Picton. Very heavy rails were laid to carry the increased tonnage, and the line was extended to the High Shore of Picton Bay. Storage bins were built for unloading the pellets directly into ore carrying ships. Freight cars were added to the train so that remaining stations were served. In 1978 the last ore train passed over the rails. All the stations were closed and the station agents let go.

Now, if the air is clear, one occasionally hears a diesel locomotive with its cars wending its way through Ameliasburgh, perhaps bearing a load of western grain for the elevator by the old decaying Consecon Station, maybe unhooking a load of farm machinery for a dealer or pulling a few cement carriers to the plant below Picton. Long gone are the coal cars, the cattle cars, the loads of fish, dripping ice water, the mail bags, and the long line of farmers waiting to unload their autumn harvest into Baldwin's grain elevator.

How much longer will these rails resound to the big diesel locomotives that have taken the place of the little steam giants— the Trenton and the Picton?

CHAPTER 20

HEATING & LIGHTING

Facilities For Heating, Lighting and Cooking

The earliest cabins were built with a container for an open fire— possibly even the crude central fireplace surrounded by stones with no chimney, only a vent in a log near the roof to allow for the escape of some of the smoke[1]. Those who arrived that first autumn of 1787 would surely have made a basic shelter or "shanty" as quickly as possible.

The earliest fireplaces with chimneys were plastered with clay to keep the fire away from the wood or stone support. Later, lime was burned to be mixed with sand for mortar between stones for a chimney and as caulking between logs.

The Rynard Brickman Home, built around 1824. Photo taken about 1870.

[1] *As described in 'The Backwoods of Canada', published in 1836 in London, England by Charles Knight.*

Some lamps prior to the Kerosene era. From left: a pottery wick-burning lard lamps; a whale or sperm oil lamp; two Flemish lamps. The small one was sometimes called a 'Sparkling lamp' supposedly used as a light and timer for the young man during his visit to his girlfriend. When the light was gone, he was supposed to be gone from the house.

Bricks were available by at least the 1820's and were used to build or line a fireplace and to make a chimney. By the 1840's stoves were available. Smith's Gazetteer of 1846 lists three foundries in Belleville, three in Kingston and two in Picton, all producing heating and cooking stoves. According to Audra Brickman, the Lewis Brickman house, located on the Gore Road just east of the house where she lives, was built in 1824 without a fireplace. It replaced an older house which incorporated a large fireplace. Doors at the front and back of the house could be opened to allow an animal, a horse or an ox to draw in a huge log to be used as a backlog.

These early settlers probably relied on the light from the fireplace to extend the light of day. This fire was kept going night and day all winter with the use of a huge unseasoned backlog which burned slowly. If the fire went out, often it meant a trip to the nearest neighbour to 'borrow fire'. This expression is sometimes heard when someone is in a hurry. Coals were carefully carried home in a container and used to kindle a new fire. Spills (tightly rolled paper

Left Back: Peg lamp made to be inserted in a candlestick. Pierced tin candle lantern. Front: Tin candlemold; candlestick with attached snuffer. Foreground: Candle snuffer and tray.

Right: A Crusie lamp. The wick burned lard or indeed whatever oil the font contained. A spike on the end of the chain allowed the lamp to be portable, and easily held wherever needed. A swivel allowed the user to direct the light.

Left: Three kerosene lamps. The centre lamp was used without a chimney. It had a fan in the base which increased the light intensity and caused it to burn cleaner. Made by Sherwood and Sons of England according to an 1840 patent specification. The other ones were made in the 1860's or 70's. Right: Candles were held in many types of containers. From left, Sheffield plate silver; brass; blown mercury glass; pressed glass; centre: spill holder and spills.

or finely cut dry splints) were used to kindle other fires or the candles or pipes used by the family. A tinder box was also very useful. It consisted of a metal box that had a rough surface under the lid. A piece of flint was drawn over this surface causing a spark which hopefully would ignite the oily wadding contained in the lower part of the box. A piece of flint and a knife blade seems to have sufficed more regularly in Prince Edward County, as few tinder boxes have survived.

Wooden matches were patented in the United States in 1836. They were the 'sulphur' match, which could be guaranteed to cause a whole room to smell of sulphur when lighted. These and other 'strike anywhere' matches were made in Canada following 1851 by the E.B. Eddy Match Co. of Hull, Quebec, and gradually came into general use.

When the first settlers arrived, lighting equipment had changed little from earliest times. The saucer and wick type lamp was still in use as it had been since the pre-Christian era. The Betty lamp and Phoebe lamp were adaptations of this principle. Candles were made in candle molds if available, or by dipping candlewick repeatedly into melted fat or wax. They used the tallow from the mutton or other lard as available. A harder and more aromatic candle was sometimes made of beeswax. Candles were displayed in candlesticks of metal, glass, pottery or wood, or in wall sconces or ceiling candelabra. The candle lantern was a portable light used both inside and outside buildings.

The first burning fluid lamps were made without chimneys and burned a purified animal oil, the best being that from the blubber of the whale, and a most-prized sperm oil from the head of the sperm whale. One or two wicks were set in a disk that fitted into the metal-reinforced neck of the reservoir of the lamp. These whale oil lamps were easily converted to receive a burner for burning kerosene, so few are found in their original state.

Kerosene or coal oil was made by a process patented by Gesner of Nova Scotia in 1846. The earliest record of an advertisement for coal oil lamps so far discovered is in the *Toronto Globe* of July 25, 1858. The coal oil era saw a great change in seeking brighter illumination with patented burners; the addition of a fan to a flame, and kerosene and later gasoline placed under pressure in the Alladin and Coleman lights. Kerosene was also used for stoves for the home, so that the necessity for a hot fire in the cookstove in summer was eliminated.

Coal oil lamps were made in a great variety of shapes and sizes and for many purposes during the era, and the affluence of 'Barley Days' was evident in the hanging lamps with their many prisms in parlor, hall, dining room and kitchen; the piano lamp to be placed by the pianoforte; the fancy lamp with its matching globe for the center table and the hand lamps to be carried by each owner to the bedrooms.

The nearest thing to the gas lighting found in the cities was the carbide storage tank which, when activated, transmitted gas by means of pipes to the lighting outlets. This system was used in Albury Church and some other public buildings. A few places had a 'Delco' system. Storage batteries transmitted direct current by wires to light bulbs.

By Oct. 1, 1930, the Picton Gazette reported 60.3 miles of rural hydro lines serving 69 hamlet and 126 farm installations. Ameliasburgh Township was in the Wellington Rural Power district, which served the west part of the county. The supply for the western district was obtained from the sub-stations in Welllington and Consecon. There were 16 miles of lines from Carrying Place to Rossmore, the second concession to Massassaga and Huff's Island had about 22 miles and the third concession about seven miles. There had to be three subscribers to a mile before lines were installed. There was a service charge at a fixed rate per month. During the depression of the 30's, many could not afford hydro installation and rural electrification did not reach a peak until about the time of the Second World War.

Marion Calnan remembers the thrill it was to have hydro finally turned on in the Mikel home on Consecon Lake. The house had been wired for a year, but inspection and installation by Hydro's office was not complete. Reg Batchellor, a fine electrician from south of Carrying Place who was severely crippled, had completed the wiring. In spite of his handicap he could climb about in all sorts of places. Some other township electricians were: Luther Alyea, Arthur and Cecil McConkey, Jay Sprague, Frank Roblin, Wm. Oliphant, Ross Snider, Donald Jones, Bob Cairns and Ron Callow. Today Gary Wetherall is carrying on the fine tradition his father, Roy Wetherall, began with his work in the township and beyond.

Today, woodpiles are seen around many of the homes in the township. Woodburning stoves, furnaces and fireplaces are making a reappearance with the high price of oil. In spite of the clearing of much of the land, woodlots are still to be found and the applewood from the trimmings of orchards makes a satisfying and aromatic fire.

CHAPTER 21

P̅EDLARS

Soon after the first settlers arrived, pedlars began to ply their calling from clearing to clearing along the bayshore. The first ones came with their packs by canoe or batteau. It was a great event to the pioneer family when the pedlar's boat came along. He usually stayed an hour or two, and perhaps the most important thing he brought was news, news of the outside world and of other families along the bay. Even when they could not buy, it was a luxury to look at the pedlar's wares. The mother and daughters looked longingly at the bright calico prints; the children at his twists of candy. He also carried pots and pans, pewter plates and spoons, ribbons, combs and tea. The settlers had no money,

The Pack Pedlar, painting by Rev. Bowen Squire.

but the pedlar would take grain or other produce in payment. Sometimes a family possession was parted with for sorely-needed goods.

Asa Wallbridge was the best remembered of the Quinte pedlars. He was an eccentric old bachelor who lived in a log cabin near the Indian camp at Meyer's Creek. One-half of his shanty was living quarters, the other half his store. He set out regularly with his wares to visit the log homes of the pioneers. He must have really loved this new land and wanted to leave a legacy to it, for everywhere he went he gave away apple seeds and seedlings, periodically returning to the States to get a fresh supply. The first apples grown in Seventh Town were on trees from Wallbridge's seedlings.

As the township opened up and rough roads were cleared, there appeared the pack pedlars who made a living by walking through the early settlements, offering a variety of wares which they were able to carry on their backs. Their goods might include needles and pins, tinware and patent medicines. They sought meals and overnight accommodation wherever they happened to be. Itinerant workmen also would come along looking for a job— the shoemaker with his kit on his back, carpenters and masons peddling their skills.

By the early 1900's there were many peddling wagons operating in Ameliasburgh Township. Harry Bisdee reminisces about some of them in the Roblin's Mills area: "Peddling wagons were a great convenience to the country folk. Farmers busy on the land, people without means of transportation, busy housewives and mothers with large families all looked forward to the peddling wagons; the children too, as the pedlar always carried a good supply of candy. In those days money was scarce, but most homes had a flock of chickens, so the surplus eggs were traded to the pedlar in exchange for needed supplies. My first experience with a pedlar was with Byron Frederick of Mountain View. My brothers and sisters and I knew the day he came and lay in wait for him. The first thing he would do was open the candy door on the wagon, grab a handful of candies and throw them over our heads into the long grass. We would all scramble for our share and did not bother him anymore. He had a horse-drawn wagon with an iron railing around its roof where he carried wooden egg crates in which to pack the eggs accepted in payment along his route. He carried groceries, canned goods, tobacco, coal oil, pins and needles, thread and bolts of cloth. It was quite exciting and fun to me then; little did I know that I would have a peddling wagon of my own someday."

"After Mr. Frederick, the next pedlar was Albert File, better known as Timmy. He had a large grocery wagon drawn by two horses. He carried a great variety of merchandise as he went to Belleville every Saturday for supplies. He would also take orders which he picked up in the city and delivered on the next trip around the following week. He had a different route each day of the week. He had a wash-tub atop his wagon in which he put the eggs he took in trade.

"Bread and baked goods were peddled by Frank Thompson, proprietor of the Maple Leaf Bakery in Roblin's Mills, first with a horse, later by car. I entered the peddling business in 1935, having purchased the Crosby bake

Albert File's peddling wagon—
Mr. File with some of his customers.
Isaylia (Alyea) Bush, Mr. File,
Pearl (Humphrey) Fulford,
Gladys (Alyea) Rowe,
Lulu (Rowe) Adams,
Hazel (Alyea) Hannah.

Harry Bisdee's peddling truck;
Gerald Fritz, driver.

shop. I started with just bread and baked goods, then added groceries in 1937 and put a larger truck on the road, peddling six days a week. I operated under the name of Ameliasburgh Bakery and Grocery. Truman Ferguson and Gerald Fritz drove the peddling wagon.

"There were several butchers peddling over the years. The first one I knew was Albert Lont. He had a horse-drawn covered wagon and carried ice in it to keep the meat cool. You could buy a shank of beef for 75¢ that would last most

Albert Lont's butcher wagon; painting by Reverend Bowen Squire.

of the week. Mr. Lont had a bell which he rang to arouse his customers. After
he retired, his son Lewis carried on the business. During the 1930's Arthur
Corfield had a butcher van on the road with routes to Huff's Island, Rossmore
and Consecon."

Grant Wanamaker butchered and peddled in the Mountain View area.
The way he got into the business is interesting. His son Loral relates: "After
working in the trade of can-making for several years for S.S. Potter of the
Union, my father was told by his employer at the end of the season that he
could not pay him the balance of his wages, as he was having great difficulty
selling much of his pack. He proposed to father that he take his horse and
democrat with a load of canned goods and go about the country selling it, thus
making up what was owing. This he soon found out was not so easy, as many
wanted the canned goods but had not the money to buy it. They offered a
trade of this and that, which father would take and then trade it with someone
else. In this way he ended up with a fat cow for killing. He took it on himself to
butcher it and sell it on the market. The story of how he killed that cow was
very amusing to those he told, but he accomplished it and took it to Belleville
market. He asked others what they were charging for quarters, and they told
him 4¢ a pound for the fronts and 5¢ for the hinds. Along in the afternoon he
still had not sold any when Bill Tufts came along and asked him what he was
charging. When he told him what the others had quoted Tufts said, "They lied

to you about the amount to ask, for they have gone and you are still here." So father at once lowered his price and sold the cow. From that time on he butchered. He killed three to four cattle a week, depending on the time of year. He peddled with a democrat with a canvas covering. He cut up very little of his meat, just in large pieces, and cut the balance on the spot for the farmer's wife. This kept the meat better than if it had been all cut up ahead. He always carried the livers, and anyone asking got some free. The hearts and tongues he usually gave away to families who could not afford to buy much meat. He also had a bell which he rang as he approached each home. I still have my father's bell and scales."

Henry Robinson of Rossmore also peddled meat. The White brothers, Joe and Stan, had a slaughter house in Rossmore and peddled meat by truck. Later Clarence Thompson of Massassaga butchered and had a peddling truck on the road.

Joseph S. Thompson had a bakery on Ridley Street in Rossmore, and peddled bread with a horse and covered wagon. Later his son George (Judd) took over the bakeshop and peddled by truck up the bayshore, down Massassaga, up the 2nd, into Huff's Island and Mountain View.

In the Rednersville area, J.M. Chislett, who was the proprietor of the general store in Rednersville, had a peddling wagon on the road, drawn by horses, with his daughters Effie and Emma as drivers. They carried a wide range of goods—groceries, coal oil, harness, bolts of cloth. Brooms hung on the side of the wagon. They bought the housewives' eggs too, 17¢ a dozen cash or a trade-in value of 20¢ per dozen. Later when Alex Gilmour ran the Rednersville store, he peddled groceries and other supplies with a truck. Will Carnrike and Loral Gerow, both of Rossmore, peddled groceries and other wares through the eastern part of the township. Like the others, they came once a week. Audra Brickman of the Gore recalls Carnrike bringing five-gallon cans of gasoline for her father after he purchased his first car. In addition to Lont with his butcher wagon, she remembers Bob Oliphant from Belleville coming through with meat.

Arthur Stewart had a bake shop in Rednersville and peddled bread in the early 1900's. Later Norman Weese from Trenton came through with a bread truck.

In the Consecon area, Jim Eaton had a horse-drawn grocery wagon, It was driven by Jack Viant and later Bert Kemp. He also took eggs in exchange and carried them on the roof of the wagon. One hot summer day as Kemp proceeded along the North Lakeside road, some of the eggs began to hatch. By the time he reached Mrs. Tomlin's (later the Earl Walt farm) he had a brood of baby chicks, so he called to her to bring a box and gave her the chickens. Later Kemp peddled meat by car. Herman Goodmurphy also had a wagon out of Consecon carrying groceries, bread and baked goods. His son Allan came into the business and carried a much larger variety. With the Goodmurphys, a truck came into use. Later pedlars in the Consecon area were Frank Brimley

Mildred and Philena Parliament, Mildred age 9, Philena 5, in dresses made of material purchased from Willie Maybee. Dresses were made by Bessie Post (later Mrs. Ray Alyea) who came to the home and did the dressmaking, staying a week or more at a time.

from Wellington with groceries and Pearsoll from Wellington with bread. There were fish pedlars too.

Pack pedlars continued to walk through the township selling their wares until the early 1930's. Willie Mabee was the best known walking pedlar. He lived at Massassaga, and later in Belleville. Several times a year he made his rounds. He carried patent medicines, toiletries, stereoscopes and views for them; he sold newspaper and magazine subscriptions; he measured up and took orders for men's suits. In the spring he carried summer dress materials, and in the fall winter dress goods. He was a small man and would be bent right over with the weight of his wares.

Two other pack pedlars of the early 1900's were Johnny Itus and William Henry Alley. Mrs. Maude Dempsey recalls Itus as a big man with a heavy mustache and a dark complexion who called regularly at her parents' fourth concession home when she was a child. She was rather frightened of him. Alley she remembers as a tall, slim fellow who sold such items as shoe laces and thread which he carried in a satchel. Ida Wood also recalls both Itus and Alley calling at her childhood home on the bayshore and 'putting up' for the night at Clarence Russell's.

Alex Lipson from Picton got his start as a pack pedlar. He walked the roads of Ameliasburgh as well as the rest of the County, selling socks, shoe laces, scarves, buttons and other notions. Lipson is quoted as saying that he always made a profit, but he never tried to make a big one.

Other pedlars people remember were the Daly tea salesman from Napanee and the Ocean Blend tea salesmen who came through spring and fall taking orders which were delivered later. Until fairly recent times men came door to door to sharpen saws, scissors and lawn mowers. And then there were those who came to buy not to sell— the Italians with their horse and wagon seeking rags, bones and bottles.

With the passage of time, the modern automobile and the supermarkets, the era of the peddling wagons came to an end. Many will remember them with nostalgia.

CHAPTER 22

GRAPE ISLAND MISSION

William Case was one of the early Methodist ministers. He was appointed as presiding elder of the Bay of Quinte circuit in 1824 and immediately became involved with Indian mission work. He enlisted the help of Peter Jones in converting the Mississaugas of the area. Jones was the son of a Welsh surveyor, Augustus Jones, and his mother was the daughter of an Ojibway chief. He had been converted in 1823 at the Grand River and became a missionary to his own people. Jones came to the village of Belleville in early February, 1826, and made contact with some of the nearby Indians. Going on to Ernestown, he met with Elder Case and attended a Quarterly meeting there, then spent two days contacting Indians in the Kingston area. At a service in the Belleville Methodist Church in May, both Case and Jones preached to the Mississaugas, and 22 adults and 11 children were baptized. The Indians were invited to attend a camp meeting at Adolphustown in mid-June, and many did so. Here 21 adults and 10 children were baptized.

The permanent settlement of the Grand River Indians had been so successful that Elder Case determined to provide similar advantages for the Belleville area Indians. He wanted the Mississaugas to abandon their nomadic way of life and establish a permanent settlement with church and school, and

Grape Island

A view on Grape Island

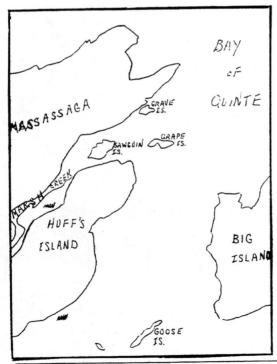

Remnants of an old foundation on the island.

to learn the "quiet pursuits of agriculture" (Canniff). Accordingly two islands, which already belonged to the Mississaugas, were leased by the Methodists for the nominal sum of five shillings. The two islands chosen were Sawguin, containing 50 acres, and Grape Island, containing about 11 acres.

A large number of the Mississaugas spent the winter of 1826 on Grape Island in bark wigwams, while the rest went hunting as usual. Instructions began immediately with William Beaver and Jacob Peters, two converted Indians, teaching the Lord's Prayer and the Ten Commandments. With the return of the hunters there were about 130 Indians on the island. In the spring of 1827, a group of 40 Mississaugas, who had been living near Kingston, joined them. A building 30 feet by 25 feet, to serve as a meeting house and school, was erected in July. It contained a small room to serve as bedroom and study for the teacher. The first teacher was William Smith who had 30 pupils in the day school and 50 in the Sabbath School. Some land was ploughed and planted that year. They had a yoke of oxen, three cows, some farming tools and building materials, all purchased through missionary contributions from Canadian and American donors. Eight log houses were completed that fall, plus a small parsonage. Solomon Waldon was appointed the first resident missionary on Grape Island, and was assisted by Indian converts such as Wm. Beaver. Richard Phelps instructed the Indians in farming and other skills. Both Elder Case and Peter Jones visited the mission often. On May 23, 1827 Case conducted Holy Communion for about 90 and baptized 20 newly-converted from the Kingston group.

Visiting Grape Island early in 1828, Case and Jones found the mission flourishing but a great need for more acreage to sustain the growing settlement. According to the Annual Report of the Missionary Society of the Methodist Episcopal church, there were "200 natives under the Christian instruction of one missionary, 120 of whom are regular communicants, and 50 children are taught in the school." A delegation of Indians went to York to petition the Governor to grant them additional land and to clarify the Mississaugas' claims to Big Island. They were told by Dr. Strachan, the Attorney General, that "His Excellency did not feel disposed to assist the Indians under their present situation with the Methodists, but that, if they would come under the care of the Church of England, they would assist them." (George F. Playter, *The History of Methodism in Canada*)

Case went to the United States in 1828 to raise money for his Indian Mission. He returned with money and enough ticking for 20 straw beds. Two women, Eliza Barnes and Hester Hubbard, came with him to teach and preach to the Indians. They instructed the girls and women in knitting and sewing. Miss Barnes later went to Rice Lake to work among the Indians there, while Miss Hubbard remained on Grape Island. Crops were good in 1828 and the Indians harvested about 300 bushels of potatoes. In October 1828 at the Canada Conference of the Methodist Episcopal Church in Ernestown, William Case was elected General Superintendent, which position he held for five years. He was also Superintendent of Indian Missions.

In 1829 a large building 40 by 28 feet was constructed on Grape Island in which the Indians were taught several trades. Hetty Hubbard and William Case were married in May of that year and made their home on the island. So little Grape Island was the home of the head of the Methodist Espiscopal Church!

The mission continued to flourish. In 1830 there were 29 buildings— a church, a school, a hospital, a blacksmith shop, a storehouse, a workshop and 23 homes. They had oxen and six cows. On Sawguin they had grown excellent crops of corn and potatoes. In the mission school, the children were taught Reading, Writing, Spelling, Arithmetic, Grammar, Geography, Astronomy and Natural Philosophy. Eunice Huff, daughter of Solomon Huff of Huff's Island, is mentioned in Peter Jones' Journal as living and working at the mission in 1830. (Eunice Huff later became the wife of Sylvanus Sprague Jr.)

Late in 1831 the Mission suffered a great loss when Mrs. Case died. Measles and whooping cough were responsible for the deaths of several children also. By 1832 the number on the island had fallen to 108, and in 1833 there were only 81. To provide enough food, they were farming Sawguin Island, Goose Island, one field on Huff's Island and Indian Island near the head of the bay.

At the 1833 Conference, the union of the Methodist Episcopal Church of Canada with the Wesleyan Methodist British conference came into effect. Case resigned as General Superintendent, and George Marsden was appointed President of the Wesleyan Methodist Church in British North America. Case was appointed to the Credit and had to leave his home on Grape Island. No missionary was appointed to the island for the 1833-34 year. S. Hurlburt, teacher of the boys' school, was "missionary in everything but name."

The number of people on Grape Island continued to decline because of the unsolved problem of insufficient land. At the Annual Conference in Belleville in 1836, Rice Lake and Grape Island were joined together as one pastoral charge, and it was decided to move the Grape Island Indians to Rice Lake. In 1837, they were relocated in the township of Alnwick on the south shore of Rice Lake, where a new village was built. It was named Alderville. Although it was a heartbreak to leave their beautiful Grape Island home, there was one happy turn of events. Case and his second wife, Eliza Barnes, made Alderville their home and he was there reunited with his "Island children." Case lived out his life at Alderville. Peter Jones died of consumption on June 29, 1856.

The Grape Island Mission lasted only 10 years, but it had a tremendous impact. It changed the lives of the Mississauga Indians; many of their descendants to-day are Christians because their forefathers were part of the Grape Island Mission.

Sawguin Island now belongs to Reg and Bill Barber and is connected to Huff's Island by a causeway they built in the late 1940's.

CHAPTER 23

CHURCHES

THE CIRCUIT RIDERS

In the early years of the 19th century, the gospel was carried to the pioneers by Methodist circuit riders. They travelled from place to place on horseback, with saddle-bags containing oats in one part and a Bible and a few articles of wearing apparel in the other. Braving privation and hardship, they laid the foundation of Methodism in Prince Edward County.

The circuit rider

Perhaps the first circuit riders to visit the north shores of Ameliasburgh Township came across the bay by canoe. But in 1817 the Hallowell Circuit was formed which included all of the County of Prince Edward. Ezra Adams was on the Hallowell Circuit in 1817 and was, according to *Case and His Contemporaries*, "the principal instrument in raising up Methodism in the Brickman neighbourhood back of Rednersville. Peter Redner became the first leader and remained faithful through a long and useful life." Adams almost perished with the cold in some of his journeys.

Calvin Flint was appointed to Hallowell Circuit in 1822. "During the year a revival took place and the first class was organized among the Dempseys on the Bay Shore. The brothers Peter, Isaac and William Dempsey were all brought in. Mr. Flint stayed several days and assisted with all his might."

In 1823 Anson Green came to the Hallowell Circuit. He went around the whole circuit of 26 appointments every four weeks. He wrote: "Our circuit takes in the whole peninsula, and is entirely surrounded by water, save the two miles at the Carrying Place... On Saturday morning I was on my new circuit, and on Sunday, the 2nd of October (1825) I commenced my work at Pleasant Bay, taking Consecon in the evening. Consecon is a small village of about 60 or 70 inhabitants. On Monday, preached in Bro. Dempsey's house. I found a lively little class of Dutchmen here, who interested me much by relating reminiscences of past days. On the 4th I rode to Mr. Redner's and preached in his house. On the 5th, in a school-house on Missassauga Point. Thursday in Bro. Snider's house. On Friday rode 12 miles to Demorestville."

Thomas Madden, George Ferguson, James Peale and W. Chamberlain were other Methodist circuit riders in the County. Through their unremitting work, armed only with a Bible, they established congregations and inspired the building of the first Methodist churches.

Churches Of Ameliasburgh Township

Consecon United Church

The first church building in Ameliasburgh Township was built in the largest settlement of the time— Consecon. It was a Methodist church. Land for the church was bought from Archibald Marsh in 1829 for £30, when George Ferguson was the Hallowell Circuit preacher. The first Quarterly meeting for the townships of Ameliasburgh and Hillier was held in the 'Chapel' in 1834. The ability to hold a Quarterly meeting— what today is called a Communion service, which was preceeded by the business meeting, usually a few days before, meant that there was now a Methodist Minister in Residence in the western end of the County of Prince Edward. For the first ones so appointed duties also included a considerable part of the south end of Murray Township as well. At quarterly business meeting, the minister was paid his three month stipend including horse keep. Thus, the Consecon church was the centre to

Consecon United Church.

which all went for 'Quarterly Service', and where business for each of the churches on the circuit was executed. The Reverend John Ryerson (a brother of Egerton) was the minister at Consecon in 1834.

To the original frame building a belfry was later added and a vestry at the rear. In 1840, sheds were built for horses and vehicles; these remained until 1951. In 1842, a parsonage of Kingston limestone was built on the back street behind the church. It served as the manse for over 100 years, until a new manse was erected in 1958.

In 1873 a Ladies' Aid was organized. By 1878 there was a flourishing Sunday School with an enrolment of 103 scholars and 10 officers and teachers. In 1953 a church hall was built, which has been an invaluable addition to

The old Consecon parsonage built in 1842.

Interior of Consecon United Church, after the fire, dedication Sunday 1981.

church and community. In 1979 a connecting corridor was built between the church and hall, also modern washroom facilities and a small meeting room.

On Sunday April 26, 1981, a blaze began in the church furnace room shortly before 9 a.m., causing an explosion which shot flames through much of the building. Due to the efforts of the Ameliasburgh Fire Department, much of the main structure was saved. Rebuilding began in June, and much of the original building was restorable. The total cost was almost $100,000. Thus, by September 1981, it was possible to hold the official reopening of an Historic building with the most up to date facilities added. This was made possible by a dedicated, hard-working congregation. Bayfield Home boys refinished all the pews as part of their donation to the cause.

Holy Trinity Anglican Church

Holy Trinity Anglican Church, Consecon.

The second church built in Ameliasburgh Township is Holy Trinity Anglican in Consecon. The site was purchased in 1847 for £10 from Reuben and Esther White, a one-quarter acre lot on Mill Street, Consecon; and a handsome stone church was erected soon afterward. The tower— a 'crown of thorns' atop a Norman Tower— is unique. The interior was renovated in 1911 and an addition to the rear provided space for a chancel and a vestry. A beautiful stained glass window was placed in memory of James A. Johnson by his widow. A new hardwood floor, a new ceiling, a brass lectern, an oak prayer desk and stall and an oak altar were added at that time. The sheds at the rear of the church were used by Sunday worshippers, but also provided shelter for the horses and vehicles of shoppers to the village during the week.

Regular services were held until 1968, and then monthly during the summer for the next ten years. However, with dwindling attendance and support, closing service of this lovely church was held on August 27, 1978, with Bishop J.B. Creeggan giving the farewell sermon. Holy Trinity was part of the Parish of Ameliasburgh, which included St. John's in Carrying Place, St. Alban's in Roblin's Mills and Holy Trinity, with the rectory at Carrying Place. In 1968 the Parish of Ameliasburgh united with the Parish of Wellington under the new name of Parish of Kente. The Reverend David Hawkins was the last rector at Holy Trinity. Township Council officially opened a portion of the church to serve the local people as a Library in February of 1979.

The Presbyterian church, Consecon

Presbyterian Church, Consecon

The Presbyterian Church stood on the Hillier side of Consecon, but drew it adherents from the Ameliasburgh side as well. It was a wooden structure covered with clapboard, topped with a belfry with a spire above it. The windows were Gothic in shape, with plain glass except for the curved section at the top which was made up of small coloured sections. There was a small balcony above the vestibule and an open shed at the rear of the church.

The congregation was small. Services were held only in the summer with student ministers serving the congregation. In 1917 no student ministers were available, and Synod regretfully decided that the Consecon Presbyterian Church was to be closed. The little congregation decided to worship with the Methodists on the other side of the creek. Thus these two congregations became one before such a national union took place in 1925. The church building was sold to the Orange Lodge for the sum of $1,200. In 1926 the trustees of S.S. 17 and 19 Hillier and Ameliasburgh rented it for the purpose of a continuation school. In 1931 Royden James bought it and used it for grain storage. In 1939 he sold it to Melvin Carnrike who used it for a garage until it burned in 1948.

Rednersville United Church.

Rednersville Church

In 1848 at a Quarterly meeting in Consecon, plans for the building of a chapel in Rednersville were discussed. Mr. Hermon promised land to the east of the store, and a subscription list was begun. When they were ready to build in 1849, the 'promised lot' had been sold so it was necessary to purchase a lot of

Rednersville United Church 1984

one-half of an acre from Richard R. Clute for the total amount of £4 9s 1½d. The original contract price was £400, but the congregation hired the stone mason Joseph Todd to lay the stone for a price of £80, and also hired H.J. Moon to dig the stone from the hill opposite. They themselves hauled the stone to the site. This reduced the contract price to £300, and final settlement saw the congregation pay Mr. George Savage an extra £25 for work he had done on the steeple and the doors. Dedication services were held on February 17, 1850 with services at '10 and 6½' with the Rev. Richard Jones, a former Superintendent as speaker.

In 1938, the church hall was added. It was the former Presbyterian church in Demorestville. At this time also, a bell was donated by Charles L. Babcock. In 1978 it was decided to renovate and add to the church hall. This has been done, with the addition of a modern kitchen, washrooms and a church office. The work was completed in 1983.

The first Albury Church built in 1850.

Albury Church

The church at Dempsey's is so listed until about 1886, when the name is changed to Albury Church. A building was built in 1850 as an Inter-denominational church on land purchased from James Peck for the sum of ten pounds. It was a stone building similar to the Rednersville church, but with three Gothic windows on each side instead of two. It was built to the east of the present church building and between the road and the cemetery which had been in use since the late 18th Century. Unfortunately, the sandy soil which made for easy interring of the dead, provided poor foundation for the

The present Albury Church built in 1898.

building. Quicksand under the building made it unsafe and unuseable not long after its construction. Mr. Peck, the owner of the land to the north of the church, constructed a hall in the upper part of his drivehouse. This was complete with a hardwood floor, and Peck's hall became a social centre, and the location for the church functions and Sunday School. Church services were held in the school built immediately west of the present Albury Church.

In 1898 the present Albury Church was built for Worship services conducted by any Protestant denomination, and for use as a burial chapel. The use of the church is controlled by seven trustees who must be resident of Ameliasburgh township. On the departure of a trustee by any means, a replacement is elected by the other six trustees. There is a story told of how a religious group, deemed unworthy by the trustees, found their platform removed and themselves locked out of the building upon their return for a second night of services. In 1967, the Annual Blossom Festival service had a priest, Rev. Terry Boyle then of St. Michael's church in Belleville as guest speaker for the first Ecumenical service held in the church. The congregation has been linked to Rednersville Circuit of the Methodist church and latterly to Rednersville Pastoral Charge of the United Church for regular Pastoral care. The building has been designated an historic site from its architectural interest, and from the fact that it is the oldest Interdenominational church in the Province.

The Methodist Church.

QUARTERLY TICKET FOR AUG., 1893.

Watch ye, stand fast in the faith, quit you like men, be strong.—1 *Corinthians* xvi. 13.

Sarah Tice .

S. A. Dupran .

Quarterly Ticket for a Methodist Church

Ameliasburgh United Church.

Ameliasburgh United Church

In 1868, Ameliasburgh church was built on land donated by Mr. and Mrs. James Coleman. The contractor was Elijah Sprague and the masons were James Spurr and Patrick McGuire. Local limestone was used for the building with the exception of the ashlars for the corners, and the window and door sills which were cut in the quarries in Kingston Penitentiary, and probably were used as ballast in ships coming to the dock in Rednersville. The copper-clad steeple is the tallest in the County. Total price of building the church was $5,000. Originally the church had a gallery on three sides, but this was removed prior to 1880.

The church was a part of the Rednersville Circuit until 1879 when a parsonage was built in Ameliasburgh and a minister was employed for the new charge. An award of Arbitration from the Conference settled the amount of equity Ameliasburgh had in the Rednersville parsonage. By this award, the Rednersville circuit were to pay the Ameliasburgh circuit $375 and "the stove in the Ameliasburgh parsonage to remain there in lieu of interest."

In June 1967, the trustees of Ameliasburgh church met for the final time and passed the following motion: "Inasmuch as the United Church at Ameliasburgh, Ontario, located in lot 82, Roblin Mills, Corporation of the Township of Ameliasburgh, and the congregation now forms a part of Wesley United Church at Mountain View, this board of Trustees unanamously supports the proposal that this historic church be sold to the Corporation of the Township of Ameliasburgh, for the nominal sum of $1, plus expenses incurred, for the purpose of a museum, to contain remembrances such as some furnishings and pictures of the former active churches in the corporation... and other historical documents and artifacts. The building to be maintained in its present state by the township council in perpetuity for this purpose. Signed by Harry Bisdee, Norris Whitney, Harry Gibson, Leo Wood, Dave Rowe, Earl Wood and Morgan Sills (Trustees). The building is now the central feature of the Ameliasburgh Museum Complex.

Centre Church

In 1868, Centre Church was built on land donated by George Roblin. It was of brick, with three windows on each side and two at the front. The entrance was unusual in that it consisted of two doors— one from either side into a vestibule. this vestibule was lighted by a window matching those on either side of the door. From the front the doors were not immediately in evidence, but rather gave the appearance of three windows. this style of entrance is noted in a few houses within the County— mostly in Picton. A

A Sunday School Convention at Centre Church Dorland Fox, care-taker, standing at the corner of the steps; in buggy in foreground are Willie Fox and sister Clara; in another buggy Edgar Redner and sister Clara; other buggies belong to Wellington Howell, Peter D. Redner and Mack Lont.

small steeple added to its attractive appearance. Inside there was a center aisle, with hand-made pine pews on either side. Stairs led to a gallery across the back. Two box stoves heated the building in the winter. In 1938 a cement block church hall was added to the back, and the horse sheds were torn down. The last service was conducted by the minister, Rev. George Ambury on Good Friday, 1966. The Centre Congregation amalgamated with the Rednersville Congregation, and the brick church was demolished in the following year.

Salem United Church

On April 24, 1850, one acre of land (part lot 89, concession 3, Ameliasburgh) was given by Roland Scriver for the building of a Wesleyan Methodist Church, but apparently members of this group could not raise sufficient funds. The Scrivers also gave the land for Salem cemetery with one of the early burials being John Scriver in 1834. A church was not built until 1870, and then it was built as a Methodist Episcopal Church on land (part lot 90) given by Samuel Simonds on December 18, 1869. The building was of brick, built very much in the style of that day. It was first on the Carrying Place circuit and changed to the Consecon circuit in 1908. The church, cemetery and school were the centre of the Salem community.

At a meeting of the Church Board in 1904, the Trustees decided to cut six inches off each end of the centre seats and to leave front and back seats loose to make it more convenient for funerals. In 1902, a Cemetery Board was organized to meet with the Church Board to draw a plan of the cemetery and allot each person interested a just and proper share of the said cemetery.

Salem Church was closed by action of Belleville Presbytery on June 30, 1967. In November 1967 the church and its contents went on the auctioneer's block. The church is now a private residence.

Salem United Church.

Wesley United Church, Mountain View.

Mountain View Wesley United Church

Land was donated on lot 68, 4th concession of Ameliasburgh, by Hulda and Cornelius Hubbs and David Sprung for the building of a church. The contract for the building of what is known today as Wesley United Church, Mountain View, was awarded to William James Davis of Belleville for $3,000. The stone foundation was laid by the local farmers and the building was erected by the builder. Dedication service was held in June 1878. In 1883 the Sunday School rooms in the basement were finished; in 1975 washrooms and an office were installed. In 1967 with the closing of several churches in the area, the congregation of Ameliasburgh and Massassaga churches amalgamated with the Mountain View congregation, and the name was changed to Wesley United Church. It is a beautiful, large building with twin towers, and the interior features a gallery on three sides.

Lightning struck the south tower of the church on June 26, 1980, doing a considerable amount of damage. Insurance covered repairs to both towers and the redecorating of the interior. Stained glass windows in the chancel were installed at the time by Mr. and Mrs. Stanley Barber.

Mountain View Church c. 1912

Left to right: back row, standing— Virgil Thompson, -- Spencer, Earl Anderson, George Anderson, George Jinks, Clement Frederick, Clark Sprung, Grace Sprung, Mrs. Ed. Hubbs, Mrs. Howard Anderson, Hazel Titus, Mrs. Wilford Potter, Adaline Sprague, Byron Frederick, Lillian Sprague, Lawrence Sprague, Charles Wood, Ira Pymer, Joshua Dodd, Howard Anderson, Alfred Post, Walter Pymer, John Tice.

Middle Row: Fred Lauder, Irene Thompson, Mrs. H.J.Parliament, Mrs. Walter Pymer, Mrs. Ira Pymer, Mrs. Greg Titus, Mrs. Frank Lauder, Henry Jason Parliament, Mrs. James R. Anderson, Mrs. Lawrence Sprague, Mrs. Clayton Sprung, Mrs. Gilford Stafford.

Front Row: Mrs. Richard VanWart. Mrs. Charles Wood, Mrs. George Anderson, Rae Eveleigh, Henry Hubbs, Gilford Stafford, Lily Anderson, Elizabeth Potter, Ruth Pymer, Percy Parliament, Hartford Parliament, Arthur Morris.

Massassaga United Church

Massassaga United Church

Massassaga was a point on the Rednersville circuit from the earliest time until 1882 when it was supplanted by Ferry Point- the present Rossmore. Later it became a point on the Ameliasburgh charge. A church was built in 1888 on lot 59 on a piece of land off the property of Robert R. Ross. All members of the congregation were urged to help pay for the church, with each child buying a brick. The church is a brick building with a vestibule and a tall tower. The steeple was struck by lightning sometime before 1920. The church was wired in the 1930's with the money being raised by the young people of the church who put on a play and presented it from place to place. Jim Broad donated an electric organ to the church in memory of his sister, Hattie Broad. After Massassaga church was closed he gave the organ to the Masonic Hall, Ameliasburgh.

Massassaga church was closed by action of Presbytery in 1967. The building was sold and has been remodelled into a private home.

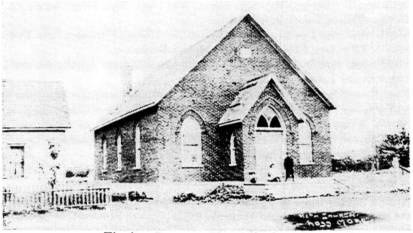

The first Rossmore Church, built 1888.

Rossmore Church

Rossmore appears on the Rednersville records for 1884 as the fourth point on that charge by its old name of Ferry Point. In 1888 a brick church was built which served the community well until 1937 when it was destroyed by fire. A new church was built on the site. Student ministers from Albert College were employed in the early days, and later it was part of the Mountain View Charge. It was closed by act of Presbytery in 1968 at the request of the congregation. The building is now a private residence.

Victoria United Church

Back row, left to right: Bruce Hennesey, J.F. Weese, Alta Adams, Mrs. Percy Catheral, Mrs. W. Bush, Mrs. Lorne Brickman, Fred Bonter, Lorne Brickman, Mrs. David Calnan, Mrs. Harry Sager, Mrs. Simon Lewis Delong. Mrs. C.G. Williams, F. Hawley, Mrs. J.F. Weese, Will Bush, Mrs. Herb Pulver, S.L. Delong, Delbert Snider, Herb Pulver.

Middle row, seated on steps: Carolla Weese, Mrs. Bruce Hennesey, Mrs. D. Snider, Mrs. S. Hennesey, Mrs. Jacob Sager, Audra Brickman,

Middle row, standing: Rev. C.G. Williams. David Calnan, Charlie Adams, Jacob Sager, Simon Lewis Delong

Front Row: Olive Adams, Ethel Glenn, Mrs. F. Hawley and baby, Mrs. Fred Bonter with Irma on her lap, Beryl Weese and Ross Hennesey, Lloyd Weese, Cecil Adams, Harold Weese

Small boys in very front: Walter and Wilfred Snider, Ceburn Adams, Arza Pulver, Melvin Pulver, Arthur Catherall

Victoria United Church

Jacob Sager and David Calnan donated land from their adjoining farms on the second Concession for the building of a church in 1897. A white frame building with a full basement was built. There were three windows on each side and a window flanking either side of the front door. Later, a cement stoop was added to the front, which housed the kitchen underneath. George Maidens was chief carpenter assisted by volunteers from the community. Dedication was held in October 1897, and as it was the Jubilee Year for Queen Victoria, the church was called Victoria Church. Members of the church became known throughout the district for the excellent chicken suppers and ice cream socials (where the ice cream was made with the hand-freezers) as well as a devoted congregation. A Sunday School had been established in the school in 1867, and this Sunday School became a nucleus of the new Congregation. The church was served from Consecon until 1915, when it became a point on the Rednersville charge. On June 4, 1967, the church celebrated its 70th Anniversary with the Rev. Verne Zufelt as special speaker.

Victoria United Church.

By action of Presbytery the church was closed June 30, 1967, and the building was demolished in 1977.

Gardenville Gospel Hall

Land was donated in November 1899 by Adam McKay and his wife Amandaville for the building of a Gospel Hall. The building, 18' by 36', was probably completed in 1900. Later a hall was added at the back. Grace Hart of Gardenville remembers Richard Irving preaching in the Gospel Hall while staying with both sets of grandparents- Mr. and Mrs. Isaac Moynes and Mr. and Mrs. John Diamond. She also recalls a Fred Peer who stayed in Gardenville one winter and preached. Previous to that he had been a missionary in

Gardenville Gospel Hall

Trinidad for some years. Wm. Hynd, who was a missionary to the Indians around Hudson Bay in the summer time, spent several winters in Gardenville. These preachers were called Plymouth Brethren. Attendance at the services was 15 to 20 persons. The Sunday School was very active. Just before Christmas, all would gather for a pot luck dinner and the receiving of Sunday School awards and the reciting of scriptures. Later the people were served from Lorne Avenue Gospel Hall, Trenton, and led by Don Sutherland. Speakers also came from Bethel Chapel, Belleville, for evening services.

In 1961 trustees Alfred Diamond and Oral Moynes handed over their trusteeship to Bill Watson of Belleville. Soon after the mission closed. The building was sold to John C. Miller who uses it for storage.

St. Alban's Anglican Church, Ameliasburgh.

St. Alban's Anglican Church, Ameliasburgh

Before St. Alban's was built Anglican services were held in the Ameliasburgh Township Hall. In 1913, land was purchased from Mr. and Mrs. Henry Duke for the sum of $100. The church was built by a Mr. Loft of Deseronto from cement blocks hand-made by John Cairns (grandfather of Bob and Alfred). It was completed at a cost of $3500. The interior is of polished tongue and groove with an intricate geometrical design on the ceiling and in the chancel. The church was consecrated on November 1, 1923 when it was finally entirely free from debt.

St. Alban's has a bell tower. Its bell was rung for over 40 years every morning at 7 a.m. as well as for church services, also on New Year's Eve by Albert File, church sexton. Mr. File purchased the lots on either side of the church, laid out the grounds, planted trees, shrubs and flowers all at his own expense, creating a beauty spot.

Regular services in St. Alban's were discontinued after Christmas 1968, but summer services are held every other week from June to September, with special services at Thanksgiving, Christmas Eve and Easter. The church is now part of the Parish of Kente, but until 1968 was part of the Parish of Ameliasburgh. In 1982 new doors were installed on St. Alban's.

In the foregoing, we can readily see the debt our generation owes to those who have gone before for the establishment of congregations and church building in our midst.

CHAPTER 24

CEMETERIES

Cemeteries of Ameliasburgh Township

Moon Family Cemetery— stones all gone ..... in Rossmore, old #14 road
Lawrence— 1 stone remaining .... Con. 1 lot 64, south of road
Post Family Cemetery .... Con. 1 lot 66, south of road
Old Pioneer Cemetery (Dempsey) .... Con. 1 lot 84, south of road
Albury— around the church .... Con. 1 lot 93
Wallbridge (Lower Massassaga) .... Con. 2 lot 53, C. Tomlinson farm
Simonds or Snider, Massassaga Road .... Con. 2 lot 61, old 14 road
Herrington— one stone, on Mac Wallbridge farmCon. 2 lot 74 south of road
Delong and Brooks Cemetery .... Con. 2 lot 92 north of road
Mountain View across from church... Con. 3 halfway up hill, old 14 road
Way Farm Cemetery .... Con. 3 lot 72 under hill
Grove Cemetery .... under hill at Ameliasburgh Village
Salem— by old church .... Con. 4 lot 90
Consecon— in the village .... Con. 4 on Wellers Bay

CHAPTER 25

EDUCATION

There were no schools and no teachers for the first settlers of Seventh Town. In fact, there were very few books. Most of the early settlers were Loyalists who, because of the haste with which they had left their homes and the long distances to be traversed, were limited in what they could carry. In many households the family Bible was the only book. For the first few years, education was neglected as the physical demands of subsistence claimed the pioneer's every thought and effort. What knowledge the children acquired was of a practical nature, the skills needed to survive, to provide a home, food and clothing. Before 1800 any children who learned to read and write did so at home, taught by their parents— if their parents were literate. Many of the early settlers themselves had very limited education.

As more settlers took up land, parents began to think of how their children could be educated. With homes few and far apart, plus the straightened circumstances of the pioneers, it was difficult for a sufficient number to unite to provide and maintain a school. There were no government funds then to assist in paying a teacher. It was up to the pioneers themselves to provide a building, pay someone to teach their children and supply board and lodging for him.

The first schools, like the dwelling houses, were crude buildings of round logs, dove-tailed at the corners. In some of the school-houses, the logs were hewn on the inside of the building and the interstices between the logs were chinked with moss and short pieces of wood split to fill the spaces, the whole plastered over with clay. They were poorly lighted, small, equipped only with rough benches without any backs, a slanting board along the wall for writing, an open fireplace, a wooden water pail and dipper, a splint broom, and a table and chair for the teacher. The teacher had the only textbooks— a speller, reader, an arithmetic and a Bible. The pupils wrote on slates.

The early teachers were often old soldiers or itinerants, of questionable fitness, possessing but a minimum of knowledge and no professional training. Sometimes they were persons with physical handicaps incapable of hard manual labour, so they were chosen to teach the young! They boarded around in the homes of their pupils. Besides their room and board they received a very small pittance which was subscribed so much per pupil by the parents.

At first the schools were open only three or four months in the winter, for the children were needed at home the rest of the year for labour in field and woods. Some of the settlers who themselves could neither read nor write thought it unnecessary for the young to be educated. "If one could read, sign his own name, and cast interest, it was looked upon as quite sufficient for a farmer." (*The Settlement of Upper Canada* by William Canniff). The pupils committed their lessons to memory and recited them to the teacher. Discipline was harsh.

There were several pioneer schools on the Bayshore in the early 1800's. Probably the first was the school at Albury, held in the basement of Captain James Peck's dwelling situtated on lot 93. This school was only kept open when a sufficient subscription was obtained to induce a teacher to come. Two years sometimes passed without any school having been kept. Reuben Potter, a surveyor, taught there, and David DeLong who later settled on lot 91, second concession Ameliasburgh. The basement was heated by an open fireplace. The seats were made of pine slabs with holes bored about a foot from each end in which the legs were inserted. Twelve to 15 children attended here. The boys sat on one side of the room and the girls on the other. Reading, writing, arithmetic and spelling comprised the entire curriculum. The teacher was paid 7s. 6d. per pupil per quarter plus his board around the neighbourhood. There were no school sections at that time, and no government grants. A few years later a log school was built to replace the Peck basement school.

There was also a log school house on lot 85 near the present Albury Community Centre, built circa 1810. It was in use for about 17 years.

In the Rednersville area, there was a log school on lot 66, owned at that time by the Post family. The pupils sat on benches with their slates on their knees. As with the others, the parents paid so much per pupil and provided the teacher with board, lodging and washing.

Consecon was another area of the township which had a very early school. There was a frame school house on the Ameliasburgh side of the village, located on the creek bank near the mill.

An itinerant teacher named Robert Laing taught at Massassaga in 1818, in a log school house on lot 60 on the hill south of the marsh, west of the Massassaga to Huff's Island road. From the Laing papers we have the following agreement:

"We the Subscribers do hereby engage and accordingly do hire Robert Laing to keep school at the school house near Mr. Essom Loveless house in Ameliasburgh on the following conditions, Vis. that he is to keep a steady day School for one quarter to commence on Friday the 8th inst. School hours to be seven hours in the day or thereabout, but in dull weather the School may be dismissed at an early hour. Every other Saturday to be a holiday— and he is not bound to keep school when there is not a proper supply of firewood. And we do promise to furnish him with board, lodging and washing for the quarter according to our several proportions.

"And to pay the Trustees for him seven shillings and six pence per quarter, for each scholar subscribed for by us severally in monthly payments.

"We promise also to pay our respective proportions to repair the school house and keep it in repair. And to furnish one cord of wood made sufficiently small by chopping or splitting for each scholar subscribed for by us or two dollars for a cord.

"We appoint Mr. John Snider to act as Trustee to receive the payments above mentioned and the supply of wood."

Ameliasburgh 6th January 1818

Subscribers Names	Number Subscribed for
Essom Loveless	2
John Snider	3
Henry Vantassel	1
David Gerow	1
John Loveless	1
William Crompton	1
-- Cross	2

Robert Laing also taught on Big Island in 1817, and in Hallowell in 1818 and 1819. He died in 1823 and his books and clothing were sold to pay his funeral expenses, with any remaining money to be divided amongst his creditors.

It was not until 1816, by the Common School Acts, that Upper Canada made a beginning in recognizing public responsibility for education. This Act made it "lawful for the inhabitants of any Town, Township, Village or place to meet together for the purpose of making arrangements for Common Schools... and so soon as a competent number of persons shall unite and build or provide a School House, engage to furnish twenty scholars or more, and shall in part provide for the payment of a teacher, it shall be lawful for such persons to meet to appoint three fit and discreet persons Trustees to the said Common School, who shall have the power and authority to examine into the moral character and capacity of any person willing to become Teacher of such Common School and being satisfied of the moral character and capacity of such Teacher, to appoint such person as the Teacher of said Common School." All teachers had to be British subjects. There was no provision made for training teachers.

Limited provincial grants were available if the school could meet these requirements. The fact that trustees are mentioned in the Massassaga contract and that a school house was provided would indicate that an effort was being made to operate the school under the act of 1816, and therefore receive a government grant. But to secure such a grant they would have required at least 20 scholars, which they had not.

In 1816 there was only one 'recognized school' in Prince Edward County, and it was in Sophiasburgh, and only nine in the whole Midland District. In

1818 there was one 'recognized school' in Ameliasburgh, with 24 pupils, teacher James Rankin, no location given in the Board of Education report. The number of the whole district had increased to 31. This report regrets the use of American textbooks i.e. Webster's Speller and the American Preceptor. The General Report of the Common Schools in the Midland District in 1829 indicated that there were 43 teachers qualified to collect part of the government grant. Only two qualified in Ameliasburgh— James Patterson, native of Ireland, 38 students in his school, second concession Ameliasburgh, texts used: Testaments, English reader, American Selection; and Patrick Jones with 28 students, no location given.

Grants, or no grants, the residents of Ameliasburgh continued to build schools. The first ones were along the Bayshore, in Consecon and at Massassaga but, as the back concessions became settled, other schools were built. In 1827 a log school house was constructed at Youngs. By 1830 both Roblin's Mills and north Lakeside had log schools; one was built at Centre in 1832, and the Snider school in 1834, on lot 74, fourth concession of Ameliasburgh. It was built on the Henry Snider farm, later owned by the Lauders. Pilewell, an Englishman, and Philip Harns were two teachers in the Snider school. Salem had a frame school house in 1833 and Victoria in 1836. Both Mountain View and Little Kingston built log schools in 1838.

The Common School Bill of 1841 provided for the allotment of money to each county, on condition of its raising an equal amount by local assessment. Each Township in each County in Upper Canada was divided into School Districts by the District Councils. It was not until 1849 that the word 'district' was changed to 'section.' In February, 1842, the Municipal Council of the district of Prince Edward in its first session passed an ordinance to divide the several townships of Prince Edward into school districts, and laid out the metes, bounds and numbers of the school districts in all the townships.

Various revisions were made in the section boundaries over the next 30 years. By the Education Act of 1871 common schools became public schools and the name 'Grammar School' was abolished. It made schools free for pupils and completely supported by public funds. It also established compulsory education for children ages 7 to 12. All townships were required to define school section boundaries, which Ameliasburgh Township Council did on Nov. 2, 1871. Ideally the school was located in the middle of the section, so no child would have more than two miles to walk.

Ameliasburgh had several union sections: #5 Ameliasburgh with #1 Murray, with the school on the Murray side of Carrying Place; #14 Ameliasburgh and #4 Hillier, with the school in Hillier (Burr's); #19 Ameliasburgh and #6 Sophiasburgh, with the Union School in Ameliasburgh (Mountain View).

School section #1 was orginally Rossmore, but later the boundaries of #2 and #6, were altered to include the Rossmore section. The number 1 was given to Huff's Island School Section in 1878.

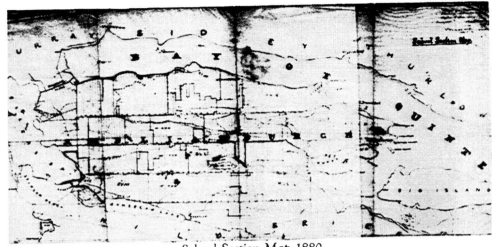

School Section Map 1880

Egerton Ryerson, as Superintendent of Education from 1844 to 1875, established the Ontario school system. He set up a strong central authority to prepare regulations, to draw up a course of studies for the whole province, to enforce the use of a single set of authorized textbooks, and to control the qualifications of teachers. In 1850 he introduced Normal School training. In 1874 a uniform entrance examination to High School was established. This set standards for public school work and a level at which High School work would start. Many residents of Ameliasburgh can recall going to the township hall to write their entrance exams.

The one-room school is a thing of the past. Most of them did an excellent job, depending on the teachers. With eight grades, the students had to learn to work alone; it taught them to be self-reliant. They learned a lot from listening to the other grades.

The schools of the 1930's were lacking in many of our modern facilities. A typical school was equipped with registers, a regulation strap, a hand bell, a box of chalk and several erasers on the chalk rail, a yardstick, clock, a globe and wallmaps and the Union Jack. Parents had to buy all the textbooks, scribblers, pencils and crayons that were used. Most schools had a few shelves of library books; any good ones were threadbare. Plasticene was used by the younger children to illustrate their stories.

A detailed time-table was on the wall. School was opened with the Lord's prayer in unison, a short Bible reading and a children's hymn. The teacher usually read aloud after the noon hour. The pupils heard many good books this way.

To make copies of maps, exercises and tests, the teacher used a gelatine hectograph. This was a shallow tray, the size of a sheet of foolscap, filled with clear gelatine. After preparing the master copy, the gelatine surface was moistened, the exercise placed on it and smoothed to all edges. With the master removed, copy after copy could be made.

Morley Dempsey,
Truant Officer for many years

Arbour Day was the first Friday in May. The morning was spent raking the yard and making and planting a flower bed. In the afternoon the teacher and pupils enjoyed a hike to nearby woods.

The Christmas concert was a big event. For weeks previous, every noon hour was spent rehearsing plays, drills and songs. All the little children had recitations. The concerts were attended by everyone in the neighbourhood.

Physical education? How did a teacher deal with it in one room with 20 to 40 pupils and an equal number of seats, a large stove and other furnishings. It consisted mainly of reaching and bending exercises by straight rows of pupils in aisles, for a few minutes as a break from lessons. Most of the pupils had walked from half a mile to two miles before school started. Also children knew how to play in those days and everyone did play at noon hour and recesses—three deep, pom-pom pullaway, baseball, hopscotch, red light, and in the winter, fox and geese.

Rossmore Schools

When the school sections were first laid out in 1842, the Rossmore area was school section #1. Its boundaries were as follows: "Commencing at Henesey's Point, and extending to the west side of lot no. 71." A small frame school house was built in 1839, location unknown. The attendance was small, and it seems to have functioned for only 15 years. In 1852 it was open for only three months. Later the school section boundaries were altered so that lots 60 to 63 were included in the Massassaga (S.S. #6) section, and the Rednersville section was extended to the east side of lot #64.

Rossmore had its own school again in the 1870's and 80's. Those were the sawmill days, and Rossmore became a booming village. The population increased enormously with the influx of millhands and their families. Many of these were French with names such as Herbert, Goyer, Laveolett and Bovineau. To provide schooling for the many children, a two-roomed frame school house was built inside the mill yard near the mill office. Burtson Laveolett, daughter of one of the mill workers, was born in Rossmore and started to school in the mill yard school. She recalls that there were about 50 pupils in the summer, but a great many more in the winter, as the boys worked in the mill in the summer. Her first teacher was Carp Howell, later George Trumpour and Lettie Welsh. Trumpour died, as a very young man, while teaching in Rossmore; he was the father of Grace (later Mrs. Sam Monroe) and Zella (Mrs. Willie Fox), and lived in Rossmore where the present Highway 14 (62) intersects the old road. The Laveoletts returned to Quebec in 1893, as the mill closed and Rossmore became almost a ghost town.

The mill school closed in 1890, and all the pupils from Rossmore thereafter went to Massassaga School. At a school meeting on Dec. 26, 1894, the school house was put up for auction and sold to Edgar Gerow for $30.50; the stove and pipes were sold to George Weese for $1.70. The school was taken down and rebuilt as a cooperage shop next to the Rossmore church. Later when the barrel business declined, the building was taken down again and moved west of the Herrington barn, west of the village, to be used as a machine shed.

Huff's Island School

School Section #1 Ameliasburgh

Huff's Island was originally part of School Section #11, Mountain View. We can understand how this would be, as at the time school sections were established in 1842, the entire east end of the island was clergy reserve, and there were few children from the island to attend the first log Mountain View School located at the corner near the present Barber's greenhouses. But when the stone schoolhouse was built in 1855 at the Union (Mountain View), it meant a great distance for the Huff's Island children to go. In 1871 Huff's Island was still part of the #11 school section. An Ameliasburgh Township By-Law of Nov. 2, 1871 reads: "School section #11 shall comprise and include all of Point B in the third concession..." Huff's Island was Point B.

In 1857 James Nightingale and John Dew purchased all the east end of Huff's Island, Nightingale settled on lot 8 soon after. Dew sold most of his to others. (See Chapter on *Huff's Island.*) By the mid 1860's there were many more families and children of school age on the island. There was an increasing concern to have a school of their own on the island. Council also was receptive to this idea. In February 1859, Ameliasburgh Township Council heard the petition of Daniel Gerow and others to divide Huff's Island and attach part of it to No. 6 (Massassaga). Council decided against, stating: "such division is not the best for the inhabitants of said island but would recommend the inhabitants of said island to build a schoolhouse and have their own school." That is just what the residents decided to do. In the Diary of Thomas

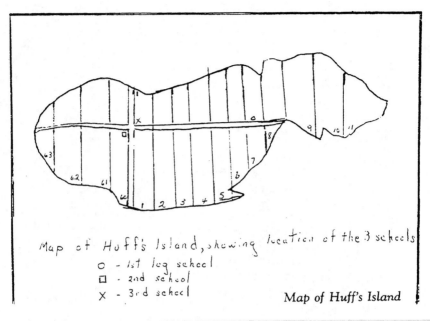

Map of Huff's Island, showing location of the 3 schools

○ - 1st log school
□ - 2nd school
× - 3rd school

Map of Huff's Island

Huff's Island school 1878-1915, Maud Conklin Young at the door.

Huff's Island school in 1923. Left to right, Mary Wallbridge, Edith Wallbridge, Mary Ellen Black, Beatrice Wallbridge, Olive Nightingale, Ethel Barber, Martha Ireland, Mabel Hatfield, Phyllis Wallbridge, Roberta Wallbridge, Teacher Edna Fleming, John Black, Allan Wallbridge, Donald Hatfield, Henry Wallbridge, Mac Wallbridge, Jack Motley.

Huff's Island school in 1959 when the Grade 3's from Mountain View were bused to Huff's island; teacher Hazel Spencer taught a total of 22 years at Huff's Island and Kente.

Seventh Town/Ameliasburgh

Nightingale under the date Jan. 8, 1868, we find the following notation: "Father, Joseph, Nash, John and I went up to the school meeting. Voted for W. Cook as trustee. W. Wood got put in as trustee. The whole of them signed a paper for us to have a branch school." Thomas, Joseph, Ignatious and John were all sons of James Nightingale. Evidently they were successful with their petition for a notation for May 11, 1868 reads: "Louisa Huff commenced to teach this morning." Louisa was an island girl, daughter of Peter Huff and granddaughter of Solomon.

This first school was a log building located on the north side of the road on lot 7, across from the present Hatfield home. Louisa Huff continued to teach the island children, for in the Nightingale Diary for July 27, 1869 we find: "Wm. Cook was here to get signers to have Louisa Huff continue her school." One other mention of the school on May 4, 1871 reads: "Joseph and Stewart cleaning out schoolhouse."

By 1878 the Huff's Island residents had been successful in having a separate school section established for the island. A small frame schoolhouse was built across the road from the present building, on the southwest corner, on land donated by Alger Huff. An old record book gives the minutes of the first meeting of S.S. 1, Ameliasburgh on Jan. 9, 1878, when trustees Joseph Nightingale, Albert Huff and James Latimer were elected. It was decided to make a contract with Lewis Conklin for five cords of "body wood and it to be dry." The first teacher, S.C. Gardner, took up her duties on Jan. 29, 1878, at a salary of $18.00 a month.

At a meeting on March 12, 1878 the trustees agreed to purchase a map of the Dominion of Canada, a map of Europe, a map of the world, a map of America, a tablet of reading lessons, a six inch globe and a numeral frame. In 1880 they built a woodshed and a fence, also purchased 15 desks. In 1879 Maggie Rowe of Consecon taught for $200.00 per annum; in 1880 Grace Rothwell was the teacher, and Ida Fox in 1881. At that time the calendar year was the school year. The Island school enrolment was never large.

In 1915 the schoolhouse was destroyed by fire and the present brick building erected that same year. It was built by William Hall on a lot purchased from Lewis Conklin for $100. It was the most modern in design of all old one-room schools and had one feature very different from all the rest. It was built with a basement and heated by a furnace. A well was dug by A. Denison. Zetta Caskey was the first teacher in the new school.

In 1940 a piano was purchased and Miss Velma Vandewater hired to teach music. The teacher received a new desk in 1944, and the school a new roof and insulation. Electricity and inside chemical toilets were installed in 1947. In 1966 after Kente School was built the Island school building was purchased by the community as a community centre, and as such it is still maintained today.

Rednersville Schools

School Section #2 Ameliasburgh

The first school in the Rednersville area was a log schoolhouse built close to the Bay on the John Post property, lot 66, concession 1. It was 12 feet by 10 feet with two windows on the east side, two on the west, and a door facing the road. The furniture consisted of a table and chair for the teacher and benches for the pupils. The blackboard was made of boards painted black. This log school was built in the early 1800's. The first teacher was Mr. Abrams, a retired sergeant of an English regiment. As the custom was, he 'boarded round'. Children only attended school in the winter months when there was no work to keep them at home. Philo Nobles also taught in this school. Fire destroyed this log school.

In 1836 a frame schoolhouse was built in the village of Rednersville. It was located south of Spurgeon Dempsey's on what was designated on early plans of Rednersville as East Street. Its dimensions were 20 by 24 feet. It served as a school until 1855 when a larger school was built east of the village. The old building fell into disrepair and eventually was torn down.

In 1855 a stone schoolhouse was erected on lot 73 on the south side of the road. The first teacher in this school was Lucy E. Morden who had an enrolment of 80 pupils— 35 boys and 45 girls. Rednersville was always a large school. In 1895 this stone schoolhouse partially burned.

Another school was built on the same site, using much of the stone and timber of the old school. Like the former, it consisted of one room with two windows and a door facing the road and two windows on each side. A small front porch was added later. The heating system was a box stove. A slate blackboard was installed in 1918, and a belfry in 1919. George Moore, the teacher at that time, had 60 pupils.

Rednersville school circa 1910.

In 1935 the school was remodelled in accordance with the new idea of having all the windows on one side, and stucco was applied to the outside of the building. Hydro was installed in 1936. In 1942, the school was so overcrowded that it was decided to use the Rednersville United Church hall as a Primary School for Grades 1, 2 and 3. Primary grades continued to use the Church hall for 14 years. In 1955 Hanthorn's Bus Service of Carrying Place was hired to pick up the primary children at the Senior School and transport them to the Church hall on the way back from his High School route to B.C.I.

By 1955 also discussion began regarding a new school because both schoolrooms were overcrowded, with about 85 pupils at this time. A lot 300 feet by 500 feet was purchased from Leon Ward for $4,500. The new school was completed in the fall of 1956— a very attractive three-room school with a teachers' room, utility room and washrooms. The old school and lot was sold to Ross Roblin in 1959 for the sum of $600 on condition that the building be torn down and the ground levelled within three months of the transfer of title.

Grades 1 to 8 attended the new Rednersville school until 1966 when Kente opened. Then Grades 1 to 6 continued at Rednersville for three years. In

Rednersville school 1940; back row, left to right: Barbara Roblin, Marguerite Boomhour, Noreen Farley, Gwen Loney, teacher William Bowerman, Jeanette Irish, Betty Landry, Fred Teney, Gordon Roblin. 2nd row— Irene Boomhour, Wilma Redner, Lois Irish, Janet Robertson, Muriel Boomhour, Laura Boomhour, Laura Farley, Bruce Smith, George Loney. 3rd Row— Lorne Bowerman, Fred Cleave, Ralph Loney, Jim Tanner, Carl Farley, Lloyd Loney, Peter Robertson, Don Farley, Ronald Post. Front row— Bill Babbitt, John Wannamaker, Bill Post, Norman Post, Lyle Wannamaker.

September, 1969, more changes were made under the County Board of Education, with Grades 1, 2, 3 at Mildred Corke and Grades 4, 5, 6 at Rednersville, and Richard McQuoid principal of both schools. In 1976, Hester Giles became principal of Massassaga, Rednersville and Mildred Corke. In 1977 Mildred Corke was closed, all the Grade 5 pupils from the township went to Kente, Rednersville became a primary school with grades 1, 2, 3. Mrs. Giles continuing as principal of Massassaga-Rednersville. With the resignation of Mrs. Giles in June 1982, Carl Wood became the principal of the combined schools.

Present Staff (1984) at Rednersville:

Kindergarten— Carole Ring, ½ time

Grade 1— Joanne Menzies

Split 1 and 2— Lynda Roblin

Rednersville School 1984

The Red School

School Section #3 Ameliasburgh

The first school was a crude log building with a roof thatched with marsh hay, built about 1810, on lot 85, just east of the present Albury Community Centre. The first teacher was a John Smith, the second Abijah Benedict. Dr. Dunn, Philo Nobles and Patrick Jones were other early teachers in this school. It served until 1827.

In the year 1827, Elias Alley gave the east half of lot 86 in the first concession of Ameliasburgh- "for the sole purpose of erecting thereon a house where a common Day School may be taught, and occasionally answer for a place of Divine Worship when any Minister of any Christian Denominational may think to make an appointment to preach the gospel in the said House, nevertheless these meetings must not interfere or incommode the school or teacher during the school hours. But with the advice and consent of John Babcock, Francis Weese and James Andrew, the present trustees who have been chosen to superintend the erecting of the aforesaid house, ... I, Elias Alley, do give, grant and confirm all that parcel of land being composed of the east part of lot number eighty-six, containing by admeasurement one quarter of an acre."

Timber for the school was cut on the property and floated down to Kingston where it was sawed into lumber for the walls, floor and benches. In 1872 the school was plastered by Thos. McMurter who received the sum of $10 for the job. In 1892 a new floor was laid. In 1895 the school was repaired,

S.S. # 3 c. 1924: Back row— Anne Bent, Helen Weese, Geraldine Allison, teacher H. Richards, Florence Dawson, Marguerite McLeod; Middle row— Summers Dawson, Vernon Thompson, Janet Adams, Evelyn Thompson, Ruth Bent, Marjorie Weese, Marguerite Dawson, Beuford Peck, Mac Thompson. Front row— Gerald Thompson, Gordon Allison, Edwin Bent, Randall Allison, Raymond McLeod, Borden Thompson, Kirby Thompson, Gerald Dawson.

clapboarded and painted red. It thus became known as the 'Red School House'. Although it was repainted in 1910 in a grey colour, it was still referred to as the 'Red School'. In 1900 a belfrey was added and a bell installed. In 1911 a quarter of an acre of the southwest corner of lot 85 was purchased from Corintha Moore for $100 to enlarge the school grounds.

At one time the school house was used for church services every Wednesday night. The ministers were Mr. Forrester (Church of England) and Mr. Pickit (Methodist).

Other items from school records:

1863— corn broom 25¢, ½ quire of paper 10¢
1866— 2 gal. soap 35¢; tablet of lessons $1.25
1885— boxstove $4.75
1887— blackboard $3.00
1889— woodshed, walk and privy screen $10.50
1890— 6 seats $1.25 each, 1 numeral frame $1.00, 1 map of Ontario $5.25
1895— 18 school seats $70.00
1897— blinds $2.25, shingled school $17.00
1899— globe $3.00, outhouse $4.96
1903— teacher's desk $15.00
1904— outhouse $7.00
1911— fence and gates $20.00
1913— school yard levelled $37.00
1917— flag pole erected $7.00
1921— porch built
1923— benches from sides taken out
1924— old desks taken out and new individual desks installed
1929— new woodshed and outbuildings, school house painted grey
1937— desks changed to west side
1938— new cupboards and Findlay stove, noon lunches prepared and served
1940— music instruction begun, Velma Vanderwater first music teacher
1943— piano purchased
1950— swings erected
1953— oil stove installed

In January 1959, the new two-room Albury Public School opened. This was a union of school sections 3 and 4, so the 'Red School' ceased to function as a school for several years. However, in 1964, the new composite school became so overcrowded that the old school was taken over again as a classroom for two years for grades 3 and 4.

Now painted white with green trim, the 'Red School' serves as Albury Community Centre. It was turned over to the Centre's Board of Trustees in 1967 for the sum of $1.00. The bell from the belfrey was donated to Albury Church and installed in its tower. The Centre is used for meetings, euchre parties, quiltings and as a voting station during elections.

Albury Schools

School Section #4 Ameliasburgh

The first school at Albury was held in the basement of Captain James Peck's dwelling. Here the children of the area received some schooling for three or four months in the winter, whenever someone could be found to teach them for his board and a small sum per pupil. This served for several years, then a log school house was built on the west side of the road near the turn on Onderdonk's hill.

According to old records, on June 13, 1833, the citizens of the area "met pursuant to notice and determined to build a frame school house to meet the growing wants of the time" on a site just west of the Albury Church. The agreement reads: "Know all men by these presents. That we whose names are affixed do each severally promise to pay Peter Dempsey, James Peck Jr., John Sager and William Dempsey, who are appointed a building committee, the sums set opposite our respective names on this paper for the purpose of building a school house in the township of Ameliasburgh, said house to stand on the premises of James Peck Sr., lot 93 1st concession at a place selected by said committee. The size of said house to be 24 x 28 feet on the ground; all money to be paid by the first of January next. Different kinds of produce will be taken in payment at the market price." Then followed a list of 31 subscribers while several others signed for four or five days work. William Dempsey contracted to build the school house and accepted the subscription list in payment of said contract. John Sager took the job of building the foundation. The building was not completed till October, and was not finished as agreed. At each school meeting for years the question of completing the

Albury School c. 1891: Back row, George Williamson, Helen Peck, Effie Peck, --, 5 Will Peck, last person in back row, Francis Peck. Middle row- 1 Roy Williamson, 2 Ida Williamson, extreme right Annie Peck. Front row- 4 Lena Sager and 7 Hessie Bryant

Albury School c. 1925: Back row— Harold Bonter, Eleanor Bonter, Teacher Mildred Corke, Bob Dempsey, Jean Allison. Front row— Dorothy Peck, Isabel Peck, Marjorie Peck, Dorothy Jean Peck, Ivy Pashley, Ruth Williamson, Evelyn Bonter.

school house was brought up by David Pierson who never lost the opportunity of reminding the contractors that they had received their pay but had never finished the contract. John Sager insisted that he had done his job. Pierson said that he had not, as there were three large openings in the foundation. Sager said they were only cat holes, and that, if you did not leave cat holes in the underpinning, the building would soon rot. Pierson said they were very large cat holes and a yoke of two year old steers could be driven through these holes.

For a time the funds for the upkeep of this school were obtained by collecting, from each resident sending children to school, a small fixed sum per month for each child, and from a tax levied on the property in the section. Each year a resident was appointed as collector in the section. Each one sending pupils to school had to furnish wood for the school, usually one-half cord each.

During the early part of 1871, the school house burned. Until a site could be chosen and a new school built, the shop of William A. Fones was rented and used as a school. A controversy arose over the site, with those living in the western part of the section determined to have the school above the Onderdonk hill in their area, and those living east of the hill objecting. Some litigation ensued and those residing in the west end of the section came out second best. A new school was built on lot 94 below the hill on the farm of William T. Dempsey. The contract for building a frame school was given to Jacob McMasters in April, 1873 with the building completed in July of that year. This building continued to function as a school until January 1959 when school sections no. 3 and 4 opened their new Albury two-room school. The old school was purchased by Bonters' Bayview Orchards and is used as a bunkhouse for off-shore workers.

Miss Mildred Corke came to Albury to teach at S.S. No. 4 in 1923, and taught there continuously until 1959 when she and her pupils moved into the new school. She taught the senior room there for three years until her retirement. On June 23, 1962, Miss Corke was honoured at a testimonial evening. She had taught at Albury for 39 years. The new two-roomed Albury school was officially named the 'Mildred Corke School' in her honour.

When Kente School opened in the fall of 1966, Mildred Corke School remained open, accommodating Grades 1 to 5. A portable classroom was added in 1968. More changes came with the County Board of Education in 1969 when Mildred Corke became a primary school with Grades 1 to 3. Due to falling enrolment, the school was closed in 1977. The property was sold to the Quinte Polonia Club in 1981.

Mildred Corke School, as it is today— Quinte Polonia.

Massassaga Schools

School Section #6 Ameliasburgh

As early as the winter of 1818, a group of parents in the Massassaga area were so concerned about schooling for their children that they provided a building and hired an itinerant teacher, Robert Laing, for three months to teach 11 children from seven families. We do not know if they hired Laing again, or someone else, in successive winters, but it would appear some attempt was being made to keep a school open for at least a few months a year.

Archival records for 1851 give 1833 as the date that a frame school, 30 feet by 24 feet, was built at Massassaga. This school gave service until 1855 when a stone building replaced it. This was located just to the west of the present school. G.W. Wright was the teacher in 1855 with an enrolment of 106. Attendance did not match enrolment, however, as many children attended only a few months of the year. There were 134 on the register in 1870, teacher James H. Benson. Teaching consisted mainly of hearing pupils recite what they had memorized.

In 1890 the Rossmore mill school closed, and all the pupils from Rossmore henceforth attended the Massassaga school.

At a school meeting held on June 15, 1901, it was moved by Alfred Anderson and seconded by Frank Hebert that a new school be built, the $1500 cost to be defrayed by issuing three year debentures. This school also was of stone, built on the present site, with the door opening to the south. During the year 1923 the attendance rose to 60 pupils so the trustees, after consultation with the inspector, F.P. Smith, decided to partition the school and make two rooms. To provide for better circulation of heat, the divider did not go to the ceiling or floor, which meant it was not much of a sound barrier. Sometimes things were hurled over the top or under the partition, as George Flower recalls. A second teacher was hired at Easter 1923. In 1925 during a severe electrical storm the school house was struck by lightning and burned to the ground. The stone foundation, the bell and the outside toilets were all that were saved from the fire.

At a meeting June 8, 1925, it was decided to use the same foundation for a new school, and the trustees called for plans and tenders. The tender of Jack

Massassaga School c. 1920

Stacey of Trenton for $12,000 was accepted. A brick school was built on the old stone foundation with two classrooms and a teacher's room on the second floor. The basement was used as a play area on rainy days and a storage place for wood for the hot air furnace. The entrance door opened to the west. There were two staircases to the upper floor, with a cloakroom at the foot of each, and a place for lunch pails at the top of each. The bell from the former school was hung in the new belfry with the rope hanging down into the teacher's room. The bell has a crack in it, which may have been caused by the intense heat of the fire. Oak desks and teachers' tables were installed in the classrooms.

On May 12, 1937, the Coronation of King George VI occurred. The Massassaga school received two little acorns from the oak tree in Windsor Forest, England which were planted in the school yard. Only one of the acorns grew; it became a beautiful oak tree which is still in the Massassaga school yard.

In 1946 a coal-burning hot air furnace was installed to replace the former one. The coal was fed to it by means of a stoker. Septic or chemical toilets were installed in the basement, and a well was drilled to the south of the school. A fire escape was built on the east side of the school in 1949, with a door opening into the larger room. Martha Bates started to teach at Massassaga in January of 1949 and continued until June 1964, and was the principal for all those years.

In January of 1952, Massassaga became a three-room school with the addition of a room on the southwest corner. A new entrance was made to the south. In September 1957, a fourth room was opened on the northwest corner, and a north door added. Baseboard radiators were installed in all the classrooms, providing heat from a new oil-fired, hot water furnace and circulating pump. Two washrooms and an office were built in the former

Massassaga School c. 1984

basement play area. Land was acquired from Mr. Beaumont, west of the school to enlarge the playground. A new well was drilled on the west side which provides sufficient water for two drinking fountains, flush toilets and washing facilities.

In September, 1963, a fifth room was added on the northeast corner of the school. These additional rooms are all of brick construction. Hester Giles served as principal from September 1947 to June 1948; she returned to Massassaga as a teacher in 1960, was principal from 1963 to 1982. A portable classroom was added in 1969 and another in 1975. The first one was sold and removed in June 1980. The second one is no longer a classroom, but is used for Physical Education and special classes and programs.

The staff in 1984 at Massassaga:

Principal— Carl Wood

Grade 5— Carl Wood (a.m.), Judy Galway (p.m.)

Grade 4— Audrey Papineau

Grade 3— Wilma Adams

Grade 2— Mary Lou Van Haarlem

French— Jean St. Jean

Special Education— Lynda Sommer

Religion (Volunteer)— Twila Langman

Caretaker— Roger Flower

Massassaga staff in Centennial Year, 1967—
J. Menzies, Helen Welsh, Iola Brummel, Edna Welsh and Principal Hessie Giles.

Centre School

School Section #7 Ameliasburgh

By Donald Spencer, Secretary/Treasurer for 27 yrs.

The first school in Centre Section was a small log building located on the corner of the lot directly across the road from the one which still stands on lot 77 on the corner of the Second Concession and County Road 23. This log school was built and in use about 1832.

In 1849 a small stone school was contructed on the present site on land rented from William Brickman. One-half acre was purchased from him in 1863 for $35. There were two windows on the north side, two on the south side and two more in the front or east side, the latter two of which were rendered almost useless by the later erection of a porch across the whole front of the school, which contained only a door and no windows. This porch was used also as a wood shed. The pupils hung their coats and hats on nails driven in the side of the wall. The window sills were used to store dinner pails and surplus garments. The floor was badly worn with knots protruding from masses of splinters. The seats were made entirely of wood and were nailed to the floor, while a row of benches ran along each side of the room. These were used by the small pupils. There was a big box stove in the middle of the school room.

Until 1863 there was practically no school yard, but in that year another half acre was bought. In 1882 another quarter acre on the south side of the lot was purchased from D.A. Howe for $25. Early records show that Benjamin Rothwell was the teacher from 1877 until 1882. His last contract was drawn in 1879 for a term of three years at a salary of $500 per annum.

On January 5, 1882, a meeting of ratepayers was held which authorized the erection of a new school. The chairman of the meeting was S.M. Herrington and the secretary John A. Howell. A new brick school was built and occupied in 1883, with Findlay Spencer as teacher. Before the new school was built the taxes on a $5000 assessment in the section amounted to $17.50. In 1902, J.E. Benson recorded in his register a notation that the worst storm in 20 years occurred the first week in February and 20 men were employed getting the stage through.

In June 1937 an interesting event occurred in the section in the form of an

Centre School

Centre School c. 1900, teacher Ed Benson, back row no. 2 Roy Giles, 4 Dora Spencer, 6 Muriel Howe, 8 Burton Fox, 9 Ray Fox. Middle row— 3 Freeman Spencer, 5 Edgar Redner, extreme right Gerald Young. Front row— 1 Marguerite Townsend, 6 Clara Redner, 7 Leonard Young.

YOU ARE CORDIALLY INVITED TO ATTEND

Centre S. S. No. 7, Ameliasburg

Back-to-School Reunion

Wednesday, June 30th

AFTERNOON AND EVENING

Roll Call at 2 o'clock. Come back and renew old acquaintances.

Lunch Served.   Special Attractions

Kindly Reply.   D. K. SPENCER, Sec., Belleville, R. 1.

Invitation to 1937 Reunion.

Old Boys and Girls reunion. The afternoon session was chaired by Douglas Redner with a former teacher, Dorland Morden, and the Hon. Nelson Parliament, former student, delivering addresses. The evening address was given by Walter Herrington K.C. of Napanee, also a former pupil. Mr. Herrington described early life in the Bay of Quinte district and especially in Centre neighbourhood. Entertainment was provided by members of the R.C.A.F. station at Trenton. An enjoyable time was spent by many old pupils renewing acquaintances.

The brick school did service from 1883 until 1966 when Kente School was opened. Then Centre School was sold to Mr. and Mrs. Elmer Young to be used as an antique shop.

Victoria School

School Section #8 Ameliasburgh

Victoria was known as Bush's in the 1800's, and the School as Bush's school. It was 1897 before a church was built. As that year was the Diamond Jubilee of Queen Victoria, it was named Victoria Church; soon the neighbourhood too became known by that name.

The first school was built in 1836. It was a frame building. Its location is thought to have been on the Weese sideroad. When it ceased to serve as a school, the building was moved to the foot of the McIntyre hill and used as a drive-house for many years.

The 1885 report of the Superintendent of the School gives the following information: teacher in 1855- Peter Stoneburgh; number of pupils— 57, 30

Pupils and teacher at the old brick school at Victoria 1895. Note bolts through the walls to keep the building together.

Victoria School 1922. Back row Joe Foley, Clarence Vanclief, Orval Taft, Roy Brickman, Harry Knox, Haviland Hubbs, Harold Wannamaker, Gerald Brickman, Gerald Pope, Clayton Wannamaker, Harmon Montgomery, John Badgley, Teacher Jim Grimmon, Geraldine Weese, Alice Hubbs, Gladys Knox, Evelyn Montgomery, Irma Wannamaker, Vivian Green. Front row— Bill Knox, Ernie Butchie, Ralph Henessey, Leslie Pope, Jack Delong, Madeline Butchie, Margaret Knox, Evelyn Calnan, Kathleen Montgomery, Florence Hubbs.

boys and 27 girls; school was open for six months and one day in 1855. From 1867 to 1870 the teacher was Henry Jason Parliament. He organized a Sunday School in 1867 in the school house. Church was also held in the school building. The first year he taught school at Bush's, Mr. Parliament recalled that a wagon drove up to the school house one morning with four men in it, all armed with guns, several dogs following the wagon. The men asked him to go with them to kill a bear which was over in the woods about a half mile away. He told them he would be delighted to go, but that his contract with the trustees did not include bear hunting. They went on without him, but were back about an hour later with a large bear, dead, in the wagon. Mr. Parliament boarded around, one week in a home, then on to another. He said it was a first-class picnic for him, eating the bountiful meals provided by the kind-hearted mothers in the homes of this section. He received a salary of $300 a year and paid $1.50 a week board.

In April, 1879, Mr. and Mrs. Albert Sager donated one-half acre of land on the north-east corner of lot 88, second concession of Ameliasburgh, on which a brick school was constructed. It was the same size as the present structure and very similar as to windows and front door, but the ceiling was lower. It was heated by a large wood-burning box stove. Scholars sat in iron-frame double desks. Some of these desks are now in the school-room at the Ameliasburgh Museum. This school was used until 1904 when it became unsafe and was torn down. Mrs. Morton Weese in 1894 received $275, and out of her salary she was expected to pay the janitor, who was one of the older boys in the school. He built the fires for about $1.50 a month. Mrs. Weese recalled giving the school a good cleaning every Friday to ready for Church in the school on Sunday.

In 1904 the present frame school building was erected. Water always had to be carried from a nearby home. In 1927 a well was drilled but the water was salty. In 1930 the school was painted inside and out, re-roofed, the foundation was plastered, new toilets and cement sidewalks built. Hydro was not installed until 1945. When Victoria School was closed in 1966 it was purchased by Harmon Montgomery.

School Section #9 Ameliasburgh

When the school sections were laid out in 1841, the plan included school section #9 on the upper second concession of Ameliasburgh. A frame schoolhouse was built in 1843 on the north side of the road at the end of the Snider crossroad. This property was owned at that time by Ezra R. Bonter whose farm extended along the west side of the sideroad.

According to the Annual Report for 1855 of the Superintendent of Common Schools, the teacher in 1855 was William A. Brickman whose salary was 16 pounds 10s. and his board supplied. He had an enrolment of 42 pupils, of whom 24 were boys and 18 girls. School was kept open for only six months that year. Later Thomas McMurter was a teacher in this school and had in his classroom nine Alyea boys. This school had only a brief existence of 27 years, for it was closed in 1869.

A new brick school was erected at the south end of the Snider crossroad in 1870 by the trustees of School Section #13 on a piece of land purchased from Ezra Bonter off the back end of his farm. The decision was made to close the little frame school in #9, with the pupils from the east side of the Bryant crossroad to the top of what is now Taft's hill henceforth to attend school in S.S. #13 (Adams School). Those pupils west of the Bryant sideroad went to S.S. #10 (Young's). We can only speculate about the reasons for closing the school, perhaps falling enrolment and the condition of the school building. It was a long walk for those pupils who had to go to #13 and, in the winter, a cold one through a sideroad which was not kept open.

Young's School

School Section #10 Ameliasburgh

The first school was a log school house built in 1827 on lot 106, on the corner of the second concession and the road now known as Highway 33, on the north side of the concession road. This log school house was in use until 1855. Annie McDonald was the teacher in 1855 with 56 pupils on the register. The seats were boards set on blocks.

The second school building was constructed of brick in 1855. It was located where the later school building still stands on the west side of Highway 33. The teacher in 1870 was Emma Hubbs. Lula Rowe Adams, now 90 years of age, recalls attending school in the brick building. The floor was worn so badly that the knots stuck up. The ink wells were iron. Smith Brown put her braids in the ink.

A third school house was erected in 1906. This was a frame building. The old bricks from the former school were sold to John Henricks for $60. The head carpenter in charge of building the new school was George Maidens at a salary of $2.25 a day with his assistant getting $1.75. On December 13, 1906 this new school was occupied by the pupils. Schuyler Humphrey supplied 10 cords of wood at $1.85 a cord. Double seats were purchased from the Preston Seat Co. and continued to be used until 1941. Prior to 1906 the pupils cleaned the school, but from then on a caretaker was hired.

In August 1924 a trustees' meeting was called at which it was decided to

Young's school c. 1890— a brick building constructed in 1855. Blake Row is child seated on grass beside teacher.

Young's School 1930, teacher Elsie Fitchett, Back row— Baden Alyea, Earl Rowe, Bessie Brown, Phyllis Brown, Norman Harris, Julia Rowe, Edward Brown. Front row— Jack Church, Harry Chase, David Rowe, Norman Humphrey, Olive Innis, Lorraine Terry, Marion Chase, Muriel Brown.

Third Young's school, built in 1906

donate $100 toward the support of Consecon Continuation School. Hot lunch necessities were installed in 1926, and were used for many years.

Music was taught for the first time in September of 1937, with Miss Flora MacDonald as music teacher. A piano was purchased for the school the following year. Electric lights were installed in the summer of 1939. Thirteen chair-type desks were bought in 1941, and the old ones sold to Blake Rowe for 25¢ each. That year also trustees purchased 40 folding chairs to be used in the school for various social functions. These were put to good use as a Home and School Club was organized in 1941 which was active for many years. Sunday School was also held in the school. A marconi combination radio and phonograph was purchased for the school in 1946 at a cost of $82.45, the trustees paying $50, the Home and School $10 and the pupils the remaining $22.45 which they had raised by a Hallowe'en party and Christmas concert.

In 1945 and again in 1946 the school won the Ontario Horicultural Association certificate in recognition of the most outstanding work in the township on the care and improvement of school grounds. Scotch pine and Carolina poplar trees were planted both in the school yard and at the pupils' homes on Arbour Day, 1949. In 1950 the school children took part in the parade at Picton Fair, winning prizes on both banner and costumes. A highlight of 1951 was going to Trenton to see Princess Elizabeth and The Duke of Edinburgh. A trip to Ottawa in 1958 was enjoyed by grades 6, 7 and 8.

Young's school was closed in 1966. Bill Hanthorn bought it, later selling to Bert Hayward who set up a small cottage industry in the building, manufacturing surgical garments. Later it was sold again and now Clark-Ad has a small business in the old school.

Mountain View Schools

School Section #11 Ameliasburgh

About 1838 a log school house was built on land given by Samuel Potter where Barbers' greenhouses now stand. Its dimensions were 24' x 24'. Pupils from Huff's Island as well as the Mountain View area attended this school. It was in use until 1855 when the Union school was built. This was a union of school section #11 with part of Sophiasburgh #6 and part of S.S. 14 Ameliasburgh. There was no school at Crofton at that time— the school was way down the High Shore, much too far to go for those children who lived north of Crofton, so that area was included with Mountain View. The Snider school in section 14 was closed; this was on the Lauder (later Norris Gibson) farm, and part of that section was also included in the Union.

The Union school house was built on lot 68, fourth concession, about halfway up the old hill on the east side of the road. This same building stands today. Built of grey limestone with walls two feet thick, it is 30 feet wide and 40 feet long. In the autumn of 1855 the school was opened with William Bly engaged as first teacher. There were more than 100 pupils enrolled! In 1879 the school was divided by a partition running north and south through the centre

Mountain View School

Mountain View School 1903. Back row— Adeline Sprague, Arnold Potter, Archie Hubbs, Lillian Anderson, Effie Cummings, Fred Lauder, Nettie Herberson, Florence Titus, Gladys Doolittle, Al Thrasher, Teacher. Middle row— Grace Sprung, Eva VanCott, Elizabeth Potter, Gladys VanCott, Maud Cunningham, Pearl Sprung, Mable Lauder, Myrtle Jones, Fred VanCott, Hazel Titus. Front row— Loral Wanamaker, Wesley Rutter, Everett Jones, Hugh Hubbs, John Black, Leonard Thompson, Clarence Cunningham, Morley Wood, Clark Sprung, Harry Cunningham.

of the school, and a second teacher was hired. Two teachers were required from then until 1915, although in 1892, teacher Mr. Rundell, salary $500, was allowed an assistant for only four months.

In 1893 a porch was added at front door of school. The rail fence around the yard was replaced by a wire fence. The grounds were square, 20 by 20 rods. In 1879 wood was bought for $2.70 a cord, in 1927 it was $14 a cord. In 1882 a pane of glass cost 5¢, and nails 3¼¢ a pound. In 1896 there were 63 pupils; it was always a big school.

In March 1940, 400 acres of land was purchased for Mountain View Airport. This land was the Sophiasburgh part of the section, from then on S.S. #11 was wholly in Ameliasburgh Township.

Inside toilets were installed in 1940. The school was wired for electricity in 1944. The school had an active Red Cross Society during the war years; 12,275 pounds of salvage was collected one year. In the fall of 1944 attendance rose to 48 and seats were rented from Huff's Island to accommodate all the pupils. In 1959 the ten Grade 5 pupils were taken by bus to Huff's Island school, bus driver Ronald Lough.

Mountain View school was closed in 1966, and the children attended Kente. The school was sold to Jay Sprague. After several years the Spragues sold it to Michael Maloney who converted it to a residence. He, in turn, sold the property to Bob Mertl who is the present owner and resident.

Roblin's Mills School

School Section #12 Ameliasburgh

According to archival records there was a school in Roblin's Mills as early as 1830. Its location is unknown. Thomas McMurter taught in this school in 1847, receiving 2 Pounds 15s. per month, plus board, lodging and washing.

The present stone structure was erected in 1848. As built then, it was 30 feet long with two windows in each wall, and a door in the centre of the east wall next to the road. The two privies were directly behind the school, separated by a board fence which extended from the back wall of the school to the fence which ran across the back of the school yard. This divided the school grounds into two parts. In 1882 the yard was enlarged by the purchase of additional land, the fence moved back and the board fence removed. The two outhouses were moved to the far corners of the grounds with a board fence around two sides of them.

At a very early date a stoop was built at the front entrance of the school grounds. This took the place of a gate. Pupils coming to school would walk up the steps, across the top of the stoop, and down the inner steps to the school ground. At that time also there was a wooden sidewalk from the school entrance to the main street of the village. In 1917 a motion was passed that the stoop be moved, as one of the pupils had fallen off the stoop and broken an arm. Two iron gates replaced the stoop.

In the 1880's an addition was put on the front of the school, adding 18 feet

We the undersigned Trustees of School Section
No 12 in the Township of Ameliasburgh Do agree to ~
Thomas Mc Murter the sum of two pounds ~~fifteen shillings~~ ~~three Pounds~~ Currecy
per month for Teaching a Common day School in the
said School Section for the term of Three or six mon~
from and after the date hereof
Board lodgeing and Washing included for which
We hereby become bound Given under our hands
This 12th day of May 1847

                    School Trustees { Simon DeLong
                                 R V Horter

Simon DeLong	1 ½	Paid	187 1847
Thomas Wanamaker	1		
William Peterson	1		
Allen Darling	2		
R V Horter	2		
Bernard Diarkenburst	1		
Ivan Roblin	2	Paid	
C H Kellogg	2	Paid	
John Terwilliger	1 ½	Paid	133 ½
Henry Symonds	1	for Quarter Paid	42
William Wanamaker	1 ½		5 5
Allen Consaul	1		

Teacher's contract, S.S. #12 1847

Roblin's Mills School

Roblin's Mills School c. 1915. Back row— Eliza Moran, Vivian Fox, Lela Fox, Cynthia Cunningham, Corintha Cunningham, teacher Charles Kinnear, Rae Ferguson, Harry Harvey, Clinton Sager, Donald Graham. Middle row— Doris Kennedy, Clair Kennedy, Dorothy Ferguson, Fred Crosby, Vivian File, Helen Nightingale, Helen File, Eva Harvey, Melinda Reddick, Truman Ferguson, Florence File, Ilene Lewis. Seated: Carman Choate, Norris Whitney, Harry Bisdee, Gerald Kennedy, Clive File, Vernon Lewis.

Roblin Mill's School, 1984, with new roof and belfry back in place.

to its length. The place where the joint was made could easily be seen both inside and out. This extension made space for one more window on each side. Two cloakrooms were added in the new entrance; previous to this coats and hats had been hung on nails on the classroom wall. Instead of one front door, pupils now entered by side doors into the cloakrooms. Some years later the windows at the rear of the school were boarded over, and a woodshed built at the back.

In 1934 the school was equipped with chemical toilets which were located in the cloakrooms. So once again the pupils hung their coats inside the schoolroom at the back. A piano was purchased in 1939, and Velma Vandewater hired to teach music. Electricity was installed in 1945. The old double desks were used until 1951 when they were replaced by table and chair type desks. A new hardwood floor was laid in 1952, cement floors were put in the porches and new sidewalks laid from doors to gate and along the south side of school to the woodshed. The exterior of the school was stuccoed over the stone by Andy Jongenotter in 1964 for $155. Along with the other one-room schools in the township, S.S. #12 ceased to be a classroom in 1966.

The old school is a historic structure which the Seventh Town Historical Society feels should be preserved. A successful Art on the Fence day is held here each summer when Quinte area artists and crafts people display their work for sale. On Aug. 10, 1980 a S.S. #12 Reunion Day brought former students and teachers together. A fire partially destroyed the school in 1981, but through the efforts of the Historical Society it is being rebuilt.

Adams School

School Section #13 Ameliasburgh

The first school in School Section #13 was a frame building built in 1843. Its dimensions were 20 by 24 feet. One of the teachers who taught in this school was Peter Story in the year 1855, with 44 pupils, 21 boys and 23 girls. When it was closed in 1870, Peter Alyea bought the building and moved it to his farm to be used as a machine shed.

In December, 1869, an indenture was drawn up between Ezra Bonter and the trustees of S.S. #13, and for the sum of $50 a part of the east half of lot 98, at the rear of the second concession, was sold for the use of a common school. A brick school house was constructed in 1870 with windows on east and west sides and on either side of the front door. There was a raised platform, about eight feet wide, across the front of the classroom. A box stove heated the school. A very long string of pipes extended the full length of the room to enter the chimney at the centre front, over the blackboards. These were exactly what the word says— boards painted black. Needless to say, an occasional chimney

Adams School 1873 examination

fire caused some excitement. Benches were attached around the walls of the classroom with wooden tables or desks placed in front of them. The school master sat at a high desk on the platform and conducted his classes by the plan of interviewing each pupil in succession. Examinations were held with trustees and parents present. A school inspector visited twice each year.

The school was supplied with 'good, hard body wood' of maple, beech and ironwood which was cut in 16-inch lengths, delivered and piled neatly in measured cords. It required about nine cords each year, plus half a cord of kindling wood to start the fire. The teacher built the fire and cleaned the school each day. In 1891 Morley Carrington was hired as caretaker of Adams' school for six months at a salary of $4.25. After that the job was discontinued, and for many years the teachers again took on the caretaking duties. Before school started in the fall, the floor was oiled, stovepipes cleaned and varnished, and the out-house cleaned.

In May, 1882, Inspector G.D. Platt wrote in his report: "The Trustees ought to have some shade trees planted about the yard without delay." In 1885, he noted, "Am very glad to see improvements in the yard in the form of a good

Adams School in 1895: Back row, left to right— Myrtle Dempsey, Ida Cummings, Leta Bonter, Lillian Adams, Lottie Alyea, Annie Carnrike, Ardella Adams, Lottie Adams, Emma Bonter, Rose Jackson, Blanche Delong, Alma Alyea. Middle row— Orby Alyea, Lancy Adams, Bidey Adams, Frank Hickerson, Aaron Adams, Arthur Alyea, Everett Adams, Arthur Carley, Leonard Weeks, Ercus Blakely, Lily Henessey, Florence --, Teacher Miss Robinson. Front row— Roy Dempsey, Floyd Bonter, Bruce Henessey, Clarence Adams, Bruce Adams, Lena Maidens, Dica Adams, Pearl Dempsey.

supply of shade trees." Today there remains, along the west side of the property, a row of large sugar maple trees. They must now be over 100 years old.

In 1911 a woodshed was built at the back of the school. A front stoop and walk were added in 1920. Ninety-six square feet of slate blackboard was installed across the complete front of the schoolroom in 1922. As with most of the schools there was no water on the school property. The 1924 minutes mention Morley Carrington being paid $10 for the use of his pump and $5 for well water for the school.

The Adams section was a large one, extending from the Blakely (now Cunningham) sideroad on the east to the highway (33) on the west, plus the pupils from the second concession from 1870 on. In 1924 the attendance rose to 47, so the school was divided by a partition and became a two-room school for four years. In 1928 with the attendance down to 32, it reverted to a one-room school.

When the school was built it was understood that the building was to be used for religious was well as educational purposes. For many years Sunday School was held in the school with an attendance of 25 to 30 persons. Ross Adams was Superintendent for 13 years and Clifford Irvine the Bible Class teacher, walking the crossroad every Sunday.

A piano was purchased in 1945, and the school wired for electricity the following year. The school was closed in June, 1966. It is now the comfortable home of Mr. and Mrs. I. Matthews.

Adams School as it is today— an attractive home.

Salem School

School Section #15 Ameliasburgh

The first school at Salem was a small, square, frame structure built in 1833 on the south side of the fourth concession road, east of Salem cemetery. It was only 22 by 22 feet in dimension. Several early teachers in this school were W.H. Bly in 1853, Thomas Anderson in 1855, Thomas Dorland 1857 and James Benson 1858. This school served until 1862 when a new school was built. Egerton Wannamaker (John's grandfather) started school in the old building in 1861, and changed to the new one the next year. The old school became the home of Mr. and Mrs. David VanCott. It was their home for many years, then home to others. The last to live in it were Mr. and Mrs. Charles Kirby. It was torn down in 1979.

In 1862 a new frame school was erected on the north side of the road on lot 89, on land given by the Scrivers. The cemetery was just north of the school, and in 1870 Salem Church was built on the west side of the school. The school house had three windows on one side, two on the other, and two windows at the front. It was painted white. The school house was used for church services until the church was built.

In 1910 a hardwood floor was laid, and a cement stoop and sidewalk added. A flag pole was placed near the school in 1917. Chemical toilets were installed in 1938.

Four generations of the Wannamaker family attended this little school at Salem and four generations of the Carnrike family. It was closed in 1966 and sold to Robert Pennell who moved it to his premises to be used as a shed to house machinery.

Salem School House

Salem School 1962, Back row— Teacher M. Redner, Judy Colton, Douglas Carnrike, Bob Hood, Eleanor Wannamaker, Darlene Cannons, Marilyn Goodman, Brenda Goodman. Third row— Patti Carter, Carolyn Goodman, Jane Colton, Edna Carnrike, Brenda Wannamaker, Mary Carnrike, Debbie Wannamaker, Jane Cunningham, Penny Weese, Arlene Goodman. Second row— Billy Colton, Roger Pennell, Roy Pennell, Ted Cannons, Fred Colton, Fred Goodman, David Wannamaker. Front row— Jimmy Colton, Richard Cunningham, Wally Colton, Wayne Colton, Gordon Wannamaker, Teddy Carter.

Little Kingston School

School Section #16 Ameliasburgh

According to archival records there was a school as early as 1838 at Little Kingston. It was a log building located on the south side of the road, on the west part of lot 100, fourth concession of Ameliasburgh. It served as school for only ten years, then was destroyed by fire.

A frame school was built across the road from the site of the log school in 1847. It was left unpainted and became very dark in colour. There were two windows on each side, and one on either side of the front door. The teacher's desk was on a platform at the front of the room. A huge box stove stood in the middle with rows of double desks on each side. There was a rail fence around the school yard. In 1855 the enrolment was 38 pupils, 20 boys and 18 girls. The school was only open for five months that year. In 1870 the teacher was Florence Zufelt. Although the enrolment was 34 pupils, the attendance was

Little Kingston School c. 1925. Girls by door Ila and Marguerite Hamilton, Lorna Phillips on right.

Little Kingston School House c. 1960.

very irregular with the average for Jan. 1 to June 30, 1870, being 17.2, and from July 1 to Dec. 31 only 13.7. Schools operated on the calendar year at that time.

In the early 1900's the school enrolment was so low that Little Kingston School was closed from 1905 to 1914, when it reopened with teacher Florence York. Changes were made over the years. In 1925 a wire fence replaced the rails. A well was drilled on the school grounds in 1928, but the water was never fit to use. A big improvement was made that year when the school was clapboarded and painted a slate grey trimmed with white. The old box stove was exchanged for a 'circular heater.' A sidewalk was laid from the school door to the road. In 1935 the small porch at the front was replaced by a much larger one in which chemical toilets were installed, and the outside privies were removed. The two front windows, now covered by the porch, were moved to the west side of the school, making four there in place of two. To ensure better lighting for the pupils, the desks were all moved to the west side; this provided floor space for a work table.

In June, 1942 Little Kingston school was closed again due to the small number in attendance. It was re-opened in January, 1946. The interior had been re-decorated by residents of the section for the occasion. It continued to serve as school until 1965. Earl Goodmurphy purchased it, tore it down and used the material to build a garage.

North Lakeside School

School Section #18 Ameliasburgh

According to archival records there was a school at North Lakeside as early as 1830, but its location is unknown. In 1843 a frame school house 20 x 20 feet was built on what is now the property of John Jinks. The school stood very close to the road, and there was no playground except the road. In 1855 there were 33 pupils in attendance at this school, 12 boys and 21 girls.

A new school was built in the early 1870's by Calvin Zufelt on a piece of land, the east half of which came off the Cornelius Huycke farm, and the west half off the P.V. Beech farm. The outside of the school was boarded up with rough planks and was painted red. Inside walls were wide pine boards painted a dull grey. Between the outer and inner boards was a mixture of lime and gravel, supposed to keep out the cold. The floor was constructured of wide planks of rough pine. Seats for the pupils were benches made by Mr. Zufelt and painted red. Each family who sent a pupil to school boarded the teacher for a week at a time. The trustees visited the school and examined the progress of the pupils.

Desks were purchased in 1898, and a hardwood floor laid. In 1908 the school was clapboarded and painted a light grey with white, inside and out. A woodshed was added about this time also, and a flag pole put up. The school was painted again in 1922, cream with a brown trim, and new desks bought.

In 1927 North Lakeside school won third prize in the County for the greatest improvement in school grounds. To improve the lighting, two front

North Lakeside School House

North Lakeside School in 1921. Back row— Teacher Mrs. Curl, Lorne Smith, Helen Walt. Front row— Dorothy Kemp, Howard Walt, Howard Peterson, John Jinks, Verne Zufelt, Arthur Jinks.

windows were moved to the west side in 1936. The desks were then moved over in two rows along the west side, and a work table put on the east side. Electric lights were installed in 1950. The next year the exterior of the school was painted white and green trim.

North Lakeside school was closed in 1965. It was literally situated on the alleged Kente Mission site, with the Reverend Bowen Squire, the discoverer of the site, living next door for many years. Fred Little purchased the school property and converted the school to a home. After a few years he built a new home. Roy Pennell bought the old building and moved it out to the third concession where it was later torn down.

Consecon School
Union School Section #19 Ameliasburgh

As Consecon was settled at an early date, the history of its schools dates back to the early 1800's. The first school was a frame structure on the Ameliasburgh side of the village, located about where the Legion Hall now stands. It served the village and surrounding area until 1843 when a new school was erected across the creek on the Hillier side. It was built below the hill, as good agricultural land in those days was not wasted on schools. It was constructed of blue limestone blocks that were shipped to Consecon from Kingston by schooner at a time when Consecon boasted of two docks on the Weller's Bay shore. The school contained two rooms with two separate entrances.

Consecon stone school, 1910. Left to right- Nellie Weeks, Miss Purser Sr. Teacher, Mabel Thompson Jr. Teacher.

Consecon had the distinction of having a Grammar School (High School) as well as a common (public) school from 1852 to 1865. In 1852 there were only two Grammar Schools in Prince Edward to receive an apportionment under the District Schools Act (1841), Demorestville and Consecon each receiving 28 Pounds 10s., Consecon with 32 pupils. From records in the Archives of Ontario we can trace the progress of the Consecon Grammar School. From 1853 to 1855 the Consecon Grammar School teacher was John Strachan. The Reverend Wm. Ormiston, Grammar School Inspector, visiting the Consecon school on Nov. 7, 1855 wrote in his report:

— only 6 in Latin, of whom 5 were absent that day,

— head master, John Strachan, a delicate man, considerable experience but quite old style.

Aug. 20, 1858

Grammar School Inspector, Rev. Wm. Ormiston, visited the Union School at Consecon— 40 present— "nearly all very young— the more advanced attended during the winter. The discipline of the school was disorderly— the master Neil Dunbar B.A. Queen's, seemed to be labouring hard, heedless of the babel around him, except occasionally when in stentorian voice he would call silence."

By 1858 Demorestville Grammar School was closed. 1859— good report on Consecon Grammar School.

1860

Grammar School Inspector George Cockburn visited Consecon Union School "good stone building of one large room and two small recitation rooms, one of which is used as a cloak room. The building is seated for 120 with desks adapted to two pupils. Headmaster B. Freer from Oxford University. 88 in Common school— 72 present; 20 in Grammar School."

Sept. 3, 1861

Inspector Rev. Wm. Ormiston visited the Consecon Union School

(1) trustees advised to provide larger quarters

(2) no more than 15 could pass entrance exams

(3) class in Algebra "knew nothing of it" and "one lad in Geometry knew a little."

(4) The school is not much more than a common school "and as such pretty well taught— Reading, Spelling, Geography all quite good"

(5) New headmaster, E. Scott, B.A. Victoria College

Aug. 29, 1862

Inspector John Ambery visited Consecon Union

"Common School held in the small anteroom, Grammar School fitted up with 31 double desks— two long pieces of blackboard, pegs for hats etc. along each side of room. Headmaster, W.E. Scott, salary $500.00, young but promising, and school kept in decent order."

Free to all within town limits, non-residents 50¢ a month. Common school teacher B. Netherby.

December 1, 1863

Grammar School Inspector, Rev. W.F. Checkley, visited Consecon. Principal, W.E. Scott, a Wesleyan; the school "an unpretentious building of stone, two rooms, furnished with plain, substantial desks, modern maps; a union school and mixed-grammar school 42 pupils.

"I examined most of the Classics in this school myself, and cannot say that I think the School has any pretension to rank among the Grammar Schools. I found that the so-called Grammar School consisted chiefly of little boys and girls too young, as well as too ignorant, for admission, and when I spoke of the absurdity of this to the Headmaster, he replied that the Trustees would have it so..." Checkley was sure it was called a Grammar School to enable them to draw two school grants and save themselves almost entirely from local taxation.

Nov. 3, 1864

Grammar School Inspector G.P. Young visited Consecon, where Wm. E. Scott was still headmaster.

"... school.. in a very low and unsatisfactory state... students all very young, older students all working. On the whole I have a strong conviction that this Grammar School ought to be suppressed. I doubt very much whether there is any proper field for a Grammar School in Consecon."

Oct. 1865

Inspector G.P. Young visited the Grammar School department of the Union School at Consecon. Scott still teacher. This was supposed to be a *classical* school with 13 in the roll for Latin, "but, the whole thing was a farce" ... mere beginners... children whom it would have been judicious and kind to have left in the Common School."

Oct. 26, 1865

"This has always, since I became Inspector, been a wretched school, and I am happy to say, that, at the date of writing this report, it has become extinct."

One of the features of the Consecon School was a belfry, and bell which sounded over the village four times a day, five days a week, ten months of the year. The school was surrounded by a decorative fence of bent iron rods. Mrs. Everett MacDonald, whose father attended the school before her, started her schooling in 1890 at the age of seven. At an Open House and Tea in 1967, Mrs. MacDonald recalled crossing the fence by means of a wooden stile, two steps up, two down. She also described how the younger children rode down hill inside the fence on barrel staves, while the older pupils used the road and, on a loaded bob-sled, sped far down it, across the bridge and even around the corner into the Ameliasburgh side of the village. Evidently the senior room was still endeavouring to provide a high school education, for Mrs. MacDonald mentioned her High School teacher was Walton McKibbon. McKibbon taught in Consecon from 1893 to 1901 at a salary ranging from $450 to $525. The teacher of the lower grades was May Osborne, receiving $250.

Continuation School inside the Presbyterian Church 1926; the four girls on right are Mabel Collens, Dorothy Kemp, Helen Bush, Audrey Alyea.

Consecon Continuation School 1924-25. Back Row: Maurice Cook, Borden Miller, Lee Cook. Front row: Nita Stinson, Edria Rathbun, Kathleen French, Teacher Russell Cole, Helen Miller, Helen Walt, Mavis Kenny, Mary Weeks.

Consecon School with frame addition and cement abutments.

In 1926 a frame addition gave the school another room which served as a continuation school. For several years previous to that the trustees rented the Presbyterian Church and it held the four forms of the continuation school. Three teachers were employed in a "teacher and a half" system- a teacher and a half for high school work, and a teacher and a half for public school work. Lily Walt taught grades 1 to 6 in the Junior room, while Barbara Mikel was principal of the public school portion with grades 7 and 8, and assistant in the high school.

At the close of the Second World War there was some concern about the safety of the old school. A crack appeared in one wall and a chimney fell down into the junior room. The two senior classes moved into the Masonic hall with a temporary partition through the middle. Mrs. Walt and her 47 junior pupils moved into the vestry of the United Church and held classes under very crowded conditions. The rows of seats were so close together, pupils and teachers could only move sideways up and down the aisles. Blackboards were hung on the wall, but often fell from their supports. This state of affairs was endured for several months while discussions and meetings were held about building a new school. In the end, cement abutments were placed against the old building to support the weak walls.

In 1949, due to the shortage of teachers, the Continuation school was discontinued, and two teachers taught the eight grades. Mrs. Walt taught in Consecon from 1946 until it closed in 1967, and was principal for 15 years. Roy Taylor was secretary-treasurer for 44 years, from 1921 to 1965, and most of that time without any remuneration.

Seventh Town/Ameliasburgh

On July 22, 1967 the old school bell rang for the last time. An open house was held to mark the Centennial year and also the closing of the school. The old school was torn down before the year was ended.

Teachers at Consecon 1967: Linda Peck, Lily Walt, Evelyn Bush.

Inspectors

Inspectors through the years:
1868-1913— Gilbert D. Platt
1913-1920— Edward Benson
1920-1927— E.P. Smith
1927-1939— Dr. C.E. Stothers
1939-1953— A.F Brown
1953-1956— H.L. Knight

Ameliasburgh had the same inspectors as the rest of Prince Edward County until 1956, at which time it became part of the South Hastings Inspectorate.
1956-1959— A. Cummins
1959-1969— R.A. Dunsmore

Directors of Education
John McNeil— 1969-1977
Harry Jacobs— 1978-1984

Teaching Days in Ameliasburgh

By Mary E. Redner

How did I, having been married for 23 years, and away from teaching for that length of time, happen to resume my former profession? I had never lost my love for working with young people, and had done a bit of supply work for several teachers when they were ill, or needed to be away for some other reason, never accepting pay for this, as I just thought of it as "helping a neighbour."

In the spring of 1947 our older daughter was teaching in her third year at Young's school. That winter she developed several colds from which she seemed slow in recovering. At the end of March our family doctor advised her to take the rest of the school year off. I had supplied for her a day or two when she was writing university subjects, and had helped prepare for Christmas concerts, therefore knew the children. The trustees, with the consent of Mr. Brown, the Inspector at that time, asked me to finish out the year. Our younger daughter was then in her third year in Collegiate, so I decided to do so. Thus I taught three months at S.S. #10, Young's School.

By the end of June, I was asked if I would consider going to Victoria School, S.S. #8 Ameliasburgh, in September. As this was much nearer home, I decided I would try, so I spent the years from September 1947 until June 1959 at Victoria School. During those 12 years we had three Inspectors— A.C. Brown, Mr. Knight and A. Cummins, for all of whom I had great respect, and from whom I received much help and encouragement. In 1956 Ameliasburgh was taken out of the Prince Edward Inspectorate and put in with Sidney and Thurlow townships to form a new Inspectorate under Mr. Cummins.

In spite of having eight grades with three sets of examinations each year from Grade 3 up, and the regular work for each day in order to cover the Course of Study prescribed and sent out by the Ontario Department of Education, we did manage to work in some extra-curricular activities.

Following the example of our Normal School (later Teachers' College) Science Master, Dr. Madill, we always managed to work in at least a spring and fall nature trip to a nearby woods. These added a great deal to Science lessons.

Victoria School joined the National Film Board Circuit in 1948. This entailed two evenings when each teacher had to go to Picton to learn to thread the projector and take care of equipment. Once a month the films were sent to each school, and passed from one school to the next by either a trustee or the teacher. During the day we had films which were educational for the pupils and which often had lists of questions for the pupils to answer later. For two dollars more per season, National Film Board also sent out, at the same time as the others, films suited to both children and adults. We used those frequently and had the whole neighbourhood in for a 'Film' evening and nice get-together with, of course, a lunch. The school would be packed for these occasions.

Then there were the Christmas concerts, which again brought the whole community, and often folk from other communities, together. These were held in Victoria Church and entailed a lot of extra work and co-operation on the part of pupils, parents and teacher. The men had to put up a platform, arrange lighting and put up curtains. The others cheerfully rallied around to help with costumes. It was a real united community effort. As I was not very musical, we were fortunate to have help with the piano playing from Nellie Montgomery, Marion Townsend and Marjorie Faulkner, to whom I was very grateful.

The mothers also rallied round when costumes were needed for the annual Music Festival which each music teacher held in the spring for his or her group of schools. They were held at the various churches in the area.

From collections at the concerts and various social evenings, Edith Townsend, the secretary-treasurer and a very faithful lady, took care of the money for us until we wanted to buy something. One year we bought a really good slide, and two years later four teeter-totters, which the men assembled for us.

At the end of the 12 years, I thought it time the school had a change, and I resigned in 1959. I thought I would now stay home and have a less active life.

Then Mr. Cummins suggested to the trustees of S.S. #15 Ameliasburgh (Salem) that they come to see me, as their teacher was leaving, which they did in the Easter Holidays. After a few days' consideration I accepted, duties to begin September, 1959. Here, also, I had all eight grades and at one time there were 32 pupils. That year we had a new Inspector, Mr. Dunsmore, another very fine gentleman who both pupils and teacher liked and respected.

Life followed much the same pattern as at Victoria, with wonderful cooperation from trustees and parents, and hard work by most of the pupils. The money from concerts and social evenings was used to pay for bus trips, usually one each spring, to Toronto, Ottawa, and one or two to Upper Canada Village. The parents only had to provide money for meals. Often several parents went with us. Our pianist at Salem for concerts was Rena Cunningham.

In both schools we made good use of the Travelling Libraries, which always contained books for all ages. We could have a new lot every three months, or oftener if we wished.

In June, 1966 Salem went the way of all the small schools, and the children went to Kente. I went to Mildred Corke for one year from September 1966 to June 1967. Here I was Principal with grades 3, 4 and 5. At the end of that year I felt that I no longer wanted to teach each day and I resigned. I did, however do supply work until 1971.

During the 20 years I taught in Ameliasburgh, my husband daily drove me to and from school, making busy years for him also, so it was a united effort.

Secondary Education

A free elementary education was available to all children in the first half of the 20th century, but getting a high school education was a different matter. Consecon had its Continuation School, which was a boon for the scholars of that part of the township. For many, Senior Fourth (now Grade 8) was the end of their schooling. Others walked, rode a bicycle, hitchhiked or boarded in town to attend high school. In the 1930's the Department of Education introduced a plan whereby First and Second Form (Grade 9 and 10) could also be taken in the public schools; many took advantage of this to get at least two years of high school. Money was scarce in the depression years, and it was sometimes a real sacrifice for parents to send their children to High School.

On Huff's Island, an unique solution was found. In the early 30's four families banded together and bought a used 1927 Chevrolet to transport their children in to Belleville High School. The oldest one generally drove. The running expenses, such as gas, were divided among the pupils riding in the car. When one family no longer had children to go, another family was ready to buy their share in the car. They drove the marsh road across to Massassaga. Those students who received their High School education by means of this car were Mary and Edith Wallbridge, Henry and Frances Wallbridge, Bill Nightingale, Doris, Lottie and Marion Wallbridge, Loreta and Betra Fairman, Wilfred Motley and Donald Hatfield. Bill Nightingale was the driver at first; when he finished school, Loreta Fairman took over as driver.

In the Centre-Victoria area, several parents took turns driving a carload of students in to Belleville High School. The riders, in this case also, changed with

The Huff's Island car with High School students in 1938; Left to right: Betra Fairman, Loreta Fairman, Frances Wallbridge, Marion Wallbridge and Wilfred Motley.

Seventh Town/Ameliasburgh

the years, but Ruth Townsend, Reta Bellyou, Evelyn and Clifford Calnan, Kathleen Montgomery, Florence Hubbs, Dorothy Hawley, Phyllis Hubbs and Jack Delong all were able to get some high school education in this way.

It was through the efforts of Clifford Barber, with the assistance of Norris Whitney M.L.A., that a beginning was made in busing secondary students to B.C.I. in 1949. The South Hastings High School Board was formed in 1949, comprising the townships of Thurlow and Tyendinaga; in 1950 Ameliasburgh joined them, with Barber appointed by Council as Ameliasburgh's representative on the Board. The South Hastings Board was a pioneer in the field of secondary school transportation, with buses hired and routes set up to transport all students who wished to go to High School. Enrolment at B.C.I. soon rose to 1300 students, with almost half of them rural students.

In 1952 the Bay of Quinte High School Board came into being, with the City of Belleville joining the three townships. Barber served as Chairman of the Board in 1953, and took a very active role on Transportation and Building Committees during the 15 years he served the residents of Ameliasburgh on the Board. Quinte was built in 1954, with two additions since, and Moira in 1959 with one addition since. In 1961 Sidney and Frankford joined the Bay of Quinte Board. Ameliasburgh was allotted a second representative, and Dave Rowe was appointed. In 1963 he was replaced by Harmon Montgomery who served on the Board for six years. Earl Price replaced Barber in 1965. A fourth high school, Centennial, was built in 1967, with Ameliasurgh students attending at all four, according to the courses they wished to take. The formation of County Boards of Education in 1969 terminated the Bay of Quinte High School Board, but, happily, education for Ameliasburgh's secondary students is purchased from the Hastings Board, and they continue to attend Belleville High Schools, the majority at B.C.I.

Hanthorn buses waiting at B.C.I. on John St., 1957

Clifford Barber, Ameliasburgh representative on High School Board for 15 years

Our School Bus Days 1950-1984

By Bill Hanthorn

Although I never attended High School as a student, I went to B.C.I. more frequently than anyone I know. As a school bus driver, I was there twice a day for many years, but did not stay to study.

It was in 1950 that my wife Edith and I both started into the school busing business. I was patching the roof on our little storage shed when a delegation of parents came to discuss school busing into Trenton High School. I agreed with them that it would be a good thing. I didn't get down off the roof. Just as a joke I said, "Why don't you ask Edith?" Since she was busily engaged with the new lunch room I had built for her on the front of our house, I didn't think she would do it. They came back and said she would if I would buy her a suitable vehicle. A 1946 three-seater Ford station wagon was purchased, and we were in the bus business.

Before we had been in operation more than a week, another group of parents from the Smokes Point Road and Gardenville also requested busing to Trenton High School. So a 1937 Pontiac three-seater was procured for me to drive. It was old and the wooden body was weather-beaten, but it was very dependable.

Apparently our service must have been dependable, for we were next approached to provide service to B.C.I. In 1951 a contract was signed with the Bay of Quinte High School Board, and an antiquated city bus was purchased from Grant Rathbun. This bus served its purpose but caused a lot of problems.

This old Ford pusher bus had the motor in the rear with long rods running the full length underneath to change the gears. These would freeze up with slush in the winter, as did also the air brakes. Before it could be used in the morning, the driver Bill Girdwood, or I or both, would have to crawl under to knock the ice off and thaw it out. Many a time while going over the bay bridge the cloth top would blow off and flop behind in the high winds. Many a time Bill and I had to work all night to patch the canvas and do other repairs, to get it ready for the morning run. We never missed a day of school.

When Edith's route to Trenton was no longer needed, Twila Langman persuaded her to get a larger vehicle to draw the elementary kids from the Carrying Place school boundary to the Rednersville boundary, and deliver them to the school at the foot of Onderdonk's Hill and the Red School while they built the Mildred Corke School. For this we traded the station wagon and got a nearly new Volkswagon. Then Jerald Anderson hired me to take the little kids along County Road 3 to the primary school in the Rednersville Church hall on my way back from the route into B.C.I.

Our bus fleet increased rapidly and we soon had a total of 10 vehicles. Throughout the years we had many requests to take charter trips at night, but we refused. Not that they wouldn't have paid but we did not feel that we, or our drivers, would be alert after a night session to properly drive a load of children safely to school in the morning. We did, however, provide free trips to Sunday school picnics, Boys Scouts, Girl Guides, local ball teams and the little hockey team that played on the rink that I made in our back yard. Also, before the school board started to pay, we provided free trips for the students as a reward for good behaviour at the end of the school terms.

In early days we were told that insubordinate pupils should be put off to walk. On one occasion one of the drivers asked me to drive his route at night and mentioned he was having trouble with the kids firing pea shooters on the bus. As the kids got on at B.C.I., I told them quite firmly that they were to put all pea shooters in the trash can and take them back out as they got off, also don't bring them on again. As we started going down Bridge St. hill, peas began hitting me until we passed Rednersville on #23 near Centre. At the top of the hill in the woods I stopped the bus and said, "Good-by, now get out," and opened the door. One of them said, "All of us?" and I said, "Everyone, and take your books." When they were all out and standing alongside (until you have seen 72 standing by a bus, you have no idea what a crowd looks like) they looked very meek and mild and one of them asked, "Have we got to walk from here?" I said, "That's up to you; if you think you can behave, get back on; if not, start walking." They got in, and there was no more trouble.

Then another driver asked me if I would drive his bus load home. The bus I had been driving had a 5-speed short shift gear handle, but this one had a long 4-speed shift with a D.P. rear axle. This was awkward after driving the other, and when I made the turn at Centre I missed the gears and made terrible grinding noise. Some of the boys hollered and said, "Where did you get your driving licence, in a bag of popcorn?" I was embarrassed but I just laughed and said, "Look, boys, this is my bus and I'll grind the gears if I feel like it." The girls laughed and clapped their hands, and I had no trouble on that bus after.

It was while driving that bus that I had a bad scare. I was going in to B.C.I. with the bus empty, when it stalled on the railway tracks. I tried to put it in a lower gear, but the D.P. rear axle points froze, and I had to run to Elliot Motors and get them to move it with a tow truck just before a train came. Another bad scare I had was also with an empty bus. At that time we always picked up B.C.I. students at the back of the school. I was going north on George St. so as to come around on John St. for my load. On my side of George St. was a great pile of leaves. I don't know to this day what prompted me to turn out and go around it. It would have been no trouble for the bus to drive over it. Just as I got alongside it, two little girls, no bigger than babies, stood up in the centre where they had been hiding!

*Line-up of school buses at.
Wm. Hanthorn's home, 1961*

*Bill Girdwood, Hanthorn bus driver
for over 30 years, washing one of the buses.*

In spite of all our problems, I always enjoyed driving a school bus. I always got on well with most of the students. I tried to be firm but fair. Throughout the years I drove on all the routes we had, mostly as a spare. I started driving regularly on the #3 route to B.C.I. when I developed an allergy to the soap necessary to clean my hands in the garage. My fingers split open till the blood ran out. To me it was a real pleasure to drive through the beautiful scenery between Carrying Place and Belleville. It seemed like a picnic to get away from the strain of garage problems. I drove bus until 1971 when I had a partial stroke. I had a lot of get-well cards from the students I had been driving; I have saved them all.

Bill Girdwood and my son Bob have been involved in the bus business for many years. Bob drove his first school bus trip on Sept. 8, 1959. Although I drove bus 21 years, Edith has put in 31 years at it. These three have stood by my side through thick and thin. Together we have worried about the weather, the roads, should we send the buses out on the icy roads or in a snow storm, or cancel? Would the buses start? Would the drivers show up? What to do when parents called to complain that the bus wouldn't wait at their gate while the kids finished their breakfast? How to get money to replace obsolete buses? The school trustees from Ameliasburgh and Prince Edward County have used us fairly, and we thank them. I am justly proud of our school bus service. I hope it will continue and prosper in the future.

Ameliasburgh Twsp. School Board 1965-1969

By Seymour Hamilton

At a Farm Union Meeting held at Edwin Carnrike's home in 1964, considerable time was given to a discussion of the problems being experienced with the Township's one room schools. Seymour Hamilton pointed out that some of the schools had as many as 45 children enrolled while others had only a handful. Overcrowding and lack of adequate water supply plagued a number of rural sections.

The outcome of this meeting was a decision to appoint S. Hamilton as a delegation of one to meet with Norris Whitney M.P.P. and discuss with him the implications of Bill 54 (a Bill dealing with the consolidation of one-room rural schools) for Ameliasburgh Township. Mr. Whitney suggested that a visit to Milford to see the South Marysburgh Township Area School, which had recently been built, would help answer a lot of the questions in people's minds. Such a visit was made with the results that a majority of the Farm Union members decided to support a lobby for a central school in Ameliasburgh Township.

On Dec. 10, 1964, the residents of Ameliasburgh Township elected the Board of Trustees which would ultimately shoulder the responsibility for seeing a new Central School built in the Township. Seymour Hamilton, John Wannamaker, Douglas Sim, Twila Langman and Angus Hannah were elected to the Board. In order to administer the educational affairs of the about 600 elementary students of the area, the Board hired George Flower as Secretary-Treasurer at a per anuum stipend of $2500. As a matter of interest, each trustee was allowed a gratuity of $20 per month and an additional $5 for expenses.

The preliminary work required before plans for a central school could be initiated was extensive. Trustees would frequently meet three times a week with each meeting opening with prayer and closing with an early morning benediction.

Even while much time was devoted to planning, the day by day education of the Township's children was not neglected. The following examples illustrate the sort of things which were done to improve the system.

(a) No teacher taught more than four grades in one room.

(b) Instruction in French was begun in all schools.

(c) Bus transportation for all students was initiated.

(d) The quality of music instruction was improved.

(e) An Opportunity Class was established under the capable leadership of Mrs. Donald Spencer. This first class was an unqualified success.

At the Sept. 8, 1965 meeting of the Board, on motion by S. Hamilton and A. Hannah, a resolution was passed to request the Department of Education to grant tentative approval for the construction of a 12-classroom, plus playroom, school. 1965 and 1966 became a time of planning and building with hopes that the new building would be ready for occupancy on Sept. 1, 1966. In anticipation of this event, the last school day in June, 1966 marked a time of historical significance for education in the Township of Ameliasburgh. On that day, the following schools closed their doors.

Young's School .... Lot 10, Gore G.
North Lakeside .... Lot 96 & 97, Con. 4
Little Kingston .... Lot 100, Con. 3
Salem .... Lot 90, Con. 3
Adams .... Lot 98, Con. 2
Ameliasburgh .... Lot 83, Con. 3
Mountain View .... Lot 68, Con. 4
Victoria .... Lot 88, Con. 2
Centre... Lot 77, Con. 2
Huff's Island .... Lot 1, Con. 3

The Rednersville School, Mildred Corke School and Massassaga School were to remain open.

On Oct. 1, 1966 after housing classes in the basement of Mountain View Church, Ameliasburgh Township Hall, and several of the one room schools, the staff and students of the township, under the leadership of the school's first principal, Douglas Trumble, entered the doors of the brand new building— a building which had yet to receive a name. Soon after, a proposal sponsored jointly by Trustee Hamilton and Principal Trumble that the new school be named 'Kente' was adopted by the Board. When the school was officially opened on Nov. 26, 1966, John R. Brant, Mohawk Chief of the Bay of Quinte, was present to explain the origin and appropriateness of the name.

In 1969, with the advent of County Boards of Education across the province of Ontario, the Township School Area Boards closed their books but not before the four-year life span of the Ameliasburgh Board had fully reflected the word of its motto:

To the Glory of God
Through Service to Youth

Ameliasburgh Township School Board, 1966. Back row: George Flower, secretary-treasurer, Seymour Hamilton, Twila Langman, Douglas Trumble, Kente Principal; Front row: Morris Pulver, Inspector R.A. Dunsmore, John Wannamaker, Douglas Sim

Kente School

Kente School was built in 1966, on the third concession of Ameliasburgh about a half mile east of Ameliasburgh village, on an eight-acre site purchased from Cecil McFaul. It was built by Miron-Wiggers Construction Ltd. of Trenton at a cost of about $400,000. Excavation began in the spring of 1966. It was supposed to be completed by the beginning of the school term in September, but was not ready until Sept. 26. The first principal of the new school was Douglas Trumble. The enrolment was slightly over 300 pupils. It brought together under one roof all the students from the one-room schools of the township. Massassaga, Rednersville and Mildred Corke remained open.

In 1966 Kente was staffed with 11 full-time teachers, a music supervisor, a part-time stenographer and a librarian. It covered Grades 1 to 8. It has 12 classrooms, a library, gymnasium-auditorium, a nurse's room, staff room, kitchen, washrooms, supply room and office. There was one full-time caretaker, Ross Shannik. The official opening was Nov. 26, 1966. Water for Kente is piped from nearby Roblin Lake. Hot water provides the heating.

As Kente became overcrowded, one portable was set up adjacent to the north door of the school in September, 1969. In September, 1971 three more portables were added at the north of the school. In the fall of 1973 approval was granted to build an addition to Kente School to relieve overcrowding and to provide home economics and industrial arts facilities for Ameliasburgh elementary students. The four portables were moved to the front of the school near the road, to make way for the addition at the back.

The firm of Jackson, Ypes and Associates Architects prepared the plans for the addition. The contractor was M.J. Finn Construction of Peterborough. The addition included an industrial arts room, a home economics room, a counselling and guidance centre, a gymnasium-auditorium, showers and change rooms, two additional classrooms, staff room and additional storage space. As well there were renovations to certain areas in the existing structure. The existing library was converted to a science room; the former gymnasium became the new library; the old staff room became a room for copying machines.

The addition was started in the early spring of 1974, and it was January of

Kente School

First portable at Kente 1969

*Donald Spencer, McGinnis
bus driver to Kente for 14 years.*

1975 when all the facilities of the new addition were available. The cost of the addition was about $400,000.

Principals of Kente School

Douglas Trumble— September 1966 to June 1967
Glenn Salter— September 1967 to June 1973
Eugene Bright— September 1973 to June 1975
David Baldwin— September 1975 to June 1982
David Lockwood— September 1982 to present

Kente Staff 1983-84

David Lockwood— Principal
Malcolm Cirtwill— Vice-Principal, Grade 8C
Doris Campbell— Kindergarten
Sylvia MacPherson— Grade 1
Judy Lambert— Grade 1/2
Laura Forkes— Grade 2
Pat Gray— Grade 3
Roman Peredun— Grade 3/4
Brenda DeCastris— Grade 5/6
Jan Munn— Grade 6B

Ann Crabb— Grade 6C
Corinne Babbitt— Grade 7B
Sony Osborne— Grade 7O
Vic Alyea— Grade 8A
Margaret Westman— Grade 8W
Shirley Allan— L.D.
Christine Yeotes— French
Leona Brady— Family Studies
Elaine Sharp— Librarian/Resource Withdrawal
Frank Foley— Industrial Arts/Spec. Ed.
Carol Dawson— Secretary
Marion Whitehead— Supervisory Assistant
Joanne MacKenzie— Supervisory Assistant
Mary Lou Frost— Supervisory Assistant
Doris Haisanuk— Supervisory Assistant

Kente Float, December 1982, with theme E.T., participated in Belleville, Wellington, Picton and Consecon Santa Claus parades.

Kente School Band in Belleville Santa Claus parade 1982

Joyce Shannik— Custodian
Ross Shannik— Head Custodian
Glenn Keene— Custodian
Rev. Maurice McLeod— Religion Grades 7/8
Twila Langman— Religion Grades KP/3
Doris Redner— Religion Grades 4/6
Kelly Dixon— Band Instructor

Presentation to Mary Huff, May 1983 at Kente School by Principal Lockwood, of all the certificates and awards at Stirling Festival of Sacred Praise, Rotary Festival, and Belleville and Picton Fairs, which she helped Kente win during the 13 years she taught there.

The winning Kente Girls Soccer Team 1982-83. Back row: L. Knox, S. Smith, L. Lukiew, S. Sopha, H. Thompson, M. Ethier, T. Keenan, Coach Miss Westman; Front Row: L. Burris, H. McCulloch, P. O'Flynn, C. Stewart, R. Patterson, C. Smit, E. Keller, J. Peck.

Winning Kente Boys Basketball Team 1982-83. Back row: D. Baker, R. Ord, M. Struyk, B. Vanghan, A. Brady, Coach Mr. Lockwood. Front row: K. Keene, A. Reid, S. O'Hara, A. Ross, B. Long.

*The 1984 Prince Edward County Board of Education: Back row, left to right—
John Wynen, Ross Foster, Robert Ord, Hugh Parliament, Edward Rutter, Lyle
Vanclief, Harmon Montgomery, Lloyd Seeley. Front row— Betty Carmen,
Arlie Nelson, Sharon Campbell, Chairman Ruth Hart, Margaret Wright, Ann
Munro-Cape.*

The Prince Edward County Board of Education

In 1969 township school boards were replaced by the Prince Edward
County Board of Education. It is a 14 member board with Ameliasburgh
having three trustees since its inception. For the first six years they were
George Flower, Jerald Anderson and Harmon Montgomery. The former
Bloomfield public school was converted into the Board Office. Ernest Shortt
was hired as Business Administrator and John McNeil as Director of
Education. A County-wide busing system was established and kindergarten
introduced throughout the County. In 1971, late busing two nights a week for
Ameliasburgh secondary students was begun.

In 1975 George Flower and Jerald Anderson retired and were replaced on
the Board by George Cunningham and Lyle Vanclief. Robert Ord became a
trustee in 1982 on Cunningham's retirement. George Flower served as
Chairman of the Board in 1971, Harmon Montgomery in 1976, Lyle Vanclief
in 1979 and Robert Ord in 1983.

CHAPTER 26

DAIRY INDUSTRY

The Dairy Industry of Ameliasburgh Township

The dairy industry began in Ameliasburgh Township with its early settlement. Fortunate were those pioneer families who owned a cow. The Dempseys, who are credited with being the second family to settle in Seventh Town, brought a cow with them in 1789. Dempsey was later offered 100 acres for a cow.

After a few years, when the first settlers had become somewhat established, steps were taken to procure stock, while those who now entered the township brought cows with them. The cows were obtained either from Lower Canada, costing about $15 a head, or animals of a superior quality from the State of New York at $20 each. They were of small size. In the summer they were turned out into the woods; in winter they fed on dry fodder.

Among the accomplishments of every housewife was the art of making butter and cheese. At first they made just what was needed for their own family's consumption. As the township became more settled and small villages sprang up, a home market for butter and cheese became a source of farm income.

It was not until the early 1870's that cheese was manufactured other than in the homes of Ameliasburgh Township. They were started by farmers to make use of their own surplus milk and that of their neighbours. Four factories were built at that time to serve the surrounding communities. Hyland and Weller's Bay factories were both built in 1872, Potters in 1873. Bayside was also operating by 1874, as records show that, in 1874, a cheese buyer named W.T. Crandall bought cheese from Bayside, cheque to J. Anderson, as well as Potters, cheque to J. Potter, Weller's Bay with cheque to Wm. Smith and Hyland, cheque to John Sprague.

The cheese business had its troubles in those early days of the factories. Generally speaking, the cows were of nondescript breeding, poorly fed and housed. They came through the winter in poor condition and freshened late in the spring. The milking season was short. The factories began operating in May and closed in September. Milk was not cared for properly, for the modern science of sanitation had not yet been developed. Germs and microbes were unknown, and the result was a large percentage of low grade cheese.

In the early 1900's conditions began to improve with the establishment of dairy schools and the appointment of Charles A. Publow in 1902 as dairy instructor and milk inspector for Prince Edward County. He persuaded cheese companies to improve their factories with cool curing rooms, better equipment and water supplies. He also persuaded the patrons to take better care of their cows and the care and cooling of their milk. Soon a great difference was noted in the quality of the cheese and a good market for it was established in England.

Milk was sent to the cheese factories in 30 and 40 gallon cans. The cans were placed on stands to be picked up, by teams and wagons at first, later by trucks. Milk drawers had a regular route to cover. The cans were returned to the farmer containing whey, which he fed to his pigs.

Hyland Cheese Factory

Hyland Cheese Factory

Hyland Cheese Factory was built in 1872 by John Sprague on his farm, lot 81, south of Roblin's Lake, on the north side of the fourth concession road. John's son, Mark Sprague, was the first cheesemaker. John Sprague operated a general store in the village of Roblin's Mills. The patrons were not paid for their milk until fall, but could go to the store and get merchandise which was taken off their milk cheque in the fall.

Mr. Sprague operated the factory for 30 years and then sold it to the patrons. In 1902 a Joint Stock factory was incorporated under the name The Hyland Cheese and Butter Co. Mr. D.S. Doolittle was the first president, Stephen Vancott vice president, Fred File secretary-treasurer, and D'Arcy Young salesman. Mr. Young was very active in the cheese industry, serving later as president of the factory, and also president of the Belleville Cheese Board. It was largely through his efforts that the factory was remodelled and put in first-class condition with an up-to-date make room and a cold room for curing the cheese. An ice-house was built on the north side of the factory. Whoever got the contract for supplying ice had to also supply a horse to draw the ice, one block at a time, up into the ice-house. There was a house for the cheesemaker just west of the factory.

A good well supplied water for the factory, supplemented by a windmill that pumped water from Roblin's Lake, with pipes on top of the ground from lake to factory. This windmill stood on three legs at the water's edge on Norris Gibson's property. Harry Gibson recalls their horses running away on two occasions, hitting one of the legs and knocking the windmill down. The pipes were taken up every fall.

Milk was drawn to cheese factories in large 30 gallon cans. They went back to the patrons containing whey, the by-product of the cheesemaking process. At Hyland any surplus whey was allowed to run down the roadside ditch, which involved the factory in a lawsuit.

Hyland Cheese Factory closed in 1936. It was sold and torn down. The windmill and pipes sold for $50.

Weller's Bay Cheese Factory

Weller's Bay Cheese and Butter Factory, Consecon

The first cheese factory was located on the east side of the road, just south of Brandy Creek, using water from the creek for its operation. Two farmers, one on each side of the road, started the factory about 1870, hiring a man to make cheese for them. Unfortunately in the second year of operation, the cheesemaker, sent to Montreal to sell off the last of the year's make, disappeared with the cheese and profits.

The Weller's Bay factory was built in 1872 by William Smith. The first cheesemaker was John E. Dingman who made four to six cheeses a day. In 1876 Lyman Smith bought the factory and operated it until 1892. Then he sold the

An early view of the Weller's Bay Factory.

factory to the Patrons, but continued as the maker. The producers applied for a charter for a Joint Stock Factory, with a capital of $15,000 divided into 300 shares at $5 each. Mr. Smith was maker and saleman until 1901, then Charlie Carter was cheesemaker for 12 years. He lived over the factory— this is where Mrs. Douglas Bush was born. Since the factory closed from November 1 to April, he moved to Consecon for the winter. In 1904 a house was built beside the factory for the maker and his family. Mr. Carter kept hogs and fed them the whey "batter" off the top of the vat. The hog yard was only a few yards from the factory. In 1909 a curing room was added to the factory. Cheese at that time was sold on the Picton Cheese Board, and was sent by train to Picton. Everett Cox was the salesman until the Picton Board closed, then the cheese was sold on the Belleville Board.

In later years, regulations under the Ontario Water Resources Commission forbade untreated wastes to be discharged into the bay, so a disposal system was installed to pipe the wastes to a field some distance from the factory. A can washer was added in 1966, and a new boiler the following year.

Weller's Bay Cheese Factory operated until 1969 when it was not economically feasible to continue. Quinte Milk Products purchased the factory milk quota and took over the 35 to 40 patrons who had been sending their milk to Weller's Bay. On January 24th, 1970, the equipment was sold by public auction, but the factory and house still stand.

Mountain View Cheese Factory

The Mountain View Cheese Factory was built in 1873. However, at that time and for the next 30 years, it was known as the Potter Cheese Factory, for it was built and privately owned by John Potter. He operated it for 20 years.

Mountain View Cheese Factory, circa 1915.

Then his son Adolphus Potter took over the factory in 1893 and carried on its operation for 10 years. A good spring supplied an abundance of water. An ice house was attached to the back of the plant. The hired help slept in quarters upstairs over the factory.

In 1903 the Potter Cheese Factory was sold to the Mountain View Cheese and Butter Association whose Board of Directors remodelled it and fitted it with all modern equipment. John Potter continued as President and Salesman for about 25 years. In 1907, James A. Mitchell, an outstanding cheesemaker, was engaged. He visited all his Patrons and persuaded them to take better care of their milk. This enabled him to produce cheese of such excellent quality that he won many prizes and honours. His accomplishments included making cheese to represent Canada at the Great Britain Exhibition in Ireland, and also for the London Exhibition in England.

John Hall was another cheesemaker at Mountain View and, with Mrs. Hall as his only helper, he made sixteen 90-pound cheeses per day. Lloyd Hicks was cheesemaker from 1923 until 1929. In 1929, 250,000 pounds of cheese was manufactured, plus whey butter. The Mountain View factory had an enviable reputation for its butter, marketed under the name of 'Gold Nuggets'. In 1939, Stirling Stewart purchased the factory and operated it for 11 years.

In 1950 Mr. T.L. Wyatt purchased the factory. It was incorporated as a company in 1955 with Glen Wyatt serving as President and maker. Many improvements were made and new equipment added. A tanker truck was purchased, with Mr. Wyatt picking up all the milk from bulk shippers. The industrial waste from the factory was discharged through irrigation.

The Wyatts specialized in making square cheese of various sizes ranging from 5 to 40 lbs. for local store trade.

Mountain View Factory closed in 1975. The Wyatts continued to sell cheese from the premises until 1980. It was the last cheese factory to operate in Ameliasburgh Township.

Glenn Wyatt's last trip; picking up milk at the farm of Seymour Hamilton.

Bayside Cheese Factory

The first cheese factory in the Rednersville area was called Bayside, and was situated at the water's edge on the property of James Anderson, lot 70, concession 1. It was built circa 1870 and operated under the management of James Anderson until 1890. For a number of years after that the building was used as a grain storehouse, as its location on the Bay made it very convenient for loading grain from the wharf to the boats.

Quinte Cheese Factory

The Quinte Cheese and Butter Company was incorporated January 23, 1891; the capital stock of the company was $3000, divided into 600 shares at $5 per share.

The first Quinte Cheese Factory was built at the water's edge below the hill in the village of Rednersville. Inkerman Kember was the cheesemaker there for the 13 years of its operation. With poor equipment, unsanitary conditions, a location which necessitated the drawing of milk and whey down and up a steep hill and the dilapidated condition of the building, a very low grade of cheese was manufactured.

At the annual meeting in 1904, the stockholders were unanimous in the decision to choose a new site on which to erect a new plant. S.B. Russell offered suitable land near the steamboat landing on his farm, one mile west of Rednersville. Both the factory and a house for the cheesemaker were built in

Quinte Factory in 1945: Albert Wallbridge is unloading at the platform; Orval Taft's truck behind. The girl in the foreground is Margaret Taft.

John Hall, Cheesemaker at Quinte Factory from 1921 to 1934. For many years he was top cheesemaker in Prince Edward County, and won permanent possession of the Bank of Nova Scotia trophy for making 100% first grade cheese three years in a row.

*Loaves of cheese before they are cut
to go through the curd mill.*

*Ninety pound cheese in the
curing room.*

1904. The new factory was 80 feet by 30 feet, built of cement at a total cost of $3000. Its sanitary conditions and equipment were second to none. Attached to the curing room was a slide, leading to the wharf, over which the cheese was delivered directly to the boat for shipment. After the completion of the new factory, a marvellous change took place in the quality of the cheese, proving beyond a doubt that, along with a good quality of milk, a first-class, well-equipped plant was essential. In 1907 an addition for the storage of ice was built on the curing room.

Clifford Peck served as secretary of Quinte Factory from 1921 to 1950, and W. H. Montgomery was president and salesman from 1927 to 1950. Quinte Factory closed at the end of the 1950 season. The property changed hands several times, and the factory was finally torn down. The house partly burned and was also torn down; no trace of the factory now remains. One of Quinte's outstanding cheesemakers was John Hall from 1921 to 1934. He won permanent possession of the Bank of Nova Scotia trophy for making 100% first grade cheese three years in a row.

Island Creamery

Elias and Annie Wallbridge came to Huffs Island from Massassaga in March, 1885, to farm on lots 9, 10 and 11. Their home was a rough-cast house built by the Nightingales for Mr. and Mrs. John Nightingale, located on lot 9 on a site behind the present stone house built by Lewis Wallbridge.

In 1894 or '95 they began a butter-making operation, building a butter factory on the east side of the old house, with Robert Welch as mason. Elias' son Lewis ran this factory for a short time, then went to Dairy School at

Guelph to learn proper methods of handling milk and cream, graduating in 1897. His older brother, James S. Wallbridge, went to O.A.C. Guelph to learn cheesemaking.

Lily (Wallbridge) Morton— the only living member of the children of Elias and Annie Wallbridge— recalls the creamery very clearly. She remembers it was a grout building with cement floors, consisting of two rooms and a cellar, with steps up into the part of the house where the family lived. She remembers the vats, churn and other equipment. The water required was pumped into the factory from a well in front of the house. She was 11 or 12 years old at this time and helped wrap the butter in 1 lb. prints which were packed in boxes about 18 inches square, with a metal insert in the centre for ice. Some of the family would take these boxes of butter at least once a week to stores in Belleville.

Elias Wallbridge died in 1896, and in 1897 the E. Wallbridge Sons received a charter from the Ottawa Department of Agriculture for cheese and butter

Application for registration
of the Island Creamery.

making. A certificate from the Local Board of Health in May of 1897 also authorized Wallbridge Sons Island Creamery to manufacture cheese and butter. At this time the family were milking a herd of 25 cows, and an old ledger gives information regarding other Patrons from Mountain View and Huff's Island who delivered milk in the years 1896 and '97. At this time Lewis Wallbridge was the butter maker; his brother Ben did the milking, while brother James was making cheese at the Sine factory near Stirling. Lewis entered a butter-making competition at the Toronto Exhibition and won first prize— a silver butter cooler.

In 1896 the family all had typhoid fever, and that ended the butter-making for a time, as all feared the dread disease. The typhoid was not passed from milk on the farm, as everyone thought, but from a Belleville cousin who came to visit the Wallbridge farm and was a carrier of the disease. From the account books of Lewis Wallbridge in the 1900's, they made butter in the winter which they sold to stores in Belleville, and in the summer sent their milk to the Massassaga Cheese Factory across the marsh from the Island.

Massassaga Cheese Factory

Massassaga Cheese Factory was built in 1900 on property purchased from Dorwin Valleau, lot 59, on the east side of the road which runs south from Massassaga church and school. It was incorporated as a Joint Stock factory and began operations in 1901, with James Robinson as the first cheesemaker and Willoughby Anderson the first President. Other cheesemakers there were

Massassaga Cheese Factory, circa 1912. Mr. and Mrs. Moore, cheesemakers, in front. Children, left to right: Zenas Palmer, Cecil Lent, Floyd Lent, Florence and Lily Mason, Tish Palmer.

William Wheeler, Mr. Copeland, Mr. Moore, Charles Bronson for two years, A. Beckwith, Mr. Ward and Mr. Hennessy. James T. Broad was the last Secretary; Edward Simonds and Valleau the last two presidents.

Massassaga Cheese Factory closed in 1925 because so much of the milk from the area was being sold as fluid milk in the City of Belleville. The shareholders kept the factory for several years after it was closed, thinking that perhaps it might open up again. As this did not materialize, the factory, property and equipment were sold by public auction. William Thompson purchased the house and moved it away. His son bought the factory and property and used it as a stable. It was later destroyed by fire.

R.J. Graham Cheese Factory

Robert J. Graham owned and operated a cheese factory, situated on lot 83, second concession of Ameliasburgh, in the late 1800's or early 1900's. The factory was built on the north side of the road near a never-failing spring which supplied plenty of water for the factory. Older residents can still recall the old factory, with a large watering trough by the roadside in front of the factory, where passers-by stopped to water their horses. Gene Fairfield and Will Elliott were cheesemakers in this factory.

Part of the building was used as an evaporator to dry apples. In 1910 the factory was destroyed by fire.

In 1913, Grant Gibson purchased the adjoining farm, along with the lot where the old factory stood. He built a large drive shed over the cement floor of the former factory.

Ridley Wallbridge
washing milk can

1909 picture of the farm of James R. Anderson showing combined ice-house and latticed milk-stand. Track leads from barn to milk-stand, and along this the cans of milk were wheeled on a flat hand-car. Mr. Anderson was a model dairy farmer and patron of Mountain View Cheese factory.

One by one the cheese factories in Ameliasburgh Township closed because they could not obtain sufficient milk to continue operating efficiently and economically. By the 1940's, the fluid milk market was demanding increasing quantities of milk, and seeking patrons who would supply a set amount of milk on a year-round basis. Those farmers who wished to sell milk to the dairies had to adopt a new approach to herd management, particularly as regards breeding and feeding policies, so that they would have cows freshening in the fall and producing heavily throughout the winter. Milk was shipped to the dairies in 8-gallon cans. Milk coolers were a necessity.

By the mid 1960's, cans became obsolete for fluid shippers as bulk tanks and tank trucks became the order of the day. Modern milk houses built to specified standards were required. In the 1970's milk houses and bulk tanks also became mandatory for industrial shippers.

By the Milk Act of 1965, all milk produced for sale on Ontario farms must be sold by the farmer to the Ontario Milk Marketing Board, and all the milk bought by Ontario processors must be purchased from the Ontario Milk Marketing Board. This Board establishes producers' quotas, the prices the processors will pay for milk they receive, and rates paid to transporters. It operates two milk supply management systems— one for the fluid milk market and one for the industrial or manufacturing milk market.

Fluid quotas, or Group I Pool quotas, are allotted in litres of milk per day to qualified licenced producers who must supply the highest quality of milk on a consistent, year round basis. If he cannot, his quota is automatically reduced. Industrial milk producers are called Group II Pool producers.

Since 1971 the Canadian dairy industry operates a national supply management programme for manufacturing milk through market-sharing quotas. The producer has an MSQ expressed in litres of milk per dairy year.

There are also a few cream producers in Ameliasburgh. This involves putting the milk, while it is still warm, through a separator. The skim milk is usually fed to pigs. Cream producers also operate under a quota.

Although some farmers are still operating with the traditional stanchion stable set-up, others have gone to free stall milking parlors and loafing barns.

Milking parlour at Goreland Farms,
Geraldine and Gerald Pulver.

Dairy Princesses from Ameliasburgh, clockwise from above left: Hetty Top, 1974-6; Jean Waterhouse, 1959-61; Jean Barber, 1957-8; Linda Hamilton 1976-7; Rebecca Pulver, 1977-8; Patti Burris, 1981-3.

PRINCE EDWARD MILK COMMITTEE

CHAPTER 27

MIXED FARMING

The Mixed Farm

by John Wannamaker

The mixed farm of Southern Ontario has become a way of life of the past. The operation of a farm of this kind is one of the most fascinating of all occupations.

There were several varieties of livestock on this kind of farm, including a herd of milk cows, the raising of the heifer calves from the best cows for replacements, making veal of others and usually one or two steers for early winter killing. The calves usually arrived beginning in early March. With the cheese factories opening in late April, this allowed a period of time when milk was available to start the calves that were to be raised for milking purposes.

Most farmers maintained a flock of sheep to run on the rough ground and they were considered essential in keeping a great many varieties of weeds under control. Cedar rails were depended upon for the most part for fencing,

Milking Time— Everett and Maude Sager milking in the barnyard, Lot 91 con. 1 c. 1910

Mrs. Lorne Brickman with her flock of New Hamsphire hens.

Flock of sheep owned by Nelson Giles, Lot 81, con. 2.

Round barn on farm of George Cunningham, Lot 78, con. 4.

and it was necessary to be regularly checking the fences for spots the sheep might find their way through or places the cattle might jump over.

Just about all farms kept two or more sows. Because it was too costly or too big a nuisance, only about one farm in 10 or 12 would keep a boar, so it was necessary for the other farmers at appropriate times to take their sows to these farms for breeding, which was done for a small fee. Driving the sow down the road, usually with a rope on her foot, was a most undesirable job usually assigned to the teenage boys in the family. Tending the sow in winter when the pigs were born was always a time of much lost sleep. If the weather was cold and windy, it was usually necessary to take the pigs in the house to get them warm. A box stall near the cows where the stable was warmest would be reserved for at least the first week of the little pigs' lives.

Much planning had to go into birth dates of pigs and lambs, as on many farms these same pens had to serve both in cold weather.

All farms had a flock of hens; some flocks consisted of many varieties where uniformity was of little concern to the farmer, and, with a different rooster each year, the variety became even greater. Many farms supported a flock of ducks, geese and guinea fowl.

All animals on the farm received care and were made as comfortable as possible in winter. Not only was this done because it tended to be eventually more profitable, but because a farmer who preferred his profession felt it was his duty to see that the animals he owned had proper care.

The many new arrivals in the very early spring made this a very busy time. Often, being present to assist would mean the difference between a dead or live calf, colt, lamb, or part of a litter of pigs, or perhaps a mother or both.

Spring seeding usually commenced well before the livestock were on pasture to add to the work day, and it was always a most welcome day when the

Preparing to disc— Beuford Peck on disc.

Sowing— Clarence Young with seed drill.

Six horse power at Herb Pulver's.

grass was good enough to 'turn out'. Spring was almost always the most exciting time of the year on the mixed farm. March would be a time for examining meadows and fall wheat, to see how they had survived the winter. Often a few freezing nights in March followed by dry, windy days would destroy a field of clover that had come through the cold months.

The latter part of April and early May was the ideal time for seeding spring grains, mostly oats, some barley or often mixed. On land inclined to be of marginal productivity, seeding was done as early as possible. Fields that were planned for corn were worked periodically from the time they were dry enough until planting to destroy as many weeds as possible. Corn planting took place the first part of June, the corn for dry cobs often in late May, with that for the silo going in a few days later. Up until the 1930's, corn was planted with a hand planter, a hill at a time. It was quite a good man who could plant two acres in a day.

Machinery requirements in the spring were, for the most part, a cultivator, spike tooth drags and seed drill. In some areas the soil was such that a disc

Allan Dempsey scuffling, man and horse both 30 years old.

Harold Young with wooden roller.

Cutting hay at Fingerboard Farm c. 1900.

harrow would be more appropriate. Other farmers preferred a spring tooth harrow. To finish the seed bed, a land roller or cultipacker was often used.

The 1930's saw a lot of the swing from horse-drawn implements to the use of tractors, in spite of the depression. Many of these tractors had been purchased in the very late 1920's but were used sparingly because hay was easier to come by for the horses than gas for the tractor. Up to this time tractors were considered to be too cumbersome for much farm work such as seeding and haying, so the horses were still considered very necessary.

Fence building would be carried out during wet times through the spring

Raking and stooking up hay (left to right)— Will Barber, Reginald Barber, Clifford Barber, Bob Bowness, Billy Brown, Stan Barber, Ben Way.

Loading Hay— Clifford Calnan and Walter Cunningham.

Unloading Hay— Painting by Rev. Bowen Squire.

Grain Binder— Elwood Spencer giving Doug Redner a hand with his knotter.

Sheaves of Grain— Bob Cannons.

Loading Sheaves— Norma Giles on load, Kathleen and Roy Giles on ground.

Threshing at the Hamilton Farm Lot 65 con. 3.

Planting tomatoes— Summers Dawson on tractor, Bill Dawson on planter which was Howard Weese's invention.

Pea Viner on the D.K. Redner farm, (left to right)— Marjorie Peck, David Brickman, Wayne Peck, Albert Bowerman, Lola Rion, Summers Dawson; standing— Orval Taft, Vernon Bowerman, Gordon Hogan, Ned McInroy.

or whenever there happened to be an hour available. About the first of June would see the cattle on pasture. Corn cultivating was done with a one-horse scuffler cultivator usually with five teeth, or a two-horse cultivator which was guided by the operator.

Before the corn was past cultivating, the early hay would be ready to cut. A wet spring would cause the hay to be so full of moisture that curing would be a difficult process. The dump rake was the machine used for a great number of years to gather the hay in windrows. From here it was put up in coils by using a long-handled three-tine fork. Then came the main process of curing. Good hay weather was a common expression, if it happened to be that kind; if too much sunshine then the grain and corn might suffer from dry weather, but at least the quality of hay would be good. A wet summer would often run the haying into the season for cutting the grain. Then the stooking and a curing process would take place again. When this came about it was often stacked about seven or eight wagon loads per stack. Some farmers preferred to put their hay in stacks and the sheaves of grain in the barn. There was always space saved in the barn for straw from threshing for bedding the animals or feed for the horses during winter months. Threshing in the barn was sometimes a nasty job; if the straw was being blown in a mow opposite where the sheaves were being pitched from, it could be almost unbearable. Then there was always the poor fellow who would have to get in and tramp the straw in front of the blower.

The later years of the threshing machine saw stook-threshing becoming popular, as it had been in the west for many years. A great amount of work was saved, but often waiting for the machine or too much rain would damage the crops and the straw would have much less value as feed.

Most crops produced on the farm were fed on the farm. Fall wheat was often an exception, and was sold shortly after harvest. Many areas where soil and climate were satisfactory, cash crops were grown for canning factories. Most popular here were green peas, tomatoes and sweet corn. These presented problems. Green peas were usually harvested when the hay was on. Picking tomatoes was backbreaking work. The birds and raccoons often did much damage in the sweet corn, and delivery was sometimes a problem if early fall rains made the fields soft.

Threshing would be followed by ploughing. In between times, special fields which had perhaps grown red clover would be ploughed and prepared for fall wheat which would be planted early in September. Autumn would be a time for many jobs, the ploughing receiving first consideration.

Filling silo was for many years done by cutting the corn with a corn binder, hauling it in sheaves to the silo where it was chopped and blown into the silo. Loading these sheaves of corn on wagons, often pulling the wagons through muddy fields, was drudgery. But this was excellent cattle feed that provided a good supply of milk from the cows when pastures would become dry and when fed throughout the winter.

Turning the furrow—
Herb Pulver with single plough.

Cutting Corn for the Silo— Hartford Parliament farm, lot 74, con. 3 c. 1918,
Mrs. Parliament holding horses.

Silo Filling at Lorne Brickman's
c. 1930.

Stooking Corn—
Painting by Rev. Bowen Squire.

Corn has always been a very important crop in Southern Ontario. Small farms which did not boast a silo made use of corn in different ways. On many of these farms, corn would be cut by hand with a sickle or short-handled hoe. Sheaves would of course be tied by hand with binder twine and stood in stooks, sometimes being drawn off the fields for stooking so ploughing could be completed. Late fall would see the sheaves stored in sheds or on the barn floor. Here on long dark evenings, men and boys would sit with a lantern and pick the cobs from the sheaves and pull off the husks. This was known as 'husking corn', and husking bees were quite common where the men of the neighbourhood would get together not only to husk corn but to visit and later in the evening to sample the cider barrel. Most farms had a corn crib, small by today's standards, but the cobs would be cured here and used to fatten hogs and poultry and other livestock. The corn stalks that were left after the cobs were taken off still made reasonably good feed for the cows.

Up until the 1930's, the stalks that were left after picking sweet corn were cut and used for cattle feed, both these operations being done by hand. Sometimes more prosperous farmers would have a corn binder to cut the stalks, but the picking was done by hand.

Most farms had a woodlot, and the frozen ground in the fall would see much woodcutting in the upland bush. Lower ground and soft maple swamps usually wouldn't be frozen hard enough to hold the horses until January.

Often the best part of the tree was used for lumber and many farmers who had large woodlots would sell logs to nearby mills for stave bolts for barrels, boxes, etc. The brush was trimmed off the top so the branches could be used for wood. The large piles of wood were sawn early in the spring and the blocks of wood split with axes.

It has been pointed out what a busy time spring was on the mixed farm, but the making of maple syrup has not been mentioned. Most farms had some hard maples, many had a number of acres of upland bush made up mostly of hard maple. As soon as the sun became warm enough in the very early spring to penetrate the surface of the frost, the sap buckets were brought out, the trees tapped and the sap shanty made ready for boiling down. The sap was carried in pails to horse-drawn sleighs which followed criss-cross trails through the bush. Milk cans were often used as sap containers on the sleigh and when filled were brought to the sap shanty where an endless fire was kept burning to boil or evaporate the water from the sap until it eventually became maple syrup, which is without doubt the most popular dessert of its kind in Canada. By popular I mean desired and sought after, not common, because of the high cost and of course a tendency to become more and more scarce, not only because of the conversion from maple trees to timber, but many farmers just did not have the time or the help required to make maple syrup. In earlier days, maple syrup and maple sugar made a terrific contribution to the farm family food supply.

Practically every farm had its own orchard where a few acres grew all the fruit required. Popular apples were Ben Davis, Pippin, Spy and Russet, and

Cutting down a tree with a cross cut saw— Jacob Sager, Lorne Brickman, Oscar Glenn.

Sap Shanty in Sager woods.

Sugaring off in Sager woods.

Wood Sawing Bee at the Waterhouse's

Barn Raising Bee at Jake and Harry Sager's in 1909, lot 88, con. 2.

Killing Hogs at Jake Sager's.

Baby foxes on the Giles farm c. 1919, left to right: Mac Giles, Jenny Wannamaker, George Wannamaker, Roy Giles, —.

Shoeing a horse— Charlie Kirby, Bob Cannons, Archie Cannons.

Ice Saw on the Bay— Albert Bowerman, Orval Taft.

Hauling Ice— Albert Bowerman, Carl Redner, Bill Dawson.

Korndyde Alcarta Sybil, First prize cow in milk at Belleville and Sr. Champion at Picton in 1936; 2nd prize in milk at Belleville in 1937-38; owned and bred by Edgewater Farm, Lot 67, con. 1.

This 3-year-old bull, weighing over 1,900 pounds, brought over $570. to his owner, Seymour Hamilton in 1951 at the Belleville Livestock Sales arena. Barton Haggerty was the auctioneer.

pear varieties included Bartlett and Clapps Favourite. Also many varieties of small fruit such as currants, raspberries and strawberries were grown.

We must not forget the family pet, the farm dog. He was on duty 24-hours-a-day, guarding the buildings from trespassers at night, rounding up the cattle for milking, morning and night, always ready to help guide the animals or even poultry to new locations. He was usually a Collie, and always a favourite with the children of the family.

The requirements of the farm family when shopping at the general store were quite different from those of today. Instead of buying a few loaves of bread, prepared cakes and pastries, one would purchase a hundred or, in early times, a barrel of flour. Instead of a five-pound bag of sugar he would likely bring a 100-pound bag. The flour sacks were used for many things, often for tea towels. The sugar sacks were heavier material and made into work shirts for the men and boys, but this was usually kept quiet.

The disappearance of the mixed farm unfortunately has brought about the disappearance of the closely-knit farm community as it has existed for years. Neighbours depended upon neighbours for many projects. When new buildings were constructed, wood sawing in the spring, or more routine work

Modern tractor and disc belonging to Roger Redner, child is Anna Redner.

Dairy Cattle on farm of Brian McFaul

Drawing Baled Hay at Hubert Townsend's, Gary Townsend driving tractor.

Loading big round bales at farm of Beecher Mikel.

Above: Purebred Hereford
Cattle at farm of Robert
Adams.

Right: Brenda Adams—
the 1980 Ontario
Hereford Queen.

such as threshing, filling silo, or butchering hogs, farmers helped each other.

Generally speaking, the average community can no longer be called a neighbourhood. This has been a sad disappointment, but can we say the same of the mixed farm? Most, by 1950, had become units where annual income was not relevant to the general economy. Rapidly increasing prices for farm equipment and government pressure on farmers to "get big or get out" soon ended a great many mixed farm operations. Whether or not this was for the best in long range terms is controversial. In this district where there is much land that is of marginal productivity, there is perhaps one farmer as compared to at least 15 about 25 years ago. He has a large income, but also a large expense and a terrific investment. The other 14 farms are not all lying idle, because the big farmer is, of course, working some of this land, but the sad part is perhaps nearly half of the total is going to weeds and brush. This in a world that is developing food shortages at such a rapid pace.

From combine to grain wagon at Alfred Cairns'.

Grain Drying set-up at Hubert and Roger Townsend's, propane fired.

Windrowing Pumpkins at Russell Thompson's.

Aerial spraying of potatoes at Willowlee Farms.

Father's and Son's— 15 month Matthew Mikel, son of Ken Mikel.

Barley Days

by John Wannamaker

Periods of war have perhaps always been a time when farmers prospered economically. Perhaps the first prosperity Ameliasburgh Township farm people experienced was soon after the beginning of the American Civil War in 1861. By 1862 the American government was buying every bushel of barley we could deliver across Lake Ontario. They soon realized our barley was superior to their own and by the time the war ended the American brewers took over purchases that continued on through most of the remainder of the 19th century.

Our area was not only close to the big Rochester and area markets, the waters of Lake Ontario and the winds that passed over them provided a cheap form of transportation in the sailing ships of that time.

It has been estimated that 15 million bushels of barley were shipped out of the County in the 30 years following 1861, and Ameliasburgh township certainly provided a large share of this. It was all cash sales, and many stately farm homes built in the late 1800's are still standing as proof of this prosperous period.

Owen Roblin had his busiest years at his mill in the village during the American Civil War. This was a modern establishment and provided a great service for the township and beyond. Elevators eliminated much of the drudgery of handling grain, but on the farms the back-breaking work continued much as it had for centuries.

A reaper of sorts was invented in the 1840's, but it did not tie sheaves like the binder, which came much later. It left small bunches of grain on the ground with heads pointing in one direction. These were gathered and tied into sheaves with a few strands of barley from the little pile or more often left to dry as the reaper left it on the ground, and picked up with a handmade, all-wooden fork with long tines. I have often been a bit fascinated at seeing my grandfather divide a sheaf into two or three parts that the binder had missed tying, and tie it himself into the smaller sheaves with a few stems of the grain we were cutting. The reaper had four arms that had short tines that reached across the width of the knife bar and table. Each one slipped the grain back from the knife bar onto the table as they revolved and about every fourth one would drop into another slot that would carry on with the grain and sweep it off the table onto the ground in little bunches.

The reaper had a setting that would permit every second or fourth arm to sweep the bunch off the table depending on the density of the crop. The operator rode on a seat which was a bit offset so he wouldn't get clunked on the head with the revolving arms. As it was, they'd come very close and the one that swept the little bunch off on the ground would come even closer. As I remember the reaper, there wasn't much to go wrong with it, and it didn't seem to give nearly as much trouble as the binder.

I'm inclined to think the reaper played a more important role in 'Barley Days' than did the binder, but I still have not found when either the reaper or the binder came into general use in Ameliasburgh. Threshing machines were a crude affair in Barley Days. The blower had not been introduced and the straw and chaff had to be carried away with forks. This was the work even my grandfather spoke of as being drudgery. The progress made in farm living from 1861 to 1900 perhaps compares with the progress made between 1944 and 1984.

My great grandfather farmed 300 acres during the Barley Days up to 1884. He had what we still call the drivehouse where he stored his barley, not downstairs, but upstairs. It has a nine-foot ceiling, so imagine the work it was to carry the grain up those stairs, which were very steep. I remember very well the grain bins. My brother took them out in the late 1930's to make way for a chicken house.

CHAPTER 28

FRUIT GROWING

Some of the early pioneers who settled in the township had left behind fine farms with good orchards. Once they had established homes and cleared the land, their thoughts turned to establishing orchards. Many of them realized that though they might not harvest the fruit in their time, the planting of orchards would supply fruit in abundance to their children.

John Alyea, whose land extended from the bay shore (the Eben James property) to the third concession, stated in his will that his son Peter was to clear 100 acres of land on the second concession and plant an orchard.

One wise pioneer lady brought apple seed with her from Hoboken, New York. She was Phoebe Redner, grandmother of James Francis Weese, who many years ago owned the Summers Dawson farm along the west side of the Weese Crossroad and extending to the bayshore. She planted the seed on Onderdonk Point and the variety was named the 'Granny' apple. Several grafts from that tree may still be found on neighbouring farms.

Ameliasburgh Township too, had its 'Johnny Appleseed', in the person of an itinerant merchant named Asa Wallbridge from Meyer's Creek. He knew all the settlers well, as he was one of the first traders to visit the western end of the Bay of Quinte. He brought to them many of the first fruit trees, as Canniff says, "which have rendered many of the old farms more valuable. He brought in the seeds from the States and planted numbers here and there, often from the motives of kindness alone." Many of the old orchards in Prince Edward County came from his planting.

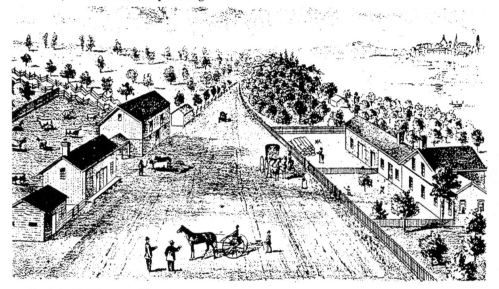

?M RES. W. E. WEESE ESQ. CON. 1, LOT 89, AMELIASBURG TP. PRINCE EDWARD CO. ONT.

FARM RES. OF JOHN S. ANDERSON ESQ CON. 4, LOT 77, AMELIASBURG TP P EDWARD CO. ONT.

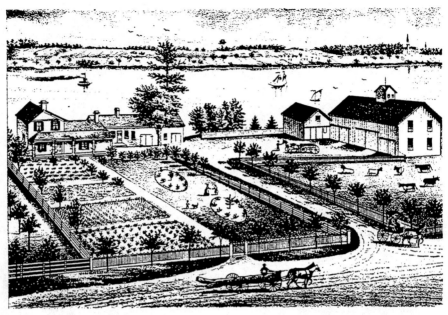

FARM RES. OF ELKANAH BABBIT ESQ. CON.1, LOT 68, AMELIASBURG TP. PRINCE EDWARDS CO.

Early records mention George Angel Weese of Albury who in 1860 set out five acres of apples. This orchard later was top-grafted by Americans who came through the area. They grafted new varieties on the undesirable trees. Through the years the poorer ones were cut out or grafted again. Brothers Allan and Lyle Weese owned and improved and enlarged this orchard which was planted by their great grandfather. Today it remains as one of the fine fruit farms of Ameliasburgh and the produce from there is sold under the label of Pioneer Fruit Farms and Quinte Orchards.

Because Ameliasburgh has sheltered areas not far from water in any place, it provides a good environment for the orchards which produce fruit of a superior quality. Some of the large growers today include the Weeses, Bonters, Dempseys, Campbells, Andersons and Onderdonks. In 1933 apple orchards all over the township froze out and many were never planted again.

In 1859 the first Ontario Fruit Growers' Association was formed "to inquire into the Agricultural resources of the Province of Ontario." From 1880-82, Peter C. Dempsey (grandfather of Gordon and Donald of Albury) was president, representing the Bay of Quinte District.

From the Ontario Agriculture Commission Report 1881, we quote Dempsey. "We grow nearly all the small fruits, apples, pears and plums. We grow very few cherries and though there are few peach trees I could recommend peach culture there. Apples are the most important crop we have." Apples are still important to Harold Bonter, who was president of the

Peter C. Dempsey
President,
Fruit Growers'
Association
1880-1882

Ontario Fruit and Vegetable Growers' Association in 1968, and his son Donald Bonter who became president in 1981.

Four Basic varieties, led by the Ontario-developed McIntosh, represent 80% of the apple production of the Quinte area. Older residents recall names of many varieties. Grace Mitts, daughter of Frank Onderdonk who owned an evaporator can list 62 varieties. In the 1881 Ontario Agriculture Commission Report, 84 varieties are recorded as follows:

Summer Apples

Red Astrachan	Sweet Bough
White Astrachan	Benoni
Early Harvest	Summer Rose
Tetofsky	Early Strawberry
Keswick Codlin	Pomme Royal
Early Joe	Indian Rare Ripe
Golden Sweet	Summer Pearmain

Fall Apples

Dutchess of Oldenburg
Gravenstein
Cayuga Red Streak
St. Lawrence
Fall Pippin
Holland Pippin
Alexander
Colvert
Hawley
Seek-no-Further
Cox's Orange Pippin
Maiden's Blush
Ohio Nonpareil
Fall Orange
Black Detroit
Taylor Fish
Porter
Autumn Strawberry
Maitland
Fall Jenneting
Blenheim Orange
Sherwood's Favourite
Sops of Wine
Kentish Fillbasket
Fatineau Belle
Hawthornden

Part of Grace Mitt's list

Wolf River	Empire
Alexander	Rome Beauty
Red Spy	Golden Grimes
Granny Apple	Cooper's Market
Starks	King David
Fallwater	Canada Red
Mother	Aikens
Red Seeks	Golden Talman Sweet
Sour Winters	Green Talman Sweet
Red Winters	Greasy Fippin
Pommigus	Cranberry Pippin
G. Mondi	Scarlet Pippin
Transparent	Russet
Red Delicious	Little Swayzie Russet
Golden Delicious	Pound Sweet
Melba	Wagener
Spartan	Red Astrachan
Quinte	(These sound more familiar.)
Ida Red	

Winter Apples

Brockville Beauty		Dora
Northern Spy	Grime's Golden	Ella
Baldwin	Peach Apple	Arnold's Beauty
Rhode Island Greening	Cranberry Pippin	Red Canada
Golden Russet	Lady Apple	Red Detroit
Swayzie Pomme Grise	Norton's Melon	Wallbridge
Montreal Pomme Grise	American Pippin	Benheim Orange
Aesopus Spitzenberg	Dominie	Ben Davis
Roxbury Russet	Belmont	Swaar
Snow Apple	Talman's Sweet	Bourassa
King	Rambo	Peewaukee
Wagener	Yellow Bellflower	Mann Apple
Newton Pippin	Wealthy	Freckled Molly
Ribston Pippin	Jonathan	Prenyea
Peck's Pleasant	Ontario	Batchelor (King of Apples)

Older residents will recall the very hard Ben Davis variety, but Dempsey said, "We have no apple that compares with the Ben Davis as a profitable market apple. Grocers prefer them to the Northern Spy as a counter apple". In 1880, the Prenyea was an apple grown only in the Albury neighbourhood and described as a good dessert and cooking apple. Today we hear the varieties Dempsey Red and Quinte mentioned.

Packing Apples

Belden's 1878 Atlas states, "there was a cooperage mill attached to Roblin's Mills, and this being a favourable locality for apples, of which large quantities are grown, a considerable trade is done at these premises in apple barrels". There was also a cooperage mill where Keith Ward's house is in Rednersville, run by John R. French. As soon as circular saws were invented about 1870, staves, hoops and heading were bought from saw mills and assembled in local cooperage mills. The staves were elm, the heading of maple and the hoops were of white ash, hand-made. The apples were picked in woven bark baskets, barrelled and shipped, for there was a brisk trade with Britain. Barrels of apples were rolled down planks onto boats that docked along the bayshore.

The Young farm at Centre; picking and packing c. 1900

Men went from orchard to orchard in the autumn to help grade, pack and head up the barrels. Sometimes apple buyers bought only specified trees and returned to harvest just those apples.

By 1930, large quantities of apples were shipped by 'box packaging', and the demand for barrels declined. A better grade of apples was marketed in boxes. Later still, apples were shipped in bulk by railway cars.

Today there are mechanical graders, which divide apples according to size. They have to be hand-sorted for defects.

The late Harry Peck of Albury said his chief interest in life was the apple business. He packed apples when he was just big enough to see over the top of a barrel. He saw most of the apples develop along the front road. By 1900 orchards were still at the height of productivity and largely free from pests.

The late Randall Weese got the first spraying outfit in the community. At first there were no pests and no need for sprayers. The first sprays were for fungus and codling moth, then railroad worm and sideworm came.

Railroad worm was introduced from the storage in Trenton, when culls from shipments of apples from Georgian Bay were dumped into the Trent River around 1904-05. The buyers who bought there were from the Trenton and Brighton area and storage facilities were better here for holding the Georgian Bay apples.

In 1925 a spray service was inaugurated among fruit growers. A person from the Agricultural Office gave full time to advise orchardists on spraying techniques, pruning, grafting and packing fruit. This service greatly improved the quality of fruit.

The first large storage facility in Prince Edward County was in Picton. This was a boon to apple growers because apples can be pre-cooled as soon as picked, then held in storage until the market is satisfactory. Earl Weese, late father of Allan and Lyle Weese, moved to Picton to manage this storage as soon as his sons could manage the orchards at Albury. Several farmers now have their own storage facilities and retail fruit on their own premises.

The Northland Fruit Supply Co. Ltd.

One enterprising fruit grower in the township was Gordon Dempsey. In 1947 he made his first trip to Northern Ontario with a truck load of about 250 bushels of apples which he peddled from door to door, and also called at corner stores. By 1960 the demand was great enough that he established a company known as Ontario Northland Fruit Supply Co. Ltd. Dempsey himself was president, Arnold Wetherall (his son-in-law), treasurer and the late Kenneth McQuarrie, secretary. Besides his own supply, apples were bought locally and also from Georgian Bay, Quebec and Michigan to meet the demand. These were packed in poly bags, baskets and paper cartons and sold to large chain stores in the northern area. In 1974 Gordon Dempsey retired. Because of rising costs it was decided to cease operations, one that through the years had provided employment for many local people.

Bins of apples

*Picking in the
Montgomery Orchard*

*Bonter's Display Case.
Your choice! What will it be?*

Hauling apples in the orchard

Orchardists of Ameliasburgh Township have had their problems too. The winter of 1933-34 was a particularly memorable one. Winter came before the harvest was gathered and by spring most orchards were lost. In 1912 the Redners at Centre, on the 2nd concession had planted an orchard that froze out. They planted another ten acre one in 1935-36. In 1960, Gerald Redner harvested his best-ever crop of 10,000 bushels.

As recently as 1981-82, orchards again suffered some winter damage, but in no way did it compare with the 1933-34 disaster.

Winter came early!
Man behind sorting table— Saylor Smith from 4th Con. (Little Kingston)

The Pick-Your-Own Excursion

The Rednersville Road orchards, including what is known as the Albury area, has become today the Pick-your-own center of Ameliasburgh and a partial solution to the labour shortage for picking fruit. Because reliable and skilled labour is needed in the orchards, some growers hire labourers from Jamaica.

New varieties of fruit are being grown and orchardists are planting dwarf and semi-dwarf trees which are easier to prune and pick. No matter how large or small the tree, the profusion of blossoms produced in the spring is a beauty to behold, and there is no drive that surpasses one taken along the Rednersville road where the dancing blue waters of the Bay of Quinte make a perfect backdrop for the pink apple blossoms.

The Damson Plum

No history of Ameliasburgh Township would be complete without mention of the Damson Plum, a variety common only to this area. In 1881 there were 32 varieties of plums, and two diseases which affected them were curculio and black knot.

P.C. Dempsey of Albury, had a local favourite plum of prolific qualities which he called the Damson. In the Agricultural Commission report of 1881, Dempsey said, "The Damson tree is thorny, is rather a slower grower and yet attains a great size. It frequently produces from four to five bushels a tree. It is very easily cultivated. The curculio takes its share of the fruit, still the tree crops abundantly. It may almost be said to grow wild with us, and often grows in the fence corners. When the tree is not overloaded it is a good dessert plum. I don't know of these being cultivated in any other section of the country."

In the fall, buyers came along the concession roads offering, on the average, $1 per bushel hamper. They shipped them to Montreal. They made excellent jam, but they were very hard to pick because of the thorns, and it took a lot of time to pick a hamper. The very best plums usually grew on the trees that were all massed in the pigyard or hen pen, because the animals and fowls helped to eradicate the curculio (or so it was thought).

For children it was a big thrill to shake the tree and watch the blue fruit come cascading down, but 'grounders' didn't sell. It never was any problem to give them away because all the family descended in Damson Plum time with offers to help pick to get some to take home.

Some Damson Plum trees still remain in the fence corners, but they are covered with black knot and not the big, healthy specimens of years ago. However they still produce fruit in some years.

Ameliasburgh Apple Blossom Festivals
(1966-1973)

In 1966 the first Apple Blossom Festival was held in Ameliasburgh, sponsored by the Fruit and Vegetable Growers' Association at Bonter's Bayview Orchards. Harold Bonter, County Warden, was chairman. The event included an Ecumenical Church Service in Albury Church, the choosing of an Apple Blossom Princess (later Queen), orchard tours, apple baking contest, and the sale of homemade apple pie with cheese.

Scenes from Apple Blossom Festivals *Pictures courtesy of The Trentonian.*

Right: Allan and Ethel Dempsey
in Centennial Costume, 1967.

Clockwise from below: 1972 Queen Janet Wetherall; 1973 Queen Debbie Rowe; 1968 Princess Vetha Connor; 1966 Princess Lorraine Adams, 1967 Princess Donna Broomfield.

Evaporators of Ameliasburgh Township
The Roblin Evaporator (Roblin's Mills)

About the turn of the century, the sawmill under the hill that was one of the Roblin enterprises, burned down. In its place they built an evaporator and cider mill which was operated by Owen Roblin's son, Roger. He bought apples from the farmers in the district which were dried for shipment overseas.

James Johnson was the watchman at the evaporator the night it caught fire. The building was destroyed, and never was rebuilt.

The Dempsey Evaporator at Albury

The apple evaporator at Albury was the oldest evaporator east of Toronto. It was built by W.R. Dempsey and run by W.C. Dempsey. It was located across from the Mildred Corke School on the north side of the Rednersville Road and east of Gordon Dempsey's home. An excellent spring provided water for use in the evaporator. There was a large set of scales in front of the building used to weigh the loads of apples.

R.J. Graham from 'Montrose House' along Highway 2 west of Belleville was involved with the drying of apples in the area. He negotiated a contract at the beginning of World War 1 with the French Government to supply dried vegetables. It so happened that W.C. Dempsey was chosen to assemble and operate machines for Graham in British Columbia. As a result he is credited with processing the first dried vegetables in Canada at Vernon, British Columbia, in 1910.

Dried carrots, potatoes, onions, turnips and cabbage mixed together as a base for soup, and named 'silky', was shipped to France in metal boxes. However this product was never processed in the evaporator at Albury.

The Evaporator at Consecon

The *Trenton Courier*, Sept. 27, 1894, stated, "Mr. Ward is having his evaporator run at full speed and doing good work and paying a good price for apples.

"The evaporator is quite a help as Mr. Ward employs about 12 hands."

It would appear that Luther Shurds of Wellington later owned the evaporator in Consecon, but R.J. Graham of Belleville managed it during the war years. He hired different men, some evaporator operators themselves, to assist him. Orbey Alyea, Harry Dempsey and Arthur Alyea were among these.

Graham negotiated a contract with the French government to provide 'silky', a dried vegetable product for export to France. Vegetables in large quantities were grown on the Mouck Farm at Niles Corners and a truck loaded with workers went many mornings to harvest the vegetables and return with them to the evaporator for drying. They used turnip, potatoes, onions, cabbage and carrots. The 'silky' was shipped to France in tin boxes as a base for soup.

Consecon— J. Gould, J. Baurlein and D. Mattis on steps f Evaporator.

Many people about the village had employment at the evaporator in its heyday. Mrs. Bob Maidens, who even now has a keen recollection of Consecon's past, was an inspector at the evaporator. Her husband went overseas and lost a leg during the war. She resided where Mrs. Roy Tripp does now. Bart Babcock of the Bayshore also worked there.

When the evaporator ceased to function as such, it was used as an ice house by commercial fishermen for some years. Not many years ago it was removed but the site remains vacant.

The Frank Onderdonk-Orbey Alyea Evaporator

On the south side of the Rednersville Road and just east of the Weese crossroad was the location of the evaporator built between 1900 and 1902 by Frank Onderdonk. After his death in 1905, the result of a tragic accident on the Bay of Quinte, it was taken over by Orbey Alyea who later married the widowed Florence Onderdonk. Alyea added another kiln and furnace to the building and carried on business as long as there was a market for the dried apples. Then, like other evaporators, it sat unused for many years. Finally Orbey Alyea's son Luther dismantled it.

Grace (Onderdonk) Mitts, who was the daughter of Florence (Onderdonk) Alyea spent many years living beside and being a part of the

Onderdonk-Alyea Evaporator. Back Row— Clarence Quackenbush, Orbey Alyea, Florence Alyea, Ida (Sager) Hubbs, Annie Shears, Pat Tyler. Middle Row- Burt Weese, Ken Weese, Child- Harold Onderdonk, Mary Weese. Front— May Quackenbush, May Broks, Morley Dempsey, Isadore Brickman, Bob Maidens, Child- Grace Onderdonk.

family who owned the evaporator. Following is her description of the operation:

An ample water supply was needed on an evaporator site. The building was always two storeys high with thick cement walls and floor. The nine-foot ceiling was supported by heavy beams to support the kilns above on the second storey. The walls of the kilns had to be strong to support a heavy roof that was vented to allow steam to escape. There were no windows in a kiln.

The kiln floors were constructed of slatted boards three-quarters of an inch apart and tapered to be an inch apart of the underside, next to the source of heat.

Huge furnaces with tall smokestacks were on the ground floor and galvanized duct-work went from the furnaces and was well secured to the ceiling beams about six inches below the floor slats. Heat was conducted through these pipes up through the slatted floor.

Soft coal (coke) or hard coal when available, was drawn by team and wagon in summer, or by team and bobsleigh via the bay ice in winter. A removable window in the furnace room was the opening through which the coal was stored and the room secured by a heavy, tight-fitting door to conserve heat.

The evaporator building had other rooms too. There was the peeling room for the women who worked from daylight to dark. Coal-oil lamps hung on wall brackets or lanterns were carried from place to place. A box stove that burned wood heated this room. The workers sat on benches during their half-hour break.

Tables of average height were equipped with hand-cranked apple peeling machines. Three prongs on the machine held the apple and a very sharp, curved knife removed a small ring of apple and the stem. There was a special technique for placing the apple on the machine to prevent accidents to the hand.

There was a hole beneath each peeling machine where the waste fell into boxes. Even this waste was dried and made into certo, jelly or champagne, depending where it was shipped.

An empty crate made a stand to hold the full crates carried in by the men. Five women peelers could keep a man constantly carrying apples. Annie (Badgely) Burshaw was the fastest peeler at the evaporator.

A slanted board carried the apples away to the trimmers who cut away bruises, peelings that remained, or deformed apples. The boxes of whole apples were then ready for bleaching.

The bleacher was a box on a cement stand. Fumes went up a pipe vented into the bleacher from a pot of sulphur, which was enclosed in a metal box equiped with a door. The sulphur was prepared by kindling a small wood fire in the pot and adding pieces of sulphur until it burned with a blue flame.

Whole apples were placed on conveyors which ran slowly for 40 minutes. A trap door in the bottom of the bleacher allowed the apples to drop on hand-cranked slicers making uniform round slices which dropped through a hole under the slicing knives into large boxes which were carried upstairs to the kiln and dumped on the slatted floors, where they were raked level to a depth of three or four inches.

The pre-heated kiln was then subjected to high-level heat from ten to 12 hours, with the apples being turned every few hours. The apples must not turn brown. The apples had to be turned in the piles even when they were removed from the kiln. Then they were inspected. If all was satisfactory, the apple slices were ready for packing in wooden boxes.

A table the size of the apple box was covered with a sheet of white paper. Overlapping rings of apples were laid on the table to form a solid thickness, then the box turned over the patterned apples which were called 'facers'. Table and all flipped up and, by dint of expertise and good luck, the whole mess fell in place. More slices were added and a person wearing a clean pair of boots, kept for the purpose, trampled them. If the boots didn't fit they were worn anyway. Fifty-three pounds had to register on the scales before the lid was nailed down. Buyers bought them and paid for 50 pound boxes. Many were shipped by boat from Russell's or Rednersville docks.

The Evaporator At Rednersville

The evaporator at Rednersville was built by Al Phillips and W.C. Dempsey in 1910 on the site of Dr. Moran's fine, large house that had burned. It was used to dry apples and, when they were finished, onions were dried. They were brought into the evaporator in large bags and peeled by hand. Ida Wood and her sister Polly Cunningham (Russell) worked there when they were teenagers and, when they were paid at the season's end, they each bought a fine, serge suit. Ida remarked that when they peeled the onions, "they just let the tears flow down".

Allan Dempsey recalls that his uncle Albert Phillips, had a Delco system in the evaporator and electrical wires ran into their house. The evaporator machinery provided power for lights. When the evaporator was closed down there was a machine near the house to charge the batteries.

W.C. Dempsey sold out his share to Phillips who ran it for some time. During the years of World War I, R.J. Graham was also involved with the evaporator. Phillips sold out and for some years the building wasn't used until Burton Osterhout put chickens in it as part of his broiler business. His father-in-law, Ray Terry, was handy to care for them as he lived just across the corner.

It was later purchased by Smith and Freeman who stored wooden patterns in it that were made by Gerald Gorsline, a pattern-maker for Stephen-Adamson Co. in Belleville. Later it was taken over by Paul Boyd, but his plans for it failed to materialize and it was torn down.

Phillips and Dempsey Evaporator at Albury.

The Carrying Place Evaporator

On the Reuben Young 'Homestead' there was a fine, strong building that was used as a tannery. It was located along a stream that now runs under the railroad tracks.

The two-foot thick stone walls of this building were field stone taken from the meadow surrounding it. The earth was scraped away, the four- or five-inch thickness of stone removed and cut into the proper sized pieces, then mortared together. The earth was then replaced on the land.

In the early 1900's, the tannery building was changed to an evaporator where apples and onions were dried. It was run by Ben Young who later went to California.

The Gardenville Young family also worked there. Keith Young's mother and grandmother helped with preparing the apples and his father Arnot fired the furnaces.

About 1920 the business ended up and the building wasn't used until Blake Young turned it into a barn for hogs. During the 1950's, Keith Young helped tear down the building and the cut stone was trucked to Trenton for flagstone for many new homes that were built on Film Street.

CHAPTER 29

HOP GROWING

Hop growing was an important industry from the 1840's to the early 1900's in Prince Edward County. In Ameliasburgh Township, hops were grown on the farm of John Howell on the lower second concession, the Manley Howell and Virgil Thompson farms on the lower third, Lawrence Sprague's on the fourth, David Stafford's at Centre and the George Williamson farm on the first concession.

As cultivated, hops are tall, perennial vines, dying to the ground each fall, and making a new growth of 30 feet or more each season. The hop is closely related to hemp, both belonging to the nettle family. Like hemp, it has male and female plants: the female plant bears the seed catkins that are of value commercially. The catkin is made up of large leaf and flower clusters called bracts. At the base of the bracts is a yellow resin-like material called lupulin. It is this substance that gives value to hops.

There was a lot of work to growing hops. They were propagated by cuttings, six or eight inches long, from the large, fleshy roots. Several pieces were planted in each hill, and the hills were usually six feet apart each way so they could be cultivated between the rows. By each hill was set a cedar pole about 15 feet high to support the vines. A special tool called a hop pitcher was driven into the ground to make the hole in which the pole would be set, and the earth was made firm around it. Fibre ties were used to fasten the vines to the poles several times during the season as the vines grew upward. The hops were mature and ready for picking the last of August or early September. The

Hop picking gang on the Williamson farm c. 1903

The Howell hop wagon made at Sam Allan's Carriage Factory, Roblin's Mills.

plants were cut off near the ground and the poles bearing the vines were taken down, laid across large bins and the hops picked off by hand.

Every large grower owned what was called a hop wagon. It had platform springs, a canvas top to keep the sun off the passengers and two seats running lengthwise. A driver with a team of horse hitched to the wagon would start out early in the morning, picking up the women who did the picking. He would return them to their homes again in the evening.

Gladys Vancott Morden, when she was a young girl, helped her mother pick hops at the Howell, Sprague and Thompson hopfields. She picked in a basket and them dumped into her mother's box. These boxes were about four feet by six feet and three feet deep, divided into four sections, each section holding about seven bushels. They were paid 50¢ per big box. Two boxes a day was good picking. The boxes were lined up at the end of the field, and the men pulled the poles and carried them to the women working at the boxes.

The full boxes were emptied into large, burlap bags and taken to the hop house for drying and bleaching, using wood and brimstone. The hop house was a frame building with two floors. In one end of the upper floor was the kiln. The kiln was constructed of narrow slats laid about an inch apart and covered with burlap. Underneath was a large box stove fired with dry wood. Brimstone (sulphur) kept the hops from becoming discoloured during drying. The green hops were piled on the kiln about two feet deep, but by morning they would have shrunk to 4 or 5 inches in depth. They had to be turned every two hours, which was a very hot job. Towards morning the hops would be shovelled into another room for storage, until the time came to bale them.

When the picking and drying was completed the hops were baled. This was done by feeding the hops down a chute into a hop press. It was a contrivance which pressed the hops down in a square box lined with burlap. The open side of the burlap was sewn with a hop needle and heavy cord.

Hops were used principally in the manufacture of beer. They added flavour to the beer and also retarded certain undesirable ferments while assisting the growth of desireable yeasts. Like all agricultural products, prices were not stable. Some years the growers made a good profit, and sometimes barely broke even.

Hops were also picked and cured by local housewives to use for yeast to bake their bread and buns. Mrs. Henry Jason Parliament of the third concession always made her own yeast from hops she gathered on Hartford Parliament's farm next door.

The 'Summer House' built c. 1905 of hop poles by Rev. J.E. Chute at the residence of W.C. Dempsey, Albury.

CHAPTER 30

CENSUS OF 1851

DOMINION AGRICULTURAL CENSUS OF 1851 - AMELIASBURGH TOWNSHIP

CONCESSION I

NAME	LOT NO.
Miller Allan	60
Miller David	60
Moon Benjamin	60
Moon John	60
Simmon John	60
Reddick Sylvester	61
Lambert Catherine	61
Cole Henry R.	62-63
Herrington Wm.	63-67
Tice Jacob	63-67
Lawrence Peter	64-65
Lawrence Daniel	64-65
Morden John	64-69
Miller Henry	65-66
Post Abram	66
VanWart Peter	66
Gerow John	68-69
Morden James P.	68-69
Cole George	68-77
Hickerson Andrew	68-77
Cunningham Thomas	70
Cunningham George	71-72
Henesy Timothy	71-72
Brickman Peter	72
Roblin Philip	73
Roblin Mary	74
Ackerman Philip	74
Redner Lewis	74-76
Herman William	75
Wright George H.	75
Makim Levi	75
Worden Franklin	75
Belake John	75
Dolman James	75
Mercer William	75
Rose John	75
Rose Daniel	75
Rose George	75
Redner Rian	75-76
Redner James	76-77
Redner Henry	76-77-78
Loveless Huram	78
Wanamaker James	78
Crouter Edward	79
Bush William R.	79-86

Fox Rinard	80
Cunningham Henry	80-84
Rush James C.	81
Rush Martin	81
Rush John	81
Hickerson William	82
Brickman James	82
Brickman Samuel	82
Wanamaker H.	82
Nix Abraham	84
Babcock John R.	84-86
Babcock John W.	85
Weese William	85-88
McMurter Thomas	85
Babcock James M.	86
Babcock William	86-87
Alley William	87
Onderdonk John	87
Weese William F.	87
McDonald James	87
Weese James H.	87-88
Weese James C.	88
Weese George Angel	89
Weese James & C.B.	89
Dempsey William	89-90
Dempsey Isaac	90
Dempsey Peter	90
Mabie Johnson	90
Sager Henry	91
Pierson David	91-92
Peck James	92-93
Peck John	93
Dempsey Peter	94
Dempsey William T.	
Lyons William	95
Mikel Daniel	96
Fones William A.	96
Bonter John	97
Shiers Samuel	98
Bryant Samuel	98-99
Masters B.	99
Bonter Peter	99
Bonter John R.	100
Shears George	100
Shears John	100-101

Shiers H.   101
Brown Alfred   101-102
Whittier Smith   103-105
Harris Henry   104
Rowe Peter   105
Rowe John   105
Hayes Richard   106
Gibson James   107
Young George   107
Lots south-west of Carrying Place rd.
Wilkins Robert C.   11-12-13
Wanamaker Wm. H.   9
Corrigan Wm.   8
Lawson Job.   6
Weller B.   3-4
Young Reuben   1-2
Young John   1-2

CONCESSION 2

Everett John   52
Higgins Brian   52
Wallbridge Asa   55
Lambert John   55
Wallbridge Samuel S.   55-59-60
Nobles James N.   56
Hunt David   57
Langdon Jos.   58
Anderson William   58
Locklin Joel   58
Ross Benjamin B.   58-59
Howell Hector   58-59
Mason Richard   59
Mason Elizabeth   59
Ballentine Simon   59
Roblin Ryan   60
Striker John B.   60
Locklin John   60
Loveless John   60
Giles Thomas   61
Snider Peter   61
Frederick Martin   62
Gerow Mary E.   62
Gerow James   63
Gerow William   63
Duggin Alex.   64
Snider George   64
Gerow Daniel   65
Way Daniel F.   66
Wanamaker Andrew P.   66-68
Snider William B.   67
Locklin Jos.   68
Locklin James   68
Zufelt Henry   69
Benson John   69-70
Cunningham Thomas   70
McGinnis Timothy   71
Brickman William   71-77
Williams Isaac   73
Redner William   73-74-75
Johnston James   74
Herrington Stillman   74
Roblin George   74-76
Platt John   75
Johnson Arthur   77-78

Giles William T.   80-81
Peterson James   81
Howard Thos. R.   82
Peterson Samuel   82-83
Crookshank Lewis   83
Bryant James   84
Charters James   84
Wilson John   85
Delong Simon   85
Glenn Robert   86
Taylor Philander   86
Burley Ephram   87
Bush William R.   87
Burley Freeman   87
Sager Jacob   88
Glenn David   89
Howe William   90
Moon John   90
Dempsey Isaac   90
Dempsey Peter   91
DeLong David   92
Masters Joseph   92
Adams Samuel   93-94
Jackson James   94
Adams Robert   95
Osborne John B.   96
Elvin Edward   96
Jackson George   96
Bonter Jacob   97
Alyea Peter   98-99-100
Wanamaker Levi   101
Murney H.   101
Mikel Peter   101
Gardiner William   103
Hunt Peter   104
Hunt Harvey   104
Chase Charles   105
Corbman Daniel   106
Mikel Duncan   106
Chase Daniel   107
Moon George   107
Head John   107
Young George   107-108
Stoneburg Peter   109
Chase Charles   110-111-112
Bonter J.A.   111-112
Stoneburg John   112
Covert John   113

CONCESSION 3

Taft Daniel   Grape Island
Rutter William S.   Grape Island
Huff Peter   60
DeLong Simion   61
Sager John   61
Bovay John
Smith William
Wallbridge Elias L.   61
DeLong Peter   62
Sprung David   64-67
Peterson David C.   65
Way George R.   66
Way Daniel F.   66

NAME	LOT NO.
Thompson Thomas	64-65
Nixon John	65
Davidson Adam	66
Tillotson John	66
Parliament Calvin	67
Fox William H.	69
Young Oliver	69
Gibson David	69
Johnson Lyman	69
Cunningham Conrad	70
Wanamaker Michael	70
Rider Joseph	70
Parliament James	71
Smith John P.	72
Sprague Sylvanus	72
Gallaher James	73
Carter Nicholas	73-74
Post Elisha	74
Redick William	74
Snider John H.	75
Quackenbush Isaac	75
Davidson Thomas	76
Massay William	76
Tice Henry	76
Terwilager John	77
Marvin Burnit	77
Haight Anthony	77
Frederick Lewis	
Lount Tobias	78
McCulloh Henry	79
Arthur James	
Scriver Cory	80
Portes James	81
Wanamaker Christopher	82
Ferguson John	82
Dulin John	82
Cotter R.C.H.	84
Spencer Asa	85-89
Carnrike Robert	86
Daniel Howe	86
Carnrike John	86
Mabie Henry	87
Snider David	88
Spencer Daniel	88
Zufelt John	90
Ockerman Nelson	91
Morrow James	91
Hopkins Joseph	91
Walt Smith	92
Knapp James	92
Parliament Henry	93
Parliament George	94
Beach H.	95
Beach George	95
Beach H.J.	95-97-98-102
Huyck Henry	96
Beech Durwillus	97
Kemp John I.	97
Kemp John C.	99
Clark James	99
Striker Jarvis	100
Clark Peter	100-107
Clark Peter G.	101
Walt Amos	101
McGrath Thomas C.	105-106
Brown Hiram	107

Sprung Richard	67
Potter John	68
Anderson William	69
Anderson John	69
Howell Griffith	70
Way William	70-71
Way Henry	70-71-72
Way John B.	71-72
Parliament George	72
Rutherford Francis	73
Lauder William	74
Lauder Thomas	74
Maybee Daniel	74
Wood John	75
Wood Daniel	75
Bates Christie	77
Consaul Allen	78-79
Tice Philip	79
Way Isaac	80
Quackenbush	80
Briant Aaron	81
Roblin Owen	81
Coleman Robert	82
Way Reuben	83
DeLong William	84-85
Howe John	
DeLong Simon	85-86-87
Glenn Robert	85
Carnrike George	86
Tice Philip	87
Jinks Mrs.	87
Spencer Daniel	88
Scriver Henry	89
Simonds Samuel	89
Jackson Robert	89
Carnrike Jacob	90-91
Blakely William	90-91
Pennock George	91
Nix Peter H.	92
Glenn Samuel	92
Walt Smith	92
Parliament Henry	93
McQuoid William	93
Adams Samuel	94
Osborne John T.	94-99
Osborne Thomas	96
Adams Robert	97
Lateur Richard	97
Oragan Thomas	98
Avery Charles	98
McWilliam John	98-99
Barringer William	99
Pennick John	99
McCabe James	101
Mastin Barnard	101
Chase Ezekiel	102
Walt Abel	103
Shuler William	103-104
Weeks Townsend	104
Weeks Solomon	104
McGrath Thomas C.	105-106
Mikel John	106
Coltman William	107
Chase Stephen	107-108
Moon Peter	107
Chase Abraham	109-110

CHAPTER 31

POST OFFICES

Carrying Place Post Office, opened April 1, 1970.

Carrying Place Post Office

Established prior to 1832 under the name of 'Murray'— Name changed to 'Carrying Place'- 1-4-1913.

Name of Postmaster	Period of Service	
Charles Biggar (Shown as Postmaster in)		-1832
Reuben Young (Shown as Postmaster in)	-1853	9-10-1856
James L. Biggar	1-1-1857	19-6-1861
Richard O. Dixon	1-10-1861	-1870
James L. Biggar	1-1-1871	27-6-1872
Peter Rowe	1-1874	4-12-1876
R.J. Corrigan	1-2-1877	25-4-1885
Theodore J. Spafford	1-10-1885	10-3-1893
John A. Preston	1-5-1893	21-12-1893
Mrs. Agnes Preston	1-2-1894	15-7-1899
Harry A. Boyce	1-9-1899	-1911
Charles Manson Westfall	17-3-1911	24-3-1949
George Vernon Westfall	14-5-1949	1-4-1970
James Hodson	1-4-1970	30-8-1983
Aileen Mountney	1-9-1983	-1984

*Vernon Westfall, Postmaster
at Carrying Place for
21 years.*

At the time Charles Westfall became postmaster, mail was moved to the area by train. The consignments for the Carrying Place post were dropped off at the C.N.R. station at Weller's Bay four times daily, and the Westfalls had to go the station and pick it up. In those days there was no route delivery, and people walked or drove to the post office to pick up letters and parcels.

At the present time there are two rural mail routes from the Carrying Place Post Office in Ameliasburgh Township.

Mountain View Post Office
Established 1-3-1862, Closed 30-1-1932
Reopened 2-11-1936, Closed 3-1-1948

Name of Postmaster	Period of Service	
W.H. Way	1-3-1862	20-9-1880
T.B. Tillston	1-9-1881	20-5-1884
John Potter	1-8-1884	1909
B.A. Frederick	9-12-1909	17-3-1913
E.M. Hubbs	24-4-1913	26-9-1913
James Grant Sprague	20-11-1913	30-1-1932
James Grant Sprague	2-11-1936	3-1-1948

Consecon Post Office, opened June 23, 1982.

Consecon Post Office

Established— 1836

Name of Postmaster	Period of Service	
E.D.S. Wilkins	-1836	6-10-1842
R.T. Biggar	7-10-1842	1849
William Kirkland	1849	1-7-1862
Abraham Marsh	1-9-1862	17-2-1879
James A. Johnson	1-4-1879	29-12-1896
James Baird	8-1-1897	6-2-1902
George H. Crane	15-8-1902	31-5-1912
W.W. Miller	23-8-1912	26-4-1928
William Vincent Zufelt	29-8-1928	30-9-1948
David John Proulx	1-1-1949	15-2-1950
William Vincent Zufelt (Acting)	16-2-1950	2-8-1950
Kenneth Alyea	3-8-1950	11-7-1959
Frederick Max Gainforth	1-11-1959	1965
Lorne O'Hara	1965	1968
Ralph Brazeau	1968	1972
David Ham	1972	1974
Mrs. (Lee) Farmes	1974	1984

At the present time there are two rural mail routes from Consecon Post Office in Ameliasburgh Township.

Rednersville Post Office

Rednersville was first called McMahon's Corners where Thomas McMahon had a wharf and steamboat landing. In Smiths Gazetteer of 1846, McMahon was named as Postmaster; perhaps the post office was in his office on the wharf. The name Rednersville does not appear until 1854 when James Redner received his appointment as Postmaster of Rednersville Post Office. Established— 6-1-1846, Closed- 28-2-1941

Name of Postmaster	Period of Service	
Thomas McMahon		6-1-1846
James Redner	1854	10-8-1863
George Roblin	1-11-1863	5-3-1867
Simon Meacham	1-1-1868	-3-1870
James Redner	1-5-1870	26-12-1883
George E. Yott	1-3-1884	12-2-1890
William H. Babcock	1-4-1890	10-4-1891
William A. Woodly	1-6-1891	27-4-1893
John M. Chislett	1-6-1893	16-7-1915
John Spurgeon Dempsey	28-12-1915	13-6-1927
Alexander Gilmour	21-6-1927	10-6-1935
Robert Keith Redner	15-7-1935	28-2-1941

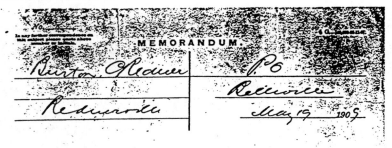

MEMORANDUM

Burton Redner   P.O.
Rednersville   Belleville   May 19   1905

We are sending you by Registered Post one equipment complete for King Edward Mail Box. Kindly have placed in position at your earliest convenience. A stenciled Letter Box is awaiting you at the Belleville Post Office where you will call for it and pay $3.00 Please do so as soon as possible as the boxes have to be placed in position at once.

Memorandum to Burton Redner

re mail box.

Postmaster.

Albury Post Office

Established 1-3-1862, Closed 1-5-1913

Name of Postmaster	Period of Service	
Isaac Dempsey	1-3-1862	7-8-1867
James H Peck	1-10-1867	11-1896
W.R. Dempsey	1-8-1897	24-1-1898
Wesley Weese	1-5-1898	30-4-1913

Gardenville Post Office

Established 1-8-1899, Closed 15-1-1917

Name of Postmaster	Period of Service	
John Dymond	1-8-1899	15-1-1917

Rossmore Post Office

Established 1-3-1876, Closed 1-11-1885
Reopened 1-3-1886, Closed 1-2-1928

Name of Postmaster	Period of Service	
William Gerow	1-3-1876	8-11-1884
Peter W. Fair	1-3-1886	10-9-1886
W.W. Post	1-7-1887	15-5-1893
Mrs. Deborah E. Post	1-8-1893	19-12-1899
John Cassidy	15-3-1900	-1907
J.E. Thompson	20-3-1907	18-11-1912
James Laurel Gerow	9-12-1912	1-2-1928

Ameliasburg Post Office

The original village down under the hill known as Way's Mill had a post office from 1832 to 1835 with James Meacham as postmaster. After 1845 the post office was on top of the hill.

Name of Postmaster	Period of Service	
James Meacham	1832	-1835
Owen Roblin	1845	8-8-1903
W.H.C, Roblin	1-9-1903	17-7-1912
Frederick C. File	16-10-1912	18-7-1927
William L. Plews	15-8-1927	8-10-1930
Frederick C. File	1-11-1930	14-1-1951
Mrs. Clara Eugenia File (Acting)	19-1-1951	24-4-1951
Norman Douglas Sword	1951-1973	
Mrs. Marie Lont Sills	1973-Present	

Ameliasburg Post Office

CERTIFICATE OF POST OFFICE REGISTRATION.

Registered this day a letter addressed to

W. R. Boker

Hamilton

Post Office Stamp and Date. }

Ameliasburg
at 7ᵈ 1867

Aron Roblin
Postmaster.

Christopher Wannamaker's receipt for a registered letter in 1867.

At the present time there are two rural routes from the Ameliasburg Post Office.

There are also two rural mail routes in Ameliasburgh Township out of the Belleville post office— a Belleville R.R. 1 route and a Belleville R.R. 7 route.

In 1851 the Provinces issued their first postage stamps.

William A. Hamilton, mail carrier on the RR 7 route in 1927 with his McLaughlin Buick car.

CHAPTER 32

A CALL TO ARMS

The possibility of American invasion of Canada was ever in the minds of the Loyalists. Upon the arrival of Col. John Graves Simcoe as Lieut. Gov. of Upper Canada in 1792, he took immediate steps to secure the country against attack by dividing the province into 19 counties and appointing a lieutenant for each county with authority to organize and train a Militia and set up regiments and companies. Every male inhabitant from the age of 16 to 50 (in time of war, 60) was considered a militia man and required to enrol. Quakers were exempted from military service by paying 20 shillings a year in peace and £ 5 sterling during a war. Notices were posted informing the inhabitants of the enrolment meetings, and they were fined if they did not enlist at the proper time. They had to assemble for training once a year in each county, and were inspected by the Captains of the various companies at least twice a year.

At first the place for training of the Prince Edward Militia was at Grassy Point in Sixth Town. No doubt the men from Seventh Town travelled there by boat. After the year 1800 the place of training was changed to Hallowell (Picton), and the men from Ameliasburgh were required to go that distance. In June 1802 in the House of Assembly of Upper Canada, a petition signed by several inhabitants of the Township of Ameliasburgh was read, praying that steps be taken to form an independent Militia Company in the said township because of the distance that the men had to go and the loss of several days during their training. This request was granted and the Ameliasburgh men were allowed to train in the township.

When the United States declared war on Great Britain in June of 1812 and prepared to invade Canada, the pioneers rallied to the call to defend this region. Having been driven from one home, they were not easily to be driven from another. The Prince Edward Militia was called out and sent to Kingston. Captain Robert Charles Wilkins, while serving in Kingston, was appointed a commissary officer to obtain supplies for the army. He immediately returned to the Carrying Place and, using his home as headquarters, took charge of the purchase of provisions and directed the movement of batteaux and supplies, troops and prisoners across the isthmus. Locally, large quantities of pork, beef and flour were supplied. Loyalists and later settlers alike did their utmost toward the war effort, and demonstrated their loyalty to the British crown.

The local Militia was again called out during the Rebellion of 1837. Some of the Prince Edward men again were sent to Kingston, but those from Ameliasburgh marched on foot to Toronto. One company was under the command of Lieutenant William Dempsey.

The 16th Prince Edward Battalion of Infantry

In the fall of 1862, two companies of volunteer militia were raised in the town of Picton. Early in 1863, five other companies were raised, one of these in the village of Consecon. The strength of each company was three officers and 55 non-commissioned officers and privates. These seven companies were gazetted in G.O. Feb. 6, 1863 as the 16th Battalion. Consecon was No. 4 Company with Captain Ed Brady, Lieut. Thomas Thurresson and Ensign G.B. Johnson.

About the same time, two independent companies were formed in the township of Ameliasburgh, one at Roblin's Mills and one at Rednersville, the former under Captain Thomas Lauder with Nicholas Peterson and Royal Hennessy as subalterns, the other under Captain William Anderson with W.R. Dempsey and James W. Anderson as subalterns. On July 10, 1863, Captain Thomas Bog of No. 1 Co. Picton was promoted to the Majority of the battalion.

In 1865, during the American Civil War, one company formed out of the 16th Battalion, a quota from each company, was placed on the frontier. In June of 1866 when the Fenians made a raid into Canada, the 16th was ordered out for active service. The two Ameliasburgh Companies were attached to the 16th, thus forming a Battalion of nine companies having a total strength of 529 men from Prince Edward. The Battalion proceeded to Kingston by train where they remained for 17 days. The Fenian raid came farther to the east, so the local forces returned home. The Fenians were Irish-Americans who hoped to force Britain out of Ireland by invading Canada and freeing it from British rule. The Fenian threat ended in 1871.

One resident of Ameliasburgh Township, John Keeble, had the distinction of being a veteran of the Boer War in South Africa. He also served in India for six years. He came to Canada in 1914 and lived in Ameliasburgh until his death in 1975.

Roll of Honour

The names of Ameliasburgh boys who lost their lives in World War I is inscribed on the Memorial Monument in Memorial Park, Picton, erected by County Council in 1920:

at Passchendaele - Mons - Ypres - Somme - Arras - Amiens

	Pte. Edward Boyce	
Pte. G. Clinton Adams	Pte. Adelbert Bush	Pte. Howard E. Parliament
Pte. W.J. Anderson	Lt. W.B. Ferguson, M.C.	Pte. Clifford (Perry) Reddicl
Pte. Charles Ayrhart	Lt. Leonard M. Frederick	Pte. W.W. Weller
Pte. Charles Bawden	Pte. T.G. Hall	Pte. Leslie Young
Pte. Clayton Belnap	Pte. Ben Juby	Pte. Ernest M. Young

Names of Ameliasburgh Boys who made the supreme sacrifice in World War
II: Pte. J.B. Genereaux   Pte. Russell Soble
          Pte. F. Harris   Pte. Clayton Young
          Pte. Ross Lough   Pte. Reginald Young
          Pte. R. Parsons

Many Ameliasburgh Township citizens have taken part in the 20th
century wars in which Canada has been involved. It is impossible to get a
complete list of all who volunteered. A few were decorated for bravery.
Perhaps the best known of these was F/O Steve Dempsey, who grew up near
the west end of the 3rd Concession. He received his commission at Crumlin
near London, and had his first operational flight over Germany on July 13,
1943. He was most efficient as a bomb aimer and survived 26 operational
flights over enemy territory. He received his D.F.C. from King George VI.

*King George VI awarding
the D.F.C. to Steve
Dempsey.*

CHAPTER 33

DOCTORS

Doctors of Roblin's Mills

Mrs. Ann Law

In 1830 there came to Canada a lady by the name of Mrs. Ann Law. Born in County Down, Ireland, in 1778, she was 52 when she emigrated to Canada. She took up her abode in Roblin's Mills in a small frame house on the farm of Isaac Way. There were no doctors in Ameliasburgh in the 1830's, but it was soon discovered that Mrs. Law had a talent for healing the sick and injured. She was called upon in many an emergency, and she was always ready to go no matter what the roads or weather. She was rugged and strong and continued to visit the sick and ailing until 1865 when Dr. Thwaites established his practice in Roblin's Mills. She was then 87. She died in 1882 at the age of 104, and was buried in Mountain View Cemetery.

Dr. James Thwaites

. Dr. James Thwaites was the first M.D. to locate in Roblin's Mills. He set up an office in 1865 in a house at the west end of the village across from the school, where the Royals now live. Unfortunately he contracted an illness that terminated his life and work in 1869 at age 35. He was buried in Christ Church Cemetery, Hillier.

Dr. S.L. Nash

Dr. Samuel Lemuel Nash also began a practice in Roblin's Mills about 1867, but it was of very short duration.

Dr. A.J. File

John Albert File was born in Napanee in 1842. He attended the Royal College of Physicians and Surgeons of Kingston, graduating in 1869. He started his medical practice in Lonsdale, but after a very brief stay he came to Roblin's Mills late in 1869 to take over the practice of Dr. James Thwaites, whose wife was File's cousin. He rode on horseback up the north side of the Bay of Quinte and crossed into the County at the Carrying Place. He spent the night at the home of Melvin Humphrey, whose wife was a sister of Dr. File's father. The following day he continued on his way to Roblin's Mills and there began a practice which lasted 60 years.

On Nov. 30, 1869, Dr. File married Catherine Barnes, and set up a home and office in the last house on the north side of the street at the east end of the village. In the early days of his practice, Dr. File made all his calls on horseback. When the roads were blocked he went on snow-shoes, and later drove a horse and buggy. He was a typical old-time, country doctor, a friend and advisor to

Dr. File

all. He treated everyone alike, the poor as well as those who could pay. He answered calls at all hours of the day or night, with Mrs. File keeping a lamp burning in the window to light his way home. Dr. File was the Medical Officer of Health for the Township, an office he held as long as he was able to drive to and fro through the countryside to put up and take down the red or yellow placards of quarantine. At age 88 he still dispensed medicines to many patients.

Dr. File was a member of the Anglican Church and instrumental in building St. Alban's Church in 1913. He also was a lover of flowers. In his garden he grew plants for the Rennie Seed Co. One year he grew a very large squash which weighed almost 240 pounds. The Rennie Seed Co. showed it many places, as far away as England. Dr. File and his son Geoffrey raised purebred Ayrshire cattle and showed them at many fairs. He also was a Justice of the Peace for many years. He had a family of nine children, all very successful in life. He died Jan. 2, 1931.

In his long practice of 60 years, Dr. File delivered hundreds of babies. Sometimes he had two births in one day. Morley Bisdee and Leonard Wood were born on the same day, with Dr. File in attendance at both births. Vera Bisdee and Myrtle Adams were also born on the same day, and Dr. File had to run his horse from one place to the other, a distance of about three miles, to be on time.

Dr. Harry Bleecker

Dr. Harry Bleecker

Dr. Harry Bleecker practised medicine in Roblin's Mills for a short time in the early 1900's. His office was at the west end of the village in the same house where Dr. Thwaites had been. He drove a horse and buggy and was always accompanied by his Dalmatian coach dog which ran between the back wheels of the buggy. Many years later, when Harry Bisdee was living in that same house, he discovered Dr. Bleecker's pine shingle up in the attic. There was also a Dr. Patterson in Roblin's Mills at one time, but nothing is known about him.

Dr. V.L. Taft

Victor Leland Taft was born Nov. 27, 1892 in Tweed. He spent his early years in Tweed, and then Picton where he completed Secondary School. When he entered Queens University in Kingston, the whole family moved there. He graduated in 1919 with his M.D.C.W. The next four years he spent in St. John, New Brunswick. He then spent a short period in Cochrane with a general practitioner, and in 1923 he came to Roblin's Mills at the request of Dr. File. He practised in the Mountain View and Roblin's Mills area until 1928 when he went on staff at Weston Hospital in Toronto.

Dr. Taft married Beatrice Mason in 1932 and returned to Ameliasburgh to live in the home still occupied by his wife. He continued his practice for 1½ years, then retired due to the breakdown of his health. He died in May 1945. Dr. and Mrs. Taft had a family of three— Mason, Harshaw and Janice.

Dr. Taft's father, John Wellington Taft, owned the house directly west of the present Taft home in Roblin's Mills and had a tailor shop there prior to his marriage and subsequent move to Tweed.

Dr. Fielding

Before coming to Roblin's Mills, Dr. Fielding had a home and office in Consecon. He came to Roblin's Mills about 1935, buying the lovely, big, brick house built by the Spragues on the north side of the street at the east end of the village. He had his shingle out for several years, then went to the States to specialize, but still maintained his home in Roblin's Mills. During the Second World War he rented the house to service people. The house burned down one night and all its contents were lost, including many valuable family heirlooms. Dr. William M. Fielding passed away in the U.S.A., Jan. 24, 1963.

Rednersville Doctors

In the late 1800's and early 1900's there were four doctors who set up practices in Rednersville. None stayed any great length of time. Dr. Moran lived in a large brick home on the corner where the evaporator later sat. His house was destroyed by fire. A. Dr. Knight practised briefly at the turn of the century. As is sometimes the case, several babies were named after him— Knight Tompkins, Glencoe Knight Wanamaker, and Douglas Knight Redner. There was also a Dr. Hiscock at about the same time, and a Dr. T.S. Farncomb.

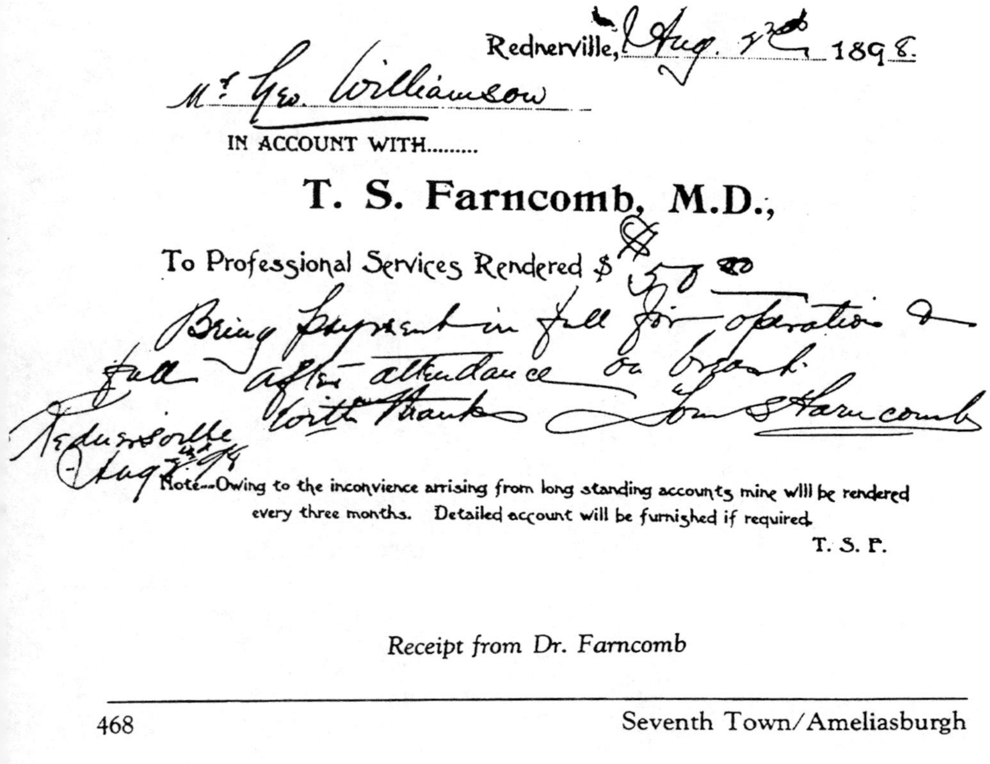

Rednerville, Aug. 1898.

Mr Geo. Williamson

IN ACCOUNT WITH.........

T. S. Farncomb, M.D.,

To Professional Services Rendered $

Being payment in full for operation & full after attendance on Wm. With thanks.

Wm. S. Farncomb

Rednersville Aug.

Note---Owing to the inconvience arrising from long standing accounts mine will be rendered every three months. Detailed account will be furnished if required.

T. S. F.

Receipt from Dr. Farncomb

Dr. Ethel Dempsey

Dr. Ethel A. Dempsey, U.E., F.R.C.P.

Dr. Dempsey was born November 1908 in the hamlet of Norval, near Georgetown, Ontario, daughter of Lieutenant Colonel Alexander Noble. She graduated from the University of Toronto Faculty of Medicine in 1933. In 1936 she took over the General Practice of the late Dr. Emma Connor in Belleville for a period of five years. After receiving her Certificate in the Specialty of Anaesthesia at the Royal Victoria Hospital in Montreal, she was on the Staff of the Ottawa Civic and the Ottawa General Hospitals up to the time of her marriage to W. Allan Dempsey of Rednersville in 1948. Dr. Dempsey was on the Anaesthetic Staff of both Trenton Memorial and Belleville General Hospitals, as well as engaging in General Practice in the neighbourhood.

In September of 1983 she was tendered a Public Reception in Rednersville Church and presented with a Silver Tray by the communities of Rednersville and Albury to commemorate '50 Years of Medicine.'

Consecon Doctors

Dr. Lougheed

According to the Canada Directory of 1851, Dr. Joseph Lougheed was a physician in the villiage of Consecon. Nothing more is known at this time.

Dr. S.L. Nash

In 1867 Dr. Samuel Lemuel Nash was a practitioner in Roblin's Mills. In 1871 his name appears as Master of Consecon Masonic Lodge, leading to the belief that he may have practised medicine in Consecon.

Dr. William Wallace Colton

Dr. Colton had his office across the lane from the Porter Hotel in Consecon. He and his wife, Diantha Jane, had a son, William Wallace, who became a veterinarian. (See veterinaries)

Dr. T.H. Thornton

The name of Dr. T.H. Thornton appears in the list of Masters of Consecon Masonic Lodge in 1875, a position he held for 11 years. He bought the practice of Dr. William Wallace Colton.

In late years, Dr. Thornton, because he was succeeded by his son, Dr. Fred Thornton, was referred to as 'Old' Dr. Thornton. He is credited with having built a fine residence across from the Methodist Church in Consecon. It was destroyed by fire. Dr. Thornton owned a strip of land bordering on the marsh and extending eastward along the Consecon Lake road. Great black walnut trees, which he had planted there, remained for many years, and in the fall the nuts were collected in many a student's lunch bucket. An orchard along the road was a haunt for Eastern Bluebirds.

T. H. THORNTON, M.D., L.R.C.P.S., K; M.C.P.S. O

Physician, Surgeon, Accoucheur

AND CORONER.

Office and Residence in the premises formerly owned by Dr. Colton,

CONSECON

Dr. Fred Thornton

It was 1911 when Dr. Fred Thornton's name appeared as Master of the Masonic Lodge, but he had been practising medicine in Consecon by 1906 when John B. Walt died of cancer, and he was present in 1912 when Frank Brimley Jr. was born in Hillier.

Dr. Fred Thornton married a local girl, Lula Sprung, who lived in a home across the street from the doctor's home where the new post-office now stands. She was the daughter of Mrs. David Sprung, who was a local midwife, who served for many years with 'Old Doc' and young Fred.

Dr. A. Moran
From the files of The Trenton Courier

March 14, 1907— Dr. Moran has purchased a lot on Front St. and intends erecting a fine residence and Doctor's Office as soon as the frost is out of the ground.

March 28, 1907— Dr. A. Moran is looking for an architect to erect his residence, office and stable for him. He and his wife moved into their home later that same year. (See also, Dr. Moran of Rednersville)

Dr. Bean

Young Dr. Bean took over the Dr. Thornton practice and moved into the fine Thornton home with his young wife and baby daughter. He was well respected and well on the way to becoming a successful country doctor when tragedy struck in the form of fire. Mrs. Bean and baby daughter, Marion, although badly burned, escaped through an upstairs window. When Dr. Bean tried to leave, the floor collapsed beneath him.

The baby was taken to Mrs. Elvira Tomlin's home, placed on one of her feather pillows and treated for burns, but she finally passed away. The young mother lingered on for some months, suffering from burns and shock, before she too died. Most of the older people of Consecon easily recall that fateful moment in history.

Dr. Wm. M. Fielding

Dr. Fielding moved to Consecon shortly after the Dr. Bean tragedy. He and Mrs. Fielding and their pretty parrot, Polly, occupied the Taylor house between the site of the fire and the Anglican Church. When one visited the office, the parrot became excited and talked. Her lingo was, "Doctor's in! Polly wants a cracker! Poor Polly!!"

Dr. Fielding remodelled the house to provide an office and waiting room on the north side. Here he practised for many years, a highly professional and most dedicated country doctor. During the influenza epidemic of 1917-18, he hired Percy Hayes to drive his horse while he slept between calls at the homes of the victims. He lost only one patient, a Mr. Deline, who resided in the 'Marsh house', which in later years was where Mr. and Mrs. Alex Rattray lived for so long.

Dr. Fielding moved way about 1925.

Dr. Holling

Following Dr. Fielding, there were several doctors who practised in Consecon for a short time. Dr. Holling was one. Roderick McLean recalls driving him in his own Star automobile to New York State to his new practice, then bringing the Star back to Canada for sale at Will Chase's garage.

Dr. Hershey

Dr. Hershey was a very young doctor who lived in what is now known as the 'honey house', on the corner nearest the Mill office. He stayed only briefly, later going to Roseneath, where he stayed for many years.

Dr. Helliwell

Dr. Helliwell had been a medical missionary in China. He and his family arrived in Consecon in September of 1924. His friend, Dr. Fielding, was leaving his practice there to specialize in the U.S.A., and he invited Dr. Helliwell to try it out, using his home and furniture and drugs just as he had left them. But the family had not been there many days when a young doctor drove into town in an old Ford flivver and challenged him for the practice. It was not a town to support two men, so the young doctor offered to pay Dr. Helliwell's moving expenses to some greener field, and he left for Springbrook where there was no doctor. His daughter, Hildegarde Wilkins, a retired teacher, lives in Trenton.

Dr. Otto Vanluven

In 1915 Dr. Vanluven graduated from Queen's University. Immediately he went overseas with the Royal Canadian Army Medical Corps, but was recalled the next year to assist in setting up training courses for RCAMC personnel. About 1927 he arrived in Consecon with his wife and mother-in-law, setting up in the former Freeman French home. Later he built a new house and office on the site of the tragic Dr. Bean fire. It was while Dr. Vanluven was practising in the village that health authorities had to cope with an epidemic of typhoid which was traced to a patron of the local Weller's Bay Cheese Factory. At the outbreak of World War II, Dr. Vanluven re-enlisted, and was Commanding Officer of military hospitals across Canada until 1946. During the war, Mrs. Vanluven sheltered refugee children sent from bombed areas of Britain. Until 1956 Dr. Vanluven served in the Department of Veteran Affairs. He died in Kingston in 1965.

Dr. Murray Bishop

Consecon's last doctor was Dr. Bishop who arrived in 1949. He had spent 1942-1946 with the RCAF. Arriving in Consecon with his wife, Peggy, and a wee son, Douglas, his first office was in the Art Ward house. For awhile he practised from the Velma Matthews house. He bought the George Bush house and continued his practice there until he moved to Trenton in 1961. When he built his new house in 1963, he took up residence just outside Trenton. Consecon's last doctor had left. But his loyalty to his patients from Consecon never wavered. There was mutual esteem. He retired in 1984.

Gardenville Doctors— Dr. Curtis

Morey's Directory for 1906 lists Dr. Curtis, physician.

Veterinaries of the Consecon-Carrying Place Area

Dr. James E. Alyea

In *The Trenton Courier*, Jan. 16, 1896, an advertisement for the practice for Dr. Alyea read:

Dr. James E. Alyea
Veterinary Surgeon and Dentist
Honor Graduate Ontario Veterinary College
Office— Consecon road, one mile from
Murray Post Office
Will attend Trenton Market every Saturday

Dr. Alyea was a brother of Rodney and Horace Alyea of the Third Concession. Most of his years as a veterinary were spent in Colborne.

Dr. Daniel Herman Rowe
Dr. John Wadsworth
Dr. James Carnrite

These three friends from about the same area went to Cornell University in the U.S.A. prior to the 1900's to learn to be veterinaries. Dr. Rowe, brother of David Henry Rowe from the farm south of the Carrying Place, remained in New York State and set up his practice in Little Falls. Dr. Wadsworth, from the former Ray Terry farm near Young's school, stayed in the U.S.A. to practice. Dr. Carnrite, son of Zaccariah and Nancy Carnrite of the former Burton Adams farm on the Third Concession, set up his practice in Amsterdam, N.Y.

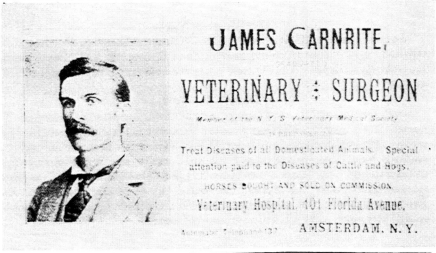

JAMES CARNRITE,

VETERINARY ÷ SURGEON

Member of the N. Y. S. Veterinary Medical Society

Treat Diseases of all Domesticated Animals. Special attention paid to the Diseases of Cattle and Hogs.

HORSES BOUGHT AND SOLD ON COMMISSION.

Veterinary Hospital, 101 Florida Avenue,

AMSTERDAM, N.Y.

Dr. Arthur Carley

Son of Phillip Carley and half brother of Wray Carley and Cecil Carley of the Third Concession, practised out of Prince Edward County.

Dr. William Wallace Colton

Dr. William Wallace Colton, M.D., and his wife, Diantha Jane, of Consecon had a son who became a veterinarian. In 1906 he and his family were farming on Concession 4, Lot 93, owned originally by the Rosebush family and later by Charles Ferguson.

Left to right: Mrs. Colton, Bill, Walter, Greta, and Dr. William Wallace Colton Jr., Veterinarian.

Dr. Burgess Weeks

Son of James and Jane Weeks, Dr. Weeks practised in Consecon. He married Lela Huycke from the north side of Consecon Lake. Sometimes he took chickens (dressed) in payment for services. He practised during the 1920's and 30's.

David W. Walt

In 1864 David Walt was living on the 4th Concession (5th line) on the present John Walt farm. Horses were the backbone of agriculture and the only means of transportation, and since D.W. Walt was a lover of animals, he studied veterinary journals and, coupled with a natural love and keen understanding, he became renowned as a skilled 'Horse Dr.', as local veterinarians were then called. He served the townships of Hillier and Ameliasburgh until he was 88 years old. Often he slept in a stable where he could administer aid to his four-footed patients.

D.W. Walt

D.W. Walt's Tools

The Veterinarians of Roblin Mills

The animal world also had its doctors. There was a veterinarian 1907 in Roblin's Mills named Dr. Pine, (Mrs. Schylar Humphrey was his sister), but he did not stay long. Following him was Dr. Herbert Fox. He was born in 1875 near Eldorado, son of Charles and Fanny Calnan Fox. In 1884 the family moved to Christian St. in Prince Edward County. Herb went on to school and trained as a veterinarian, establishing a practice in Roblin's Mills. He was married twice, his first wife being Alice Brooks who died at age 34 leaving two daughters. Vivian died as a young woman and Lela married Gerald Noxon. Dr. Fox's second wife was Aletha Lont of Roblin's Mills. He had one of the first cars in the village. After a time he retired from veterinary work and took the job of bridgemaster of the Bay Bridge at Rossmore. He served as Deputy-Reeve of Ameliasburgh Township in 1919 and 1920, and Warden of the County in 1919. He died at an early age in 1922.

CHAPTER 34

F̄AIRS

Ameliasburgh School Fairs

The first Ameliasburgh School Fair was held on Friday, Sept. 20, 1912. It was, in fact, the first rural school fair in Prince Edward County. It was held under the auspices of the Ontario Department of Agriculture, through the County Agricultural Representative, A.P. MacVannel. The purpose was to stimulate among rural children a deeper interest and pride in farming, and to put the study of Agriculture into a practical form by enabling young people to conduct enterprises of their own and learn at first hand many of the details they would later need to know.

Mr. MacVannel asked the schools of Ameliasburgh to give the new venture a try. In the spring of 1912 the pupils were requested to make their choice of

Pupils and mothers from Mountain View School at Ameliasburgh School Fair in 1913. Note exhibit tent behind wagon. The teacher, Mabel Kinnear (later Mrs. Lewis Wallbridge) is in centre front with large hat. Two children at back are Cecil and Marjorie Wood; woman at front holding child, Mrs. Dave Dehaney; behind her, Annie Vanwart and Vivian, Driver of wagon, Oral Lee Lauder.

crops from a list submitted; the choice was not too large in this trial year—Banner oats, barley, early Ohio or Delaware late potatoes, Golden Bantam or ensilage corn. The seed was supplied, free of charge, by the Department of Agriculture in time for sowing. Each pupil was required to take at least one variety of seed, to plant and tend his own plot, harvest his crop and exhibit at the school fair. MacVannel and his staff inspected each plot during the summer and prizes were awarded at the fair to the pupil in each section having the best kept plot. Their prize list also included collections of insects, weed seeds and apples. Both heavy and light colts, born after Jan. 1, 1912, were halter broken by pupils and exhibited at the fair.

A report of this first fair in *The Picton Gazette* reads: "The results of their work reached culmination in the town hall at Ameliasburg at which place an exhibition was given of their work. The specimens of their handiwork were truly wonderful. Speaking to the crowd of pupils, parents and visitors, A.P. MacVannel suggested the desirability of extending the work to other townships, and thought that such results could not fail to develop among the pupils a deeper love for farming."

The first fair had been so successful that the prize list was extended in 1913 to include essays and drawings, collections of vegetables, poultry, calves, cooking and sewing, and a bouquet of flowers. As well as seeds, the Department of Agriculture supplied eggs for hatching to those children who wished them, at a nominal charge of 25¢ a dozen. All chickens hatched from these eggs and alive at the time of the School Fair had to be exhibited. Also in 1913, the Department began the practice of supplying a large tent for the

Tug-of-war at Ameliasburgh School Fair.

A huge tent on the fairgrounds.

school exhibits and wire cages for the poultry. While the judging was taking place, a programme of sports was held with races for the various age groups, sack races, three-legged races and a tug-of-war.

By 1916 a school fair was held in each of the seven townships. Judges were supplied by the Department of Agriculture free of charge. Each School Board was requested to give a grant of $3.00 towards the prize money.

By the 1920's more vegetables, flower and fruit classes were added. School parades, drills, marching competitions and Strathcona exercises became a feature of the fairs, with schools vying for originality of designs, drills and uniforms. The competitions varied from year to year. In 1931 there were stock-naming and apple-naming contests, public speaking, sports and Strathcona exercises. In 1935 there was an adding contest, stock judging, school choirs, public speaking and sports. New classes appeared on the prize lists, as neatest patch on grain bag, hammer handle and collection of six named knots in 1932, and model of a bird, footstool, tie rack and rope halter in 1935.

A shield was awarded to the school winning the highest average number of points in proportion to the number of pupils, to be retained for the following year. Any school winning the shield for three years, as S.S. 8 Victoria did, kept the shield permanently. The Department also awarded a certificate of honour to the pupil winning the highest number of points in each school. The winners in 1932 were: S.S. No. 1— Douglas Black, S.S. No. 2— Gladys Mullin, S.S. No. 3— Harold Russell, S.S. No. 4— Doreen Bryant, S.S. No. 7— Ronald Giles, S.S. No. 8— Ross Vanclief, S.S. No. 11— Alex Bass, S.S. No. 12— Connie Wood, S.S. No. 13— Steve Dempsey, S.S. No. 15— Edna Carnrike, S.S. No. 16— Ruth Hickerson, S.S. No. 18— Olive May.

MANGELS—YELLOW LEVIATHAN

Sec. 1. Best 6 roots selected from plot.
Six Prizes—50c, 40c, 30c, 20c and Ribbons.

Class IX.
TURNIPS—HARTLEY'S BRONZE TOP

Sec. 1. Best 6 roots selected from plot.
Six Prizes—50c, 40c, 30c, 20c and Ribbons.

Class X.
POULTRY

All chickens hatched from eggs supplied by Department and alive at time of Fair must be exhibited.

Flocks or single entries may win but one single prize. Entries winning other than First prize may compete in the other sections.

Sec. 1. Best Flock, any number, Cockerels and Pullets, exhibited by one pupil.
Six Prizes—$1.00, 75c, 50c, 25c, and Ribbons.
Sec. 2. Best Pair, Cockerel and Pullet.
Six Prizes—75c, 50c, 25c, 10c, and Ribbons.
Sec. 3. Best Single Cockerel.
Six Prizes—50c, 30c, 20c, 10c, and Ribbons.
Sec. 4. Best Single Pullet.
Six Prizes—50c, 30c, 20c, 10c, and Ribbons.

Class XI.
LIVE STOCK

All stock must be halter broken and exhibited by the pupil.

Sec. 1. Best Heavy Colt, pure bred or grade, born after January 1, 1916.
Six Prizes—75c, 50c, 25c, and Ribbons.
Sec. 2. Best Light Colt, pure bred or grade, born after January 1, 1916.
Six Prizes—75c, 50c, 25c, and Ribbons.
Sec. 3. Best Beef Calf, pure bred or grade, born after January 1, 1916.
Six Prizes—75c, 50c, 25c, and Ribbons.
Sec. 4. Best Dairy Calf, pure bred or grade, born after January 1, 1916.
Six Prizes—75c, 50c, 25c, and Ribbons.

Class XII.
COLLECTIONS

Sec. 1. Collection of not less than 20 Weeds, pressed, mounted and correctly named, and collected in 1916
Sec. 2. Collection of not less than 20 Insects, mounted and correctly named, and collected in 1916 by exhibitor.
Six Prizes—50c, 40c, 25c, 10c, and Ribbons.
Sec. 3. Collection of not less than 12 Weed Seeds, correctly named and collected in 1916 by exhibitor.
Six Prizes—50c, 40c, 25c, 10c, and Ribbons.

Class XIV.

Best kept plots in each Township. Three prizes will be given for each kind of plot. First Prize 50c, Second and Third Prizes, Ribbons.

Class XV.
ESSAYS AND DRAWINGS
(Senior III. and Upwards)

Sec. 1. Essay, "Growing Corn for Ensilage."
Six Prizes—20c, 20c, 10c, 5c, and Ribbons.
Sec. 2. Essay, "How to Cure and Make Hay."
Six Prizes—30c, 20c, 10c, 5c, and Ribbons.
Sec. 3. Essay, "How I Reared My Flock of Chickens."
Six Prizes—30c, 20c, 10c, 5c, and Ribbons.
Sec. 4. "Menu for Farmer's Dinner."
Six Prizes—30c, 20c, 10c, 5c, and Ribbons.
Sec. 5. Drawing "Plan of Basement for Farm Barn suitable for 100 Acre Farm."
Six Prizes—30c, 20c, 10c, 5c, and Ribbons.
Sec. 6. Drawing, "Floor Plan for Poultry House for 100 Hens."
Six Prizes—30c, 20c, 10c, 5c, and Ribbons.

Class XVI.
GIRLS' SECTION

Sec. 1. Loaf of Bread, made by pupil.
Six Prizes—40c, 30c, 20c, 10c, and Ribbons.
Sec. 2. Dozen Cookies, made by pupil.
Six Prizes—40c, 30c, 20c, 10c, and Ribbons.
Sec. 3. Apron, hand sewn, made by pupil.
Six Prizes—40c, 30c, 20c, 10c, and Ribbons.

1916 Prize List, Ameliasburgh Township Rural School Fall Fair.

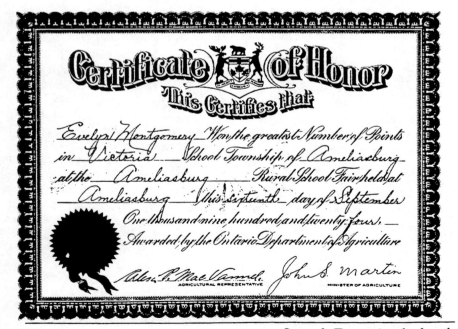

The T. Eaton Co. donated a silver trophy each year to the pupil scoring the greatest number of points at the fair. Winner of this cup in 1927 and again in 1928 was Kathleen Montgomery, Ruth Hickerson in 1931, Joyce Bonter 1935, Jean Conklin 1937, Alfred Cairns 1938.

1939 was the final year for the rural school fairs. The Department of Agriculture was by then pursuing a different approach to the development of agricultural knowledge and skills among rural youth with the 4-H programme. The onset of the Second World War also was a factor in the decision to discontinue the fairs. But, for Ameliasburgh Township from 1912 to 1939, the school fair was a most successful and rewarding venture.

Boys of Victoria School at the fair; Department of Agriculture tent in background. Front row left to right: Gerald Brickman, Harold Wannamaker, Roy Brickman, Joe Foley, Jack Delong. Back row: Harmon Montgomery, John Badgley, Dick Foley, Clarence Vanclief, ——, Ralph Hennesey.

Victoria school pupils doing calisthenics under the direction of teacher Jim Grimmon at 1923 School Fair.

A History of Ameliasburgh Fair

An Ameliasburgh Agricultural Society was formed, and the first Ameliasburgh Fair was held, in 1855. It became an annual event, and was usually held early in October. A fair was held every year from 1855 until 1941. A letter to the editor on Oct. 22, 1856, comments favourably on the recent Ameliasburgh Fair and said the sheep and horses department and the vegetable entries were very good. "The perfect sobriety, good order and kindly feeling which characterized the proceedings of the whole day were particularly observable."

There is no record of where these early fairs were held for the first 20 years. Township Council did not purchase, from David Coleman, the five acres of land on which the Township Hall was built until 1874. From that time hence, the fairs were always held on the township property behind the hall. We can only speculate that Coleman, or some other resident of the village, allowed the Agricultural Society to use some of his land for the livestock judging and some of the exhibits. According to the reminiscences of old-time residents of Roblin's Mills, the Sprague Carriage Factory showroom was used for the exhibits of roots and vegetables, and horse races were held on Main Street.

On Feb. 23, 1875, at the Ameliasburgh Township Council meeting, a motion was passed that: Council do authorize the Agricultural Society to fence the grounds south of the Town Hall suitable for such purposes as they may require, and this Council do agree to hand over to them $100 when such fence is built and also agree to draw up a By-Law allowing the use of the grounds for 10 years for the use of the society. Following is the by-law:

(a) that Elijah Sprague, Francis Peck, Ed Roblin, Peter Bonter, Lewis Brickman, N.A. Peterson, G.H. Sprung, Elias Wallbridge, George Fox, John S. Carnrike, Edward Delong, Directors of the Agricultural Society and their successors, are granted use of the public lands lying south of the town hall for two days each year for ten years, from 1 June 1875 to 1 June 1885.

(b) to pay Ed Roblin, Treasurer of the Society, to fence the grounds.

(c) that the days for use by the Society are Dominion Day and the day of the annual fall show.

(d) that the proceeds from the use of the grounds are for the Society.

(e) that all fences, pens, stands and improvements on the grounds at the expiration of the ten years remain and become township property.

(f) to let the Society use the town hall on the same days.

In 1879 Dr. A.J. File presented to Council a petition signed by 300 people, requesting that two acres of land adjacent to the township grounds be acquired from Edward Roblin, as more space was required for the fair. Council agreed and the two acres were duly purchased for $200.

From the *Intelligencer* of Oct. 12, 1881:

AMELIASBURGH CENTRAL FAIR

The annual Fair of the Ameliasburgh Agricultural Society was held at their grounds, Roblin's Mills on Saturday, Oct. 8, 1881. The exhibit was as good as we have ever seen. The crowd was small due to the bad weather, only about 1500 people on the grounds.

A quilt patched by Mrs. Delong, mother of D.H. Delong, in her 97th year and done without glasses, was a source of interest to all visitors. Line of machinery: fanning mills from the establishment of W.I. Dingle, Oshawa; plough and corn cultivator from Empire Works, Montreal, Wm. and J.G. Peck agents; D. Gibson showed combined seed drill from Masson & Co. Oshawa; 2 reapers manufactured by L.D. Sawyer, Hamilton; fanning mill and 2 ploughs from G.J. Brown, Belleville, shown by agent John Garbutt. An excellent display of carriages and wagons— a covered phaeton trimmed in leather, and a covered family wagon with 2 seats, finely got up, from the carriage shop of Hatch and Allen, Mountain View; 3 lumber wagons, an express wagon with 2 seats, and a richly got up covered buggy were from the carriage shop of the late E. Sprague.

A complete prize list was given.

Among the winners in the fruit class were: S.J. Dempsey, W.R. Weese, W.R. Delong, W. Peck. S. Dempsey, H.Weese and G.A. Weese.

For cattle: Ayrshire— Dr. File, W.K. Burr

Durhams— C. Giles, John Nightingale, Dr. File

Poultry: K.C. Burr, J.L. Clapp, W.K. Burr, D. Clapp, G.A. Weese

Hogs: W.K. Burr, W. Anderson, Dr. File, C. Wannamaker

Sheep: Garbutt Bros., E. Wallbridge, M. Morden, Joseph Nightingale.

The Ameliasburgh Brass Band was upon the grounds during the afternoon and enlivened the proceedings by a few favorite selections. Amount taken in at the gate $160. (last year $180.) Taking into consideration the state of the weather, the show was better than could have been expected."

In 1884 the Agricultural Society again approached Council asking that additional land be purchased. This time Council bought land from David Coleman and George Consaul for $100. The Society leased the grounds for another ten years at $1 per year.

In 1888 the Agricultural Society decided to build an exhibition building, and borrowed $500 from Council for this purpose, the money to be repaid at the rate of $50 per year plus 6% interest. A round, two-storey exhibition building was erected by John R. Cunningham. The second floor consisted of a balcony completely around a central opening. This new building was a great asset. Quilts, embroidery, knitting and other ladies' work was displayed all around the balcony with the vegetable exhibits below. The township hall was always used for exhibits too. Livestock were judged on the grounds- horses, cattle, hogs, sheep, also poultry. Exhibits of machinery, carriages, buggies and wagons were a centre of interest for the large crowds attending this annual fall event.

Cattle judging at Ameliasburgh Fair with round exhibit building in background. The crowd appears to be watching one class being judged while the next class awaits its turn.

The Ameliasburg Agricultural Society
1907 Roblin's Mills, Ontario 1907
ENTRY TICKET

No..........

....

....

....

Class ....Div............ ...Sec............

☞This Ticket must be fastened securely to the article or animal
and remain there during the Exhibition.

1907 Entry Ticket

In 1894 the Agricultural Society paid annual rent of $5 for use of the grounds, and was instructed to keep them free from pasturing stock. In 1896 Council warned the Society not to drive any nails into the woodwork or plaster in the town hall, and to take good care of the chairs and furnishings in the hall while the fair was on.

The 56th Annual Exhibition held in 1911 had an attendance of 1400 persons. The sun shone brightly, the entry lists were large, booths plied their trade, and the Ameliasburgh Band enlivened the proceedings with musical numbers. It was in the feathered creatures that the fair excelled that year with

Dinner Ticket 1914

an entry list of 65 and superior specimens of geese, turkeys and all varieties of barnyard fowl. There were some good horse races on the track.

Mrs. Loral Wanamaker recalls the fairs with nostalgia: "When we were children, this was a great day in our lives. It seems to me this was the only time we would see peaches and grapes, and they were a great treat. Our parents would buy several baskets to preserve and a few to eat. The taffy pulling and band playing and horse racing made a grand spectacular day for us all. It seemed the place to meet all your friends and relatives."

A prize list for 1922 gives Saturday, Oct. 7 as the date for the 67th Annual Exhibition on the Society's Grounds, Roblin's Mills. All livestock was to be on

Mr. and Mrs. Morley Dempsey in open buggy with team of roadsters.

Canadian Bank of Commerce
Trophy won by P.B. Hamilton
in 1929 at Roblin's Mills Fair
for the best team of three year old colts.

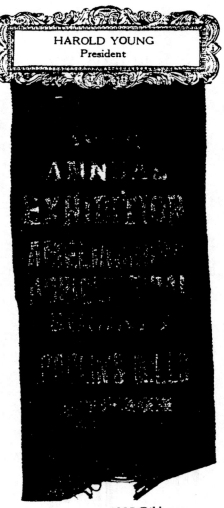

HAROLD YOUNG
President

1927 Ribbon.

the grounds by 10 a.m. There were classes for agricultural horses, general purpose horses, roadster and carriage horses, driving horses and a "best lady driving" section. Cattle classes included Durhams, Ayrshire, Jerseys and Holsteins; there were sheep classes for five breeds. The fruit class listed sections for 31 varieties of apples and five of pears. Some sections not likely to be found on a present day fair list were: butter 5 lbs. in 1 lb. prints, lard 5 lbs. in pail, home rendered, one dressed duck, raspberry vinegar one pint, home-cured ham, buttonholes, darning on wool socks, home-made hand soap 2 lbs in cake, home-dyeing 3 different materials, rag carpet 5 yards, a mended garment, drawn thread work.

By 1928 the round exhibition building was in such a state of disrepair that it was torn down. Council erected a rectangular building that same year in which to store machinery, and allowed its use to display exhibits for the annual fair. Council also gave a yearly grant of $100 to the Agricultural Society.

From the *Daily Ontario*, Nov. 21, 1930, the following: "Huff's Island gardener, Fred E. Motley wins Eckardt Trophy at the Ameliasburgh Fall Fair in 1930 with 1027 points. Runner-up was Charles L. Babcock with 995 points. Announcement was made by W.H.C. Roblin, secretary of the fair board. A condition of the Albert John Herrington Eckardt award is greatest number of points in all classes at the fair. Two qualified at Ameliasburgh Fair. Exhibitors of livestock must be bona fide owners at time of fair, and must show in at least three classes of farm produce; all produce must be from farm of exhibitor. The prize was a four-piece silver tea service, lined with 24-carat gold."

In 1931 the Gananoque Band furnished music during the afternoon, and in the evening there was a concert in the town hall given by the Gilbert Orser Dramatic Co. In 1932 Johnson's Pipe Band marched back and forth several times during the afternoon, "attractive in their kilts." There were some good horse races on the track. The County Calf Club exhibit was one of the most interesting of the events. Nineteen boys had brought their calves and displayed them in the ring, while a great number of people watched the judging. The Gananoque Band was back for the 1934 fair and also provided the music for a dance in the town hall that evening. One of the features of the 1934 fair was a Baby Show with nine babies weighed, measured and examined by Dr. Thompson of Wellington, the winning babies being Donna Casson and Charlie Pickells. There was a ball game between the Mountain View Girls' Softball Team and the (inte Inn girls, and one between the Rednersville boys' team and Victoria. Two Siskins from Trenton Airport gave a display of fancy flying, and a dance was held in the evening.

There were 21 calves shown by the County Boys' Calf Club in 1934. A bicycle race and a slow auto race were two new events. By 1936, as well as the County Calf Club competition, the Girls' Home Garden Club displayed vegetables and record book. In 1938 the 45-piece R.C.A.F. Band entertained and 25 boys from the Ameliasburgh Calf club showed their calves.

By the late 1930's, attendance and exhibits at the fair began to slip, and 1939 was the last fair under the direction of the Ameliasburgh Agricultural Society. For 84 years the Society had held an annual fall fair. The fair did continue for two more years under the auspices of the Hillier and Ameliasburgh Agricultural Society. The 1941 fair was held on Friday, Oct. 10 with the War Emergency Branch of the Red Cross providing a dinner. There was a dance in Idlyewilde Hall in the evening. That was the 86th and final fair.

Presidents and Secretary-Treasurers of the Ameliasburgh Agricultural Society
(Unfortunately there is no record of the officers for the first 12 years)

Year	President	Secretary-Treasurer
1867	Wm. G. Stafford	James Austin
1868	Joseph Nightingale	Irvine Diamond
1869	William DeLong	”
1870	Hugh Brodie	”
1871	Hugh Brodie	Edward Roblin
1872	R.R. Ross	”
1873	Edward DeLong	”
1874	S.M. Herrington	”
1875	Elijah Sprague	”
1876	Francis Peck	J.G. Johnston
1877	William DeLong	”
1878	N.A. Peterson	Edward Roblin
1879	G.H. Sprung	”
1880	John G. Peck	”
1881	Elijah Sprague	”
1882	A.J. File, M.D.	”
1883	S.G. Way	”
1884	Jacob. R. Wood	”
1885	W.E. DeLong	”
1886	H. Welbanks	”
1887	John Nightingale	”
1888	D.T. Stafford	”
1889	J.H. Parliament	”
1890	John Roblin	”
1891	W.R. Weese	”
1892	C.H. Osborne	”
1893	Wesley Weese	”
1894	R.W. Herman	”
1895	John Barber	”
1896	C. Bonter and E. Babbit	”
1897	George Williamson	”
1898	H.W. Weese	”
1899	D.M. Howell	”
1900	F. Onderdonk	”
1901	L.F. Sprague	W.H.C. Roblin
1902	A.M. Weese	”
1903	John A. Howell	”
1904	F.C. File	”
1905	A.J. Huff	”
1906	A. Weese	”

1907	G.B. Sprague	"
1908	D.A. Anderson	"
1909	J.M. Giles	"
1910	Alex H. Anderson	"
1911	C.E. Lauder	"
1912	Everett Sager	"
1913	C.G. Sprague	"
1914	J.W. Gibson	"
1915	C.C. Wannamaker	"
1916	W.J. Barber	"
1917	H.F. DeLong	"
1918	M.B. Weese	"
1919	A.G. Roblin	"
1920	Roy Williamson	"
1921	C. Roy Parliament	"
1922	H.E. Redner	"
1923	E.E. Wallbridge	"
1924	Harry Jose	"
1925	C.W. Ferguson	"
1926	W.H. Montgomery	"
1927	Harold Young	"
1928	G. Ross Roblin	"
1929	G. Ross Roblin	"
1930	C. Ray Jackson	"
1931	James Barber	"
1932	James Barber	Harry Redner
1933	John Weese	"
1934	John Walker	"
1935	Korah Ackerman	"
1936	Francis Wood	"
1937	Milton Wood	"
1938	Merritt Adams	"
1939	Earl Onderdonk	"
1940	Ignatius Nightingale	"
1941	Ignatius Nightingale	"

The 1982-83 Ameliasburgh Fair

By Lee Farmes

1982 was a "red letter" year for Ameliasburgh Township! It was the year the Township Fair was revived after a lapse of over 40 years.

It was first suggested in 1980 that the Fair should be revived. However, it was not pursued until 1981 when a series of meetings were held in conjunction with the Recreation Committee of the Ameliasburgh Township Council. Subsequently, an executive committee of the Fair Board was elected. The idea was to keep it as much a rural fair as possible. The date for the first Fair was October 2nd and 3rd 1982.

The first executive committee was: Robert Bell, Chairman; Dean O'Hara, 1st Vice; Ron Carter, 2nd Vice and Treasurer; and Debbie Ruston, Secretary.

The first Fair in over 40 years got under way to a colourful start with a large parade of 32 separate entries, under the direction of Art Corfield.

Included in the exhibits were ladies crafts, baking and preserves, and junior crafts and baking. There were school exhibits and floral exhibits; cattle, horse and poultry competitions. The Womens Institute and church groups set up food booths on the grounds. There were donkey rides and a petting zoo; local vendors displaying and selling their wares; a police safety display; a small ride for children. There were pony pulls, as well as stage entertainment. The Junior Farmers provided the entertainment for the young folks. The museum was also open during the Fair on a no-charge basis for those attending the Fair. The volunteer fire department operated a game-of-chance booth and also brought along Resusci-Annie to practice mouth to mouth resuscitation. They also displayed newly-purchased extrication equipment. The Trent Valley Five Watters Radio Association provided excellent security on the grounds for the two-day event as well as communications for the parade.

The 1983 Fair was bigger and better still. Robert Bell again took the

Ameliasburgh Fair executive 1982: Ron Carter, Roy Pennell, Debbie Ruston and Robert Bell.

Shaving a balloon contest, Dave and Lee Farmes and Robert and Joan Bell.

Some of the exhibits inside the hall.

Harry Bisdee and his train in the opening parade 1983, Angela Price his passenger.

Poultry exhibits outside.

The Albury choir entertaining at the 1983 fair.

responsibility of Chairman of the Fair Board. Roy Pennell was 1st Vice Chairman; Ron Carter was 2nd Vice and Treasurer, and Lee Farmes was Secretary. There were more exhibits and competitions. The number of classes in which people were able to exhibit and compete were expanded to include flowers and fruits and vegetables. The horse classes were also expanded, and the school division was opened up to competition this year.

The members of the Masonic Lodge provided a lovely chicken barbecue just before the Old Time Fiddlers' Association came on stage to fill the evening hours with their toe-tapping music. Many of the people attending the fair stayed to enjoy the Street Dance on Saturday evening.

The committee feels that the great success enjoyed by the Fair in 1982 and 1983 was due, to a great extent, to the support given to them by the residents and service and volunteer groups in the community. The committee also feels quite sure that with this kind of support, there will not be another 40-year lapse!

CHAPTER 35

BANDS

Bands of Ameliasburgh Village

Ameliasburgh village had three bands over the years. The first was called the Ameliasburgh Brass Band and was very active during the 1880's and 1890's. John Irvine Coleman was a member of this band for 17 years, playing a bass horn. One of the summer activities of this band was furnishing the music on excursion steamer boats going to the Thousand Islands, boarding at Rednersville dock. They also played for many local events, Dominion Day celebrations, Twelfth of July parades and fall fairs. An account of the Ameliasburgh Agricultural Fair of 1881 mentions the Ameliasburgh Brass Band playing "a few favorite selections."

The second Ameliasburgh band was organized at the turn of the century. Coon (Conrad) Delong was the bandmaster, and the members included Fred and Albert File, Charles Palmer and Gil Choate. Their uniforms consisted of dark trousers and vests with white jackets and caps.

Albert File is the first man in back row, and Fred File the third in middle row. Bandmaster Coon Delong is on the left along the side.

The third Ameliasburgh band was active from about 1910 until 1918 when it was disbanded. Bandmaster was Jack Arnold. As well as playing for many events through the year, the band would put on an open-air concert every Saturday night in the summer in front of File Brothers store in the village. Smartly uniformed in white duck trousers and blue jackets and caps, they presented a fine appearance. They had a large, portable acetylene light standard with two arms extending out at the top bearing the light jets to illuminate the surrounding area. Harry Bisdee recalls the young men and their girl friends driving up and down, before and after the band concerts, with their buggies and harness all polished up. The Saturday night band concerts were a great attraction, and it was quite an honour to be in the band.

Ameliasburgh Band— 1911 taken by C. Roy Parliament. Standing: Grant Crosby, Milton Crosby, Earl Spencer, Herb Maybee, Ralph Stafford, Arclan Blakely, Arthur Parliament, Harold Maybee. Kneeling: Albert Crosby, Arthur Beardmore, Albert File, John A. Arnold (Band Master). Sitting: Fred Russell, Harry Crosby, Frank Thompson, Geoffrey File. Little boy at front: John Arnold's son.

The Rednersville Band

The Rednersville Band was organized on Aug. 1, 1919. Ralph G. Stafford was the moving spirit behind it. His was the idea; he organized and trained the band. It consisted entirely of local men, none of whom had ever played in a band before; in fact, most of them had no previous musical training. It says much for Stafford's teaching ability, as well as musical talent, that he could take a group of 15 men and teach them how to play several different instruments, so that in a few months' time they were proficient enough to start playing at various public functions.

Rednersville Band, Ralph G. Stafford, Band Master. Back row: William R. Russell, Sherman F. Babbitt, Elgin Herrington, Melvin Pulver, George Clapp, Ross Roblin, Douglas K. Redner. Front Row: Otho Herrington, Ernest Russell, Roy Anderson, Ralph Stafford, Bert Covert, Rae Roblin, Donald K. Spencer, Clifford Hillman. The picture was taken at the old Belleville Fair Grounds.

The first officers of the newly formed band were: President, the Reverend L.M. Sharpe; Secretary-treasurer, Alfred Hillman; Bandmaster, Ralph Stafford. From a Toronto firm they obtained 15 excellent, reconditioned, second-hand instruments (later buying two more) which looked like new, but cost considerably less. Melvin Pulver recalls paying $28 for his E flat alto horn. Each member of the band paid for his own instrument and, later, his own uniform. They purchased military type uniforms, also from a Toronto firm. They were dark blue, trimmed with red and brass buttons. The peaked caps had gold braid trimming on the front. The uniforms were of a heavy material and were lined as well, so they were extremely hot on a warm summer day. So summer uniforms with white duck trousers were purchased during the summer of 1920.

Band practices were originally held in Mr. Stafford's grist mill, and later in the upper storey of Adelbert Roblin's drivehouse with a wood stove supplying the necessary heat in the cold weather. The following were regulars: William R. Russell, snare drum; Bert Covert, bass drum; Douglas Redner and George Clapp, bass horns; Ross Roblin, baritone; Harold Babbitt, trombone; Sherman Babbit, Elgin Herrington and Arza Pulver, tenor horns; Melvin Pulver, alto horn; Donald Spencer, Rae Roblin and Roy Anderson, cornets; Ernest Russell, E flat cornet; Otho Herrington and Clifford Hillman, clarinets, with Bandmaster Stafford on occasion playing clarinet too.

The band had 13 engagements during the summer and fall of 1920. They played in several parades and celebrations- on the 1st of July, the 12th of July, the I.O.F. picnic and the Ameliasburgh Fair. They also played at ice-cream socials and other events, and gave a concert on the Roblin lawn. The usual fees charged were $15 for socials and $25 for fairs. On the church circuit there was no charge. The money was used to purchase music.

At their second annual meeting held on Jan. 15, 1921, the following officers were elected: President, Adelbert Roblin; Secretary, Douglas Redner; Treasurer, Rae Roblin. Adelbert Roblin was presented with a smoking set from the boys of the band in appreciation of the band room he had supplied, fuel and light for same, and his generosity in lending a helping hand in time of need.

Melvin Pulver remembers the band playing at Rossmore on July 1, 1921 when the Bay Bridge was formally declared toll-free. He also recalls the band going on an excursion to a U.E.L. celebration at Adolphustown by steamer, leaving from Belleville. The band played on board the boat, as well as at the afternoon programme at Adolphustown.

The Rednersville Band continued to play at all manner of events until 1929 when they disbanded.

CHAPTER 36

CANNING FACTORIES

The History of The Canning Industry

By Jane Elizabeth Sprague

The publication of this book recognizing the 200th Anniversary of the arrival of the United Empire Loyalists to the Quinte region coincides with the 100th Anniversary of the food processing industry in the area. Since the first canning factory was built in 1885, the industry prospered and grew rapidly. As canned goods became more and more popular, the local industry had a significant input into the Canadian market.

When the first United Empire Loyalists arrived on the soil of Prince Edward County, they had to overcome many hardships in establishing homesteads. As they worked with their families and neighbours, their first and most important priorities were clearing the land and producing enough food to last throughout the long and cold winter months. Survival was the paramount concern of these early pioneers during the first years of settlement.

Over the years however, as the farms and communities developed they were able to produce more food than was required within the immediate area. From that time until the present, the agricultural community has continuously searched for methods of reaching further markets with an ever-widening variety of food products which lends itself to cultivation in the area.

The first crop grown in the area for shipment to other areas was barley.

Original Sprague Canning Factory, Mountain View, 1928. Still being used as a warehouse.

Soon after, other cereal crops were being shipped. This was followed by the production of cheese which resulted in a very intensive cheese manufacturing industry in Prince Edward County and indeed the rest of eastern Ontario. This industry thrived and was a major source of income for the area until the post-World War II era.

The preserving of fruits and vegetables in various types of containers was a technology developed to enable Napoleon to feed his troops when he invaded Russia. This skill had therefore been available for about 100 years before becoming commercially utilized in this area. When the equipment and technology necessary to process and properly seal containers on a commercial basis became available here, it made it possible to produce preserved fruits and vegetables.

Soon after technology was available, one after another enterprising resident established manufacturing plants to enable fruits and vegetables grown in Prince Edward County to appear on store shelves thousands of miles away. This combination of agricultural and manufacturing capability immediately expanded the markets for food products of the area.

The first canning factory in Prince Edward County was built in Picton by Wellington Boulter in 1885. Within three years, canned goods from the area were being shipped to western Canada by rail and within ten years whole trains of Prince Edward County canned goods were being transported west.

In the early 1900s, canned goods were being exported to all parts of Canada and to England. This paralleled the long established cheese trade routes. Shipment by boat was the most popular means by which earlier shipments were made. With about 500 miles of shoreline and several harbours, Prince Edward County was well suited for exporting its products by this means.

Potter's Canning Factory at The Union

By Loral Wanamaker

The first canning factory in Ameliasburgh Township was the Potter factory built in the 1890's. I was born in 1896 and I am sure the factory had

Canadian Canners Factory at Rednersville

been going for some time then. In 1898 Mr. Stanley Potter hired my father, Grant Wanamaker, to assist in the making of cans along with Fred Potter, a cousin of Mr. Potter's. The cans were made during the winter months and right up until the canning season began. The cans of that day were all hand-made and of a much heavier tin than the cans of today. Mr. Potter bought the tin in sheets and the cans were made up on the third floor of the factory with the help of some machinery. First the large sheets of tin were cut into can-size strips which we then put through a roller to make them round. Next they went on another machine which turned a hook edge and the side seams were float-soldered with solder and resin. Other hand machines pressed or, as they said, 'knocked out' bottoms and tops for the cans. Each top had a round hole in it through which the can was filled when completed. First the top was snapped on and soldered on the inside through the open bottom. The bottom was then snapped on and soldered on the inside through the cap hole in the top.

The canning season began with asparagus, then peas, corn tomatoes, followed by pumpkin and pork and beans. The men who had made the cans were then kept busy sealing the cans after they had been filled by the local women, who were picked up by a covered wagon sent by Mr. Potter. At first the shelling of the peas was done by the women, but Mr. Potter soon bought a viner. The corn was husked and cut off by hand until he bought cutters and a corn gun. My father and Fred Potter would be given the filled cans on trays that carried a dozen cans. They had a little engine which pumped air into a fire-box where their solder irons were heated. They placed a cap over the hole in the top of the can with solder and a round soldering iron made it air-tight. The final drop of solder went on the vent or air-hole in the cap. Then the cans went down to the basement where there was a large retort for cooking.

I know that local women would remove the cap by the use of a hot coal from the stove or a hot ring placed on the cap. Then when the contents were emptied, they would wash these cans through the hole in the top, dry them and re-use them when canning their own produce.

Eventually, as more canning factories were operating, there was a glut of canned goods on the market and Mr. Potter had difficulty in selling his produce and was forced out of business by the big canners. This was quite a loss to the local women in work and also to the local farmers for their produce.

The second canning factory in Ameliasburgh Township was the Rednersville Canning Company built about 1910 by three founding families named Parliament, McFaul and Haight. The factory was operated by the owners for several years until it was taken over by Canadian Canners Limited, who operated the plant until it was destroyed by fire in 1951. This plant canned tomatoes and employed up to 70 people during the peak season.

The third canning factory in Ameliasburgh Township was a factory at Consecon built in 1912 on the shore of Weller's Bay directly across the road from the Consecon Railway Station. A spur line of the railway serviced the plant. The document entitled *Prospectus and Statuatory Information* dated May

During World War II the Brickmans gave the use of their factory to the Rednersville W.I. one day a week to make jam for the Red Cross. 8,800 pounds of jam were made and sent overseas. This picture was taken in 1940. Back row left to right: Mrs. Alex Gilmour, Mrs. McLean, Mrs. Harry Peck, Mrs. Harry Cunningham, Mrs. Will Hubbs, Mrs. B.L. Redner. Front Row: Mrs. L.R. Brickman, Mrs. Jack Scott, Mrs. Roy Williamson, Mrs. W. Simpson, Miss Audra Brickman.

Lorne Brickman with a trailer load of jam for the Red Cross.

23, 1912 reports that its registered name was Consecon Canning Co. Ltd. Its manager and president was Arthur Allan of Frankford who obtained 40 shares of $100 each from the local farmers. To become a director one had to own at least one share. Adam S. Burr who owned the mill at Consecon was a shareholder, as was Cyrus Humphrey on whose farm the factory was built, and M.B. Trumpour of Hillier.

The Consecon Canning Co. was later taken over by the Dominion Canners, and following that became a Canadian Canners factory. Peas, corn and tomatoes were processed there. Harold Clarke and Jim Mattis of Consecon can recall husking corn by hand at the factory. Farmers who grew peas for the factory took the pea straw back to their farms and hung it over rail fences to dry before storing it for winter cattle fodder. Tomatoes were peeled in large aluminium dishpans. William Hamilton (Bessie Smith's father) grew tomatoes for the princely sum of 17¢ a bushel! To make matters worse, the loads of tomatoes were graded at the factory and docked anywhere from 20% to 50%

Robert Young was manager of the factory during the 1920's when it was a Canadian Canners Plant. He was followed by Leo Gosleigh. Then Charles Carter and his nephew Edmund Carter from the Stinson Block managed the factory together for a number of years until it closed in 1932. The factory was later torn down.

The Howard Weese Canning Factory
by Frances Weese

In 1924, Grant Sprague built a canning factory at Mountain View. After three years, he decided that this was not to his liking and turned the factory over to his son Jay who operated it for 40 years until his untimely death in 1967. Following Jay's death, his elder son Roger Edward took it upon himself to continue the operations. The following year he had constructed a new canning factory to extend the seasonally operated business into a year-round operation. Over the years, the main production has been canned tomatoes, although pumpkin, corn and raspberries were also processed. Most recently the mainstay of production consists of a wide variety of canned beans. This plant remains as the only canning factory still operating in Ameliasburgh Township.

The next plant to appear in Ameliasburgh Township was built in 1930 by Alex Lipson at Consecon. This was the first plant to operate under the name United Canners. Tomatoes and peas were the first crops processed with corn production starting later. Cream style corn was the only crop processed during later years. Upon the death of Alex Lipson in 1978, operations ceased.

The last plant to be established in Ameliasburgh was opened in 1947 by Howard Weese, west of Rednersville near Albury. This plant operated until 1955 processing tomatoes, tomato purée and apple sauce.

Many of the canning factories in Prince Edward County originated as a result of expanding home canning industries. In Ameliasburgh Township, the Brickman Home Canning Company on the Gore and Eddy Hall's plant on Huff's Island were two such cottage industries which began in 1934. Eddy Hall's business ceased in the early 1940's while the Brickman Home Canning

---

Six row tomato planter devised by Howard Weese.

Company continued on until the death of the founder Lorne Brickman in 1959. The Brickman plant canned a variety of locally produced foods including green and yellow beans, tomatoes, pumpkin, asparagus, corn, peas and chicken.

In 1946 the canning factory was a steel barn, about 35 by 120 feet, with the ceiling of the main floor 8½ feet high. It had not housed the 50 Hereford steers, its former occupants, for a number of years, but was an attractive building. By 1948 it was still attractive, but had undergone a great transformation. It was now a tomato canning factory, owned and operated by Howard Weese.

Howard had purchased that property, Lot 91, east half, Concession 1, Township of Ameliasburgh, from George Hardy and sold his small canning factory at Crofton in Sophiasburgh in 1946. He spent much time planning his new factory, enjoying every minute of it. Then came the searching for used equipment, buying it when possible (e.g. the water tube boiler with auger) and ordering new equipment. Some equipment he designed himself.

One piece of equipment he designed was the flume. He built it with the help of his friend and right hand man, Jack Dawson. It was erected on the platform west of the building, running down the middle of this platform. On both sides of it the crates of tomatoes were piled, and water was piped into the flume at the south end. The tomatoes were dumped into the water, accomplishing two things— it prevented crushing the tomatoes, and, at the same time, they were pre-washed. This flume was about 70 feet long, turning at the north end on a 90 degree angle going into the rotary washer. A stainless steel belt conveyed the tomatoes through the scalder and past the sorters, who picked out the best for the cans of whole tomatoes. The others went on to be processed for juice or purée. Howard received compliments from various inspectors, and produced a high quality pack of tomatoes. He had a contract with the Toronto General Hospital for salt-free tomatoes. The regular tomatoes he sold to Canada Packers and to brokers.

Actually this was the third of Howard's canning enterprises. The first one was in the basement of what became Quinte Inn. It was under the north verandah, which was supported by cement pillars at that time. The workers could view the beautiful bay when their eyes were not focused on tomatoes. There was only one retort sunk in the ground near the west end. To heat the water for the retort, Howard had a steam engine from an old threshing machine. Fortunately for the Inn, this lasted only one season; then he bought the small factory at Crofton. The barn-factory building still remains as a workshop and storage, and has had a new roof since factory days.

CHAPTER 37

FISHING & TRAPPING

Fishing In Ameliasburgh

Ameliasburgh Township has many miles of shoreline bordering on the Bay of Quinte and Weller's Bay and as well, two lakes in its environs. In days gone by, these waters teemed with fish; bass, pickerel, pike, salmon, perch, carp, suckers, eel and maskinonge. In the fall of the year, whitefish and herring were plentiful. In the spring spawning season, every inlet, creek and marsh seemed to be alive with fish.

In the summer, whitefish, the most valuable, were caught in nets that were set in the bigger bodies of water and in the fall by seines. In 1830, William Whittier was a fish buyer in Consecon. In 1805-51 the Directory noted that 3000 pounds of whitefish were shipped from Consecon, and that Brady and Young, merchants in Consecon, handled whitefish and salmon trout from Consecon fishermen. Mrs. William Robinson, who came to Consecon in 1852,

Morley Bisdee with fish caught in Roblin's Lake (1920's).

Left: Net Winders; Right: Clark's Fishing Camp at Consecon on Weller's Bay.

reported that in one catch of two nets, as many as 16,000 fish, were landed. They were packed in 200-pound barrels and shipped to the States. In fact, prior to that, Consecon was so noted for its Indian name for Pickerel or Big Fish that it was decided to keep its Indian name.

In those days herring and whitefish were cleaned, cured in brine, packed in half barrels and sold for five dollars per hundred pound barrel. They were shipped to New York or Buffalo.

Rossmore was an important fishing area and in early days fishing was good. Nets were set in the bay and when lifted they often contained a ton of fish. The Belnaps of Rossmore often lifted their nets three or four times a day. Herring, pike, perch and bullheads were caught in quantity. For many years the Bay of Quinte Fisheries buildings stood just across and at the north end of the Bay Bridge and Ameliasburgh people both bought and sold fish there.

Gardenville, on Weller's Bay, had its share of fish and fishermen. Harry Young was a dealer, and Marshall, Arnot and Keith, three generations of Youngs, were commercial fishermen. O.G. Moynes and Stanley Hart also fished and likely many others. They packed their fish in boxes with ice and shipped them from the Gardenville train station.

Smoke's Point had its generations of Bonters who were commercial fishermen. When Weddell Bonter wasn't fishing, he guided fishermen and duck hunters who holidayed here.

Farmers, like Blake Rowe who had a creek on his farm that emptied into the bay, got into the act. With a pitchfork he loaded carp on his democrat and shipped them. Young lads, as soon as school was over, waded the creeks in their hip-rubber boots, spear in hand, and threw out the big ones. When the ice left the lakes the young at heart went 'Jack-lighting'. A light was attached to the front of the boat which attracted the fish so they were easily caught with a long-handled spear. Eels were so plentiful they ignored them, as one a year was

George Offen and Robert J. Hanthorn with 87.5 lb. sturgeon taken in Ameliasburgh Township waters of Bay of Quinte in Spring of 1947. Bob was 16 years old. George was a great hockey player for the Consecon team of that era in the Prince Edward League.

sufficient to provide the boot laces made from eel skin.

Enterprising mothers canned some fish in jars. The raw fish were cut in pieces, packed in the jars, salt and some vinegar added to soften the bones, processed for three or more hours in boiling water and the end product was much like the pink salmon that we buy tinned from the store.

The *Trenton Courier*, Feb. 26, 1885 noted— "Fishermen at Consecon Bay have huts on the ice and catch from one to two dollars worth of pike, pickerel and bass a day". Ice fishing has again become a popular sport and some excellent catches were reported in the winter of 1983-84.

Commercial fishing on a large scale waned and brought changes to families where fishing seemed hereditary, like the Clark family in Consecon. Now all that has changed. They have turned to sport fishing and guiding, running a fishing camp and catering to the tourist trade.

The Fur Industry

by Roger Redner

Isn't it wonderful that one can still work with Canada's Heritage in the Fur Industry? It dates back to some 400 years ago, when man began to play a part in a developing world in which food and fur was important for existence.

Well, there's another beaver on the board; some 125 nails and about 1½ hours later, it is ready to dry. I am not the fastest beaver skinner and flesher, but I like to do a good job. When the animal is removed from the water, it is the best it will ever be, and it is up to us to maintain that quality with proper handling of the pelt, which we hope will reward us with the best possible price.

The trapping season opens in mid-October and runs to the end of March. Animals harvested in this area are Muskrat, Raccoon, Beaver, Mink, Fox, Coyote, Ermine, Red Squirrel; these species are all present in Prince Edward County.

The Fur Harvest in this area is essentially a part-time occupation, which works in well with my cash crop farming operation, as well as for those who have seasonal employment. There are about 250 trappers in Prince Edward

Roger Redner with a folding underwater trap for muskrat or mink.

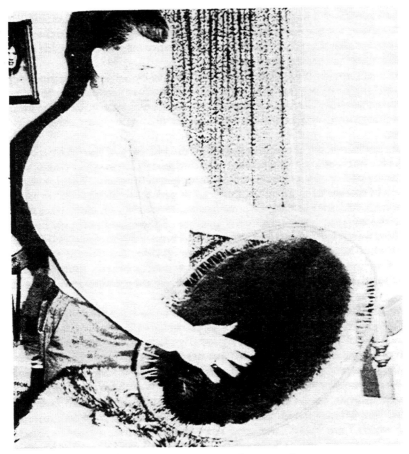

Roger Redner with a beaver pelt.

County, which is part of Napanee District of Ministry of Natural Resources.

Times are changing from the days when trappers were loners, hiding their secrets from each other. Now workshops, open to trappers and the public, are common and well-attended events. In 1947 the Ontario Trappers Association was formed.

I started to trap when I was a boy in public school and, despite years of experience, I find there is always something to learn from fellow trappers. One device that I have made some modifications to is a two-cell Duracell flashlight used as a test device to detect if the circuit has been broken in an underwater 330 Conibear, set for beaver. If it has, you can suspect a probable catch and, with your ice chisel, go to work to remove it. Otherwise you are saved the time and effort and go to the next trap.

I am very much aware that many people are opposed to trapping, and I agree that the industry could do with more research to make the fur harvest as humane as possible. In fact, during the past few years I assisted in designing a leg-hold inground snare thrower for one of the major trap companies in Canada.

Furs are harvested under the control of the Ministry of Natural Resources, and the fur harvester is an asset to farmers and society in general. Animals such as raccoons and coyotes cause loss of farm crops and livestock. There is also the problem of disease such as rabies. It costs this province alone about six million dollars each year for the control of rabies, and it would be a lot more if it were not for the trapper who controls the number of animals in his area. Trappers keep close watch for signs of any diseases and keep wildlife agencies informed.

But what happens to the carcasses when all those fur pelts are removed? Little, if any, is wasted. For many animals, especially beaver, there is a ready market for the meat. Other carcasses are used as food for animals such as sled dogs.

The means for getting around trap lines are as variable as the weather. Trappers may use hip waders, snowshoes, all-terrain, three-wheeled vehicles or snowmobiles. A trapper must have signed permission from landowners for his trap lines to get a Ministry licence. Running the trap line is only part of the work. Each animal must be skinned, stretched and dried, and the quality of a pelt may often count on the skill of the trapper in those three areas. To become a licensed trapper, one is also required to take the province's mandatory Fur Harvest, Fur Management, Conservation course which is offered annually, and of which I am Head Instructor with special experts in various areas to assist me. Instruction includes the types of traps and their uses, and hands-on experience at skinning the species available locally— raccoon, beaver and muskrat. There is a field trial for a full day in which each student must make five sets of traps. The student is judged on finding the right locations and setting the traps properly and most humanely. Minimum mark to pass the course is 75 percent.

A trapper must also take the safe gun handling course to qualify for a small game hunting licence before he can qualify for a trapper's licence.

With the Ministry of Natural Resources supporting the Fur harvester and working close together, it is hoped that Canada will continue to be looked upon as the best in fur quality and fur management the world over.

Left: Seymour Hamilton with Canada Goose. Above: Muskrat house in marsh. Below: Muskrat pelts stretched on forms. Everett Jones & Bill Vanwart.

Trapping On Huff's Island Marsh

By Seymour Hamilton

About 1840 Mr. Osborne of Arnprior purchased 1,000 acres of marsh land from the Crown, to be used as a cranberry marsh. At that time the area was covered with marsh hay. In 1876 it was surveyed from the Bay of Quinte to lot 65 on the third concession of Ameliasburgh.

The marsh generally sat idle except for some duck hunting and a little trapping until 1921, when farmers, with land bordering the south side of the marsh, found out that they did not own it, even though they paid taxes on it. So the farmers purchased the marsh for the sum of $1,000 from Osborne and his descendants. Each farmer received a clear deed to the marsh bordering his property. This action was disputed hotly by poachers who took the farmers to court. However, the farmers won the case because of their clear deeds. The court hearing was held in Ameliasburgh Township Hall. Francis O. Flynn was the poachers' lawyer while Walter Herrington defended the farmers.

About this time muskrat pelts were bringing $5 each and trappers often got 50 pelts in a day.

In 1927, Lee M. Brown bought some of the marsh with the plan of raising the water in the marsh and selling live muskrats for export and breeding purposes in Europe. In fact, Walter and William Hamilton sold a considerable number of live muskrats for $5 a pair. However, Brown's plan fell through because of low water levels in the dry years of the thirties.

In 1940 the rats began to come back— slowly at first. Examples of catches follow:

> 1943— 185 muskrats, price $1.85 a pelt.
> 1947— 915 muskrats, price $3.25 a pelt.
> 1956— 145 muskrats, price $1.85 a pelt.

Between the years 1943 to 1956, the writer caught 5,462 muskrats, at an average income of about $1,000 per year.

The marsh provided the farmers of Huff's Island a second crop each year. Heavy trapping seemed to actually increase the muskrat crop since it conserved their food supply.

In 1983, rats again are scarce. As a result of the trapping seasons, Seymour Hamilton was able to take a 30-day trip to Australia on the proceeds of his trapping.

There are a few beavers in the marsh now, along with the odd mink, coyote, fox, deer, raccoon and snapping turtle. On June 29, 1949, there appeared the first snowy egret to visit the marsh. The following day two egrets were observed. Later their nest was discovered on lot 65. In the autumn, four egrets were seen— the parents and two young ones. Six African Ibis came in on a strong south wind and remained for a week. Blue herons are common visitors along with many wild ducks. In May, 1983, at least a thousand Canada geese stopped to feed on lots three, four and five during their migration northward.

The marsh provides a home for fish, the most common being bass, perch, mudcat and carp. In all it is a paradise for naturalists.

CHAPTER 38

Museums

Ameliasburgh's First Museum

Edited from an article by the late Blake Young

The CHADD MUSEUM was the first museum in Ameliasburgh Township. It was located on the shore of Young's Cove at the Carrying Place on property now owned by the Hancock Lumber Company.

Across Weller's Bay on the lake side is a strip of beach which was Indian stamping ground or settlement. The Indians called it Nee-we-gee-waum, but to us it is Bald Head Point. They probably used it as a short cut from Brighton to Consecon. It was logged off early in the century, leaving it vulnerable to wind and weather and by 1851 the Waters of Lake Ontario cut a wide channel through the beach.

An ardent antiquarian, in the person of George J. Chadd, was appointed Customs Inspector at Young's Point. Very often after work he crossed over to Bald Head to explore and gather articles he found there. He filled two rooms in an old boarding house there that had been built by the McMullen Brothers, near their iron ore dock, with one of the finest collections of relics and curios in the country.

George Chadd collected flint arrow heads, tomahawks, bayonets, muskets, muzzle loaders, Indian beads, Indian skulls, one with an arrow head still buried in it, and upon discovery of an Indian grave, he found the body had been buried in a sitting position and many trinkets interred with it. His discovery of artifacts of a religious nature led to the supposition that the Kente Mission may have been here, a theory later discounted. Mr. Chadd's collection also contained stuffed birds and animals such as ducks, loons, owls, hawks and a flying squirrel. His fascinating egg collection included one ostrich egg.

During the summer, many people came to view Chadd's relics (for which he charged a small fee) and then went fishing. It was a common sight to see horse-drawn vehicles filled with people with long fishing poles protruding from the rear. If you had no pole you cut a tag alder, tied a cord to it with a hook and something for a sinker, baited the hook with a fishworm, dangled it from the iron-ore dock nearby and were rewarded with a good catch.

When the Prince Edward Railway became the Central Ontario Railway, George Chadd was appointed stores keeper for it, no doubt because his slogan was "Waste not, Want not". He moved to Trenton where he constructed a building on Stanley St. to display his collection.

Mr. Chadd had, in addition to his own collection, artifiacts from other local people. One such addition came from Crooked Creek Farm, owned by the Robinson family of Consecon Lake. At one time he refused $20,000 for his exhibits.

Sometime after Chadd's death, the Royal Ontario Museum in Toronto acquired his collection and you may see it there today.

G.J. Chadd

The Ameliasburgh Museum

by Harry Bisdee

It is snowing to-day after a lovely winter, this March 11, 1983. I sit in my window and look across the road at a building with a past. Built in 1868 by our ancestors, also with a past, but with a longing look at the future, it is a building of stone with a very high steeple pointing upward to heaven and looking down on us.

Ameliasburgh Museum complex.

It was first built as a Wesleyan Methodist Church, became a United Church in 1925, and served the community until 1967 when it was closed and the congregation went elsewhere to worship. Then the great question arose, "What will we do with the House of God?" Some churches had been closed and turned into other purposes that were not befitting a place of so many fond memories. Many ideas were brought forth until Norris Whitney, our member of Parliament in Toronto, suggested a museum. He waited on Township Council with the idea, also thought that, if Council would go ahead with the plan, he might get a grant from the Ontario Government. George Cunningham was the reeve at the time, and was very enthused. From then on, plans began to formulate. The money was made available, and someone had to be put in charge to build a museum. I, being a life-long resident of the village and also a member of the Church, was called upon to get the show on the road. Peter Styrmo, Head of the Ontario Museum Association, and his assistant came from Toronto with ideas and plans. We also visited the Wellington Museum for help and layouts. Home we came, full of zeal, and started to work. First the church had to be stripped of its original furnishings, material ordered, and help spoken for. Walter Humphrey, my brother-in-law, was willing to give a hand, and also my son, Eugene. Soon everybody was eager to help.

A Museum Board was set up consisting of: Harry Bisdee— Curator, William Nightingale— Secretary-Treasurer, Grace Whitney, Mac Wallbridge, and Laird Adams and Arnold Wetherall— Members of Council.

Work progressed at full speed from the first day. A floor plan was drawn

Harry Bisdee, curator of the Ameliasburgh Museum for nine years. Courtesy: The Trentonian.

up, consisting of a school, chapel, kitchen, parlor, bedroom, blacksmith shop, and also an Indian display, along with paintings by the Reverend Bowen Squire of life in the early days of Prince Edward County that were purchased by the Township. Then came the time to fill the cases and floor displays, with nothing in sight. I contacted Mr. Styrmo for advice, "Will I advertise?" He said, "Never! You will get things you will never want, but will have to display. Just pass the word to a few people and then let things take their course."

On June 30, 1968, Opening Day, we were full of everything that we were set up for, and of the best that the Township had to offer. Some cases were changed as many as three times to satisfy the donors. Reverend Maurice McLeod came on the scene to help, and was a tower of strength as he had experience in antique displays in Kingston in his college days. On Opening Day, people came from far and wide. Elmer Bonter had given us good publicity by sending in progress reports and pictures of the museum from day one. Many notables came, as well as a crowd of well-wishers, and it was off to a good start.

One evening my wife and I were on a drive through our township when we spotted a log house about five miles from home. She said that we should have it for a museum. I told the board; they were all for it, and Mac Wallbridge offered to interview the owner, Vince O'Hara. He donated the building to the museum. In the spring of 1969, Wm. Knox with trucks and backhoes from the Township Road Department and many willing helpers had the house down

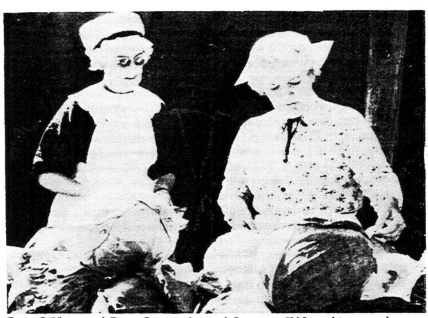

Betty O'Hara and Rena Cunningham of Consecon W.I. making sauerkraut at a 1983 Activity Day. Courtesy: The Trentonian.

The log cabin on the Museum grounds.

and delivered in two days, along with the stone cellar at the rear which, when restored, became the fireplace and stone chimney. The house was put on display in June of 1970 with Rev. McLeod, now on the Board, in charge of setting it up for viewing. Many lovely old things came to the log house from the Norris Whitney home.

In 1970 the first display barn was built and furnished, and also a large display shed with farm machinery. Then a blacksmith shop followed with hand-pump bellows and a forge in working order. A full-scale saphouse with evaporator and furnishings for a maple sugar display were donated by Elmer Young. In 1974 a second barn was built, bird pens and animal compounds. A stone mill was built in 1975, and a milk house followed. Many artifacts were donated and set on cement slabs on the grounds. A windmill was donated by Reginald Barber and restored to working condition. A martin house was donated, and a large number of martins have made it their home ever since. We also added a smoke house from which great gusts of smoke and some lovely edible delights come every Activity Day.

I can't begin to name and thank all of the people who gave of their time to help at the museum, but will mention Bill Nightingale who so capably looked after our finances.

In the beginning the staffing was donated. One day Ellen Cunningham, one of the guides, came up with the idea of an activity day. We tried it, and it was such a success that it has continued three times each season ever since with large crowds attending. By this time we were growing and Reg Barber and Frances Young were added to our staff of museum board members. Many schools came to the museum with busloads of children to see how our ancestors lived and what they had to work with. Travelways of Toronto also had us on their route.

In 1975, a second floor was added to the museum with many rooms made available for further displays. A rock display was set up upstairs, and an 1854 Fourth Division Court room with the original Judge's chair and bench, and a set of hand cuffs from the original jail in the Ameliasburgh Township Hall in 1874.

I retired as curator in 1977. Vivian Swain became the new curator, in whose capable hands the museum carried on. In the following years a log barn was moved in, a carpenter's shop established, a pea viner, weaver's cottage, canteen, two old-fashioned corn cribs and herb shop added. The unsightly electric wires were put underground. Three flag poles were erected, many flower beds established, a vegetable garden and herb garden planted and improvements made on the grounds. In 1982 many trees were donated and planted throughout the grounds. Since 1968 many changes have come, and many faces of the original crowd have gone, but, with many capable hands available, the Museum will still carry on and, I hope, never look back.

Licence plate collection at the museum.

Upstairs in the Museum, 1968.

Photos courtesy The Trentonian

The Rev. Maurice McLeod making butter at a 1977 Activity Day.

Bill Cannons making cider at a 1977 Activity Day.

The blacksmith shop at the museum, 1968.

Ameliasburgh Museum grounds at an Activity Day in 1977.

Harry Bisdee's little train at a 1982 Activity Day.

CHAPTER 39

Dutch-Canadians

Ameliasburgh's Dutch-Canadians

As much a part of Ameliasburgh's history as the United Empire Loyalists are the Dutch immigrants who came here in the 1940's and 50's, escaping because they had suffered from German and Russian hostilities. Few of them spoke English, but they were sure they would find a better life here than they had left behind.

It was largely due to the efforts of Jan VanderVliet that so many Dutch immigrants settled here. Some of the names that come to mind are Banga, Veltman, Andeweg, Kuiken, Westerhof, Devries, Werkhoven, TenHove, Westerveld, Vandervelde, Fledderus, Zandstra, Kuipers, Voskamp, VanVliet, Vanzoeren, Hoekstra, VanRhyn, Korver and Teerstra.

The VanderVliet and Voskamp Families

Jan VanderVliet had come to Canada from the Netherlands in the late 20's and his family settled in Trenton in January, 1948, when he was appointed by the Christian Immigration Centre as an agent to look after and find sponsors for the Dutch citizens wanting to emigrate. In the early days an immigrant had to be farm-oriented in order to come.

Every area had a fieldman working with VanderVliet who spent time travelling across the country. From 1958-1966, Jan VanderVliet was Vice Consul for the Netherlands, appointed by Queen Julianna. For meritorious work he was awarded the Olivier Van Noort medallion and certificate from the Netherlands government.

In their home, Jan and Alida VanderVliet spoke English, French, German and Dutch with guests. He was active in beginning the first Dutch Credit union, the Christian School and was editor of a Dutch newspaper, *Calvinist Contact.*

After retirement in 1966, the VanderVliets bought a large home on the north shore of Consecon Lake where they enjoyed fishing and entertaining their family and friends. They celebrated their 50th wedding anniversary in 1973. Both have since that time passed away.

The VanderVliet's had three daughters, but only Alida has remained in Ameliasburgh. She is married to Leonard Voskamp, who when he was 20 years old emigrated to Canada from Holland with his parents, five brothers and two sisters.

Alida and Leonard Voscamp came to the Gore in Ameliasburgh and bought the farm previously owned by John Black. Here they began a poultry business raising broilers. Here they raised their family of two sons and four daughters. On the same farm, Leonard and Alida in 1982 built their retirement home and their son Peter and his wife Cathy (Carlisle) have taken over the farm and poultry industry.

CHAPTER 40

N̄OSTALGIA

Cars Of My Youth

By Harry Bisdee

The first car I can remember was a 'Mitchell', owned and driven by Albert Carley of Melville. It was a large car with high wheels. William Black, who was my wife's uncle, also had one. He started from his home near Dead Creek with a full tank of gasoline and ran out before he had gone the 12 miles to Belleville. The choke was out, which he didn't notice, but he thought it was a rather expensive trip.

My first ride in a car from Picton, which had stopped at my father's, was quite exciting. S.A. Vancott had the first car in our community, and I think in the township. In later years, Mr. Vancott bought a new car which he was not used to. He drove it into his garage and on out the west end hollering, "Whoa! Whoa!" when he couldn't find the brake.

Many years ago, a new road was built south of Roblin's Mills, as the village was called then. People with cars would come there to test the speed their cars would travel. A Claude Carnrike came to the village, picked up his uncle and

A postcard view depicting the joys of automobiling.

Zetta Caskey, a teacher at Huff's Island in 1915 with an old car.

Roy Giles with his brand new Model T. Ford.

took him for a ride. When they got to the far end of the road Mr. Thompson was very scared. He said to Claude, "If you are trying to scare me, well, you have!"

I once traded a spring calf and a two-burner electric hot plate for a model T Ford Coupe. It was in our courting days and Hilda, my wife-to-be, another couple and I started out for Presqu'ile to attend a dance. We arrived just as the dance ended. On the way there and home again we had 17 flat tires!

A rich farmer near home had a new Ford. Farther along the road another man, a not-so-rich farmer, also bought one. The first farmer was heard to comment, "Well there are Fords and can't affords."

Joe Nightingale had a Hudson with carbide lights that had to be lit with a match. The tail-light was a separate lamp that burned coal oil, but was also lit with a match.

The first car I ever drove belonged to Fred Russell, with him sitting beside me. The first time I ever drove by myself was Horace Calnan's Model T Ford, taking a load of Victoria neighbourhood ladies to a church meeting in Consecon. Going up Taft's hill on the second concession, I stalled the car and Mrs. Calnan got out and put a stone behind the back wheel to hold it while the women all got out. I started the car again, the women walked up the hill, and I picked them up again and we went merrily along.

My most exciting ride was going out to Weese's hill on the front road to watch the explosions of the munitions factory in Trenton. It was 1918 and they went on all night.

Fingerboard Hill was the proving ground for all new cars in those days. If you could go up it in high gear you had something to brag about. If the gas tank was in the back of the car with the gravity feed and the tank was low in gasoline it was necessary to come up in reverse.

The biggest car I ever drove was a 16-cylinder La Salle owned by a stock broker from Toronto. It was so long that the police in Belleville wouldn't allow him to 'diagonal park', because the end was out too far in the road.

A lot of engineering has gone into the building of cars since I was young.

All the Joys
of the Season

A 1909 Christmas card, with a common greeting for those days.

1918 PRICES

From a newspaper clipping:

The price of transportation begins to climb with Dodge posting the biggest increase with its luxury models now nearing the $1,000 range. Ford is in the middle with $750 priced cars while Chevrolet remains the bargain with cars as low as $460, brand new.

"Autoists" in Trenton were fined for parking their cars on the street at night without a warning light on them. Others were fined for not showing government plates on the cars.

Mr. and Mrs. Jacob Sager, Mr. and Mrs. Wm. Glenn, and Rhoda Sager in the back seat of an early car.

Treats of my Childhood

By Harry Bisdee

When I was a boy, a treat was something that was a 'real treat,'— spring after a winter of salt pork, or fresh fruit after months of canned fruit. We lived near a lake. In the spring when the ice started to go out from shore, father would get his spear and a clean lantern globe and go spearing. We children would all stay up. As soon as he got a fish, he would come in and clean it and mother would fry it. How good it tasted! We ate and ate till it was all gone.

When I was young we only had oranges at Christmas time. How delicious they were! We ate the pulp, sucked the seeds and chewed on the rind. Peaches and sweet grapes came only at Roblin's Mills Fair time, and Mother had to keep a real sharp eye on them with seven kids on the loose.

In the fall we would get fresh cider; Mother would boil it and sweeten it and have it for a treat in the winter time. Fall also was the time for hickory nuts and butter nuts which Father would gather in the gully north of the village. Mother would make candy with nutmeats in it. The leaves of the horehound plant were gathered at the same season, also in the gully. The juice was boiled down in a sweetened syrup and then put out in the cold to harden. It was supposed to be kept for colds, but many pieces were hooked for candy. Mother also made hickory nut cake using broken pieces; the unbroken halves were saved to decorate the top. How lovely it looked! We kids would try to get the piece with the most nuts on top.

Christmas was a happy time as there always seemed to be extra treats. The tree was dressed up with fancy paper cutouts that we would colour with crayons, and strings of popcorn. On Christmas Eve we would light real candles, but had to be very careful on account of fire, so always had a pail of water and some older person close by. The small children had orders to just look and keep away from the tree.

Mother baked her own bread and finished up by baking buns which also were a delicious treat. We would pick wild strawberries, bush berries, blackcaps, chokecherries and green apples, which always gave us a stomach ache. Still it was fun, and they were a treat, or so we thought.

Books

By Harry Bisdee

When we get in the relaxing years of our sojourn on this earthly planet, we like to reminisce of the good old days, and also of times that had their drawbacks. Maybe it was a time of testing.

I always like to read, so my thoughts turn to books. I suppose I had the books that all small children of my day had, but the first book that comes to mind was Eaton's catalogue. What a wonderful book for a child— toys, candy, clothes, so many good things. I remember that my mother had to hide the book to save its life; with a family of seven all wanting to look at once, the pages were torn. When the new one came out, we got the old one, but that did not suit, we had to have the new one. So when mother's back was turned, the hunt was on. We knew we would be in for a scolding when caught, but the pleasures outweighed the dangers involved.

Then came school and learning to read. To me the primer had wonderful stories, then we progressed through the other grades and could read better. Some of the stories still come to mind; the old Ontario Readers had such good poetry and stories. I can still remember Somebody's Mother, My Shadow, Two Little Kittens, How I Turned the Grindstone and The Hare and the Tortoise. There were short verses and proverbs all through the readers. I still remember many of them yet:

A stitch in time saves nine."

Whatever you do	*Work while you work,*
Do with your might;	*Play while you play,*
Things done by halves	*That is the way*
Are never done right.	*To be happy and gay.*

I recall other stories of my childhood, such as *Jack the Giant Killer*— how my hair would stand on end! And *The Night Before Christmas*— I could almost see Santa and the reindeer leaving the chimney and going off in the great blue yonder. At that age, all was peace. Then as I grew older and read the newspapers with their accounts of the grave happenings in the outside world, all my small world got a great shattering. The First Great War came with all its horrors. My brother went; we went to Kingston to see him off.

In time the war ceased, and I grew up and went out into the world, but my love for Eaton's catalogue still stayed with me. Then came the Joke magazines, the wild west books such as Zane Grey's, and the detective stories. Ralph Connor's *Glengarry School Days* was a boy's delight. Sunday School supplied us with good papers, which made better reading than some others. The Bible was always there, but so often left unread.

Then I got married and set up a home with my wife. The depression came and no money was available. Books came into their own again. Lloyd C. Douglas' *The Robe* has been a favourite book which I have read many times, also *The Big Fisherman* and almost all the books he has written. *How Green was My Valley* by Richard Llewellyn was another very good book, the A.J. Cronin books, and many, many more. Our son came along, and with him a new set of books, so different from ours of 25 years before. The baby books were new, and all his public school books as fully intended to do the job as the old Ontario Readers. But gone were the books of my childhood which were such a delight to me. Many more books have come into my life, but none can take the place of those of my youth— or the Eaton's catalogue, which is no more.

Barn-raising at Albury

From the *Trenton Courier*, July 6, 1905— Last week one of the largest barns in this section was successfully raised on the premises of Charlie Dempsey, Albury, nobody being hurt. Eighty-two men were at the raising. The barn is 45 X 80 feet on a 9 foot stone wall. Miss Grace Hutchinson, Trenton, christened the barn with a bottle of champagne naming it the "King Edward".

Old Time Remedies

Peno-dine healing oil— good for rubbing on or taking as a medicine.

Sweet Spirits of Nitre— for kidney infection.

1 oz. cream of tartar and 1 pint of water to relieve discomfort from small pox or chicken pox.

Pioneer Medicine

by Edith Cairns

In order to ease their suffering, pioneer families made good use of the healing properties of certain plants known to be medicinal. Along with a simple chemical substance or two, they steeped and stirred and came up with a salve or syrup that was good for man or beast. One such remedy found in an old Dr. Chase's celebrated Recipe Book goes thus: "White pine turpentine and lard ½lb each; honey and beeswax ¼lb. each; melt all together and stir in ½oz. of very finely pulverized verdigris". Verdigris is the greenish deposit found on copper or brass and is usually known as copper sulphate. This ointment was reputed to be good for chillblains, a frequent and painful trouble of feet and hands in cold wet weather. Horses experiencing cuts on their feet from stepping over corn stubble in spring ploughing were cured with the same remedy.

Leafing through old recipe or 'receipt' books often indicates to the reader the nature of the more common ailments as check marks are found beside cures for rheumatism and asthma and kidney stones.

Snake bite was alleviated by drinking a strong concoction of white ash bark. Green asparagus shoots, eaten raw, was reputed to help cure hydrophobia (rabies) in any stage of canine madness. Poultices of raw potato, scraped fine, applied frequently, should cure inflamed eyes. Narrow-leaved dock root, sliced and soaked in vinegar does wonders when applied to ringworm. An oil for deafness is collected from milkweed seeds allowed to sit in the sun in a glass jar. A drop of the oil is put in each ear. A coal of fire sprinkled with sugar gives off smoke that eases earache when held under the ear. Horehound, the bitter medicinal flavour familiar to many even today was a favourite lozenge. Horehound tea was a cure for chills. Balm of gilead buds, chewed and held under the tongue ease asthma distress. My favourite, because of its ease and availability is a teaspoon of apple cider vinegar stirred into a glass of water. Any stomach discomfort is quickly dispelled by this pleasant drink.

Somewhere near the back of the old hand-written recipe books was usually found a recipe or two for a fermented fruit wine or a fruit drink fortified with a cup of strong liquor. Even the most downcast spirits would be revived by this medicine.

The world of medicine has changed beyond the pioneers' wildest imaginings, but the need for medicine is with us yet.

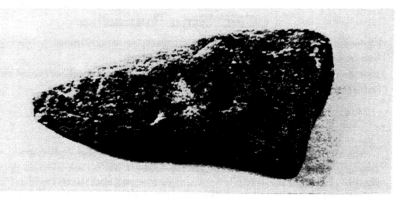

Indian Artifact

This Indian artifact pictured was discovered in 1983 in the garden of Robert J. Hanthorn, Lot 106, Carrying Place. Many arrow heads and other relics have been found here. Indians, apparently, camped here in this spot beside the creek, sheltered from the cold winds. Sand dunes nearby have yielded many weapons of various sorts. The piece pictured is unusual in that it has holes through the stone.

Bottling plant

Quinte cheese factory was closed in 1950 after which a man by the name of Scott used the building to operate a soft drink bottling plant for a time and marketed his product under the trade name of Lushy Cola. The business was closed down by the department of health, as he was using the water from the Bay of Quinte without it being purified.

A Teenager's Impression Of Present-Day Ameliasburgh By The Bay Of Quinte

By Jane Inglis

The southern shores of the Bay of Quinte is the only real home for me. It has so much to offer, if only one has the eyes to realize its special charms. This area has the ability to magically transform its character depending upon the season.

During the summer months, many recreational activities can be found right outside of our doorstep, such as swimming, boating, water-skiing, sailing, fishing, picnicking, hiking and other enjoyable summertime events. Living in this locality, one does not have to travel a great distance to find a quiet beach, because they are readily found in many backyards.

The winter season, like the summer, also has a lot to offer. During these colder months, ice-boating, skating, snowmobiling, ice-fishing, downhill and cross-country skiing are enjoyed by many. The remaining two seasons allow one to view the breath-taking transformation of the waters and the surrounding environment.

I know about all of this because I have witnessed this for nearly 15 years. When I was at the early age of three, my father's occupation brought us to the Belleville area and we decided to build our home in this part of Ameliasburgh Township. We chose this vicinity because we wanted to live by the water, with the added advantage of living fairly close to the nearby cities. Although we are not farmers, a short drive takes us into the farming community, where we are able to purchase fresh fruits and vegetables when they are in season.

The homes along Old Orchard Road and County Road 3, known as the Rednersville Road, are part of this scenic atmosphere. Every drive I take along this way, I find myself viewing something different, which wasn't seen on the journey before. The variation of seasons also adds an extra pleasure to the tour. There is the splendid appearance in Spring of lilacs, fragrant orchards of apple blossoms, garden flowers in summer, the reddish-gold leaves in Fall and of course the cozy blanket of snow covering everything in Winter.

I have a chance to observe the changes in nature five days a week when I travel to Belleville to attend my Secondary School. Another impressive sight to be mentioned is the new Norris Whitney Bridge, which was just completed within the last year (1983), linking this County with Belleville.

As the years pass and I gradually become older, I realize how fortunate I am. I presume this feeling originates due to the fact that my years to reside in this part of Ameliasburgh are becoming fewer, because my near future lies elsewhere. I shall always recall special moments at this place where I have lived for many years. My special memory will always be times spent by the water, listening to and watching the motion of the waves, the flapping of the sails as they pass by in the channel which hugs the shoreline.

In my eyes, this is definitely one of God's beautiful gifts— to live on the southern shores of the Bay of Quinte.

Ameliasburgh Recollections

By Kenneth Alyea, as told to Marion Calnan, 1984

The eldest son of Morris and Sarah Cronk Alyea was named after his two grandfathers— Kenneth Jacob Randall Alyea. He was extremely fond of his two grandmothers and often visited them. It was a real adventure to go with his maternal grandparents to the 15-acre Cronk Island (Indian Island) which they owned near the head of the Bay of Quinte. There was a barn there and a house with a woodshed and the soil grew good vegetables and berries.

To get to the island, his grandparents for a long time used a rowboat, then they got one with a motor. They either took a horse across on the ice or swam it across the water to the island for it was needed to work their land. The produce they grew was taken to Trenton by boat. They docked, where the Cold Storage is now, and then took it by wheelbarrow to market. His grandmother owned two houses on Quinte St. where Zellers and Woolworths stores are now.

Ken loved the trips to the Island so much that he hoped that one day it might be his; a dream that never came true.

When he was very young his parents rented the David Rowe farm on the Consecon Road and Ken began school. It was being reconstructed in frame by Geo. Maidens in 1906. Being only six years old, and among so many new people and surroundings, he was unconsciously taking it all in when, WHAM! the pointer, wielded by his teacher, "who wore funny clothes," broke it into pieces over his desk. Ken, frightened half to death, took off out of the school, but not before leaving the sleeve of his shirt dangling in Miss Armour's hand. He ran down the road and hid under the bridge until the other children came along to accompany him home. Next day he returned with a note assuring his teacher he would be a better boy henceforth.

Kenneth recalls that at this time a Marchmont Home boy from England named Neville Gooding came to work at their place. Shortly, he returned home and brought back his two brothers and a sister— namely Claude who became a teacher, Spencer, an Anglican Minister, and Lily, who married Elbro Sprague in Roblin's Mills. Together they bought a farm on the Fourth Concession where Neville and his wife Pearl (Rosebush) farmed for many years.

The Alyeas left the Rowe farm and moved to the Bayshore, two farms west of the Williamson place, where they stayed nine years. Ken attended the Onderdonk School at Albury and went to Sunday School and recalls that Dolly Onderdonk taught and played the organ.

Ken fondly recalls the trips his dad arranged for them aboard the steamers Varuna, Leitha or Brockville. He had his own ice boat in winter.

When he was older, he worked at the cheese factory on the Bay, where Eugene Van Dusen was the cheese maker. Apples, plums and cheese were loaded on boats that called at Barton and Herb Russell's dock. The cheese was easy to load, for a slide went from the curing room right onto the boat.

In 1918 they were moving to their new farm on the Second Concession but still milking cows at the old place, when the British Munitions plant exploded. The barn doors blew out, the window glass shattered, the cows were jolted to their knees and Ken spilled the milk he had in his pail. Everyone was anxious that night, and it seemed everyone was walking away from Trenton.

When Ken came to the Second to live, he was close to his Grandmother Alyea and his Uncle Clayton who was still at home. They had fun together especially in the early spring when the great bush was tapped. They had a shelter of juniper outside the sugar shanty to protect the horses and he would stay there for three or four days boiling down the sap. Clayton brought back meals and they sometimes stole eggs to boil in the sap for a snack.

One day he and Clayton tried to repair the root cellar where the winter's supply of vegetables was stored. They dug it out, loaded stone on a stoneboat which was pulled by a horse with 'springhalt' to the site, and were beginning to put the stone in place when the horse dropped dead, falling fair into the root cellar. They were awhile getting out of that predicament, and the horse belonged to Peter Nelson Alyea.

At this time a lot of gravel was being taken from the pit under the hill, especially when the time came for the farmers "to do their statute labour." The Alyeas always kept an extra team of horses to help pull up every load taken, because of the steep hill.

Ken recalls when the deep well was dug behind the farmhouse. A tripod was set up over the spot, and the earth and rock as it was removed by pick and shovel was pulled up. He enjoyed looking down in the hole that Horace Alyea and the boys were making.

Ken easily recalls the Jerry Kemp family and later William White who lived in the log house that is now at the Museum. He remembers the bountiful supply of vegetables from the garden behind his Grandma's house and seeing them stored away in the root cellar and the beautiful St. Lawrence apples that grew in the orchards, along with the different varieties of plums and gages. He laughingly recalls the Hallowe'en pranks they enjoyed in those days before he was married to Irene Burris and settled down on their own farm on the 2nd Concession.

They have retired in Consecon, and they probably have many more memories to share with friends.

Bee-Keeping in Ameliasburgh

Sugar was an expensive and rare commodity in early settlement days and maple sugar and honey were in great demand for sweetening foods. Naturally, when a swarm of bees could be captured and enticed to enter a hive, there was rejoicing. The children helped too, with their pan-tapping and repeated chanting of "Come back bees" and "Light Low". Of course when the bees were safely hived, they were convinced that they had made it happen. There was also a verse about swarming bees that went—

A swarm of bees in May is worth a load of hay,
A swarm of bees in June is worth a silver spoon,
A swarm of bees in July isn't worth a fly.

Henry Stafford, who lived on lot 76, concession 3, Ameliasburgh in 1885 had kept bees for 25 years. He had as many as 190 colonies. He shipped as much as give tons of honey to Montreal in a season. He must have made a business of it, as he manufactured comb foundations, made hives and kept bee

Many farmers had a bee-yard in days gone by.

supplies on hand. Ameliasburgh family stories reveal that many of the farmers had bee-yards, or apiaries as they were called.

John McLean of Consecon, had one of the largest apiaries in the area in the early 1900's, when a fungus type disease attacked. There seemed no cure for 'Foul Brood,' as the virus was named. The McLeans disposed of a hundred 'skips' by drawing and discarding them in the marsh at the back of their farm where it bordered on Consecon Lake. All bee-keepers then decided to call in experts and the result was a Bee Convention held at the McLean farm, to try to discover why the brood failed to hatch.

Not many Ameliasburgh farmers now have bee-yards. Donald and Eleanor Garretsee of Consecon have the largest apiary, in fact they have bee yards in several locations on farms in the area. Bees are their business.

CHAPTER 41

SPORTS

Athletic Activities of Ameliasburgh

From material made available to W. D. Hanthorn

Although Ameliasburgh Township has no indoor hockey rink, throughout the years many players have practiced on local ponds and the Bay of Quinte but gone to Wellington, Trenton, Brighton and Belleville to play. As can be seen by the pictures, they have given a good account of themselves.

While other sports have had to be played outside, the Ameliasburgh ball players are quite well supplied with playing facilities. Three parks complexes, supported by grants from our council, are being used all summer long. They are quite strategically situated, one being in Rossmore, one on Roblin's Lake and one in Carrying Place. This is the largest and also serves the south end of Murray Township, which helps support it. It boasts two ball diamonds (one with lights), a tennis court, and another ball diamond and rugby field may be contemplated, also a 'T' ball diamond for beginning players.

The land for this 'Westfall Memorial Park' was donated mostly by Mrs. Vernon (Elsie) Westfall with separate strips of land donated by Mr. and Mrs. Klingspon in order to enlarge the ball fields to permit league play. This land was originally a cow pasture and local boys used to play there with a rock, a stick of wood, or a dried up cow cookie for bases. We used to get a good crowd of spectators even then, and foremost among them were Charles and Vernon Westfall in whose memory this park was named.

The Carrying Place Recreation Association was formed to support sports activities. Some people worthy of mention were Doug and Dorothy Burns, Fred Yardy, Gwen (Smith) Herrington, Rodney and Georgette Green, Don and Marilyn Wright, Fred and Joan Rollins, Bob and Marilyn Hanthorn, Bill Jr. and Helen Hanthorn, Helen Milligan and Frances Taft.

1976, Leola Doxtator— *Winner of Ontario Provincial Archery Championships held in London, Ontario. She was also winner of Field and Hunter Mailmatch Rounds.*

1981-82-83, *Heather Kuzmich* of Carrying Place, age 17, currently attending high school in Brighton. She is reigning Ontario Junior Golf Champion and only winner of the international trophy at Junior world in San Diego.

1978 Carrying Place Girls Softball Team
Back row, left to right: Coach, Fred Peterson, Kim Selman, Sandra Wright, Margo Stewart, Bernie Cote and Statistician Don Taylor.
Middle row, left to right; Jan Cheverie, Carolyn Hanthorn, Kathy Walsh, Tracey Miller and Martha Vincent.
Front row, left to right: Jane Leedham, Kelly Green and Anita Taft. Missing are Carolyn Over, Joanne Milligan and Laurie Mack.

The first Ameliasburgh Firefighters Horseshoe team.

1955, Consecon— 'Alyea Motors Team'
Back row, left to right: Chuck Acker, Larry Clark, Gerry Mattis, Glenn Offen, Al Tripp, Graham Burris, Lawrence MacDonald, Lavern Phillips.
Front row, left to right: Bob Adams, Burt Garattsee, Ron ?, David Larue, Chuck Phillips, Name Unknown?

1953, Hanthorn Bowling Championship Team
Left to right: William Girdwood, Clarence Taft, Tim Church, John Taylor, Jim Kingyens, Fred Moynes, William Hanthorn.

Track and Field Day at Massassaga School

The Mildred Corke Public School Mixed Ball Team, coached by Twila Langman. This team was never beaten.
Back row, left to right: Sharon Dunely, Judy Wetherall, Nancy Graham, Bonnie Murray, Sandra Dempsey.
Second row, left to right: Stephen Weese, Peggy Blakely, Louise Miller, Rita Higgins, Larry Muxworthy. Boy in front: Paul Stanton.

1980, Carrying Place Ball Team

The all Ontario MacDonald's Esso Bantam Team winners of 1980 trophy for first place after a hard fought battle with Seiberlingville at Sharbot Lake.

Back row, left to right: Wilfred Whitehead, Pete Selman, Paul Lundin, Chris Hanthorn, Scott King, Joe Veenstra, Terry Salisbury, Doug Schalley, Rick Morris and Pat Whitehead. Front row, left to right: Ken Keene, Sherwood Mindell, Brad Mahar, Scott Empey, Tim Veenstra and Tony Hanthorn.

1980, Ameliasburgh's Firemen's Championship Horseshoe Team.

Left to right: Tom Noyes, Bob Frost Jr., Jim Seymour, Bob Frost Sr., Bill Taylor, Bob Hanthorn Sr. and Jim Vader.

1934-35 Consecon Millionaires, Prince Edward Hockey Champions
Back row, left to right: Fred Bolte, Leonard Philips, Bill Zufelt, Wesley Kaiser, Bill Bolte, Dr. Otto Van Luven.
Centre row, left to right: Earl Burris, Carman O'Hara, Jack Clarke, Cecil McConkey, Ernest Hayes, Frank Pearson.
Front row, left to right: Bill Storms, Roydon James.

July 1982, Lee Hamilton's Motorcycle Club, Ameliasburgh Township

1922, Carrying Place First Softball Team
Left to right; Gyn Martin, Garrett Orser, Vernon Westfall, Stan Hart, Bill Latour, Bill Weese (crouching), Eckerett Pearsall, Bill Hanthorn and Ball Martin. (This team began playing hardball but due to many players unable to afford gloves, they changed to softball whereby only the catcher and the first baseman were allowed to use gloves.

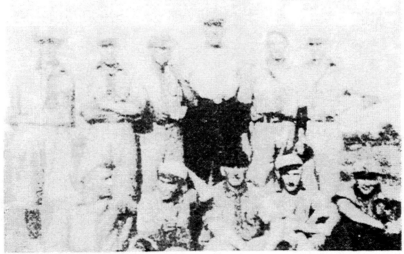

The Consecon Baseball Team, *taken in about 1922. From left to right standing: Gillie Goyer, George Spriggs, Nap Goyer, Herb McCabbe (manager), Leonard Phillips, Roderick McLean. Sitting: George Lazier, Clarence Vanwart, Fred Clarke, Harold McConkey and Barney Clarke.*

Albury Hockey Team, about 1962.
Back row, left to right: Bill Hanthorn Jr., Keith Dickey, Jim Redner, Everett Doxtator, Norm Post, Bud Reid, Doug Weese.
Front row, left to right: Jim Hatfield, Royce Doxtator, Bob Hanthorn, Billy Genereaux, Benny Brown, Gary Genereaux, Gerard Genereaux, standing.

1982, Carrying Place Fire Department Hockey Team
Back row, left to right: Tom Noyes, Stu Carter, Bill Hanthorn Jr., Dean O'Hara, Harold Peck. Len Bedford.
Front row, left to right: Bob Hanthorn, Bill Bedford, Lyn Thompson, Mac Certwell, Tom Hanthorn.

1981, Bishops Seeds Ladies Softball Team
Back row, left to right: Linda McDavid, Chris Dobson, Mary Lou Vos, Susan Wetherall, Lori McConkey, Frances Generaux, Jean Bedford, Fay Wetherall and Roy Wetherall (Coach).
Front row, left to right: Mary Jane Ellis, Sandy Anderson, Brenda Francis, Marion Whitehead, and Ellen Wetherall.
Coach- Dean O'Hara and Asst. Coach Sharron O'Hara absent.

1981 Hanthorn Motors Ameliasburgh Twp. Ladies Softball Team-Winners
Back row, left to right: Bob Hanthorn Jr. (Asst. Coach), Joyce Stewart, Helen Hanthorn, Patti Frost, Janice Hanthorn, Martha Vincent, Aloma Bennett, Kitty Noyes and Bill Hanthorn Jr. (Coach).
Front row, left to right: Cindy Neal, Kelly Green, Cheryl Speight, Mary Lou Frost, Barb Quinn and Caroline Hanthorn.

Albury Athletics Softball Team 1960

Winners of Prince Edward Northshore Softball League. 1960 was first year for league which continued on until 1982. The first year there were four teams, Albury, Ameliasburgh, Rossmore and Consecon. Through the years the league expanded up to eight teams. The trophy was won seven times by various Albury teams.

Back row, left to right: Norm Post, Keith Dickey, Ron Denyes, Gary Genereaux, Doug Weese, Jim Redner.

Front row, left to right: Bob Hanthorn, Arnold Wetherall, Everet Doxtator, Royce Doxtator, (player and coach), Gerard Genereaux.

1983-84, W.R. Bonter Landscaping Hockey Team

Back row, left to right: Steve Doxtator, David Bonter, Russel Smidt, Tom Donavan. Front row, left to right: Andy London, Glen Middleton, Dwayne Doxtator, Paul Latchford, Andre Chabot, Gerry Inglis, Terry Clark, Rick Cartright, Glen Watson, Joe Bonter. Absent- Brian Dawson

1937, Quinte Orchards Hockey Team

Back row, left to right: W. Latour, Manager, Bruce Graham John Anderson.
Middle row, left to right: Don Anderson, Ed Davis, Ken Davis, Don Vandervoort,
Charles Drake.
Front row, left to right: Bill Miller, Bernard York, Walter Bowen, Wilfred Lemoire,
Norm Johnston.

This team was sponsored by Bob Dempsey and his father-in-law George Hardy.
This unselfish and generous man also literally, kept many of the local residents from
starving in those mean years of poverty in the early Thirties. He provided work for the
unemployed. He used his equipment and paid to clear the snow-blocked roads. He
even paid the Anglican Minister's Salary. He also headed a committee in 1944 to
obtain the necessary funds to provide Trenton with its own Hospital. Bob drove
many miles collecting donations for this worthy cause.

1974-5. Tom Hanthorn and
Coach Chuck Phillips with the
high score trophy for most goals
scored while a player in the
Wellington House League.

1972, Winning Team, Carrying Place Bantams Softball
Back row, left to right: Jeff Leavey, Barry Hanthorn, Rob Selman, Rod Mountney and Bob Hanthorn Jr.
Front row, left to right: David Johnson, Paul Lunt, J. Weller, Gerry Luxton and Kevin Genereaux. Rear- Chuck Macaulay and Bob Hanthorn, Coaches.

1975-78, Bayview Orchards Prince Edward Northshore Softball League
Back row, left to right: Royce Doxtator, coach, Don Bonter, Gerry Inglis, Bob Casselman, George Foote, Doug Mason, Bill Minaker, Mike Reddick.
Front row, left to right: George Chapman, Steve Doxtator, Rob Roblin, Gary Mason, Todd Doxtator, Bob Jones 'Bat Boy', Buch Stevenson, coach.

Carrying Place Recreation Association Committee Members
On the occasion of the opening of Westfall Memorial Park, Carrying Place. Left to right; George Vincent, ?, Elsie Westfall original donor of park, Rod Green, ?, Wayne Leavey, Bob Hanthorn, Jim Seymour, Fred Rollins, Art Butler.

Opening of Westfall Memorial Park, Carrying Place. *Fred Rollins, Committee member, left, and Fred Yardy, President, Recreation Association.*

CHAPTER 42

FIRE DEPARTMENT

The Ameliasburgh Fire Department

By Fire Chief Arnold Wetherall

In early 1968, Reeve George Cunningham suggested to his council members who were Deputy Reeve Russell Thompson and Councillors Norman Post, Arnold Wetherall and Lyle Vanclief, that, as costs for buying fire protection from Belleville in the east and Trenton in the west end of the Township were steadily increasing, we should have our own fire protection system. Also, any residence within a five-mile radius of a fire station was eligible for an insurance reduction of about 45%.

So in 1968 the land was purchased in the Rossmore area for Fire Hall #1. Then in 1969, Hugh Murray Construction Company was awarded the contract for the erection of a fire station. As Russell Thompson was elected Reeve in 1969, he and Township Clerk William Nightingale, assisted by Norris Whitney, M.L.A., met with the Clerk of the Session at the Ontario Legislature to assure Council that everything was in order for a private member's bill to provide the municipality with the borrowing authority of up to $50,000 for capital expenditures.

The fire hall was opened for use in September 1969 and Council passed a by-law appointing Arnold Wetherall as Fire Chief. On Feb. 14, 1970, the hall was officially opened by Past Reeve George Cunningham, assisted by Reeve Russell Thompson and the Warden of Prince Edward County, Gordon Lloyd. The building was dedicated by Reverend Maurice McLeod. Total expenditure for the 40' X 60' building, two 1500 gallon tank trucks and a new 1969 Class 'A' pumper was $50,000. Eighteen volunteer firemen were recruited and trained at Mountain View Airport. Roger Flower was made Deputy Fire Chief and Jim Lynn and Roger Fleming were made Captains. The first fire was a tractor fire at the home of Carl Boyle, R.R. 7, Belleville on Sept. 16, 1969.

The fire marshall's office in Toronto had recommended a fire hall at the western end of the Township and also one in the centre at Ameliasburgh (Roblin Mills). The Township already had land available at Carrying Place, so in 1971 council decided to erect Fire Hall #2. Tenders were called and Robert

1st fire 1969: Carl Boyle's tractor.

Roger Flower, deputy fire chief, with the hydraulic jaws which are part of an extrication unit.

Official opening of Fire Hall #2 1972 James Taylor M.L.A., Reeve Russell Thompson, Warden Ross Benway, Don Southorn.

Ronald Carter and Fire Chief Arnold Wetherall. Courtesy: the Trentonian.

Official opening of Fire Hall #1, 1969
Left to right— Rev. Maurice McLeod, Roger Redner, Reeve Russell Thompson,
Warden Gordon Lloyd, Past Reeve George Cunningham. Children in front were
winners of a school poster competition on Fire Safety.

Frost of Carrying Place was awarded the contract. This fire hall was officially
opened on Feb. 12, 1972, by Reeve Russell Thompson assisted by Prince
Edward County Warden Ross Benway. Also present were the chairman of the
fire committee, council member Donald Southorn, and M.L.A. for Prince
Edward-Lennox, James Taylor. The firemen had already purchased an old
1941 pumper to be used for parades and promotional activities. This was
stationed at Carrying Place Hall with an 1800 gallon tank truck.

Ten more part-time firemen were taken on and trained to operate all
equipment. Since captains Jim Lynn and Roger Fleming had resigned their
positions, new captains were appointed. These were William Bedford, Neil
Peck, Howard Lockwood and Howard Brant.

In 1980, a new Class 'A' pumper was purchased for the sum of $47,000 and
housed at the Carrying Place Hall. The old 1941 pumper was now used for
parades and social functions only. In 1982, Township Council purchased a
new utility van to carry supplies and equipment for accidents, fires and
anything else that may come along.

As some residences were still not within a five-mile radius, the Council

Deputy Reeve Ron Carter and Fire Chief Arnold Wetherall of the Ameliasburgh Fire Dept. officially open the doors of the new #3 Fire Hall during the Ameliasburgh Fair, Oct. 1, 1983.

The first fire truck rolls out of the #3 Fire Hall in Ameliasburgh, Oct. 1, 1983.

decided in 1983 that it was time that Ameliasburg village had a fire station. Reeve Daniel Brady along with Deputy Reeve Donald Carter and Councillors Ross Kerwin, William Bonter and Stewart O'Brien found enough money in the budget, with no extra burden to the taxpayer, to modify the existing Township barns to accommodate one truck with provisions for future expansion. So, on October 2, 1983, Fire Hall #3 was officially opened by the Deputy Reeve Ronald Carter, Council's representative on the Fire Committee. At the present time, one truck is stationed there and about 10 firemen will be working out of this hall.

The firemen are fully trained in all types of fire fighting, including techniques of wearing Scott Air Packs used when going into smoke-filled rooms or wherever there is a danger of poisonous gases.

In the past year, auto extrication has been turned over to the Fire Department. So, when any accidents occur that involve victims being trapped in vehicles, the Fire Department is called to get them out.

The firemen hold a bingo once a week and the proceeds from this go to help charitable organizations and to buy fire fighting equipment.

To be a fireman you must be 18 years of age or older and have a medical certificate from your doctor. Being a fire fighter has its bright side when the boys get together at meetings or attend field days to see which fire department can win the most events. But, there is a side when all is not so bright— such as carrying a body from burned ruins and wondering who that person might be, or going to remove someone from a vehicle, not knowing if that person is your next door neighbour or maybe even part of your own family.

CHAPTER 43

PERSONALITIES

Tom Hiscock

If you follow a picturesque, winding road along the shore of Weller's Bay it takes you through one of Ameliasburgh township's newer subdivisions known as Hiscock Shores. It is here that Tom Hiscock and his wife Thelma live on a beautiful one-acre lot. A retired quality control tool inspector with MacDonald Douglas Aircraft in Toronto, Tom and his wife moved to Trenton to aid his uncle in developing the area where they now live.

Tom Hiscock creates poetry and has two books of his poems in print. They are *There's One For You* and *Loosen Up and Laugh.*

Hiscock creates poems which are based on circumstances true to life and depict a special appreciation of a power greater than man. He really has a poem of every nature to suit everyone.

His interest in writing began when he was about 12 years old and was attending school. He has many unpublished articles. His writings have appeared in various newspapers and one of his Christmas songs was sung by a church choir in New Zealand.

Tom pursues other hobbies too, such as furniture refinishing, fishing, gardening and keeping the grounds in shape about their home.

The Pencil

A pencil stub once softly said,
I've not much time, I'll soon be dead,
And all because the life I've led.

Since I first saw, the light of day,
I've had an awful lot to say,
And thus it is, I'm worn away.

But with my passing, you may find,
Some message I have left behind,
Creation of the human mind.

If it achieves some useful plan,
Or worth has been, the life I span,
And so it is, with mortal man.

By Tom Hiscock

Lilian Leveridge

Lilian Leveridge was born near the village of Hockering in Norfolk County, England in 1879, one of seven children. The family emigrated to Canada in 1883 and homesteaded on 100 acres about six miles north of Coe Hill. As there was no school for several years, Lilian's mother taught the children. Later some of them did go through public school and Lilian also attended Normal School. She taught school for seven years in Manitoba and Ontario then took up office work in Toronto.

Lilian's mother, Anna Leveridge, had a gift for writing poetry, and Lilian inherited the talent. She was always a gentle person and a great lover of nature. She knew all the birds and flowers and loved to walk in the woods. She was a quiet person but her poetry revealed the depths of her thoughts. She wrote prolifically, and many of her poems, children's stories and others appeared in both Canadian and American publications. The *Family Herald and Weekly Star* published several of her stories in serial form. *The Picton Gazette* often published her poems.

Her most famous poem was "Over the Hills of Home" written during World War I after her youngest brother died of wounds received in the fighting. This poem struck a responsive chord in so many hearts that it was called "The Poem that Circled the Globe."

Never too strong physically, ill health made it necessary for Lilian to give up office work and come to live with her sister, Gertrude Clarke in Carrying Place. She spent her later years helping her sister in their garden and writing poetry. In 1950 she slipped on some ice and broke her hip. Due to complications she was never able to walk again. She died in 1953 and is buried in Carrying Place Cemetery. Mrs. Gerald (Marjorie) Trounce is a niece, her mother being a sister of Lilian's.

Invitation
by Lilian Leveridge

How sweet, how fleet were the old days
When all of us were young!
'Twas then our dreams were rosiest,
Our blithest songs were sung.

Come, visit again the old scenes
Where youthful years were spent,
And taste again the rare delight
Of hearts ease and content.

The dear old home, the church, the school,
The old friends tried and true,
Across the miles, across the years
To-day are calling you.

Written for Old Boys and Girls Re-Union,
Carrying Place, July 1, 1941

Reverend Bowen P. Squire Family

Reverend Bowen P. Squire is a man of varied talents: artist, Baptist Clergyman, archeologist, historian, lecturer and farmer.

Born in Hendon, England in 1901, he began to study painting at an early age. In May 1915, Bowen Squire came from England with his parents to Ameliasburgh township. His father, Thomas Squire, an English Baptist Clergyman, was for many years the pastor at Crofton in Prince Edward County.

Squire went to Toronto in 1922, where he studied art and continued theological studies. He lived in Bronte and served briefly the church there and in Toronto.

In 1928, he was ordained in a church in Rhode Island, where his father had

Rev. Bowen P. Squire, son Philip and Mrs. Squire.

been preaching before his birth. Here, he met and two years later married Eva Fishe, the daughter of a senator. A son, Philip, was born to them in 1932. Four years later, the Squire family went back to England where he served the church in London and briefly in Holland. When World War II began they returned to the United States with the Southern Baptist Convention. Here Rev. Squire preached in the mountains of Virginia where the women carried their shoes to and from church and wore them only during the service, while the men who came to the mission packed along their guns and hound dogs. When Christmas came that year, one old lady in the parish shared her one chicken with the minister and his wife- Bowen got the head and Eva, the feet.

Transportation in the mountains wasn't always easy and when a stream had to be forded, the parishioners attached ropes to their car and hauled them across. The Squires recall a wedding between two feuding families in their mission in Wyoming. Forewarned of trouble pending, Rev. Squire performed the ceremony with a revolver in his hip pocket. However, all went well and later he was invited to christen their child. They recall many humorous and tragic events during their southern mission.

In 1946, the Squire family returned to Ameliasburgh to take over the ministry of the Baptist church at Crofton from which his brother-in-law Lorne Burr was retiring. Burr had married May Squire, and his brother Val Squire lived in the same neighbourhood too. His sister Celestia, (Mrs. George Valleau) lived nearby in Melville, so he was back home among them when they purchased the Karl Woof farm on the north shore of Consecon Lake.

The Squires raised sheep and farmed the land and Mrs. Squire taught in the small school (S.S. 18) for a few years before becoming Secretary

Some of Squire's humorous cartoons.

receptionist for many years for Dr. Murray Bishop, both in Consecon and Trenton. Philip graduated from High School, remained for awhile on the farm and was involved in Junior Farmer and 4H activities and Barber Shop singing, which he taught. Philip left the farm for a college education in Pennsylvania and now lives with his family in California.

The Squire farmhouse, 1949.

After many years spent in research, excavating and locating what is thought to be the lost Kente Mission, on his own farm, and on the shores of Consecon Lake, as well as additional sites in Ameliasburgh Township, the Squires sold the farm and moved to Carrying Place where they spent 11 years.

They visited California a few times and spent the winter of 1979 with their son Philip and his family there. Upon their return they settled in Trenton, where they still reside.

Reverend Bowen Squire still paints. His work appears in many schools and books, including the grade eight history text for schools of Ontario. His paintings are in many museums, in the Public Archives of Canada, the Ontario Government Art Collection, and in private collections in England, Canada, Australia and in the United States. Rev. Squire has also worked with charcoal and pen and ink. His series of cartoons which have been published in the *Trentonian* are delightfully humorous.

It is a pleasure to visit the Squire home, for everywhere hang his fine framed masterpieces, with a great many more stored away; while Mrs. Squire's crafts— delicate bead work, handmade jewelry, broomstick lace, crocheted flowers and felt favours enhance their home. No matter how involved in their hobbies the Squires are, they always have time for a friendly chat.

Malcolm Harvey Gunter (Malley) Maybee— Clairvoyant

Ameliasburgh Township is fortunate to have had as a part of its history one of those rare people reputed to be a clairvoyant or fortune teller. This man, Malcolm Maybee, known as Malley Maybee, was born in St. Ola in 1867. He claimed to be the seventh son of a seventh son and born with a caul or veil over

Left: Malley and his grandson Floyd.
Above: Floyd reflected in his grandfather's crystal ball.

his face. He remarked that he had this particular gift because the veil when being removed was lifted upward.

Maybee's earlier years were spent as a wood ranger and prospector for the lumber company of Gill and Fortune of Trenton at Gilmour. He knew the north country like a book. Although he always had rocks around his house he never discovered any valuable minerals. He often wandered through the woods in search of wild herbs such as ginseng, the root of which was used in medicine.

Malley married Lucy Ann Birkett in 1890 at St. Ola. She was a Quaker. In 1922 they moved to Trenton and resided for three years with their son and family. In 1925 he purchased a farm on the Second Concession of Ameliasburgh two miles east of Highway 33. He died there in 1937. Lucy then moved in with their son and family in Trenton and did some practical nursing. She passed away in 1949. Malley and Lucy are buried in the Carrying Place Cemetery.

Malley was a short stalky man with a moustache, who was known far and wide for his predictions and his ability to tell people where to find lost possessions. Neighbours recall the many cars owned by visitors who came to make use of Mr. Maybee's strange gift. Maybee never told fortunes on Sunday. He had two crystal balls which he would turn in his hand and study. Many people report that they had great faith in his predictions and would bring their friends from the U.S.A. and other places across the country to consult with him. It is reported that he was consulted about the disappearance of the Charles Lindberg baby. Ross Snider, a neighbour, reported helping some callers start their balky cars upon occasion at the Maybee's house. Mrs. Thomas Thompson recalled that she and her son walked from a mile west of Rednersville to the Maybee home in the winter of 1933-34 to get his assistance in locating the body of her husband who had drowned in December. The body was found in April in the spot where Maybee predicted.

Lost animals, stolen produce and missing valuables were some problems that Maybee helped solve. Others were more light-hearted. How did Mr. Maybee know that Bob and Mabel Bowness' foster son was sitting under a tree on the edge of a hill (which turned out to be Mountain View) talking with a friend about running away from home, using the neighbour's grey horses, all the time while smoking cigarettes? It is also said that he tried in vain to coax Clarence Vanclief to look into his crystal ball to see the faces of two girls, one of whom he would someday marry. No one will ever know if it was Jean's face or not that appeared there.

Malley and Lucy had two children, a daughter Phoebe born in 1892, who died at age three, and a son Arthur John born in 1897. Arthur joined the CNR in 1915 and 1918 married Elizabeth Bessie Moon. He worked for the CNR out of Trenton, and later Belleville, for 47 years as a conductor, retiring in 1962. He passed away in 1971. Bessie is now a resident of Trent Valley Lodge in Trenton.

Arthur and Bessie had two children, Floyd, who lives on Smoke's Point Rd. in Ameliasburgh Township and is the current Building Inspector for the Township; and Audrey who is married to Arnold Cronkwright. They live in Trenton. Floyd and Audrey each have two children, and Audrey and Arnold have four grandchildren.

After Malley's death the farm was sold and the house eventually burned down. A portion of that land is now a part of the property of Rece Selman.

The W-B Stables
Their Hobby was Horses
The Campbell Wannamaker/Rejean Boily Connection

The late Campbell Wannamaker, son of Mr. and Mrs. Claude Wannamaker, was born on the family farm on the fourth concession of Ameliasburgh. His wife was Irene Bulpit and it was the death of their only child, a daughter Marilyn, in a tragic accident that changed the course of their lives.

Feeling very depressed, the Wannamakers took a small trailer and drove just beyond Toronto to Long Branch where Campbell found work as a carpenter at a race-track, so they remained there for the summer.

When they arrived back home, the Wannamakers decided to get a race horse of their own and from then on it was racing— near and far.

Racing brought another unexpected pleasure to the Wannamakers. During racing time they met a young lad named Rejean Boily from Mont-

Campbell Wannamaker (center) and Rejean Boily (right) accept one of the many trophies won.

morency Falls, Quebec, who became their driver. Rejean became very close to them and when he was married he brought his wife Nicole home to the farm where they still live. When a young son Claude was born into the Boily home there was great happiness.

The Wannamakers have had many good horses and some very special ones. Their most special was R. Yankee Wann, the winningest ($208,000) and fastest (1:57.1) native-bred pacer in Canadian harness racing history. His highest purse of $20,000 was won at Yonkers Raceway, New York City; his share of the winnings was $10,000.

R. Yankee Wann died a winner at the age of seven years one Sunday morning at the Ameliasburgh Township farm. Rej Boily was there when Campbell traded a brood mare for the six month old colt and he had been the only driver of R. Yankee since he bagan racing him as a two year old. Rej was also there when the prize pacer died on Oct. 18, 1970.

R. Yankee Wann was buried beside the Wannamaker-Boily stables and a suitable engraved monument erected on the grave. For his driving success with R. Yankee Wann, Campbell Wannamaker gave to Boily as a Christmas present that year, a half brother of R. Yankee named J.J. Wann— himself over the $100,000 lifetime earnings mark.

Officials and fans at the raceways respected Campbell Wannamaker. His horses won many lovely trophies. He, along with two other horsemen from the Kingston area, received the special certificate for 'Pioneer Horsemen' for

Eastern Ontario because of their promotion of the Montreal and Toronto Raceways. Campbell also received a plaque from the Quinte Raceway in Belleville for his contributions and assistance.

In 1969, after racing finished, the family decided to come home, with the exception of Rejean who raced in Batavia and other raceways during the summer but returned in the winter to look after their stable of 20 horses.

In 1970 Campbell Wannamaker suffered a heart attack and was never well again. Rejean continued to race summers only until 1974. Now he has some horses, and a public stable and fertilizer business. Campbell Wannamaker passed away on Oct. 12, 1981.

Ameliasburgh's Historians and Genealogists
Mr. and Mrs. Loral Wanamaker

Loral Wanamaker was born December 29, 1896 at Crofton, Sophiasburgh, the son of Grant and Letta (Vancott) Wanamaker. He attended the 'Union School' at Mountain View until he completed his high school entrance examinations, then moved to Bloomfield where he joined the staff of the old Standard Bank.

After more than two years of banking he went to Belleville to attend the Ontario Business College in 1913-14. Upon graduation, Loral tried to enlist, but being under age was rejected. Later, when he joined the Canadian Forces he spent three years in France and Germany. Immediately after graduation, Wanamaker went to Toronto and worked for a rubber company.

Emma Mildred Parliament, daughter of Hartford and Luella (Hodgen) Parliament of Concession three, was born on December 25, 1904. She too attended the 'Union School' at Mountain View. Upon completion of her

C. Loral R. Wanamaker U.E. S.A.R.
Emma Mildred Parliament Wanamaker U.E.

education there, she worked for some time for the Sprague Telephone Company, in their office at Mountain View.

Loral Wanamaker decided to return from Toronto to work on his father's farm (but probably with the urge to be nearer to Miss Parliament, which part he didn't relate to us, for they were married on April 5, 1921, at Trenton).

Following two years of employment with the Sprague Canning Company, the Wanamakers moved to Belleville where Loral painted and papered, Mildred kept a tidy home and became, as Loral fondly says, "a good house wife". He tried Civil Service examinations at that time and went to work at the Post Office where he was employed for many years and where in time he was appointed Supervisor of Letter Carriers.

The Wanamakers have one daughter who was four years old when they left Mountain View. She is now Mrs. Jean Reid and works in a law office in Belleville. They have two grand daughters: Lola Symington is a commercial pilot and flying instructor in Thunder Bay and Lynn Reid resides in Toronto and is an Honour Graduate of Loyalist College in Advertising. They also have a great grandson, Brandon Melton.

When a family relative came to visit one time, the Wanamakers questioned her on family history. They drove her to some cemeteries to check information about their 'roots', and gradually they became hooked on family history. Genealogy, became for both a fascinating hobby which they have pursued for many years. They used vacation time to search for information at the Dominion Archives in Ottawa. Because they recognized they had this unusual talent and enjoyed working at it, they signed themselves as

Genealogists, and people from far and near sought their assistance.

Naturally, they began their hobby by compiling the genealogy of the Wanamaker family which consists of six brothers who remained loyal to the Royal Cause and came to Upper Canada, one being Andrew Wanamaker, Loral's ancestor, and two other Wanamakers who had Rebel ancestors, yet one family intermarried with the other in 1810 and 1815.

Their second project was the history of the Parliament (Mildred's) family, 250 pages long. However, their 540-page book, listing the names from all the cemeteries in Prince Edward County, was a colossal undertaking. It was done by townships, listing names, dates, lot numbers and concession. Many of these books were presented to local libraries and museums.

Families which the Wanamakers have researched and recorded are as follows: Roblin, Babcock, Allison, Vancott, Gerow, Loveless, Hodgen, Sayers, McTaggart, Cole, Redner, Alyea, Canniff, Wallbridge, Weese, Peck, Whitney and Sprague. More records are being compiled at this time.

For the Genealogical Society of Ontario, the Wanamakers have rewritten the Registers of Rev. John Langhorn and the Reverend Robert McDowall. Copies of all these reports may be found in the Ottawa Public Archives.

One of the Wanamakers' unique projects is the compilation of a book of old wills, recording the names mentioned in the body of the will, the date made and date of probation.

During the past 25 years the Wanamakers have researched and compiled histories of families from all over U.S.A. and Canada by correspondence. There are few residents living in Ameliasburgh who have not sought information from our congenial and talented team of Genealogists.

It is a pleasant experience to visit their cosy bungalow, located on the Bay of Quinte shores at Rossmore. It is a veritable Archives and the amount of information these people can relate 'off the cuff' is astounding and reflects their marvellous power of memory.

We are indeed privileged to have Mildred and Loral Wanamaker as active participants in this ambitious project of recording some of the Township of Ameliasburgh's 200 years of history.

A Tribute To Malcolm Wallbridge

A grandfather clock that didn't work and finally sold for $100 more than he wanted to pay at a Brighton auction gave Mac Wallbridge the idea of making one for his wife Velma (Cook). The only machinery he possessed at that time was a table saw. He obtained some butternut lumber and a set of plans. His first Grandmother-style clock was a success and orders for more started rolling in.

His clock-making hobby gathered momentum as locally grown wood, mostly walnut, was cut, dried and shaped into timepieces. The clockworks, faces and hardware were purchased. The pendulum alone for one of his larger clocks cost $198.00

Mac Wallbridge

Our prolific hobbyist added some machinery including lathes and a sander and began turning out numerous items such as bowls, cedar chests, boats and furniture. He made items from ironwood burl, elm, red cedar, birdseye maple and even honeysuckle.

Mr. Wallbridge had hobbies other than working with wood. For more than 20 years he collected Indian arrows and axe heads from his farm land. His prize possession was a skinning stone with an edge as sharp as a razor which he found in marshland nearby.

An avid rock hound as well, he and his wife collected rocks from Newfoundland to Alaska. They panned gold at Bonanza Creek in the Yukon on their travels.

Time and talent passed away, as on Feb. 7, 1983, Ernest Malcolm Wallbridge passed away very suddenly at his home on the Second Concession of Ameliasburgh at the age of 67. During his lifetime in the township, Mac, as he was known to all, by his endeavors and personality, built up a vast store of good will that remains in the hearts of those who knew him.

Mac Wallbridge, although classified as a farmer, was always interested in business adventure and sound financial planning. For many years he was a director of the Bay of Quinte Agricultural Mutual Fire Insurance Company.

Norris Whitney

Norris Elson Howe Whitney, son of Dave and Ida Whitney, lived his entire life on the family farm, just west of Roblin Lake in Ameliasburg. Almost 30 of his years were spent in politics at both the municipal and provincial levels. Politics were inborn; his father had taken him to nomination meetings when Norris was 10 or 12 years old. His maternal grandfather was Elson Wycott who participated in politics in Picton. His ability to relate to his constituents and their problems inspired the Hon. James Auld to remark, "Norris was, in the truest sense of the word, a people's representative."

Mr. Whitney studied to become a chartered accountant, but before finishing his course, he chose to begin his career with an auditing firm in Toronto. In the 1930's, during the Depression, he returned to Ameliasburgh to farm; also, he did bookkeeping and accounting locally.

His first election to public office was in 1943 when he became a councillor for Ameliasburgh. The office of Deputy Reeve followed, then that of Reeve of Ameliasburgh from 1946 to 1951. When he was Warden of Prince Edward

County in 1951 he was managing about 400 acres of farmland on which he kept a large flock of sheep.

It was in 1951 he was approached to run in provincial politics. His success at the polls kept him in the Ontario Legislature for 20 years until his retirement in 1971. At the provincial level he was instrumental in the replacement of the army at Prince Edward Heights, Picton, with a department of the Ministry of Health. The Quinte Skyway Bridge connecting Prince Edward County and the mainland was built during his office.

Mr. Whitney's wife was Grace Donnelly, a Belleville nurse, who predeceased him in 1979. His tragic death at age 71 in a fire that swept his home in 1980, shocked the community.

Norris Whitney was a conservationist, interested in various conservation problems, especially concerned with water levels in Consecon Lake. In his honour the Prince Edward Region Conservation Authority named the dam at Consecon the 'Norris Whitney Memorial Dam'. Also, on the opening of the new bridge connecting Rossmore and Belleville, it became known as the 'Norris Whitney Bridge'.

Lady Rose Anne

Born in Picton, Prince Edward County of U.E.L. and Irish ancestry, Lady Rose Anne is the daughter of Meleata and Arthur De'Nyke.

Married to Surindar Parmar, she is the mother of four and a psychic. A transmedium, she is capable of communicating mentally with every living thing in the Universe. Lady Rose Anne uses a high frequency mental vibration which enables her to talk with trees, animals and discarnate spirits who have left the earth's plane.

A psychic since age 6, she gives individual life readings on health, status, family and future. Karmic (past life) readings are also part of her repertoire. Spirit contacts are usually with deceased loved ones who may wish to make contact with families, with ghosts, alter-egos, inner selves and Universal Councils. Part of her work lies in investigating haunted houses to alleviate problems; interrelated Ouija phenomena; poltergiest activities and other psychic phenomena.

Well-versed in ancient mystical and religious history, she is a firm believer in positive parapsychology. Lady Rose Anne and her husband, a psychic healer, work hand in hand to instill the truth of the psychic side of the individual. "It is time to bring forth the truth of psychic phenomena; to inform people that it is not a gift but rather an integral part of the human brain and must be understood in order to benefit mankind," she states. "The darkness of medevial mysticism and witchcraft has cloaked this topic in fear and superstition for too long. In order to understand God and His Universe, each of us has to ascertain the truth of their psychic potential and the benefit it serves unto self and others."

A resident of Mountain View, Lady Rose Anne and her family enjoy their Century farm house and numerous hobbies. A member of the Mountain View Women's Institute, the Quinte Irish Canadian Society and the Belleville Writer's Club, she also shares a Television series with her husband called 'Beyond Truth,' shown bi-weekly on Quinte Cable 4.

Her aim is to continue working with her husband helping to enlighten others on the positive aspects of psychic awareness via their teachings, healings and future books.

The Singing Post Family
Ameliasburgh's Down Home Country Folks

Norman Post, descendant of the Ameliasburgh pioneer John Post and son of Charles Post and his wife Uldene Babcock of Rednersville, was born with a musical talent that has inspired his children to become professional entertainers.

Norman in 1951 married Jean Corfield, daughter of Arthur and Helen Corfield of Ameliasburgh. Her grandfather was Fred File, long time clerk of the township and her great-grandfather was Dr. File.

In 1953 Elizabeth Joanne, named after the Queen, was born to Norman and Jean. While they lived and worked in Toronto their second daughter Debra Jean (named after the movie star Debra Kerr) was born. In 1962 their only son Kenneth Norman arrived to make their family complete.

As very small children the girls loved to sing, and their father recalls having listened to them sing as they waited for the school bus. In the evenings they kept having their little family sing-songs and playing their guitars until Norman Post entered the family in the Ameliasburgh talent contest March 31, 1966 at Tobe's County Gardens at Rossmore, and they won.

In 1967 a Centennial Talent Show was held in the Ameliasburgh Town Hall and the Singing Post Family won first place. In that same year, five-year-old Kenny entered a contest in Toronto and won first prize.

In 1967 two other musicians and Post formed 'The Cross Country Jamboree' dedicated to the promotion of Canadian talent. Participants who have benefited include Carol Baker, Donna Moon and Karl Elliott.

For the Belleville Centennial Celebrations, a program including a variety of musical talent was staged with the Singing Post Family winning the first

The Singing Post Family— left to right: Debra, Jean, Joanne, Norman and Kenneth

place— a trip to New York City to appear on the Ted Mack Television show. The winners were judged by ballots sent in by viewers. Before the votes were tallied, Ted Mack died and the show was taken off the air, so they never knew how well they fared.

To their credit as entertainers, there are eight Singing Post Albums. Their Country Gospel Album has been the biggest seller in their 12 years together, and in that time they have toured Canada three times from St. John's, Newfoundland, to the west coast and back. Several more times they toured Eastern Canada and appeared on TV with The Family Brown and Orval Profit, both on C.T.V. and C.B.C.

The Posts engaged Billy Walker from South Marysburgh Township as lead guitar player, to strengthen their group and have been onstage with Gordie Tapp, Stompin' Tom Connors, Hank Snow, Wilf Carter, Tommy Hunter, Carol Baker and Bobby Bare.

One tour from here to New Brunswick ended in Dresden, Ontario, with the ambassador of Country Music of the World, George Hamilton IV. They made friends all over the country.

Through the years, Jean Post made all the costumes used on stage. She drove for hundreds of miles while the family rested, helped as a stage hand and was their business manager.

Joanne was the first to be married, but after two years left the group. She and her husband have two sons, Jeremy and Charles. Debra has her own show and is owner of Creative Records. Kenneth plays with top country bands across Canada after beginning with a little Prince Edward County Band called 'Sundown'.

Both Norman and daughter Debbie are composers of songs, and Norman feels two of Debbie's beautiful songs are sure to achieve hit parade popularity.

Music is hereditary in their family, because Norman organized several bands in his early years and was the oldest member, at 18, of a band that played in support of the March of Dimes.

The Post home, built by Norman, is on the last lot in the incorporated Village of Rednersville. He has served on schoolboards at the local and township level; and was involved in municipal affairs for nine years. During this time he was instrumental in the planning of the H.J. McFarland Home in Picton.

Norman Post's philosophy is: "Each child is a professional in his own right, but if we can't use our Senior Citizens equally as well as we do our Junior Citizens, we might as well throw in the hat".

For three years Norman Post's own television show, County Country Time was aired and he has done many radio shows.

As if Norman wasn't busy enough with music and municipal affairs, he sponsored and coached both baseball and hockey in the County. Prince Edward Northshore Softball league won the championship when he was their coach. (See the Sports chapter.)

Harry Bisdee

The name Harry Bisdee has become synonymous with public service to his community. To many he is 'Mr. Ameliasburgh' because he has such a wide range of interests. All his life has been spent within sight of Roblin Lake— all 78 years of it.

During his working years, he has had several occupations, as a farm hand, a baker, shopkeeper, building inspector, Curator of the local Museum, but mainly as a carpenter during the war and post-war years until his retirement.

Harry Bisdee was instrumental in the organization and the establishment of the United Church into what we know now as the Ameliasburgh Museum, under the guidance of the council in 1967-68. He, along with his wife Hilda (Humphrey), contributed many volunteer hours in its early beginnings. The size and growth of the Museum has largely depended on his ideas and his conception of what a museum could and should be.

Harry Bisdee's energies serve his fellow man in many ways. He took an active part in church and Sunday School, in the Masonic Order and of late years organized the first Senior Citizens' Group in the Township and became its founding President. In January 1982, the Ameliasburgh Garden Club was initiated under his leadership. This club has actively participated in the revival of the Ameliasburgh Fair in 1982 and 1983.

Harry Bisdee has countless ideas to contribute to other local events and often attends parades in the Bay of Quinte area, where he enters the floats he has built. Harry's latest project is the beautification of the Mill Pond in the valley beside Grove Cemetery. As President of the Garden Club he continually inspires others to participate just as he does.

In 1977 Harry Bisdee received the Queen's 25th Anniversary Award, a Commemorative Medal. In 1981, he was the recipient of the first 'Service to the Community Award' by Dan Brady, then Reeve of the Township.

Harry and his wife Hilda have one son, Eugene, who lives in Ottawa, three grandchildren and one great grandchild. In the late fall of 1983, the Bisdee's decided to sell their attractive home on the large lot on the main street of the scenic hamlet of Ameliasburg, and move to an apartment in Belleville, but due to pressure from their many friends and with a feeling of deep loyalty and devotion to their community they decided to build a smaller home on their lot across the street, and truly, that is where Hilda and Harry really belong.

Honourable

Nelson Parliament

Nelson Parliament was the son of Mr. and Mrs. Adam Leslie Parliament. He was born and grew up on the family farm in Centre neighbourhood, Lot 79 2nd Con. of Ameliasburgh. He was M.L.A. for Prince Edward from 1914 to 1919 under the premiership of Sir William Hearst. He was re-elected for a second term in 1919 and was chosen as Speaker of the House under the premiership of Ernest Charles Drury. Nelson Parliament was a Liberal, but Drury's United Farmers of Ontario party came to the office without a single one of its supporters being a suitable occupant for the Speaker's Chair from sheer lack of experience with standing order. So Parliament was drawn from the opposition side of the house. He discharged his parliamentary duties in such a manner as entitled him to the respect of his fellow members of the provincial house. He also had the distinction of being one of the few farm Speakers.

Nelson Parliament was the last Speaker to be given his Speaker's chair at the conclusion of his term. He donated it to Centre Church where it remained until the church was torn down in 1967, then it was given to Lake Lodge A.F. and A.M. No. 215 at Ameliasburgh.

Wally Williamson (Julian Gallo)

Wally Williamson (Julian Gallo)

Supper club entertainment in the form of a revue is becoming popular in the Quinte area because of Wally Williamson, also known as Julian Gallo, the stage name he acquired in 1967. He lives on County Road 23 near Rednersville.

Wally was born in Long Branch, a suburb of Toronto. He was educated there and fortunately his talent was discovered by a teacher who encouraged him to take voice lessons. His studies led him to a four-year scholarship at the Royal Conservatory of Music at the University of Toronto.

His early touring began with the Canadian Opera Company from 1957 to 1967. During those years he travelled all over Canada and the United States. He has appeared in 70 Broadway shows.

In 1967 Wally joined forces with actor Mickey Rooney doing shows and night club acts all over the United States. His favorite was 'George M'— the story of George M. Cohan.

Wally has made several T.V. appearances, has been in talk shows and sang for Art Linkletter. His favourite operatic role was that of 'Eisenstein' in Der Fledermaus while with the Canadian Opera Company.

'Don't Look Back', an L.P. for R.C.A. is another accomplishment. This includes four songs by writer Johnny Cowell. This could be coming up for release under a new label. Wally contemplates a revival of many favorite love songs of a few decades ago.

For two seasons he appeared in Stratford in the musical programs of the theatre schedule there, and has starred in the following musical comedies: Student Prince, Carousel, King and I, Brigadoon, New Moon, Great Waltz, South Pacific, Most Happy Fella, Fiorello, Carnival, Fledermaus, Bells Are Ringing, Damn Yankees, Camelot, Merry Widow, Guys and Dolls, Show Boat, Oklahoma, Fanny, Pajama Game, Gypsy Baron, Mahogony, Silk Stockings, Happy Hunting, Red Mill, My Fair Lady, and ten others.

Ross MacDonald— Seaway Pilot

Charles Way and his wife Ellen moved to the 2nd Concession from Actinolite and farmed for many years. Of their nine children only two remained in Ameliasburgh. Their daughter Gertrude married Victor Kleinsteuber and they farmed for a long time on the 3rd Concession before retiring in The Carrying Place. Daughter Emily married Lorne Orser and they farmed on lot 99, concession 2 before moving into Consecon where they retired. Another daughter, Blanche Way, married Alfred Beckwith and moved away, but their daughter Betty, with her husband Ross MacDonald, a Seaway Pilot, have lived for several years on the edge of Consecon Village.

This is the 41st Season that Captain Ross MacDonald has been on the water. He has been a Seaway Pilot for ten years. Not many people in Ameliasburgh know there is so much activity on the Great Lakes.

Ross boards ships on their westward journey at the Cape Vincent, N.Y.

Pilot Station. He is on the Lake Ontario section, which means he services the lake to the Welland Canal, then changes places with Canal Pilots. Also Ross is a harbour Pilot for the ports of Lake Ontario.

Pilotage is split up into districts starting at Escoumins, P.Q. and extends throughout the Lakes. On the eastern journey Seaway Pilots relieve the Welland Canal pilots or they may be dispatched to one of the harbours. A ship's pilot boards a vessel as an advisor to the Master, in local waters with which he is unfamiliar.

Ross began his career in 1944 and served on many 'lakers' running in the Great Lakes and along the east coast. He was a Master for nine years before writing his Pilot's licence examination and was accepted.

He works for Great Lakes Pilotage Authority Ltd., with head office in Cornwall, a Crown Corporation of the Federal Government. The ships he serves come from all over the world and many of them have as many as ten nationalities on board, because the vessels are registered under 'Flags of Convenience' (Tax convenience). The vessel may be owned by any country except Russia and Cuba.

For Ross it is an enjoyable occupation, as shipping is a changing industry. Cargoes are different, ships are bigger, better and fewer.

For another enjoyable season, Ross has joined his ships.

Helen B. Anderson

The late Helen B. Anderson (1865-1956) was born Helen Blakely, of Loyalist background. She lived many years on the south shore of Consecon Lake. She was a teacher and taught her first class at Victoria School, S.S. #8 Ameliasburgh. She was paid $275.00 per annum and board cost her $1.50 per week. After one year she moved to Salem, S.S. #13 where she taught for two years.

Helen Blakely Anderson was a noted poetess. She composed a great many beautiful poems, and some were published in book form. Locally, her work appeared in the *Belleville Intelligencer* as, "Wayside Thoughts By The Wayfarer", and in *The Picton Gazette* under "Thoughts By The Way". Her poems brought delight and pleasure to many readers. The following poem shows the pleasure she took in viewing Consecon Lake.

A September Morning

How blue the lake this calm September morning,
Where shrouding mists have spread their vapors gray.
How calm the stately trees the shores adorning,
With light and langour opes the autumn day.
The fervid heat of summer days is over,
The fret and flurry of the anxious year.
So wings of peace will o'er the aged hover
When youth is past— its tests— its toil and tears.

Al Purdy— Ameliasburgh Poet

On the south side of Roblin Lake is the home of Al Purdy, a well-known Canadian poet. He built his chalet-style home here in the late 1950's. Since then he has travelled extensively, writing about the places he has visited. Some of his early works are about Roblin Lake and the solitude of his surroundings, in his words, he "does not enjoy rubbing shoulders frequently with other poets and writers." Al Purdy's writings about Ameliasburgh, *In Search of Owen Roblin, Wilderness Gothic,* and *Roblin's Mills (2)* make us aware of our rural heritage.

Purdy has written many books and poems and was honoured in 1966 by receiving the Governor General's Award for Literature. In 1967 he won The Centennial Medal. Another award was The Queen's Jubilee Medal, also, an award from the University of Western Ontario for the best poem describing the country north of Belleville.

Roblin's Mills (2)

The wheels stopped
and the murmur of voices
behind the flume's tremble
stopped
    and the wind-high ships
that sailed from Rednersville
to the sunrise ports of Europe
are delayed somewhere
in a toddling breeze
The black millpond
turns an unreflecting eye
to look inward
like an idiot child
locked in the basement
when strangers come
whizzing past on the highway
above the dark green valley
a hundred yards below
The mill space is empty
even stones are gone
where hands were shaken
and walls enclosed laughter
* * *

but they had their being once
and left a place to stand on

Wm. D. Hanthorn of the Carrying Place

Born in 1904 on a farm 6½ miles north of Coe Hill, in Hastings County, one of nine children, Bill describes the Hanthorn family as "poor but happy".

The potato blight in the 1840's in Ireland, with its subsequent famine, drove many Irishmen to North America. The Hanthorns were among these. Two young brothers, John and James, settled at Rice Lake. John, great grandfather of Bill, was a skilled carpenter and had brought with him his chest of tools to do fine carpentry. His son, Robert, learned the trade too, but there was little demand for fine carpentry in the wilderness, so he built barns and houses. Robert's wife, Bill's grandmother, was Amanda McNutt of Dutch ancestry.

Bill's father was Joe Hanthorn, son of the above. Joe left Rice Lake and went to 'Coe Hill to apprentice with his older brother, Will, who was a blacksmith. While there he met his future wife, Florence Leveridge, whose family lived in the vicinity.

Bill's Grandfather and Grandmother Leveridge had come from England. They had a farm of 100 acres, called 'Park Farm' after the home they had left in England, and located along the survey for the railroad to Bancroft. Grandfather Leveridge worked by day in the mines and on the railroad. Along with his sons, they cleared the trees and stones from a large section of his acreage. Bill recalls stone piles and stone fences everywhere, with plots of grain and hay, and space for a large vegetable garden. Picking potato bugs was a job for the grandchildren.

When Joe Hanthorn and Florence Leveridge married, they made their home at 'Maple Farm' north of Coe Hill and near the Leveridge farm. Using his oxen, 'Buck' and 'Bright', Joe was able to clear only about 10 acres of their 100-acre farm. It became impossible to support the family on such a meagre holding, so they moved to Coe Hill, and Joe resumed blacksmithing. Young Bill helped in the shop, blowing the bellows and holding the lantern for his father to see. When Bill was 10 his father embarked on a bad business venture. He had a contract to carry the mail and run a transportation service twice a day from Brinklow to Coe Hill. To replace his canvas-covered stage coach with a Model T, he mortgaged his home and shop. Rural conditions of the north and corduroy roads were not suitable, even for a Model T. The house and the blacksmith shop went first, and the family returned to the farm in the woods in 1916.

When Bill passed his Entrance Examinations, poverty was knocking, so it was necessary for him to help support the large family. Ever since, a major regret has been his lack of further education. He was an avid reader from an early age, and whenever possible he read Dickens, Horatio Alger and papers sent from his mother's English relatives. When about 10, he had read the Bible from cover to cover. He could produce poetry with ease! Once at school, when he and a friend had been strapped for being late, they later sang some of Bill's poetry out-of-doors and loud enough so that the teacher could hear them: "Oh, Lord of Love, Look down from above, And pity us poor scholars. They have hired a fool, To teach the school, And they paid him 600 dollars." Another strapping followed. Bill's Aunt Lilian Leveridge, whose poetry introduces the Carrying Place section of this book, may not have been amused, either.

The year Bill was 17, in 1921, his father and mother moved to the Carrying Place, partly in order to educate the family. Already his Leveridge grandparents were there, living with his Aunt Gert Clark and his Aunt Lilian

Leveridge. His Grandmother Hanthorn came too, and died shortly after arrival at age 90.

The first task was to convert the barn behind the house in Ameliasburgh Township into a blacksmith shop for his father to ply his trade. One of Bill's first jobs in the Carrying Place was janitor of St. John's Anglican Church. For 50¢ a week, besides looking after the stoves each Sunday, he would clean, fill, light and snuff innumerable kerosene lamps, sweep and dust. Also, he tolled the bell for funerals, climbing the belfrey and banging the clapper by hand at measured intervals.

His Aunt Gert, who operated a private lending library in Trenton, and for whom Angus Mowat worked, supplied books for Bill to read and egged him on toward self-improvement. Another source of his reading materials was the home of Charles and Alfreda Westfall, who kept the store and post-office. Bill was invited to dinner frequently; each one would sit quietly reading books, then a discussion of the books followed during the meal.

In the 1920's it was very hard to find work, so Bill took a course in motor mechanics. His father offered to divide his blacksmith shop, which had been established in Murray, and Bill opened up his 'Car Repairs' in one half. One year a gas pump was added to their business when a detour, by-passing Hwy. 2 between Brighton and Trenton, re-routed cars past their location. The Hanthorn Garage was born. Business expanded and presently they have a modern garage, a car agency and a fleet of school buses that are seen regularly on Ameliasburgh roads.

Bill married Edith Montgomery of Colborne in 1935. They have a family of four, and all have attended college. Of late, with spare time at their disposal, Bill has penned many a story and rhyme, laced with humour, and products of a fantastic memory of nearly 80 years.

The Minakers of the Third Concession

By Barbara Minaker

In 1919 there came to Prince Edward County from Edville, north of Brighton, a family by the name of Minaker.

In the raw January weather of that year, Walter Minaker with his wife, Ethel Jane (Knox) Minaker, and their five children, packed their belongings onto a bob-sleigh and headed for their new home. The packing had not gone without incident for the stovepipes fell while they were taking them down and hit the baby, Douglas, cutting his lip. He wears the scar to this day. The cattle had been driven on foot by neighbours and friends two days previous to the family's departure. At the end of the first day of travel, the family arrived in Trenton where they spent the night with an uncle and aunt, Bruce and Alma Morrison. The next day they crossed the ice of the Bay of Quinte and proceeded to the home of another uncle and aunt, William Sr. and Ardie (Mildred) Knox in Ameliasburgh. On the third day they continued the few miles journey to the site of the present Minaker homestead which is on the east

The Minaker Family, 1984. Back row: Iva, Hazel, Doris, Bernice and Eileen; Front row: Douglas, Grant and Arthur.

half of lot 70-71, Lower Third Concession, Ameliasburgh.

Their home was a large red brick one with a central hallway and staircase separating parlour and dining room. A veranda went across the entire front of the house. A wooden garage was attached at the back beyond the kitchen. Surrounding this home were orchards. An L-shaped barn stood north of the house. The Third Concession road divided the 106-acre farm almost evenly. Across this road a never-failing spring still provides cool water for drinking and home use. It certainly looked like an ideal spot for raising the family.

Tragedy dogged them from the very beginning. In 1921 their fourth child, Herbert, a blond, curly-haired boy of five years, died of mastoids, an ear infection so easily cured today. These were hard times. Mr. Minaker had procured a milk route. With a team and wagon he collected the cans of milk from neighbourhood farmers and transported them to Rednersville's Quinte Cheese Factory. This helped their finances since the family had increased. Now there were eight children to clothe and feed. In the fall of 1927 tragedy struck again. Mr. Minaker had a new Ford car. Langstaffs, neighbours of the Minakers, asked Mr. Minaker to drive them to their hunting camp on Papineau Lake. He was not, however, a hunter or a boatman, but when they asked him to row a boat across the lake he agreed. He was never seen alive again. His body was discovered in May of 1928, just a few days before the birth of his daughter, Eileen.

Then the eldest son, 15-year-old Everett, had to fill his father's shoes. It was up in the morning, and away on the milk route, while younger members of the family helped at home with chores, ten or 12 cows to milk by hand, pigs that

The Minaker home, built to replace the one destroyed by fire.

required grain which had to be ground weekly at the grist mill, and whey carried in buckets to them, chickens to feed, and eggs to gather. In the fall our 15-year-old lad could be seen cutting grain using three horses to draw the heavy binder, or ploughing for next spring's crop. Then there were apples to pick and horseradish to dig, clean, and grind for Saturday market to make money for buying sugar and flour.

During that fateful winter of 1927, the eldest daughter, Iva, was attending Normal School (now Teachers' College) in Toronto. When she finished, teaching positions were very scarce and it wasn't until Easter that she received one at Crofton. She was married the next year, and since married ladies were not allowed to teach in those days, she was forced to resign in June.

Another misfortune happened during Iva's teaching year. On Hallowe'en night the family was awakened by the constant tooting of a car horn. The garage was burning and the flames were licking their way into the brick portion of the house. It is thought that a short circuit in the motor of the car started the fire. Fortunately, there was time for the entire family to escape. However, all furnishings except a settee and two matching chairs were lost, as well as family pictures. In the hurry to get out of the inferno, Douglas couldn't get his trousers on, and so was, possibly, Ameliasburgh's first 'streaker'. Mr. Hicks, the cheesemaker at Mountain View, gathered the children in his car and took them to safety.

That winter the Minakers lived in a vacant house owned by John Waterhouse and just a stone's throw away. Neighbours, friends and relatives came forward with help. When spring came, the burned site was cleared. The bricks that remained standing at the corners of the house were reclaimed and taken by Grant Sprague, who used them around the boiler in the original

Sprague canning factory at Mountain View. The Way house which stood vacant in the Hubbs crossroad was moved to the cleared site. It was a two-storey structure with a parlour and dining room, three upstairs bedrooms and a store room. A tenant house which stood across the road was pushed against the back of the Way house and served as kitchen and woodshed. Another portion of the tenant house was re-located nearby and became the garage. After much repairing, painting and papering, the Minakers returned to their 'new' home.

Again misfortune struck. In 1935, just six years after their dad's tragic death, Mrs. Minaker went to the dentist who extracted several teeth in one sitting. She was not strong enough to cope with the shock of such extensive dental surgery, and within two weeks she died at the age of 51 years.

Now the Children's Aid intervened, saying that the younger children would have to be placed in foster homes. It was not realized the stubborn opposition that would be encountered; Everett and Hazel were determined to keep the family together. And they did just that! Through the influence of Mr. Sprague, the Mothers' Allowance was obtained in Hazel's name. In the years that followed, Everett acquired the nickname 'The Colonel', and a good colonel or boss he proved to be. He implemented such rules as "We *all* work; then we *all* play", or if there was something to be divided, the one who did the dividing had to take last choice. Each member had a duty.

Every one of the Minaker family is married. The 'Colonel', so lovingly nicknamed by his brothers and sister, slipped away very suddenly at the supper table in 1974 at the age of 61. Iva, the teacher, married George Rikley and lives near Foxboro. George died very suddenly the day after Everett's funeral in 1974. Hazel married Andrew Harris whom she met while he was teaching at Mountain View school. They live in Trenton. Douglas married Doris Trumpour. They farmed at Black Creek and continue to live there. Doris and her husband, Charles Watering, live at R.R. 2, Ameliasburgh. Grant worked with the County Highway Patrol and married Muriel Burkitt. Bernice and her husband, Floyd Adams live in Campbellford. Arthur married Marie Nagloren, a teacher from Alberta. He graduated in Electrical Engineering from Queen's University. They live in Burlington. Eileen married Donald Wannamaker and they farm near Eldorado.

I did not mention the "Colonel's" wife. The reason? I, the writer, Barbara (Mikel) Minaker married the 'Colonel', Everett Walter Minaker, in 1949. We lived on the home farm. With the help of his five daughters and me, Everett built a new house in 1972-73, but enjoyed it for only five months before his death. All of our daughters have graduated from various universities, three from Queen's, one from Western, and one from Guelph. All five are married. I retired from teaching in 1983, just in time to put the Minaker story in writing.

The George Frederick Keller Family

In October 1975 at a dedication service in St. John's Anglican Church in Carrying Place, two brass collection plates were received. They bore this inscription:

Given in memory of George Frederick Kellar 1896-1937
By his wife and children

After having served in the Canadian Army in World War One, Kellar was invalided home in 1918. He brought along his English war bride, Ethel Maud Parsonage, and they settled in Kingston. Their first son died of meningitis at 16 months.

Since Kellar had tired of his job as an upholsterer, they moved to a small farm at Odessa, with the assistance of the Soldiers' Settlement Board. Here a daughter, Margaret, was born, but when she was three months old a chicken brooder exploded and their small, log farmhouse burned to the ground. The baby was wrapped in a blanket and thrown into the arms of a neighbour. A new frame house was built on the site.

1925 brought them twin sons, but both died at birth. In 1927 the Kellars were blessed with a baby daughter they named Ruth.

The Kellar family moved to Ameliasburgh township in 1927 and located on what is now Old Orchard Road where they took up mixed farming. Here, a daughter, Winnifred, and a son, Arthur, were born. They raised cattle, sheep, gardened and cultivated fruit, all the tilling being done with horses. With his team he helped build the cement road along the bay from Carrying Place to Rossmore. It was dubbed the 'Bonter Sidewalk' because it was only one lane wide.

Later, George bought a Chevrolet truck. One day he was backing it toward his barn on which he had built new doors. He became confused with the braking system and the truck went through the doors with him calling, "Whoa, back! whoa, back!"

Once, Kellar left his team of horses at Hanthorn's Blacksmith Shop in Carrying Place to be shod while he walked on to Trenton on business. Bill Hanthorn, busy as he was, got round to the shoeing job so late in the day that his wife had to hold a lantern for him to see. One horse, probably weak from hunger, lay down, but Bill shod it anyway— the only horse he ever gave new shoes while it was in a reclining position.

About this time the Soldiers' Settlement Board was selling land to returned soldiers and the Kellars took advantage of the offer. Much of the land they obtained was on top of the hill, and it would grow virtually nothing. Still, they were forced to pay on time and in the Dirty Thirties very few had any money at all.

On March 11, 1937 Kellar walked across the ice on the Bay to Trenton rather than go the seven miles around by Carrying Place. Just before six o'clock in the evening he left the Trenton shore to return home. A few yards from shore he went through the ice into seven feet of frigid water. He broke the ice for ten feet around in an effort to save himself, but died of exhaustion before help arrived. He was 40 years of age.

Upon his death, every cent he had paid toward the farm was retained by the Settlement Board. The stock and farm implements which were in Mrs. Kellar's name yielded pitifully little for her to carry on with four children. The family left Ameliasburgh in 1937, but all of the children embraced worthwhile careers, Margaret becoming a teacher, Ruth taking up nursing, Winnifred an accountant, and Arthur a salesman. Ethel Kellar died in 1981.

Elmer Bonter's Story

In the Albury area of Ameliasburgh Township the name Bonter has been prominent in fruit farming, municipal affairs, as fishermen and the military for almost two centuries.

The first Bonters arrived in Canada about 300 years after Christopher Columbus discovered the New World in 1492. Earlier they had migrated to the New England Colonies, settling around Schraalenburgh, in the present New Jersey, and were known by the name Banta. There is a story that some Bonters owned land in the Manhattan area, including the site on which the prestigious Trinity Church was built. Their heirs have been trying for years to claim the church property as their inheritance, worth millions today. Much money has been spent on the case, and they still remain hopeful.

Menfolk of the earliest Bonters in North America served in the military, and it is reported that a Captain Bonter was among the leaders of the pioneers seeking new homes in a strange and harsh environment. Men and women through the generations have answered the call to arms in every major war since then. In World War I, Metta and Mabel, daughters of Jacob Randall and Victoria (Orser) Bonter, volunteered for active service as nursing sisters. The latter was decorated for extraordinary duty. At a Canadian hospital bombed by Germans at Etapes in Belgium, she was gassed. At a hospital in Cairo, Egypt she nursed casualties from the Dardenelles. On returning to Canada, she was a nursing supervisor at Kingston General Hospital for 22 years. The Bonter sisters were born in Ameliasburgh and became familiar and well-known figures in the community as they grew older, with a permanent summer residence on the farm acquired by their grandfather, Peter Bonter, in 1832.

In Township and County affairs the Bonters have shown leadership. Orchardman Earl Bonter and his son Harold both officiated as Reeve of Ameliasburgh and Harold was Warden of Prince Edward County. Presently, William Bonter, L.A.C., son of Elmer and Pat Bonter, serves as Deputy Reeve of Ameliasburgh. Along with two younger brothers, he is operating a landscape service in the Quinte region.

The grandfather of the three Bonter landscapers, William Riley Bonter, nicknamed 'Wisdom Willie', would be considered an entrepreneur nowadays. As a young man he bought hay from farmers locally, then shipped it to the United States for horse feed. His bonus one year was a one-cylinder 1907

Cadillac open-touring model with shifting levers on the side and brass carbide headlights. By the time he was 40, he was regarded as one of the top insurance salesmen in Canada. In the Great Depression he raised the capital to finance the sinking of a shaft at an impressive talc deposit in North Hastings. After the spending of $100,000, it was learned that the ore was contaminated with iron.

William Riley Bonter's son, Elmer, lives with his wife, Patricia Holland R.N., on one of the original Bonter farms near Carrying Place. A writer and photographer for 40 years, he represented *The Toronto Telegram*, *The Toronto Star* and *The Intelligencer* of Belleville. He was named 'Scoop' following a tornado that hit the Trenton Air Station in 1936, with winds over 100 mph, killing two, sucking out the fronts of two airplane hangars. He had 'scooped' the story for *The Toronto Telegram*, the first newspaper in Canada with the headline and photos.

In World War II, Elmer Bonter served with the Army Film and Photo Unit in London, England. A qualified paratrooper, he was assigned to cover the activities of the First Canadian Parachute Battalion. One of his assignments took him to Normandy to photograph a series of the first airborne Canadians who landed in Europe and secured the Allied drop zone. In 1944 he was issued the same credentials as a war correspondent, a three-language pass in English, French and German, signed by General Dwight Eisenhower, the Supreme Commander.

Jack and Cecilia Longstaffe of Onderdonk Point

We enjoy living on Onderdonk Point, Carrying Place— the spectacular view embraces the Bay of Quinte for as far as we can see.

In 1953 we needed pull-out facilities for a 65' sailboat and we were told about the Onderdonk Farm. There were ten heirs involved who had to be satisfied for their 125 acres, including the Onderdonk home, which is famous for its hand-carved main staircase. Our greatest fear is that a tenant will choose to paint it without permission. Over the years we increased our land holdings by purchases from Mrs. Ruth Peck, A.J. Barrick, Howard Weese and Mr. Pederson giving us a total of 700 acres.

When we bought the original Onderdonk farm, the area was all in farming. Then residential people started buying and, after many complaints, threats of law suits, complaints about the odours of farming, plus the help situation, we decided to end our bovine operation and now rent our totally tiled field to Willowlee Farms. We are happy to be collecting the rents without the hassels and headaches of farming.

The escarpment is all very shallow land and grew red cedar trees which made good cedar chests but unfortunately they never grew large enough for big businees. However, Knechtel Furniture did use some of them. The back fields and swamp have some water ponds, and great numbers of geese and ducks rest here while waiting for the northern lakes to thaw. Also, if you are lucky, you can spot deer cavorting in the fields.

Farming did have its highlights. On Oct. 23, 1964, we held a Corn Day here at Onderdonk Farms. Hundreds of farmers from the four counties of Hastings, Prince Edward, Lennox and Addington, and Northumberland took in the program including reports of field trials and the various yields obtained. Special speakers from the Ontario Agricultural College of Guelph spoke on corn production and on corn-growing machinery. There were many other speakers, some of whom included George Jones, Crop Science Department of Ontario Agricultural College, G.S. Maggach of the Ontario Department of Agriculture of Clinton, and G. Rendell, president of the Quinte District Soil and Crop Improvement Association and vice-president George Buchanan. The Albury United Church ladies provided very good food at the noon-day luncheon and the Longstaffes hosted a reception/dinner after the festivities were concluded.

In 1958 the Longstaffes held a family reunion (the neighbours all thought that a circus was coming when they saw the marquees being erected just west of the original house). We had fun but the elements were not kind. A howling wind blew down Old Orchard Road churning up the bay, blowing down the marquees, breaking all the glasses and china, starting a fire and Southwind had to put out to sea. A seaplane carrying some of the guests also put out to sea hoping to get into the air, but was capsized in Onderdonk Cove. There were no serious mishaps in all this excitment except that one guest lost all his money and it was fun wading through the shore waters after the storm trying to find $10.00 bills— we did find some.

Our family reunions were held usually ten years apart with a mini-reunion at the intervening five-year mark. The reunion we held in 1967 coincided with Expo 67 and was well-attended by nearly 100 people. In 1983 we again held our reunion over the July-August holiday weekend. It was a four-day event, was well-attended and included a church service at St. Alban's, Ameliasburgh, two dinners at the Ramada Inn, one dinner and three luncheons here at the farm, a disco dance and a barbeque. People came from as far away as Los Angeles, Vancouver, Winnipeg, Montreal, Toronto, etc. as well as many local relatives, all of whom are looking forward to the 100th celebration in 1988.

Jack Hazard, a Carrying Place Personality

Jack Hazard, the typical 'modern-day pioneer' must be allotted a space in the history of the Carrying Place. He was the son of Maud Fitzgerald who died at the Carrying Place in 1966, aged 87. She was a member of a local family whose husband was a chef and restaurant-keeper near Detroit, at a place called Bad Axe, where Jack was born.

He was a thrifty lad; at age nine he began breeding and selling Easter bunnies, coloured them with vegetable dyes, and then displayed them in store windows. He banked his money from the project. When he was 18, he married number one of his five wives, went to Los Angeles, built a service station and began a parking-lot business. By age 28 he was a millionaire. His operation became known as System Auto Parks, and spanned the U.S.A., including Hawaii.

His mother, Maud Fitzgerald Hazard Zimmerman, returned to the Carrying Place to live with her sister, Daida Weese, and Jack came to visit her frequently. He took a personal interest in improving the village. He bought 440 acres of land and built or bought 18 houses. When he rented the homes, the stipulation was they must be kept tidy. He was proud of the village and he wanted others to be, too.

This "cigar-chomping leprechaun", as he was called by a *Toronto Telegram* reporter in 1967, began his "pilgrimage to refurbish the Carrying Place in Centennial Year." Touring around in his Cadillac, he cast a watchful eye for untidiness and for weeds, Blue Devil in particular.

Vernon Westfall remarked, "If there is any real trouble with Jack it's just that we wants everyone else to be just as hepped up about the place and as proud— but how can you fault him for that?"

Douglas K. Redner

D.K. Redner is an author, historian, philatilist, former farmer and friend. For decades he has been recording family stories, events and articles pertaining to the experiences of local people and places from pioneer times to the present. He is endowed with the ability to narrate information in a fascinating manner. We are indebted to him for the support he has given us for this publication.

Douglas was born on Ameliasburgh's 2nd concession where his grandfather Nelson Giles lived. A short time later his family returned to the farm a mile south of Rednersville to what has been termed "Ameliasburgh's only ghost-town," Eatonville. Here he has remained and still lives with his retired school teacher wife, Maimie, and next door to his daughter, Elizabeth.

Mr. Redner attended school at Centre, then Belleville High School and the Ontario Business College. He returned home to farm and in the 1930's became a correspondent for *The Picton Times*. Those were depression years and his often humourous writings bore the nomme de plume of, 'Cy Hardup'.

When *The Picton Times* was discontinued, Redner wrote news for *The Picton Gazette* in a column called 'From the Farm Window.' Later, he penned a series of articles on pioneer families, places and personalities. Some of these he has published in two books by Mika Publishing in Belleville. His first was *It Happened in Prince Edward County*, and his latest, *It's Good to Get Home*.

Mr. Redner enjoys tending his flower and vegetable gardens, has travelled to the British Isles and Europe and is an avid stamp collector. He has stamped envelopes from each of more than 130 countries around the world, and still has time for visits with friends. Douglas K. Redner is indeed a man with forethought and one who has in his own way made a real and treasured contribution to the Township of Ameliasburgh.

CHAPTER 44

H̄OMES

200 Years of Progress
'Greystones'— Home of Mr. and Mrs. Eben James

'Greystones' was designed by architect Robert Creighton in 1962. He followed the plans of Gwendolyn James, who wanted a traditional house facing Old Orchard Road and a modern house overlooking the Bay of Quinte.

The house is built on the Bryant farm which was deeded from the Crown to Isaac Alyea in Nov. 1837. Isaac Alyea appears to have been a relative of the Bryants. In 1958 the Bryant property was bought by Eben James.

The house is constructed of Queenston limestone. The interior trim was cut from the original farm and the fireplaces are of Kingston quarry and Tennessee marble.

Of interest to 'Greystones': on the property were found two grey stones, one bearing the inscription Robert Adams d. Oct. 17, 1866 age 60 years. 5 . 7 days; the other stone was inscribed Isabel Adams d. Nov. 10, 1861 age 48 years, and 22 days. It is not known where the graves are located on the farm, It was the custom in those days to bury where they lived.

Home of Eben James, on former Bryant farm.

The Deserted Log Cabin by Rev. B.P. Squire.

Carpenter David Rowe, Consecon built his house, to shelter Rowe generations for a century.

Delong-Glenn-Mastin-Veltman
House, Third Concession

Owned by Mike Levine,
Third Concession.

Jas. Barber, at the end of second
concession.

Hubert Campbell, on former Bryant
farm, first concession.

Home and Gardens of R.A. Wilcox,
first concession, where once an
orchard grew.

Quinte Inn

When Everett Sager died in 1932, the Sager home was purchased by Howard Weese who converted the west part of it into a dance hall called Quinte Inn. It was opened in March of 1933 and all through the 1930's was a popular spot. Mrs. Howard Weese has a letter dated Feb. 1, 1935, from Jack Denmark of Deseronto who had an orchestra, asking to play at Quinte Inn for $15 a night— 6 men at $2 each and $3 for the taxi.

Quinte Inn

The Management
requests the pleasure of yourself and lady
at the opening dance of the
Quinte Inn

situated 3 miles west of Rednersville, on front road

Friday, March 31st., 1933

music by the Commodores

An invitation to
opening dance at
Quinte Inn

Admission 75c Plus Tax.   *Extra lady 25c*

Quinte Inn

A place for those who love to dance
Upon a floor as smooth as glass,
An orchestra with lots of pep
Plays tunes it seems you can't forget.

And when they turn the lights down low,
And play a slow, romantic waltz,
The shadows dance around the floor
To hold you in their magic spell.

On the veranda we often sit
To talk and rest our weary feet;
And many a time we quench our thirst
With soda pop and cherry cream.

But when they played "God Save The King"
We know our fun has met its end.
So with happy hearts we leave for home,
To wait for a dance the following week.

In 1949 Quinte Inn was turned into an apartment house and is now known as Weese Apartments.

The Hamilton Home on Huff's Island Rd.

Lot 65- Con. 3

The Hamilton Home

Historical

The Hamilton Home is one of the older homes in Prince Edward County. It was built in 1853 and has been continuously lived in by the succeeding owners to this day.

The original owner of the land was The Honourable Richard Cartwright, grandfather of Sir Richard Cartwright, so prominent in Canadian political scenes during the administration of Laurier. He was born in Albany, New York, 1759. In 1784, he settled in Upper Canada at Niagara and Kingston. He entered into partnership with Robert Hamilton and became one of the foremost merchants of the province. It is believed that the Hon. Cartwright obtained 3,100 acres of land as a Crown grant around the year 1791, which would mean that it was one of the first grants to be awarded in this area, then passed on to his son the Rev. Robert Cartwright. In 1853, Thomas Knox built the lovely stone house on Huff's Island Road.

Succession of Ownership

After the Cartwrights, the next owner was Thomas Knox, and this deed dated 1853, and signed by Mr. Cartwright's wife Harriet, still exists. The son, Robert Knox, purchased it from his father about 1855. The next owner was a Mr. Armistead. In 1917 Philip B. Hamilton bought the place, and it was purchased by his son Seymour Hamilton, the present owner, in 1942.

The Farm

One excellent No. 1 government-tested drilled well 40 feet deep supplies the whole farm and house. It was drilled in 1936.

At the present time the farm is registered with the Canadian Government as an Elite Seed Farm producing Breeder Seed under contract to Her Majesty the Queen. It also produces Clover Seed for the Department of Agriculture and Forestry of the Government of Japan, and Foundation Seed for the Province of Prince Edward Island. There is also a 30-cow dairy herd with quota... The farm that flows with milk and honey.

CHAPTER 45

GROUPS & ORGANIZATIONS

Lodges & Fraternal Organizations

The first lodge to officially receive recognition as far as records are available, was at the Carrying Place. In 1818, a group headed by Col. Richard Bullock, a hero of Queenston Heights, applied for a Dispensation to form a Masonic Lodge. On Feb. 11, 1819 a dispensation was granted to form a Masonic Lodge on Lot 10 (a clergy Reserve lot which is located just east of the present store), the Carrying Place, Upper Canada. In 1822 when enough Masons had signed the Petition, a Charter was granted for the Establishment of Lodge Number 16 on the Registry of the Grand Lodge of England. Later, the lodge became dormant, possibly due in part to the imminent formation of a lodge at Consecon. In 1855 the Lodge was revived, and the place of meeting was moved to Brighton. Following the formation of the Grand Lodge of Canada in 1858, this Lodge was granted a Charter under that body, and was numbered 29 on the Registry.

Consecon Lodge of Masons met for the first time on June 24, 1854, in a building which was situated between the stone store and the Ward home. The charter was number 947 on the Registry of the Grand Lodge of England. In 1859 Consecon Lodge became part of the Grand Lodge of Canada and was given a charter by that body, and numbered 50 on their registry. Membership came from most of Ameliasburgh and Hillier Townships. On March 26, 1904, the original building burned, and meetings were held in the 'Red Store' and R.R. station. On Jan. 3, 1905, the present building was dedicated. The lower hall from the time the building was first dedicated has been used as a Community Centre. In 1979 and 1980, this hall was extensively renovated with the installation of a new kitchen and washrooms also. A new hardwood floor was laid, and cloakrooms and newly panelled walls have made a very attractive and useful meeting place.

On May 8, 1869, a dispensation was granted by the Grand Lodge of Canada in the Province of Ontario permitting the formation of a lodge of Masons in Ameliasburgh Village. Arrangements were made to lease the upper storey of the west wing of the Roblin Mill— the carding mill— for use as a lodge room. This arrangement went on for several years, and the first meeting was held on the 26th day of May, 1869, almost two months before the charter was granted on July 16, 1869. Subsequent meetings were held "on the Monday on or before the full moon at 7 o'clock in the evening from September through March, the meetings to be on the same day but at 8 o'clock all the other months of the year." In June 1903, the present Masonic Hall was dedicated.

On April 14, 1919, a motion was passed in Lake Lodge, Ameliasburgh, that the order of the Eastern Star be granted the use of the East Room— now the cloakroom and kitchen— for the Establishment of the Eastern Star. This organization was begun in the United States under the direction and guidance of Dr. Rob Morris. The first Grand Chapter had been Inaugurated in the State of Michigan in 1867. Quinte Chapter Number 59, which was thus formed, was the second chapter to be established in Ontario east of Toronto— the first being Belleville, Number 55. It is an organization where female relatives of masons and masons themselves are eligible to belong.

Quinte Chapter is unusual in that there has always been an appeal in it to the men, and often it is the husband and wife who join at the same time. This Chapter meets on the second Thursday of each month, except for the months of July and August.

During the years, some members of the lodges and the Eastern Star Chapter have been elected to district positions. In 1898, Gilford Stafford served as District Deputy Grand Master. He was a member of Lake Lodge, Ameliasburgh. In 1936, Harry E. Redner of the same lodge served the same office. In 1948 Stewart C. Wood of Consecon Lodge was given the same honour, and in 1963 A. Clare McFaul of Hillier Township and a member of Lake Lodge was District Deputy. In 1966, Rae Spencer of Consecon Lodge was Masonic District Deputy Grand Master. In 1980 Richard Hall of Hillier Township and a member of Lake Lodge became district deputy, and in 1983, Victor Alyea, also of Hillier Township and a member of Consecon Lodge, received this honour and responsibility. The Order of the Eastern Star serves the area covered by both lodges. Over the years several members of the Chapter have been honoured in their appointment as District Officers. Helen Cross of Bloomfield and Eleanor Silver of Consecon are two that have so served. Adeline Anderson of Ameliasburgh Township was the first to be given this honour.

Other lodges have met for a time in the township. We know that the Loyal Orange Lodge was active in Consecon, and purchased the Presbyterian church in that village following the closing in 1917. Following the fire of 1889, the store in Rednersville was renovated to include a 'Community Hall' on the second storey. The Loyal Bayside Lodge No. 124, Canadian Order of Foresters, Rednersville, met there. This Order had been revived and put on a sound financial footing by Dr. Peter Martin of Frankford— better known as Oronhyatekha. He later became consulting physician to the Mohawks.

This hall also was the meeting place for Bayview Loyal Orange Lodge No. 889, whose meeting on July 9, 1926 was marked with the tragedy mentioned in the chapter on Rednersville Village. The Black Preceptory of the Orange Lodge met in this hall also. In 1934 or before, when the Hall was changed into a residence, another place of meeting had to be found. Many of the members of the Orange Lodge transferred their membership to Belleville or Allisonville.

It is beyond the scope of this volume to go into the history of these fraternal organizations in depth. Such a study might produce a large volume of information and certainly would prove rewarding. The attitude and the moral quality of the citizens of the township have been influenced both by the members of these fraternal organizations and also by their influence in the community. These organizations tend to emphasize and enforce the principles inculcated in the teachings of Christianity, and as such have directed the thinking of many and the actions of many toward a higher plane.

Ancient Order of United Workmen

Ancient Order of United Workmen, Lodge 262

Seated: John Camrike, James Glenn, Albert Lont

Standing left to right; 1. Dorland Fox, 2. Dr. File, 7. Lewis Lont, 9. Moran Lont, 11. Fred File, 12. Gil Choate, 13. Jesse Choate, 14. Byron Frederick, 15. Ferris Wood, 16. Francis Wood, 17. Jake Ferguson.

Counting back from right to left: 1. Duff File, 3. Fred Lauder, 4. Edgar Redner, 5. Will Reddick, 6. Ab Crosby, 7. Jesse Sprung, 12. Wm. Bisdee, A.O.U.W. Lodge Hall, Roblin's Mills, in background.

The Ancient Order of United Workmen was a fraternal organization for the mutual benefit of its members and their families. It embraced in its membership men of every vocation, profession and occupation, workers of all classes, whether their labour was mental or physical. It had no connection with any religious sect, political party or labour union, but was designed to promote fraternity, mental and social improvement and mutual assistance.

The AOUW was organized Oct. 27, 1868 at Meadville, Pennsylvania, by John Jordan Upchurch. In 1926 a merger was struck between the 152,000 members of the Independent Order of Foresters and the 8,300 members of the AOUW. Its mission— to aid its members in sickness and distress, to unite men in the bonds of Fraternal Fellowship, to pay widows and orphans of its deceased members the sum of one or two thousand dollars.

The letters CHP on the members' blue and gold badges stood for Charity, Hope and Protection. A small gold-coloured Bible hung from the top of the badge.

The Ameliasburgh Lodge was No. 262. On Dec. 20, 1909 there was a recorded membership of 40.

Rednersville Women's Institute

Rednersville Women's Institute was organized Jan. 20, 1909 at Rednersville Church by Miss Gertrude Grey of the Ontario Department of Agriculture. It was decided to hold regular meetings on the fourth Thursday of each month, and that meeting date has continued for 75 years. There was a membership of 53 the first year.

The programs in those early years were varied to meet the needs of the

Rednersville W.I. Nursing Class c. 1926

times, just as they are today: Bread making, Cooking for Hired Help, Care and Training of Children, Canning and Preserving. They had Departmental speakers every year and short courses in Sewing, Millinery and Home Nursing. They started and staffed a library at Rednersville. The year 1914 found everyone sewing for the Red Cross, which was repeated during World War II, also making jam for overseas at the Brickman Canning Factory. In 1942 alone over a ton and a half was sent to Britain.

Down through the years the Rednersville W.I. has sponsored Girls' 4-H Homemaking Clubs. Following the motto, "For Home and Country," the programs still are educational and timely, with yearly short courses provided by the Ministry on such topics as quilting, crafts, cooking, sewing. Compiling a Tweedsmuir book on the history of the area is another accomplishment. A boy in Hong Kong was adopted through the Foster Parent plan and provided with schooling. Bus trips to various places of interest are an annual event.

Rednersville W.I. is celebrating its 75th anniversary in 1984 by entertaining all the W.I. branches in the District.

Consecon Women's Institute
by Mrs. Clifford Smith

Consecon W.I. was organized April 22, 1913 by Mrs. Johnathon Talcott of Bloomfield at the home of Mrs. Fred Ward. Ten ladies joined and Mrs. Ward was made President and Mrs. George Maidens secretary. From the beginning the W.I. met local needs such as helping families in the community.

In 1914 war broke out and the W.I. sent boxes to 18 boys who went overseas. The money for this work came from a monthly canvas in the community. The Bush girls, Dorcas, Caroline and Annie, knitted over 100 pairs of socks. When the Armistice was signed the W.I. was left with a good bit of money, and since Picton Hospital was coming into existence at that time, a room was furnished with the money in memory of the boys who gave their lives. Donations were given annually for years toward this project.

In 1920 the W.I. purchased street lanterns for the village of Consecon. The first bill of gasoline for the lamps was paid in Jan. 1921, with Elias Weeks looking after lighting the lamps. These were used until 1928 when electricity became available.

First aid kits were supplied in Consecon school in 1923. Consecon W.I. held a nursing course in the early 1930's which was well attended. This was just one of the many courses supplied by the Home Economics Department. In 1936 the W.I. started catering to the Masonic banquet, and this has been carried on each year since, their only money-making project.

In World War II, 33 boys answered their country's call from the Consecon area. When they returned in 1945 a reception and banquet was held in their honour in the Masonic Hall and the W.I. presented each boy with a signet ring.

When the Porter Hotel was torn down in the centre of the village. the land was made into a park and the Institute planted three flowering almond trees and bought several flags for the park.

The W.I. has sponsored a 4H club since 1955, and each year the girls and leaders are presented with gifts. They also have participated in most of the Senior Training projects. Bus trips, pot luck dinners, visiting museums and entertaining other branches are part of their activities. A Tweedsmuir Tea was held in 1979 in the home of Mrs. Clifford Smith.

Consecon W.I. has had three District presidents, namely Mrs. W.W. Ward, Mrs. Ross Bush and Mrs. Clifford Smith, and one District Secretary, Mrs. George Cunningham. They have two life members, Mrs. Clifford Smith and Mrs. Howard Walt.

In February 1984 they purchased a bench for outside the Post Office, and are planning another Tweedsmuir Tea as a bicentennial project. Consecon W.I. for 71 years has carried out the Motto: "For Home and Country."

Mountain View
Women's Institute

Women's Institute members visiting Hastings County Museum in 1966. Left to right, Back Row: Evelyn (Barber) Thompson, Annie Barber, Alice Johnson, Sheila Woodall, Margaret Barber, Jane Werkhoven, Florence Wood, Margaret Wallbridge; 2nd Row: Lottie Green, Carol Farmer, Lily Anderson, Millie Burkholder, Eva Lough, Beth Nightingale, Myrla Motley; Front Row: Adeline Anderson, Blanche Sprung, Edith Burkitt, Dorcas Motley, Evelyn Hamilton, Verna Roblin.

There has always been a large Women's Institute in the area. It was organized at Mountain View Church in 1908— among the first in the County. The Institute included ladies from Massassaga, Huff's Island and Mountain View. The Motto of the Institute is "For Home and Country". The Institute has sponsored 4-H Homemaking Clubs since they were first introduced. When the Institute first began, a committee was formed to clean up the cemetery. It has served the community by organizing clean-up drives, donating money, sponsoring money raising events and hiring caretakers. Now there is a Cemetery Board which administers to the needs of the cemetery.

During the war years, the ladies made jam and quilts and knit socks to send overseas. Donations of clothing and food were sent to the dried out areas of the west during the 30's. Help has been given to needy families and fire victims as well as donations of money for special Institute projects in under-developed countries. In June of 1983 the 75th Anniversary was celebrated by entertaining members from neighbouring Institutes.

As in most organizations, there has been much gained through the social contact, especially in the beginning years. The interesting and timely topics discussed have made the Institute top priority for many rural homemakers.

The Consecon Charge A.O.T.S. Men's Club

by Ross Adams

The Consecon Charge (United Church) A.O.T.S. Men's Club is an organization for men and is recognized by the church as a group such as the U.C.W. This organization is affiliated with the National A.O.T.S. Organization, with head office in Toronto.

The Consecon Group was chartered on Oct. 5th, 1960, by the King St. A.O.T.S. Men's Club of Trenton. The Consecon Club, in turn, chartered a club in Wellington, in April 1961 and in Rednersville in 1963.

Consecon charter members were: Rev. Donald Pipe, Ross Adams (Charter President), Frank Root, Max Gainforth, Frank Wilson, Melvin Carnrike, Charles Brooks, Joffery Beecroft, Victor Kleinsteuber, Everett MacDonald, Edward McIntyre, Arthur Kinnear, Howard Palmer, Joe Rollins, Bert Eggleton, Russel Forsythe, Donald Southorn, Gordon Lloyd, Donald Terry, Donald Charlton, Ross Goodmurphy, Albert Fox, Frank Hickerson, Stanley Hart, Douglas Williamson, Gary Wilson, Douglas Palmer, Lyle Clark, Edwin Carnrike, Ross Bush, Gerald Bush, Cecil Blakely, Reg. Batchelor, Cecil Andrus, Lieuvernie Drummond, Charlie Kent and Everett Ketcheson.

The Presidents of the Club, now in its 23rd year, are as follows:

Ross Adams— 1960, 1961, 1980	Isaac Smith— 1966, 1975
Frank Root— 1962	Russel Forsythe— 1967
Gordon Lloyd— 1963	Frank Wilson— 1968, 1979
Donald Southorn— 1964	Gary Wilson— 1969, 1978
Corey Burris— 1965	Ross Goodmurphy— 1970, 1976

Fred Clark— 1971	Rodney Green— 1974, 1981
Earl Burris— 1972	Delbert Bush— 1977
Clifton Gamble— 1973	Lloyd York— 1982, 1983

The Consecon A.O.T.S. Men's Club meets at the Consecon Church in Kingerly Hall on the first Thursday of each month, except July, August and September, with a supper at 7 p.m. served by the ladies of the U.C.W.

Annually, some members attend the Ontario Roundup of all Ontario Clubs, held in Geneva Park. Here there is an average attendance of 160 men. Each year the Consecon Club members attend the Belleville Presbytery Roundup hosted by a voluntary club within the Presbytery. This is held in November with about 100 men in attendance. Some of the Members and their families attend the National Biennial convention in a different city in Canada each time. Calgary hosted for 1981, St. John's, Newfoundland in 1983 and the 1985 Convention is to be held in Sudbury, Ontario.

Club projects include a pancake supper in March, an auction sale of donated articles in May, a strawberry and ice cream and cake social in June. For many years nuts were sold as an autumn project, but rising prices prohibited continuing.

Funds are donated to the local charge annually. Donations were made to Operation Crossroads Africa, as long as help was needed. Support goes to the Mission and Service Fund, The Salvation Army, trophies to graduates of The Bayfield School in Consecon, and assistance was given to purchase a movie projector for the charge and a movie screen for the Sunday School. Donations of $500 have been given to both the building fund of Carrying Place United Church and to the Consecon re-building fund following the fire. For some years the attendance of one or two younger members has been donated in full enabling them to attend the Geneva Park Conference.

The name A.O.T.S. is taken from the 22nd chapter of St. Luke, verse 27, where Jesus said to the disciples, "I am among you, As One That Serves". The aim of the organization is to promote Christian Fellowship, to deepen the spiritual life of men, and to develop an effective programme of Christian service.

The Royal Canadian Legion, Branch 509
Consecon, Ontario

Edited from article by Dorothy Goodfellow

Branch 509 was originally formed at The Carrying Place, Ontario on Dec. 7, 1949 and was known as the Quinte Branch 509 of the British Empire Service League.

The first president was Nostrand Sprague and there were about 35 members. Their meetings were held at the Anglican Church Hall in Carrying Place, which was also used by the Boy Scouts and Girl Guides, as well as by the church as a meeting hall.

Unveiling Ceremony Oct. 3/81
New Cenotaph Consecon Legion Hall

In early 1951 the Branch tried to purchase the Church Hall for their own use, but their tender was turned down, and later that same year, arrangements were made to purchase a solid stone two-storey building, which was about six miles south of the Carrying Place at Consecon, Ontario.

This old stone building held many different businesses over the years, including a hardware store and a furniture store, but there were no conveniences and it was heated with wood stoves. Purchase of this building was finally made and the Legion took over, and on Jan. 8, 1952, held their first meeting in their new hall.

Almost immediately, plans were made to erect a cenotaph on the grounds in memory of their fallen comrades of both World War 1 and 2, but it was not until July 1956 that the cairn was finally complete. This was a beautiful memorial, but it was made of field stone and gradually over the years, with the weather conditions and vandalism in the village, it had to have many repairs, until in 1981 it became beyond repair and was torn down and a new cenotaph was erected by Campbell Monuments in Belleville.

In 1957 Honor Rolls were obtained and Rev. E.M. Cook entered all the names of our fallen comrades from the Village and surrounding area and was assisted in this task by the President at the time, Comrade Dorwin Smith.

Our records are almost non-existant until 1968, at which time they had only 21 regular members. To date, they have a total of 135 members made up of Life, Ordinary and Associate and Fraternal Affiliates, and are becoming more active in Legion Affairs and in sports, especially Darts.

The Ladies Auxiliary has contributed much to the branch over the years, both in contributing funds to many projects and in being there to lend a helping hand when needed. They have always been willing workers and it is due to their unswerving loyalty to the branch that they have progressed so well over the years.

The unveiling ceremony of the new Cenotaph on Oct, 3, 1981, was attended by members from all the Branches in the Zone, as well as several other branches in Ontario and was a very impressive service.

Over the years they have had several Presidents, and today among the active members are two of the original members, James Colton and Robin Adair, who are Life Members of the Branch, as well as Stan Boudreau, who served as President in 1974 and is now serving, and the branch's first lady President, Dorothy Goodfellow, who served in 1981 and 1982.

Helen B. Anderson, in a fine and fitting tribute to those who gave their lives in World Wars 1 and 2, penned the following lines:—

May We Be Worthy

May we be worthy of the victory, Lord,
That Thou hast given by Thy powerful hand,
And may our voices blend in sweet accord
To sing Thy praises in this freedom land.

And may we not forget the sacrifice
Of those who fought and suffered, bled and died,
Who flung their youth away in war's abyss,
That we at home might still in peace abide.

And may we strive to build a better world,
Where greed and gain will find no more a place,
Each despot from his lordly seat be hurled,
And brotherhood, the triumph of our race.

The Seventh Town Historical Society

The Ameliasburgh Township Council on April 28, 1969, called a meeting for the purpose of initiating an Historical Society in the township. As an outcome of that meeting, The Seventh Town Historical Society was formed with the following executive: President— Loral Wanamaker, 1st Vice-President— Martin Hamelink, 2nd Vice-President— Reginald Barber, Secretary/Treasurer— Sharon Vanclief. Members enthusiastically began researching and preparing papers of village, church, school, cheese factory, farm and family histories, with the objective that eventually these could be incorporated into a history of the township. By the end of the first year the society had a membership of 56.

One of the first projects of the society was the erection of a plaque at the site of the Roblin Mill. This was achieved on June 27, 1971. The first bus trip was taken that year also, to several historical spots in the Kingston area. This was so successful that bus trips became an annual event. Pot luck suppers for the June and November meeting have also become an enjoyable tradition. As well as many papers by the members, guest speakers, slide presentations, demonstrations such as stencilling and weaving, and displays of collections such as bells, music boxes, buttons, clocks, guns and bottles, have provided varied and interesting programs.

Realizing the historic value of the old S.S. 12 school, the society has worked toward its preservation and restoration under the dedicated leadership of Daisy Wannamaker and a very energetic building committee. Another committee is working on the original objective of the society, that of publishing a book concerning the history of the township. This is the Bi-centennial project of the Historical Society.

Officers of the Historical Society since its inception are the following:

Year	President	Secretary-Treasurer
1969-70	Loral Wanamaker	Sharon Vanclief
1970-71	Loral Wanamaker	Sharon Vanclief
1971-72	Mac Wallbridge	Susan Beevor
1972-73	Frances Young	Nora Barber
1973-74	Frances Young	Edna Jones
1974-75	Frances Young	Nora Barber
1975-76	Mildred Wanamaker	Nora Barber
1976-77	Mildred Wanamaker	Edith Cairns
1977-78	Bruce Graham	Edith Cairns
1978-79	Daisy Wannamaker	Edith Cairns
1979-80	Daisy Wannamaker	Edith Cairns
1980-81	Ron Dickens	Nancy McNaughton
1981-82	Ron Dickens	John Wannamaker
1982-83	Rev. Maurice McLeod	John Wannamaker
1983-84	Rev. Maurice McLeod	John Wannamaker

S.S. #12 AMELIASBURGH

At the west end of Ameliasburgh village stands a fine example of an early stone structure, the oldest public building in the township. The main part of the school was built in 1848 with an addition of 18 ft. towards the east end added in the early 1890's. Education took place in this building until 1965 when rural schools were amalgamated.

In 1969, Township Council offered the building to the Historical Society but it lacked sufficient funds to undertake necessary upgrading and repairs. In the late 1970's and early 1980's the building was used during the summer for the Society's meetings, plus 4-H and W.I. training courses. A most successful event was the reunion of former students and teachers, held in August 1980 with 120 attending a Pot Luck Dinner, with a schedule of events during the afternoon.

'Art On The Fence', has been a most successful event for the past ten years. It is a display and sale of art and crafts held on the school grounds and attracts many visitors to Ameliasburgh.

A fire of unknown origin destroyed the interior of the school on Sept. 12, 1981. The Society petitioned Township Council not to demolish the building until assessment could be made as to its reconstruction, as the basic stone work was structurally sound.

Volunteer work began in earnest in October of 1981 and with money that had been donated and the insurance money from Council, the roof was completed before winter arrived.

Just previous to the fire the Council had designated the structure as an Historic Building. In September 1982 an application for a Wintario Grant resulted in an award of $22,000 to cover a two year building programme.

The interior reconstruction which began in the summer of 1983 is in its first phase. In 1984, a kitchen, bathroom and disposal system remains to be completed.

The cupola which housed the school bell was rebuilt and painted under the guidance of the late Mac Wallbridge and his assistants replaced it early in 1983. Fund raising events have been held to assist with the reconstruction and as a requirement for receiving the Wintario Grant.

The Ameliasburgh Garden Club

By Robert J. Kendall

On Jan. 25, 1982, the Ameliasburgh Garden Club was organized, with Harry Bisdee, Bruce Graham and Rev. Maurice McLeod providing the initiative and Allen Gardiner and Harry Lambourne, District Director and Assistant District Director, District 3, Ontario Horticultural Association, providing assistance and direction. A slate of officers was elected with Harry Bisdee to serve as president.

Meetings are held on the last Monday evening of each month. These feature, guest speakers, coloured slides, plant sales and exchanges. Door prizes have proven popular and refreshments are served.

Ameliasburgh Garden Club members have attended horticultural meetings at Belleville, Trenton, Picton and Kingston. Each spring a car cavalcade visits local greenhouses, as a learning experience.

Among the highlights was a bus trip to Ottawa at Tulip time, a visit to the Dominion Experimental Farm, RCMP horse stables, the Museum at Rockcliffe and the National Collection of Aeronautics display.

Yearly projects include the vegetable garden at the Museum, flower beds at Centre, SS 12 School house, Huff's Island School, Ameliasburgh Township hall, Roblin Mill plaque and at the west end village sign.

Ameliasburgh Fall Fair provides the club with the opportunity to 'strut their stuff', with their fine displays of fruit, vegetables and flowers. Their float in the procession drew applause. Decorated by Phyllis McFaul, Glen White and helpers, it was also entered in the Consecon Santa Claus Parade. President Harry Bisdee was at the throttle of his 'Ameliasburgh Flyer' in each parade.

Henry Lambourne, a member of the Royal Rose Society of Great Britain said, "Adopt a policy of reaching out for new gardening ideas and advanced horticultural technology... and your club will enjoy sustained success."

The Ameliasburgh Garden Club welcomes new members and looks to the future with enthusiasm for its growth.

Ameliasburgh Seniors' Club #948

By Marjorie Trounce

On June 15, 1978, the Ameliasburgh Township Seniors' Club was organized at a meeting in Ameliasburgh Town Hall. Lavina Hamilton of Bloomfield Seniors' Club came to the meeting along with Wilfred Sager and together offered information and answered questions. The first slate of officers was: President Harry Bisdee, First Vice President Charles Pratt, Second Vice President Marjorie Faulkner, Secretary Marjorie Trounce, Treasurer Beatrice Taft, Advertising Secretary Douglas Redner.

Forty-two Seniors attended the initial meeting, with 34 becoming members. Ameliasburgh Township Seniors' Club became the Club name.

The Club meets on the third Thursday of each month at 8 p.m. in the Township Hall. It is affiliated with the United Senior Citizens of Ontario and has the charter number 948. This charter was presented to the Club by Lavina Hamilton along with a tri-coloured flag: gold for age, white for serenity and security, and blue for true-blue for Canada. The gold-edged blue maple leaf in the center is for loyalty and the satisfaction of recognition as senior citizens, and respected as such. This flag is displayed at all meetings. The Ontario Constitution for Senior Citizens is: non-racial, non-sectarian, non-political.

Euchre parties, open to all Seniors are held on several Wednesday evenings a month. Special movies for Seniors are shown and well-attended at the Quinte Mall in Belleville.

Through a New Horizons (Health and Welfare Canada) Grant in 1980, new equipment was procured for social activities, including a public address system, card tables, folding picnic tables and chairs, coffee maker and flatware. All supplies are housed in a cupboard built by volunteers.

Club membership has grown to 70. Presidents through the years have been: John Jinks, Ross Adams and Betty O'Hara. Co-operation is the key and brings pleasure to all. The Charter Members are: Harry Bisdee, Hilda Bisdee, Charles Pratt, Eva Pratt, William Faulkner, Marjorie Faulkner, Marjorie Trounce, Beatrice Taft, Douglas Redner, Earl Onderdonk, Mabel Onderdonk, Ralph Redner, Belle Redner, Marjorie Adams, Ross Snider, Mary Snider, Harry Knox, Josephine Knox, Douglas Williamson, Addie Williamson, Gordon Waterhouse, Charles Bedford, Gertrude Bedford, Clarence Vanclief, Jean Vanclief, Frank Roblin, Verna Roblin, Harry Gibson, Ann Gibson, Margaret Wallbridge, Ruth Peck, Hugh Weese, and Grace Fritz.

The Salvation Army Camp— Ameliasburgh

by Daisy Wannamaker

The two storey, limestone home of the Roblin family in Roblin's Mills had sheltered a fair number of residents. Owen Roblin who built it died there in 1903, aged 97 years.

George Symes Wallbridge (1883-1957), a more recent owner, in 1944 donated the property to the Kiwanis Club in Belleville of which he was an active member, for use as a fresh air camp for underprivileged children. From 1945 to 1948 the Club spent nearly $20,000 to make it suitable for summer use. The camp was operated by the Kiwanis Club until 1951, then purchased by the Salvation Army through the generosity of the late Senator W.A. Fraser and other interested citizens, with the agreement that the camp would continue to be operated for the same purpose.

The Salvation Army has spent thousands of dollars adding needed facilities. At the moment there are eight summer cabins for 116 campers, six cottages for staff, a hospital, an eight-room lodge and a recreation room.

On July 3, 1978 the stone house was destroyed by fire with the loss of two lives. Rebuilding took place on the same site and a Conference Centre Facility replaced the home. Some of the stone from it was incorporated into a large fireplace which dominated the Centre. With a modern kitchen and dining hall, 200 people can be served at one time.

NEWS ITEM: THE LATE SENATOR W.A. FRASER LEAVES $325 000² TO CHARITY, INCLUDING SALVATION ARMY'S ROBLIN LAKE CAMP, TRENTON NURSES 'RESIDENCE.

"....Charity vaunteth not itself, is not puffed up." (Corinthians XIII).4

Courtesy The Trentonian

Suitable engraved plaques were presented by the Kiwanis Club President and Directors on July 28, 1960 and June 20, 1961 to commemorate the generosity of Kiwanian George Wallbridge and Senator W.A. Fraser and other interested citizens. The auditorium is designated 'Fraser Hall'.

Victoria Athletic Club

by Evelyn Thompson

Those of us who grew up in Victoria neighbourhood in the 1920's and 30's had no reason to be concerned about some form of entertainment. We didn't have cars as most young people do now, so our recreation had to be close to our homes. We were lucky in that Mr. and Mrs. George Wannamaker related to young people. George and Jennie, as we knew them, had a tile and cement plant on their farm which had considerable flat land on top of the hill behind the tile house. They called us together and asked us if we would like to form an athletic club and use their field for ball, tennis and other field games. We had to have balls, gloves, raquets and such, and provide them for ourselves; however there was so much enthusiasm that in no time at all the Victoria Athletic Club was formed with President and Secretary-treasurer, and we were on our way.

Mr. Wannamaker had been a hardball player, so we had an excellent coach for ball, and in time there were teams all over the township. We played softball as the equipment was not so expensive, and girls could enjoy the sport also. Many people helped along the way, and our V.A.C. became a popular meeting place for a great many young people.

In the winter months we had a pond where we skated. We even had a small shed with a stove where we could change into our skates. We also had euchre and crokinole parties at the members' homes in winter. The girls took along some sandwiches or cake, and an evening of fun and laughter was enjoyed. Sometimes, when there was room, we ended up with dancing.

Our boys' softball team won the championship on a couple of occasions. I remember my parents, Mr. and Mrs. Henry Montgomery, made and served a chicken dinner with all the trimmings to the team and their wives or girl friends; such was the spirit of the community.

The V.A.C. continued for many years. As each of us grew up and were married, we were given a charivari and presentation. I still have the floor lamp, and it is in use some 53 years later. Looking back, I feel we were very fortunate to have lived in such a caring community with such wonderful people as George and Jennie Wannamaker and others, who cared enough about the young people of our day to think of the idea of the Victoria Athlete Club. I am sure there are many who have similar fond memories of the healthy, happy times we spent together in Victoria Community.

CHAPTER 46

ARTS & CRAFTS

Ameliasburgh's pioneer settlers had to craft things out of necessity. They knitted warm clothing from sheep's wool, that they carded and spun into yarn, wove wool blankets and cloth, and stitched quilts for the warmth they provided. They braided rag rugs to provide a bright warm spot on a cold floor. From primitive workshops came furniture, wooden cradles, sap buckets, handsleighs, building blocks, wooden bowls and many other essentials of housekeeping.

Today many residents craft articles as a hobby in their spare time. Some of the same patterns and techniques used long ago are employed today, not out of necessity but for the sheer pleasure of creativity.

'Log Cabin' pattern often used by the early pioneers, used small pieces of material. It was pieced by hand and was Brenda Wannamaker's first quilt. She won $150 first prize at Picton Fair in 1979.

An antique brass bed with homemade quilt. Note the intricate and vast amount of quilting done on the border by Mrs. William Hubbs (nee Ida Sager). These are in the home now owned by Malcolm Hubbs, Gore Road.

A Hair wreath

Hair Wreaths

The ladies made hair wreaths sometimes as memorials and framed them under glass. Such a wreath is today a prized possession of Mrs. Gordon

Waterhouse (nee Florence Hubbs). It was given to her as a remembrance of her Grandparents, William Emery Hubbs and his wife Matilda Ann (Babcock). By trade he was a carpenter and became very crippled so the wreath dates back to before the turn of the century.

Mrs. Hubbs would cut locks of hair from family, relatives, friends and everyone saved combings from their long hair in those days. A special container had its place on the bedroom dresser to receive these combings. These gave the different shades of colour that were woven into the flower designs.

The Shell House

William Emery Hubbs and his wife Matilda Ann (nee Babcock) made two shell houses. One is a replica of the home of Haviland Hubbs on the Rednersville Road, while the second is of the home of Malcolm Hubbs, Gore Road.

Matilda Ann would take her horse harnessed to a buggy and go either to the bay shores or to the shores of the lakes and gather snail shells for her project. They had to be washed and polished.

William Emery, who was an excellent carpenter, built the houses in sections. His wife papered the walls, carpeted the several rooms, and even put lace curtains on the glass windows, before her husband finally assembled the house. The shells were glued on last. It was a true work of art, and a craft not seen anywhere else. The Hubbs family lived in Rednersville, across the road from the present church.

```
Family Record July The 21 1846        Demorestville &c

George    Boulter born    December 5 1799

Sarah     Boulter born    September 29 1798

Nathaniel James   Boulter born    November 24  1821
Charlotte Sophia  Boulter born    February 13  1823
George    Henry   Boulter born    July    17   1826
Theodore  Hacraft Boulter born    May     2    1827
Sarah     Elizabeth Boulter born  March   7    1829
Emily     Maria   Boulter born    May     12   1831
Mary      Matilda Boulter born    October 14   1833
Emily             Boulter born    November 5   1835
Wellington        Boulter born    Febuary 14   1838
Collingwood       Boulter born    June    22   1842
Maria             Boulter born    September 18  1843
Edward            Boulter born    March   23   1845
Nelson            Boulter born    Febuary 14   1847
Wilson            Boulter born    December 15  1848
Franklin          Boulter born    February 12  1851
Franklin          Boulter born    September 15 1852
Alice             Boulter born    March   ?    1854
Florence Nightingale Boulter born  December 26  1855

Worked by Emily Boulter aged 9 years  Demorestville &
```

This Sampler was done by Emily Boulter, later wife of Wm. Ryerson Dempsey M.L.A.

Samplers

In early days 'Samplers' were worked to maintain family records or record proverbs etc. and were hung on the walls of the pioneer homes.

Vivian Green... Needlecrafts.

Enter the cosy bungalow on Gorsan Farm, on Ameliasburgh's second concession, and immediately one is impressed with the fine handcrafted articles which are in use throughout the home. There are fine hand crocheted table cloths gracing the tables in the dining room and kitchen, intricate macramé lampshades in colours that blend beautifully with the decor, pretty cushions and handmade quilts with myriads of tiny stitches.

The Carter family, consisting of Gordon, his wife Sandra (Green), their daughter and son and Sandra's mother, Vivian Green live in this pleasant home, where needlework seems hereditary.

When Vivian was very young, she learned from an aunt the art of tatting. She has many shuttles and still tats beautiful doilies. Because there were fewer social events to attend then, Vivian spent many evenings doing crocheted pieces which she almost always gave away. Now her daughter Sandra is crotcheting beautiful sweaters and it is she and husband Gordon who excel at macramé.

Vivian's mother (Lottie Fox) made many quilts in her lifetime. Frequently, she quilted alone or had a 'quilting bee', when neighbourhood ladies came to help quilt. Center Church was in need of a hall and Wellington Howell, a church member, loaned the church women the money to have it constructed. In order to repay the debt, they served potluck dinners and quilted for anyone who wished to pay $8 for the quilting. Mrs. Ida Rathbun from the upper second concession made several quilt tops from men's discarded neckties, using as her pattern, "mother's flower garden". When these were quilted she took them to the United States.

Like her mother, Vivian knitted, but admits it's not as pleasureable a hobby as crochet. This winter she has crocheted another beautiful tablecloth of fine linen thread.

When Vivian's children were grown and she quit helping with the farm work, she began quilting for other people. She sews intricate designs in tiny stitches, so that the back of the quilt is often more beautiful than the patterned front. She has quilted dozens of quilts for people who request special creations, and many have won awards at fairs and exhibitions.

Vivian Green is a charter member of Rednersville Women's Insititute. She has been involved in nine W.I. courses and has led several of them, the latest having been a quilting course in 1982-83. She also tailors and sews especially well, but we must credit her with the title, 'Master Quilter'.

Frank Keene—Wood Carver

From the time Frank Keene was a child he liked to whittle with his jacknife. He never produced anything to brag about until one day he was helping to gravel a lane at Percy Carnrike's farm on the fourth concession. Between loads of gravel which he spread as it arrived, he cut a piece of cedar

Frank Keene uses
spruce or pine wood
and a carving knife
to create his chains.

from a fence rail and started to whittle. He made three links of wood, separating each link and releasing it, with absolutely no glue being used. He gave the finished carving, with a bolt fastened to it, to Ronald and Gordon Carter who received first prize for it at a local fair.

In 1959 Frank went to work for the Department of Highways and was given a job on the swing bridge at Rossmore. Frank, with time on his hands, began carving more and more as a pastime. The first chain he produced on the job there, he gave to William Burkitt, another bridge employee. During the fall when there were few boats, Frank carved longer chains. He retired from the bridge job in 1975.

Frank Keene has not enjoyed the best of health and many times he has been a patient in hospital. On one occasion he was in Kingston General under the care of Dr. Connell who belonged to a Scottish Club in the city. He asked Keene to display his chains and other carvings on the other bed in the room and many doctors and club members came to see them. For the club, Frank later carved an Indian, a chunk of chain and a Scottish Piper. He has made three extremely long chains similar to the one in the picture, which have each taken about 150 hours to carve. He has also made necklaces of tiny links and carved names on them for every female member of his family. Recently, he has fashioned a chain that hangs in Turner's Variety Store at the Murray Canal Bridge.

Frank admits great satisfaction from his unique hobby and confesses that there is a knack to it.

John and Margaret Black
Their Business and Their Hobbies

John Latimer Black was born in Ameliasburgh Township at Massassaga. When he was eight years of age, he moved with his parents, Willet and Mary (Latimer) Black, to a former DeLong farm on Huff's Island, next door to where Mrs. Black's mother and brother John Latimer lived.

John farmed and took an active part in agricultural affairs. He was a member of the Prince Edward judging team at the Royal Winter Fair. He participated in ploughing matches, winning several classes.

In 1936 John Black with Clarence Thompson of Massassaga began a butcher business and from then it was Black's Meat Market. He recalls hard times during Depression Years, and the big flood.

Margaret Beatrice Fox, from the Gore in Ameliasburgh, became John's wife in 1939. They bought a home in the city, moved the shop to larger quarters and purchased a slaughter house on the Cannifton Road. He installed modern equipment for handling, curing, cutting, and smoking meat. In the 1970's the city of Belleville purchased this property and today it is the site of the Quinte Sports Center.

In the 1940's the Blacks bought the Wilson farm on the Gore in Ameliasburgh, and named it Victoria View Poultry Farm. Here they kept 6,000 laying hens and, also, beef cattle. John bought a team of show horses from Senator Fraser which he showed at fall fairs. The work at the farm, along with the business in Belleville was too much, so the farm was sold to Leonard Voskamp, whose son still operates a poultry business.

John Black was, and is, a builder. They enjoy trips in a 37-foot cruiser, one of four he has built. In 1959 they built a home on the north shore of the Bay of Quinte, west of Belleville. A boat house on the same property houses their cruiser.

In 1960 a fire destroyed several stores on Bridge Street in Belleville, and Black's Meat Market was severely damaged, so the Black's bought the former Imperial Bank building on Front Street. This proved to be an ideal location, and seven employees worked along with Margaret and John.

After 36 years in business, the Blacks sold out, and in summer enjoy boating, fishing, and gardening, but when winter comes they have a hobby like no other. John began making miniatures. His first one was a single plough to which he attached a team of horses (Royal Doulton figurines). There followed: carriages, wagons, carts, landeaus, the Queen's carriage, an eight-horse team of Budweiser show horses. Now, the collection consists of 75 different displays, all with harness made by John, and costumes of the people (dolls) made by Margaret.

Another pleasure of the Blacks is reminiscing— their special memories are of years spent in Ameliasburgh Township.

William Campbell

The Campbell Monument Company has served the Quinte area for nearly a century. John Campbell, grandfather of William, apprenticed under his brother-in-law Mr. Moore, in Stirling before leaving to open his own Trenton business operation in the early 1900's. Unfortunately, he contracted tuberculosis because of the stone dust, so his son Arnold took over and carried on the business until his father recovered.

In 1931 Arnold Campbell began a monument operation in Belleville and the firm served the memorial needs in the district, including the County of Prince Edward, until 1950. The following year Bill, Arnold Campbell's son, started working full time with his father. His apprenticeship consisted of learning the basics of the trade and about six years each in the field of layout, design and hand cutting of stone. The mastery of the trade includes sandblasting, hand cutting and the use of pneumatic tools. In 1979, Bill bought out the business.

The Campbell Monument Company has branches in Peterborough and Pembroke as well as the Belleville operation and employs 23 fully-trained staff members.

Stone is shipped to Montreal from all over the world, then forwarded to Beebe, Quebec, where it is cut and made ready for shipment to the company's branches. Tractor trailer loads weighing 25 tons, provide labour for the staff during the winter months.

The Campbell Monument Company construct mausoleums, cenotaphs, and any other type of stone work desired. This is the only company to totally service the industry. The firm provides a free restoration service to cemeteries and has done so for the past 90 years.

The Campbell family moved into a new home beside Roblin Lake, Ameliasburg, in May 1979, and they have been active participants in community affairs since their arrival in the township.

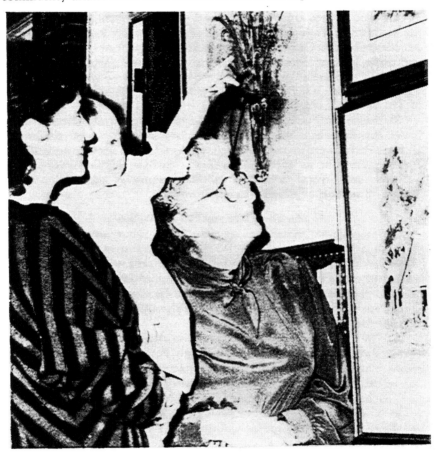

Donnah Cameron and daughter Donnah II with daughter Kirstin.

Donnah Cameron— Artist

There are few people in Ameliasburgh Township who have not heard of Donnah Cameron, her talented family of four daughters, and the work she has accomplished in the field of pen and ink drawing and in oils and watercolours. Her work has been shown continually, either at public exhibitions or at her own gallery for many years.

Donnah and her husband Allen had their first exhibition at St. Andrew's Presbyterian Church in Belleville in 1967. Then she began teaching classes in local schools under the night school programme, and later instructing, from its inception, for the Extension Department of Loyalist College. When classes concluded in the spring, Donnah organized 'on the spot' painting classes on her own property and travelled around the County, too.

Donnah and her daughter Donnah II, a graduate of the Ontario College of Art and also a gifted artist in pottery and painting, began classes in the open in the Madawaska Valley. Back at their own home on the Rednersville Road in Ameliasburgh, the Cameron family hold open house once a year featuring arts and crafts, watercolours, oils, and special handmade quilts.

In 1970, Donnah Cameron won the Lake Ontario Cement 'Artist of the Year' award with her *Picton Harbour,* and again in 1980 with her watercolour of *The Gore* (Ameliasburgh).

She has in fact become famous as an artist. Her paintings grace the walls of many Ameliasburgh homes. A trillium watercolour hangs in Toronto's Queen's Park. In the Banker's Association building in Toronto and in the Art Planning Consultants' office of New York City hang samples of her paintings. Galleries and private collections in many countries feature the work of Donnah Cameron of Ameliasburgh Township.

Marjorie Mitchell (nee Walker)

Marjorie Walker Mitchell was born in Toronto, but came to the County in 1957, when her father purchased Walker's Camp on the Stinson Block in Hillier Township. After receiving her education, she returned to Toronto to work, and at that time became interested in ceramics. For four years she attended Harrison Bell seminars where she learned the basics of the craft, before returning to Walker's Camp where she and her sister began teaching the craft full time to adults.

In 1980 they exhibited their ceramics at the Toronto Home show. The following year they moved to Ameliasburgh Township, where Marjorie gave lessons from her home as well as instructing seniors at the Belleville Recreation Centre and in two of Picton's nursing homes.

From her home on Ameliasburgh's third concession, Marjorie teaches two classes of ceramics per week to help finance her current full time post-secondary education at Loyalist College.

Marion Casson

Marion G. Casson is a native of Peterborough, where her parents still reside. While her husband Richard was attending university, she began two years of pottery lessons at the Potters' Workshop in Waterloo.

In 1970, the Cassons moved to Prince Edward County. At this time they live on the Rednersville Road with their three children and Richard is a Secondary School teacher at Bayside. Marion has taught pottery lessons to children in her own home, and adults through the Loyalist College programme.

Marion Casson at her loom.

After having taken weaving lessons from the Nurcombe's in Cherry Valley, Marion taught the craft at the Recreation Centre in Belleville in 1983 to children. In her home she has three looms, ranging from 22 inches to 45 inches. The largest is a 60-inch loom and often she has them all in operation. She prefers weaving ornamental pieces and has a special interest in design.

Marion learned the art of spinning much later than that of weaving, and she owns a small portable wheel. Like most spinners and weavers she has been involved with the Belleville Weavers' and Spinners' Guild, acting as President in 1979-80. For ten years she has participated in the Quinte Arts Council Shows. Three times her pottery and weaving have been displayed at Century Place in Belleville.

Marion Casson is currently a member of both the Ontario and Canadian Craft Councils. She is participating in a course at St. Lawrence College in Brockville, sponsored by the Ontario Hand Weavers and Spinners which involves six weekends per year for three years for the Master Weavers' programme. Upon completion of this, she will become a Master Weaver and intends to concentrate on the art of weaving.

Mrs. Bessie Cornell

Bessie Cornell was born in Belleville and attended school there. For many years she worked for Bell Telephone in the city as a Supervisory Clerking Staff member, retiring in 1967.

A lady with varied and many talents, Bessie taught millinery for awhile and also made hats. She did leathercraft, candlemaking and weaving, which was her preference. Her sister from St. Catharines sparked her interest in this craft and she studied many books on the subject before joining the Belleville Weavers' Guild.

This opened a new door for Bessie Cornell, as she became involved in the setting up of a loom at Glanmore House in Belleville (The Hastings County Museum). She then began to teach children the old art of weaving rag rugs. She began instructing adults in the same craft at the Recreation Centre and has often been a volunteer for Activity Days at the Ameliasburgh Museum, where she set up the loom in the Weaver's Cottage to show how rag rugs were made.

Bessie Cornell and her husband moved to Ameliasburgh Township in 1938 where she continues to carry on other hobbies but invariably she returns to the art of weaving, which gives her great pleasure.

Tremeer's Treasures

Harvey and Jan Tremeer and daughters of Rednersville enjoy a craft which has captured the imagination and fantasies of many people of all ages. It is the hobby of making miniature house furnishings on a 1/12 scale. One of their activities was to provide Glanmore House Museum in Belleville with a display for the Christmas season. They have also displayed their miniatures at the Corby Public Library. They enjoy displaying their treasures in their home or anywhere for those who are interested. They agree that a visit to a miniature show is a great experience, if only to see the variety of articles and the creativity that they involve.

The Tremeer family especially enjoys making accessories in the needlework line for the miniature home. They make petite point carpets on 22 canvas, which means that every square inch has 484 stitches. Patterns are taken from authentic Persian or Indian carpets and worked in wool as the originals are, or Orientals which are done in floss to represent silks. To work one square inch takes from one and one half to two hours, depending on the complexity of the pattern.

Tremeer's Treasures include embroidered bedspreads, braided rugs, cushions and place mats. With a miniature wood lathe they produce bowls, plates and covered dishes of wood, native to Ameliasburgh Township.

Verna Roblin, mother of Jan, has become involved in the venture too. Because of her skill in the use of a crochet hook, she has made exquisite table cloths and bedspreads using very fine sewing thread.

Because of this unique hobby, the Tremeer family has derived pleasure, relaxation and new friendships.

Spinners & Weavers— Joy and Jim Sutherland

Joy Sutherland has been spinning for the past 10 years, but weaves as well. An elderly lady taught her the basics when she lived in Barrie, and since then she has moved twice, from Barrie to Lanark then to the east end of Ameliasburg village.

Joy has been teaching at her home for two years, both nature dyeing using

Joy's Display at Weavers' &
Spinners' Guild.

Jim Sutherland. Expert in
Canoe Repairs.

weeds and plants found locally, as well as spinning, using wool mostly, but even some dog hair. Joy also has been a volunteer at the museum and taught classes during the summer of 1982, as well as being available on Activity Days. Joy is presently on the executive of the Belleville Weavers and Spinners Guild which has a membership of 80.

The Sutherlands have three children who seem to be interested in learning from their mother, who claims the motion of the spinning wheel has a calming effect on the children, especially the 2-year-old.

Joy's husband, Jim, has a unique talent: he is becoming an expert in repairing canoes, especially cedar strip and canvas canoes. He is a woodworker and a craftsman by trade, and has been picking up this new trade over the past four and a half years.

Marjorie Rinearson

Marjorie Rinearson was born in Kansas City, Missouri. She came to Canada when her husband was transferred to Oakville, Ontario. She enrolled at the Ontario College of Art to study portraiture and has been doing portraits for 25 years. She also does small sculptures, paintings of floral scenes and batik.

When Marjorie Rinearson and her husband cruised through the Bay of Quinte, they were so impressed by the beauty of 'The County' that they decided to retire here. They chose Ameliasburgh township and built a new home on the Rednersville Road in 1974.

From 1975-83 she taught portraiture at night school at Trenton and also at Barbara Whelan's Art Studio.

For two years she served as president of the Belleville Arts Association. She has been displaying her work at various local shows and has won several awards: 'Best in the Show', Mill Gallery, Bowmanville, plus an Honourable Mention, Tom Thomson Gallery, Owen Sound, Oakville East Central Ontario Association, Belleville Art Association and also at local fairs.

Madeline Hope-Jobin, Photograph by Ian S. Robertson, courtesy County Magazine.

Mountain View Miniatures— Madeline Hope-Jobin

Madeline Hope-Jobin's delight in little things originated with *The Friendly Giant* on CBC television, who would set out tiny chairs "to curl up in" before his miniature fireplace. An article in an American magazine about 12 years ago led her to the discovery that dollhouses and miniatures had become a bona fide hobby for adults and were not simply considered playthings for children.

Madeline was then living in Montreal and, not able to find the miniatures she wanted locally, she began making her own. When she later moved to Toronto, and had become more proficient in miniature building, she found that there were collectors who were interested in buying the pieces she made. Since she had been a college teacher in Montreal, it was a natural step for her to begin teaching her new skills in miniature workshops.

About three years ago Madeline's family purchased an old farmhouse in

Mountain View. She and her husband Larry soon decided that County life was for them and soon made it their permanent home. They now operate a mail order business dealing in dollhouse building supplies. They have also set up a small shop in their home where they sell supplies along with their handcrafted dollhouses, miniature furniture and accessories, dolls, toys and gifts.

Madeline and Larry are planning to offer workshops again as soon as they have cleared enough space in the midst of their full-size house renovations.

Eugene Moshynski

Mr. Moshynski was born in Lodz, Poland in 1923. When he was 17 he was arrested and placed in Dachau Concentration Camp for five years. He was liberated by the United States Army.

Moshynski was married in 1947 and came to Canada in 1948. He moved around from Penetang to Midland, Toronto, Trenton and finally to Carrying Place, where he has a home on the Rednersville Road.

In Moshynski's early childhood, his artistic ability had been discovered and he had attended art school in Poland until his arrest. However, he survived the years in the concentration camp mainly because of this talent and it also earned him extra food and tobacco. After the war he worked for the U.S. Army painting cartoons and pin-up girls on the walls of mess halls and dance halls.

He became a professional in commercial art in Canada and his work is found in many countries and coast-to-coast in Canada. He is also known for his cartoons and caricatures which often appear in local newspapers.

The Moshynskis have two children and their daughter is also an artist. Mr. Moshynski has added a gallery to his home and plans to devote his time to his art.

Barbara Whelan

In Grade 4, Barbara Whelan took her first award in drawing and painting, and she never looked back. She has participated in public and private teaching of students of all ages including senior citizens under the Belleville Recreation Department and Loyalist College.

Her family have a cottage on Roblin Lake and Barbara admired S.S. No. 12 at the west end of the village while driving back and forth from Belleville to the cottage. She undertook to approach council with a view of setting up a studio there and for awhile it was called the 'Schoolhouse Studio'. For years she conducted oil painting classes, and with fellow artists, instruction was given in batik, portraiture and sculpture. As an outcome of these talents, a one day show was created in June of each year called 'Art On The Fence'. Large crowds and great interest have made this show an institution in the village of Ameliasburg.

Barbara has travelled extensively across Canada as well as abroad in Spain and Italy. She is a member of the Belleville Art Association, Burlington Fine Arts Assoc., Central Ontario Art Association, East Central Art Association as a founding member, Quinte Arts Council as well as Visual Arts, Ontario.

Her awards are numerous: 'Best in the Show' 1972-78 and 1982; in 1977, the Belleville Art Association Dora Purdin Award (ECOAA). She has had several one-person shows in Wellington, Oakville, Delaney Gallery, Corby Library, Belleville, plus a group show, 'Portraits of Spain', 1973, in Burlington.

Barbara has also been commissioned to do work for the city of Belleville and for that has received many commendations.

CHAPTER 47

F̄AMILY HISTORIES

The Adams Family

Originally of Omagh, County Tyrone in northern Ireland, William Adams and his wife Sarah left that country early in the 1800's, with their six children (one married) for Canada. The parents died enroute and were buried at sea. The surviving family eventually reached the Melville area in Ameliasburgh-Hillier Townships, Prince Edward County, on land which was later known as the W.H. Kinnear farm on lot 83. The surviving family was:

1. James Adams m. Fanny Baxter... the family moved to London, Ontario.
2. Robert James 1806-1866 m. Isabella Brooks 1813-1861. Their tombstones were removed from Albury Cemetery and their names placed on a new stone. The former ones were returned to the farm where their descendants were living. (ref. *Greystones, the Eben James home*)
3. Samuel 1809-1888 m. Susannah Burley 1818-1874
4. Jane m. Thomas Bonter... the family settled near Marmora
5. Mary Ann m. William Ellis... the family settled near London, Ont.
6. William m. Jane Hunt... the family settled near London, Ont.

The Robert Adams Family

By Shirley Adams Mikel

In the year 1822 Wm. and Sarah Adams and their six children left their home in Omagh, County Tyrone, N. Ireland to begin a new life in Canada. During the voyage they both became ill, died and were buried at sea. They had six children, four boys and two girls.

Two of their sons, Robert and Samuel, settled on the 3rd Con. of Ameliasburgh where they cleared some land and built a log house. Robert

Adams and his wife Isabella settled on Lot 95 Con. 2 Twp. of Ameliasburg, adjoining his brother Samuel's farm. This farm has continued as an Adams family farm and is in 1984 owned by Everett and Dianne Adams and their two children Scott and Michelle, Everett being the sixth generation.

One of Robert and Isabella's 12 children was Joseph, nicknamed 'Big Joe' to differentiate between him and another Joseph Adams 'Little Joe'.

'Big Joseph' married Vellena Urquhart. They had five children: Isabel, married John Onderdonk; Earl who died at age 12 yrs.; Grace married Clarence Petherick; Everett married Carrie Parliament; Burton married Maude File in the year 1902, Dec. 3rd. Maude was the daughter of Dr. Albert J. File, Ameliasburg.

In 1904 Burton and Maude bought 100 acres being the West half of Lot 100, Con. 2, Ameliasburgh, from Joseph Adams (Little Joe) who was moving to western Canada.

This property was formerly owned by Zachariah & Nancy Carnrite. Inside the house under the window sill was a groove 8 in. long and ¼ in. deep, where Nancy Carnrite had scratched her matches to light her pipe which she smoked while sitting in her favourite chair.

In 1920 Burton and Maude purchased an adjoining 42 acres being the east half of lot 101 from Marcus, a bachelor and his mother Armetesia Carnrite. Before the business could be settled, lightning struck the Carnrite barn while

The Robert Adams Family:
Joseph (Big Joe) Burton,
Ross, Reginald, Larry—
Four Generations

Marcus was milking the cows, the barn was destroyed, and Marcus died. Later the deal was finalized with Armestesia and another son, Ross.

To Burton and Maude were born four children: Ross, who married Gladys Pope, in 1927; Wilma married Eber Alexander; Kathleen married Howard Alyea and Mildred married Joseph Dempsey.

In 1927 Burton and Maude built a new house on the 42-acre piece of land. Their son Ross and his wife Gladys moved into the original house. In 1932 Ross and Gladys' house burned so with their two children they lived with his parents until their new home was finished in the spring of 1933.

Ross and Gladys had three children, Reginald, Shirley and Robert. Ross and his father Burton farmed together until 1940 when Ross fell while riding a horse and severely injured his back. He then accepted employment at Benedict-Proctor Manufacturing Co., Trenton, makers of silverware, and worked there for 30 years (until 1970). He drove a bus for Grant Rathbun Bus Lines and later Travelways until 1980.

Burton died in 1959 at age 80 and Maude died in 1978 at age 96.

Robert married Florence Redcliffe and they have three children, Allan, Brenda and Tracey. They reside in the home where Burton and Maude lived and raise registered Hereford cattle.

Everett Adams (son of 'Big Joe') and Carrie had five children: Eldon who married Marjorie Wood, Evelyn m. Cecil Moreland, Gordon m. Aletha Thompson, Laird m. Hilda Alyea, Marion m. Allen Alyea.

David B. Adams, son of Robert and Isabella, had a son Hiram who married Mary Louise Cunningham. Issue: Harry who married Marie Weese, Issue: Marilyn Adams.

Rebecca Matilda, daughter of Robert and Isabella, married John Bryant, Issue: Bert and Hester, who married Pembroke Peck.

Robert Scott, son of Robert and Isabella, had a daughter Blanche who married Delbert Snider. They lived on the Ezra Bonter farm on th upper 2nd Con. Issue: Roy, Wilford, Walter and Ross.

Roy married Marion Allison had a daughter Ann and lived for years where Rece Selman lives.

Wilford married Margaret Sutherland R.N., one of three daughters. Sally m. Roy Pennel and they have a farm and mail-route in the area. Wilford farmed on the homestead until his death.

Walter married Kathleen Giles (Ref. *Giles* family).

Ross, farmer and electrician on the lower Third married Mary Bristol, their son Delbert lives near home.

The Samuel Adams Family

Samuel Adams (1809-1888), son of William and Sarah Adams of Omagh, Co. Tyrone, N. Ireland, married Susannah Burley (1818-1874). Samuel became owner of more than 300 acres in the second and third concessions of Ameliasburgh on lots 93, 94 and 95. Samuel and Susannah had 12 children who married into many of the pioneer families of Ameliasburgh Twp. Space does not permit mentioning but a few who live (lived) in the area.

Charles Adams, son of Samuel and Susannah, married Sophronia Brooks. Four of their 10 children were: Lottie who married Roy Williamson, Alta m. Smith Brown, Olive m. Percy White, and Ceburn m. Irene Weese.

Ephraim Adams, son of Samuel, married Martha Coleman. Their son Byron married Bessie Hamilton; two of their four children are Helen who married William Jose, and Howard who married Orris Foster.

John Adams, son of Samuel, married Laura Way. Two of their six children were Anne Laura who married Willet J. McFaul, and Merritt who married Ada Doolittle.

William Henry Adams, son of Samuel, married Eliza Jane Glenn and they had 11 children. Their daughter Minnie married Mac Giles; daughter Laura, Fred Cunningham, father of Clarence and Harry; Daughter Mary D. married Francis Wood, father of Morley. Their son Albert married Laura Brason; two of their five children were Nina who married Frank Osterhout, and William who married Audrey Reddick.

12 children of Samuel and Susannah Adams. Two pictures on wall: Wm. Henry Adams, Stephen Adams, Back row: Joseph, Sarah, Samuel, Mary Ann, Charles, Front Row: Alzina, James, John, Ephraim, Catherine.

Alyeas of Ameliasburgh

A French Huguenot, Nicholas d'Ailly came to America from Manheim, Germany aboard the ship 'Faith' in 1680. By 1693 he was living in New Jersey. There were many spellings for the name— Alje, Elya, Alee, Ally, Aliee, d'Ailly. The son of Nicholas was Jan Aliee. Jan's son was Peter Aliee (or Allee). Peter's son, Isaac Alyea, was baptized March 19, 1732 and married Annatje Mors (Demorest?).

The fifth generation of Alyeas, John of Worch, N.Y., married Mary Banta (Bonter) in 1790. They had a family of eight. Their fifth child, Peter,is the ancestor of the Alyeas of this area. They came to Prince Edward about 1790, and by 1798 had grants of 300 acres at the Carrying Place, and according to the 1851 census are shown on Lots 98, 99, 100, 101.

The sixth generation, Peter, born in 1802, married Elizabeth Shears b. 1804 and they had 14 children. He was known as Peter, 'The Great'. This family was:

    John Alyea 1823-1893 m. Elizabeth Ann Brown
    Henry F. 1825 m. Catharine Moon
    David 1827 m. Almira Alvin
    Samuel 1830-1896 m. Margaret Moon
    James 1832-1899 m. Mary Elizabeth Sager
    Phoebe Ann 1833-1917 m. Robert Maidens
    Hannah Maria 1836 m. Wm. Benjamin Weese
    Peter 1839-1913 m. Mary Carnrite
    Elizabeth Catharine 1841-1914 m. John Hunt
    Margaret Jane 1842-1921 m. Elisha Moon
    Jacob Smith 1845-1905 m. Augusta Moon
    Sarah Eliza 1846 m. Jacob Moon
    Isaac 1848 m. Elizabeth
    Alzina Samantha 1850-1908 m. Cory Baker

First Alyea home in Ameliasburgh on the First Concession, located on the property of the present Eben James home.

Smoke's Point Alyeas

Henry F. Alyea and his wife, Catharine Moon, lived on Lot 101. Their son, Henry James (Sam) married Catharine (Kate) Parliament. They had a son, Lewis Ross. When Ross (Slim) was 9 months old, his father died. Kate bought a house on Smoke's Point Road and raised her six children there. Son Fred died of wounds after World War II. Ray went to Massassaga, Archie, Gertie and Violet left the area. Ross married May Goldsmith and they had two children, Burton and Shirley. Shirley's son, David Grosjean, owns the Kate Alyea house. Shirley recalls her father trapping muskrats, painting houses, market gardening, picking blueberries in the North. Her father called for square dancing at house parties, laid up the car for winter, bought the children 5¢ ice cream cones on their rare visits to town. A Christmas treat was apples and an orange in a sock. Every fall the entire family plucked feathers from about 50 chickens for a whole day, and then they canned the meat for winter. Another son, Ray Alyea, b. 1891, married Bessie Post and they had Gordon b. 1919 who married Mavis Lord, and Catharine Maude b. 1921 who married Gordon Dempsey. Two Dempsey children were Dennis and Dale. Gordon and Mavis had one son, Brian Alyea.

Third Concession Alyeas

James Alyea and his wife, Mary Elizabeth Sager, had a family of nine: six boys and three girls. Their home was on Lot 99 on the Third Concession. The oldest son, William, married Sarah Lont and settled on the Second Concession near her sister Ida Rathbun; their daughter, Aletha, married Bert Bellamy. Son Herman, born 1864, and his wife, Elda Kemp settled in Consecon; their son Lorne, born in 1899, married Hilda Burris and they had one daughter, Gwen, married to George Southorn. Gilbert and his wife, Sarah Spencer, had a daughter Carrie. Alma married Austin Reddick and their daughter, Viola, is the wife of Gerald Ward. George Alyea and his wife, Jennie Pymer, settled on the James Alyea homestead on the Third Concession where Dean O'Hara resides today. Edgar and his wife, Emma Stoneburg, settled a little to the east of George on the Third Concession. Melissa, the youngest of James and Mary's family of nine, married Fred McConnell and lived in Wellington. Annie never married, and one son died young.

Peter Alyea married Mary, daughter of Zachariah and Nancy Carnrite, who lived on the Third Concession. They moved onto Lot 102 close by her parents. There was a family of five. Rodney Orlando, 1862-1930, the oldest, married Julia Russell, 1868-1911, from Rednersville, for his first wife. Their two daughters were, Isaylia b. 1890 who married Biard Bush of Consecon with their family Adelbert and Mildred; and Gladys b. 1898 who married Lee Rowe from the Carrying Place with their family Julia and David. Rodney Orlando's second wife was Perditta Farrell. Two more children were Fern b. 1913, who married Robin Adair and had a family of four, Nancy, Robbie, Lionel and

Sharon; Rodney W. b. 1918, married Edna Smyth and had two sons, Damon and Cory. Rodney and Edna's son, Damon, has a son, Matthew, born in 1982 who is the 11th generation of Alyeas in America. Another son of Peter and Mary Alyea was Horace who married Lettie Young and lived across the road from Rodney. Their daughter Hazel married Russell Hannah, daughter Vivian married Thomas King, son Keith was killed in an accident. A third son of Peter and Mary was Edward, who became a veterinary and practised in Colborne. With his wife Mary Harris from the Carrying Place he had two sons, Norman, who died of the flu in 1918, and Clifford. A fourth son of Peter and Mary, Delbert, died young. Besides four sons of Peter and Mary, there was one daughter, Cynthia Hester (Nin). She married Wesley Weese of Rossmore; their only child, Cyril, died when struck by lightning while travelling in the Murray Canal. When Peter Alyea died in 1913 he was taken to Albury Cemetery in the first motorized hearse owned by Thompson's of Belleville.

Sarah Elizabeth Alyea married Jacob Moon and they lived in the Bryant Crossroad where Clifford Irvine lives now. Their daughter, Sarah Adelia Moon married Andrew Tyler. Sarah's and Andrew's son, Herchimer Tyler married Edith Massey b. 1885; they lived on the Third Concession with their family of Norman (Duke) b. 1906, Lewis, Paul b. 1910, Albert and Mary. Paul Tyler stayed on the homestead and never married. The others moved away.

First Concession Alyea Connections

Hannah Maria Alyea married William Benjamin Weese. There were four children. Their daughter Francina married William Wesley Sager and remained in Ameliasburgh. They have a large family connection. (See *Sager* and *Hubbs* family stories).

The Alyeas of the Second Concession

Jacob Smith Alyea (1845-1905) and his wife Augusta Moon, came to the farm (lot 98) which his father Peter had bequeathed to him, provided he plant an orchard, and settled into the home on the south side of the road, far back in a field by a never-failing spring. Here, the Alyeas raised a family of eight. They were twins, Morris and Morley, Orbey, Ardella, Lottie, Arthur, Walter and Clayton.

The Alyea family left their home one Sunday morning to attend church in Adams School and the house burned down. The family set up housekeeping in a part of their good L-shaped barn until such time as they could get another house built.

Jacob, had a nephew who was a good carpenter named George Maidens, so with his expertise and the families' help, a large six-bedroom home was built half the distance from the road, to where the former house had been. A well had to be dug behind the house and a huge cistern was made in the basement. However, Jacob Alyea died in 1905 at age 55 and the house wasn't finished until 1907. Augusta Alyea moved into the new house with some of her younger children.

1. Morris married Sarah Cronk and they farmed lot 104, Con. 2. Their daughter Pauline went to the U.S.A., daughter Clara married Ray Spencer of Salem, Kenneth married Irene Burris, Howard married Kathleen Adams and Baden married Greta Bishop. All lived and farmed on the Second Concession for many years. Clara and Ray Spencer moved to Consecon where Ray took over Melvin Carnrike's garage business while he was overseas, Howard and his wife Kathleen (Adams) farmed and had a daughter Doreen. He died suddenly at the farm. Kenneth and Irene (Burris) retired from farming and moved into Consecon, while Baden and Greta (Bishop) left for Wellington. None of Morris Alyea's family remain in Ameliasburgh today.

2. Morley Alyea and his wife Gertrude Pickle lived in Trenton and their family was Muriel, Chalmers (a Jeweller in Trenton) and Glenn.

3. Walter left home, went out west and died in Vancouver.

4. Ardella, married an Alyea, a very distant relative but they had no family.

5. Mary Lottie married John Frederick Chase and their farm was along the east side of the Consecon Road. They carried on mixed farming and kept bees. He was interested in municipal affairs in the township. They had a daughter Elsie who with her husband Roy Tripp, an excellent carpenter, remained in the area and retired in Consecon. Their children were Freda, organist of Consecon United Church, Earl, Wayne, Alan(deceased), Eleanor, present Bank Manager of Scotiabank in Consecon, the only bank in Ameliasburgh Township, and Winston.

6. Clayton went to live in the U.S.A.

7. Orbey Alyea took over the home farm lot 98, but when he married the widow Florence (Garbutt) Onderdonk they settled across the road from the big house on the knoll, in what was known as the Maidens house. Mrs. Jacob Alyea was still living. They farmed with hired help, and also ran the Onderdonk Evaporator at the bottom of the Weese Hill, Con. 1. Besides the two Onderdonk children, Grace (Jamieson) Mitts and Harold Onderdonk, they had a daughter Audra and a son Luther.

In 1929 the "Maidens" house as it was known, burned down. Clifford Irvine, who was ploughing for the Alyeas with a team of horses in the sand field under the hill, recalls leaving the team harnessed to the plough, scrambling up the steep hill, and fighting the fire. When it was over, the team was still awaiting his return, standing on the same spot.

It was Orbey and Florence Alyea's son Luther, who married Evelyn Calnan from the Victoria Community, daughter of Horace and Maud Calnan, who took over the Jacob Alyea farm that had come down now, through four generations. They settled into the house on the knoll. Audra, the Alyea's daughter became a teacher and for several years taught in Ameliasburgh at Little Kingston. She married the Reverend Alvin Keeler and they retired near Ottawa.

Luther (1914-1972) and his wife Evelyn had a family of five children. The tragic death by drowning of two of their sons, Donald (7) and Clare (6) in May 1944, resulted eventually in their departure from the farm to Belleville. After being home to five generations of Alyeas, it became home to Luther Alyea's brother-in-law Clifford Calnan and his wife Marion (Mikel) Calnan who lived in the large home for 27 years, before building a smaller house on the site where the 'Maidens house' had burned in 1929.

The Calnans still farm the land where the basements of three former Alyea homes remain, reminders of, in all probability, one of the largest of Ameliasburgh's families.

Jacob's son Arthur married Allie Babcock and had two children, when she passed away he married Mary Weese and they moved away from the Township. Years later their son Douglas, returned to work for his uncle, Howard Weese, in his canning factory on the Bayshore. Douglas married Betty Bongard of Hillier Townhip and their son Victor is a teacher at the Kente School in Ameliasburgh.

The Rossmore Alyeas

Samuel Alyea (1830-1896) m. Margaret Moon (1835-1915)
Samuel Alyea and Margaret Moon had five children:
John Smith Alyea 1857-1940 m. Catherine Gerow 1860-1921
Stephen H. m. Marion Wood (1st) Mrs. Wm. Alyea nee Sarah Lont (2nd)
Mary E. 1860
Angenetta (Nettie) 1863-1942 m. Clayton Sprung 1863-1939
1. John Smith Alyea and Cathy Gerow lived in Rossmore on the bayshore side of Ridley St. He was a carpenter. When his mother was a very old lady she put corn on a fish hook, let it dangle under the fence inside a neighbour's chicken yard and had herself an occasional chicken pie.
Their children were:
Arthur Carleton known as Carter 1881-1954 m. Nellie Caroline Jarvis 1889-1917
Earl Delbert 1885-1960 m. 1st ?
   m. 2nd Sarah Hebert
Kitty Mae 1891-1973 m. Manley Belnap 1889-1942. Everyone called her 'Aunt Mae'. She lived in Rossmore, beside her Father's house. All her five children, Verna, William, Laura, Fern and Joan live outside Ameliasburg.

Carter Alyea fished Lake Ontario and lived in the summers in a cottage at North Bay near Consecon.

Arthur Alyea, had two sons
1. John Jarvis 1909-1980 m. Freda Bloom. They had two children Wayne and Sandra. Jack was a fisherman at Rossmore and he and his father built boats. In 1982 Jack and Freda's grandson Terry, son of Wayne was killed in a car accident.   2. Arthur Rexford 1919-1973 m. Florence Hill and had a

family of 3- all live in Belleville- they are Monty, Sherry and Connie.

2. Angenetta (Nettie) m. Clayton Sprung of Mountain View. Their children were:
   1. Pearl m.Roy Vancott
   2. Clarke b. 1898 m. Blanche Doxsee and he resides in the home where he was born in Mt. View.
   3. Marjorie m. Edward Hall

The James Way Anderson Family
By Gordon Babbitt

James and Jane Anderson of County Monoghan, Ireland, emigrated to New York c. 1792. One of their children, William (1786-1869) came in 1803 to Ameliasburgh Twp, and settled at Massassaga. On July 1, 1806 William married Mary Way (1791-186). This union produced 12 children but two boys and one girl died very young.

James Way Anderson, (1832-1914), the youngest of the 12 children, resided on Lot 70, Con. 1, Ameliasburgh. This property had been purchased by James' father William, c. 1852 from George Cunningham, who had received it from King George III in 1803. In 1857 James married Theodocia Brickman. They had four children: Edward born 1859, Frederick born 1862, Mary born 1865, and Harry (1872-1931). Both Fred and Mary died prior to their 30th birthdays.

James, a considerable entrepreneur, established a cheese factory called the 'Bayside Cheese Factory' in 1870, built a ferry boat (with Captain Porte) in 1879 called 'The Mary Ethel', raised purebred Percheron horses and patented several appliances. He was also a lieutenant in the 16th Battalion, Rednersville Co. for over 20 years.

James' son Harry farmed the east half of Lot 70, Con. 1, Ameliasburgh, while his brother Ed farmed the west half of Lot 70. Harry married Gertrude Peck (1876-1955) c. 1900 and this union produced one child, Mary Eleanor. I never knew my grandfather Harry, however I have been told he was a kind, compassionate, quiet humoured man, well respected in the community.

Mary Eleanor Anderson married Francis Sherman Babbitt (1905-1973). This union produced two sons, William Sherman and Harry Gordon. Mary Babbitt resides on Lot 69, con. 1. The younger son Gordon resides with his wife Corinne (Fargey) and three children, Mary Jane, Julie and James, in the original James Way Anderson homestead on Lot 70. William with his wife Shirley (Wagner) and their three children, David, Marion and Donald, live on the bayside, where James had his dock and berthed the 'Mary Ethel.'

The Willoughby Anderson Family

By Jerald Anderson

William Willoughby Anderson (1862-1928) was born on the third concession of Ameliasburgh, west of Highway 14, being the eldest son of Squire William and Mary (Potts) Anderson. In 1885 he purchased a 100-acre farm bordering on the Bay of Quinte, Lot 69, Con. 1, Ameliasburgh, which was originally crown land, owned by John Morden, a pioneer settler. On Feb. 28th, 1886 he married Anna Margaret, daughter of Mr. and Mrs. John White, M.P. of Roblin. To this marriage was born a daughter, Muriel. His first wife deceased, in 1897 he married Edna Jane, daughter of Mr. and Mrs. Marshall Burr. To this marriage was born one son, Jerald, who still resides on this farm.

In 1908 Willoughby demolished the old barns and erected new ones, and 1916 built a new home. The original Morden house built around 1800 still occupies an important spot among the farm buildings. Willoughby took a keen interest in community affairs, serving as Justice of the Peace, tax collector, assessor, councillor, reeve, and in 1917 Warden of the County. Politically he was a dyed-in-the-wool Conservative. His hobby was the raising of Percheron horses and showing them at Fall Fairs. For several years he acted as government Judge of horses in various parts of Ontario. His livelihood was obtained from mixing farming, including 25 acres of orchard.

Jerald Anderson married Gladys Wells in 1932. To this union were born two daughters, Margaret and Meribeth. Both Jerald and his father were very active in the Masonic Order. Gladys Anderson died in 1979. Jerald has since remarried, to Dorothy Lidster.

W. Jerald Anderson,
Worship Master of Moira Lodge
A.F. & A.M., No. 11,
G.R.C. Belleville 1934

Celebrated 50 years as a Past
Master in Feb. 1984

Babbitt Family of Ameliasburhg Township

By Gordon Babbitt

The first Babbitt (also spelled Babbit) to emigrate from England to Massachusetts was a young man of about 12 years. The year of emigration was 1639. The first Babbitt's tombstone can be found at the Taunton Historical Society building, Taunton, Massachusetts, along with a number of items attributed to Babbitt, including a very thick Babbitt book.

The War of Independence, 1776, created many a family rift; the Babbitts were no exception. The Babbitts who remained true to the Crown emigrated to the Maritime provinces. One of the Babbitt girls married Sir Charles Tupper, and apparently there is a museum in Gagetown, N.B. exhibiting various Babbitt articles.

The Babbitts came to Prince Edward County c. 1810 and settled in Hillier and Picton. Elkanah Babbitt (1837-1908) married Ellen R. Morden (1836-1913). Elkanah was the first Babbitt to settle in Ameliasburgh Township, and he located on the property of his father-in-law, James P. Morden, east half of Lot 69, concession 1, Ameliasburgh.

The union of Elkanah and Ellen produced two children, Charles Herbert (1870-1945) and Alma Blanche (1865-1939). Alma Blanche married Alex Anderson and they had one daughter, Clara E. (1888-1955) and one son, M. Roy (1891-1979). Clara never married. Roy and his wife, Pearl Fox, had no

Ellen & Elkanah Babbitt

children. Charles H. married F. Mabel Huff in 1899. They had two sons, Harold (1900-1967) and Sherman (1905-1973).

At one time Charles and Mabel lived on Lot 69, East half, con. 1. Blanche and Alex lived on Lot 68 West half, con. 1, and Elkanah and Ellen lived on Lot 68 East half con. 1. Harold married Louise Hinds, and two children, Barbara and Charles, were their offspring. Sherman married Mary Eleanor Anderson and this union produced two sons, William Sherman and Harry Gordon. Mary still resides on the (original Morden) Babbitt property, East half Lot 69. William and Gordon reside on the Anderson (original George Cunningham) property, East half Lot 70 Con. 1, Ameliasburgh.

The Early Babcocks of Ameliasburgh
By Earle W. Elliott

The earliest member of this branch of the Babcocks is John Babcock Senior. He seems to have been a descendant of those Babcocks who emigrated from Essex County in England to Rhode Island, one of the original Thirteen Colonies. Over the years Babcock descendants moved into Connecticut, Massachusetts and eastern New York.

The first known record of John Babcock Sr. is when he joined a Provincial Regiment, the 4th Battalion of the New Jersey Volunteers, as a Ensign in 1776. On Dec. 21, 1776 he was taken prisoner in Bergen County, New Jersey by troops of General George Clinton. After that he does not appear on the rolls of the New Jersey Volunteers. His wife was carrying their fourth child, John Jr. at the time. As the rebel forces did not have facilities for prisoners, John Sr. probably was released shortly after being taken prisoner.

John Sr. appears next as a farmer in Franklin township, Bergen County, N.J. He is recorded on the assessment rolls of that township from 1778 until 1790, at which date the record indicates that he was in the process of ceasing to farm there. In 1778 he had 70 acres of land, two horses, five horned cattle and five hogs. When he entered Canada in 1791 he stated he was a carpenter. His will, dated Dec. 14, 1804 at Ameliasburgh, divides his carpenter's tools equally between his sons, William and John. The small number of livestock owned would suggest he was a part-time farmer.

In early 1791 John Sr. and his family, excluding daughter Catherine who by then had married, moved by boat up the Hudson River to Albany. Then they moved overland to Fort Stanwix and thence along the Oswego River system to Lake Ontario and across to Kingston. Here he made application for a single lot of land, as did his son, William, on June 29, 1791.

The Mecklenburg Land Board minutes of June 29, 1791 show the following:— "603. William Babcock, son of John Babcock, applies for and receives a Certificate for 200 acres of land, after administering the Oath of Allegiance. 628. John Babcock late of New Jersey applies to be admitted as an Inhabitant and to receive a portion of land. Mr. Babcock appears to have been a loyal subject during the late War and to be a person of good character; he has a wife and five children, by trade a carpenter; a Certificate for 200 acres of land is granted him and the Oath of Allegiance is administered."

These same Land Board Minutes dated June 29, 1791, show Certificates for 200 acres of land granted Andrew, Thomas, Peter and Hermanus Wanamaker, as well as to Henry Redner, a weaver with five children.

The land granted to John Sr., his son William, plus a later grant to John Jr. and Wm.'s late wife, Huldah Cole, was all in Percy township, Northumberland County. Wm. spent the remainder of his life in Percy Township.

John Sr. purchased a location ticket from the original grantee for the West half of Lot 86, Con. 1, Ameliasburgh Twp. This was registered to him from the Crown on Dec. 31, 1798.

John Sr. established a sawmill on the creek below his residence on Lot 86. By 1816 John Jr. found he was cutting timber on land he did not own i.e. on the rear west half of Lot 86. He was granted this by the Crown and continued cutting. This sawmill ran for many years. Mrs. Morton Weese remembered the sawmill as, at times, the noise of the saws disturbed her teaching of the pupils at Victoria School.

Over the years Lot 86 was cleared and tilled. By 1847 John Jr. owned parts or all of lots 85, 86, 87. Originally these landholdings extended northerly to the Bay of Quinte. By the time the remaining land was sold in 1942, some years after the death of the last Babcock owner, Letitia Babcock Wilson, the acreage had been much reduced.

The six children of John Babcock Sr. were: Catherine (m. Abraham Bonter), Mary (m. Andrew Wanamaker), William (m. 1. Huldah Cole and 2. Elizabeth Skinkle), John Jr. (m. Mary Hubble), Phoebe (m. Henry Weese), Margaret (m. Francis Weese).

The Bedford Family

By Evelyn Peck

A blacksmith and toolsmith by trade, William Bedford came to Canada in 1905 from Cardiff, Wales. He worked in London, Ontario, for a time and then got a job at the Belleville Rolling Mills. In June 1907, William's wife, Maryann, and their three small children joined him in Canada and made their home on Charles St., Belleville.

When the Rolling Mills closed, William opened a blacksmith shop on Lot 86, Con. 1, Ameliasburgh. (This is now the home of a granddaughter Evelyn and her husband Neil Peck.) He walked the nine miles each morning and night. Because many customers paid by barter, there were some days when he had barely enough money to pay the toll to cross the bay bridge.

In the spring of 1908 the William Bedford family moved into Ameliasburgh township. They lived in several rented houses in the Red

William Bedford and daughter, Mrs. Nellie Mains on Belleville market.

School area. When they moved to the Hitchon house on lot 81, William also relocated his shop building and contents. In 1917 the family moved to the Will Giles farm, lot 74, 2nd Con. Again the blacksmith shop was moved. In the fall of 1925 William Bedford bought the Aaron Adams farm, lot 71, con. 1. The blacksmith shop was moved once more.

William's son, Charlie, who helped his father with the farming and blacksmithing, recalls making sleigh runners and many other things. They respoked many wheels. People came from as far away as Brighton and Napanee to have the Bedfords shoe their driving horses. A few times each year, William and Charlie would spend a couple of days in the garage at what is now the Weese Apartments, Albury, shoeing horses from that area.

The Bedfords also were well-known market gardeners with Mr. Bedford attending Belleville market for more than 50 years.

William and Maryann had nine children. At his death in 1969 William was survived by 23 grandchildren and 45 great-grandchildren.

Charles, who stayed on the family farm, married Gertrude Bradshaw in 1938. They have six children. Their two sons, Leonard and William, have both built homes on the family bayshore farm. Although both have full-time jobs off the farm, they help with the growing of cash crops. Both are volunteer firemen for the Ameliasburgh Fire Department, with Bill being a captain. Charlie's two oldest daughters, Audrey (Mrs. Ronald Carter) and Evelyn (Mrs. Neil Peck) are also township residents.

Seventh Town/Ameliasburgh

The Beitel Family

By W.D. Hanthorn as told by Edward Beitel

During years 1909 and 1910, Martin Beitel, Wesley Hanoski and other residents in the area of Bucovina, Austria, became very alarmed at the frustrating and belligerent actions of the Romanians who had swarmed into and taken possession of their district. Also vying for power were Germans and Russians. Higher taxes and conditions imposed on Austrian farmers became intolerable. A meeting was held and it was decided they should pack up and leave.

They chose to emigrate to Canada to avoid communist rule. After a long and tedious journey they finally arrived at Spring Valley, a little hamlet about 50 miles from Moose Jaw, Saskatchewan. With very little money left, they dug holes in the hillsides and erected the often-mentioned Sod Shanties of the plains. Working hard on the unbroken land allotted to them and living on the bare necessities, they began to prosper.

Two of the children, Kasper Beitel and Elizabeth Hanoski, grew up, got married and eventually acquired a fine new house. They had six children, Gertrude, Emma, Jack, Kasper, Edward and Doris.

All seemed to be going well until disaster struck. First it was lack of rain, creating a virtual 'Dust Bowl'. The topsoil blew off the fields causing terrible dust storms in the 'Dirty Thirties'. Conditions became so bad with swarms of locusts (grasshoppers), army worms, cut worms, rust and blight that five families decided to pull up stakes once again. They accepted an offer of government assistance and moved to Ontario.

In July, 1937 they arrived at Brighton Railway Station with all their worldly goods; cows, horses, sheep, goats, hens and all household and prairie farming equipment formed a large, strange caravan enroute to Cedardale.

Five families moved into the vacant Seward house at the corner of the road to Stoney Point. They were the Beitels, Hanoskis, Nagels, Schicks and Ottenbrites.

The then 12-year-old Ed Beitel remembers that the house was very crowded, and the excitement among the children as they drove the livestock from Brighton and got severe belly-aches from the green apples they pilfered along the way.

One unexpected knock on the door of the Seward house sent all the little children to huddle behind their mother's skirts. The men and older boys were all out looking for work or checking on the properties the Ontario Government was making available through agent Frank Bulles. A smiling Gilbert Waite stood at the door with a basket of good eating apples. We presume this was to discourage the children from eating his green apples. This friendly gesture made a lasting impression on the newcomers. They had feared being treated with resentment.

The Beitel family soon moved into the Wilson Stoneburg place on the

Second Concession of Ameliasburgh. They quickly became popular and were accepted into the social life of the area. Their home was where Ed Miller presently has his farm repair business. Mr. Beitel gradually replaced his prairie farm machinery with more suitable equipment for Ontario farming. William Hanthorn and Bruce Graham recall sharpening the long plough share used by Mr. Beitel for breaking prairie sod.

These families from Western Canada were a fine and welcome asset to our rural community. Some of the younger ones have strayed but most still reside in this area, though not in Ameliasburgh Township.

The Bisdee Family

William Bisdee was born at Weston Super Mare in England. He came to Canada as a Barnardo Home boy at the age of 12, and stayed at the Marchmont Home in Belleville. Mirancy Redner, a farmer from the 2nd concession of Ameliasburgh, took him, as was the custom, to live and work at his place. He grew to manhood and married a local girl from Roblin's Mills by the name of Flora Hart. He lived in Roblin's Mills and Bisdee worked for farmers in the area during the summer and hunted in the winter. They had a family of eight children, three boys— Morley, Harry and Gerald, and five girls— Pearl, Rosellia, Flossie, Vera and Marjorie. Rosellia died at a very early age. Morley went overseas in the first World War, on his return married Amelia Johnston of Tamworth. Pearl married Durwood Conklin of Huff's Island; Flossie married Frank Cross; Harry married Hilda Humphrey from Consecon; Vera married Elwood Demille of Doxsees; Marjorie married Jack Fitzgerald; and Gerald married Hilda Belnap of Rossmore.

Harry and Hilda Bisdee ran a bakery and general store for a few years. Then Harry worked as a carpenter until his retirement, and for 20 years served as Ameliasburgh Township's building inspector. He was the curator of the Ameliasburgh Museum from 1968 to 1976. The Bisdees have one son, Eugene, who married Jean Foley; they are now living in Manotick.

The Bonter Family

The first generation on record here is Jacob Epke— whose son Cornelius Epke— made the second. The third generation of the family was Abraham Epke (1712-) married in 1735 and moved to Rockland County New York State. It was Jacob Banta who married Rachael Smith, who came after the Revolutionary War to Prince Edward County, where he was a farmer and a miller. His descendants spelled their name Bonter, which was the Dutch pronunciation for Banta. It was 1796, when Jacob and Rachael came here along with their son Abraham Bonter (1770-1841), who was a farmer and a distiller.

Jacob (Banta) Bonter and his wife Rachael had seven children:
1. Abraham born 1770 married 1. Catherine Babcock 2. Lucy McCarthy
2. Maria (Mary) born 1771 married John Alyea
3. Annatie (Anna) born 1774 married Abraham Cole (b1789)
4. Cornelius born 1776 married Sarah Wilkins
5. Lanna (Magdelana) married Peter Weese
6. John Sylvannus (1783-1876) came to Canada in 1795 from Paramus, New Jersey where he had been born and had married Margaret Dempsey b. 1790. She was the daughter of Thomas Dempsey U.E. and Mary Lawson.
7. Altjie (Letitia) (1786-1871) married Samuel Peck (1787-1866) son of James and Elizabeth Peck and they were first cousins.

Abraham and Catherine (Babcock) Bonter, had six children and it was their fourth child John who married, 1. Rachael Covert and 2. Mary Chase (widow Church) who got the deed for the Smoke's Point property, he being of the fifth generation. His family intermarried with the Coverts, LaTours, Fitzgeralds, Churches, Wannamakers, Stapletons, Chases and others, about the Carrying Place.

The Bonters of Smoke's Point by John Bonter

Smoke's Point was named after an Indian named Smoke. Great, Great Grandma Bonter would make homemade bread and butter it, for the little Indian children who stood outside waiting for a sample, and in return they would bring her woven baskets.

Our Grandmother, Mary Ann Bonter, told a story of how that poineer, John Bonter left home with 25 cents in his pocket to go to Toronto to get the deed for his land. He slept in a farmer's barn the first night. The next day while walking along, he found a horseshoe. By helping the farmer the next day, he was allowed his supper and to sleep in the barn. He finally arrived in Toronto and secured his deed. On his way home he met a man whose horse had thrown a shoe, so he sold him the horseshoe he had found. When he returned home he had 50 cents.

Smoke's Point is usually buried in snow in winter due to the winds that sweep across Lake Ontario. Catherine Bonter LaTour, told her grandson, George LaTour Sr., how as children they would slide on sleighs from the upstairs window. The Bonters would be snow bound for weeks.

Generations of Smoke's Point Bonters have made their living from the waters. Our father Weddell Bonter was a commercial fisherman, when Lake Ontario and Weller's Bay were rich in white fish, mudcats and herring. He also trapped muskrats and sold their pelts. He guided the fishermen and duck hunters who came from Toronto and the U.S.A. and lodged at Mary Bonter's home. They were treated to hearty old time meals and spotless bedrooms.

Weller's Bay has been a friend and also an enemy to many area families, but in particular to the Bonters. For years it provided a living for us, until one day, on a return trip from selling his catch, our father Weddell drowned, not far from home. Also in checking our family tree, we have discovered that our great grandfather, Gilbert, was also drowned when our grandfather Rupert was just a young boy.

The Bayshore Bonters

John Sylvanus Bonter (1783-1876), son of Abraham Bonter, married Margaret Dempsey, and they had 12 children. One of them was John R. Bonter (1818-1870) who married (1) Fanny (1824-1850) and (2) Mary Ann Shears. A son of John R. Bonter and Mary Ann Shears, George Sylvanus Bonter (1864-1940) married (1) Jessie Chase (1866-1913) and (2) Hattie Wells (1873-1935). To the union of George Sylvanus Bonter and his first wife, Jessie Chase, were born five children: John, Ernest Earl, Bert who married Flossie Adams, Ewart who married Bernice Arbuckle, and a daughter who died in infancy. For years George Bonter ran a drygoods store in Trenton, and here the children were born and attended school. Later he returned to the Bonter homestead on Lot 100, Con. 1, Ameliasburgh.

George's son Earl Bonter (1889-1944) married Grace Evelyn Peck (1888-1970) youngest of the five daughters of William Peck and Sarah Ann Dempsey. They bought the Stephen Peck farm, part of Lot 93, Con. 1, just west of the Wm. Peck farm. They had a family of four: Eleanor who married Allan Weese, Harold who married (1) Evelyn Stevenson and (2) Helen Miller, Evelyn who married Howard Holmes, and Joyce who married David Brownlee.

Harold and first wife Evelyn had two daughters— Dianne and Carole. He and Helen have a son Donald who is now operating the greatly expanded Bonter farm, well-known as Bayview Orchards. With the purchase over the years of the Ben Dempsey farm, the Bert Bryant farm and the former Wm. Peck farm, the Bonter holdings now comprise 450 acres of which 120 acres are in apple orchards, 15 acres in a 'pick your own' strawberry operation, five acres in asparagus, and 10 acres in sweet corn and other vegetables to supply the farm market outlet on the premises. Both Harold and Donald have been very active in the Ontario Fruit and Vegetable Growers' Association, of which Harold was President in 1968 and Donald in 1981.

The Brickman Family

The Brickman family came to America in 1710 from the Palatinate on the Rhine with the Redner, Wanamaker and Pulis families, and settled in New Jersey. Lewis (Lodewyk) Brickman's birth and his marriage to Mary (Marytje) Wanamaker, also the birth of several of their children, are registered in Paramus, Bergen County, N.J. They came to Canada and settled in Seventh Town in the 1790's on Lot 82, Con. 1. Lewis and Mary had seven children. Mary died and Lewis married again, to Olive (Aule) Crouter. There were two more children by this marriage. The first home was a log cabin on the bay shore.

Lewis Brickman's will of May 5, 1813 wills 400 acres of land: 100 acres, west ½ of lot 82, 2nd con. to oldest son Rynard; 100 acres, east ½ of lot 82, 2nd con. to second son William; 100 acres, west ½ of lot 82, 1st con. to 6-yr. old Peter; and 100 acres, the east ½ of lot 82, 1st con. to son Henry. Peter and Henry were children of Lewis and second wife. Lewis left each of his five daughters $50, and his wife $60.

Rynard Brickman built a log house and barn on the limestone ridge north of the present Gore Road. He married Margaret Peck, and they had six children. Another log house was later built on the south side of the road where the present home of Audra Brickman stands. This one boasted a cellar, not much more than a hole in the ground, but a place to store fruit and vegetables. Rynard's second son was named Lewis after his grandfather. He married Margaret Jane Cole and they built a frame house east of the log home. It was built of wood cut on their own farm and sawed at the William Babcock mill on the creek about a mile and a quarter west of them. This house years later became the Brickman canning factory. Lewis and Margaret had four children. Their second son, Rynard, remained on the farm. He married Alzina DeLong and they had one son, Lorne. Lorne married Emma Ainworth in 1899. In 1902 they built the present spacious home where their daughter Audra lives on this century farm.

Samuel, third son of Rynard and Margaret, married Catherine Jane Sager.

Audra Brickman home

They lived west of Rynard and Lewis on lot 83. Their oldest son, Wm. Francis Brickman married Mary Annie Bonter and they built a house on the east half of lot 82, (present G. Trounce home). Their children were Everett and Vera. Everett married Flossie Weese; to this union were born Gerald and Roy. Gerald married Gladys Page, and Roy married Luella Holmes. Vera Brickman married Frank Bedell.

The Brooks Family

The Brooks family came to Canada from Albany, New York. David Brooks (1785-1865) married Catherine Delong (1794-1864) in 1815. They had a family of 10 children, three of whom were born in Prince Edward County after 1829. In 1834 David purchased 169 acres of Lot 92, Con. 2, Ameliasburgh from Jacob Corbman. Both David and Catherine are buried in the Brooks-Delong family cemetery located about 300 yards back of the Brooks farmhouse on Lot 92 on the north side of the road. Also a little grandson, child of David and Catherine's son Charles Wesley and his wife Nancy Jane Gibson, died at age 6 and was buried there. Members of the Delong family who lived just over the line fence on the adjoining farm also were buried in this cemetery.

Anthony Brooks (1825-1901), son of David and Catherine, purchased 21½ acres from his father in 1858 at the rear of the farm, later buying another 5 acres also. Anthony married Content Way (1827-1897). Issue: Charles E. Brooks who married Alzina Adams, Lodicea, and Sophronia who married Charles Adams. Charles E. and Alzina had 4 children: Charles, Herbert, Anthony, Alice who married Herb Fox, and Stanley who married Lily Maud Way. The family of Stanley and Lily Maud were: Gerald Brooks who married Helen Green, May who married Earl Rathbun, and Charles who married Lela Campbell.

Charles Wesley Brooks, son of David and Catherine, purchased 134 acres of his father's property in 1865. He and Nancy Jane had nine children who mainly moved to other areas. One daughter Etta married Freeman French of Consecon; they were married in Victoria Church, Dec. 22, 1897 soon after it was opened. Her brother Frank Brooks helped draw the lumber to build the church; he married Mae Mary Westfall and settled on the 2nd Con. of Sidney. After Charles Wesley Brooks died, his widow Nancy Jane sold the farm and bought a home in Roblin's Mills.

The Burkitt Family

By Muriel Minaker

Francis (Frank) and Hester Burkitt lived in Marmora after their marriage on June 24, 1891. To them were born two children, Ida May and William Edwin. The family moved to Prince Edward County in 1912, purchasing a farm in the Burr community from a Frank Shorey, which was formerly the Peter Burr home. On March 12, 1912 Frank Burkitt, his brother John from Springbrook and his son William drove two span of horses drawing two bob sleighs loaded with moveables to the new farm. When they reached Rossmore they drove the ice to Rednersville, then proceeded south and up the Fingerboard Hill. They drove fields the rest of the way as the roads were full of snow.

Frank and his brother went back and William stayed alone at the new home for one week. He was to get some wood cut, draw out manure, etc. before the rest of the family and livestock arrived. A neighbour, Jesse Harns, sent his son Ewart to invite Will to dinner and to spend the nights at his home until the rest arrived.

Frank, Hester and Ida came by train to Consecon Station about March 20. Will and his new friend and neighbour Ewart Harns drove to meet them. On their way home they upset their load consisting of sheep, chickens and pigs at North Lakeside in front of the home of George Ridley Mikel. He had them put one sow, which was due to have pigs very soon, in his barn and leave her because of the cold. She raised ten pigs thanks to his kindness.

Mr. and Mrs. Frank Burkitt lived and farmed for 33 years on that place. In 1945 they sold it to Hugo Diggins and retired to an apartment in the home of their daughter Ida who had married Ewart Harns and lived in the same community.

William married Edith Muriel Lauder in 1919. He farmed with his father until 1929 when Edith's mother died, then they moved to the home and farm of Edith's father, Charles E. Lauder, to assist him. They had two children, Harry and Muriel. Muriel married Grant P. Minaker and they are still living in the Charles Lauder home. Besides farming, Will Burkitt worked for the Department of Highways for 23 years, 15 of them as bridgemaster at the Bay Bridge. He died February, 1984 at age 91.

The Burr Family
By Allene Burr

The Wesley K. Burr Home

William Burr the pioneer came to Canada in 1820 as a boy of 14. He worked in Sophiasburgh Township for 10 years, then in 1830 bought 100 acres in Hillier Township in what is now called the Burr neighbourhood. It was dense forest at that time and he lived in a small log cabin. He married Sophia Redner in 1834 and to them were born six children. He cleared the land and built a fine home, large barn and wagon-house on this property— later the farm of his great-grandson Ewart Harns.

Wesley Kenton Burr, youngest son of William Burr, married Mary Catherine Valleau in 1863 and was given 200 acres of land directly north of his father's farm, lot 75 Ameliasburgh Township. Here he built a large brick residence and enhanced its grounds with a mile or more of ornamental wooden picket fences and gates. The gate posts were topped with huge hand-turned cedar ornaments. There were six single picket gates and six double picket gates, the central gate highly ornamental. The home grounds and driveways were bordered by hedges. The lawn was laid out in paths bordered with many shrubs. The barn also was of a singular appearance with its diagonal set windows and large dovecote atop. Its south side was open originally for the cattle to run under. Later it was made into a basement using stone from the old Disciple Church which was dismantled in the 1920's.

Wesley K. Burr and his wife had five children. One son, Kirwin Carroll Burr, married Aurelia Ainsworth Trumpour in 1896. To them were born two sons, Lorne and Ross. Lorne married May Squire in 1920. They had three children: Carol married William Soble, Rodney married Ellen Schmidt, and Pauline William Dempsey. Ross Burr married Allene Werden in 1919 and they have one son, Ronald.

Kirwin Burr built the large frame house across the road from his father's home c. 1900. He and his wife both died at age 51. His son Ross occupied the homestead until 1961 when he and his wife moved to Belleville.

The Bush Families of Ameliasburgh

Sometime before 1800, John, Robert and Henry Bush came from the province of New York to Hay Bay. Henry went west and was never heard of again. Robert settled on the north shore of Consecon Lake. The history of the family is vague. John, 1775-1858, settled near Frankford.

Zenas, 1820-1889, one of the Pioneer John's younger sons, moved from the Hay Bay area to Murray Township where he lived for eight years. In 1874 he moved to Lot 101 Ameliasburgh Township on the north shore of Consecon Lake, settling on this farm previously owned by Amos Walt. Zenas married Hannah Lines from England in 1837. They had 12 children.

David B. Bush married Fanny Walt and remained on the homestead. Their stone house was built in 1839. In an older wooden section attached to one end, lived David's spinster sisters, Dorcas (1851-1938), Charlotte (1855-1877), Caroline (1853-1923) and Annie (1860-1943). In Zenas Bush's will in 1889, the small house by the road is referred to as the hired man's house. Three sons were born to David and Fanny. Ross married Florence Titus and farmea east of Consecon Railway Station. They had one daughter, Margaret, who lives in the U.S.A. Adelbert Bush was killed in World War I. Biard stayed on the farm, married Isaylia Alyea, and had a son Adelbert, who married Dorothy Skinkle, and a daughter Mildred, who married Earle Rowe. Today David and John, Adelbert's sons, remain on the Century Farm. In addition to their farming operation, they have established a trailer camp on their shoreline on Consecon Lake. David married Karen Leigh, and their son, Graydon Biard, is the sixth generation of Bushes on the farm.

George Bush's (1862-1936) wife was Louise Webster (1876-1959) from Napanee. Her father was a carriage-maker. There was a family of four. Ross married Hazel Fox, and their children were Earl, Donald, Gerald and Shirley. Douglas Bush married Evelyn Carter and there was one daughter, Marilyn. Marion married Mr. Storey. Helen married Lyndon Thompson, then a Mr. Giles, and has two daughters.

Samuel and his wife, Alice DeLong, of Ameliasburgh Township had four daughters: Beatrice married Cleave Blakely of Wellington, Charlotte (Lottie) married Ray Fox (see Fox-Green Family), Gladys married George McCurdy, Bernice married Reginald Gilmour.

The Cairns Family

John Cairns and his wife and three children, Johnny, George and Mary, came to Canada from South Berwick, Scotland in April 1911. Cairns had been manager of a 1300 acre farm in Scotland where Cheviot sheep and Shorthorn cattle were raised. When he decided to come to Canada, he secured Canadian employment through the Department of Immigration in Edinburgh and came to this country to work for George Anderson on his farm near Mountain View. He stayed there one year, then bought a house and 2 acres in Mountain View where the family lived for three years. Selling this place, Cairns rented a farm for five years from Howard Anderson (present Harold Werkhoven farm). Son Johnny enlisted in 1917 and went overseas, returning in 1919 to find his father had purchased the Mahlon Eckert farm, the west half of Lot 75, 2nd Con. Ameliasburgh in 1918, and his brother George had died of the flu.

Johny married Florence Cook in 1921. In 1923 they went to Detroit where Johnny worked in the Ford plant and on the Ford farm at Dearborn. In 1926 Johnny, Florence and children Robert and Isabel returned to Canada, and Johnny worked with his father until 1930. Then Ernest VanAlstyne who had married Johnny's sister Mary took over the farm and Johnny moved again. He worked for Fred Hubbs for one year, and for Homer White for three years. Daughter Isabel died of scarlet fever at age 7 while they were at the Whites.

In 1934 Johnny bought his father's farm and two years later bought another 45 acres on Lot 76 from Owen Kehoe. In 1940 during the Second World War he joined the Veterans' Guard and served as guard at Government buildings in Ottawa and at internment camps at Montreal,

Farnham and Sherbrooke. In 1942 he was sent to the Bahamas and helped guard the governor's residence (the Governor at that time was the Duke of Windsor) and other vital buildings. As his oldest son Robert had joined the airforce, Johnny returned home to the farm in early 1944.

In 1946 Johnny purchased the adjoining Townsend farm on the east half of Lot 75, and in 1950 the next farm to the east (west ½ Lot 74) was also purchased, where Robert and his wife Barbara Ferguson live. Johnny's son Alfred and his wife Edith Foster live in the former Townsend home, while their daughter Margaret and husband Keith Stather live in the Mahlon Eckert home. Johnny and Florence's youngest son Donald married Alma Wannamaker; he is a teacher in Sault Ste. Marie. Johnny died September 1983. Alfred presently farms the entire Cairns acreage, which now also includes 142 acres of Lot 76 lying along County Road 23 which he purchased in 1966.

The Calnan Family

The early history of the Burley family is traced from the pioneer David Sager in other family stories. (Ref. *Sager* and *Weese*), so we will begin with David Gilbert and Catharine Sager whose daughter Mary Elizabeth born in 1790 married John Burley (1782-1820). He was a son of Freeman Burley U.E. and his wife Susannah Weese, daughter of John Weese U.E. and his wife Mary Rees of Ernestown.

Mary Elizabeth and John Burley had four sons, David, Freeman, James and Ephraim. Freeman Burley (1820-1886) married Elizabeth Scholler (1823-1891) and lived on the west half of lot 87, Con. 2, which he inherited through his mother in 1866, and on which he built the present house. The farm still remains in the family. Ephraim Burley lived next door on the east half of lot 87.

Freeman and Elizabeth Burley had three daughters and an only son John, who when four years old was killed by a colt. Two of their daughters, Elizabeth and Emily married Calnan brothers.

In County Cork, Ireland, Richard Calnan and his wife Sarah lived with their young son Richard Jr. When he was still very young his father drowned. When he was 21 the inheritance he hoped to get went to his older brother. Richard met Sophia Hurren, whose father had been a bodyguard to King George III, and when he retired they had moved to Ireland. Sophia was 17 when she married Richard Calnan.

In 1832, when their baby daughter Margaret was three months old they sailed for Canada. The late W.K. Burr in 1929, wrote, "on their arrival in Kingston, they had only one English pound in money and their clothes." They walked from Kingston and carried their baby. They worked on a farm in Hillier for a year, then came to Ameliasburgh and bought a farm on the 3rd concession. In 1849 they moved and farmed on Con. 5 Hillier. They had a large family of 12. Richard (1803-1892) and Sophia (1812-1901) buried in Burr's Cemetery, were the pioneers of the Calnan family.

The Pioneer Richard Calnan Family

Back row: James Calnan, David Calnan, John Calnan, William Calnan, Oliver Calnan. Front row: Elizabeth (Mrs. Colborn Bonter), Fanny (Mrs. Chas. Fox), Edward Calnan, Margaret (Mrs. William Pyne), Richard Calnan, Hannah (first Mrs. Anson Maybee, second Mrs. Philip Haight), Sarah (first Mrs. John Young, second Mrs. George Tice).

Elizabeth Burley (1849-1935) married Edward Calnan 1858-1939. Their son Allen married Alma Babcock (from the Gore, now Fox farm). Their daughter Aileen Calnan Foster is the author of *The Calnan Family*, Printcraft, Bloomfield 1981.

Emily Burley (1854-1935) married David Calnan (1847-1925) and since there was no Burley son, David Calnan and his wife Emily inherited the homestead. Here they raised nine children;

1. Barton Calnan (1877-1931) -m- Annie Stoneburg
2. Rosa M. Calnan (1875-1920) -m- Burton Weeks (1871-1935) no issue
3. Minnie Calnan (1881-1939) -m- Lieuvernie Drummond (1878-1965)
4. Niles A. Calnan (1879-1880) died in infancy
5. Azella Calnan (1884-1952) -m- Fred Maisennbacher
6. Horace B. Calnan(1886-1950) -m- Maud Cunningham
7. Dora Pearl Calnan (1888-1950) -m- Frank Hickerson
8. Leonard Calnan (1900-1915)
9. Maud Calnan (1891) -m- Grant Gibson

It was David and Emily Calnan and Jacob and Mary Margaret (Brickman) Sager who each gave land for the building of Victoria church, which was named and dedicated in 1897. The first wedding solemnized in the new church was that of Minnie Calnan and Lieuvernie Drummond in 1901. The congregation gave them a large leather-bound Bible and school was let out for the day to celebrate. They had one son Orville, a teacher, who married Bernice Thompson. They live in Kingston.

Barton and Annie Calnan lived for some time on the Stoneburg farm on the upper 2nd, and had two children Harold and Beatrice. They went to live in Rochester. Another sister, Azella went to Rochester, married and remained. Rosa and Burton Weeks lived in Consecon. They had no children and she died at an early age. Dora and Frank Hickerson, went to live on his farm on the 4th concession at Little Kingston. They had two daughters, Eva, who married Douglas Williamson, and Ruth who married Jack Chatterson and live in Rossmore. They have four children and their daughter Elaine married Allan OHara and with their two children; James and Christine live at Massassaga. The youngest child Maud, married Grant Gibson (Ref. *Gibson* family). They farmed for years on the 2nd concession where Gary Adams now lives, then moved to Belleville and eventually to Rochester. When they retired, they came back to their cottage on the Gibson homestead on Roblin Lake. They had one daughter Dorothy. They now reside at Westgate Lodge in Belleville.

It was Horace Burley Calnan and his wife Maud Cunningham who remained on the homestead, and shared the house with his parents until they passed away. They had two children, Evelyn who married Luther Alyea, from the upper 2nd, lot 98. Luther farmed and trucked, and was Township Road Superintendant (1940-1942). They have five children, Shirley, Donald, Clare, Melvin and Elmer. In May, 1944 Donald and Clare were drowned while taking a short cut home from Adams School. The double funeral was from Victoria Church. In 1947 the Alyeas moved to Belleville. Luther passed away in 1972. Clifford, remained on the homestead and with his father, worked both their own and the Alyea farm. In 1947 Clifford bought the Alyea farm and he and his wife Marion Mikel, moved there. They have one son, David Mikel Calnan, the only descendant to carry on the Calnan name, and a foster son Edward Preston, who lived with them for 22 years.

Horace Calnan passed away in 1950. His widow Maud, in 1956 married Morley Dempsey, and the Calnan house has been rented since. Clifford works the land.

The Richard Calnan Family

Richard Calnan (1860-1904), the youngest child of Richard Calnan Sr. and his wife Sophia, married Jennie Lafferty (1867-1952). They moved to the east half of lot 87, next door to his brother David. The farm had belonged to Ephraim Burley, brother of Freeman, so once more two brothers owned the farms. For a time Richard was a tax collector in Ameliasburgh.

In 1889, Richard and Jennie's only child Ruby was born. She grew up there and married Bruce Hennesey in 1906, and went to live on lot 91 a few farms west of her father's farm. They had two sons, Ross and Ralph. Their mother Ruby passed away with pneumonia in 1922 at the age of 33. Bruce, with the assistance of his parents Mr. and Mrs. Sidney Hennesey, who lived in half the house, cared for his sons. Richard Calnan, the youngest was the first of the 12 to pass on. His widow Jennie remarried to Mr. Harris and moved to Madoc. Ross Hennesey in 1937 married Hazel Thompson, who taught for many years in Trenton. They have a daughter Donna Kay. Ralph remained on the farm for many years, then in 1971 he moved to Belleville, and is married to Nora Baldwin.

The Elizabeth Calnan Bonter Family

Elizabeth Calnan (1842-1922), the sixth child of Richard and Sophia Calnan, in 1867 married John Colborn Bonter (1845-1896). He was the son of Jacob Bonter and their home was on lot 96, Con. 2, Ameliasburgh. Their son Fred married twice and by his first wife Nettie Pearsall had no heirs. She died in 1901. His second wife was Calista Ainsworth, and they had a daughter Irma. After her mother's death she lived for many years with her first cousin Audra Brickman on the Gore Road. She passed away in 1980, the last of the Elizabeth Calnan Bonter family.

The John Calnan Family

John Calnan (1834-1907) eldest son of Richard and Sophia, married Elizabeth Morden (1836-1930) and it was their son Herbert (1861-1940) and his wife Matilda Gorsline, who have descendants living in Ameliasburgh. Oral Calnan of Picton married Elfleda Zufelt, daughter of Mr. and Mrs. Herbert Zufelt, from the north shore of Consecon Lake. She was a sister of Rev. Verne Zufelt. Their families live outside our township. Norma Pearl Calnan daughter of Herbert and Matilda, in 1910 married Roy Giles and came to live on the 2nd concession at the Giles farm. They had three children (ref. *Giles Family*) but only son Ronald remained, and married Hester Cook of Rossmore. Their two sons Larry and Wayne have left the township. Norma Giles has celebrated her 95th birthday, and is one of Ameliasburgh's oldest residents.

The Oliver Calnan Family

Oliver Calnan (1852-1932) was the tenth child of Richard and Sophia Calnan. Ben Smith and his wife Phoebe Wannamaker kept store at Mt. View and their daughter Helena, (1837-1921) married Oliver in 1879. Oliver and Lena had a family of two sons and one daughter. It was their son Arthur who married Edith Allison Hall of Bayside who were the parents of Marjorie Calnan who married William Faulkner and reside on a farm in the Victoria neighbourhood. Marjorie Faulkner taught school for many years in the township and retired from Kente School in 1981. None of their four children remained in the area.

Hannah Calnan (1840-1915) married Anson Mabee (1827-1879). He had bought a farm of 100 acres on lot 60, 2nd Con. of Ameliasburgh on the upper Massassaga Road in 1853. They had two sons William and Wilbert. Mabee died at 52. Wilbert married and lived on the home farm. Mr. and Mrs. Anson Mabee and William were buried in the Simonds Cemetery at Massassaga.

The Robert Cannons Family

We'll begin our story of the Robert Cannons family with Mrs. Robert Cannons (Sarah) who eventually was instrumental in bringing Bob to Canada.

Sarah Ann Stephens came to Ameliasburgh and to the William and Huldah Roblin octagonal house at the age of 13 in 1900, as a Barnardo Home girl. She worked in the home and was able to attend the stone school at the west end of the village. She stayed with the Roblins for five years, received $5 a year pay, then went back to England at age 18. She was 23 when she married Robert George Cannons at Romsey Abbey in 1909.

They returned to Canada to live in the Roblin Tenant house (Rose Cottage)— where Charlie Cannons lives now. Sarah went back to work at the Roblin house- the 'Round House', as she called it. Bob went to work at the Roblin Mill.

Bob began farming as a hired man to Bert Redner on the Gore. Their first child, Martha Blanche, was still born in 1916. They moved and hired out to Wellington Howell on the second concession, where their second daughter Dorothy was born in the tenant house which still stands. The family then came to the Dolan farm which first they rented then bought, where their only son Archie was born. Bob was able to begin farming on his own 50 acres in the third concession, Lot 86 where Marjorie was born. During this time one of his brothers (Charlie) came to Canada and Bob provided him with a home for a short time, and in the meantime moved to the Kemp farm next to Salem

Left to Right: Robert Cannons, Sarah (Annie) Cannons, Marjorie, Archie, Dorothy.

School where the family stayed for four years. His last move was to Lot 85 in 1928 where Dorothy Istead lives now. He kept from one to three hired men, milked 14 cows, drew milk with a team, grew canning factory crops, kept four horses, did custom threshing and farmed, in general having a viable farm operation. At this time he owned 450 acres in all, having bought part of Lot 88 which he later sold to Frank Cannons.

The Cannons' son, Archie, enlisted and went overseas in 1941 and was there until 1945. Daughter Marjorie joined the WRENS in 1942.

Bob had his share of mishaps. When he worked for Bert Redner he was taking a load of pigs to Belleville market across the Bay ice, when the horses broke through the ice. Pigs and horses were all swimming in the cold water but all came through unscathed. Another time, Bob was taking a load of tomatoes with a team to Consecon canning factory, and because he was deaf in one ear, he didn't hear the train whistle and the train struck the wagon, killed the horses and threw Bob on the cat walk between the engine and the coal car. He came through this with only a broken wrist.

Bob was instrumental in bringing out to Canada from England his brothers and sisters, who for the most part settled in the township. Many of their descendants are still in the community. Bob died in 1953 and Sarah in 1960.

The Carnrike Family

By Nancy Carnrike Baldwin

"I'm Canadian! Fifth generation of Carnrike's to be born and raised in 'The County'. How much more Canadian can you be?" I'll never forget that argument. A professor was irate with me for answering 'Canadian' to the question of nationality. She was trying to insist that there is no such thing as a true Canadian.

The Carnrike family of Prince Edward County was first established here, in Ameliasburg Township, in the early 1800's. Jacob Carnrike came to settle, with his father George (1782-1860) and mother Charity (1781-1870), apparently from the United States. From what I have read and discovered, his background was Pennsylvania Dutch (German). He came as a young man and established himself on Lot 91 of the fourth concession of Ameliasburgh. The first building was a log cabin built on the south side of the present road.

Shortly after his arrival, he married a local girl, Mary Parliament (daughter of Jacob Parliament who lived along Consecon Lake) in 1825 at the village of Ameliasburg. (Her brother also married a Carnrike.) Then Jacob was granted a Crown Deed to Lot 91 on July 15, 1856. He also purchased Lot 90. From the old documents that are still kept in the antiquated safe at the farmhouse, he was on the land as early as 1842. He had borrowed money from a Mr. Parliament, who was a neighbour. The I.O.U.'s, marked 'Paid in Full,' are still in existence. As their family grew to the grand total of ten children, so did the farm of Jacob and Mary. The present farmhouse was built in 1844 and added to later on. Jacob must have been very proud when he made out his last will and testament in 1874. He left each of his four living daughters (Sarah Ann Henesey, Margaret Ferguson, May Clark, Lovilla Lundy) equal amounts of money, as well as some to each of his grandsons.

Lot 91 was passed on to a son and his wife. The Crown Deed was signed over to James Albert Carnrike on June 24, 1874. Lot 90 was left to another son, Selim Carnrike.

James, born April 3, 1844, had married Matura Jane Terwilleger on Oct. 17, 1869. The goldbound Family Bible presented to them at that time contains a great deal of family information. They moved into the expanded family home to raise their offspring; and so a second generation took over. Jacob died in 1882 and Mary in 1887; both are buried in Salem Cemetery.

Among the crinkly old papers in the old safe, I found James and Matura's church membership cards for 1900-1901. As I held them, I transported myself back almost 100 years. I could picture this young couple placing their three children into a horse-drawn buggy for the short ride to Salem Church for Sunday service. How I wish at least one ancestor had kept a diary or journal so that I could get to know them better. Their children were Lona Carletta, Charles Leslie and Jennie Alberta.

Charles, my grandfather, married Inez Humphrey on Oct. 4, 1899 at Ameliasburg. W.H. Buckler was the minister, the witnesses were Henry Black and Ida Humphrey (Inez's twin). Charles and Inez moved into the farmhouse. The settee, two straight chairs, two arm chairs and a corner chair, that were given to them by her parents, Mr. & Mrs. Noel Humphrey, are still at the farm, some pieces still in the parlour. Not only was furniture built to last in those days, but it also was proudly preserved. The Crown Deed was signed over from James to Charles in 1916.

I was named after my grandmother, and I have a linen tea-towel she made for her trousseau— still sparkling white, with INEZ crocheted along the bottom. She died suddenly at the age of 41, leaving a growing family for Charles to raise. How I wish I had known her! There's a picture that shows I inherited her round face and general features, as well as the tea-towel.

Charles and Inez had seven children— Verna Marie, Percival Lorne, Eva Belle, Melvin James, Nina May, Edna Minerva and Edwin Allan. All except Nina settled in 'The County' after marriage.

The Carnrike family has always been active in the community; involved in Church work, 4-H, Junior Farmers, local fairs, etc. My Dad, Melvin, has told me numerous stories of showing prize animals at fairs, taking fresh produce to markets, and hitching a good horse to a new buggy for an evening of fellowship with neighbours.

As the fourth generation of Carnrike's grew, their interests did too. Percy, married to Leta Brason, purchased the farm next to Salem Church and School; Melvin started his own business in the village of Consecon as a mechanic, with three years out while he was overseas during World War II.

1920— *Eva and Nina Carnrike*
Home, 4th Con.

On his return he married Marion Mumby, November 22, 1945. He retired just five years ago, now. Edwin, the youngest, married Keitha Van Clief in 1947, and they settled on the family farm. The Crown Deed was signed over to Edwin in 1952, just two years before his father's death. Edwin and Melvin each have a son to perpetuate the family name; Douglas, married to Cheryl Baldwin June 5, 1971, has two sons— Ronald and Donald. They live near his father's farm on the fourth concession of Ameliasburgh. Dennis, Melvin's son, is living at home, working and continuing his education. Hopefully, he too will have sons to help preserve the Carnrike family traditions. Edwin and Melvin each have a daughter living in Alberta (Edna Heibert and Jane Brandon); this is the furthest away any member of this family has moved in over a century. The husbands out west enjoy teasing the cousins about being 'stubborn German-Canadian girls'. Maybe there is a little truth in that, but it is a proud heritage that we should all pass on to the sixth and seventh generations.

The Carter Family

The Carters were of English descent, but had emigrated to America before coming to Canada in 1812. The obtained a grant of land from the Crown at Holloway in Thurlow Township where Thomas Carter, a descendant of the pioneer, was born and grew up. He became a cheesemaker at Holloway. His son Edward married Jennie Maines. They lived at Holloway for a few years, them moved to Demorestville in Sophiasburgh Township where they operated a general store and a peddling wagon which served all the surrounding area. They had seven children. One of their sons, Floyd, married Ethel Vanclief, daughter of Mr. and Mrs. Nelson Vanclief of Victoria community. Floyd and Ethel lived in Sophiasburgh for several years, then purchased Lot 81, 2nd Con. Ameliasburgh, where they still reside. They have five children, Ronald, Gordon, Harley, Terry and Darlene.

The Chase Family of Concession Two

A son of Daniel Chase and Aletha Gordon of Oswego, New York State, Charles Chase came to Canada from Vermont, U.S.A. about 1822. His wife was Emily Hawes, and together they had a family of five sons and two daughters. These seven offspring chose their spouses from local families of Mikels, MacDonalds, Montgomerys, Walts, Herringtons, Orsers and Corbmans. What a staggering figure when one considers the number of cousins there must be within the community today!

Ross and Florence Chase

Mr. Chase secured from the Crown Lot 105 and Lot 106 on the Second Concession of Ameliasburgh. Part of Lot 106 which extends along the present Highway 33 was a cedar woods. In the vicinity was a mill which made cedar shingles, in great demand at that time. Eventually, this industry doomed the cedar woods. Stories of the period tell of religious camp meetings there, and also, of the illegal sport of cock fighting being carried on. Doubtless, bets were wagered while participants were concealed among the trees.

Charles Chase obtained more land in the area, and two of his sons occupied farms near him. Son Jewett and his wife, Martha Orser, married in 1871 and lived on the farm owned in later years by Lee Rowe and presently by Alex Wright. Son Phillip and his wife lived on the farm with the stone cottage on Highway 33, in later years owned by Blake Rowe, and then his daughter Ethel Andrus.

Today Harry Chase and his wife, Jean Moreland, occupy the original family farm, inherited from Harry's father, Charles Ross Chase, son of Jewett. In 1928 Ross Chase replaced the original brick home, which had become too costly to repair. Part of the first brick house remains today as a useful storage. There have been two barn structures; following a fire, a new barn was built in 1913 for $4,000. In early days, apples were packed from the farm's orchards each autumn. Too, the making of maple syrup was an annual process. One may assume that oxen were used for farm labours, since a yolk for oxen has been a Chase heirloom throughout the years. Today it graces a fireplace mantel; wouldn't our ancestors be amused!

Harry's father, Ross Chase, married Florence Hayes, sister of Amelia Hayes of Trenton. Harry's Aunt Amelia was born in 1875, and was renowned for birthdays, having managed 106 of them. His mother, too, made her mark; after reaching the age of 90, she died on July 19, 1969, the date of man's first landing on the moon.

All of Harry's and Jean's family of four are married with families of their own. These grandchildren are the sixth generations of Chases from the earliest Ameliasburgh settler.

The Coleman Family

By Mrs. Verna Sills

The Coleman family was of Gaelic stock, the family name of old being O'Coleman. It has been anglicised into various forms including that of Coleman. The original name is derived from the Gaelic word "Colm" meaning "dove".

Robert Coleman (1787-1848), patriarch of the Roblin's Mills branch, came from Ireland and settled in the United States, date unknown. Finding that country still turbulent and uncongenial for those of Loyalist Gent, he migrated to Canada and settled at Roblin's Mills in 1834. He was accompanied by his wife Sarah (1784-1857) who was also born in Ireland, and his five sons and one daughter.

The eldest son David (1813-1892) lived in the village and became a millwright and grist mill operator. He was a member of the Prince Edward County Militia, and was in action at Carrying Place during the Rebellion of 1837, marching to Toronto. For a number of years he was Tax Collector and also taught school for several years. In 1842 he married Sarah Gilmore (1819-1967) and in that year he built the house located directly across the street from the Township Hall. In 1870 he married Mary A. Howe. He had three daughters and two sons by his first wife and a son by his second.

David's eldest son Isaiah (1846-1938) also lived in the village for many years. He was a harness maker and also a photographer of note. In the 1870's he delivered the mail to Belleville. In 1871 he married Margrett Johnston (1844-1911) and had five sons and a daughter. David's daughter, Martha (1845-1905) married Ephriam Adams; they had three children— Alberta, Ardella and Byron.

Charles (1815-1869), the second son of Robert Sr., also lived in the village and was a carpenter and wagon maker. He married Ellen Lauder. They had two sons who both died in their 20's and a daughter Margaret who married William Henry Kinnear and settled in Hillier. Their wedding was the first in the church across the street from their home.

James (1818-1897) was the third son of Robert Sr. He built and operated the blacksmith shop at the west end of the village. In 1852 he held the rank of Ensign, in 1854 he was promoted to Lieutenant, and in 1862 he became Captain and Commanding Officer of the Roblin's Mills company of the 2nd battalion, Prince Edward Militia. James married Jane Gilmour and had four children. John Irvine Coleman (1851-1936), son of James and Jane, married Catherine Frances Morgan. He was an undertaker and was in the business from 1892 until 1912. They had one child Anna Verna Jane who is still living in the house built by James in 1844 at the west end of the village.

John (1819-1900), the fourth son of Robert Sr., was a photographer, and also a woodworking and furniture shop in the village. He was twice married, first to Mary Clegg, and then to Eliza Butler.

Jane Ann (1824-1898) Robert Sr.'s only daughter, married Thomas Lauder. They had three children— Robert Wm., David C. and Sarah Jane.

Robert Jr. (1826-1910), the youngest son of Robet Sr., continued to live on the homestead and operated the farm. He married Sarah Ann Way. They were childless.

Mr. and Mrs. Arthur Corfield

By Arthur Corfield

I was born in Madeley, Shropshire, England, in 1900, son of Percy Corfield, who worked at the original Coalport China factory. On many occasions his work included china for the Royal Family. During a visit to Toronto a few years ago we came across a huge vase in Simpson's china department. Engraved in the glazed base was my father's number (8).

I practically grew up in the butcher business and served three years apprenticeship in that trade. This was during the First World War; my job in the services was in the meat department. In 1922 I decided to come to Canada where I thought chances for advancement would be better. I left England on 22nd of April 1922, arriving in Canada 10 days later at Quebec. As I had just left Wellington, England, I saw on the Quebec platform a list of people wanting to hire help and noticed one place was Wellington, Pr. Ed. Co., so I chose that as my destination.

Arriving in Wellington, I was met by a farmer named Robert Blakely of Gilead Road. I enjoyed working for him. I met a young man named Blake Conley and lived at his home during the winter. I worked for several farmers but was not satisfied as I wanted to get back into the butcher business. Many farmers hired me to kill their beef for winter.

Living in the vicinity of Consecon, I met a young lady by the name of Helen File who was teaching school at Pleasant Bay. She was daughter of Mr. and Mrs. Fred File and granddaughter of Dr. A.J. File. We were married in 1927 and moved to Ameliasburg Village where we have happily lived ever since.

I got back in the butcher trade in 1932, opening a shop on Front St., Belleville, in 1933, and also had a truck on the road peddling meat door to door. Finding it hard to make a living, I went into business with Wallbridge and Clarke. I owned the meat department. They went out of business, so I moved back to Ameliasburg. I also owned a grist mill and ground grain for farmers and manufactured Shur-Gain feeds. Nothing at the time was very profitable in the Depression Years. I struck out with my tractor and plowed for many farmers in the area. Then I purchased a threshing machine and did custom work. Later I bought a combine and did custom work. I bought Geoffrey File's herd of Ayrshire and milked them until 1944 when I sold them and joined the army. I went overseas in 1944 with the Reinforcement Unit with the Hasty Pees. Upon arrival in England I was transferred to the Royal Canadian Army Service Corps. Returning home in December 1945, I bought Fred File's farm. When he died we took over File Bros. Store, sold it in 1960. We have four children: Jean married Norman Post, Margaret married Clifford Foster, William married Jean Smith, and Harold married Marlene Blackburn.

Mr. & Mrs. Harold Corfield

By Marlene Corfield

Harold and Marlene Corfield live on lot 79, concession 3, on the eastern fringe of Roblin's Mills. Their property was part of the land obtained by Philip Choate from the Crown in 1862 and willed to his son Joseph Walter in 1872. In 1880 Joseph deeded 1 acre to Anna Choate on which a two-story home 24' by 24' was built. In 1884 this lot was sold to Wm. Quackenbush for $200. It must have changed owners again, for Wm. Henry Wood left the house and lot to his daughter Ella Maud Lont. She sold it in 1942 to Thomas Keene, who left it to his daughter Dorothy Tanner. She in turn sold it in 1949 to William and Edith

(Corfield) James, who sold it to Harold and Marlene Corfield in 1967 along with a ¼ acre plot across the road on which stood a small barn.

Harold and Marlene have made many changes and renovations. The barn was torn down. A large family room with attached garage, woodworking shop and two bedrooms have been added to the house. During the renovations, pine boards up to 22 inches wide and 24 feet long were found. The beams under the floors were as good as when first put there.

Harold and Marlene have three sons— Randy, Paul and Steven.

The Corrigans of The Carrying Place

Until 1964 the Miskin-Weller house was owned continuously by descendants of Asa Weller. His daughter, Sarah, had moved in as a young bride, having married Richard Miskin, who built her this new red brick Georgian home in 1828. After only 13 years in their new home, her husband died in 1841. By this time her sister Hannah's daughter, Hannah Marie Sloan, had married William Corrigan and, indulging in speculation, we may assume the couple moved in with Aunt Sarah Miskin, or Aunt Sally, as she became known. Their daughter, Ann, married Mr. Sherriff of Bloomfield, daughter Sarah married Cap't John Rowe of The Carrying Place, and son Richard, born in 1841, fathered the six Corrigans who were reared at the family home from the late 1800's into the 1900's. During most of its years, probably 100, the house has been owned by Corrigans, hence the local label 'The Corrigan House'.

This final family of six Corrigans, who would call Asa Weller's daughter, Sarah Miskin, their great-great aunt, graciously tended their inheritance. Only two of the family married, Edith who went to British Columbia, and Martha (Mattie) who went to St. Catharines. Mary (Mame), 1876-1954, a nurse, was employed in New York and then retired at The Carrying Place. George, 1885-1962, a travelling salesman, would come from Washington, D.C. to visit his brother and sisters. But it was Maria, 1877-1934, and William, 1880-1948, who were the anchors for the family, remaining in the place of their birth for their entire lives, and always there when the relatives came home.

Wm D. Hanthorn lived near the Corrigans for over 40 years. He has some recollections of them. Will Corrigan might have been called a 'squire', considering his manner and style. He maintained his farm buildings in perfect order, a place for all things and everything in its place; one could say he kept his whole farm in apple-pie order. Always he had a hired hand who lived in and helped with the farming. His herd of dairy cattle was quality stock; he was one of the first to have a milking machine, and he had a cooling tank for his milk. He was so proud of his horses that he carefully picked their blacksmith. One could say he farmed scientifically, studying plants and their requirements for a healthy growth, fertilizing accordingly, generally with success. His acreage included a sugar bush, which he kept free of fallen branches and debris. Yearly he tapped his maples and also treated the local school children to a taffy pull and a demonstration of the making of maple syrup. One of The Carrying

Place's upright citizens, he could also be called a philanthropist, making many generous donations in his quiet, unpretentious way.

Maria Corrigan complemented her brother in her management of the home, discreetly preserving their inheritance, everything done graciously with an old-world charm. She employed a girl who lived in and helped with the housekeeping. A meal was always an occasion even when the threshers and wood sawyers went for their dinner. The table would be set as if for company, with a linen cloth, napkins, lots of cutlery, often a fire sputtering in the fireplace, and flowers on the table. There seemed to be a standard of excellence that they always upheld.

The Corrigans loved their gardens, including both vegetables and flowers, and throughout the growing period there was a profusion of seasonal flowers. Even in his fields where he worked, Will Corrigan often found a patch to plant some flowers. As W.D. Hanthorn recalls, "They even trimmed their lilacs while the rest of us just let ours grow". Miss Corrigan, like her brother, had a deep interest in the welfare of the community, was generous, hospitable, and ready to help wherever needed. Indeed, Asa Weller would have been proud of his Corrigan descendants.

It was on Dougall Morrison, the only son of Mattie (Corrigan) Morrison of St. Catharines, that the family had pinned its hopes for its future and survival. He was a pilot in World War II, and when he was killed in action a pall descended. Finally, in 1964, his mother, the last member of Richard Corrigan's family, found it necessary to sell the Carrying Place property. There were no more Corrigan connections in The Carrying Place.

From *The Trenton Courier*, April 30, 1885— Mr. R. Corrigan of the Carrying Place, having sold off his stock, the enterprising firm of Wamsley and Spafford, Belleville, have purchased the stand and have stocked it with all new and fresh goods, groceries, dry good and boots and shoes. Mr. Spafford takes charge of the business and offers bargains.

□ R.J. Corrigan is doing a driving business in the Maple Syrup line. I know it is good and so will you, Mr. Editor, if he sends you a sample.

Three Cunningham Brothers

Three Cunningham brothers, George (1774-1843), John and Robert came from County Fermanagh, Ireland in 1792 to Philadelphia, Pennsylvania, and on to Canada, circa 1795. George applied for and was granted land in Haldimand, but lost it to land agents. He helped Peter Smith from 1795 to 1798 and received a new grant for lot 71, Concession 1, Ameliasburgh. This is the original Cunningham homestead where a descendant, Marilyn Adams lives now.

The George Cunningham Sr. Family

The pioneer George Cunningham (1774-1843) married 1. Catherine Crouter (1786-1827) and 2. Catherine Campbell. The children were:

Henry Cunningham (1805-1877) m. Sarah Weese (1803-1875)
George Cunningham (1810-1885) m. Phoebe Babcock (1812-1869)
James Cunningham (1813) m. Elizabeth Wallbridge (1819-1894)
Thomas Cunningham (1824)
Mary Cunningham (1816-1808)
Jane Cunningham (1816-1840) m. John Babcock (1811-1895)
Elizabeth (Bessie) (1819) . George Landerkin
John (1820)

The George Cunningham Jr./Phoebe Babcock Family

George Cunningham married Phoebe Babcock and had a son, Henry (1836-1926), who married Huldah E. Redner. Their daughter Ada married Herbert Dempsey and moved to the 3rd concession to farm on lot 86 (2nd con.) Here their son Morley was born. He married 1. Pearl Whaley 2. Bessie Hillman and their daughter Betty Dempsey married Bryan Cronk and moved to Wellington. George Cunningham and Phoebe had a son John and a daughter Victoria who never married. Another daughter, Mary Louise, married Hiram Adams and became the parents of Harry Adams who married Marie Weese. Their daughter Marilyn Adams lives on the original Cunningham homestead.

The Robert Cunningham Family

Conrad Frederick U.E. married Elizabeth Rush, daughter of Martin Rush U.E. who received land on lot 81, Concession 1 and it remained in the family until 1919. Conrad Frederick and Elizabeth had a daughter Margaret who married Robert Cunningham.

The third generation Cunningham was Conrad (1812-1862) who settled on lot 69, Concession 4, Ameliasburgh and married Esther Merebe Babcock (1818-1873), the daughter of John Babcock Jr. and Mary Hubel. Their son was John Ridley Cunningham (1840-1889) who married Cynthia Jane Consaul (1840-1903). She was the daughter of Allan Consaul, of the north side of Roblin's Lake, and his wife Jane Tice.

They went to live on the south side of the lake on lot 79. J.R. Cunningham became a major in the militia. He was a millwright and was at work setting up a mill (see Mills) when he drowned in Roblin's Lake in 1893. He built a round barn on his farm and also the round Agricultural building on the fairgrounds in Ameliasburgh. For many years they stood strong— a tribute to a fine builder and soldier.

George and Corintha Cunningham when first married.

They had a family of five children.

Amarilla (1864-1929) married Charles Lauder (1861-1935). Their son Fred married Clara Redner and there were three daughters, Marion, Clela and Mildred Edith Lauder married William Burkitt and they had Muriel and Harry. (Ref. to *Burkitt Family*)

George Cunningham (1866-1933) married Corintha Pierson (1867-1953), the daughter of John Pierson and Sarah Carnrike of the Salem area. They had a daughter Maud, born in 1893. She married Horace Calnan in 1911 and they lived for awhile on the third concession before moving to the Calnan farm on the second concession. With the exception of a short stay in Rochester, they remained on the Calnan farm until Horace passed away in 1950. They had two children, Evelyn married Luther Alyea and Clifford married Marion Mikel. In 1956, Maud Cunningham married Morley Dempsey.

George and Corintha Cunningham had a son Thomas who died in infancy, and in 1901, another son Walter Clifford, who married Marybelle Black from the township. They farmed with his father and they also bought the farm next door from Charles Wood. But Walter passed away in 1943 and his wife sold their farm and moved away.

In 1903, the George Cunningham family was completed with the arrival of twin daughters, Cynthia Jane and Corintha Estelle. A year later at a Medicine show in Roblin's Mills, the Cunningham twins won first prize as the most popular babies in Ameliasburgh Township and their prize was a set of china dishes for 12. Today each has half of the set. The twins grew up and married; Cynthia to Harold Wright and they live in Belleville. They had a son Douglas. Corintha married Edward Parliament and they lived in Wellington until his death. Their two children were Howard and Lois. Corintha married Clayton Cruickshank and they reside now in Trenton.

In 1933, George Cunningham passed away and the farm was operated by Walter until his death, then sold to Milton and Mary Wood. Corintha Cunningham then moved into Ameliasburg, where she resided until her death in 1953.

Fred (1869-1935) was the third child of J.R. Cunningham and his wife Cynthia Jane. He married Laura Adams (1871-1937). They had two sons, Harry who married Corolla Weese who farmed on the 2nd concession at Victoria and Clarence who married Polly Russell and their farm was on the lower 3rd. Neither family had children.

Frank Wilson Cunningham (1871-1937) went to Minneapolis. He married and remained there.

Thomas Cunningham went to Gary, Indiana. He married Lily --- and they had two daughters. Mable married Virgil Clark and they had a daughter Lois who was a teacher. They all passed on in Florida. Lillian married Roy Meader and they had two daughters. They live in Chicago. The Clarks and the Meaders returned to visit the Cunningham families through the years.

The Dempsey Family

By Allan Dempsey

Major William Dempsey, U.E.

William Dempsey, born 1799 in the 7th Town (Ameliasburgh) was the third and youngest son of Thomas Dempsey, second permanent settler and the first Assessor of the Township which included Hillier Township until 1823. At the tender age of 12 years he drove a team to 'Muddy York' (Toronto) in the War of 1812. In the Rebellion of 1837 he marched his Company to Toronto, and rose to the rank of 1st major in the Second Battalion of the Prince Edward Militia 1858 with James Peck as 2nd Major and Lt. Col. Samuel Peterson the Commanding Officer. In 1842 he was apooited a member of the first Prince Edward County Council and was the first Reeve of Ameliasburgh Township Council 1850-51. In 1822 a Methodist Revival took place and the first Class in

William Dempsey   Wm. Ryerson

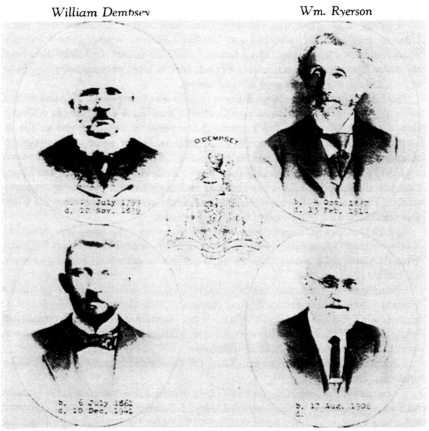

William Charles Dempsey   Allan Dempsey

the Hallowell Circuit was organized among the Thomas Dempsey family. The brothers, Peter, Isaac and William "were all brought in." These Class meetings continued to be held in the Dempsey home until 1849 when the Rednersville Church was built. William died in 1879.

Captain William Ryerson Dempsey, U.E.

William Ryerson Dempsey, born 1832 at Albury, second son of Major William Dempsey, school teacher, exporter of barley on a large scale to the U.S.A. in the 1870's and a Justice of the Peace. In the Fenian Raid of 1866, Capt. Ryerson Dempsey took his Company No. 9, 16th Battalion, Prince Edward Infantry to Kingston. He was Warden in 1876 and represented the Riding of Prince Edward in the Legislative Assembly of Ontario in 1898. Masonically he was the first candidate initiated into Lake Lodge A.F. and A.M., No. 215 G.R.C.

William Charles Dempsey U.E.

'Willie C.' Dempsey, born 1861 at Albury, 2nd son of Capt. W. Ryerson

Dempsey, pioneer and first manufacturer of dried apples east of Toronto, first manufacturer of dried vegetables in Canada 1915), called the 'Asparagus King' by Officials of the Dominion Fruit Branch, Ottawa. A pioneer Holstein Friesian breeder in Ameliasburgh Twp., erected the first hollow block cement silo in Prince Edward Co. His younger brother Harry was Warden of the County in 1909. Deceased 1941.

William Allan Dempsey U.E., B.S.A.

Son of 'Willie C' and Lorena Smith, 1924 U.E.L. Courier Belleville to Toronto, Graduate of the University of Toronto 1930 with specialty in Horticulture at O.A.C. Guelph where he was outstanding in Track, Field and Wrestling, breeder and exhibitor of Hostein Freisian cattle and Chantecler poultry, grower of asparagus and apples, active service in the R.A.F.V.R. as a Physical Training Instructor and administrative duties with five years in England and two years in India (1939-1946), 23 years service with the Canada Department of Agriculture as a Greenhouse Technician following World War II, Life Member with outstanding attainment in all four branches of the York Rite of Masonry and 32 degrees Life Member of the Scottish Rite of Masonry.

Harry Dempsey (1876-1948) youngest son of Wm. Ryerson Dempsey and Emily Boulter, married Josephine Dakin Issue:

   Gordon who married (1) Myrtle McInroy (2) Maud Alyea
   Gerald who married Olive Ryder
   Donald who married Lillian Hayes
   Charles who married Marguerite Dawson

Thomas Dempsey (1818-1895) son of Isaac Dempsey and Elizabeth Brickman, and grandson of Thomas Dempsey, the pioneer, and his wife Mary Lawson, married (1) Hannah Babcock (2) Elizabeth Ann Peck

Three of the children of Thomas and Elizabeth Ann Peck were:

   Aaron who married Cinda Rilla Adams
   Herbert who married Ada Cunningham; they had 1 son Morley
   Spurgeon who married Mary Ann Pitcher; one of their four children was

Gladys who married Roy Wannamaker.

Morely Dempsey married
(1) Pearl Whaley
(2) Bessie Hillman— 1 daughter Betty who married Bryan Cronk
(2) Maude Cunningham Calnan

The DeLongs

The *Belden Historical Atlas* of 1878 lists 10 different properties, totaling almost 2000 acres, with the name of DeLong as owner. It is interesting to note that the last of these properties to pass from the DeLong name in the early

1970's, Lot 91 on Con. 2, was probably the first one to be settled by pioneers of that name. This farm was taken up shortly after 1800 and remained in the family for nearly 170 years.

The origin of the DeLong name is French Huguenot, and variations in the spelling in the early New York State were De Longe and De Lange. Still, today, there are DeLongs living in Holland.

The DeLongs in Prince Edward County are all believed to be descended from Arie Fransen DeLong, who was born in Amsterdam in 1650 and came to Kingston, N.Y. in 1671. The names Arra, Simon, David, Peter and Henry were common among his descendents. They became prosperous landowners in Duchess County, N.Y., and were British supporters during the American Revolution. Some fought actively for the British and came to Canada as Loyalists. Some others were , apparently, pacifist Quakers who tried to keep a low profile after the war to retain their farms. Due to their known sympathies, however, they were ousted from their lands, some violently, and made their ways northward to start lives anew.

Henry (Henrik) DeLong, a descendent of Arie, and most of his family came to Prince Edward County from the Albany N.Y., area shortly after 1810. His second son, David Henry, must have come over several years before as he was married and settled on Lot 91, Con. 2 in Ameliasburgh in 1811. Family history relates that he acquired land in York County in an area now occupied by Metropolitan Toronto. He married Sarah Cole. Sarah's mother was Mary DeLong, her father Daniel Cole U.E., and she and her husband were with VanAlstine's band of refugees when they landed in Adolphustown, June 16, 1784. Sarah claimed to be the first white child born in Adolphustown. We are told that she refused to leave this comparatively civilized part of the country to settle in the wilderness of York County, so David traded his holding there for Lot 91 on Con. 2, Ameliasburgh. Of course, at that time the Carrying Place seemed more likely to develop than York, and was even considered as the capital of Upper Canada. As history developed, this did not appear to his descendents to have been a very good deal.

Sarah DeLong, born 1785 and died 1883, used to walk great distances to church. Audra Brickman of Rednersville has in her possession a quilt which was made by Sarah and given to her grandson, Lorne Brickman, Audra's father.

The largest holding in Ameliasburgh seems to have been that of William DeLong on Con. 3, just west of Roblin's Mills, now known as Ameliasburg. At one time this consisted of 800 acres with a large stone house. In the early 1900's this place was acquired by Dr. A.J. File who raised purebred Ayrshire cattle. The large stone house had an upstairs room with a raised platform at one end, it is said this was used as a classroom for the children in its early days. It had particularly high ceilings, thick stone walls and deep recessed windows. The house was demolished by W. Knox, who built a new one on the site, using some of the original stone.

Only a few of the original DeLong homes remain. Three are on Huff's Island, the former Clifford Barber home, the present Douglas Black one, and that of David Farmer formerly owned by Ross Fairman. Another former DeLong home is the Gordon Waterhouse residence at Victoria. The former Arnold Mastin house on the Third Concession was a DeLong home. These houses are fine examples of those built in the Quinte area in the mid-1800's. It is said that the cost of building and maintaining these large houses was a factor in many changes of ownership.

Frank DeLong was the last of the DeLongs to live on Lot 91, Con. 2. His wife was Mabel File. They had three children, Bernice, Gladys and Jack. Bernice married Daniel Pope and lived in Corbyville, later moving to Palmerston. Gladys, a registered nurse, married Elgin Herrington of Rossmore. Jack, a school teacher, married Peggy Runnalls and lives in Trenton. Their three daughters are married, and there are three grandchildren.

The Dawson Family

By Marguerite Dawson Dempsey

Clarence William John (Jack) Dawson was born in Grenville, Quebec, and was the son of William Edward Dawson of Quebec and the grandson of Sir William Ernest Dawson of Ireland. Dawson was brought up on a farm in Grenville, but went out on his own as a contractor in 1907. In 1909 he married

Dawson family c. 1955— Back row, left to right: Gerald, Summers, Bill, Tom; Front row: Florence, Enid, Jack Dawson, Don, Marguerite.

Margaret Jane Tompkins of Ottawa. They settled in New Liskeard, Ontario, when it was just a small village, so small that the drug store was a tent. Dawson helped build many houses in New Liskeard, Cobalt, Latchford, Timmins and North Bay.

In 1916 the Dawsons moved to Trenton where he operated a meat and grocery store on West St. until 1918 when the T.N.T. plant blew up. Dawson then rented a farm on lot 86, concession 1 of Ameliasburgh from Carson Jeffery. His only means of transportation from Trenton to the farm was by bicycle in summer and by crossing the Bay of Quinte in the winter with a team of horses and sleigh. In 1920 he bought a Model T Ford truck, and moved his family to the farm the following year. For several years he rented local farms and finally in 1930 bought his own home situated on lot 87, con. 1.

Dawson's nickname 'Jack' came from the phrase 'Jack of all Trades,' for he was a carpenter, stone mason, farmer, as well as other trades. Along with running a farm, he started a small greenhouse which grew to be quite a size, as did his family of eight. He lived in what is known as the Albury Community until his death at the age of 79 in June, 1962.

The Files of Ameliasburg Village

Village

The hardest thing you ever do
Is worrying about it;
What makes an hour resemble two
Is worrying about it;
The time goes mighty slowly when
You sit and sigh and sigh again
And think of work ahead, and then
Keep worrying about it.
Just buckle up and buckle in
A task is easy, once begun,
It has its labor and its fun,
So grab a hold and do it, son
Quit worrying about it.

Albert Barnes File

The File Family

No history of Ameliasburg would be complete without a story of the File family. Dr. File, the patriarch of the Files, was responsible as a doctor, for bringing many of the residents into this township.

Malchier 1773-1825 and his wife Rachael Jinks m. 1776 came from near Albany N.Y. bringing with them their Bible which contained family records. It was badly worn because Malchier carried it whenever he left home. They settled on a farm in Fredericksburg Township, near Napanee. Their son John File was born there, 1807-1885. He married in 1828 Catherine Maddon 1803-

Left to right, back row: Lorne, Albert, Geoffrey, Herbert, Dufferin, Frederick; front row: Maude, Dr. A.J. File, Luella, Catherine Barnes File and Mabel.

1882 and they became the parents of Dr. Albert John File.

Dr. File 1842-1931 was born in North Fredericksburgh. His secondary education was at the Royal Military College where he obtained the rank of Captain. He enrolled in the Royal College of Physicians and Surgeons in Kingston and graduated as a medical doctor in 1869. On Nov. 30th 1869 Dr. File married Catherine Barnes (1842-1933) of Kingston, where her father had been sent from England to manage a bank. It is interesting to note that Catherine was born two days before their ship landed.

Dr. File started his first practice in Lonsdale, then came to Roblin's Mills on horseback and took over a vacant medical practice. He became known as Canada' oldest practicing physician and at 88 years of age he had been a doctor for 60 years.

Dr. & Mrs. File had nine children; all prominent in the village. In spite of a busy medical practice, Dr. File was active in church affairs helping to build the Anglican Church of St. Alban the Martyr. For many years he was Medical Officer of Health in the township and acted as Justice of the Peace.

Their six sons were: Fred C. File 1870-1951— who was township clerk for many years. He had his office in his home as long as he served. His wife was Clara Cunningham and they had a daughter Helen who married Arthur Corfield and lives in the village. (Refer to *Corfield* family) Albert 1872-1959- was a teacher, merchant, postmaster for 35 years and deeply involved in the work of the Anglican church of St. Alban the Martyr, where he was sexton and caretaker, free for many years. He purchased Idlewilde to be used by the church as a hall.

Stanley Dufferin married Mabel Crosby of Ameliasburg and moved to Oshawa where he worked at General Motors.

Herbert John married Estella Choate. He taught school before moving to Toronto where he worked for Weston's.

Geoffrey E. File was the farmer of the family. On Con. 3 Lot 84, a mile west of the village, he specialized in Registered Ayrshire cattle and won major awards. He drove cattle to Picton Fair in those days and also to Ameliasburgh Fair. Geoffrey was a gardiner and pedalled strawberries from a special wagon that resembled a milk cart used in the city.

Lorne K. File 1879-1969 attended Toronto University and married Clara Hunter. They had three children. He was employed by the Canada Life Assurance Co. and remained in Toronto. Mabel Lousie married Frank Delong of Con. 2, Lot 91. They had three children (Refer to the *Delong* history).

Catherine Maude File (1883-1978) married Burton Adams d- 1959 of Con. 2, Lot 100 in the Adams Community. (Refer to *Robert Adams* family story).

Luella May 1884-1968 remained at the homestead in Roblin's Mills and kept house for her brothers, Albert and Geoffrey until her death. Today their niece Gladys (DeLong) Herrington owns the former File Home.

Dr. File and his wife suggested that the Files, always a close-knit family, should have an annual family reunion. In the 1890's the Napanee and the County Files began meeting annually at Massassaga Park. When the excursions by steamer like the *Ella Ross* were stopped, the picnic was held at Idlewilde, Albert File's hall in Ameliasburgh. About 1962 the reunions lapsed. About 1972 they were revived and once again the Files hold their annual family reunion.

Gibson Family

Earliest records show that Jane Gibson (1762-1850), who was born in Ireland, came to Canada with two sons, David and Patrick. In 1800, David was born in Ireland, came to Canada, and married Elizabeth Huff and built the house where Elmer Young lives on the 2nd Concession. Patrick, born in 1783 in Ireland married Catherine Simpson and they emigrated to Canada and settled at the west end of Roblin's Lake. David had two sons and a daughter. They were David, Robert and Ellen.

David Gibson (1825-1907) married Catherine Wannamaker (1831-1903). They settled at Mountain View and moved to the south side of Roblin Lake in 1865. They had seven children, four girls and three boys. Ann (1822-1922) married John Tice (1850-1927). Deborah (1859-1949) married Joseph Adams (little Joe) (1858-1915). Ellen Marie (1860-1931) married George Wood (1855-1925). Mary (Maim) Catherine (1863-1941) married Sam Adams (1860-1928).

The sons were John Wesley (1854-1944) married Madilla Adams (1859-1952). Charles (1857-1894) married Myrtle Chase. David Andrew born in 1866 went to Portage La Prairie and was never heard from.

John and Madilla Gibson had a daughter Grace (1882-1943) who married Charles Wood (1880-1956). They had four children: Everett who married Flossie Ainsworth then Beryl (Covert) Welch; Marjorie m. Eldon Adams; Cecil went to the U.S.A., and Ila who married Howard Bovay.

Edgar Gibson (1884-1956) married Florence Elliott (1888-1971) and moved to Willowbunch, Saskatchewan. They have five daughters and one son.

*Grant & Maud Gibson married
72 years. Sept. 4, 1984*

Norris William Gibson (1886-1964) married Mable Kathleen Lauder (1894-1975). They had one son, Harry Alton and a daughter Merle. Harry married Martha Ann Colden.

Grant Andrew Gibson, born in 1890, married Maud Calnan born in 1891. They have one daughter Dorothy, married to George Brown, with their five children have the Gibson cottage on Roblin Lake, formerly owned by her parents, who celebrated their 72nd anniversary, Sept. 4, 1984.

Harry Gibson and his wife Ann live on the homestead on the south side of Roblin Lake. They have four daughters and one son. They are Katherine, Carol, Cecila, Valerie and Alton. There are six grandchildren. The original home on the farm of David and Catherine, burned in 1860 and they built the home where Harry and Ann live. Although it is covered with wide vinyl siding, it has the appearance of the original home. Another house built by John and Madilla Gibson in 1881, was of frame and now covered with stucco and is known as the tenant house.

The Giles Family

The Giles family was of English descent, but had emigrated to America from whence members of the family came to Canada. An 1825 map of Ameliasburgh shows a Thomas Giles leasing Lot 61, Con. 2. The Giles family remained on that lot for over 50 years, for in 1876 Thomas Giles sold the property to Samuel Simonds. This is the farm on which the Simonds cemetery is located, and in the cemetery is a stone bearing the names of Thomas and

Four generations of the Giles family— Malcolm, Cyrus, Ronald and Roy.

Mary Giles. The Giles name also appears in Sophiasburgh Twp. at an early date.

William T. Giles (1797-1882) received the Crown Patent to Lot 80 Con. 2 Ameliasburgh in 1848. He married Maria Baker (1802-1874). Their children were Nelson who married Martha Jane Graves, John Wesley, Cyrus who married Mary Ann Adams, Catherine who married John Lauder, and Letty who married John Sprague. William T., his wife and son John Wesley are all buried in the Simonds Cemetery.

Nelson Giles (1835-1924) and Martha Jane Graves lived on Lot 81 just west of his father's farm. Their children were: Sarah who married David Wright Redner, Will who married Carrie Barber, Mary unm., May who married Charles Tumelty of Madoc, and a daughter who married Ed Bristol.

Cyrus Giles (1841-1934) took over the farm on Lot 80 from William. He and Mary Ann had a son Malcolm and two daughters, Annie who married David Stafford and Frances who married Eben Fox. The original home of William and Maria was on the south side of the road. Cyrus and Malcolm built the present large Giles home on the north side of the road in 1897. After Mary Ann died in 1915, Cyrus remarried. He bought a small house and lot a short distance to the east on Lot 79, and he and his second wife lived there.

Malcolm (1872-1947) remained on the home farm. He married Minnie Adams. They had one son, Roy (1889-1954). Roy married Norma Calnan b. 1888, and they lived in the first Giles house on the south side of the road until 1941 when they moved to the big house. They had three children— Kathleen married Walter Snider, Dorothy married Herbert Coukell and Ronald married Hester Cook. Ronald and Hester have two boys, Larry and Wayne. The Giles farm was designated as a Century Farm in 1967.

The Fox-Green Family

The Fox Family— Back Row: Lottie Fox, Mac Lont, Neva Lont, Ray Fox, Margaret Fox, Stanton Fox, Nellie Clough. Front Row: Kenneth Green, Jane Anne Fox (Mrs. Stanton), Vivian Fox

Brothers William and Henry Fox came from Dutchess County, N.Y. State, in 1791 and settled in Sophiasburgh. Henry, 1762-1822, came to Ameliasburgh and bought land from John Redner in 1817. Of his 11 children, three were by his first wife, Catherine Brickman. One of his sons, Rynard, married Charity Brickman. They settled in Ameliasburgh and had five children.

One of the five children, Stephen, was the ancestor of the Fox-Green family. Stephen married Annie Maybee. There were two sons, Wilbert Stanton and Walter. Walter married Naomi Pearsoll, settled on Lot 80 on the Gore, then left for the Picton area. Stanton married Jane Ann Lont. They lived awhile in Murray Township, then returned to farm on the Gore. Their only son was Morley Ray Fox.

Stanton Fox built his brick home in 1897, to replace an old frame one located across the road to the west. The bricks were brought from Deseronto by sleigh. To this day the original metal shingles remain on its roof. A Masonic emblem is embedded in a sidewalk. In 1938 Stanton Fox died.

Ray Fox and his wife, Charlotte Bush from the north side of Consecon Lake, married in 1909, and moved into the big brick house on the former Clayton Pulver farm. Interesting features about this house include its hand-hewn woodwork, handmade doors still stained naturally, and a winding

The Green Family— left to right: Wilbert, Vivian, Ronald, Sandra, Kenneth.

stairway with applewood banister. After Stanton died in 1938, Ray and his wife moved back to the farm where Ray was born. Ray died in 1950, and his wife moved to Belleville with her mother-in-law, who died in 1952.

Ray and Lottie Fox had two daughters, Vivian and Margaret. In 1929 Vivian married Kenneth Green, and they continued to live with her parents. Margaret married John Black in 1939. (See John and Margaret Black).

Vivian and Kenneth Green had a family of three, Wilbert, Ronald and Sandra. Wilbert married Marion Stickle and moved to the Stanton Fox farm. Ronald, who married Sandra Wood, remained on the original Pulver farm. The two sons farm together; their farming enterprise is known as Wilron Farms. Daughter Sandra married Gordon Carter and lives on Concession 2. Their father, Kenneth Green, died in 1955, and their grandmother, Lottie Fox in 1983.

Hamilton Family

Philip Burgess Hamilton and Alice Jane Tufts were married in Thurlow in 1902 and moved to Ameliasburgh Township the same year. First they purchased a small farm at Massassaga, and in 1917 they purchased Lot 65, 3rd Con., Ameliasburgh, where Seymour Hamilton and family now reside.

When Philip first moved to this township he did a lot of trucking with horses. When he wanted a telephone, Mr. Sprague told him, "Sure, if you put up the poles I'll wire them." The first telephone call was for a job doing roadwork, value $7— one year's phone bill. Philip raised Percheron horses and took many prizes at Shannonville and Roblin's Mills Fairs.

Alice Hamilton was Superintendent of Mountain View Sunday School for 30 years. Her leadership and teaching, taught the children that God and the Church would be the mainstay of their lives which made a lasting impression on her students. Alice Hamilton was the first Life Member of Mountain View Women's Institute having been a very active member. Mrs. Hamilton was born May 1, 1873. She passed away in 1954. Philip predeceased her in 1952.

The Hamilton children were:

Stephen Alexander— born 1903, died in infancy

William A.— born 1904

Mary S.— born 1906, deceased in 1978

Frank— born 1908, decased in 1952

Pearl— born 1911

Walter— born 1915

Seymour— born 1919

William drew mail in Ameliasburgh for eight years and now lives in Napanee. He has a son Pte. Francis Hamilton, born in Ameliasburgh and is a veteran of the Korean War.

Mary graduated as a nurse in 1932.

Frank homesteaded in Peace River, Alberta. He is buried in the Military Cemetery, Wetaskiwin.

Pearl graduated from Belleville General Hospital in 1932. In 1952 she married Otho Herrington of Rossmore. He passed away in 1968. Pearl did regular nursing for 50 years.

Left to right: William Hamilton, Walter, Seymour, Evelyn, Lee, Seated: Pearl, Linda.

Walter lived in Belleville. In 1943 he married Maude Denyes also a Registered Nurse. Walter did road contracting all over eastern Ontario and is now retired in Belleville.

Seymour Hamilton married Lieutenant Nursing Sister Evelyn Potter of Bridgetown, Nova Scotia in 1954. They have two children, Philip Lee a graduate of Kemptville Agriculture College, 1977. Lee lives at home and owns Lot 4, Con. 3, Ameliasburgh on Huff's Island. Linda Alice graduated from Guelph Agricultural University with Bachelor of Science degree in Agriculture. She is now with the Dept. of Agriculture, Alberta.

Seymour was born in the house where he now resides and attended S.S. No. 11, Ameliasburgh. He was an Ameliasburgh Twp. trustee for a number of years, also a director of Pedigreed Seed Growers of Ontario, and the Quinte Co-Operative Health Insurance.

The Edward Hamilton Family

Edward Hamilton (1884-1963) was born in Madoc, the son of Robert Hamilton and his wife Matilda Lafferty. She died very young when her daughter Bessie was born. James Broad from Massassaga went to Madoc and brought the baby home with him and she made her home there. Young Edward stayed with his mother's sister Jenny Calnan at Victoria.

In 1905 Edward Hamilton and Bessie Mabel Pymer (1884-1960) of Mountain View were married. They lived for many years on the 4th concession, where he farmed and their children attended Little Kingston School.

The Hamiltons had seven daughters:

Marguerite, the eldest married Ernest Hayes and lived on the 3rd Con. They had two children, Frances and William who married and still farm in the area.

Ila, married 1. William Carter and 2. Harold Kenny. Her son Ted is a merchant in Consecon. He married Jean Armstrong of Trenton and their family of 11 have left the area with the exception of Karen and Chris who live at home.

Viva married Carman O'Hara and they live on the 4th Con. in the Little Kingston area. They have no children.

Jean married 1. Donald Ellis 2. Pat Soucier. Their home is also in the Little Kingston area. Their children are Lynn who married Robert Keene and Lee married Mary Soucier and they live on the 4th concession in a new house on the Ellis farm.

Irene and Ilene— twin daughters of the Hamiltons also live nearby. Irene married Rex Weese and Ilene married Robert Keenan.

Betty, the youngest in 1944 married Harold O'Hara. They have farmed on the 3rd Con. near Adam's school for many years. In 1970 they built a new home east of the school and have retired there. Their son Dean, an auctioneer, and his wife Sharon have taken over the farm. A second son of the O'Haras, Donald lives on the 4th Con. at Salem

The Bessie (Hamilton) Adams-Boyle Family

Bessie Hamilton (1883-1969) married 1. Byron (called Bida) Adams and 2. Gordon Boyle. For many years they lived on the Samuel Adams homestead on the 3rd concession. By her first marriage there was Howard -m- Oress Foster, Helen -m- William Jose, Elmer -m- Alice Diamond (their daughter Elda married James Sopha, Rednersville), and Lorna married Floyd Locke. He passed away in 1969.

Their son Robert married Ann Mawdsley and they live at Massassaga. Ronald Locke also has a home there.

The Boyle children were Delbert who married Ruth Ainsworth, Edith married Elmer Forsythe who died young. Carl married Audentia Cross and they took over the Boyle Farm at Massassaga. Their daughter Janice recently married and lives in Northumberland County. Their son John married Jane Bailey and they remain on the Boyle farm. One more Boyle daughter Hazel married Edward Sills and they had four children. He passed away in 1984.

The Hattie (Hamilton) Dyer Family

Hattie Hamilton was one of the six children of Robert and Matilda Hamilton of Madoc. She also, came to Ameliasburgh township and married 1. Eskert Dyer and 2. Herman Goodmurphy. Her children were Ralph Dyer who married Luella Ferguson daughter of Charles Ferguson from the 4th Con. They moved to Arizona. Kathleen Dyer married Ernest Groves and Hilda married Leo Haberfellner. Neither family remained in the township.

The William Hamilton Family

William Hamilton married Hattie Doughty. They came from Madoc and settled on the farm where Earl Goodmurphy now lives on the 4th Con. They had a family of 11 children. They were Mabel, Merle, Bessie, Earle, Laura, Roy, Allan, Kenneth, Jack (Murray) Ruth and Velma. Their father died while the four younger children were still very young. Mrs. Hamilton moved into Consecon where the children completed their education and moved away. In later years she remarried to Charles Carnrike at Salem and lived there until her death.

Her children who remained in the township were Bessie who married Clifford Smith, son of Saylor Smith. They lived for many years on the Smith farm on the 4th Con. When Bessie and Clifford retired they moved into Consecon. Roy, the son, married Phyllis Palmer and they farmed for many years in Hillier. They had two children, Roger and Marilyn. When they sold their farm in Hillier, they built two new homes in Mountain View at the top of the escarpment. Roy and his wife occupy one while Roger, his wife Norma and their children reside in the other. Marilyn moved away from Ameliasburgh.

Jason Harns

Jason Harns (b. 1771- --) son of Thomas Harns, U.E. and his wife Rebecca of Fredericksburgh twp.

By his fathers will which was probated 1803, Jason Herns received Lot #71 in Concession 1 of Ameliasburgh, Prince Edward County where he settled with his wife Rebecca and where their children was born.

1. Thomas Harns b. 1800 d. 1848— married Catherine Tice, the daughter of neighbour Henry Tice of Ameliasburgh twp. On the Militia list of 1822 we note Thomas Harns gives his age as 22 years. Thomas and Catharine had three sons of whom two died as young men. The third son Jesse W. Harns was born 1834 and died 1856- married Naomi L. Burr 1836-1909. Some time after 1850 the widow Catharine and son Jesse W. Harns moved to Lot 76 on the 4th Concession of Ameliasburgh twp. and here Jesse Wellington Harns was born in 1855- d. 1917. He married Catharine Denike and had four children— Blake, Vera, Gladwin and Ewart. The Harns family continued to live on this homestead until the decease of Gladwin (Gladdy) in year 1975.

2. Abigail Harns b. 1803- d. 1856 m- Frederick Post b. 1799-1866 of Thurlow twp. He was son of John Post of Ameliasburgh twp.

3. Deborah Harns b 1806- d 1857 m John L Wannamaker, 1808 d 1847.

The Howell Family

The Howell family was of Welsh extraction. Richard Howell b. 1715 emigrated to Sussex County, New Jersey some time before 1750. His son John b. 1753 was the pioneer of the family in Canada. He served throughout the Revolutionary war and rose to the rank of Sergeant Major. After the war he settled in Fredericksburgh for 12 years, then moved to Sophiasburgh near Northport for a time, and later moved to Big Island.

A grandson of Sergeant Major John Howell, Griffith, married Phoebe Allison and settled in Ameliasburgh on lot 70 on the Third. They had seven children: Jacob who became a Methodist minister, John A, Manley, James, Catherine, Wellington and Cyrus. Wellington (1857-1926) stayed on the home farm, while John A. and James bought a farm on lot 73 on the 2nd Con. from Irvin Diamond in 1871. James never married; he lived with John and his wife Sarah Fox. The present large brick house was built by John and James in 1883 on the same foundation as former house. They raised Durham cattle and grew hops.

John and Sarah had four children: Sarah M. married Cyrus Hancock, Phoebe and Minnie were unmarried, and Wellington who married Muriel Howe. The Howells named their farm Spring Brook Farm. Carl and Velma McFaul are the present owners.

The Hubbs Family

Robert Hubbs was born in 1624 in Gloucester, England. After 1700, several of his descendants were living in America.

The pioneer in Prince Edward County was Robert Hubbs, born in 1753 and married first to Mary Fowler (died in 1780) and to Jane Haviland.

Robert and Jane Hubbs with their eight children arrived by batteau in Picton Bay, Dec. 27, 1797. In the cove where they landed, Robert built a log cabin and a canoe and this home was later replace by a red frame house. When the Danforth Road was built (1798-1801) it passed by their door. It is interesting to note that the child Amos Hubbs, an infant when his parents arrived, sold the homestead and later the True Blue Orphanage was built there.

The Robert Hubbs family of 11 grew up and William, the eldest son, settled in Hillier at Hubbsville. Other family members went to other townships. It was Robert's son Benjamin who was the ancestor of the Ameliasburgh Hubbs family.

Robert's son, Benjamin Hubbs (1783-1861) had married Sarah Way (1784-1841) and they settled in Hallowell. One of their children John Hubbs (1820-1902) married Matilda McDonald and one of their eight children, a carpenter, William Emery (1844-1909) married Matilda Ann Babcock (1847-1928) and came to Ameliasburgh township.

Wm. Emery Hubbs and wife.

To this couple was born, Effie May Hubbs (1874-1948) married Ernest Adams (1873-1959).

Emma Jane Hubbs (1879-1954) married Gilbert French (1878-1944). They had one son Malcolm killed in action in 1918. and Wm. John Hubbs (1884-1943) married Ida Sager (1883-1974).

William Babcock, a brother of Matilda Ann, owned part of lot 85 Con. 1 in Ameliasburgh. In January 1911, he had crossed the ice on the Bay of Quinte. As he came off the ice and while crossing the railroad tracks, a train frightened his horse. He was thrown from the cutter and received severe head injuries. He was taken to the nearest home, a doctor called and there he made his will leaving his property to his nephew Wm. John Hubbs. Some heirs debated his fitness to make a will but the doctor verified it. In order to keep the farm, Wm. John had to pay the court fees. This is now the Malcolm Hubbs farm on the Gore Road.

A few years after Will Hubbs and Ida Sage (ref. *Frederick Sager* story) were married, they raised the house to two storeys, cut off 40 feet and moved it for a machine shed, that is still in use. They installed a bathroom, probably one of the first in the area.

The William Hubbs Home on the Gore. Lady with hat in hand is Ida, Wm. next.

Four of the six children of Wm. and Ida Hubbs remain in Ameliasburgh. Haviland lives on the Sager homestead on the Bayshore, while Malcolm who married Evelyn Mikel has the Babcock farm. Florence married Gordon Waterhouse and they live on the 2nd Concession at Victoria, Helen married Harvey Brown and lived on the upper second— Alice married Rev. Robert Wragg and left the area. Elton died at age 2.

Florence (Hubbs) Waterhouse had a family of three, Raymond, Jean and Ida. Raymond married Joyce Whyte and they have two children Lisa and Scott. Helen's family left the townships. Only Malcolm's sons Robert and Ronald, who married Karen Graham, remain in the township. Their son Elton is in B.C. while Perry who married Rhonda Smith lives in Belleville and Barbara Ann and her husband Glenn Payne live near Stirling.

The Humphreys

Noel Melvin Humphrey 1835-1905 was the son of Melvin Humphrey and Margaret File. He married Sarah Adams 1838-1901, and according to the 1864 *Ameliasburgh Directory* they were living on Lot 109, Con. 2, the Smoke's Point Road, on the farm known as the Fred Taylor farm. This was the family homestead for their family of eight:

Cyrus Humphrey 1872-1949 married Annie Main. Their daughter, Hilda, who married Harry Bisdee, was born on the homestead, but her parents moved soon to their own farm on the Consecon Road by Weller's Cheese Factory. There was a son, Walter, who never married and lived on the farm for most of his life.

John married Etta Taylor. In the *Morrey's Directory of 1906*, he is listed as owning Lot 106, Con. 2. His son, Harold, and wife, Bertha Wilson, along with their son, Norman, lived on Wellers' Bay at the foot of the road known as "Humphrey's Lane", and more lately, the 'Blakely Sideroad'. Another son, Orin, and his wife, Ethel Bedal, had a daughter, Vivian, and lived on the Consecon Road, then moved to Trenton.

Schulyer married Melissa Snider. *Morrey's Directory of 1906* located them on Lot 2 in Gardenville; later they moved to the Humphrey homestead on Lot 109. There were four children. Ray c. 1891 married Pearl Marvin, Pearl b. 1893 married Cyrus Fulford, Beatrice c. 1895 never married, and Kenneth c. 1897 died young.

Samuel married Ella Hutchison; there was a family of four. Two girls were Blanche and Minnie. Earl 1884-1933, married Mary Helen McCurdy b. 1886 and lived on Lot 97 on the Third Concession. Their daughter Flossie married Winston Pulver, John never married, and Lorne died young. Samuel and Ella's other son, Adam, born in 1887, is celebrating his 97th birthday this year; his wife, Ethel Irvin, born in 1890 in now 94 years of age. This year they celebrate their 73rd wedding anniversary. They live in Trenton now.

Edna Humphrey married William Black. Of their three children, Zelda married Rev. Osborne, Greer married Helen Haines. and only Lela settled in

Ameliasburgh. She married Cecil Blakely of Consecon.

Inez b. 1883 was a twin sister of Ida. Inez Humphrey married Charles Carnrike in 1899. Their family were Eva, Nina, Edna, Verna, Percy, Edwin, and Melvin. All except Nina settled in the County. (See *Carnrike* family story).

Ida b. 1883 was twin sister of Inez. She married George Elmy. They lived on Stinson's Block. There were six children. Earl and his wife Bernice Hogle, Arnold and his wife Marguerite Milligan, Marjorie and her husband Earl Brooks, all moved away. Only three remained in Prince Edward County: Vernon and his wife Ruth Dorland, Melvin and his wife Evelyn Miller, and Ernest with his wife Jean Goodmurphy.

Harriet Humphrey never married.

The Irvine Family

John Irvine immigrated from Scotland in the late 1800's and went to work on the farm of Jewett Chase on the Second Concession of Ameliasburgh.

At the age of 12 years Mary Taylor and her sister Margaret, aged eight, landed at Quebec, sent to Canada from an orphanage in Glasgow, Scotland to find a new home. They went to live with a doctor in Perth, Ontario. From there Mary went to work for Ezra Bonter who lived on what was later the Delbert Snider farm. While living here, Mary met and married John Irvine. Their first home was a small house located on part of Riverside farm east of Ed Miller's Garage.

John worked for Ben and W.C. Dempsey on the Front Road and lived in a tenant house there.

About 1911 John and Mary purchased a 35 acre farm, on the Bryant

The John Irvine Home— left to right: Clifford, Mary and John Irvine

Sideroad, from Jake Moon. They ran a small self-sufficient farm and had a large garden, whose produce they sold on the Trenton market for a number of years. John worked by the day for neighbouring farmers, and during World War I he collected scrap and sold the iron to a dealer in Belleville. He served as a trustee for S.S. 13 Ameliasburgh and cleaned the school for 36 years. Mary did housecleaning and laundry for several neighbours as well.

They have five children, Bruce, Albert, Ethel, Ross and Clifford.

Part of Bruce's family, Albert's only son and Ross's family now live in the United States. Ethel's only surviving daughter lives in Chatham, Ontario.

Clifford, a retired civil servant, lives with his wife, Kathleen Harvey, on the farm his parents purchased. His family, except for one son who lives in Orangeville, live within a ten mile radius of his home, three in Ameliasburgh Township.

The Ray Jackson Family
of the Upper Second Concession
(1842-1915)

Charles Jackson and his wife, the former Victoria Maidens, (1855-1924) farmed on the Second Concession of Ameliasburgh. Her father and mother, Phoebe Ann Alyea b. 1833 and Robert Maidens b. 1824, lived on the Second, too. Charles and Victoria had three children, David, Rose and Raymond. David moved to Toronto, Rose to Cleveland, Ohio, and Ray, the youngest, remained at home.

To the family farm in 1916, Charles Raymond Jackson brought his young bride, Kathleen Pierson of Pleasant Bay in Hillier. They became the parents of two children. A daughter, Marguerite Kathleen, became a teacher and married Olaf Goodsell of Trenton; they have a daughter, Olga, a teacher. The son, William Raymond (deceased), was employed for many years by Bell Canada.

Ray and Kathleen Jackson were active in community and township affairs. She remains a charter member of Consecon Women's Institute. Ray had a special interest in the Ameliasburgh Fair. He claimed never to have missed a fair from the year he was born until it was discontinued.

Community activities with neighbours and friends were always happy events. These included taffy-pulls, corn roasts, birthdays.

Beekeeping was part of the family farming operation, as was gardening and the traditional Saturday market.

A point of interest on the farm is the falls— named Jackson Falls. The unusual land and rock formation with a drop of about 80 feet becomes a spectacular rushing torrent in spring and a frozen splendour in winter. The source of the water is the run-off from the fields and woods. For many years a log house sat above the falls, and near the road. Charles and Victoria Jackson and family lived in the log house before they built their new one. Victoria was a beekeeper; on her death Ray took over and turned the log house into a bee-house, using it for his extracting.

Myrtle Helena Delong Johnston

daughter of John Gilbert Johnston, born and raised in Roblin's Mills (Ameliasburgh).

This was her Official Identity Card to enable her to enter Rathbun Air Force Camp, Deseronto during the First World War. Note the British Coat of Arms. Canada was not granted Arms until Nov. 21, 1921 at the Court of Buckingham Palace.

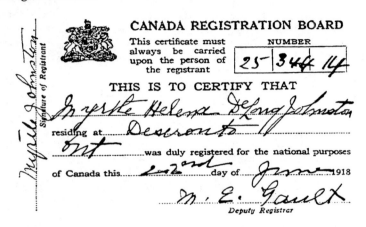

The Keene Family

Frank Keene, his wife Helen (Mastin) and baby son Robert, moved to Ameliasburgh Township in 1939 and lived on Concession Three where Keith Burris now lives. Later they moved into what was known as the Blakely house in what is now called the Cunningham Sideroad. In 1942, their second son Larry was born there. The house burned down but the foundation is still visible.

In 1945 the Keenes moved to the Fourth Concession, lot 92, where P. Holden now resides. The original house into which they moved was destroyed by fire in 1947, when a grass fire went out of control. It was early spring and Mr. Keene lost 190 skips of bees, one-half ton of bees' wax and all associated equipment in the fire. As a result of the fire, Frank's father Tom Keene died of a heart attack.

There was an unoccupied house in the Dempsey Sideroad that the Keenes moved to the location of their former house and when renovated and the grounds landscaped, it made an attractive and comfortable home for the family until 1976. After Helen Keene's sudden death Frank sold out and moved by the Murray Canal.

Both of the Keene sons remained in the township where they grew up. Robert Keene married Lynn Ellis and with their four children, live on the

The Keene Family— Mr. & Mrs. Mizen, Helen and Frank Keene, Annie Mastin, Larry Keene & Robert Keene.

former Levi Terry farm by the old Consecon Station. Robert is the newest member of Ameliasburgh Council.

Larry and his wife Pat (Clapp) and their two children live on the Second Concession on the former Peter Badgely property.

The Knox Family

Three brothers by the name of Knox came to Canada from Scotland. One of the three was John W. Knox (1855-1898). He farmed first in Sidney Township on land which is now part of Trenton Airport. Later he moved to the Mount Carmel neighbourhood along the Murray Canal. Knox married Ella Jane Black from Murray Township; they had a daughter Ethel who married Walter Minaker. Ella Jane died at age 26, and Knox married her sister Annie Black (1868-1892). To them was born a son, James Wilmot. Annie also died, at age 23. Knox married a third time and had a daughter Alma, who married Bruce Morrison. Knox himself died as a young man of 43.

James Wilmot Knox (1890-1968), known as 'Bill,' married Mildred Ardie Crosby b. 1890, daughter of James Crosby and Mary Louise Ferguson. Crosby was a carpenter and lived in Roblin's Mills just west of the Methodist Church. Bill and Ardie lived briefly in Murray, then moved to Belleville. When the first World War broke out, Bill immediately enlisted and served all through the conflict with the 155th Regt. When he came home in 1919 he purchased the east half of Lot 86, 2nd Con., Ameliasburgh, from a Mrs. Covert, and moved his family there. Bill and Ardie had a family of four: Harry who married Josephine Sampson, Gladys who married Howard Robinson, Margaret who married Denis Keegan, and Wilmot who married Helen Coe. Harry purchased the Knox farm in 1963, and his parents retired to a home in Belleville. Wilmot (Bill) and Helen live on the former File farm, lots 84 and 85, 3rd con. Ameliasburgh.

The La Tour Family of the Carrying Place

By W.D. Hanthorn, Gladys and George La Tour.

Richard La Tour (1803-1886) married Debra Van Cott and they lived on the 4th Concession near the Salem church. They had a family of five children, namely Charlotte, Benjamin, Louis, Sarah and Lucy. It was Louis (1839-1895) who went to the Carrying Place and married Catherine Bonter (1842-1935) whose family lived in the area of Smoke's Point. She was known as Kate to everyone, and she and Louis owned a hotel straight across the road from the present store. This hotel, one of three in the place, burned down, with the Empey House being saved, as it was across the road on the Ameliasburgh side.

Louis and Kate La Tour had a son George Ross and a son Harry. Wm. Bruce Urquhart and his wife Angelina Rose had a daughter, Annie Lena Urquhart (1886-1958), who married Harry. Her father was a blacksmith in the Albury area at the time. Harry and Annie had two sons, George and William.

Harry La Tour and his wife Annie had gone to Point Anne where he operated a steam shovel at the cement plant. Matt Quinn, another Carrying Place resident, had been assistant to La Tour and "the best helper he ever had." However, the La Tour returned to the Carrying Place, bought the Methodist church parsonage and were living there when their son, William, was born. In 1921, the Hanthorns bought the house, and the La Tour family went to the farmhouse formerly owned by the Biggars, alongside another known as the Bingley house. These homes have long gone and a fine new home is owned and occupied by George La Tour and his family.

When the Hanthorns had changed the old parsonage drive shed into the blacksmith shop, Bill began to hew timbers for Harry La Tour's barn, which is still in use. Since Harry was frequently away operating a steam shovel, Bill Hanthorn, besides blacksmithing with his father, worked the La Tour farm on shares. He and Bill La Tour became real pals and trapped muskrats together, played ball and shinny and Bill Hanthorn recalls all the meals he enjoyed there, for "Annie was a good cook and I can never forget her pancakes," he says.

The La Tours had the first Victrola and the first new Overland car in the village, and Harry loved the four horses that he owned. But in 1933, for some undetermined reason, the horses sickened and died, in spite of all the medical attention they received by family and neighbours.

William La Tour married Gladys Miller of Trenton, a dental assistant and they had a son Robert and a daughter Joy. His ability as a coach of a team sponsored by the Courier Advocate, then Quinte Orchard, sponsored by Bob Dempsey and George Hardy, filled the old Trenton rink with spectators.

William La Tour enlisted with the Hasty P's in World War II and was wounded in Sicily. After his return from Overseas, he became the Area Representative for Veterans' Affairs. He died in 1975. Both Harry La Tour and Bill Hanthorn's father passed away in 1953, with Annie soon after. The La Tours and Hanthorns had been inseparable friends for two generations.

George La Tour works for the Ontario Department of Agriculture, Livestock Branch. He and his wife Betty have three children, Ann, Scott and George Jr.

The name La Tour, so many years synonymous with the Carrying Place, will not soon be forgotten.

The Lauder Family

William Lauder (1788-1866) and his wife Margaret came to Canada in 1828 from Lauder, Roxboroughshire, Scotland. They settled on lots 73 and 74 in the 3rd and 4th of Ameliasburgh. They had four children— Thomas (1812-1875) who married Jane Anne Coleman, John (1819-1888) who married Catherine Giles, Franklin (1821-1868) who married Melissa Huff, and Euphemia b. 1828. Thomas and Franklin lived under the hill on the lower third, while John lived above the hill on the fourth concession.

The children of Thomas and Jane Ann were: Robert who married Susan Platt, David who married Mary Black, and Sarah. Franklin and Melissa had one daughter Ella who married Howard Anderson; they had two sons, Donald and Ross.

The children of John Lauder and Catherine Giles were Franklin, Charles, and twin girls Margaret and Catherine. Franklin (1858-1906) married Martha Doxsee. To this union were born two children, Mabel who married Norris Gibson and Oral Lee, unm. Charles (1861-1935) married Amarilla Cunningham; they had two children— Fred who married Clara Redner, and Edith who married William Burkitt. Margaret (1867-1929) married Greg Titus; their children were Florence who married Ross Bush, Hazel who married Howard Young, and Grace who married Percy Wilson. Catherine

Lauder log house across road from the new Charles Lauder home. Edith Lauder (Burkitt) with cousin Clella Meadows & niece Marion Lauder (Arnott)

died at 16.

Franklin Lauder lived on lot 74 on the 4th con. and Charles on lot 73. The first Lauder house on lot 73 was a log home on the south side of the road. In 1902 Charles built a new frame residence on the north side of the road on property he purchased from lot 73, 3rd con. His granddaughter Muriel and her husband Grant Minaker are the present owners.

The Lough Family

George Lough of Marmora and Sarah Victoria Barlow were married in 1915 in Bonarlaw. In the fall of that year they purchased the farm from the Way family located at Lot 66, Con. 3, Twp. of Ameliasburgh, Huff's Island Road.

They brought down with them a few cows, calves, four horses and two democrats. It took two days to make the trip, staying over night with a relative near Foxboro. There was a gas well on the farm which supplied the fuel to light lamps at different locations around the yard.

In 1917, Mrs. Lough received a new 1917 Ford Auto, with instructor, a gift from her parents.

The family of George and Victoria was comprised of eight children from the oldest down— Percy, Helen, Ross (killed in World War II), Howard, Doris, Leslie, Mary and Ron who has continued on the family farm.

This picture taken in the early 1900's shows a verandah around the large brick Lough house.

The Madigan Family

By W.D. Hanthorn

Patrick Madigan and his wife Rachael moved into Ameliasburg Twp. from the Deseronto area about the turn of the century. He settled on a parcel of land alongside the Bay of Quinte about two miles east of Carrying Place village. It was very shallow soil, hardly suited for farming, but this suited Pat very well. What he needed was pasture, for he was a horse trader. A 'gypsy', so described by his grandson, Jack Madigan, who supplied most of this family history. According to Jack, Pat's 'string' of horses was brought into Ameliasburgh Township tied 'head to tail'.

Pat's children grew up, married, and moved out. Pat rented the house to the David Leveridge family who later moved to the Carrying Place.

Fred (1871-1931) and Bertha Madigan (1875-1955), parents of Jack, lived in the Carrying Place house that was later sold to Chas M. Westfall for a store and Post Office in about 1910 after the Boyce building burned. The Murray Post Office, as it was known then, changed postmasters every time the government changed and residents hardly knew which side of the road to go to for mail pick-up.

Fred Madigan moved his family to Gardenville across from the store. He had four children, William, Clarence, Gladys and Jack. Horses were his life. His team of matched Clydes was always groomed to perfection with braided tails and manes, shining harness with ribbons and in winter strings of sleigh bells. He made his living with his team. In the 'Dirty Thirties' some illegal seine fishing was done off the bar in Weller's Bay. Madigan transported the white fish and herring by the wagon load to Gosport before daylight.

Fred and son William bought two teams of horses, drove to Oshawa and scraped out a foundation for a new truck plant at General Motors. William and his brother Clarence also worked on the road from Carrying Place to Trenton with horses, which they stabled in a shed where the Empey Hotel had been. While Highway 2 was being paved, all traffic was routed past the Madigan home where there were great mud holes. Day and night cars got stuck and Bill made a bundle hauling them out. The boys accused him of pouring water in the holes. He would laugh and joke but the holes did seem to get worse overnight.

William married Goldie Turner (mother of Pete) and they built a new home which Pete and his family now occupy. Clarence remained on the family farm and married Ella Sine from across the road who worked for the Corrigans. The Madigan family, once well-known in Ameliasburgh Twp., is no longer represented by any member, as sister Gladys, Jack and Clarence moved away.

From *The Trenton Courier*, Aug. 10, 1905— West Ameliasburgh: The Gypsies have been located for some days at the Centre and considerable horse dealing is taking place. They are in a position to furnish almost any kind of horse one may require from a 'go-a-head' to standstill.

Buchanan and MacDougall Families

For generations these two families have been part of the history of The Carrying Place.

The Buchanan family came to Canada from Ireland in the late 1800's. They had three sons, James, Thomas and John. James was killed by a runaway team of horses, Thomas lost his life while helping to build the Murray Canal. John worked on a dredge on the canal and later supervised the paving of what is now Highway 33 to Trenton. They were Anglicans by faith and farmed just west of the Anglican Church on the Murray side.

The MacDougall family came to Canada from Scotland and settled directly across the road from the Buchanans on the Ameliasburgh side. Wm. MacDougall was married to Arwilda Brown, whose family lived on the Second Concession east of Young's School.

MacDougall was an enterprising farmer who milked a herd of holstein cattle and drew milk to Weller's Bay Cheese Factory. They had a young daughter, Helen, and all was going well with them until 1918 when Wm. MacDougall suddenly succumbed to influenza. His good friend and neighbour, John Buchanan, promised to care for his family, but didn't know that in a short few months there would be another little MacDougall to care for. On June 3, 1919 Wm. MacDougall III was born.

John Buchanan cared for his friend's family and farms, and finally married Arwilda MacDougall. They had one son, John Jr. In 1946 the Buchanans moved to Picton leaving the farm to her son, Wm. MacDougall III, who married Eileen Wickens. They had two children, Wm. Douglas George and Judy Helen.

The MacDougall farm is owned and operated by the fourth generation Wm. MacDougall who raises Hereford cattle and is a Toronto banker. He has

Left to right: Bill MacDougall Jr.,
Helen MacDougall, John Buchanan Jr.

a daughter, Stephanie, and son, Michael Charles, and they hope to keep the farm in the family name for a long time. The widow of John Buchanan Jr. still lives on the family farm.

The McFauls of Fingerboard Farms

By Phyllis McFaul

Years ago a fingerboard pointing directions to the traffic stood at the top of the hill. Thus it was called Fingerboard Hill. From this the farm was named and has been our prefix for many years.

Willett Jackson McFaul bought 100 acres of lot 77 from Daniel Howe in 1893. Willet was one of seven sons of Haskell McFaul of Allisonville who was a great grandson of Robert McFaul who came, with his family, from Duchess County, N.Y. and settled at Colborne. Willet married Annie Adams, daughter of John Adams in 1893 and they moved to their new farm. They had two sons, Allen who went to Toronto to work and live, and Cecil who remained on the farm his entire life. There were no telephones when Willet and Annie were married, so Willet's father sent messages from Allisonville tied to his dog's collar. Willet told of one occasion when he was boiling sap in the bush late at night and the dog came scratching at the door with a message. The message was answered and the dog told to take it home, a distance of five miles.

Cecil McFaul married Phyllis Wallbridge in 1928. A small addition was made to make the house a comfortable two-family home, heated by five wood stoves. Cecil and Phyllis had four children— Elda (Mrs. Roy Brooks), Florence (Mrs. Leo Wood), Carl who married Velma Vancott, and Brian who married Donna Rae Row. Willet died in 1944, and Annie in 1947.

More land was purchased. First 20 acres just south of the 2nd concession was bought from the Estate of Wm. F. Brickman. Then in 1939 the Fred Cunningham farm on lot 75 and 76 on the 3rd concession was bought. This 160 acres had a narrow lane running to Roblin's Lake to allow cattle to water there.

Fingerboard Farms has a large maple bush on the side hill, and about 300 trees are tapped. At first boiling down was done in two pans but now an evaporator is used. Plastic tubing now has replaced most of the sap buckets of yore. In 1958 the barns were destroyed by fire. Ridley Wallbridge and Reg. Barber took the cattle to board for their milk until the next spring when a new aluminum barn was finished and christened by about 200 people at a barn dance.

In 1960 Cecil bought 150 acres from Mrs. Clinton Sager. This farm runs to Roblin's Lake and building lots had been sold and 15 cottages built on the shoreline. In 1966 ten acres of land from lot 78 with a right of way for a waterline to Roblin's Lake was sold to the school board on which Kente School was built. In 1970 9½ acres was bought to enlarge the school grounds.

Carl, being very mechanically-minded, went into the construction business. He and Velma purchased the Wellington Howell farm on the second concession. Brian went into partnership with his father. After his marriage to Donna Rae they took over the family home and Cecil and Phyllis moved to the Sager home. In 1982, 70 acres was purchased from Wm. Corfield, part of lot 79 in the 3rd con. May of 1983 brought the passing of Cecil McFaul, and the farm was passed down to his son Brian.

The Mikel Family

Godlove Mikel U.E. lived in Germany and when he was discharged from the German troops, he came to Quebec. In 1782 he joined the second battalion of Sir John Johnson's Royal Regiment of New York. In 1784, he received 100 acres of land in Third Town, Fredericksburgh. He married Elizabeth Lott who had come to the Midland district with her parents after their farm in the province of New York had been confiscated.

To Godlove Mikel and his wife Elizabeth were born nine children:—
1. Duncan Mikel (1788-1865) m. 1. Hannah Chase, 2. Mrs. Henry McWilliams
2. Catherine Mikel m. William Chase
3. Margaret Mikel 1793-1847 m. David Covert
4. Elizabeth Mikel m. Alfred Brown
5. Charles m. Margaret Maria Fones
6. Sarah Ann 1800-1876 m. William Dempsey
7. Peter Mikel 1804-1868 m. Abagail Chase
8. Eva Mikel m. John Stoneburg
9. Daniel 1810-1882 m. Sarah Ann Pierce

Many descendants of these families reside in Ameliasburgh today.

On July 10, 1801, Godlove Mikel received the Crown Deed for lot 96 Con. 1, Ameliasburgh where they remained until their death when they were buried in Albury Cemetery. Godlove Mikel U.E. born 1758 died Oct. 25, 1830 and his wife Elizabeth Lott D.U.E. born 1760 died March 15, 1831.

It was Daniel Mikel who married Sarah Ann Pierce who remained on the property longest and his sons sold it in 1867 to John Burley Williamson.

John Mikel, son of Duncan and his wife Hannah Chase and grandson of Godlove, married Sarah Ann Herrington. Her father, Zachariah Herrington, owned several lots of farmland and John and Sarah Ann lived for awhile on lot 96 Con. 4. They had a daughter Abagail who was buried in 1843 in the Carrying Place Cemetery and then it appears that they, along with other Ameliasburgh families went by way of the corduroy road along the Trent River to the German's landing area. Names of some who settled there were Buryea, Zufelt, Bush, Walt and Osterhout.

Their son George Ridley Mikel (1847-1914) was the only descendant of Godlove who returned to Ameliasburgh for many years, and he settled on the east half of lot 96, on the north shore of Consecon Lake. He married Mary Little (1847-1920). Their two sons died in infancy and their daughter Annie Melissa, born in 1878 died at age 16. They were buried in Salem Cemetery. Being very lonely, they took a lad, Jack Hutchison, from the Barnardo Home

GODLOVE MIKEL CREST

WORK, FIGHT, STUDY, SAVE,
IMPROVE EVEN DUNCE OR KNAVE.

and he grew up with them and inherited one of their farms (the Kente Mission Farm). Later, he sold it to Karl Woofe and went to Oshawa.

George Ridley's deceased brother Johnson Hope Mikel in the 9th of Murray had a large family. His wife, the former Philona McMurter, was lucky to have two sons teaching school and three other sons who were able to carry on the work at her farm. It was Thomas, that his Aunt Mary and Uncle Ridley asked to take over the farm. He came down from Murray in 1911 and remained until his death in 1968. George Ridley Mikel died in 1914.

In 1917 Thomas O. Mikel (1887-1968) and Sybil W. McGillis (1894-1979) were married in Brighton. They lived in half the house until after Mary Mikel's death.

It was a picturesque place, with 40 hard maples bordering the road by the lake the full width of the farm and up the laneway. The lawns were bordered by picket fences and the buildings were neatly kept. Thomas and Sybil extended their Aunt Mary's perennial garden and shared flowers and especially peony roots with friends and neighbours. Thomas made cedar shingles to roof the house that lasted for many years. It is probable that he was Ameliasburgh's first genealogist. He compiled a book which was printed in 1934 listing the descendants of Godlove Mikel, under the sponsorship of his cousin W.C. Mikel K.C. of Belleville. He compiled family data on the DeMille, Way and Herrington families as well.

Thomas and Sybil Mikel had five children— Marion, an elementary teacher, married Clifford Calnan. Their son David and his wife Susan live in Ottawa. Their foster son Edward Preston is in Trenton. Evelyn, second daughter is married to Malcolm Hubbs of the Gore. Their five children are Elton, in B.C., Barbara Anne married Glenn Payne, Ronald married to Karen Graham lives at Albury; Perry married Rhonda Smith. They reside in Belleville while Robert is at home.

Barbara, also a teacher married the late Everett Minaker of Mountain View. Their five daughters all university graduates are Jane, Suzanne, Nancy, Peggy and Sally. All live elsewhere (Ref. *Minaker* story).

Beecher taught school for two years at Salem and decided then to take over the farm. He married Shirley, daughter of Ross and Gladys Adams. Their three children are Ann, Katherine and Kenneth. Ann, a Queen's graduate left the township as did Kathy. Kenneth married Janice Blaind and farms in partnership with his father. They have a large dairy herd and have bought neighbouring farms. Their farms are known as 'Mikeldale Farms'. Shirley Mikel R.N. is the youngest child and lives next door to the farm, but in Hillier, as the township division is 'there'. Her husband is Noxon Foster and they have four children, Mikel, Laurie, Jon and Lezlie who all attended Ameliasburgh schools.

The Mikel farm on Consecon Lake was always a family gathering place, and still is the center of a tightly-knit family.

The Montgomery Family

The Montgomerys were of Irish descent. They came to Canada in 1829 from Derrybeen, County Cavan, Ireland. The pioneer William Montgomery obtained a Crown grant to a farm in the Township of Drummond, Lanark County, near the present village of Lanark. That same farm and an adjoining one still remain in the Montgomery name, now owned by another William, a great, great grandson of the pioneer William

William Henry Montgomery, a great grandson of the pioneer, met Mabel Weese when she was visiting an aunt and uncle, Mr. and Mrs. W.C. Delong, in Lanark village. W.C. Delong had operated a tailor shop in Roblin's Mills, then moved to Lanark to continue his trade there. His wife, Minnie Babcock, was a sister of Mabel's mother, Jennie Babcock Weese. Mabel's father was Harmon Wellington Weese, a great grandson of the pioneer John Weese U.E. Mr. and Mrs. Harmon Weese lived in a stone house on the Weese side-road. They had four children— Morton, Eugene who died at age 9, and twin girls Minnie and Mabel.

William Henry Montgomery and Mabel Weese were married Jan. 22, 1908. The lived for a few months with his parents at Lanark, then purchased a farm, the east half of Lot 89, 2nd Con. Ameliasburgh from Wm. H. Glenn. Their three children Harmon, Evelyn and Kathleen were born there. They sold that farm in 1919 to Harry Cunningham and purchased the east half of Lot 88, 2nd Con. from Harry Sager. Harmon and his wife Nellie Werden still live on this farm. Evelyn married (1) Clifford Barber (2) Dan Thompson. Kathleen married Howard Walt.

The Harry O'Hara Family

In 1912 Harry O'Hara married Amanda Etta Hawley. Both were born in 1912. They moved from Madoc to Trenton where some of their 11 children were born. Harry worked on the railroad. They went to Glen Miller and lived on a farm for a while before coming in 1929 to the Wellington Miller farm near Consecon Station. It is now the Mindle property. After nine years of farming there, the family moved to the third concession in 1938, to their own farm. Harry continued to commute to Toronto to work on the railroad.

Harry and Amanda O'Hara had eight sons and three daughters. Already deceased are Carl, Phyllis, Keith and Dorothy who was the wife of the late Dave Kelly of the 3rd Concession. They had a daughter Patricia.

The O'Hara sons: Carman married Viva Hamilton and Harold, married Viva's sister, Betty Hamilton. Harold and Betty have two sons Dean and Donald living here. James married a local girl, Dorothy Cross and their son Allan married Elaine Chatterson of Rossmore. They live in Massassaga. Lorne and Norman O'Hara served overseas during W.W. 2. Lorne afterward married Cecily Hawley and bought the General Store in Consecon from Max Gainsforth. Years later he sold out to Ralph Brazzeau and they moved away. Norman married Alice Jinks, daughter of Charles and Norma (Post) Jinks of Consecon Lake. None of their four children stayed in Ameliasburgh. Ralph O'Hara married Bessie Dillon and went to Belleville as did Betty O'Hara who married Reginald Adams. (Ref. Robert Adams family).

The Onderdonk Family

By Mabel Onderdonk

John Onderdonk came to Canada in 1832 at the age of 20, from Sodus, N.Y. He was the son of Andries Onderdonk and Maria Smith. He bought land on lot 95 concession 1 Ameliasburgh, now known as Onderdonk's Point and Hill. In 1836 he married Mary Jane Dempsey who lived on the next farm. They had a family of six. In the diary of John Onderdonk, which was begun in 1868, there were interesting notes as to weather, crops, prices and social activities including trips to 'the States' by crossing the lake from Brighton and also crossing the Bay on the ice to visit friends and shop. One entry in 1871 relates the following trip: "Started to the States end of February, went to Kingston the first day, to Henderson's Harbour the second day, to Oswego the third, to Sodus the fourth, in all 180 miles with a span of horses; returned in three weeks by way of Kingston."

John Onderdonk was elected to Council in 1869. He died in 1894 and his wife in 1900. He left the farm to his son John Ryerson Onderdonk who continued the diary. In 1898 he mentioned selling Spy apples for 20¢ a peck. The same year they set 226 apple trees— Cranberry Pippin, Stark, Baldwin, and Sutton Beauty, bought from Mr. Reid in Belleville Nursery. In 1900, 100 Smith Spy trees were set.

The original house is still there. As there is no mention of the 'new' brick house in the diary begun in 1868, it must have been built before that. After John Ryerson and his wife died, the farm was sold to J.R. Longstaffe who still owns it.

William Andrew, oldest of John Onderdonk's children, was born in 1840. He married Mary Weese, daughter of W.F. Weese. She died in 1884 and he married Jenny (Garbutt) Babcock. William Andrew had five children. John

Home built by John Onderdonk on Lot 95, con. 1, later owned by John Ryerson Onderdonk

Home & barn on lot 86, con. 1, owned by John Jay Onderdonk and later Earl Onderdonk

Jay, born 1875, was left the farm on lot 86, concession 1 by his mother's father, W.F. Weese. He married Isabel Adams, daughter of Joseph Adams. They had two sons, Earl and Keith. Earl married Mabel Lloyd and they have two daughters, Joan and Margaret. Earl and Mabel reside on the farm in a new house built in 1971. The original house is now owned by daughter Joan Foster.

The Osterhout Family

By Evelyn Osterhout

William Osterhout, son of David (born 1799) and Elizabeth (born 1802) Osterhout, cleared and settled a farm on the 9th of Murray Township, Northumberland County. William was married twice and had nine children, two of whom settled in the Canadian West. William's son John remained on the homestead on the 9th of Murray. He married Emma Westfall; to this union were born eight children. Many descendants of William Osterhout remain in the Frankford and Trenton areas. A son of John and Emma, Arthur, remained on the homestead, while another son, Frank came to Prince Edward County.

Frank Osterhout married Nina Adams, daughter of Albert W. Adams and Laura Brason. They had four sons: Allan who married Marie Chase, Elmer who married Jean Baitley, Burton who married Lorraine Terry, and Donald who married Evelyn Richards. Frank and Nina bought a farm on the 5th concession of Hillier in 1921, and lived there the rest of their lives. Their youngest son Donald and his wife Evelyn were married October 1944, and the following year bought the farm across the road, lot 77 of the 4th concession of Ameliasburgh, from Mrs. Egerton Cook, where they still reside. They have four children: Brenda (Mrs. Gary Townsend), Daryl who married Linda Elliott, Noreen (Mrs. Jack Elliott) and Lynne (Mrs. Randy Ellis).

In 1955 Don and Evelyn bought his father's farm across the road. Daryl and his family now live there, and he farms in partnership with his father.

The George Parliament Sr. Family

The Parleman family came to America from Partenheim, Paltz Germany in July 1709 and settled first at Hackensack, New Jersey and in March 1714 moved to the Ramapo Tract, N.J. John and his first wife had ten children, and by his second wife Catherine Stier he had George, Bapt. 17th Feb. 1723. He married Susannah Garnier and had two children. His wife died and he married 2nd Mary Garnier and had a family of nine who came to Canada in 1788 with their parents. The father died within six weeks and the widow Parliament married John Parcells, a widower. They lived for a short time in Adolphustown before moving to Sophiasburgh just west of Northport where the family grew up. George Jr. (1780-1875) married in 1807 Mary McTaggart, (a daughter of Corporal James U.E.) of Sophiasburgh twp. They lived on land on the 4th Con. of Ameliasburgh (leased) before buying in 1815 west half of

Lot 72 on the 3rd Con. from his step-father where he lived until his death in 1875. His wife Mary died 1832 leaving a family of nine children. In 1836 George married Sarah Mason; James Harvey, the eldest son, was born 1810 and died 1852. He married Hannah Tice; of this marriage seven children were born. The eldest Marshall Roblin (1836-1904) married Philena Tice; they had six children but only two grew up, Emma Jane and Hartford Clayton who married 1896 Luella J. Hodgen and had three children Percy, Mildred and Philena. Percy married Myrtle Spencer; they had one son Ralph. Mildred married Loral Wanamaker; they have a daughter Jean. Philena married John Thompson; to this union were born Elmer, Donald, Shirley, Lyle and Mervin.

The Jacob Parliament Family

Jacob Parliament (1778-1857) married Margaret Fox (1782-1847) both buried in Consecon Cemetery. He was an older brother of George Jr. He lived first in Sophiasburgh with his mother and step-father. In Oct. 1823 and April 1826 he bought 200 acres, pts lots 93 and 94 Con. 4. They had a family of 11 children but four appear to have died young. The rest married and lived mostly around the old homestead, expect George who was born 1814 and died 1892 and had married Elizabeth Wait and moved to Rose City, excepting his youngest daughter, wife of Samuel Alyea who remained in Ameliasburgh twp. The other 11 children all settled Rose City and West Branch Michigan where they were farmers, druggists and one a doctor.

Henry (1804-1882) married Mary Carnrike; they had eight children; all lived in Ameliasburgh twp. Arthur and Roy Parliament and Edward and Ernest Parliament were grandsons. Arthur's son Donald and wife Mary Ellen Black live near Bloomfield they have five children, Margaret, Gertrude, Arthur, Hugh and Lyle. The other son, Ross, is deceased. He had two daughters, and Roy's family live in Toronto. Edward had two children, Howard Parliament M.A. and Lois Scribner.

Jacob Parliament (1819-1863) married Agnes Huycke and had eight children, three sons and five daughters. Peter A. (1852-1932) married Alice I. Beach; they had one daughter Gertha May (1878-1975) who married Harry J. Chase.

The Peck Heritage

By Lorene R. Reid

The heritage of the Pecks of Albury is embedded with tales of the ilk which frequently inspires movies. A sampling of tales recalls the nature of this pioneer family of Albury.

In 1798 James Peck Jr. and his wife Elizabeth arrived in Sophiasburgh Twp., Prince Edward County from New Jersey with four children in tow. Born in Harrington, New Jersey, they were first cousins. Their respective fathers James Peck Sr. and his brother Samuel, were sons of Jacobus Peck of New Jersey, one of the founders of the Dutch Reformed Church, and descendants of 17th century Dutch pioneers. The fathers possessed intriguing pasts as secret service agents for the Royal cause during the Revolution. In 1783 the two families had been transported by British ships from New York harbour to Nova Scotia where they endured great hardships and deprivation. James Jr. and Elizabeth were married in Nova Scotia, and three of their children were born there, one dying at age four. They returned to the States and two more children were born there.

According to story, James Jr. and Elizabeth then came to Canada overland with a decrepit blind mare and her colt. Elizabeth, a very shrewd and apparently wealthy woman, decided not to leave the family future in the hands of Upper Canadian government grants. She successfully outwitted the American authorities and spirited all her gold money over the border in the bottom of a large tub covered over with lard. James and Elizabeth did not remain long in Sophiasburgh Twp., where James Peck Sr. had preceded them in 1796 and settled on Lot 22, Con. 1, west of Green Point. According to family tradition, the parents had not entirely blessed the marriage of first cousins. In fact, James Jr., the eldest son, was at his father's death, bequeathed only "the large Dutch Bible," a long gun and any wild lands that might be granted to his father after his death. In any case, in 1800 James and Elizabeth bought, perhaps with some of the tubfull of gold, Lot 93, Con. 1 of Ameliasburgh from John Blaker. A child had been born in Sophiasburgh, and five more were born in Ameliasburgh. Here the family remained and became pillars of the

Pioneer board and batten Peck home, Albury where Isabel (Peck) Hatfield now lives.

community, and their descendants over the years have continued to take the same prominent role.

A church, cemetery and school were established on land bought from James Peck. The original stone church was replaced in 1898 by the present one, now a Heritage site. While the new church was being built, services were held in Peck's Hall, a building erected by John Grier Peck, Justice of the Peace, and grandson of James and Elizabeth. The hall was also a popular spot for dances and bees, since the bottom floor was a drive-shed and the top story sported a hardwood floor. John Grier's father, James 'Cos' Peck and uncle, William Peck, were important members of the community in their time.

A granddaughter of John Grier Peck, Isabel Hatfield, now lives in the old homestead while the name of Peck and other descendants can be seen on many mailboxes in the area.

The Peck Family

Space does not permit tracing all the descendants of the Peck family in Ameliasburgh Twp. They intermarried with Weese, Bonters, Brickmans, Dempseys, Allisons, etc. Many who live in the Albury area and all along the bayshore are descended from James 'Cos' Peck (1803-1882), son of James Jr. and Elizabeth. 'Cos' was short for Jacobus. He married Anna Weese in 1826 and they had nine children. His second son Franics was father of Clifford Peck who married Gretta Weese and bought a farm on Lot 85, Con. 1. They had two sons, Beuford and Wayne. Beuford married Ruth Williamson, and she is still living in the original home on the property which in the 1890's had a race track for racing horses.

William P. Peck, another son of 'Cos', married Sarah Ann Dempsey and they had five daughters— Hattie, Gertrude who married Harry Anderson, Blanche who married Ernest Redner, Florence who married Rev. Geo. Rowland, and Grace who married Earl Bonter.

James "Cos" Peck

Another son of 'Cos', John Grier Peck married Nancy Jane Weese. Their son, Pembroke married Hessie Bryant and they had two daughters, Isobel and Dorothy. Harry Woodruff, son of John Grier married Lena Sager and they had four daughters— Bernice, Lorna, Myra and Marjorie.

The Phillips Family of Consecon

George Phillips and his wife Henrietta Herrington of Bloomfield had four sons: Charles, Erban, Harry and Dorland. Charles came to Consecon and married Rose Clark daughter of James and Melissa Clark. To them were born seven chilren: James Leonard, Theodore, Pearl, Nina, Gladys, Leo and Stanley.

James Leonard grew up in Consecon and enlisted and served overseas during World War one. Upon his return he became a commercial fisherman and boat builder. On his property which fronted on Weller's Bay, there were fine docking facilities and he manufactured boats from rowboat size to big lake fishing boats.

In 1921 Leonard married Addie McMaster from the Stinson block, west of Consecon. They built three cottages and Addie cooked and served meals while Leonard acted as fishing and hunting guide to the tourists who visited there. Addie also seamed nets for fishermen. This was the process of putting on lead sinkers and cork floats, for which she was paid by the pound. The last net she seamed (pronounced simmed) was for Chuck Phillips and Nig (Leo) Mattis for carp fishing under the ice. She recalls the huge fish they caught and took to Brighton for shipping.

Leonard and Addie had four children, James Lavern, Jean, Charles Wesley (Chuck) and Muriel. Their eldest son Lavern was overseas during World War two. He married Jean Weller of The Carrying Place. None of their five children live here. Lavern was killed in a car accident. Jean married Vernon MacDonald. They live in Wellington, Charles Wesley (Chuck) married Doreen Mastin and they remained in Consecon. Their son Barry married Christina James daughter of Everett James whose parents owned the grist mill and his wife Della Holland whose parents lived on the Cunningham Crossroad. Chuck's and Doreen's other three children left Consecon.

Leonard and Addie's fourth child Muriel married Orliffe Kemp, son of Bert and Pearl Kemp of Northlakeside. Of their three children, the two sons Brian and William have remained in Ameliasburgh.

Leonard Phillips passed away in June 1955. In 1972 Addie Phillips married Douglas Williamson and they have a home a short distance from where the Phillips Fishing and Tourist Camp was located. Now, Chuck Phillips resides in the house which his parents built. The cottages are gone, a break-water holds back the water of Weller's Bay and it is a beautiful place to live.

Leonard's brother Leo and Stanley remained in Consecon too. Leo was overseas with the army during World War 2. He married Donna Mattis and their children are Cathy and Brenda.

Stanley Phillips married Ruby Clark daughter of Mr. and Mrs. Lee Clark of Consecon. They had two children, Loraine and Myron. Loraine married Gerald Mattis and had a son Donald, who married Arlene Spriggs, daughter of George Spriggs and his wife Arlene Mattis. Myron and Arlene had five children but only George Phillips remains in Consecon. Stanley is also deceased.

The Pope Family

Jonas Pope came to Canada from England. He was married twice and had nine children from each marriage. The children from his first marriage were William, Charles, Ernest, Susan, Elizabeth, Henryetta and Jonas.

William Pope who became a cheesemaker married Lily Langabeer in 1900 and they had five children— Maude, Roy, Gladys, Gerald and Leslie. When daughter Gladys was born in 1906 in Thurlow Township, Con. 5, Lot 26, they were living in one end of the cheese factory which had been made over into living quarters. This property is situated across the road from what is now Gilead Hall. The factory which was named the Bronk Cheese Factory, is now gone, but the cement floor still remains.

When Gladys was a preschooler, they went farming. They rented a farm on the 4th Conc. of Sidney Township, owned by Nathan Vermilyea. She started to school while living here. They lived down a long lane and in the winter, Gladys and her brother Roy would ride a horse down the lane to the 4th Con., turn the horse around and it would go back home.

Then they moved and rented a farm owned by George Frost situated on the 5th Conc. of Sidney Township now owned by Mr. & Mrs. Maurice Mallory.

In 1918 they bought a farm on the 2nd Con. of Ameliasburgh Township, east half of Lot 88 formerly owned by George Sager and his sister Alma. This property is now owned by Mr. & Mrs. Wm. Faulkner. They moved in winter, driving their herd of cattle from Sidney Township across the Bay of Quinte, landing at Bill Way's farm (at the end of the Weese crossroad), now occupied by Anna Way. When they brought the cattle, they also came with two sleigh loads of people to assist them. They were pleased and excited to move into a home with gas lights and a wood furnace in the Victoria neighbourhood. The neighbourhood boys, Bill Knox, Gerald Fox, Clarence Vanclief, Haviland Hubbs and Peter Badgley often came in the evening for cards and Bagatel, because Gerald, a victim of polio at an early age, was handicapped and drawn to school in winter on a hand sleigh.

Directly across the road from the house was a steep hill where many young people in the area gathered for sleigh riding. Unfortunately, an accident claimed the life of James Loney as his sleigh hit the fence and he died the same night. No one cared to ride after that.

Many activities were centered around Victoria Church which was situated in the midst of the community. There were church services, chicken suppers, pancake suppers, Christmas concerts and plays. The ice-cream socials were fun

The Pope Family. Left to Right: Front, William and Lily, Back, Roy, Maud, Gerald, Gladys and Leslie

tor the children for with homemade ice-cream, "It was great fun to lick the paddles." The Victoria Athletic Club was formed by George & Jenny Wannamaker who donated their property for the use of outdoor activities such as tennis and baseball. Next to this property was a farm pond owned by Edgar Storms. Many young folks would gather for skating parties. Several lanterns would be placed around the pond for light. They even had a change house!

When the family grew up, Roy moved to the States, Maude married Stanley Wetherall, and she and many of her family reside in Ameliasburgh Township. Leslie married Mary Mangold, a teacher at the Victoria School. Gerald married Ida Lewis and kept post office for years at Corbyville. Gladys married Ross Adams in 1927 and moved to the 3rd Con. of Amel. They are the parents of Reginald of Foxboro, Robert at home and Shirley (Mikel) of Consecon Lake.

The John Post Family

John Post, b. 12/7/1771 in Bergen County New Jersey. He came with his father who settled in 3rd Town (Fredericksburgh) U.C.

John Post married Eunice Alger dau. of Elisha Alger of Cramahe., twp. They first settled on Lot 64 con. 1 Bayside and later purchased Lot 66 in same where he resided until his death in 1863 at 92 years.

John Post and Eunice Alger on this homestead raised 10 children— Frederick Post, b. 1799-1866 -m- Abagail Harns, 1803-1866; William, b. 1802-1861 -m- Mary Gerow; Mary (Polly) 1808-1881 -m- Benj. Gerow 1809-1850; Jacob 1812-1855; Elisha, 1816-1871 -m- Mary Morden; Sarah, 1818-   ,John Tice Post, b. 1821-   -m- Amelia Fretts 1841-1912; Rinard, b. 1823-

Abraham b. 1825-1895 -m- Catharine Hamilton; Eunice 1824-1912 -m-(1)Philip Choate (2) William Wickett.

Abraham Post retained the homestead and raised five children of whom the youngest Silas Oscar Post 1866-1907 married Julia Etta Taft 1877-1922. At the death of Oscar Post the property left the Post family after over 100 years. A cemetery on this farm has a number of the Post family and their relatives, and is kept in fine condition.

The Charles Post & Uldene Babcock family are descendants.

The Pulver Family

The Pulvers were originally from the Palatinate on the Rhine. They came to America and were living on Long Island, New York at the time of the American Revolution. David Pulver Sr., born 1773, came to Canada, and with him his son John Pulver (1806-1856). John Pulver married Elizabeth (Betsy) Wannamaker, daughter of Henry P. Wannamaker. They lived in Rednersville. Five children were born to this union: Henry b. 1843, Hannah Eliza b. 1845, twins Sarah Parthana and Bethana b. 1850, and David b. 1853. In 1856 they paid Ameliasburgh Township taxes of One Pound 10 shillings. John Pulver died in 1856; Betsy remarried, to a Mr. Austin. Hannah Eliza (Biddy) married Alpress Ashton; she died and he married her sister Sarah Parthana. Bethana died at age 22.

David Pulver married Sarah Emily Tompkins (1862-1883). They had two children— Arthur Herbert (1879-1960) and Alberta Evelyn. After his first wife's death, David married Sarah Ann Rose by whom he had a daughter, Mabel Lillian. His second wife also died and he married Catherine Wannamaker; they had a son Donald Roy. David died in 1894 at age 41.

David Pulver lived on the west half of Lot 81 on the Gore Road. His older

Herbert and Emma Pulver

brother Henry lived on the east half of Lot 82 adjoining David's farm. Henry had a son Clayton. When David died, his son Herbert was only 15; by his father's will he was to obtain ownership of the farm at age 21. An agreement was worked out that Clayton would have the use of the land until Herbert came of age, providing he kept Herbert and his two sisters.

Herbert married Emma Clista Pymer in December 1900 and they took over the farm, as he was then 21. They had three sons— Melvin, Arza and Winston. In 1916 a second farm was purchased from the estate of Fred Redner, and the family moved down the road in the spring of 1917 (Winston and Flossie Pulver live on the former Fred Redner farm). When Melvin married Annie Price in 1925 he assumed ownership of the original Pulver farm. In turn, when Melvin and Annie's son Morris married Mae Brooks in 1950, he took over the homestead and Melvin and Annie bought and moved to another farm on the Gore Road on Lot 84. Morris and Mae have eight children— Linda, David, Roger, Ann, Rebecca, twins Gerald and Geraldine, and John.

Arza married Bessie Profit and they had a daughter Sheila Margaret. Arza died in 1946. Winston married Flossie Humphrey; they have two children, Beverly and Howard.

The Rathbun Farm— Riverside Farms

Originally the 200-acre farm on Lots 103 and 104 on Concession Two, Ameliasburgh Township was owned by Isaac and Adelaide Lont. On their deaths the property passed to their two daughters, Ida Jane and Sarah. When Sarah married William Alyea and left the farm, newlyweds Ida Jane and Henry Rathbun bought Sarah's share and commenced farming about 1879. Henry Rathbun was living with his mother, Martha Oliver Rathbun on a farm east of Victoria on Concession Two. He had a brother, Jacob, who lived in Trenton. Their father, James, died young.

The Henry Rathbuns had a family of four, three girls, Lulu, Nora (Peg), and Edria, and a son, Earl. The girls moved to the U.S.A. Earl remained on the farm. In 1931 he married May Brooks from Melville, and here on the farm they raised their children, Jean and Ronald.

The present home was built by the Lonts, who had lived in a log house on the property. The present barn was built in 1944 following a disastrous fire the year before that burned three large barns.

Earl and May Rathbun sold in 1964 to Walter Terry who carried on a traditional farm operation. With Walter's purchase of another 150 acres, the property totalled 350 in all.

The farm was sold in 1979 to the Quickert family of Trenton. Further acquisitions of 50 acres from S. Klemencic, and 72 acres on the Snider crossroad enlarged the 'Riverside Farms,' as it is known today, to 472 acres. There, a herd of beef cattle utilizes whey products from the 'Trenton Riverside Cheese and Butter Co.' plant, as vital feed.

The Rathbun Home

The Quickert family came to Canada in 1951, after fleeing the communist regime in Prussia, now a part of Poland. Arthur Quickert was manager of dairy in Prussia and, altogether, numbers more than 50 years in the business. Since 1964 the family has operated the Trenton company. Presently a son, Dr. Nick Quickert, is president and general manager at the Trenton site, and another son, Armin Quickert, manages "Reid's Dairy" a 'sister company' in Belleville.

Philip Reddick, U.E.

Philip Reddick-Riddick— on land board of Mecklenburgh 1792 as a settler from U.S.A.

Philip Reddick of Adolphustown— 1796 Muster Roll 1. man, 2 women: 4 males; 3 females; total— 10

Philip Reddick— At the Council Chambers, York July 1st, 1797 applied as a Loyalist settler. Recommended for 200 acres.

Philip Reddick- on the early map of Ameliasburgh we find him living on W. ½ lot 63 and later on Ameliasburgh map of 1863 the Reddicks (Samuel) on lot w. ½ lot 65, and east ¼ lot 66. There is an old Cemetery on lot 64 today and another (now gone) on lot 65 which is known as the Raymond Roblin farm where no doubt the early Reddicks were buried.

Philip Reddick of Ameliasburgh— wife unknown.

Issue

David Reddick b. 1790-1864 -m-   buried in Salem Cemetery in Cramahe
George Reddick -m- Catherine Frederick of Smithfield
Thomas Reddick b. 1792
Philip Reddick b. 1793 -m- Mary ? 1799
Polly (Mary) Reddick -m- Perez Cooper of Cramahe
Margaret Reddick -m- (1) Isaac P. Glover (2) Essom Loveless
Catharine Reddick b. 1797-1887 -m- Capt. Robt. Morgan
John Reddick b. 1798-1861 -m- Clara Wanamaker
Ann Reddick -m- Able Hubble of Cramahe
Abigail -m- ? McConnell
Nathan b. 1803-1846 -m- Unice Tice 1817-1868
Sylvester Reddick b. 1805 -m- Polly Ann Herrington 1817-1852

Miss Helen Reddick of Rossmore is a descendant of Sylvester and Polly Ann Reddick.

The Redner Family

The Redners originally came from the Palatinate on the Rhine to America. They were living in Bergen County, New Jersey, at the time of the American Revolution. Henry Redner b. 1738, married Maria Bielsfeldin, b. 1746. They had a family of seven children. Redner was loyal to the Crown and served as a private with the New Jersey Volunteers. The family came to Canada in 1791, applying for land at Cataraqui on June 29, 1791. The Henry Redner family is listed on the Adolphustown muster rolls for the years 1794 to 1798.

In 1798 the Redner family settled in Seventh Town, purchased lots 76 and 77, con. 1, lot 76 from the Widow Hurd and Peter Phillips, and lot 77 from the Widow Lucas. They held the land by 'Location Tickets,' but Redner received the 'Crown Patent'. Their first home was a log house near the water. Their descendants are still on much of the same land today, and the village of Rednersville took its name from the Redner family.

Both Bernard and Ralph Redner are great, great, great grandsons of the pioneer Henry Redner, descendants through Henry's oldest son, Henry 2 (1769-1852), and his son Henry 3 (1801-1861). Henry 1 and 2 both lived on the bayshore at the front of their property, but Henry 3, when he reached manhood, moved to the back of the farm and built a stone house on what is now known as the Gore road. His brother James remained on the front and also built a stone house (where Bernard presently lives). Henry 3 eventually divided his land between his two sons, James settling on the west portion where his son Fred and grandson James Edgar also lived (it is now the Winston Pulver farm), and William Henry remaining on the east portion. Wm. Henry had three sons— Harry, Burton (Ralph's father) and Ernest (Bernard's father). Wm. Henry assisted his Uncle James in the grain business and James, being childless, left him his property. When the stone house on the Gore burned in 1905, Wm. Henry and his wife moved to the Rednersville stone house where his son Ernest and grandson Bernard followed him as owners.

Burton remained on the Gore. After the fire he and his wife, Lena Pearsoll, built a small frame house where they lived until 1909, then built a large frame house on the site of the former stone one, where Ralph and his wife, Belle Black, still live.

The gravel pit on the north end of Ralph's farm was opened in 1856. In 1972 Ralph started a stone quarry. There used to be a roadway going back by the house to the gravel pit, then east out to the main road. It was a short cut in winter for people going to Rednersville. Long ago it was an Indian trail. Many Indian artifacts have been picked up on the knoll east of Ralph's house; it is believed there may have been an Indian village there.

As well as raising purebred Holsteins registered under the name Rednerholme, Ralph and Belle specialized in raspberries from 1930 until 1968, starting with two acres and increasing to ten. Their son Roger is now farming the original acreage and several other farms as well.

The Redner antique baby carriage.

The Stone Redner Home on the Gore built by Henry 3.

There are three Redner Century rarms, belonging to Bernard, Ralph and Douglas. Douglas is great, great grandson of the pioneer Henry Sr., but he is a descendant through Peter (1790-1864), the youngest son, and Peter's son Rynard, and Rynard's son David Wright Redner who married Sarah Giles.

Harry Redner and his son Gerald who lived on Lot 78, 2nd Con. were also descendants of Peter Redner through the line of his son Lewis, and Lewis' son Mirancy. There are many other descendants of Henry Redner living in the area.

The Roblin Family

The Roblins were of English or Welsh ancestry. At the commencement of the Americn Revolution there were Roblins living in both New York and New Jersey. As a result of the revolution four branches of the Roblin family came to Canada. One of the four was Philip.

Philip Roblin U.E. (1750-1788) a Loyalist in the struggle for Independence in America, was at Sorel, Quebec during the winter of 1783 with his wife Elizabeth Miller, one son over 10, two sons over 6, and two daughters under 6 years of age. He said his old home was at Smith's Clove, Orange County, N.Y. where he had 15 acres with a grist mill and saw mill on it. He received land near Hay Bay; died at age 38 leaving a wife and eight children.

Philip Roblin II (1775-1848) son of Philip the pioneer, married Prudence Platt; they had 10 children. He built the Roblin's Mills near Green Point in Sophiasburgh.

John P. Roblin (1799-1874) son of Philip II, married Nancy Langhorn Conger; in 1830 moved from Sophiasburgh to Lot 79, Con. 2, Ameliasburgh where he built a flour and grist mill on the creek running south from the mill pond on which the John B. Way mill was already located. He was for four terms a Member of the Upper Canada Legislature representing Prince Edward. In June 1846 he was appointed Registrar of Prince Edward County, which position he held until his death. He moved to Picton after his appointment as Registrar.

Owen Roblin (1806-1903) son of Philip II and younger brother of John P., married Hulda S. Conger. He came to Ameliasburgh in 1832 where he took up 400 acres of land which his father had purchased two years previous, Lots 76 and 77, Con. 3, located on either side of the road which runs from Rednersville to Fingerboard Hill. In 1838 he traded Lot 76 for John B. Way's Lot 81 whereon was located a mill, post office and several houses. Owen Roblin built a large stone mill on top of the hill and initiated various other enterprises (as outlined in the chapter on Roblin's Mills). None of his descendants live in Ameliasburgh today.

Owen P. Roblin (1774-1845) third son of Philip Roblin I, married Mary Dulmage, issue 12 children. Owen P. settled on Lot 73, 1st Con., Ameliasburgh, Crown Patent March 5th, 1804, where a great, great, great

Nora, Helen and Theodore Roblin c. 1914

grandson, George Roblin now resides. Owen P.'s seventh child was Philip who married Nancy Vandewater. The oldest of their four children was George E. who married Angenora Manuela Baker. Second son of George E. was Adelbert who married Ardella Sprague. Adelbert and Ardella had twin boys, Ray and Ross. Ray married Cora Weese and they had two children, George and Muriel. George married Marjorie Ellis and Muriel married Leon Ward. Ross Roblin married Cordelia Simonds and they also had two children, Marjorie and Gordon. Marjorie married (1) Allen McCoy (2) Ronald Caterer; Gordon married Barbara Kyle.

The oldest son of George E. and Angenora Roblin was Theodore Baker Roblin (1859-1936) who married Mary Emma Yott. Issue: Raymond Roblin who married Doris Reddick, and Angenora who married Norman Duetta. Raymond and Doris Roblin issue: Theodore John Roblin (1908-1966) who married Hazel Hawley, Helen who married Emile Masse, Nora who married Orville Landry, and Norman d.y.

The Rowes of The Carrying Place

By Julia Rowe Sager

One wonders whether or not this is an ancestor of mine and whether or not I might boast of it, but I have seen on Nell Gwynne's house in Windsor, England, a proclamation signed by some 60 men for the execution of Charles I, duly carried out on Jan. 30, 1649; one of these 60 men being named Owen Rowe. Some 100 years later, John, my great-great-great grandfather, the earliest Rowe of whom I am aware, came from England by way of the American Colonies to the Niagara Peninsula around 1780. He was engaged in soldiering and farming on the Niagara Frontier in Upper Canada. He was a sergeant in Butler's Rangers, then promoted to a captain with the Grenadier Company of the Lincoln Militia, finally fought in the War of 1812-1814, and was killed in 1814 at the Battle of Chippewa. All this is greatly removed from the execution of Charles I in England but one wonders about Owen Rowe's descendants.

This great-great-great grandfather of mine, John Rowe, had two wives and 13 children. His seventh child was my great-great grandfather John Rowe Jr., born in 1791. He married, farmed for awhile in Peel County, then moved to The Carrying Place, locating on land granted by the Crown on the Bay of Quinte. There was a family of ten children. One of them was John, born in 1841, a sea captain, and father of a life-long resident of The Carrying Place, Miss Ella Rowe, who lived her entire 79 years on lot 105, passing away in 1961.

As a child I marvelled at her interests and accomplishments: she knit and gave away baskets of socks, she was the organist for St. John's Anglican Church it seemed forever, she possessed a camera and made our first family snapshots, I admired her handwriting, she corresponded with other Rowe relatives in such remote places as Winnipeg, Clarkson and Cornwall and related the family news, she had a spinning wheel which she willed to me, a roll-top desk with lots of books, and in her upstairs she possessed wonderful chests and paraphernalia of her sea-captain father. One family heirloom that met with disapproval was a picture of Ella's grandmother, Sarah Vail, wife of John Rowe Jr., and my great-great grandmother. She was scowling so that Ella's mother turned the picture to the wall.

Of particular interest to me is the story of descendants of another son of John Rowe Jr., that of my great grandfather, David Rowe, an older brother to Ella's father, Captain John Rowe. David Rowe was born in 1825, was a carpenter, and built several houses and barns in The Carrying Place area. One pattern predominated with its Gothic window and brick exterior as seen presently in the homes of the late Morris Alyea, the late Fred Chase, and that of my father Lee Rowe. While he was a carpenter, Great Grandfather was also a farmer, occupying the 'Century Farm' recently sold by Earle Rowe. The front of the farmhouse on this farm is also attributed to the carpentry of my great grandfather, and as a child I was aware of a great chest of carpenter's tools that rested upstairs in the drive house. Still these remain in the family, the possession of Earle Rowe.

Here on Highway 33 between The Carrying Place and Consecon, my grandfather, David Henry Rowe, born in 1861, was reared, and he and my grandmother, Deborah Jane Ferguson, brought up their family, my father Lee Rowe born in 1897, my Uncle Blake, and my aunts, Alice Hayes and Lula Adams. My grandfather accumulated two more adjacent farms, one of which became my home and was known as the Jerry Kemp farm. There was another son, Earle, whom I never saw, but I have always referred to him as Uncle Earle. He died in 1911 at 21 years of age from an unfortunate accident. When he had gone to the chip yard to get a sharp stick for use in putting a ring in the bull's

David Henry Rowe and wife in surrey with the fringe on top

nose, he stepped on a nail. The wound healed, but two weeks later he became ill. Three doctors, Dr. Farncomb, Dr. Kidd and Dr. Thornton came and were unable to diagnose his illness. Finally, when my grandparents recalled the nail wound, the doctors recognized lockjaw. They sent to Montreal for serum, but it was too late. He died the day it arrived.

My grandfather, David Henry Rowe, was a good horseman and raised horses for sale. His only brother, Daniel Herman Rowe, my great uncle, left early in life for the U.S.A. to attend veterinary college, after which he set up his practice in Little Falls, N.Y. My grandfather had a ready market for his horses since his brother developed a consuming interest in them for competition and show. To transfer horses from The Carrying Place to Little Falls, N.Y., they would wait for winter when they could make a short-cut, driving by cutter over ice to Wolfe Island, Cape Vincent and finally to their destination, returning by train to Trenton, cutter and all. Annually my father and grandfather made trips to race courses to watch sulky races, often locally, then on occasion to Syracuse, N.Y. where Uncle Herm was racing his horses. Two of his racers were 'Belle Wilkes' and 'Audacity'. It was from the sale of some of Grandfather Rowe's horses that a piano and an organ were purchased in order that my aunts could take music lessons.

My father's sister, my Aunt Lu Adams, born in 1894, recalls some excursions from the farm at The Carrying Place when she was a young girl. She tells of pleasant Sunday buggy rides that would go by way of Consecon, up Stinson's Block Road to Lake Ontario, follow the sandbar between Lake Ontario and Weller's Bay to Bald Head, down Smoke's Point Road and home. On a trip in 1911 she took the side paddle-wheeler Alexandria from the

Murray Canal to Quebec City, one-week round-trip for $20. Then in 1907 she and my grandparents journeyed by train to Chicago to visit cousins. One of these far away cousins used to come regularly to visit at my grandfather Rowe's. She was Aunt Lu Heron to us children, though actually a cousin to my grandfather, and she would stay for long periods of time renewing her Canadian ties.

But time passes and the descendants of those Chicago cousins are unknown to us now, along with most of the descendants of those early families of my great-great-great grandfather John Rowe with his 13 children in the Niagara Peninsula and of my great-great grandfather John Rowe Jr. who first came to The Carrying Place and had a family of ten. And still one wonders whether Owen Rowe, collaborator in the execution of Charles I, may be an ancestor in this veritable web of North American cousins.

The Sagers of Albury
By Lorene R. Reid

The community of Albury in Ameliasburgh Township is one of the oldest and finest settlements in Prince Edward County. Among the very early settlers was David Gilbert Sager, a pioneer with two little-known, but fascinating, claims to local fame.

David Sager was born Dec. 5, 1765 at Rhineback, Duchess County, New York, to parents David Sager and Elizabeth Waldemeyer. The young Sager was fortunate in also having as sponsors, or godparents, his uncle and aunt, John and Mary Waldemeyer. John was none other than the colourful character later known as Captain Meyers, the pioneer of the Belleville area, who possessed a flamboyant and sometimes alarming personal and military history.

Tradition holds that David travelled to Canada with his Uncle John in 1787, first settling in Adolphustown, then Sidney Township and finally Ameliasburgh Township. He was a blacksmith who, with Cornelius Benson, made nearly all the utensils essential to pioneer existence: ploughs, shovels, hoes and other tools.

In 1789 David married Catherine Weese, daughter of John Weese Sr. here lies David's second claim to fame; David and Catherine enjoyed the prestige of being the first couple married in the township. Elder Winer, a Baptist minister at The Carrying Place received one York shilling for performing this noteworthy ceremony.

David bought the west half of Lot 91, Con. 1, Ameliasburgh from John Finkle in 1803. A portion of the land remains in the possession of Albert Sager, great, great grandson of David. The old homestead remained in the family until 1932. Though greatly changed, the house is still standing on its beautiful bayshore location, and locally known as Quinte Inn because for a brief time it was used as a dance hall. The Sager land originally fulfilled a more becoming and historically relevant role. According to an old Sager Bible, in the early

Lena and Claude Sager, children of
Albert and Mary Ann Sager, with rocking horse.

West part of Sager home at Albury,
showing the belvedere.

1800's training of the Militia was held on Sager's land, and David eventually held the rank of colonel.

One of David and Catherine Sager's nine children was John who, with his Irish wife, Harriet Gaffield, lived on the homestead and was a prominent member of the Albury community. John's position and interest in the development of Albury was subsequently inherited by his son, Albert, a steward and trustee of Albury Church, to the construction of which he generously contributed.

A descendant of David Sager, Lorna (Peck) Bowerman, whose mother was Lena Sager Peck, still lives near the old family land in Albury. She fondly remembers her gracious grandparents, Albert and Mary Ann (Knox) Sager. She recalls the stately brick home with the central feature of a spiral staircase that ended in a belvedere on the roof, a special and irresistible place for a child where treasured things evoked memories and a heritage: heirlooms, china, a doll house and an old rocking horse.

The Sager Family

David and Catherine Sager had nine children, but only three settled in Ameliasburgh Twp.— Elizabeth who married (1) John Burley and (2) Wm. Rosebush, John who married Harriett Gaffield, and Jacob who married Anna Rogers. Catherine, as the daughter of John Weese Sr. U.E., received a Land Board Certificate for Lot 87 in the 2nd Con. which she sold to son John in

1844, and he sold to Wm. Rosebush in 1861. An 1823 map of Ameliasburgh shows David Sager as leasing Lot 88 in the 2nd Con. which was Crown reserve. It was acquired by his son Jacob with a Crown Deed in 1848. The first home on the property was built by Jacob Sager to the north-west of the present house.

Jacob and Anna had eight children. The second son Joseph bought the west 100 acres from his father in 1860. He married Mary Ann Parliament. They built a home on the west hundred and raised their family there— Jacob, Melissa, George and Alma. Melissa died at age 15. George never married. Jacob married Mary Margaret Brickman. Alma kept house for George after their parents died, marrying James Reid late in life.

Jacob Sager died in 1869. By his will his youngest son, Albert Lemuel, received the deed to the east 100 acres of Lot 88. Albert married Mary Ann Vanwoort. They built the present home in the early 1870's. In 1874 they sold ½ an acre on the north-east corner of their farm on which a school was built. They had two children who both died in childhood. They sold the farm to Joseph and his son Jacob and moved away. Jacob, his wife Mary Margaret and son Harry, then three years old, moved down into the house on the east hundred. When Joseph died in 1892 he left the east half on Lot 88 to Jacob and the west half to George.

In 1897 Jacob Sager and David Calnan each gave 7500 square feet of land where their farms adjoined on the south side of the road, and here Victoria Church was built. Harry Sager married Rhoda Bryant; they had no children. Jacob died in 1914. William Pope bought the west half of Lot 88 in 1918, and in 1919 Harry sold the east half to William Henry Montgomery, and he and his wife and mother moved to Belleville.

The Frederick Sager Family

Frederick Sager Sr. U.E., a soldier, served with Butler's Rangers. He settled first at Niagara, later moving to Richmond Township, with his wife Barbara. His son Frederick came to Ameliasburgh in 1816. He lived on the Weese sideroad and married Mary Babcock. They settled on lot 87, Concession 1, then left for Warkworth, because it appears that Mary Babcock had received land there, in the right of her mother Huldah (Cole) Babcock, daughter of Daniel Cole U.E. After 1878 they came back to Ameliasburgh. Florence Hubbs has a china tea-set that has been passed to her from Mary Sager.

Frederick Sager Jr. (born Oct. 15/1790, died March 31/1847) and his wife Mary Babcock Sager (born Oct. 5/1793, died April 16/1853) had six children. Their daughter Barbara Ila (Allie) born in 1810, married Sandford Blanchard. Their descendants are unknown. William Sager (1821-1887) married Margaret Smith (1842-1912). Their family story is recorded under the title *The William Sager Story*. Catherine Sager (1825-1896) married Lewis Swenor (1823-1926) and her sister Maria Sager (1827-1893) married George Teller

(1820-1891). Another sister Fanny (1829) married Peter Weese (1829) and yet another, Mary Jane (1838-1920) married 1. -- Urquhart, 2. Francis Brickman (1843-1905). These latter four daughters of Frederick Sager Jr. lived on Ridley St. in Rossmore.

The Rossmore Sager Connection

Catherine and her husband Lewis Swenor had three children. Annie married Jesse Sprung, and they had Grace Sprung who married Clement Frederick, whose daughter is Noreen Frederick, now of Belleville. Maretta Swenor married John Belnap and their daughter Hazel became the wife of William Riley Brickman. They raised two sons Asa and Clayton Brickman. Another Belnap daughter Mabel married 1. Frank Reddick and 2. Bart Russell and they had one daughter, Maretta Russell. The Swenor's third daughter Margaret married Lewis Wesley Gerow and they had a son Stanley who moved to Cleveland, Ohio, but his daughter visits here.

Fanny Sager and her husband Peter Weese kept store in Rossmore. Their children were Mary Catherine who married William Campbell; Sarah Margaret who married William Switzer and Lucy Ann married Charles Reid. Their children were Bertha Reid who married Charles Brickman. Bertha had two sons, Stanley Brickman married Annie Hill and Glencoe Brickman married Helen Louise Weese. Another daughter of Fanny and Peter Weese was Emily Maria. She married John Francis Bondhead (called Bonny) Gerow. Their children were:

Lillian May 1879-1925 -m- Ross Onderdonk 1887-1950
Howard Richard died young.
Frederick Clayton 1884-1914 was drowned
Annie Grace Gerow 1891-1969 married Frank Belnap 1888-1968
Kenneth Morris Gerow married 1. Mina Hunter 2. Stella Barriage (Hunter)
William Ross Gerow married Mildred Drake
Marjorie Gerow 1895 married Percy Clapp 1893-1972
Bon Gerow 1899-1967 married Alice Rittwage 1898-1972
Myrtle Maud Gerow married Myron Carl.

Fanny and Peter Weese had a son George Washington Weese. He married Ellen Gray. Their four children were George, Clinton, Roy and Ellen.

Mary Jane Sager and -- Urquhart Family

Mary Jane Sager and Mr. Urquhart were the parents of two children, a daughter Vellena Urquhart 1858-1932 married Joseph Adams 1854-1949. (For the family story refer to the Robert Adams Story, the Onderdonk Family, the File Family.) Their son William Bruce 1854-1905 married Angelina Victoria Rose 1858-1941 William Urquhart drowned in the Bay of Quinte along with Frank Onderdonk in 1905. (Reference *The La Tour Family*).

The William Sager Family

Sager House, Pt. Lot 83, Lightning struck, house gone. Left to right: 1. Unknown, 2. Bessie Sager, 3. William Wesley Sager 4. (seated) Francina (Weese) Sager, 5. Ida Sager, 6. Lady & child unknown, 7. (seated) Grandmother Weese.

William Sager (1821-1887) married Margaret E. Smith (1824-1912) and they settled on part of lot 83 which contained 94 acres between Rednersville and Albury in 1864. They had three children, Maretta (1849-1875), who died when young, Mary Emily (1853-1936), a spinster who became a fine seamstress and later settled in Rednersville, and William Wesley (1861-1940) who married Marrietta Francina Weese. After their marriage, instead of going for a honeymoon they returned home and dug and picked up potatoes all afternoon.

William Wesley Sager and his wife lived on part of lot 78, Concession 1 until January 1911. Prior to this move, lightning had struck their house, shattered the stove pipes, splintered their bedposts, bored a hole in the floor downstairs, then went to the basement where the posts of the swing table were shattered and the butter bowl of freshly churned butter was thrown across the room into the shelf containing the canned goods. This house was across the road from Marcenko's store.

The Sagers had two daughters, Bessie (1882-1958) and Ida (1883-1974). Bessie never married and when Ida was six years old she went to live with her grandmother Margaret, whose home was where Haviland Hubbs now lives. When Ida Sager and William John Hubbs were married in 1911, her parents

Now, the home of Haviland Hubbs. Bessie Sager with chickens.

moved up the road to live with grandmother, Margaret, but she lived only a short time. Ida left the Sager home by the bay and moved with her husband to the Gore, the home now owned by her son Malcolm Hubbs.

Ida Sager and William John Hubbs had six children. Their eldest, Alice Pearl married Rev. Robert Wragg, William Haviland grew up on the Gore and left to take over the grandfather Sager's farm and his aunt, Bessie Sager remained there with him until her death. Ernest Elton Hubbs, died young, Florence May Hubbs married Gordon Waterhouse and lives on Concession 2 of Ameliasburgh, Helen Hubbs (1) married Harvey Brown also of Concession 2 and after his death (2) Rev. Robert Wragg. Malcolm Linford, who remained on the farm on the Gore married Evelyn Mikel from the North shore of Consecon Lake. From these unions there are several grandchildren and great grand children but no descendant bears the name of 'Sager'.

The Soble Family

By William Soble

Richard Soble was born in Germany and came to Canada at age seven months with his parents in 1887. They settled in Monteagle Township, Hastings County, in a German settlement east of Maynooth. In 1914 Richard married Maria Smith, born 1893 at Lake St. Peter. He took up the trade of blacksmith and continued at his occupation all his life. To Richard and Maria were born nine children, the first seven in Monteagle Township and the last two when they moved to Coe Hill. They had seven sons— William, Allan, Russell, Lloyd, Kenneth, Carl and George, and two daughters— Hazel (Mrs. Howard Gunter) and Janet (Mrs. Del Latchford).

In 1932 the Sobles moved to the village of Roblin's Mills in Ameliasburgh Township. They rented the large stone Roblin home for a time, then purchased the Marsden House where Richard and Maria lived until their deaths, both in 1959 within three months of each other. Richard bought the blacksmith shop at the west end of the village (originally the Coleman smithy) and pursued his trade there until the shop had to be torn down to widen the road. Then he moved his Smithy down behind the Marsden house. This large old hotel was an ideal home for his big family. One son, Russell, lost his life in the Second World War. Some of Soble's blacksmith tools are in the Ameliasburgh Museum.

The only member of the Soble family now living in Ameliasburgh Township is William who married Carol Burr, daughter of Lorne and May Squire Burr. They have three children— Elsie, Wayne and Dale; both boys are Baptist ministers. William is a carpenter, recently retired, and living on County Road 23 south of Rednersville.

The Spencer Family

The Spencers came to America from Great Britain, a John Spencer settling in Rhode Island. At the time of the Revolutionary War a grandson, Benjamin Spencer was living in Durham County, Vermont, possessed of 300 acres, dwelling house and barns, 42 head of cattle, 12 horses and 60 sheep. Benjamin and his wife, Mercy Potter Sweet, had five boys and two girls. In 1777 Benjamin and one of his sons joined the British army under General Burgoyne. Later that year Benjamin died on his way from Ticonderoga to Montreal. In 1778 his land was confiscated and sold by the rebels, and all of his livestock seized and sold, leaving Mrs. Spencer only two cows. A son, Augustus, U.E. received land in Marysburgh and Sophiasburgh. In 1797 he was granted 1200 acres as a magistrate (J.P.), including a former grant of 200 acres.

Augustus Spencer married Sarah Conger first and Mary Jane Miller of Athol as his second wife. A son, James Potter Spencer, lived at Salmon Point in Athol. He married Catherine Rankin. Their son, John Augustus Spencer (1832-1920), married Phoebe Minaker. John and Phoebe moved to the Centre neighbourhood of Ameliasburgh Township in 1870 and settled on the rear of lots 73, 74 and 75 of the 1st concession. They had three children— Findley, Elwood and Dora who died at age 3. This property had been purchased from Lewis Redner in 1869 by Phoebe's brother, Sanford Minaker. A sister, Sarah, married James Redner and lived nearby.

There were only about ten acres of the farm cleared in 1870. The woods were maple, beach and pine. When cleared there were enough pine roots to build all John's half of the line fence surrounding the 83 acres. Their house was a small frame building with low ceilings. The present house was built by Elwood, partly on the foundation of the old house, which was torn down. Elwood married Sophia Burr, daughter of W.K. Burr. To this union was born Dora, Freeman and Donald. In 1917 a purebred Holstein calf was purchased which was the beginning of the purebred herd registered under the farm name of 'Elm Knoll'. In 1938 the William Redner farm was purchased, adding 122 acres. Donald married Hazel Horton; they have two children, Lloyd and Donna. Lloyd and his wife Myrna Dickens and their children now live in the Elwoood Spencer home while Donald and Hazel reside in the house across the road on the former Redner Farm.

The Sprung, then Anderson— Werkhoven Farm

David and Richard Sprung, brothers, moved to the farms owned by Henry Murney of Kingston in 1822. Records show that it was 1832 when they received the title to the place for some 200 Pounds and ten shillings. The Sprungs always farmed together.

James R. Anderson bought 200 acres from David and Richard Sprung and there now were two houses on the property. Later he purchased part of the Potter farm, where his eldest son Earle, who had married Nellie Werden and their two children, Douglas and Lillian lived.

James' Anderson's son Ben married Adeline Sprague and they lived in one of the two houses on the farm. They had no family.

John; the youngest and his sister Lily lived with their parents on the home farm. Earle Anderson died very young and the property was sold to his brother John, who rented the house until the time it was sold to the Burkholders.

In 1923 the *Farmers' Advocate* published an article on the Anderson Farm, describing how they cropped the land, gave special mention of the dairy herd and the careful handling of milk and the good condition and cleanliness of the buildings.

This picture was taken when the Andersons lived in the house. Now the home of Klaas Werkhoven.

When John retired from the farm, he built a new retirement home for himself and his sister Lily, south of the cheese factory.

The farm, known as Spring Valley Farm on the third concession east of Highway 14, now belongs to Klaas Werkhoven and his son Harold. Klaas had the misfortune to lose the barn by fire. The barn on the adjoining farm where his son Harold lives was prepared to house the dairy herd. The Werkhovens carry on a mixed farming operation with dairying as the mainstay.

The Townsend Family

By Hubert Townsend

The first record we have of the Townsends is of Samuel Townsend of Rumny Marsh in England who was born in 1637 and died in 1704. His son Jonathan came to Lynn, Massachusetts where he married Elizabeth Walton and resided there until his death in 1718. His son Rev. Jonathan Townsend was born in 1697 and received his later education at Harvard. He married Mary Sugar and they had seven children. He preached at Lynn, Nantucket and Needham, and died there in 1762. One of his sons was Samuel who married Ruth Tolman; they resided at Tyrinham, Mass. They had eight children, one of which was Jonathan, their third child and second son.

Johnathan married Lois Scripture and they had nine children, the eighth one named Asahel. Lois Townsend died in 1809; Jonathan them married Elizabeth Foster and they had four children. Asahel Townsend, born in Berkshire, Mass., drove mules along the Hudson River towing the barges when in his teens. He later came to Canada. In 1838 he and Nancy Palmer were married at Hillier. In 1846 he purchased from John Vancourt 50 acres of Lot 102 on the 3rd concession of Ameliasburgh for the sum of 100 Pounds. In 1852 he moved to Lot No. 28 on the 2nd Con. of Hillier which lies along the south shore of Pleasant Bay. This property he purchased from the Clergy Reserve of Upper Canada at the time of George IV for 57 Pounds, 9 shillings and two pence. Asahel later sold it and purchased Lot 83 on the 5th Con. of Hillier, east of Melville, where he resided until his death in 1888. Asahel and Nancy had four children, three girls born in Ameliasburgh and one son Jonathan born in Hillier.

In Sept. of 1888 Jonathan married Frances Nethery of Hillier whose family were of Irish descent. They resided on Lot 83 in Hillier until 1899 when they sold it and purchased Lot 75 on the 2nd Con. Ameliasburgh which is the present home of Edith and Alfred Cairns. They operated a mixed farm, also growing barley and made maple syrup. They had two children, Frank and Marguerite. Frank married Edith Allison and Marguerite married Floyd Huff. Frank and Edith when married purchased from Wes Coulter Lot 79 on the 2nd Con. Ameliasburgh and resided there until 1942, raising four children Asahel, Ruth, Clifford and Hubert.

In 1942 upon the marriage of Hubert and Marion Wallbridge, the Townsends sold their farm on lot 79 to Clarence and Jean Vanclief and bought the Morton Weese farm on Lot 87 and 88 1st Con. (Gore Road) where there were two houses to accommodate the two families. Frank died in 1959 and Edith in 1974. Hubert and Marion still reside on this farm with their son Roger, who married Faye Brooks, occupying the second home and farming with his father.

The Trounce Family

By Marjorie Trounce

In July 1984 we will have lived on the former Everett Brickman farm on the Gore Road, Ameliasburgh township, for 37 years. This is the longest time either Jerry or I have lived in one place in our lives.

Gerald Trounce was born in London, England, getting most of his schooling in a large boarding school there. He came to Canada in April, 1922, with a group of young people, to the Marchmont Home in Belleville. The plan was to place these young people on farms where they could help with the work. They were supposed to be provided with further education, but very few seemed to have the opportunity for that. Mrs. Orser and her son Ernie took Gerald to their home on the second concession of Ameliasburgh where he worked on their farm. He stayed with them for two and a half years.

I, Marjorie Tivy, was born on a farm six miles north of Coe Hill in Hastings County. My parents were Charles and Katherine Tivy, and I had three brothers older than myself. My mother's maiden name was Leveridge. When I was two months old, our father was kicked by a horse and fatally injured. With her brother's help, Mother carried on with the farm for five years, working very hard. She then sold the farm and tried to make a living running a local store and post office in Northern Ontario. This was not satisfactory, so she moved to a farm near Carrying Place where she and James Wilson were married. After one year on this farm, they bought the Leveridge homestead

Marjorie and Gerald Trounce

north of Coe Hill, and lived there until 1924. Then they rented the Stoneburgh farm on the 2nd Concession of Ameliasburgh. That was when I met Gerald Trounce, as we were across the road from the Orser farm.

After Jerry left Orser's he used our home for several years as a base, in between the places he worked— other farms, twice out west on harvest excursions, lumber camps, etc. In 1934 Jerry and I were married and lived in Trenton where he worked at the Benedict-Proctor Silverplate factory. In 1937 our son Richard was born, and in 1939 Jerry joined the army, soon after World War II started.

Jerry developed bronchitis so was not sent overseas. He was in the army all through the war, helping to train recruits at first. When the Officers' Training Centre began in Brockville in 1941, Jerry went there and was one of the instructors until the war ended. Most of the time during the war, Dick and I lived with my parents on a farm just west of Cobourg. When the war was over we rented a house in Cobourg. Jerry became a brakeman for the C.N. Railway. Our daughter Beverly was born in 1943.

Later my mother's health began to fail, so in 1947 we looked for a farm with a double house. We found the ideal house on the Brickman farm on the Gore Road. James Wilson worked the farm for several years before he retired from farming. It was a satisfactory way of life for both our families. Our daughter, Patricia, was born here in 1951. Our children enjoyed growing up in this neighbourhood and we all feel fortunate to have made our home here.

The Vanclief Family

By Jean Vanclief

In 1842 John Vanclief was born in South Marysburgh Township. He and his wife, Irene Smith of Hillier, moved to Coe Hill where they purchased a farm. To them were born four sons and a daughter. One of the sons, Nelson, born 1891, married Minerva Vader, daughter of Garret Vader & Eliza Boomhour in 1912. They purchased a 200-acre farm north of Coe Hill with five cows and a team of horses. They began farming, while Nelson continued to make cheese at a factory about two miles from the farm. He drove his faithful horse, Maude, to the factory each morning, turned her around and headed her home. Minerva watched for her return and later in the day drove her back to the factory to assist.

In 1921 the Vancliefs sold this farm and purchased 100 acres on the second concession of Ameliasburgh from Miss Ethel Glenn. On March 1st they and their three children, Clarence, Ross and Ethel (now Mrs. Floyd Carter) moved from Coe Hill. Their possessions were put in two train cars and brought to a siding at Gardenville. They arrived after dark and Clarence, then 7 years old, drove the team of horses on the wagon while his father walked behind with the cattle to their new home. Sidney Hennessy and his son Bruce, one of their new neighbours, met them at Gardenville and assisted with the cattle.

Two years later their home burned, but the Vancliefs rebuilt immediately on one end of the foundation. A fourth child, Keitha (Mrs. Edwin Carnrike) was born. In 1936 Nelson began work as a bridgemaster on the Bay Bridge at Rossmore. He was on duty 12 hours a day, seven days a week, and started at 25¢ per hour.

Clarence married Jean Blackburn in 1936 and an addition was put on the remaining foundation for them. Clarence stayed on the home farm until 1940, then started farming for himself on a small rented farm on the 2nd which was owned by Fletcher Hawley. He supplemented his income by working two winters as a carpenter building Mountain View Airport, working 10 hours a day at 40¢ per hour. In 1943 he and Jean bought the Frank Townsend farm. Their house burned in 1951 and was rebuilt the same year. They purchased the adjacent farm from Nelson Parliament.

Aerial picture of Vanclief farm in strawberry time.

Clarence and Jean have two sons. Allan graduated as a funeral director and now operates his own business in Belleville. Lyle graduated from the University of Guelph and returned to farm with his father. He married Sharon Hall and they have two children. In 1968 Clarence and Jean built a home on a farm purchased from Roy Wannamaker one mile east of Rednersville. Lyle and Sharon live on the home farm on the 2nd. The business was incorporated and became known as Willowlee Farms. The neighbouring Redner farm was purchased in 1981 to make a total acreage of 260 acres at the home location.

The farming business in 1984 consists of 1500 acres of crop. The livestock portion of the operation has 160 sows in a farrow-to-finish enterprise that markets 2800 hogs per year, and a small beef feedlot finishing 75 to 100 cattle per year. The cropping program includes strawberries which are sold as pick-your-own, fresh market, and processed on the farm, potatoes, peas, sweet corn, green beans, tomatoes, cauliflower, broccoli, zucchini, pumpkin, squash, grain corn, wheat, barley and soybeans. Willowlee Farms is a very busy place with four full-time employees, many part-time workers and up to 300 daily seasonal helpers.

The Walt Family

Some time in the early 1700's, Oswald Walt came to the colonies aboard the S.S. Britania. He is supposed to have been a Deutch Hugenot who settled in Pennsylvania where many persecuted groups found refuge.

His son Augustine Henry Walt was born on Aug. 15, 1754 in Northampton County, Pennsylvania. Augustine was to become the father of a large family of ten boys and two girls. The youngest, Hiram (1806) was born in Leeds county after they immigrated to Upper Canada. In 1811, for the yearly sum of 1 Pound, 12s., 6d. Augustine leased a clergy Reserve portion— Lot 101, Con. 4, Ameliasburgh. That Land is now proudly owned by Adelbert Bush and sons, David and John of the seventh generation.

Amos Walt, son of Augustine, married Phoebe Wannamaker, daughter of a Loyalist, Sgt. Peter Wanamaker and so won the right to Lots 107 and 108, Con. 2, Ameliasburgh where the original stone smokehouse still stands.

David Walt, son of Amos and Phoebe, began married life in Cramahe township, Northumberland County. Bears destroyed his few animals, so with his few articles of furniture on a flat rack, he came to Lot 100, Con. 4, Ameliasburgh next to the lots of his grandfather Augustine, now in the possession of his uncle, also named David. For a time he and his wife, Caroline Butler, occupied a tiny log cabin already on the lot; but as he was to become the father of 12 children, a larger house was necessary. It is now occupied by John W. Walt, great grandson of the original owner. David Walt had a natural inclination for treating animals, and as Doc. Walt served as local horse doctor until well over 80 years of age. He is also remembered as being a Methodist of the first trustee board of Consecon Wesleyan Methodist Church, built in 1829.

David Walt's sons, Leslie, John and Robert, took up farms along North Lakeside. Leslie's home is now occupied by his grandson, Howard Elliot Walt, son of Eldon. John, who received the adjoining farm left it to his son, Earle, father of John W. Walt. The original homestead was to become the property of Robert who had one daughter, Helen Roberta. It is now operated by John Walt, great grandson of the original owner with his two sons, Bruce and Brian.

One daughter, Fanny, did not move far from home when she married David Bush, both of Augustine's lineage. She became the mother of Biard and thus grandmother of Adelbert.

Among the Walt stones in Consecon cemetery is the name of Reuben Walt, another son, who died of consumption at the age of 30. He was part of the Wolseley Expedition which at the time of the North-West Rebellion walked the whole distance from Upper Canada to Winnipeg and arrived just as the rebellion was quelled.

It is to be noted that in locating their homes on Con. 4, Ameliasburgh it was the aim of the homesteaders to be near Consecon Lake. They were actually on the rear end of their farms. The road was not surveyed and originally followed a crooked deer path leading to a salt spring on the Walt homestead.

My 'Wanamaker' Family

By C. Loral R. Wanamaker U.E., S.A.R.

Their home town was Leeheim, Darmstadt, Germany. They were a poor Protestant family who, with other thousands, were being driven out of their homes by Louis XIV's army under his Marshal Louvois, who had orders to lay the land a waste. These people fled down the Rhine river valley to the city of Rotterdam on the sea. Here they found ships provided for them by our good Queen Ann of England and were taken to a temporary home in tents on the Common near London where they found food and clothing, in 1708. A Rev. Kocheral had been given permission to gather together a shipload of these poor refugees and transport them to the British Colonies of America. Here he found work for the Wanamaker's and others in New Jersey and they survived and multiplied and were baptised in the Dutch Reformed Church N.J. and the Rampo Lutheran Church of New Jersey, and they continued to live here along with other families of our local names of Brickmans, Redners and Crouters when the American Revolution came upon them in 1776. Here Harmanus Wanamaker b. 1721 in the Rampo N.J. married one Susannah and had issue of 7 children of whom John was killed in the Revolution, three served the Colours— Sgt. Peter W., Pte. Henrick and Corp. Jacob W. along with Andrew, Thomas & Harmanius Wanamaker who were too young to serve the Colours. The six brothers all came in at once and asked for their free Land in 1791 at Kingston by petition which they received and disposed of in different ways. Sgt. Peter W. b. 1/10/1753 of N.J. sett. Lot 79 con. 1, Ameliasburgh married Mary Jones who had issue of 2 sons and 3 daughters. Abagail b. 1790-1836, married Zachariah Herrington 1782-1843 whose family takes in the Thomas Mikel family of Consecon Lake with the Herrington family of Rossmore and the Jack Sills family of Rednersville Rd. William b. 1792, married Ann Dempsey and had issue William H. and Thomas and he married again and had issue of 4: Mathew, Manley, Reuben and Lucy Ann. William H. married twice and Thomas married Sarah Covert and their grandson is no other than Roy Wanamaker of the Rednersville Rd. who is now 92 years and married Gladys Dempsey in 1913 and have issue Eva, Marion and Lyle.

Andrew Wanamaker b. 1766, married Mary Babcock (daughter of John Babcock, U.E., they lived on lot 78, Con. 1, and both were deceased by 1851 they had 11 children— Catherine, John 1796, Peter B. b. 1799. James B. b.

1800, Phoebe, 1803-1872, Margaret 1805-1882, Clara 1807, Anna 1814-1882, Clarinda 1824-1898. Two girls' names unknown. Peter B. married Catherine Schollar and had six children. Jacob married Mary Taft, Sarah and Jane married Bovay Bros. William and John Bovay, Phoebe married Ben Smith and John H. married Margaret McQuoid and they had two sons Grant and Ralph, Grant married Letta VanCott and they had two sons, C. Loral and Glencoe.

James B. Wanamaker married Eliza Ann Moon and their family consisted of four sons and six daughters. One son James Andrew lived at The Carrying Place and Andrew lived in the Trenton area.

Harmanus Wanamaker 1769-1858 and wife Dorothy Steward on lot 78, Con. 1, had seven children— Susan, Dorothy, Jacob, Peter, Harmon, Catherine and John. Susan married John Fox and the Rose family of Rednersville and Urquart family of Carrying Place are descendants. Jacob married Mary Wanamaker (daughter of Henry P. Wanamaker of the Gore most of their descendants live in Hastings County. Peter Wanamaker married and went to Bruce County. Harmanus' first wife was Elizabeth Tice they had two sons Henry and Jacob. Catherine married Henry Way (son of John. B.) they had 10 children who married into the Weese, Brickman, and Tompkins families of Rednersville. Harmanus and Dorothy are buried in Albury cemetery.

Andrew Pulis Wannamaker

Wannamakers have lived in Ameliasburgh Township continuously since 1797. They were of good Loyalist stock, and closely related to Andrew Pulvis Wannamaker who was born in 1784 and came to live in Ameliasburgh in 1810, along with his wife, Maria Litchult, and their two children, John L. born 1808, and Esther born in 1805. His father, Peter, born 1743, had taken an active part in the American Revolutionary War as a rebel, and the feeling had rubbed off on Andrew P. The Wannamakers, Andrew P. and his wife Maria, had two more children after coming to Ameliasburgh— Levi, born 1815, and Isaac born 1820. About 1816 they purchased 200 acres at Massassauga where Fenwood Gardens is now located and farmed there with Isaac until 1868. Maria died in 1862 and in 1868 Andrew P. at 84 years of age, with feelings still in favour of the American Revolution, returned to the United States, this time with his son Isaac who had married Mary Ann Way of Mt. View and their four children. They all lived in Missouri the remainder of their lives and are buried there.

John L. married Deborah Harns about 1830 and they pioneered on Lot 82 in the Fourth Concession of Ameliasburgh on land taken up from the crown in 1817. They had five children, Christopher the eldest 1831, married Elizabeth Howe. Then three daughters who married William Valleau, David Gibson and William Smith Wood, all names still familiar in this area. The youngest, Andrew, was born in 1842 and died in 1861. He was riding in a buggy at Massassaga Point, along with two of his cousins when someone threw a stone at the buggy striking Andrew in the head. He died less than a week later after only partially regaining consciousness. John L. died on Lot 82 of a kidney ailment at 39 years of age. He believed in baptism by immersion. Realizing he had only a short time to live and that he had not received his sacrament, neighbours hollowed out a large pine log so that the ceremony could be performed. The water was warmed by using heated stones.

John L.'s sons Christopher and Elizabeth Howe had four children, Edgerton born 1855, married Melinda Mitchelson, John born 1860 did not marry, Alma born 1866 married Henry Benson, Walter born 1870 married Zella Trumpour. Christopher moved from Lot 82 in 1857 to Lot 87 on the same road where he bought 300 acres in one block, including 200 acres in Lot 88. Edgerton farmed the east half of Lot 88, following his marriage in 1882 and John farmed the west half. Walter later took over the 100 acres in Lot 87 and Christopher bought 100 acres in Lot 85 which is the only part of the mentioned land remaining in the Wannamaker name.

Edgerton's son Claude, married Margaret Fox in 1909 and purchased the west half of Lot 88. They had four children- Campbell, Douglas, John and Ruth.

Campbell married Irene Bulpit and their only child Marilyn died accidentally. Douglas married (1) Lila Haggerty and (2) Hazel Cannon. Their daughter Elaine lives in Toronto. John married Daisy Vet and they have four children- Catherine in Collingwood, Eleanor, in Toronto, Brenda in Haliburton, and Christopher in Kingston. Ruth married Charles Margetson and their children are Gail, who lives in Kingston, and Brian, in Toronto.

Andrew P. Wannamaker must have had an exciting life. He lived his first 26 years near the New York/New Jersey border then 58 years in Ameliasburgh and the last 13 years in a very fertile area of north central Missouri.

The Waterhouse Family

Thomas Waterhouse came from Londonderry, Ireland to Canada during the potato famine in the 1840s. He settled at Moneymore, east of Roblin in Hungerford Township. His son, Henry Kirkpatrick Waterhouse (1846-1911) was twice married, first to Eliza Jane Charlesworth and later to Catherine McLaren. They owned a store at Moneymore and Henry was a master carpenter. He built the L.O.L. 836 lodge hall there. His son, John McIlwayne Waterhouse (1871-1961) married Mary Letitia Blanche Wilson (1878-1965). It was this family that came to make Ameliasburgh their home.

John and Mary Waterhouse, along with their children, Gordon, Katherine and Margaret, moved from Thurlow to the Third Concession of Ameliasburgh in 1925. A neighbour, who helped move the family possessions

The Waterhouse Home

was surprised to find upon arrival that his seat for the journey had been a cheese box containing homemade grape wine.

In 1934, the Waterhouse family bought Lot 84, Second Concession, in the Victoria neighbourhood, and have lived there now for 50 years. During the first year they tore down a barn and with the material from it, they remodelled their present barn. The large brick home was one of the huge DeLong houses. Will DeLong married Arvilla Roblin and her father promised to furnish her new home, but when he saw the huge place, he refused to keep his promise. Years later, part of it was destroyed by fire. The part that was rebuilt was still larger than those constructed today. During the remodelling of the house, Gordon and his wife Florence (Hubbs) have found charred, hand-hewn beams and square cut nails. It was in this large house that Mr. and Mrs. Waterhouse Sr. and son Gordon, his wife Florence and family resided until the death of Gordon's parents.

Gordon and Florence Waterhouse are the parents of Raymond of Ameliasburgh's Second Concession, who married Joyce White and they have two children, Lisa and Scott. Jean is married, has two sons, resides in Illinois, while their youngest daughter Ida resides in California.

The Way Family

Anna (Mrs. Lawson) Way lives on a small farm consisting of 14½ acres on the east half of Lot 88, concession 1, Ameliasburgh township. This property was purchased from Moses Shears in the year 1895 by Lawson's father, William E. Way. Part of the acreage comprises the east half of Salt Island. This island was so named because of the existence of a salt well there. This salt was probably of considerable importance to the Indians in the early days, and tradition has it that Champlain stopped at Salt Island on his expedition through this area with the Huron Indians in 1615. The house was built in 1860, of timber. Although many improvements have been made, the original house still remains. A small orchard was planted in 1886. At one time a grist mill operated on this farm. An old stone wall remained until a few years ago.

William E. Way was born in 1864, died in 1945. He married Mary Russell

Lawson and Anna Way

(1864-1941), and operated a threshing outfit purchased in 1886. To William and Mary were born two children, Lawson and Florence (Mrs. Ed Pine). Lawson married Anna Hogan, and they had one son, John. Lawson was a great, great grandson of John B. Way who came to Ameliasburgh in 1815 and settled on the east half of Lot 72 on the lower third concession, and built the first flour mill on the pond under the hill called Way's Mill, at what later became the village of Roblin's Mills. John B. Way and his wife are buried in the small Way family cemetery on the old Way farm.

Since Lawson's death in July 1982, Anna lives alone in the old Way home. Their son John married Shirley Belch and they reside in Ottawa with their children, Christopher and Lisa.

The Weese Family

The Weese family came to America from the Palatinate region of Europe. At the time of the American Revolution they were living in Herkimer County, New York. John Weese (1742-1797) married Arrientlje Hogel in 1761 and they had five children. Arrientlje died and Weese married her sister Juliana Hogel Pellum (widow). It was the second wife who came to Canada with the family. John Weese supported the Royal cause; he was in the 1777 campaign with General Burgoyne. His oldest son, John Jr., though just a boy, also served two years in the Royal Regiment of New York. They were disbanded in 1784 and each drew 100 acres of land on Oct. 6, 1784 as discharged privates of the Royal Regiment of New York. Each was allotted ½ of Lot 6, Con. 2 Third Town (Fredericksburgh). They lived on this land, cleared and improved it to get their deed to it. As his family land, Weese was also given 300 acres in Lot 89, 1st con. of Seventh Town, so, in 1787 the family moved from Fredericksburgh to Seventh Town. A John Hough had been granted the 200 acres in Lot 88, Con. 1, lying just east of Weese's 300 acres. The Weeses traded their 200 acres in Fredericksburgh for this 200 acres of Hough's in 7th Town. This gave them 500 acres on the shores of the Bay of Quinte. They were the first permanent settlers in Seventh Town.

Three of John Weese's children lived out their lives in 7th Town— Catherine, Henry and Francis. Catherine married David Sager; Henry m. Phoebe Babcock, and Francis married her sister Margaret, both daughters of Ensign John Babcock, U.E. When John Weese died in 1797, he left son Henry the 198 acres of Lot 89, and his beloved granddaughter, Elizabeth Sager, daughter of Catherine and David Sager, the 200 acres of Lot 88. Henry Weese had 11 children, and Francis nine. Their children and grandchildren intermarried closely with the other pioneer families in the area and cousins married cousins. Henry and Phoebe's son, George Angel Weese, married Phoebe Ann Weese, granddaughter of Francis and Margaret. Their son William Randall Weese married Nancy Jane Brickman, issue: Earl who married Bessie Onderdonk, Viola who married Harry Allison, and Elton who died young. Earl and Bessie had two sons— Allan who married Eleanor

Bonter, and Lyle who married Verna Dermot. Allan's two sons, Robert and Charles, and Lyle's children, Mildred Ann and William, are the seventh generation of Weeses on Lot 89. In 1987 the Weeses will have been there for 200 years.

William Francis Weese, another son of Henry's, married his first cousin, Mary Jane, daughter of Francis. Their son Wesley Weese married Harriett Bryant; two of their children were Kenneth and Howard. Many other descendants of John Weese U.E. live in Ameliasburgh Township today.

The Westfalls of Carrying Place
By Andrew Harris

Charles Manson Westfall

No story of Ameliasburgh Township and especially the hamlet of The Carrying Place would be complete without an account of the contribution made by the late C.M. Westfall, longtime postmaster and general store keeper.

Charles Manson Westfall was born in Sidney Township in 1872. After his schooling, he and his wife Alfretta Harris (eldest daughter of Mr. and Mrs. Amos Harris) lived and worked in Rochester, N.Y. They returned to Canada and the Carrying Place where their son, Vernon, was born in 1903. Vernon was born in a little log house owned by the McCruddan family. At this time his grandparents, Mr. and Mrs. Amos Harris, were living there. This house was situated in Murray Township west of the C.N.R. tracks near the Murray Canal.

Shortly after Mr. Westfall returned to Canada, he was appointed Postmaster for Murray, Ontario. The original post office for the Carrying Place had been in Murray township across the highway (now Hwy. 33) from the cairn which marks the site of the famous Gunshot Treaty. As the fire had destroyed this first post office, the Boyce family had moved it to the Middle House in Ameliasburgh township. One of the first acts Mr. Westfall did as the new postmaster was to have the office name changed to the Carrying Place Post Office. The new post office was located where the village store stands.

At first Mr. Westfall operated the post office and did some farming on a tract of land which his father-in-law had given the Westfalls as a wedding gift. This particular land now is known as the Vernon Westfall Memorial Park and Sports Complex.

In a few years, Mr. Westfall added a grocery store to the Post Office. This proved to be a very successful venture. The Westfall store handled groceries, soft drinks, candies, tobacco, patent medicines, paints, kerosene, gasoline, some hardware and other sundry merchandise. Here was one of the few places in the early days of motoring where one could buy gasoline and oil. The writer can remember vividly Mr. Westfall measuring gasoline into a gallon measure from a large tank (about 500 gal.) and pouring it into the Model T Ford tank, one gallon at a time. The fuel was kept in a shed in the Westfall's back yard. About 1920 a pump to dispense gasoline at the front of the store was installed.

C.M., as he was affectionately known by his friends, was a kind, gentle and generous man. During the great depression in the 1930's he allowed many unfortunate families to buy groceries on credit. At one time he had several thousands of dollars on the books. It is interesting to note that when times improved, about 1937, most of these debts were repaid.

As Westfall's health deteriorated in the late 30's his son Vernon became Assistant Postmaster and he assumed most of the duties associated with the business. In addition to this, a flour and feed business was added and Vernon did general trucking of farm produce and livestock for local farmers. In the late 30's and early 40's Vernon also ploughed many of the roads in the winter months for Ameliasburg township.

An interesting anecdote is told about Vernon when he was a young lad of about seven or eight years. He was quite fond of his uncle, George S. Harris, and often visited the Harris farm on the second concession of Ameliasburgh. He sometimes stayed with his uncle and grandparents for a night or so and was allowed to sleep with his Uncle George. In 1910 George Harris married Luella Brown and one of their first visitors after the honeymoon was nephew Vernon. When it came time for bed, probably about 9 o'clock, Vernon was told he would have to sleep by himself as Uncle George now shared his bed with Aunt Luella. Without hesitation he gathered his suitcase and took off for home. Later, when it was discovered that he had disappeared, his Uncle George harnessed a horse and set out to overtake him. Although Vernon was a small boy and short of stature, he arrived home before the horse and buggy got there.

Charles Westfall died in 1950 and his wife Alfretta in 1956. They are buried in the Carrying Place cemetery. Vernon Westfall married Elsie Fitchet in 1956. Elsie had been a teacher and later principal of the Carrying Place school.

In the early 1960's, Vernon enlarged the store and made it into a modern supermarket. Fresh fruit and vegetables were added plus a meat counter and a complete line of frozen foods. Gone were the old egg crates on which many a local citizen had passed the evening discussing the weather and local news. The new supermarket was a huge success and three or four clerks were added to serve the many customers.

Vernon died in 1970 and soon after, the new Carrying Place post office was opened. Mr. Westfall continued to operate the store for a year or so when it was sold to James Little of Trenton. It is now owned and operated by Mr. and Mrs. Elvin Higgins and is known as the Village Store.

As a memorial to her husband Vernon, Mrs. Westfall donated land to the Ameliasburgh Township to establish the Westfall Memorial Park and Sports Complex. The township paid a nominal amount of $1.00 to Mrs. Westfall to make the land belong to the Township legally. This was part of the same land that had been originally given to the Westfalls by Vernon's grandfather, Amos Harris. There could have been no more fitting memorial to Vernon and his father as they were both great boosters of local sports. Vernon had been active as a player for local teams and for many years had furnished transportation for the teams going to out-of-town games.

One can see from this account that the Westfall family provided a great service to the community of Carrying Place for 50 or more years.

The Williamson Family

John Burley Williamson (1827-1906) came to Canada from Adam Centre, N.Y. near Watertown and made his home with Charles Dempsey and his wife Sarah (McMurter). They had a son Fred and their home was the one now owned by Mr. and Mrs. Jacob Vandervelde on the Bayshore.

Lighthouse on Bay of Quinte, built in 1911 on the Scea Farm.

The Williamson Home: 1885. In rocking chair and back right— Mr. and Mrs. John Burley Williamson; standing left back: Mr. & Mrs. George Williamson; Lady seated in middle: Fercy Crouter's Grandmother; Children— Ida and Roy Williamson

At the year's end Dempsey gave John a horse and saddle and he left for the ninth concession of Murray where he took up Crown land.

In 1852 John and Sophia Peck (1831-1906) were married and their son George was born in 1853. By 1867 they were able to buy a farm of 130 acres, the west half of lot 96 on the first concession, the original Godlove Mikel land, from his grandson James R. Mikel for $3000.

On June 24, 1873 George (1853-1939) married Mary Catherine Weese (1854-1924) and the whole family lived in the old house behind the barn overlooking the bay. Father and son, John and George made an agreement to work the farm on shares and they built a new brick house into which they moved at the end of the year 1875.

In the year 1877 George Williamson ploughed on Dec. 28th and the steamer Utica ran from Trenton to Picton the same day.

To George and Mary Williamson was born a son Roy (1879) and a daughter Ida in 1883. That year they began to grow hops and continued in the business until 1895. They hired 20 or more pickers per day to harvest the crop.

In the years between 1895-1900 they built their large barn.

Roy Williamson (1879-1960) and Lottie May Adams (1879-1970) were married in 1901 and their son Carl Adams was born in 1902. Another son John Douglas was born in 1906 and during that year both great grandparents John and Sophia passed away. Both funerals were held in Albury church which was built in 1898.

Roy Williamson capsized in a sailboat on the bay on March 28, 1903 but luckly survived. He and his father received domestic fishing licences in 1909 for $2. The following winter he helped build the first lighthouse on the bay which was on the Scea property next to the Williamsons. The first light in the lighthouse was march 19, 1911 and Mr. Allison lit the light for many years. Buoys with lights were installed in the 1940's and ten years later the lighthouse was sold to Mrs. Hanley of Toronto and moved to the Weese property just west of the Will Allison farm.

In 1913, Ida, Roy's sister, married George Young of Trenton. It was April 1917 when George Williamson bought his first car, a Ford and on April 28, 1917 their daughter Ruth was born.

In 1921 Roy Williamson sold 1000 baskets of plums. He drew milk to Quinte cheese factory and was President of Roblin's Mills Fair, and a director for several years.

In 1924 Carl married Hattie Russell (1900-1984) and their two children were Mary and Ronald. That year, the grandmother Mary passed away. In 1926, Douglas married Eva Hickerson (1909-1971) and they left for Rochester. They returned to Consecon. In 1972 Douglas married Addie McMaster Phillips.

Hydro came in 1930. Roy cut all the holes in the metallic ceiling at Albury church for hydro to be installed there. The same year Bonter's sidewalk, as the cement road along the bay was known, was built. When the cement was laid the Williamson's days of statute labour, drawing gravel from the Alyea pit out the Bryant Sideroad, ended.

1939 was the year Ruth was married to Beuford Peck, and the year her grandfather George passed away. Ruth and Beuford had four children, Eric, Neil, Linda and Douglas. Her brother Carl passed away in 1949, her father in 1960 and mother in 1970. Douglas of Consecon and Ruth sold the brick home to Kenneth and Barbara McAdam of Port Credit in 1971.

The McAdam Years in the Williamson Homestead

Ken and Barbara McAdam formerly of Montreal and latterly of Port Credit bought the property in 1971 as a retirement home. The house had been unoccupied for several years and renovations were begun with the help of their son and daughter-in-law.

Old plaster went out, insulation and new wall-board went on in every room. The beams from the barn were used in the cathedral ceiling of the livingroom, formerly the woodshed, and a garage was added and covered with the barn boards, in keeping with the old house. The pine floor boards were stripped and new floors laid in the dining room and kitchen. The bathroom was fitted with pedestal basin and long footed tub. The transformation with wall paper and paint in every room was completed in 1983. The McAdams have made it a most comfortable home.

Outdoor the swing built by Roy Williamson hangs from the horse chestnut tree and is used by the neighbourhood children.

Locustwood Farm

Century Farm of the Abraham Wood Family

'Locustwood' is appropriately named for its tall locusts that surround the stone farm house of the Wood family on lot 80 on Con. 4, Ameliasburgh Township, with a Crown patent dated May 23, 1817. Abram Wood Sr. (1816-1896) registered 122 acres in 1857. He had come from Scotland and brought with him a gold medal he had won in a ploughing competition. His wife was Margaret Rutherford (1823-1898). They had five children:

Thomas (1853-1925) married Isobel Morton (1852-1920)
George (1855-1925) married Ellen M. Gibson (1860-1931)
Marybelle (1856-1942) married 1. Daniel Black 2. David Lauder
Margaret (1859-1937) married Arthur Sprung (1859-1949)
Abraham J. (1862-1922) married Bertha Darling (1872-1916)

In 1896 the farm was given to Abram Wood Jr. who married Bertha Darling and again the land was passed on to son, Leonard, in 1918. Leonard married Eva VanCott in 1919. More land was acquired to the west by Leonard in 1932, from William Cave.

On the home farm was a log house (part of the present day granary). The stone house was built in 1872 by the Wood family and a carpenter named Rutherford. Stone came from the farm, except for the cornerstones which were brought from Kingston by boat to Rednersville dock, where they were unloaded and drawn by horse and wagon to the farm.

The Wood farm passed from Leonard to son Leo, who with his sons Lyle and Dale, farm a total of 370 acres, along with additional rented land. Son Lyle owns lot 83, the former Norris Whitney property, but lives with his wife Nancy, and their two children on the farm next door.

In the 1950's, 12 cows were milked. Today, three silos, a feeder, and a pipeline milker serve a herd of 50 cows, plus 50 head of young cattle. In 1981, Carl McFaul, brother of Florence, Leo's wife, blasted a cattle pass under the road. He also built a road across the marsh. The farm produces corn, soybeans, hay and oats, plus pasture for the cattle.

Dale, second son of Leo and Florence Wood, has been active in 4-H and has completed a record of 38 Agricultural Projects. A daughter, Joyce married John Lazenby.

Mr. & Mrs. Leonard Wood
50th Ann. plaque

The Thomas Wood Family

1. Rilla Wood m. Sam Stewart
2. Milton Earle (1887-1967) m. Mary E. Rathwell and their children are: Harold married Faye Vanclief and they live near Roblin's Lake. Connie, in Toronto and Joan, who taught in Ameliasburgh, before going to Toronto.
3. Mable Pearl 1888-1956 married Burton Fox. Their family is, Arnold (1915-1976), Winfield and Raymond.

The George Wood Family

George Wood and his wife Ellen M. Gibson had Ella, Edna, Ethel (m. Wellington Nelson) and Edith (1886-1958) who married Fred Calnan (1888-1963). They also had a son Charles, a hotel-keeper in Colborne. He died in 1984.

The Marybelle Wood Family

Marybelle Wood (1856-1942) married 1. Daniel Black 2. David Lauder and her children were John Black who married Irene Unger and Marybelle Black (1897-1980) married Walter Cunningham (1901-1943)

The Margaret Wood Family

Margaret Wood married Arthur Sprung, and they had one daughter Vera (1849-1982) who married Everett Jones. For many years they lived on the lower third concession. Their only son Donald married Edna Carnrike.

The Wood Family of the Lower Third

This Wood family came from New Jersey. There were two brothers, Daniel (1808-1896) and John (1809-1896).

Daniel Wood married Laura Jane Washburn and they moved from Sophiasburgh to Ameliasburgh and settled on west half of lot 75 Con. 3. John Wood married Ann Osborne and they settled on the east half of the same lot and today Ronald Wood lives on that farm.

Daniel Wood and his wife had eight children and most of them moved away in later years and there are none here.

John Wood and Ann Osborne (1809-1894) had a family of eight. They were (1) Amarilla, married Wm. H. Davidson, (2) John Wesley married Lydia Whitney, (3) Catharine married Joseph Allison, (4) Jane married Hiland Root (father of Milton the teacher for many years at Mountain View), Descendants of his son, Stillman Roat, still live in Rossmore, (5) Finley, (6) James Wilbur, (7) Ellen married Walter Choate. The Choate children were Jessie, Gilbert, and Stella who married Herb File. They lived in the stone house below the hill in Roblin's Mills, (8) William Henry married Margaret Cunningham and they had four children and remained on the farm. About 1850 they built the house where Ronald and his family live. Previous to that there was a log house on the property.

Francis, the son of Wm. Henry was born there. They also had Ferris, Charles and Maud. (1) Francis married Mary Adams and their son Morley married Ida Russell daughter of Wm. R. and Hannah Russell of Con. 1, Bayside. Morley and Ida Wood lived for many years on Con. 2. Their only son Earl, who married Jean Blakely, is deceased. (2) Ferris Wood married Annie Sager and they had no children. (3) Charles Wood married Grace Gibson (Ref. Gibson family). They had five children. The youngest, Ronald, married Olive Mackey and they had six daughters. They still reside on the original home farm. (4) Maud Wood married Moran Lont. They had no children.

The Charles Young Family

In 1802 Stephen Young (1778-1849) and his half brother Asa Weller came to Murray Township in Northumberland County from East Dorset, Vermont. He married Lucy Marsh, daughter of Mathias Marsh, and they lived on lots 6 and 7, 1st Con. of Murray. Their seventh child was Reuben who married Elizabeth Hendricks; they also lived in Murray. Charles Gilbert was one of their seven children. He married Cassie Hall; part of her dowry was two sheep. Charles bought a farm, lots 72 and 73, 2nd concession of Ameliasburgh from Mrs. Nell Dick in 1875. This farm was at one time Clergy Reserve. It was bought from the Crown by David Gibson for 75 pounds and later owned by

Charles Young home c. 1880

his daughter, Mrs. Dick. Charles Young worked for Mrs. Dick before he bought the farm. The farm consists of 100 acres including 20 acres of mountain. This rock formation is Precambrian rock (granite). There is supposed to be a cave on the mountain. Because the mountain extends right across the farm, David Gibson had purchased a road allowance from the Howell farm to the west for access to the barn and land back of the mountain.

Charles and Cassie Young's family were Harold, Clarence, Florence, Lorne, Gerald, Percy and Leonard. Charles died at an early age when Harold, the eldest, was only 14 years of age. For a few years Harold and Clarence were partners on the farm, then Harold bought Clarence's share, and Clarence purchased a farm by Centre School. The four younger sons and daughter Florence all attended O.B.C. Belleville, and then went to Winnipeg to live, their mother accompanying them. Florence invented and patented 'Kleerex' for eczema.

The stone house was built c. 1840 as a one-and-a-half storey with a cottage roof. In the 1860's it was changed to a two-story house. It has three fireplaces— one with a bake oven. Charles Young had two stump pullers and cleared his own and other farms in the area. There were two orchards at one time, one over the mountain and one in front of the house. Maple syrup was made for many years and some of the old wooden sap buckets still remain.

Harold Young married Ada Reid. They had one son Elmer who still lives in the stone house by the mountain. He married Frances Wallbridge and they have gone into the antique business.

Ending

The following prayer is framed and hangs in the Covenanter's Church in Grand Pré, Nova Scotia. It is a fitting tribute to the pioneers of our country, who carved their homes out of the wilderness and gave to us our heritage.

It was quoted in the sermon of Rt. Wor. Bro. John Jordan, Assistant Grand Chaplain, Grand Lodge A.F. & A.M. of Canada in the Province of Ontario, at the Prince Edward District Church Service on Sunday, April 15, 1984. The service was under the direction of Rt. Wor. Bro. Victor Alyea, District Deputy Grand Master of Prince Edward District, and held in the United Church of Consecon, built in 1829.

Father God, we keep forgetting all of those who lived before us;
We keep forgetting those who lived and worked in this community;
We keep forgetting those who prayed and sang hymns in this church before we were born;
We keep forgetting what our fathers have done for us.
We commit the sin, Lord, of assuming that everything begins with us;
We drink from wells we did not find;
We eat food from farmland we did not develop;
We enjoy freedoms which we have not earned.
We worship in churches we did not build;
We live in communities we did not establish.
This day, make us grateful for our heritage.
Turn our minds to those who lived in another day, and under different circumstances,
Until we are aware of their Faith and Work.
Today, we need to feel our oneness, not only with those of a recent generation who lived here;
But those of every generation and in every place, whose Faith and Works have enriched our lives.
We need to learn from them in order that our Faith will be as vital, our commitment as sincere, our Worship as alive, our Fellowship as deep as many of the devout and faithful,
Who lived in other times and places.

BIBLIOGRAPHY

Manuscripts:
Ameliasburgh Township Council Minutes and By-Laws
The Tweedsmuir Histories of Consecon, Mountain View and Rednersville Women's Institutes
Records of the Building of the Rednersville Church 1848-1853

Records of the Rednersville Circuit 1879-1901
Richard Boehme, The Grape Island Mission
Indians of Ontario, Indian Affairs Branch, Queen's Printers 1967
Kingston Historical Society, Volume #7 Nov. 1958— The Indian site at Consecon by Rev. Bowen P. Squire. Volume 27— The Failure of the Sulpician Mission to Kente in 1681
Canadian Historical Association booklet #30— Bruce and Trigger, The Indians and the Heroic Age of New France.
Scrapbooks of Barbara Phillips, Gladys Adams, the late Blake Young and the late Thomas Mikel.

Periodicals:
The Intelligencer
The Picton Gazette
The Trentonian
County Magazine

Books:
Gerald Ackerman, *History of Cheesemaking in Prince Edward County* (The Picton Gazette, 1971)
H. Belden, *Historical Atlas of Hastings and Prince Edward Counties 1878*
Gerald E. Boyce, *Historic Hastings* (Ontario Intelligencer Ltd. 1967)
William Canniff, *History of the Settlement of Upper Canada* with Special Reference to the Bay of Quinte (Toronto: Dudley and Burns, 1869)
J.M.S. Careless, *Canada— a Story of Challenge* (Macmillan Co. Toronto)
G.P. de T. Glazebrook, *Life in Ontario- A Social History* (University of Toronto 1968)
Jane B. Goddard U.E., *Hans Waltimeyer* (Haynes Printing Co. Cobourg, 1980)
Edwin C. Guillet, *Pioneer Days in Upper Canada* (University of Toronto Press, 1973)
W.S. Herrington, *Pioneer Life Among the Loyalists in Upper Canada* (Toronto: The Macmillan Co. of Canada Ltd., 1915)
Morrey's Directory 1906 Vol. XIV (Union Publishing of Ingersoll)
James Plomer, *Desperate Venture* (Mika Publishing 1979)
Prince Edward County Old Boys' Reunion— *Picton's 100 Years 1837-1937* (The Picton Gazette)
Smith, *Canada: Past, Present, and Future*, 1850
Malcolm Wallbridge, *The Diary of Thomas Nightingale* (The Picton Gazette 1967)
T.C. Wallbridge, *On Some Ancient Mounds upon the Shores of the Bay of Quinte,* Canadian Journal 1860

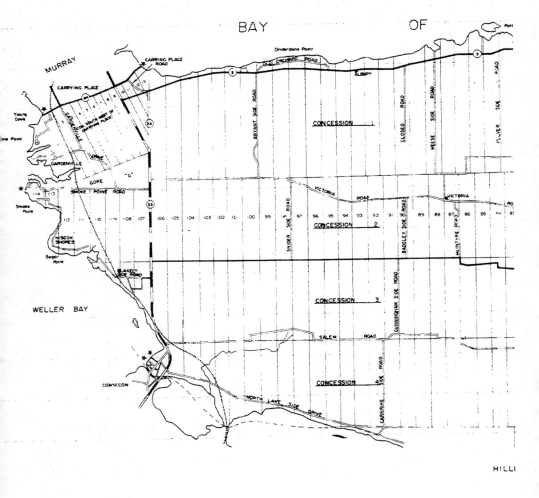

★ Right-of-Way to water

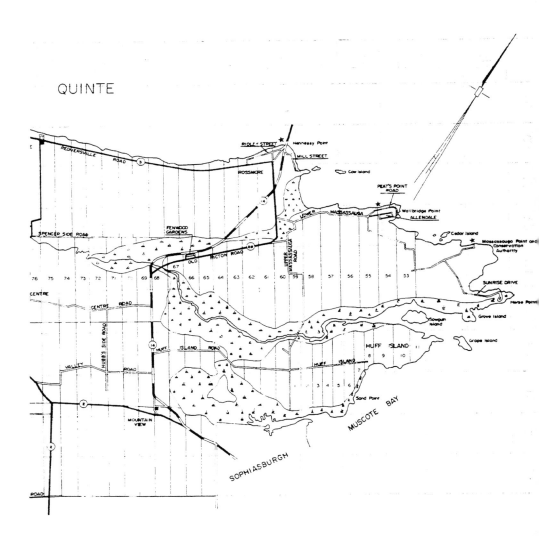

QUINTE

Modern Map of Ameliasburgh

Index

Index Compiled by
Murray Clapp

Data Entry by
Larry McQuoid